Excel 4 for Windows:
The Complete Reference

Excel 4 for Windows: The Complete Reference

Martin S. Matthews
Stephanie Seymour

Osborne **McGraw-Hill**

Berkeley New York St. Louis San Francisco
Auckland Bogotá Hamburg London Madrid
Mexico City Milan Montreal New Delhi Panama City
Paris São Paulo Singapore Sydney
Tokyo Toronto

Osborne **McGraw-Hill**
2600 Tenth Street
Berkeley, California 94710
U.S.A.

For information on software, translations, or book distributors outside of the U.S.A., please write to Osborne **McGraw-Hill** at the above address.

Excel 4 for Windows: The Complete Reference

1234567890 DOC 99876543

ISBN 0-07-881836-2

To the next generation of Excel users:
Tara, Jaimeson, and Michael

Publisher ——————————————
Kenna S. Wood

Acquisitions Editor ——————————
William Pollock

Associate Editor ——————————
Vicki Van Ausdall

Editorial Assistant ——————————
Judy Kleppe

Technical Editor ——————————
John Cronan

Project Editor ——————————
Nancy Pechonis

Copy Editor ——————————
Deborah Craig

Proofreader ——————————
Zoe Borovsky

Indexer ——————————
Julie Kawabata

Computer Designer ——————————
Lance Ravella

Cover Design ——————————
Bay Graphics Design, Inc.

Contents

Part II
The Excel Dictionary

Part III
Appendixes

A
Installing Windows and Excel   833

B
The Excel Character Set   843

Acknowledgments

John Cronan did an excellent job of technically reviewing all of this book—a long, painstaking task which he always managed to get done on schedule even though he had been shorted some (and more than once, most) of his allotted time. Not only did John provide good ideas and find some of the most obscure errors, but he also always did what it took to get the job done.

Erik Paulsen jumped into the breach when Marty was pulled away on another project. Erik ended up writing the majority of Chapters 3, 4, and 5. Erik's willingness to take this project on with no notice, and then to do whatever was necessary to get it done (including more than one sleepless night) is very greatly appreciated.

Jane Seymour, Stephanie's mother, has an office equidistant from Stephanie, Marty, and John; she therefore provided a most valuable exchange point for portions of the manuscript going from one person to the other.

Maureen Jones, Amana Fisher, and Gary Seymour provided Stephanie with practical and emotional support essential to the completion of this book. Their contributions are greatly appreciated.

Carole Boggs Matthews and Michael Matthews provided Marty with all that it took to allow this book to be finished. Their love, patience, and understanding are without parallel.

Introduction

Excel for Windows has long had a popular following. With the release of Excel 4 this popularity has expanded, and Excel now easily outsells both major competing spreadsheet packages. Such dominance is well deserved, given Excel's ease of use and the features it provides.

About This Book

Excel 4 for Windows: The Complete Reference has two purposes: first, to allow you to put the full power of Excel to work in the easiest possible way; and second, to provide an in-depth reference so you can easily find what you need to know for expanding both your knowledge of Excel and your use of it.

This book uses a very simple structure, offering a comprehensive reference work that is also easy to use. It is meant to be a primary supplement to the Excel documentation. In the documentation we have found it very easy to get lost in the pine needles and not be able to find the trees, let alone the forest.

How This Book Is Organized

Excel 4 for Windows: The Complete Reference is divided into two major sections, in line with its twin purposes. The first section, The Excel Basics, provides a quick and easily read introduction to the product. The second section, The Excel Dictionary, provides a concise, easy to use reference to every concept, every menu command, and every function and macro function. These two sections work together to give you the basics you need to get started with Excel, as well as an in-depth reference source to help you keep growing with the product. They are complemented by two appendixes that provide useful information about software installation and about the Excel character set, and by two handy Excel command supplements.

The Excel Basics

The first section of the book is made up of five chapters that introduce Excel and its three main components: worksheets, charts, and databases. These chapters are meant to be easily and quickly read so you can get started using the product.

The first chapter, *Overview of Excel 4 for Windows,* describes Windows and Excel, focusing on their on-screen characteristics and how they are used with both the mouse and the keyboard. The chapter then goes into the basic features of Excel, covering cells and ranges, formulas and functions, and toolbars and menus.

The second chapter, *Producing Worksheets,* discusses the basic skills that are fundamental to using Excel worksheets. Included in this chapter are entering and editing data; getting around, changing, formatting, and printing a worksheet; saving and loading a worksheet; and leaving Excel.

The third chapter, *Creating Charts,* gives you the tools necessary to use Excel's charting features. The chapter shows how to create charts from worksheet information, then describes the types of charts that can be created, and how to customize, format, and edit charts.

The fourth chapter, *Using a Database,* shows you how to place and use a database on a worksheet. The chapter covers building and maintaining a database, as well as organizing, manipulating, and analyzing information in a database.

The fifth chapter, *Working with Macros,* provides an introduction to the use of macro commands, an often overlooked but very powerful feature of Excel. This chapter describes what macros are; discusses how to record, edit, and run them; and examines the classes of macro functions. Finally, the chapter leads you through building and running both a command macro and a function macro.

The Excel Dictionary

The second section of the book, as you might guess from its name, is structured like a dictionary. It is meant to provide a very simple, convenient reference to all facets of Excel. The section's high usability has been carefully thought out and is based on these features:

- **Alphabetic structure** This simple structure enables you to quickly locate what you are looking for without having to figure out which section to look in.

- **Categorized entries** There are four types of entries, each clearly marked: concepts, menu commands, functions, and macro functions.

- **Consistent layout** Each entry includes a complete description, as well as the following information: type (concept, menu command, function, or macro function), identification if an item is new to version 4 of Excel or not available in version 4, associated commands, associated functions, associated concepts, keyboard shortcuts, tools, and mouse tricks. This information is formatted into a consistent and easy-to-use layout. The title of each entry includes both the item name and any arguments it uses. Often there are one or more examples of how the item is used.

- **Comprehensive cross-referencing** The Excel Dictionary is designed to help you easily find an item even when you don't know exactly what a macro or function is called, or can't recall the full name of a menu option. For example, if you wanted to print, but didn't know that the Print option is on the File menu, you could easily find this out by reading the entry for Print (the concept), which cross-references File Print (the menu command).

- **Dictionary style page headings** At the top of every page is a heading, similar to those in language dictionaries, that indicates what topics can be found on that page.

- **Alphabetic thumb tabs** The Excel Dictionary includes alphabetic thumb tabs—again, like a language dictionary—to make it easy and fast for you to find the right spot in the book.

Appendixes

Appendix A provides detailed instructions for installing Excel, as well as valuable background information. It describes what equipment you need and explains how to start and use the Excel Setup program. In addition, it discusses how you prepare to store the data you will create with Excel, and how to start and leave the program. Appendix B provides a handy reference to the Excel character set.

Excel Command Supplements

Near the back of the book are several supplemental pages listing the many keyboard shortcuts available in Excel. These pages are followed by a toolbar command card that can be removed and used as an instant reference. The card combines pictures and descriptions of the many tools that appear on Excel's built-in toolbars.

Using Various Versions of Excel

Excel, for the most part, has maintained an upward compatibility among its different releases. In other words, the majority of the commands and functions available in older versions can be used in newer versions.

Most of the features new to version 4 of Excel have been identified in this book. Therefore, if you stay away from the sections that address these new features, you can easily use the book with versions 3.0 and 3.5.

Conventions Used in This Book

Excel 4 for Windows: The Complete Reference uses several conventions designed to make the book easier for you to use. These are as follows.

- **Bold** type is used for text you are instructed to type from the keyboard.

- Keys on the keyboard are presented in small capital letters (RIGHT ARROW and ENTER, for example).

- When you are expected to enter a command, you are told to *press* the key(s). If you enter text or numbers, you are told to *type* them.

Part *I*

The Excel Basics

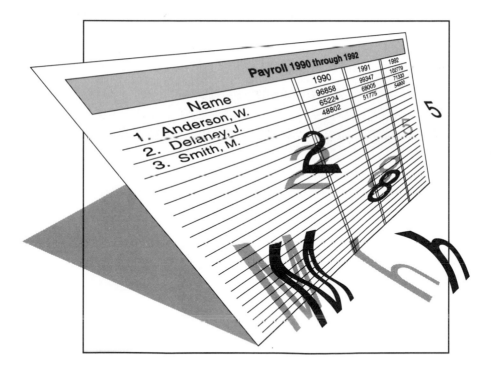

Chapter *1*

Overview of Excel 4 for Windows

Excel is a spreadsheet program—a program in which you can enter numbers in rows and columns and perform arithmetic on those numbers. However, Excel is also much more. Excel includes a full charting module that lets you display spreadsheet numbers in graphic form, and a database module that lets you specify a section of spreadsheet data to use as a database. In addition to these features, Excel includes a large number of mathematical and statistical functions; a complete language for automating Excel operations; and many commands and tools for manipulating, formatting, storing, and retrieving information.

Although Excel can do so much, it is very straightforward and easy to use. Keep this in mind as you learn Excel: the intuitive approach will often be the one that works.

This chapter will introduce Excel 4 and the Windows environment under which Excel operates. It assumes that you have Windows and Excel on your computer and have them operating. If you need help installing or starting Excel, see Appendix A. If there is a particular command, function, or concept on which you want more information, see the Excel Dictionary later in this book.

The Windows Environment

On IBM and compatible personal computers, Excel runs under Microsoft Windows. *Windows* is an extension to the MS-DOS operating system that provides a graphical, or visual, interface between you and your computer. Since Excel for Windows uses this visual interface, the first step in learning about Excel is to learn about Windows.

The Windows Screen

The most obvious part of the Windows visual interface is what you see on the screen. Figure 1-1 shows an Excel screen. Many parts of this screen are features common to all Windows applications.

The Excel screen is composed of two windows, one inside the other. A *window* is an area of the screen with a border around it. The outer window is an *application window*, in this case the Excel application window. The inner window is a *document window*, in Figure 1-1, it contains a spreadsheet, or *worksheet*. (If you cannot see a distinction between the application window and the document window, your document window has been maximized. To get your screen to look like Figure 1-1, move the mouse pointer to the small box with two arrows in the *second row* from the top on the far right side and press the left mouse button.) The application and document windows contain the following features common to all windows:

- Across the top of each window is the title bar, which contains the window name. For application windows, the name is generally the name of the application; for document windows, it is the name of the document.

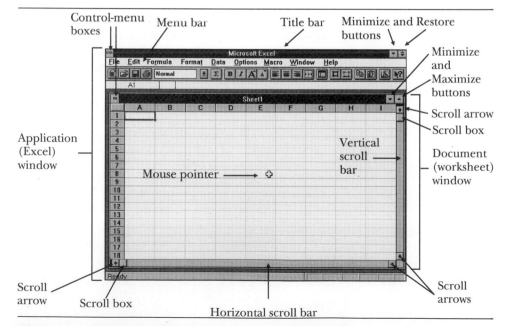

Figure 1-1.   *The common Windows elements on the Excel screen*

- In the left corner of the title bar of most windows is a box with a bar in it. This *Control-menu box* displays the Control menu, which is used to size, position, and close the window. The Control menu will be discussed further under "Using the Keyboard" later in this chapter.

- In the right corner of the title bar of most windows is a pair of boxes containing arrows. The left box with the downward-pointing arrow is the *Minimize button*, which reduces the screen to an *icon* like this:

The box on the right can be one of two buttons. In Figure 1-1, the Sheet1 document window has a Maximize button with an upward-pointing arrow. The *Maximize button* enlarges the window as much as possible. When a window is maximized, the Maximize button becomes the Restore button, as shown in the Excel application window. The *Restore button* returns the window to the size it was before it was maximized.

- Beneath the title bar is the *menu bar*, which contains the current set of menus for the active application. Only application windows have menu bars.

- Down the right side and across the bottom of the document window are the vertical and horizontal scroll bars. The *scroll bars* allow you to position the contents of your windows, either vertically or horizontally, when you can't see the entire contents on the screen at once. Each scroll bar includes two *scroll arrows,* one at either end, for moving the window contents a small amount. Each scroll bar also contains a *scroll box* that tells you what part of the window contents you are currently looking at. If the scroll box is in the middle of the scroll bar, you are in the middle of the data. You can also drag the scroll box to move the window contents. The scroll bars, arrows, and boxes will be discussed further under "Using the Mouse on Windows" later in this chapter.

- In the center of the document window is a cross that is the mouse pointer. The *mouse pointer* tells you where the mouse is currently pointing. The cross is only one of several shapes the mouse pointer takes depending on its location. The mouse and its pointer are discussed further in the next section.

While Figure 1-1 shows only one application window and one document window, you can have several of each on the screen at once. You will see multiple document windows in later chapters.

Using the Mouse

It is possible to use Windows and Excel with the keyboard alone. A major ingredient in the Windows visual interface, however, is the mouse. Just as the screen allows Windows to communicate with you visually, the mouse allows you to communicate with Windows visually. For this reason, the mouse is generally the fastest and easiest way to select things on the screen and to tell Windows or Excel what to do. The keyboard still has a place for data entry, and there are some handy keyboard shortcuts, but the mouse has superseded the keyboard in most other areas. For that reason, this book will assume that you have a mouse and are using it in all cases where it's easiest to do so.

You use the mouse to move the mouse pointer on the screen. In other words, if you move the mouse to the right the mouse pointer will move to the right, and if you move the mouse to the left the mouse pointer will move to the left.

A mouse can have one, two, or three buttons. When you press one of the buttons, you tell Windows and Excel that you want to do something. Usually, only one mouse button is used by Windows and Excel. It is called the *mouse button* in this book. The left mouse button is used by default, but you can change this default with the Windows Control Panel. If a second mouse button is called for, it will be described as the *right mouse button*. The third mouse button is generally not used; when it is, it often has the effect of holding down the left button.

Mouse Operations

To indicate that you want to do something with an object on the screen, move the mouse until the tip of mouse pointer is *on top* of the object and then press the mouse button. There are actually a variety of terms which describe using the mouse. These terms are used throughout this book, and are described here:

Term	Meaning
Press	Hold down the mouse button
Release	Quit pressing the mouse button
Click	Quickly press and release the mouse button
Double-click	Press and release the mouse button twice in rapid succession
Point on	Move the mouse until the tip of the mouse pointer is on top of item you want
Click on	Point on an item and click
Drag	Press and hold the mouse button while you move the mouse
Select	Point on an item and click (same as click on)
Choose	Click on a menu option to indicate that you want it carried out

If you find yourself at the edge of your desk or work surface when using the mouse, pick up the mouse (don't roll it) and set it down where you have more room. You can then continue to use the mouse normally.

Using the Mouse on Windows

There are a number of window elements, detailed below, that are designed to be used with a mouse:

- You must click on the Minimize, Maximize, and Restore buttons to minimize, maximize, or restore your windows.

- You can use the mouse to change the size of a window. When you position the mouse pointer on the window border, it turns into a two-headed arrow that you can drag (press and hold the mouse button while moving the mouse) to change the size of the window. You can drag on the sides of the window to change its size either vertically or horizontally, and you can drag on its corners to change the size of both sides at once.

- You can move the mouse pointer to the title bar and drag to reposition the window on the screen.

- Clicking on the scroll arrows moves the window contents by a small increment—one row or one column when the window contains a worksheet.

- Clicking on the scroll bar moves the window contents by a larger increment, usually the width or height of one window. If you click on the vertical scroll bar beneath the scroll box, you will move the contents down the height of one window. Similarly, if you click on the horizontal scroll bar to the right of the scroll box, you will move the contents to the right one window's width.

- You can drag the scroll box to move the window's contents an amount proportional to the amount and in the direction that you drag the box.

- Double-clicking on the Control-menu box closes the window.

- Double-clicking on a window icon restores the window to its previous size.

Using Menus and Dialog Boxes

The Excel menu bar (just below the Excel title bar) contains nine words—File, Edit, Formula, and so on. These words are the names of *menus*, the primary device used to give instructions to Windows and Excel. When you click on a menu name, you select or open a menu, as shown in Figure 1-2. An open menu lists a series of menu *options* from which you can choose. An option often is a command like Save or Print.

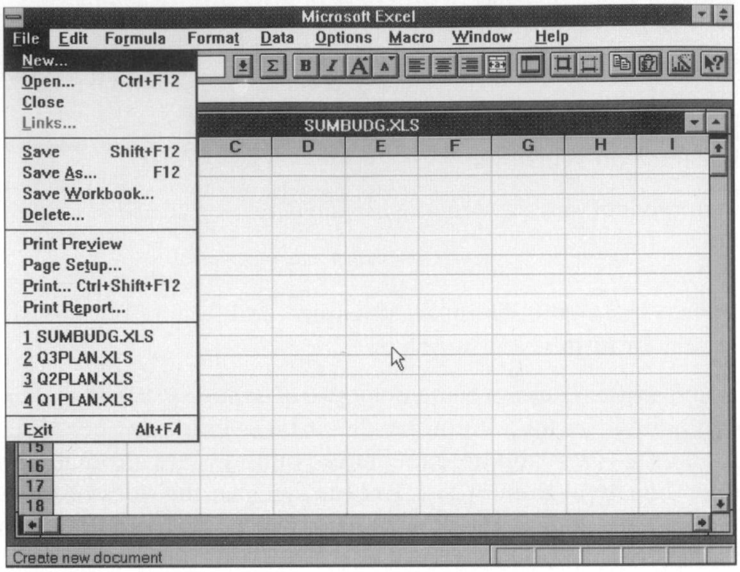

Figure 1-2.   *The Excel File menu*

In other cases, an option is a means for you to choose among several alternatives—for example, to choose among several open documents or to tell Excel how you want your screen to look. To choose a menu option you click on it. As you can see, the mouse makes it very easy to use menus: you click on the menu name to open a menu and click on an option to choose it.

Notice the ellipses (three dots) to the right of many of the options. This tells you that choosing that option does not immediately carry out the command but instead opens a *dialog box* which Excel uses to obtain further information or allow additional choices. For example, when you save a file you need to tell Excel the filename and possibly the drive and directory to use. Excel uses the dialog box shown in Figure 1-3 to elicit this information.

As you can see in the figure, a dialog box is a window, complete with a title bar with which you can reposition it and a Control-menu box with which you can close the dialog box. A dialog box also has several special devices for gathering information and presenting you with choices. Some of these devices are shown in Figure 1-3 while others are shown in Figure 1-4. Each dialog box element is described here:

Device	Use
Text box	To enter text, such as filenames.
List box	To present a list of items from which you can choose.

Device	Use
Drop-down list box	To present a list box in limited space. (Click on the downward-pointing arrow to display the list.)
Command buttons	To take some action, such as leaving the dialog box, opening another dialog box, or getting help.
Check box	To present an item which you can choose. A check mark appears when the item is chosen, and you can choose as many check boxes as you want.
Option buttons	To present a set of items, from which you can choose one. A black dot appears in an option button that has been chosen. (These are also called *radio buttons*.)

Most dialog boxes include at least three command buttons: an OK button that completes and closes the dialog box, a Cancel button that closes the dialog box without taking any action, and a Help button that opens a Help window for that dialog box. Occasionally you will see other devices in dialog boxes; such devices will be described throughout this book.

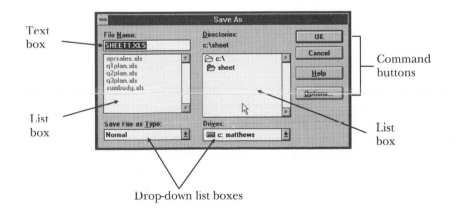

Figure 1-3.   *The Save As dialog box*

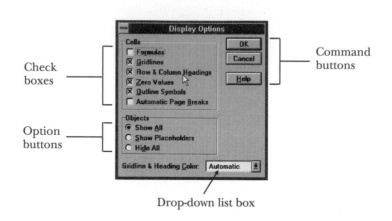

Figure 1-4.   *The Display Options dialog box*

Using the Keyboard

Although Windows was designed to support the mouse, it has many features that facilitate keyboard use. Also, just about anything you can do with the mouse, you can do with the keyboard although often it is not as easy. You can use the keyboard to make menu selections and to work in dialog boxes. In addition, there are many keyboard shortcuts provided in Excel, and you can use the keyboard with the Control menu. Each of these areas is discussed in the following sections.

Using Menus with the Keyboard

Windows provides two ways to get to the menu bar with the keyboard: pressing ALT and pressing F10. Excel adds a third alternative tailored to ex-Lotus users: pressing / (the backslash key). Once you are in the menu bar, you can type the underlined letter in a menu name to open that menu or use LEFT ARROW or RIGHT ARROW to select a menu and then press DOWN ARROW or ENTER to open the menu. When a menu is open, you can type the underlined letter in an option to choose it or press DOWN ARROW or UP ARROW to highlight an option and then press ENTER to choose it. If you want to close a menu without choosing an option, press ESC to return to the menu bar. If you want to leave the menu bar and return to your work, press ESC again.

In summary, the fastest way to use a menu with the keyboard is as follows.

- Press ALT or F10 to get to the menu bar

- Type the underlined letter in the menu name you want

- Type the underlined letter in the option you want

- Press ESC twice to cancel a menu selection after starting

Using Dialog Boxes with the Keyboard

In a dialog box, one of the command buttons (usually the OK button) has a darker border around it. This is the default button, and pressing ENTER will select it. In addition, you can normally select the Cancel button (which closes the dialog box without taking any action) by pressing ESC.

To get around in a dialog box, press TAB or SHIFT-TAB, or hold down ALT while pressing the underlined letter in an item's label. You press the SPACEBAR to select or deselect check boxes. (In this context, SPACEBAR acts like a toggle. If the check box is selected, pressing SPACEBAR deselects it, and if the check box is not selected, pressing SPACEBAR selects it.) You can also use the arrow keys to move around within a group of option buttons and check boxes.

Shortcut Keys

Several menu options have one or more keystrokes to their right. For example, in the File menu CTRL-F12 is opposite Open and F12 is opposite Save As. These keystrokes are *shortcut keys* that perform the same action as opening the menu and choosing the option. Shortcut keys are the one keyboard feature that is faster than the mouse. Some of the more commonly used shortcut keys are listed here:

Option	Shortcut Key
Absolute/mixed/relative	F4
Add to current selections	SHIFT F8
Bold style	CTRL-B
Calculate all documents	F9
Clear	DEL
Copy	CTRL-C
Cut	CTRL-X
Edit cell	F2
Extend selection	F8
Fill down	CTRL-D

Option	Shortcut Key
Fill right	CTRL - R
Find next	F7
Format commas	CTRL - ! (CTRL - SHIFT-1)
Format date	CTRL - # (CTRL - SHIFT-3)
Format dollars	CTRL - $ (CTRL - SHIFT-4)
Format percent	CTRL - % (CTRL - SHIFT-5)
Goto	F5
Help in context	SHIFT-F1
Help Index	F1
Insert AutoSum	ALT- =
Insert cells	CTRL - + (CTRL - SHIFT - =)
Italic style	CTRL -I
Menu	ALT or F10
New chart	F11
Next pane	F6
Paste	CTRL-V
Save As	F12
Undo	CTRL-Z

Many other shortcut keys are described in the Excel Dictionary section of this book.

Control Menu

The Control menu, which opens from the Control-menu box in the upper-left corner of each window, allows you to perform many functions with the keyboard. The Control menu for the Excel application is shown here:

Restore	
Move	
Size	
Minimize	
Maximize	
Close	Alt+F4
Switch To...	Ctrl+Esc
Run...	

There is some difference among Control menus, but most allow you to move, size, and close a window. The options in the Excel Control menu are as follows.

Option	Purpose
Restore	Restores the window to the size it was prior to being minimized or maximized.
Move	Moves the window with the arrow keys.
Size	Sizes the window with the arrow keys.
Minimize	Reduces the window to an icon.
Maximize	Enlarges the window to full-screen size.
Close	Closes the window and the application.
Switch To	Switches to another running application.
Run	Allows you to run the Clipboard, Control Panel, Macro Translator, and Dialog Editor applications without leaving Excel.

You open the Excel Control menu by pressing ALT-Spacebar, whereas you open a document Control menu by pressing ALT-Hyphen. In the sizing and moving options, press one or two arrow keys (using two keys is like dragging the window from the corner instead of a side) until the window is in the desired location or of the desired size and then press ENTER to complete the operation. If you decide to cancel the operation, press ESC.

Getting Help

Windows and Excel include a lot of online assistance all built around the Windows Help system. You can select the Help menu, shown here, and get into the Help system in several ways or run a tutorial.

You can also select a Help command button in a dialog box to get specific help about the dialog box. From the keyboard, you can press F1 and get the same Help table of contents that is available from the Help menu. You can also press SHIFT-F1 and get specific (context-sensitive) help about what you are doing. If you have a dialog box open when you press SHIFT-F1, you will get specific help about that dialog box. Otherwise, pressing SHIFT-F1 transforms your mouse pointer into a question mark. At this point you can click on anything, including a menu option, to receive specific help on that item. For example, if you pressed SHIFT-F1 and clicked on the Edit menu and then the Cut command, you would get the Help screen shown in Figure 1-5.

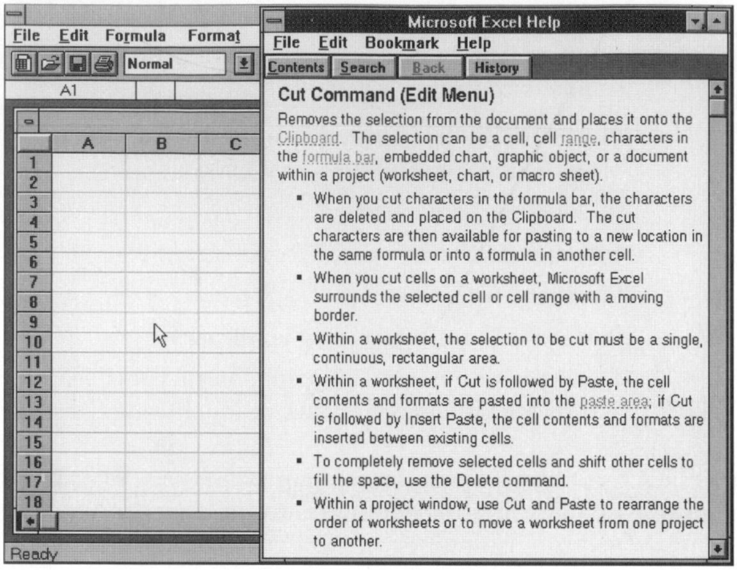

Figure 1-5.   *The Help window for the Cut command*

Most Help screens, including the one in Figure 1-5, contain cross-references or *jump terms* to other related help topics. These jump terms are underlined and are green on a color monitor. When you move the mouse pointer to a jump term, the mouse pointer turns into a *grabber hand.* Clicking the mouse button at this point will take you to the reference topic. In addition, Help windows have a series of buttons that allow you to easily get to the Help table of contents, search through Help topics for a specific subject, and see a history of your most recently selected Help topics.

Excel Basics

Although Excel handles charts and databases as well as worksheets, the underlying structure of Excel is a worksheet. A *worksheet,* in its simplest form, is an area that has been divided into rows and columns. The computerized concept came from the accountant's multicolumn pad of paper. However, an Excel worksheet is much larger—up to 256 columns and 16,384 rows.

The row and column structure of Excel provides a powerful framework for financial analysis. Figure 1-6 shows just one of many alternative layouts for financial plans. Each row is an element of cost or an account and each column is a period of

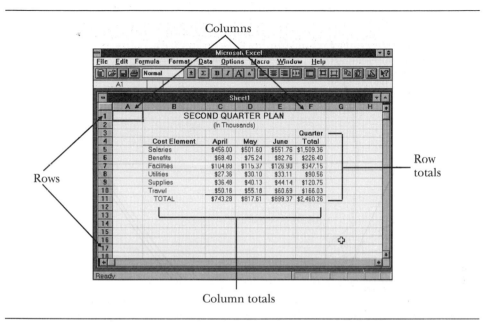

Figure 1-6.   *A financial plan*

time—months, quarters, or years. If you sum down a column you will get the total cost for a single period and if you sum across a row you will get the total for all time periods for a single element of cost.

Addresses and Cells

The rows and columns form a two-dimensional grid. Each row is numbered 1 through 16,384, while the 256 possible columns are labeled A through IV (A through Z, then AA through AZ, BA through BZ, and so on through IV). This allows you, for example, to add across row 16 from column D through column H, or to chart column AB from row 215 through 220.

When information is entered into a worksheet it is stored in a specific location. You can identify that location by its row and column coordinates, which can be considered an *address*. For example, if you put something in column C, row 3, Excel gives it an address of C3. Each cell can contain up to 255 characters, including numbers, letters, or a mixture of the two.

A single address, the intersection of a row and a column, is called a *cell*. An Excel worksheet, then, is a collection of over four million cells addressed from A1 in the upper-left corner to IV16384 in the lower-right corner.

Text and Numbers

A cell may contain either text or numbers. Numbers are anything on which you can do arithmetic, including dates, times, dollars, percentages, and formulas that result in numbers. Text is everything else. Text includes numbers entered as text as well as titles, labels, and notes.

Excel considers an entry to be a number if it only contains the following items:

- The numbers 0 through 9
- The numeric symbols: $+ - ( ) ., : \$ \% / E e$ (scientific notation)
- A date or a time in a standard Excel format
- A recognizable formula that results in a number

Numbers can be entered in a number of formats and Excel will automatically attach the closest standard Excel format to the cell. Examples of this automatic formatting are shown here:

	A	B	C	D	E	F	G	H
1								
2								
3								
4		4.52	4.52%	$4.52	4 2/5	4,520,000	4.52E-02	
5								
6								

When it applies automatic formatting, Excel is limited to two or no decimal places for dollars, percents, and numbers formatted with a comma as a thousand separator. For example, if you enter 4.3% you will get 4.30% and if you enter $1,234.5 you will get $1,234.50. Also, Excel makes some assumptions when you enter dates. If you enter only a month and a day, Excel adds the current year (according to your computer's clock), and if you enter a month and a year, Excel adds the 1st as the day.

Ranges and Range Names

Often in formulas and in Excel operations you need to work with a group of cells. When you want to do this, you need to select a *range* or a rectangular group of adjacent cells. There are four kinds of ranges: a single cell, a row of cells, a column of cells, and a block of cells. Examples of these are shown in Figure 1-7.

A range is defined by the cells in the upper-left and lower-right corners of the range separated by a colon. For example, the ranges in Figure 1-7 are B3:B3, D3:G3, B7:B17, and D7:G17. You can also name a range if the name you create follows these conventions:

- Begins with a letter or an underline character

- Contains only letters, numbers, periods, and underlines

- Uses periods and underline characters rather than spaces as word separators

- Is less than 256 characters long

- Does not look like an address such as A13, R4C5, B$3, or CD247.

Range names are usually easier to remember than the range coordinates. For example, if you want to add a set of sales figures, the formula =SUM(SALES) has more intuitive meaning than the formula =SUM(F32:H44). Also, if you make changes to your worksheet that change a range, changing the definition of its range name automatically changes every formula that refers to that range by its name.

Formulas

All arithmetic in Excel is performed through *formulas*. Excel formulas combine data on the worksheet with constants using arithmetic operators to produce a result. Formulas normally begin with an equal sign (=), but you can enter a formula beginning with an at sign (@), a plus sign (+), or a minus sign (−). Excel will automatically change the at sign and the plus sign to an equal sign and place an equal

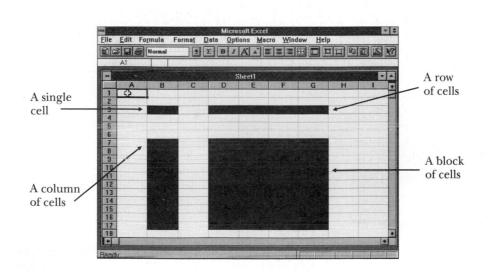

Figure 1-7.   Types of ranges

sign in front of the minus sign. Formulas can be up to 255 characters long, but cannot contain spaces except within quotation marks. Anything in quotation marks is called a *literal*.

There are four kinds of formulas or expressions that use four different kinds of operators. There are numeric formulas that use numeric operators, logical formulas that use logical operators, text formulas with the text operator, and reference expressions that use reference operators.

Numeric Formulas

Numeric formulas are what you normally think of when you think of a formula. Numeric formulas can contain numbers, cell references (such as B23 and A16), range names (like SALES and TAX), and functions (such as SUM and PI). Examples of numeric formulas and their results are shown here:

Formula	Result Displayed in the Cell
=356+219–56	The result of adding or subtracting the three values
=1278*.25	The product of multiplying 1278 by .25
=B4–C18	The result of subtracting the contents of C18 from the contents of B4
=D3	The contents of D3
=tax*amount	The product of a range named "tax" times a range named "amount"

All numeric formulas contain one or more of these six numeric operators:

$$+ \quad - \quad * \quad / \quad \wedge \quad \%$$

These symbols represent addition, subtraction, multiplication, division, exponentiation, and percentage. Exponentiation is taking something to a power. For example if you want to square the contents of cell E12 you would use the formula =E12^2. Percentage is the same as dividing by 100 to create a percentage. For example, if you wanted to express 45 percent, you would write =45% and the result would be .45, which can be displayed as is or formatted as 45%.

Logical Formulas

Logical formulas compare two things and return a logical value of either TRUE or FALSE depending on whether the comparison is correct. All logical formulas use one or more of these six logical operators:

=   <   <=   >   >=   <>

for equal to, less than, less than or equal to, greater than, greater than or equal to, and not equal to. Examples of logical formulas and their results are shown here:

Formula	Result Displayed in the Cell
=B7=C2	The logical value TRUE if B7 is equal to C2, or the logical value FALSE if they are not equal
=date<=today()	The logical value TRUE if a range named date is less than or equal to the Excel function that provides the current date, otherwise the logical value FALSE

Text Formulas

Text formulas combine text with the single text operator & for *concatenation* or joining two items. You can think of text as a *string* of characters. Concatenation simply involves joining two text strings. For example, the formula

="Dear "&C3

combines the literal string "Dear " with the contents of cell C3 as you might do with a form letter. A literal string is anything in quotation marks used literally character for character. The space after the word Dear is significant in this case because it supplies the separator between Dear and the contents of C3.

Reference Expressions

A *reference* is an address on a worksheet. It can be a single cell, a range of cells, or several ranges. Reference expressions are used in other formulas and produce a reference either from individual cells or from other references. Reference expressions use one or more of three reference operators. Each of these are explained here.

Operator	Purpose
:	Creates a *range* from two cells resulting in a single reference for all the cells between the first cell, which is in one corner of the range, and the second cell, which is in the opposite corner of the range. An example of a range is D7:G17, which is a reference for all the cells in the rectangle formed by D7 and G17. (Other ranges are shown in Figure 1-7.)

A space   Creates the *intersection* of two ranges. An intersection is a reference to the cells that are common between two given references. For example, the expression D4:E8 B5:G7 produces the reference D5:E7 for the intersection, as you can see here:

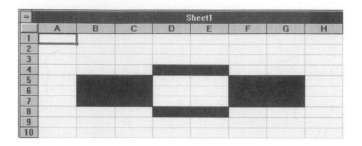

Creates the *union* of two references. The union is a single reference to all the cells contained in either of the two original references. You may or may not be able to express this as a single range. For example, the expression A4:C8,D4:E8 would produce the single range A4:E8, but A4:C8,E12:F15 is a multiple-range reference that can only be expressed as A4:C8,E12:F15.

A reference expression can generally be used anywhere a reference is called for.

Order of Calculation

When Excel evaluates a formula and produces its result, it does so using a specific set of rules. Of primary importance among these rules is the order of calculation or *precedence* of the operators within the formula. Excel assigns a precedence number to every operator, as shown here:

Operator	Description	Precedence
:	Range of cells	1
A space	Intersection of cells	2
,	Union of cells	3
–	Negation	4
%	Percentage (divide by 100)	5
^	Exponentiation	6
*	Multiplication	7
/	Division	7
+	Addition	8

Operator	Description	Precedence
–	Subtraction	8
&	Concatenation	9
=	Equal to	10
<	Less than	10
<=	Less than or equal to	10
>	Greater than	10
>=	Greater than or equal to	10
<>	Not equal to	10

Operators with a lower precedence number are evaluated earlier in the calculation. When two operators in a formula have the same precedence, they are evaluated sequentially from left to right.

You can change the order of calculation with parentheses. Calculations within the innermost set of parentheses will be evaluated first. For example, if you want to add two numbers and multiply by a third, you cannot use the formula =A1+B1*C1. Due to Excel's established order of precedence, the multiplication will take place before the addition. However, if you use parentheses for the addition operation, changing the formula to =(A1+B1)*C1, the addition will take place before the multiplication. You can use up to 20 sets of parentheses. You must add parentheses in pairs. Excel has a handy feature that shows you the matching left parenthesis as you enter a right parenthesis. This way you know your parentheses match without having to count them.

Functions

A *function* is a predefined or built-in formula that comes with Excel. Functions can stand alone as an independent formula or they can be used in another formula or even within another function. There are many kinds of functions, including mathematical, statistical, financial, informational, date and time, lookup, logical, database, and text. The Command Reference section of this book describes all of the Excel functions. Some examples of functions are shown here:

Function	Description
=SUM(A4:A7,A9)	Adds A4, A5, A6, A7, and A9. Note how the union operator allows you to have a reference containing two separate ranges.
=NOW()	Produces the current date and time.
=PI()*G3^2	Calculates the area of a circle whose radius is in G3.

Function	Description
=PV(C4,F6,B1)	Calculates the present value of a series of equal payments whose amount is contained in B1, at an interest rate in C4, for the number of periods in F6.
=RIGHT(T22,5)	Displays the rightmost five characters of a text string contained in T22.

In a function, the items within parentheses are called *arguments*. There can be no arguments or many arguments, depending on the function. If there are no arguments, you must still enter the parentheses. If you have only one pair of parentheses in a function, you do not have to enter the right parenthesis—Excel will do it for you. As you enter arguments, you cannot include spaces except within a literal enclosed in quotation marks. The Formula menu's Paste Name option will help you construct a function; it even reminds you of the appropriate arguments.

The Excel Environment

The Excel environment is an extension of the Windows environment, tailored to worksheets and charts. All of the screen, mouse, menu, and dialog box features that are common to Windows and were described in the first part of this chapter are carried over to Excel. To this Excel adds three additional bars in the application window, four different document windows, and its own menus.

The Excel Application Window

In the Excel application window, shown in Figure 1-8, there are two unique bars at the top of the window under the menu bar. These are the toolbar and the formula bar. In addition, at the bottom of the window is a unique status bar.

The Toolbar

The toolbar provides a set of buttons or *tools* that you can click on to accomplish tasks that would otherwise take several steps with the menus. You can only use the toolbar with the mouse, so if you don't have a mouse you can hide the toolbar and use the space on the screen for other purposes. (Use the Toolbars command listed on the Options menu.)

The toolbar in Figure 1-8, the Standard toolbar, is one of nine toolbars available in version 4 of Excel for Windows. (Previous versions included only one toolbar.) You can turn on other toolbars, turn off the standard toolbar, change the tools, and even add custom tools to an existing toolbar or to a new toolbar you create. You accomplish

Toolbar

Formula bar

Workaheet document window

Status bar

Application window

Figure 1-8.   *The Excel application window*

all of these tasks through the Toolbars option on the Options menu and the Customize button. The Toolbars entry in the Command Reference section explains the over 130 tools available in Excel and describes how to create your own tools.

You can size toolbars; move them around the screen; and arrange, add, or delete tools by dragging them with the mouse. Toolbars are fast and flexible and make working with Excel very efficient.

The Standard toolbar tools are described here:

Tools	Description	Purpose
	New Worksheet	Creates a new worksheet.
	Open File	Displays the Open File dialog box.
	Save File	Saves the active document.
	Print	Prints the active document.
	Style Box	Applies styles to selected cells, or defines a new style based on the selected cells.

Tools	Description	Purpose
Σ	AutoSum	Creates a SUM function in the active cell with a reference to the contiguous range of numbers (either in the column above or in the row to the left).
B *I*	Bold and Italic	Apply and remove bold and italic type styles, respectively.
A▲ A▼	Increase/Decrease Font Size	Respectively enlarge and shrink selected text by one font size.
	Alignment	Apply left, center, and right alignment, respectively, to selected cells.
	Center Across Columns	Horizontally centers text in the leftmost cell across the selected columns.
	AutoFormat	Applies predefined formatting to the selected range.
	Outline Border	Applies a border around the selected cells.
	Bottom Border	Applies a border to the bottom edge of the selected cells.
	Copy to Clipboard	Copies the selected range to the Clipboard.
	Paste Format	Pastes the formatting of the most recently copied range.
	ChartWizard	Assists you in creating charts.
▲?	Help	Changes the mouse pointer to a question mark. Clicking with the question mark on a command or screen area displays context-sensitive help.

The Formula Bar

The formula bar, which is beneath the toolbar, has two main areas: the reference area on the left and the edit area on the right, as you can see in Figure 1-9. The *reference area* generally displays the current cell address. When you are selecting a range, however, it tells you the number of rows and columns being selected. For example,

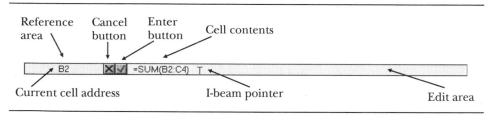

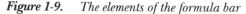

Figure 1-9. *The elements of the formula bar*

while you are selecting the range C3:E4, the reference area will display 2RX3C for two rows (3 and 4) and three columns (C, D, and E). The reference area also has some specialized uses in charting and during several operations.

The *edit area*, which normally displays the contents of the active cell, is used for entering and editing those contents. During data entry or editing, two buttons appear between the reference and edit areas. The left button, with an X in it, is called the Cancel button. Pressing this button is like pressing ESC while editing; it stops editing and ignores any changes made to the cell. The right button, with a check mark in it, is called the Enter button. It has the same function as pressing ENTER while editing; it completes editing and saves any changes in the cell.

When you move the mouse to the edit area it becomes an *I-beam* pointer that you can insert between characters. When you click the I-beam pointer you set the *insertion point.* This flashing vertical line indicates where the next characters you type will be placed. While editing, you can also move the insertion point with the arrow keys. (See Chapter 2 for more information on editing.)

As you enter information into a cell, the information is displayed both in the formula bar edit area and in the cell itself. Often the cell is not wide enough to display all of the information, but the edit area will expand to the full 255 characters that a cell can hold. During entry and to the limit of the cell width, the cell and the edit area will display the same information.

When you complete the entry by pressing ENTER or clicking on the Enter button, the edit area will continue to display the cell contents. The cell will also display the contents if the contents is text or numbers. If the contents is a formula, however, the cell will display the resultant value of the formula, while the edit area will display the formula itself.

The Status Bar

At the bottom of the Excel application window is the *status bar.* It displays messages on the left and the keyboard status on the right, as shown here:

| Edit | | EXT CAPS NUM SCRL OVR FIX |

The message area on the left side of the status bar has several uses. As you are selecting a menu option, the message area displays a brief reminder of what the option does. Similarly, as you select a tool from the toolbar, the status bar displays a brief reminder of what the tool does. When you have a dialog box or an alert message on the screen, the message area tells you how to get help. At other times the message area tells you what Excel is doing by displaying a *mode indicator*. There are 12 mode indicators, the most common of which is Ready mode which means that Excel is ready to receive data or a command. The mode indicators are explained here:

Mode	Meaning
Calculate	The worksheet needs to be calculated.
Circular	A cell is referencing itself.
Copy	Copying is in process; a destination needs to be selected.
Cut	Cutting is in process; a destination needs to be selected.
Edit	Editing is in process.
Enter	Data entry is in process.
Find	A database record has been found and is highlighted.
Help	A help window is being displayed.
Point	A cell or range needs to be selected for use in a formula.
Ready	Excel is ready for a command or an entry.
Recording	The macro recorder is recording what you are doing with Excel.
Split	A window is being split; the column or row on which to make the split needs to be selected.

The keyboard status indicators on the right of the status bar tell you that a certain key has been pressed or that a certain condition exists. The status indicators are explained here:

Indicator	Meaning
ADD	SHIFT-F8, the Add key, has been pressed to select multiple ranges in a single reference.
CAPS	CAPS LOCK has been pressed for entering uppercase characters.
END	END has been pressed, and an arrow key needs to be pressed to move the active cell to the last occupied cell in the direction of the arrow.
EXT	F8, the Extend key, has been pressed to extend the current selection.

Indicator	Meaning
FIX	The Fixed Decimal option has been chosen from Options Workspace. This adds a fixed number of decimal places on all numeric entries, like an adding machine.
MI	The Macro Interpreter has been started to run Lotus 1-2-3 macros.
NUM	NUM LOCK has been pressed for numeric entry with the keypad on the right side of the keyboard.
OVR	Ins has been pressed during editing of a cell to turn on overtype mode instead of insert mode.
SCRL	SCROLL LOCK has been pressed, causing the arrow keys to move the entire worksheet instead of just the active cell.

The Excel Document Windows

Excel has six types of document windows. These display worksheets, charts, macros, cell information, slides, and workbook contents. All the figures and illustrations so far in this book have displayed worksheet document windows similar to the one shown in Figure 1-10.

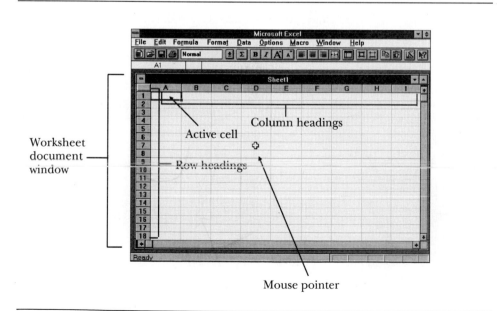

Figure 1-10.   *A worksheet document window*

The Worksheet Window

The worksheet window is divided into rows and columns and has headings on the top and left side of the window that label the columns and rows. One cell in the worksheet has a dark border around it. This cell is called the *active cell* and is the cell you are currently working on. You can move the active cell by clicking the mouse pointer on another cell or by using the arrow keys.

When you initially start Excel one worksheet window is displayed, the active cell is in cell A1, and rows 1 through 18 and columns A through I are displayed (your screen may be slightly different depending on your video display). Besides moving the active cell, you can move the worksheet with the scroll bars or by pressing SCROLL LOCK and using the arrow keys.

While normally you use only one worksheet, you can also have multiple worksheets on your screen. If you do, the worksheet you are currently working in is called the *active worksheet*. It has the active cell in it and has a dark title bar as you can see in Sheet2 of Figure 1-11. The window arrangement in Figure 1-11 is called *tiled*. It is just one of several possible arrangements when you have several worksheets open. Another popular arrangement is the overlapped pattern shown in Figure 1-12. You can control how multiple windows are laid out by dragging the window border, using the Window menu, or using the Control menu.

In addition to opening multiple worksheets, you can split one worksheet vertically or horizontally into two *panes*, or both ways into four panes. Figure 1-13 shows a window split into four panes. By splitting a window, you can look at two or four

Figure 1-11. *Three tiled windows with Sheet2 active*

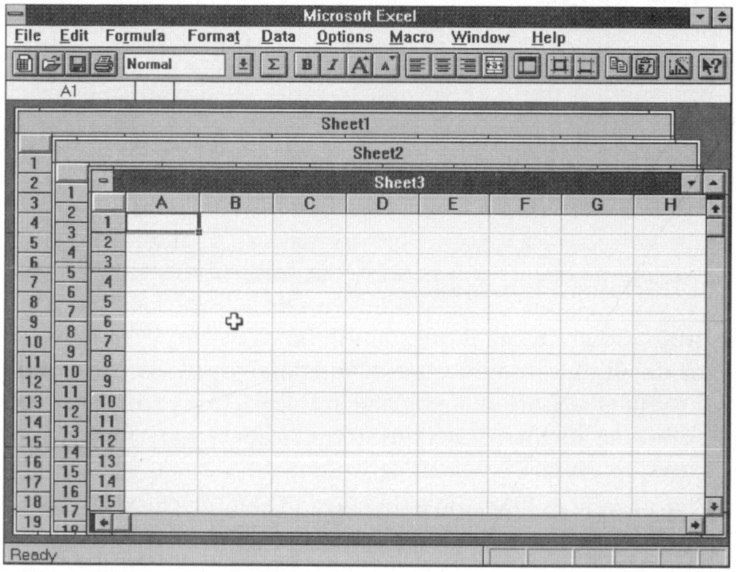

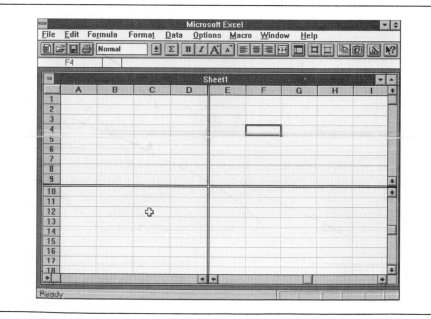

Figure 1-12.   *Three overlapped windows*

Figure 1-13.   *A worksheet split into four panes*

different, perhaps widely separated parts of a single worksheet at the same time. To split a window into four panes, choose Split from the Window menu. If you want only two panes, you can drag one of the pane's center borders off the screen or you can drag the center borders to size the panes. To move from pane to pane, click on the desired pane, press F6 to move clockwise, or press SHIFT-F6 to move counterclockwise. To return to a single pane, you can drag both center pane borders off the screen or you can choose Remove Split from the Window menu.

Other Excel Document Windows

Most of the time you are using Excel you will be using the Worksheet window. It is where you will do all your numerical, text, and database work. You can even use the ChartWizard to build a chart on a worksheet. Excel's five other document windows provide the following ancillary functions to the primary worksheet functions:

- The Chart window allows you to create and change charts. It has both its own set of menus and its own toolbar. Charting and the Chart window are discussed in depth in Chapter 3, "Creating Charts." You create a new Chart window by selecting Chart from the File New dialog box.

- The Macro window displays a macro sheet, which is used to store and edit macro commands. (Macro commands allow you to store keyboard and menu commands to automate a worksheet.) The macro sheet is very similar to a worksheet with the same menus and tools but the cells display formulas rather than their results, as on a normal worksheet, and the normal cell width is wider to facilitate this. You create a new Macro window by selecting Macro from the File New dialog box.

- The Info window displays information about the current cell. The information includes the cell reference, formula, value, format, protection status, names, precedents and dependents, and notes. You open the Info window by selecting the cell for which you want to see the information and then selecting Info Window check box from the Options Workspace dialog box.

- The Slide Show window displays a special document included with Excel and used to produce slide shows. A *slide show* is a series of computer screens (they cannot be printed) that contain charts, graphics, or pieces of worksheets that you create in Excel or import from other applications. You can add special transition effects as well as sound to a slide show. You open the Slide Show window by selecting Slides from the File New dialog box.

- The Workbook window allows you to select various documents (worksheets, charts, and macro sheets) to save as a group. If you repeatedly work with a group of documents, it is handy to open and save them as a group. You open the Workbook window by selecting Workbook from the File New dialog box.

Excel Menus

The normal Worksheet window includes ten menus. Two of these, the Control and Help menus, were discussed in the section "The Windows Environment" earlier in this chapter. The Chart window has three unique menus and the Info window has one unique menu. Therefore Excel has 12 unique menus in addition to the two already discussed. Each of these menus is introduced in the following sections. Specific menu options are discussed more fully in later chapters and in the Excel Dictionary section.

File Menu

The File menu enables you to create, open, close, link, save, rename, delete, and print worksheets, charts, and macro sheets and lets you save combinations of these documents. The File menu also allows you to see a preview of and set up your printed page, set up your printer, structure a printed report consisting of several print ranges, and exit Excel. Finally, you can open one of the last four documents you saved by choosing them from the bottom of the File menu. The File menu is shown here:

```
File
New...
Open...            Ctrl+F12
Close
Links...

Save               Shift+F12
Save As...              F12
Save Workbook...
Delete...

Print Preview
Page Setup...
Print... Ctrl+Shift+F12
Print Report...

1 Q4PLAN.XLS
2 Q3PLAN.XLS
3 Q2PLAN.XLS
4 Q1PLAN.XLS

Exit                 Alt+F4
```

Edit Menu

You can use the Edit menu to undo or repeat the last thing you did, to copy, move (cut and paste), or clear (delete) the contents of a cell or range of cells, to insert and delete rows or columns, and to insert objects. Besides pasting a cell's contents, you can paste just the formula, value, format, or note associated with a cell. The Fill options at the bottom of the menu allow you to quickly copy to a range of cells. The Edit menu is shown here:

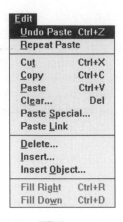

Formula Menu

You use the Formula menu to construct formulas. This includes creating, using, and deleting range names, adding functions, and switching between absolute and relative references. Also, through the Formula menu you can add notes to cells, go to a particular cell, find cells based on their contents, search and replace text, and select cells of a specified type. Finally, the Formula menu provides access to Excel's Outline, Goal Seek, Solver, and Scenario Manager functions. The Formula menu is shown here:

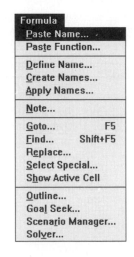

Format Menu

Through the Format menu you determine how a cell entry looks. If it contains a number, you can format it as dollars or percents, with commas, or as scientific notation and then set the number of decimal places. For both text and numbers you can left, right, or center align them in a cell; place a border, pattern, or shading on the cell; protect a cell from being overwritten; and determine a cell's height and width. Finally, you can apply a predefined format to a range, justify text, and manipulate graphic and text objects placed on the worksheet. The Format menu is shown here:

```
Format
  Number...
  Alignment...
  Font...
  Border...
  Patterns...
  Cell Protection...

  Style...
  AutoFormat...

  Row Height...
  Column Width...

  Justify

  Bring to Front
  Send to Back
  Group
  Object Properties...
```

Data Menu

The Data menu is used with databases to define them; to determine selection criteria; to find, extract, or delete selected records based on the criteria; to view and maintain them as a form instead of a table; and to sort them. Also, the Data menu is used to fill a range of cells with a series of numbers or dates, to create a table, to divide or parse a text string into individual cells, to consolidate several data ranges on one or more worksheets, and to summarize data into a crosstab table. Chapter 4 discusses each of the Data menu options more fully. The Data menu is shown here:

```
Data
  Form...

  Find
  Extract...
  Delete
  Set Database
  Set Criteria
  Set Extract

  Sort...

  Series...
  Table...
  Parse...
  Consolidate...
  Crosstab...
```

Options Menu

The Options menu is the catchall menu. It provides the means for specifying the area of a worksheet to be printed, to identify the repeated titles on a printout, and to set manual page breaks. You can also determine how your screen will look, which tools and toolbars are displayed, display a color palette, and protect a document or a window from being overwritten. The Options menu also provides the control of add-in programs; determines how a worksheet is calculated; allows the immediate calculation of a worksheet; and sets workspace defaults like the display of scroll bars, the status bar, the formula bar, the Info window, and whether Drag and Drop is on or not. (Drag and Drop is the capability to copy and move cell contents with the mouse alone. It is described in Chapter 2.)

Finally, with the Options menu you can spell check your document, make changes to a number of documents at once, and access a number of analysis tools. The Options menu is shown here:

Macro Menu

The Macro menu allows you to record a macro function as you carry out commands on a regular worksheet, to run a macro function once it is recorded, and to set several options of recording macros. Chapter 5 fully describes this process. The Macro menu is shown here:

Window Menu

The Window menu is used to open another window on the current active worksheet, to arrange all open windows so they can be seen, to hide and "unhide" a window, and to save a particular view of a worksheet by saving various display and print settings. Additionally, you can split a worksheet into horizontal and vertical panes, freeze a worksheet pane so it stays fixed while the other panes scroll, and enlarge or reduce a view of the worksheet. Finally, you can select from among open windows. The Window menu is shown here:

```
Window
  New Window
  Arrange...
  Hide
  Unhide...
  View...

  Split
  Freeze Panes
  Zoom...

  1 Book1
  2 Q1PLAN.XLS
  3 Q2PLAN.XLS
  4 Q3PLAN.XLS
  5 Q4PLAN.XLS
√ 6 Sheet1
```

Info Menu

The Info menu is available only on the Info window. It allows you to select which items you want to display in that window. The Info menu is shown here:

```
Info
√ Cell
√ Formula
√ Value
√ Format
√ Protection
√ Names
  Precedents...
  Dependents...
√ Note
```

Gallery Menu

The Gallery menu, which is only available on the Chart window, allows you to choose from among 14 chart types and from four to ten alternatives of each type. You can also set a preferred chart type and alternative and return to it after choosing another type and alternative. The Gallery menu is shown here:

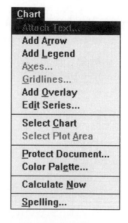

Chart Menu

The Chart menu, available in the Chart window, enables you to add text, arrows, a legend, grid lines, and an overlay to a chart. It also allows you to turn the axes on or off, edit the formulas that produce the chart, select the chart or the plot area, protect the chart from change, define a color palette, calculate the underlying worksheet and redraw the chart, and spell check the chart. The Chart menu is shown here:

Chart Format Menu

The Chart Format menu in the Chart window allows you to change the patterns, font, text, scale, and legend on a chart. You also can select either the main chart or an overlay, change to a three-dimensional view, and move and size an object on the chart. The Chart Format menu is shown here:

Shortcut Menus

In addition to the regular menus that open from the menu bar, version 4 of Excel for Windows adds shortcut menus that open at the current mouse pointer location when you press the right mouse button. Shortcut menus combine options from several regular menus and provide a fast way to get the most heavily used menu options for the current object.

Three examples of shortcut menus are shown here. You can display the Cell shortcut menu by clicking the right mouse button on any cell.

You can bring up the Toolbar shortcut menu by clicking the right mouse button on any toolbar.

```
√ Standard
  Formatting
  Utility
  Chart
  Drawing
  Microsoft Excel 3.0
  Macro

  Toolbars...
  Customize...
```

You can access the Chart shortcut menu by clicking the right mouse button on any chart.

```
Clear    Del

  Gallery...

  Attach Text...
  Axes...
  Gridlines...
  Edit Series...

  Patterns...
  Main Chart...
  Overlay...
  3-D View...
```

Chapter 2

Producing Worksheets

Although Excel has many uses, the most common is to create tables of numbers. Most Excel users produce such tables—or *worksheets*—repeatedly, using the basic skills that you'll learn in this chapter. Mastering these skills is important to any user of Excel, and prepares you for working with more advanced features of the program.

Using Excel begins with simple data entry. Somehow the information has to get from your mind, or from a piece of paper, to a worksheet. Once you put information into worksheet form, you need to be able to move around within that worksheet, change its contents or its overall structure, save the worksheet, and print it. This chapter teaches all these tasks: entering data, navigating the worksheet, editing, saving, formatting, and printing your work.

Entering Data

Chapter 1 explained that data in Excel is either numbers or text; it can't be both. Numbers are information on which you can perform arithmetic, including dates, times, and formulas. Text is everything else, including numbers on which you don't want to perform arithmetic, such as phone numbers and numbers in titles.

Entering Numbers

To enter numbers, type only numbers and the symbols associated with numbers (see "Text and Numbers" in Chapter 1). You can enter numbers either on the keys above the regular keyboard or on the numeric keypad.

The Numeric Keypad

The numeric keypad is on the right of most keyboards. (This keypad is not available on most laptop and notebook computers.) To use the numeric keypad, press your NUM LOCK key—you will see NUM in the status indicator on the right of the status bar. (This key is a toggle; you also press NUM LOCK to turn this feature off.)

If you can use a ten-key adding machine, the numeric keypad may be very convenient for entering a lot of numbers. If you have enabled the NUM LOCK feature, you cannot use the arrow keys located on the numeric keypad without pressing SHIFT; however, most recently designed keyboards include a second set of arrow keys.

Entering Numbers as Text

If you want to enter numbers as text, you must include a nonnumeric character in your data. This cannot be a space at either end of the number, because Excel will ignore those. It can be a space in the middle of the number, or even what you might think of as a numeric symbol. For instance, a telephone number such as 555-1234 is treated as text. (You'll learn more about this in a moment). When Excel thinks you have entered a number, it right-aligns the data; if it thinks you have entered text, it left-aligns the data within a cell, as shown here. (You can also change the default alignment, as discussed later in this chapter.)

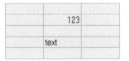

Entering Formatted Numbers

If you want numbers formatted to contain punctuation or special characters, such as commas separating thousands or percent signs following percents, enter the formatting with the numbers. For example, if you want numbers with commas, enter the commas; if you want percentages, enter the percent signs following the numbers. Excel will use its closest standard format to what you entered. Normally, you only have to change the number of decimal places. If you enter the formatting incorrectly or if Excel misinterprets your intent, you can change a cell's or range's formatting after entry in several ways, as you will learn later in this chapter under "Formatting the Worksheet."

Fixing Decimal Digits

If you are entering many numbers, possibly with the numeric keypad, you can fix the number of decimal digits for all entries. You do this with the Fix Decimal Places option on the Workspace Options dialog box, which is shown here:

If you select this option and set the number of decimal places, every number you enter will have the specified number of decimal digits. For example, if you choose 2 decimal places and enter 45 the result will be .45, and if you enter 346 the result will be 3.46. This feature can come in handy if you are used to it; however, it can produce unanticipated results if you forget that it is on. (Excel displays a status indicator in the status bar to remind you.)

Entering Formulas

Formulas are a mathematical expressions for calculating a result. For example, you could use the formulas 4500*.07, PRICE*RATE, or C17*B6 to get the commission paid on a sale. Formulas allow you to extract new information from existing information on a worksheet.

If you want to enter a formula, you must precede it with an equal sign (=), an at sign (@), a plus sign (+), or a minus sign (–). If you forget to do so, Excel will treat your entry as text. For example, if you enter 555-1234, the phone number mentioned above, Excel will treat it as text. However, the formula =555–1234 will give you a number, as you can see here:

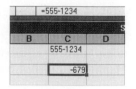

Entering Formulas by Pointing   Although you can type formulas, there is an easier way to enter them: You can point to the cells you want to use in a formula and Excel will capture the cell address in the formula. To use this method, start a formula by typing an equal sign (=), use the mouse or arrow keys to point to the first cell in the formula, and type one of the following arithmetic symbols:

+ – * / ^ % & : , ( )

Then point to the second cell, and so on. To complete the formula, press ENTER. For example, to enter =A12+B14 you would type =, click on A12, type +, click on B14, and press ENTER. You cannot use an arrow key to complete the entry because the arrow key would change the address B14, *not* complete the entry and move to the next cell.

Large Entries

If you enter a number that is larger than the width of the cell, the number will change to ######## or to scientific notation (1.23E+09, for example) in the cell but you will still be able to see the number in the edit area. If you enter text that is longer than the cell is wide, it will spill over into the next cell on the right if that cell is empty. If the next cell contains data, the text will be truncated within the current cell's width, although the edit area will show the complete cell entry. You can see the various effects of entering large numbers and text here:

In the section, "Changing Column Width and Row Height" later in this chapter, you'll learn how to change the width of a cell to accommodate a large entry. Remember that no matter what you see in the cell, your full entry (which can be up to 255 characters long) is still there. You can view your complete entry by selecting the cell and looking in the edit area.

Completing an Entry

You can complete an entry in several ways. If you want to remain in the cell containing the entry, press ENTER or click on the check mark in the Formula bar. (If you activate the Move Selection after Enter option in the Workspace Options dialog box, pressing ENTER will complete the entry and then move the cursor to the next cell on the right; however, this is not advised. As you are about to see there are other ways to do this.)

If you want to go to another cell when you complete an entry, you can press one of the following keys: an arrow key, TAB (which is the same as pressing RIGHT ARROW), HOME, END and an arrow key, PGUP, PGDN, CTRL-PGUP, or CTRL-PGDN. For example, to complete an entry and go to the next cell on the right, press RIGHT ARROW or to complete an entry and go to the next cell below, press DOWN ARROW. (See "Getting Around in the Worksheet" later in this chapter to find out more about these keys.) The three most common entry completion keys, besides ENTER, are LEFT ARROW, DOWN ARROW, and TAB.

Mapping Out a Path for Data Entry

If you're entering a great deal of data, it is worthwhile to map out a path you will follow and then use the appropriate key at the completion of each entry to follow that path—you will save a lot of keystrokes.

For example, if you are entering data in columns, you would press DOWN ARROW after entering a number. If you are entering data in rows, you may use TAB or RIGHT ARROW. If you are entering data and remaining in the cell, perhaps to perform another function, such as to copy the newly entered number to another column, you would use ENTER.

Getting Around in the Worksheet

Remember, the cell you are currently working with—where the data will go when you enter it—is called the *active cell*. This cell has a dark border around it; in addition, its address is displayed in the reference area of the formula bar. Before you enter data, you must activate the cell in which you want the data to be placed.

The easiest way to activate a new cell is to click on it. You can also you use any of the arrow keys, with or without CTRL, and the four other direction keys (HOME, END, PGUP, and PGDN), again with or without CTRL. Many of these keystrokes are intuitive

(RIGHT ARROW moves you right one cell), but others are more subtle and are worth becoming familiar with. The following table summarizes how you can activate a new cell (referred to as *moving the active cell*) with the keyboard.

Keypress	Moves the Active Cell
RIGHT ARROW or LEFT ARROW	Right or left one column
UP ARROW or DOWN ARROW	Up or down one row
PGUP or PGDN	Up or down one window height
CTRL-PGUP or CTRL-PGDN	Left or right one window width
CTRL or END and an arrow key	In the direction of the arrow, to the next occupied cell located before a blank cell
HOME	Left to column A in the row containing the active cell
CTRL-HOME	Up and/or left to cell A1
CTRL-END or END-HOME	Down and/or right to the lowest, rightmost cell containing an entry

CTRL and END Key Combinations

One of the more subtle and useful keystroke combinations is CTRL or END plus an arrow key. CTRL and END do exactly the same thing in this context. If you have come to Excel 4 from earlier versions of Excel, you are used to using CTRL and an arrow key. If you have come from Lotus 1-2-3, you are accustomed to using END and an arrow key. If you are new to worksheet packages, try both methods, and then use the one you find most comfortable.

Pressing CTRL or END and an arrow key quickly moves the active cell around the edge of a block of data. To use the CTRL key and an arrow key, you hold down CTRL while pressing the arrow key. To use the END key, you press and release END and then press one of the arrow keys; you do not have to hold down END. Look at the pattern of data in Figure 2-1. If you started in cell A4 and took the following actions, you would end up in the cells indicated:

1. Press CTRL or END and RIGHT ARROW to go to B4. (As mentioned, you must hold down CTRL while pressing RIGHT ARROW but you can press and release END and then separately press RIGHT ARROW.) B4 is the next occupied cell that is next to a blank cell.

2. Press CTRL or END and RIGHT ARROW again to jump to G4; do this a third time to jump to I4.

3. Press CTRL or END and LEFT ARROW to return to G4.

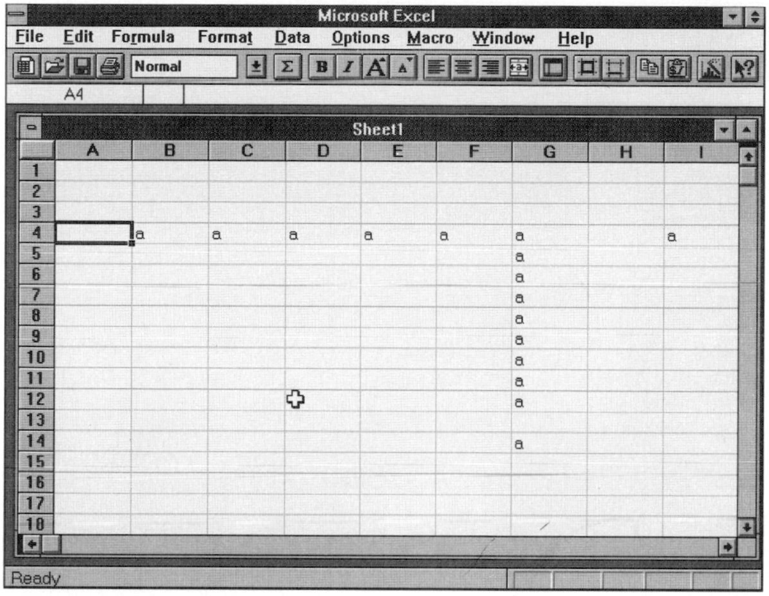

Figure 2-1.   *Using* CTRL *or* END *with arrow keys*

4. Press CTRL or END and DOWN ARROW to jump to G12; do this again to jump to G14.

5. Press CTRL or END and UP ARROW twice to jump first to G12 and then to G4.

Jumping with the Mouse

You can also use the mouse to move the active cell to the last cell in a block. You do this by double-clicking on the active cell border on the side facing the direction in which you want the active cell to move. Using this technique, you can activate a cell not currently visible on the screen. Drag and Drop must be turned on for this mouse procedure to work. (Drag and Drop is turned on by default and is indicated by the very tiny cross in the lower-right corner of the active cell border, as shown in Figure 2-1. If it isn't on already, you can turn it on by selecting Cell Drag and Drop in the Workspace Options dialog box.)

Notice that, with the mouse, you don't always jump to an occupied cell as you do with CTRL and END. Also, from a cell adjacent to a group of cells, such as cell A4 in Figure 2-2, double-clicking the cell border will move the active cell all the way to the opposite end of the group.

For example, if you had the pattern of data shown in Figure 2-2, and if A4 were the active cell, the following actions would move the active cell to the cell indicated:

1. Double-click on the right border of the active cell to move the active cell to G4.

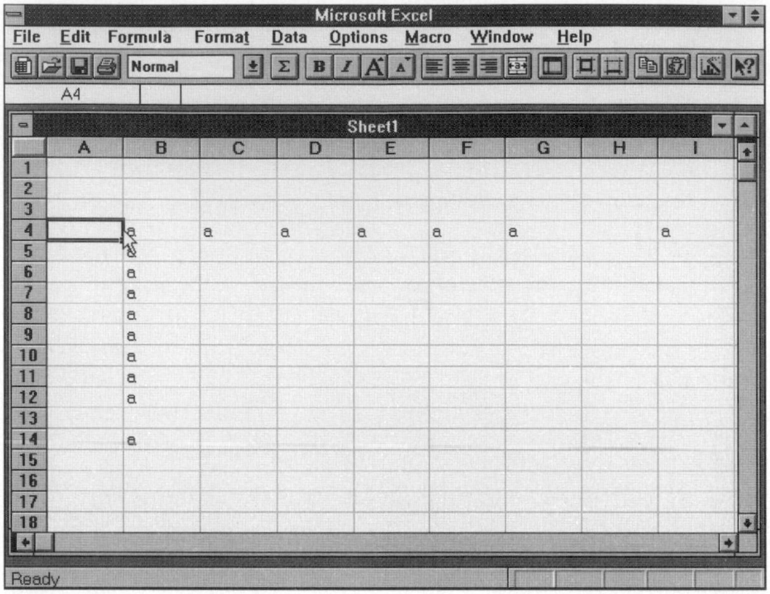

Figure 2-2.   *Doubling-clicking on the cell border*

2. Double-click on the right border of the active cell again to move the active cell to H4.

3. Double-click on the left border of the active cell to move the active cell to B4.

4. Double-click on the bottom border of the active cell to move the active cell to B12.

5. Double-click on the bottom border of the active cell again to move the active cell to B13.

6. Double-click on the top border of the active cell to move the active cell to B4.

Of course, in a real data pattern as small as that in Figure 2-2, you would never use this technique because it is far easier just to click on the cell you want to activate. The mouse techniques covered here are most useful in large worksheets when you must move to areas that are not visible on the screen.

Using the Scroll Bars

Often, when you move the active cell you need to move the part of the worksheet that is being displayed so you can see the new cell. If you use the keyboard to move the active cell, the part of the worksheet being displayed moves with you. If you want to use the mouse in the normal way—by clicking rather than double-clicking—you either have to use the keyboard or scroll bars to move the worksheet.

You can use the scroll bars to move the worksheet in the active document window either up, down, left, or right. As you learned in Chapter 1, to do this you can click on either scroll bar at any of three areas:

- **Scroll Arrows** There are four scroll arrows, one at either end of each scroll bar. By clicking on one of these arrows, you move the active worksheet so you can see one more row or one more column in the direction of the arrow.

- **Scroll Boxes** There are two scroll boxes, one in each scroll bar. You can drag a scroll box to move the active worksheet in the same direction. If you drag a little, the worksheet will move a little; if you drag a lot, the worksheet will move a lot. The scroll boxes also show where you are in a worksheet. If the vertical scroll box is at the top of the scroll bar, you are viewing the top of the worksheet; if it is in the middle, you are viewing the middle of the worksheet.

- **Bar Area** You can move around in the worksheet by clicking on a scroll bar at an area other than the scroll arrows or scroll box. If you click on the vertical scroll bar below the scroll box, you will move the worksheet the height of one window so you can see the area below that previously displayed. If you click on the horizontal scroll bar to the right of the scroll box, you will move the worksheet the width of one window so you can see the area to the right of that previously displayed.

The scroll bars give you three levels of control. You can move the worksheet the greatest distance with the least time and effort by clicking on the scroll bar area itself. Dragging the scroll box lets you move the worksheet by small or large distances, but may not offer the precision you need. Clicking on the scroll arrows moves the worksheet in the smallest, most exact increment: one row or column at a time.

Using Zoom

Beginning with Excel 4, you can magnify or shrink the worksheet to see more or less of it on the screen. This function is handled by the Windows Zoom option and its dialog box, which is shown here:

Zoom works like a camera lens: it allows you to increase or decrease the magnification of the worksheet. You might want to use this feature to see the entire worksheet on the screen, or to verify formulas in one segment of the worksheet, for example. From the dialog box, you can choose five preset magnifications from 25% to 200% (100% is the default) or you can enter a custom magnification from 10% to 400%. Finally, you can select an area of the worksheet and have the worksheet sized to display the entire selection. Zoom only changes the amount of the worksheet that is displayed in a given window; it does not change the window size. Figures 2-3 and 2-4 show the same window, first with a worksheet magnified to 200% and then with the same worksheet reduced to 50%.

Editing Data

When you enter data into a cell, you are in Enter mode. (The word "Enter" appears on the left side of the status bar at the bottom of the screen.) In Enter mode, you can only make changes by pressing BACKSPACE until you reach the error and then retyping what you removed, or by pressing ESC to remove the entire cell contents and retyping it. Also, if you notice an error immediately after completing an entry, you can press ALT-BACKSPACE or select Undo from the Edit menu to restore the prior contents to the cell and then, if desired, retype the desired contents. In all cases, you cannot do

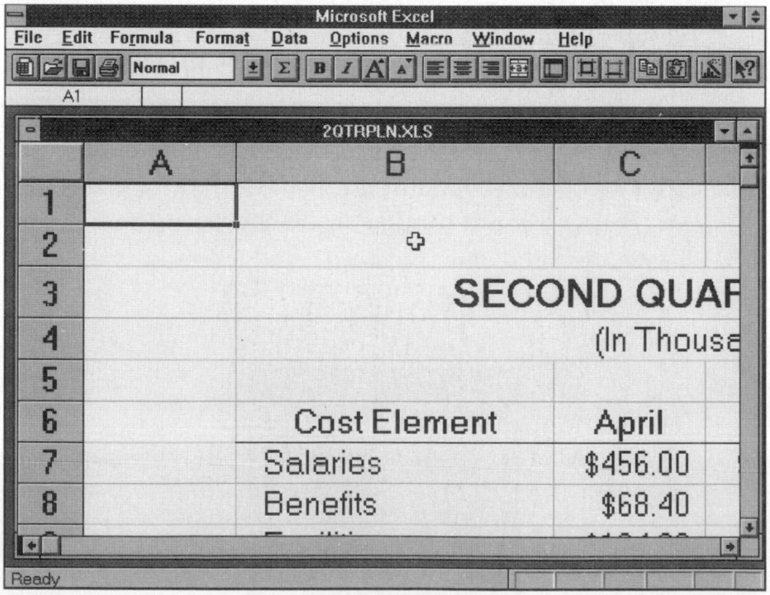

Figure 2-3.   *Worksheet magnified to 200%*

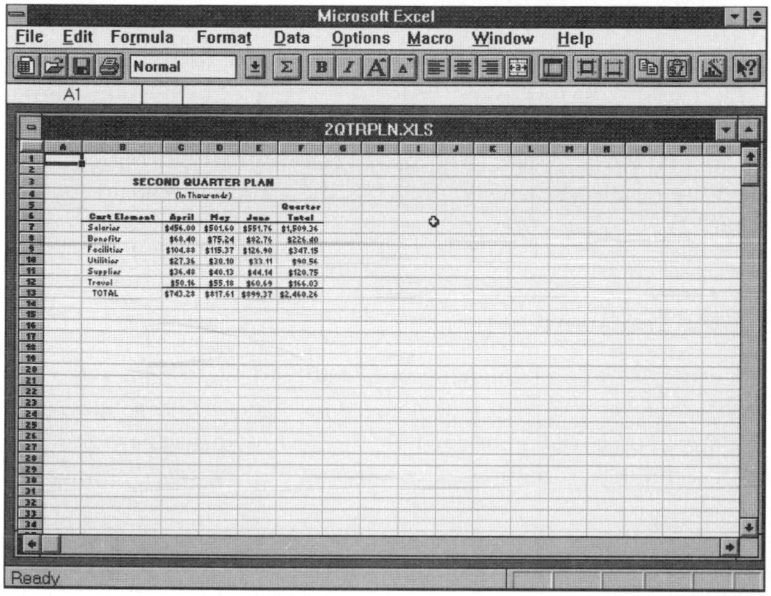

Figure 2-4.   *Worksheet reduced to 50%*

character editing and you must do a lot of retyping unless only the last letter or two are in error.

If you want to change a long cell entry in some small way, you need to switch into Edit mode. (The word "Edit" will appear on the left side of the status bar at the bottom of the screen.) In Edit mode, you can change one or more characters anywhere in the entry without affecting the other characters. To edit a cell, you must first activate it by clicking on it or using the arrow keys. Once the cell is selected, you can either click in the right side of the formula bar or press F2 to activate the edit area and go into Edit mode. You can also use either of these methods to switch to Edit mode while you are entering data.

The I-Beam Pointer and the Insertion Point

While you are entering and editing data, several things are different in the edit area, as you saw in Chapter 1. Moving the I-beam pointer and clicking the mouse places a vertical line, or insertion point, in that location. New characters that you type are added at the immediate left of the insertion point, so if you know where you want to add characters, you can just click there and begin typing. If you want to delete or replace some characters, simply drag across them and either press DEL or type the replacement characters. You can also select characters to delete or replace by pressing SHIFT-LEFT ARROW or SHIFT-RIGHT ARROW.

Insert Versus Overtype Mode

Under normal circumstances, characters that you type at the insertion point are added to the text already in the cell; they don't replace the current contents of the cell. This is called *insert* mode and is the default in Excel. You can also press the INS key to switch to *overtype* mode, where characters you type replace any existing characters in their path. (When you press INS, the OVR status indicator comes on in the status bar.)

Editing with the Keyboard

Although the mouse can perform many important tasks relating to editing and entry, much editing requires that you type some data. Since you are already using the keyboard, many people find it handy to use the keyboard to get around the edit area and perform some other functions. The keys you can use while editing are summarized here:

Keypress	Function
BACKSPACE	Deletes the character to the left of the insertion point.
CTRL-LEFT ARROW or CTRL-RIGHT ARROW	Moves the insertion point one word to the left or right in the entry.
CTRL-DEL	Deletes text from the insertion point to the right end of the current line.
CTRL-'	Inserts the formula from the cell above.
CTRL-"	Inserts the value from the cell above.
CTRL-;	Inserts your computer's current date.
CTRL-:	Inserts your computer's current time.
DEL	Deletes the character to the right of the insertion point.
END	Moves the insertion point to the right end of the current line in the entry.
ENTER	Completes editing, closing the edit area without moving the active cell.
ESC	Cancels any changes made during editing, closes the edit area, and returns the original contents to the active cell.
F2	Activates the edit area so you can edit the active cell.
HOME	Moves the insertion point to the left end of the current line in the entry.

Keypress	Function
INS	Switches between insert and overtype forms of data entry while in Edit mode.
LEFT ARROW or RIGHT ARROW	Moves the insertion point one character to the left or right in the entry.
UP ARROW or DOWN ARROW	Moves the insertion point one line up or down if the entry occupies more than one line.
SHIFT and an arrow key	Selects data being edited in the direction of the arrow.

Spell Checking

A final way to edit your worksheet, if you have Excel 4 and above, is to check your spelling. You check the spelling for your worksheet text by selecting the Spelling option from the Options menu. You can choose to check a word, a selected range, an embedded chart, or the entire worksheet depending on what is selected when you start the spelling checker. (The entire worksheet is checked if only a single cell is selected.) You can also check the spelling of the text on a chart document by selecting the Spelling option from the Chart menu. If you do a lot of spell checking, you can display the Utilities toolbar and use the Spelling tool on that toolbar or move the tool to another toolbar you normally display.

On a worksheet, the spell checking starts with the active cell. If a word in the cell does not match a word in the dictionary, the Spelling dialog box opens, as shown here. In this case, an alternative is suggested and several other possibilities are shown. (If a similar word cannot be found in the dictionary, Excel may not be able to present any alternatives. In that case, you may have to resort to another source, such as a printed dictionary.)

Just click on the Change button if you want to replace a misspelled word with the suggested word in the Change To box. If you prefer one of the words in the

Suggestions box, click on the word and then click on the Change button. You can change the present use of the word or you can change all instances throughout the worksheet.

Excel will sometimes stop to check the spelling of words that are not necessarily misspelled, but which do not appear in its spelling dictionary. Such words may be acronyms, abbreviations unique to your work, or other words that you commonly use; you can add them to the custom dictionary by clicking on the Add button.

Finally, after you have corrected the misspellings from the active cell to the end of the worksheet, Excel will ask you if you want to continue spell checking from the beginning of the worksheet or stop spell checking. If you select a word or phrase in the edit area or a range on the worksheet, the selected item is checked, you are notified of the outcome, and the spell checking operation is completed.

Saving and Opening Worksheet Files

When you create a new worksheet or a chart, it resides in your computer's temporary memory (RAM). If you want to save the document so you can leave Excel and then come back and work on it later, you must store the document as a disk file. You do this with the Save option in the File menu.

Naming Files

To save a file, you must give it a name. The full name of a file has three parts, a path, a filename, and an extension. The path is made up of a disk drive letter followed by a colon (for example, C: or A:) and one or more directory or subdirectory names of up to eight characters enclosed within backslashes (for example, \EXCEL\ or \EXCEL\DATA\). You can create a tree structure of subdirectories within directories such that a full path might be C:\EXCEL\PLANS\SALES\1993\.

A filename is one to eight characters long. It can consist of any combination of letters, numbers, and the following special characters:

~ ' ! @ # $ % ^ & ( ) - _ { } '

A filename may *not*, however, include blanks or any of these characters:

< > , . ? / " ; : [ ] | \ + = *

Filename Extensions

An optional extension may follow the filename. It begins with a period and can be up to three characters long, not counting the period. Unless you override it (which is not recommended), Excel automatically creates an extension for all the files it creates. This automatic extension helps Excel and other applications tell what kind of file they are working with. The extensions that Excel can read and/or write are listed here:

Extension	Type of File
.CSV	Comma-separated values text files
.DBF	dBASE II/III/IV database files
.DIF	VisiCalc worksheet files
.FMT, .FM3	Lotus 1-2-3 format files
.SLK	Multiplan worksheet files
.TXT	Text files
.WKS, .WK1, .WK3	Lotus 1-2-3 1A, 2.*x*, and 3.*x* worksheet files
.XLA	Excel macro add-in files
.XLB	Excel toolbar files
.XLC	Excel chart files
.XLL	Excel commercial add-in files
.XLM	Excel macro sheet files
.XLS	Excel worksheet files
.XLT	Excel template files
.XLW	Excel workbook files

Storing Related Documents in a Workbook

Often your Excel projects may include several Excel documents: one or more worksheets, several charts, and possibly a macro sheet. Each of these documents can be stored in its own file. However, in that case you must open all of the files one at a time when you work on the project. It is easy to forget or misplace a file, and, since charts are dependent on worksheets for their data, you may find yourself with only part of what you need to get the job done. Microsoft has solved this problem in Excel 4 with a new document type called a workbook. A *workbook* stores a group of related documents in a single document so you only have to open and close one document and no documents can get lost.

You can attach a document to a workbook in one of two ways: It can be *bound* into a workbook, in which case it is stored with the workbook and not as a separate file. (A document is bound in the workbook by default.) Alternatively, a document can be *unbound,* in which case it is referenced in the workbook but is stored as a separate file. If a document is unbound, it can be referenced in several workbooks; however, bound documents cannot be referenced in another workbook.

A workbook provides a table of contents that lists all of the documents that are bound and unbound into the workbook. Figure 2-5 shows a sample workbook in

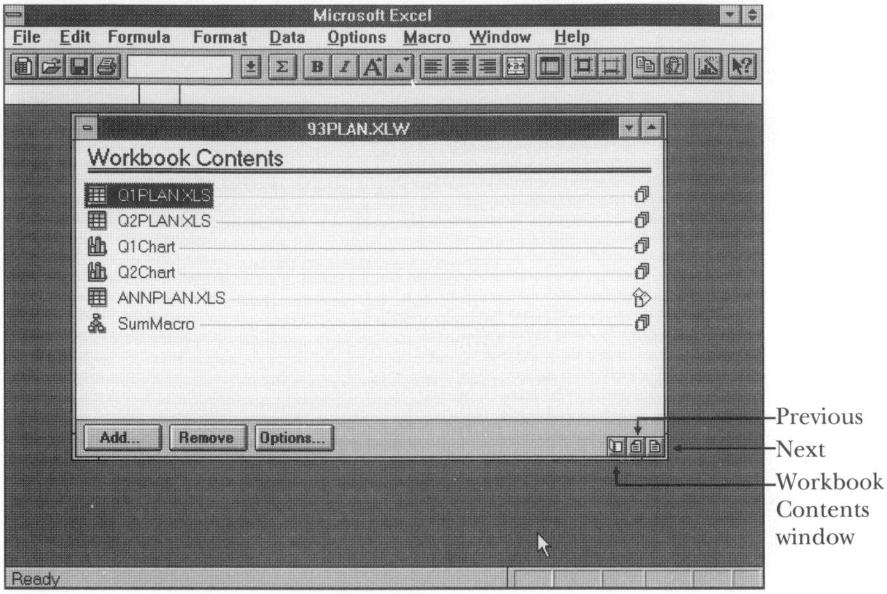

Figure 2-5.   *The Workbook Contents dialog box*

which all of the documents are bound into the workbook except ANNPLAN.XLS, which is unbound. Note the different icons to the right of the file names.

If you want a document to be unbound in a workbook or if you want to give a long description (up to 31 characters) to a document, select the document and click on the Options button in the Workbook Contents window. The Document Options dialog box shown here will open:

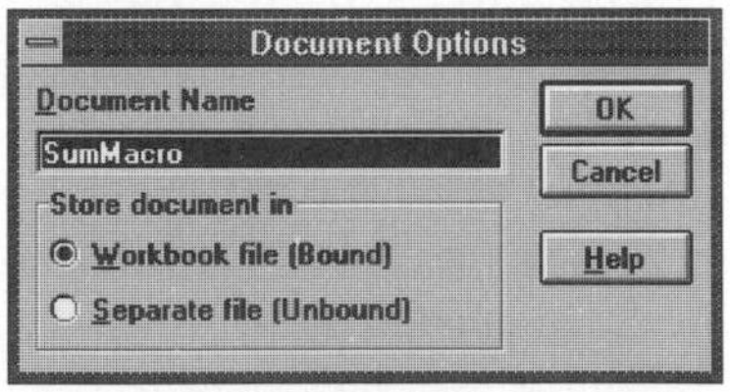

Type the long description in the text box and/or click on the Separate File option button for a document to be unbound.

Creating a New Workbook

To create a new workbook, choose New from the File menu, then select Workbook from the File New dialog box. If you then want to create a new document within the workbook, click on Add, then New, and select the document type. If you want to add an existing document that is not currently open, click on Add, then Open, select the document, and click on OK and Close. If the document is already open, you can identify the document either by dragging the Select All button at the intersection of the column and row headings to the Workbook Contents window, or by clicking on Add. If you click on Add, then select the document from the displayed list. Click on OK if there is only one such document, or click on Add and select the next document if there is more than one, as shown here:

NOTE: If the document you want to add to a workbook is a chart, it does not have a Select All button and you must choose Select Chart from the Chart menu and then drag one of the square selection boxes to the Workbook Contents window.

Within the Workbook Contents window, you can rearrange documents simply by dragging them to their new location.

You can remove a document from the workbook by dragging it outside the Workbook Contents window or by selecting the document and clicking on Remove.

All documents associated with a workbook have three icons in the lower-right corner. These are, from left to right:

- The Contents icon, which opens the workbook contents window when you click on the icon.

- The Previous icon, which displays the previous document in the workbook.

- The Next icon, which displays the next document in the workbook.

Opening Files

Once a file is saved, you can work with it again in the future. To do this, open the file or the workbook that contains it by choosing Open from the File menu. The Open dialog box appears, as shown here:

To use the File Open dialog box, first select the disk drive and directory in which the file resides. Then select the file you want to open from the list that Excel presents. If you open a workbook, you can then select the desired document from the Workbook Contents window.

In addition to Excel files, Excel will directly open files from Lotus 1-2-3 (all versions), dBASE (II through IV), Multiplan, VisiCalc, and two kinds of text files (pure text files and comma-separated text files). You can then work with these files in Excel with the same or more extensive facilities than are available in the original applications.

Leaving Excel

When you are done working in Excel, you can exit the program in several ways. The easiest way is to double-click on the Control-menu box in the upper-left corner of the Excel application window. From the keyboard, the easiest way is to press ALT-F4. Using either the mouse or the keyboard, you can also select the Exit option in the File menu.

As Excel is shutting down, it checks whether there are any unsaved files. If there are, Excel warns you and allows you to save these files before returning to Windows.

Manipulating Data on the Worksheet

Entering and editing information in Excel, which chiefly involves typing, is laborious and should be minimized. Fortunately, Excel provides many ways to manipulate and reuse existing data on a worksheet to save you from having to reenter it. These time-saving techniques include copying and moving data and formulas, inserting and deleting rows and columns, and changing the cell width and height.

Copying Information

Excel provides several ways to copy information from one location to another on a worksheet. Among these are the Drag and Drop technique with the mouse, CTRL-C or CTRL-INS with the keyboard, and the Copy option on the Edit menu.

Using Drag and Drop

The Drag and Drop technique, which was introduced with Excel 4, is the easiest and most intuitive copying method. For this technique to work, Cell Drag and Drop must be turned on (checked) in the Workspace Options dialog box. You can tell if Drag and Drop is turned on if there is a small cross in the lower-right corner of the active cell border. (This cross appears in most figures and illustrations in this book.)

You can perform two types of copy operations with Drag and Drop: you can copy one cell or range to another cell or range of the same size (one-to-one copying), and you can copy one cell or range to a larger range (one-to-many copying).

One-to-One Copying   The simplest form of copying is from one cell to another or from one range to another range of the same size. Use the following steps do this:

1. Select the cell or range you want to copy.

2. Hold down the CTRL key while moving the mouse pointer to the cell or range border on the side closest to where you want to copy the cell or range. The pointer becomes an arrow, as shown here:

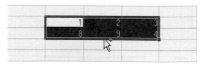

3. While holding down the CTRL key, hold down the left mouse button and move the mouse in the direction in which you want to move the cells to be copied. As you move the mouse, a rectangle the size of original range moves with the mouse. This rectangle indicates where the data would be copied if you released the mouse button at that point, as you can see here:

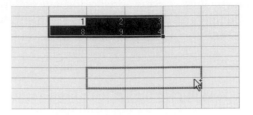

4. When you get to the location where you want to insert the copied material, first release the mouse button and then release the CTRL key. If you release CTRL first, you will *move* the range instead of copying it. A successful completion of the copy looks like this:

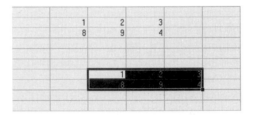

Inserting While Copying   In normal copying operations like the one you just did, any data in the destination cells is replaced by the information being copied. If you immediately choose Edit Undo or press CTRL-Z, you can recover what has been overwritten, but otherwise it is gone.

Instead of copying over cells, you can insert copied material between two rows or two columns. To do this, hold down SHIFT and CTRL while selecting the destination for the copied material. When you hold down SHIFT and drag the range to be copied, the rectangle representing the destination area becomes an elongated I-beam. In this example, information is being inserted between "Top Row" and "Bottom Row":

You can insert the copy between two columns by pointing on a column border (the vertical segments) and you can insert material between two rows by pointing on a row border (the horizontal segments). When Excel thinks you want to insert material between two rows, the I-beam is horizontal, like the one you just saw. The I-beam is vertical when the copy will be inserted between two columns, as shown here:

If the I-beam is horizontal, place it at the intersection of the two rows between which you want to insert the copied information; if it is vertical, place it at the intersection of the two columns between which you want to insert the copy. When the I-beam is in place, release the mouse button *before* releasing SHIFT and CTRL.

One-to-Many Copying   Copying one cell or range to a larger range is called *filling*; Drag and Drop allows you to do this with the mouse. There are four types of fill operations: copying one cell to a row of cells, copying one cell to a column of cells, copying a row of cells to a block of cells, and copying a column of cells to a block of cells. Figure 2-6 illustrates each of these types of filling.

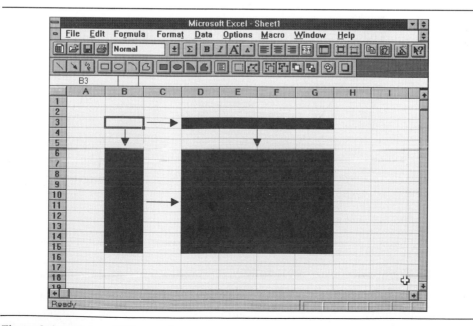

Figure 2-6.   *Types of fill operations*

You can fill with the mouse by dragging on the small Drag and Drop cross in the lower-right corner of the active cell or range. Use the following steps:

1. Select the cell or range you want to copy.

2. Move the mouse pointer to the lower-right corner of the cell or range you want to copy; the mouse pointer will become a crossbar like the one shown here:

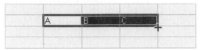

3. Hold down the left mouse button while dragging the mouse in the direction you want to fill. As you are in process of filling, the active range border expands to show what area will be filled, as you can see here:

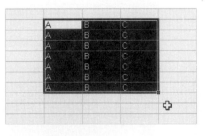

4. When you have highlighted the area you want to fill, release the left mouse button. The area will be filled, as shown here:

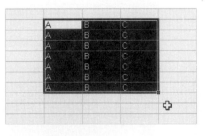

Using the Keyboard

You can copy with the keyboard by using CTRL-C or CTRL-INS. Either of these two key combinations make a copy of the currently selected cell or range. CTRL-INS is a

Windows standard and is common to most Windows applications; CTRL-C is unique to Excel and several other applications. You can use either of these *shortcut keys* for either one-to-one copying or filling (one-to-many copying), as outlined here:

1. Select the cell or range to be copied, and then press either CTRL-C or CTRL-INS. A flashing dashed line, or *marquee,* will appear around the selected area, as shown here:

2. Select the cell to copy to (for one-to-one copying), or the range to fill, as shown here:

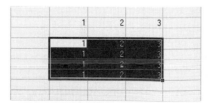

3. Press ENTER to complete the copy or fill operation. A completed fill might look like this:

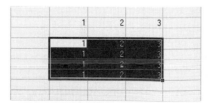

Notice that in the fill operation you just completed, you copied a row to a column and got a block that measures the width of the original row and the height of the column you highlighted. This illustrates an aspect of one-to-many copying: the source range provides one dimension, and the destination range that you highlight provides the second dimension.

Using the Menu

The Excel Edit menu provides several options that you can use for copying. These include Copy, Paste, Insert Paste, Paste Special, Fill Down, and Fill Right.

Using Edit Copy and Copying to the Clipboard   Using the Copy option on the Edit menu is the same as pressing CTRL-C or CTRL-INS. This same Copy command is also available on the Shortcut menu, shown here, that you open by positioning the mouse pointer on a cell and clicking the *right* mouse button.

Also, the Copy tool, the fourth tool from the right on the Standard toolbar, performs the same function as the Copy option on the Edit menu. After selecting a range to be copied, you can start a copy operation in four ways: with the CTRL-C or CTRL-INS shortcut keys, with the Copy option on the Edit menu, with the Copy option from the Shortcut menu, and with the Copy tool. When you use any of these methods, you are placing a copy of the selected information on the Clipboard. The *Clipboard* is a Windows feature that provides temporary storage for *one* item that is being copied. When you copy a second item, the first item is replaced by the second.

Using Edit Paste to Paste from the Clipboard   Using the Paste option on the Edit menu is similar to pressing ENTER at the end of the copy process. However, when you press ENTER to complete the copy, the Clipboard is emptied. If you want to make another copy of the same cells, you must again copy them to the Clipboard. If you use the Paste option or one of its shortcut keys, CTRL-V or SHIFT-INS, you can copy from the Clipboard repeatedly. The marquee will stay around the original cells copied to the Clipboard until you perform another operation or press ESC.

Edit Insert Paste   The Insert Paste option only appears on the Edit menu when you have just copied something to the Clipboard. This option is similar to inserting while copying with Drag and Drop. However, you use the Insert Paste dialog box shown here to determine if you want to insert the material between rows (Shift Cells Down) or between columns (Shift Cells Right).

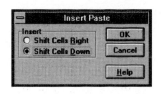

To copy material by using the Insert Paste option from the Edit menu, follow these steps:

1. Select the cell or range to be copied.

2. Copy the selected cells to the Clipboard using any of the four possible methods: Copy from the Edit menu, CTRL-C or CTRL-INS, Copy from the Shortcut menu, or the Copy tool (fourth from the right on the Standard toolbar).

3. Select the cell or range above which or to the left of which you want to insert the copied cells.

4. Choose Insert Paste from the Edit menu, determine whether you want to insert the copy between rows (Shift Cells Down) or columns (Shift Cells Right), and then click on OK.

The current cells will be shifted and the copy will be inserted as specified.

NOTE: Only the cells directly affected by an insert operation are shifted, not entire columns or rows. If you want to shift entire rows or columns, you must use the Insert option on the Edit menu, which is described later in this chapter.

Edit Paste Special   When you perform a normal copy operation, you copy everything in the cell: the value, any formulas, formatting, alignment, and notes. The Paste Special option on the Edit menu allows you to select which of these items you want to copy, with the exception of alignment. Selecting Paste Special displays the dialog box shown here:

In some cases, you may want to copy both the value and the format. If you don't want the formulas and notes, you must choose Paste Special twice, once each for value and format. Otherwise, use the normal Paste option or use Paste Special and click on All. The alignment always goes with the formatting; if you copy the formatting, you'll get the alignment.

The Paste Special option on the Edit menu also allows you to mathematically combine the current cell contents with what is being copied, assuming that they are both numbers or formulas that evaluate to numbers. To do this, follow these steps:

1. Copy the first value to the Clipboard.

2. Select the second value.

3. Choose Paste Special from the Edit menu.

4. Select the mathematical operation desired, and click on OK.

Edit Fill   The Edit menu has four Fill options, two when you open the menu normally (Fill Right and Fill Down) and two more when you hold down SHIFT and open the menu (Fill Left and Fill Up). To make these options work, you must select *both* the originating cells containing the information to be copied and the cells to be filled, as shown here:

The information in the left, top, right, or bottom cells— depending on whether you are filling right, down, left, or up—is copied into the remaining highlighted cells. As in most copy operations, the original contents of the cells receiving the information is replaced by the information being copied.

You can fill cells with Edit Fill, Edit Copy, or Drag and Drop. Drag and Drop is faster if you have it turned on. However, Edit Fill is faster than Edit Copy because you have only one cell selection and one menu selection compared to two of each with Edit Copy.

Copying Formulas

When you copy a number or text from one cell to another, you copy the exact contents, letter for letter or number for number, to the new location. A formula such as =A1+A2 that is in A3 is not of much value when it is copied to B3 unless it is changed to =B1+B2. Excel knows this, and unless you tell it otherwise, it automatically changes a formula to fit the new location into which it is copied.

Relative and Absolute Addressing   This ability to adjust a formula when it is moved from one location to another is called *relative addressing*. The formula is always adjusted relative to its location. For example, if you have a formula =A1+A2 contained within cell A3, and move the formula to cell B3, Excel would interpret the copied formula as:

="the cell 2 cells up"+"the cell 1 cell up"

In other words, the copied formula in cell B3 becomes =B1+B2. Such a formula will work anywhere on the worksheet. Of course, sometimes you want to fix one or more parts of an address so that it cannot be changed. If the entire address is fixed—locked on to a particular cell no matter where you copy it—the addressing is called *absolute addressing*. A cell address, like A1, is made up of a row component, the 1, and a column component, the A. If one part of the address is fixed and the other part is relative, the addressing is called *mixed addressing*.

To make an address absolute or mixed, type a $ in front of the address component you want to be fixed. If both the column and row portions of the address are fixed, you place a $ in front of each, as shown below. In other words, if you copied the formula =$A$1 from C3 to D3, it would remain =$A$1 instead of changing to =$B$1.

You can also press F4 to make an address in a formula absolute or mixed immediately after you type it. For example, if you type =**B1** and then immediately press F4 before completing the entry, Excel will change the formula to =$B$1. You can continue to press F4, and Excel will cycle through the all four possible combinations of addresses, as shown here:

If You Have	Pressing F4 Will Yield	Type of Address
B1	$B$1	Absolute
$B$1	B$1	Mixed (fixed row)
B$1	$B1	Mixed (fixed column)
$B1	B1	Relative

F4 always cycles through the alternatives in the same order, independent of where you start.

Moving Information

Moving information is the same as copying that information to a new location without leaving a copy in the original location. With Drag and Drop, moving is just like copying except you *don't* hold down the CTRL key. You still press SHIFT to insert the information being moved instead of replacing information on the worksheet. With the keyboard, you use CTRL-X or SHIFT-DEL to begin a move operation; with the Edit or Shortcut menus, you initiate a move operation by selecting the Cut option. You complete a move operation by pressing ENTER or choosing the Paste option from the

Edit or Shortcut menus. In this context, however, you cannot paste multiple copies and you cannot use Paste Special.

Moving with Drag and Drop

The steps involved in moving a cell or a range with Drag and Drop are listed here:

1. Select the cell or range to be moved.

2. Move the mouse pointer to the selected cell or range border on the side facing the destination of the move operation.

3. Hold down the left mouse button while dragging the cell or range to its new location. (If you want to insert the moved information between existing cells, hold down SHIFT while pressing the left mouse button.)

4. When the border representing the range to be moved is in position, release the mouse button to complete the move operation. (If you are inserting rather than overwriting, release the mouse button *before* releasing SHIFT.)

For further information on using Drag and Drop, see "Using Drag and Drop" earlier in this chapter.

Moving with the Keyboard or the Menus

Moving a cell or a range with the keyboard and with the menus involves the same steps, which are listed here:

1. Select the cell or range to be moved.

2. Use one of two methods to cut (transfer to the Clipboard) the information to be moved: Press CTRL-X or SHIFT-DEL or choose Cut from either the Edit or Shortcut menu.

3. Select the destination for the material to be moved, the cell in the upper-left corner of the receiving range.

4. Use one of three methods to complete the move: press ENTER, press CTRL-V or SHIFT-INS, or choose Paste from either the Edit or the Shortcut menu. (If you want to insert the information being moved, choose Insert Paste from the Edit menu and then select either Shift Cells Right or Shift Cells Down and click on OK.)

Deleting Information

It's easy to delete information from the worksheet: you select the cell or range, press DEL, and click on OK. The Clear option on both the Edit and Shortcut menus does the same thing as pressing the DEL key. When you choose the Clear option or press DEL, you'll see the following dialog box, which lets you choose what to clear:

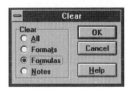

The Clear dialog box options are as follows:

Option	Result
All	Erases everything (contents, formats, and notes) from the cell and returns it to the General format.
Formats	Erases only the formats of a cell, leaving the contents and notes. The cell is returned to the General format.
Formulas	Erases only the contents of a cell, leaving the formats and the notes.
Notes	Erases only the notes in a cell, leaving the formats and the contents.

The Formulas option is the default and the one that is normally used.

Inserting Cells, Rows, and Columns

Instead of moving information on a worksheet, it is often easier to insert cells, rows, or columns around and even within existing data. For example, if you have a worksheet that lists sales or expense categories and you want to add a new category, you could move down the categories that you want to be positioned below the new one. However, an easier approach that accomplishes the same thing is to insert a cell, shifting down existing cells beneath it, or to insert a row, shifting down all rows beneath it.

Inserting Rows and Columns

To insert rows or columns, follow these steps:

1. Select the number of rows or columns that you want to insert by clicking on the row or column labels at the left or top of the worksheet, beginning with the row that you want to be directly beneath the inserted row or the column that you want to be directly to the right of the inserted column.

2. Choose Insert from the Edit or Shortcut menu. The rows or columns will be inserted.

Inserting Cells

Inserting cells is similar to inserting rows or columns. However, you must select not only the number of rows or columns you want to insert, but also that portion of a row or column that you want to move. For example, if you wanted to insert a block of six cells in two rows above B4:D4, you would select the cells shown here:

Once the desired range is selected, choose Insert from the Edit menu. Since it is not obvious how you want to shift the original cells when you are inserting cells, Excel presents a dialog box, shown here, that lets you specify how you want the insertion performed.

In this case, you want to shift the cells down, which is what Excel guessed, so you can just click on OK. When you do, the result will look like this:

Deleting Cells, Rows, and Columns

Deleting cells, rows, and columns is much like inserting cells, rows, and columns. When you delete rows or columns, you select the ones you want to delete by clicking on their labels and choosing Delete from the Edit menu. To delete cells, select them, choose Delete from the Edit menu, select between Shift Cells Left and Shift Cells Up, and click on OK. The Delete dialog box looks like this:

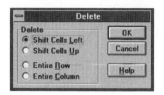

Inserting and deleting cells, rows, and columns can sometimes affect formulas on the worksheet. For example, if you delete column B and cell B4 is referenced as an individual cell (not in a range) in a formula elsewhere in your worksheet, you will get a #REF! error where B4 was referenced since that reference is no longer valid. Excel has gone to some length to prevent this from happening, but you should still check your formulas immediately after an insert and especially after a delete operation. If you find an error at that point, you can use CTRL-Z or Edit Undo to reverse your steps.

Ranges are almost totally immune to errors resulting from inserting and deleting. Not only can you insert and delete cells in the middle of the range, you can also delete the named first and last cells in the range and the range will be correctly adjusted. The only possible problem is that if you insert one or more cells at the first cell in the range, the inserted cells will go before (either to the left or above) the first cell and will not be included in the range.

Changing Column Width and Row Height

The final way to change the structure of the worksheet is to change the column width and the row height. You can do this by using the mouse or the menu system.

Using the Mouse

It's easy to use the mouse to change the column width and row height: You point to the intersection of two rows or two columns in the row or column headers at the left or top of the worksheet. When the mouse is in the right position, the mouse pointer changes into a crossbar with arrows on the top and bottom for changing the row height, as shown here:

The mouse pointer changes to a crossbar with arrows on the right and left side for changing the column width, as shown here:

When the mouse pointer is in the correct location, you simply drag the row or column intersection with the mouse. The row height or column width will change as you move the mouse, and you will see the size change on the left side of the formula bar. If you want to change several rows or columns at the same time and by the same amount, select them all and then change any one of them. The rest will also change by the same amount.

Using the Menus

To change the column width and row height using the menus, you must first select the rows or columns to be changed. Then open the Format menu and choose Row Height or Column Width. Choosing Row Height opens the dialog box shown here:

Choosing Column Width opens this dialog box:

In either dialog box you can enter a new row height or column width, return to the standard height or width, or hide or unhide the selected rows or columns. With columns, you can also specify a new standard width, or use the Best Fit command button to set the width to fit the widest information in each column being changed.

Formatting the Worksheet

The previous section explained how to change the structure and contents of the worksheet; this section describes how to change its appearance. You can change your worksheet's appearance in several ways. You can align text and numbers, format text and numbers, and add borders, patterns, and color. Each of these topics will be discussed in the upcoming sections.

Aligning Text and Numbers

When you enter any information into Excel, it is given the *General* alignment. As you saw earlier in this chapter, Excel normally aligns text on the left of a cell and numbers on the right of a cell. Excel also centers error values like #REF! and logical values like TRUE. While this alignment style is fine for a default, you will often want to change the alignment. You do this by selecting the cells to be aligned and clicking on the appropriate tool (right, center, or left aligned) in the toolbar, or by choosing Alignment from the Format menu to open the dialog box shown here:

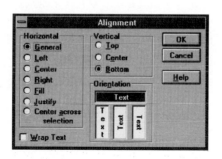

The Alignment dialog box also enables you to align information in a cell vertically and to change the orientation of text. The Justify button permits you to evenly distribute over a block of cells text that is in several cells. Finally, the Fill button allows you to fill the cell with whatever character you enter in the cell.

Centering Text over Several Columns

The Center Across Selection option in the Alignment dialog box, which is new with Excel 4, allows you to center a title over several columns. You do this by entering the title (any text) in the left-hand column, selecting the columns over which you want the text centered (including the one it's in), and then selecting the Center Across

Selection option. Alternatively, you can click on the Center Across Selection tool, the eighth tool from the right in the standard toolbar.

Formatting Numbers

Excel uses many forms of numbers, including dollars, percentages, times, and dates. Not surprisingly, Excel provides many different number formats as well as different ways of applying formatting.

Earlier in this chapter, you learned that the easiest way to apply formatting is to enter it as you enter the number. In other words, if you want numbers to include dollar signs and commas, type them as you type the number. The only problem with this approach is that you must enter a number in a format recognizable to Excel (it must be the same or similar to one of Excel's standard formats, which are discussed shortly), and you must accept the standard number of decimal places. If you want other formatting, you must use the Number option on the Format menu.

Using the Format Number Menu Option

The Number option on the Format menu offers a variety of standard formats and lets you customize these formats to suit your needs. Choosing Number from the Format menu opens the Number Format dialog box shown here:

This dialog box provides eight different format categories—such as Currency, Date, and Percentage—and a number of different formats for each category. If you highlight a number before opening the dialog box, Excel uses that number to illustrate what the selected formatting will look like. This enables you to try several alternative formats before making a final decision.

If you want to use a nonstandard format—for example, a percentage with a single decimal place—you can create it in the Number Format dialog box. Just above the sample at the bottom of the dialog box is a text box labeled Code in which you can edit the current format. To use this text box, select the closest standard format and edit it to meet your needs. To create a percentage with a single decimal place, select the Percentage format with two decimal places and delete one of the decimal places.

The codes used in formatting are explained under the FORMAT NUMBER entry in the Excel Dictionary section of this book.

Formatting Text

Formatting text involves changing the appearance of both text and numbers. You can change the font and size and apply styles such as bold, italics, or underlining. You format text by selecting the text to be formatted and then either using the Format Font dialog box or the tools on the Standard or the Formatting toolbar.

The Format Font dialog box, shown below, allows you to choose the font, the font size, and the font style for currently selected text. You can also choose a text color and can determine whether text is underlined or has a line through it. The fonts that are listed in your dialog box are dependent on your printer and what has been loaded into Windows so they probably differ from those shown here.

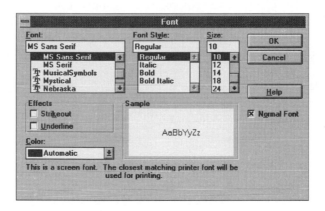

Five formatting tools are available on the Standard toolbar. These are the Style box, the fifth tool from the left, and bold, italic, increase font size, and decrease font size, the seventh through tenth tools, respectively. When you click on one of these tools, its formatting is applied to the selected text. The tear-out card at the back of the book shows and describes each of these tools.

Using the Style Box

The Style box in the Standard toolbar includes a series of predefined formatting styles. Clicking on the arrow next to the box opens the list. At this point, you can click on a style to apply it to the currently selected text. You can also define a new style by selecting text on the worksheet that includes the desired formatting, clicking the mouse on the Font Style list box, typing the style name, and pressing ENTER.

Using the Formatting Toolbar

The Formatting toolbar, shown in the Tools tear-out card at the back of the book, contains several tools that are the same as the Standard toolbar. In addition, you can select the font name and size, and apply either an underline or a line through the text. The Formatting toolbar also has tools for justifying text; applying the standard Currency, Percentage, and Comma number formats; and increasing and decreasing the number of decimal places. Finally, the Formatting toolbar lets you apply light shading to areas of the worksheet and apply the currently selected AutoFormat format (which you can designate with the Format AutoFormat option).

Adding Borders, Patterns, and Colors

You can add borders, patterns, and colors to a worksheet. You can do this with either the Border or Patterns options on the Format menu or with the AutoFormat option or tool.

The Border option on the Format menu opens the Border dialog box, shown here:

This dialog box allows you to apply a border of any of eight line styles either all around the selected cells (the Outline option) or on any of the four sides. Also, you can make the border any of a number of colors and you can add shading inside the border.

The Patterns option on the Format menu opens the Patterns dialog box, which you can see here:

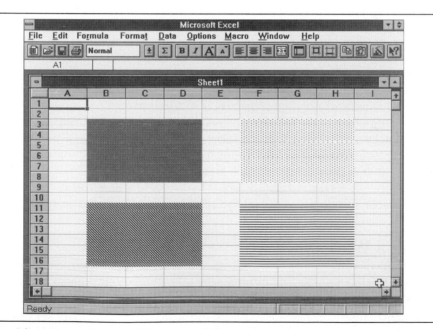

This dialog box allows you to choose among a number of patterns to apply to the selected cells and then to apply both a foreground and background color to the patterns. If the pattern is solid, only the foreground color shows. Figure 2-7 shows four of the 18 possible black-and-white patterns applied to a worksheet.

Figure 2-7.   Four patterns applied to a worksheet

Using AutoFormat

Excel 4 has added an easy method for applying some professionally designed formatting to your worksheet. The AutoFormat option on the Format menu brings up a dialog box that lists 5 formatting styles and 14 formatting schemes, as shown here:

Each of the formatting schemes provides a combination of number formats, fonts, alignment, borders, patterns, colors, column widths, and row heights, allowing you to format your entire worksheet with one click of the mouse. Additionally, the dialog box displays a sample of each of the formats so you can preview the results.

To use AutoFormat, select the area of the worksheet that you want formatted, choose AutoFormat from the Format menu, and select the formatting you want. If you change your mind immediately after applying the formatting, you can use Edit Undo or CTRL-Z to reverse the process.

You can also customize the application of AutoFormat by clicking on Options and then selecting which of the following formatting areas you want AutoFormat to apply to: number format, border, font, pattern, alignment, and width or height. Finally, after using AutoFormat, you can manually change the formats you've applied by using the other options on the Format menu.

Once you have formatted the worksheet to your satisfaction, you are ready to print it out on paper.

Printing a Worksheet

Before it can print a worksheet, Excel must have information about what and how to print. The "what" is the area on the worksheet that you want printed, and the "how" is the many parameters such as margins and headings that you can set to control printing. If you set up your printer in Windows, you can print using Excel's initial defaults. To produce more polished output, however, you need to set some parameters.

Defining What To Print

If you do not define an area of the worksheet to be printed, Excel will print all of the occupied cells. This is an area from A1 to the cell in the lower-right corner formed by the row containing the lowest occupied cell and the column containing the rightmost occupied cell. You can press END-HOME to view this cell.

If the default area just described is not what you want to print, you need to define a print area. You do this by selecting the area on the screen (point to the upper-left cell and drag with the mouse to the lower-right cell). Then choose Set Print Area from the Options menu.

If you want to redefine the print area, simply repeat the previous steps with the new area. If you want to restore the default print area, choose Define Name from the Formula menu, select Print Area from the Names in Sheet list box, click on Delete, and then click on OK.

Setting Up a Printed Page

To enter margins, headers, and other parameters for a printed page, you need to use the Page Setup dialog box that you open from the File menu. It is shown here:

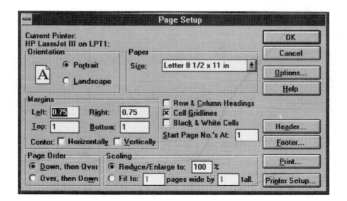

The Page Setup dialog box allows you change the print orientation from *portrait,* where the long side of the page is vertical, to *landscape,* where the long side is horizontal. Also, you can turn on and off row and column headings and grid lines, and you can force items in color to print in black-and-white instead of in grey patterns. You can stipulate that cells are printed by column (Down, then Over), which is the default, or by row (Over, then Down). You can also enlarge or reduce the size of the printed information or scale it to fit on a given number of pages.

Setting Margins

Margins are the distance in inches from the edge of the page to the printed data or chart on four sides: top, bottom, left, and right. You determine the maximum width of a printed line by subtracting the left and right margin from the page width. For example, using the default 3/4-inch left and right margins and the standard 8 1/2-by-11-inch page, you can print a line that is 7 inches wide.

The top and bottom margins are the distance from the top and bottom of the page to the start or end of normal printed worksheet information, *not* the header or footer. The distance from the edge of the page to the header or footer is approximately 1/2-inch. Also, the header and footer always use the default left and right margin of 3/4-inch.

Under the Margins text boxes are two check boxes that allow you to center your worksheet or chart horizontally and vertically. This can save you a lot of time by making Excel calculate the width and height of your print selection and subtract it from the page width and height.

Adding Headers and Footers

The Page Setup dialog box has two command buttons on the right that allow you to open separate dialog boxes for entering headers and footers. The Header dialog box, which is very similar to the footer dialog box, is shown here:

A *header* is a line of text that is included at the top of every printed page. It often contains a page number, date, and a descriptive line of text (like a company name or the name of a report). A *footer* is a line of text added to the bottom of every printed page. As a default, the header contains the name of the current worksheet file and the footer contains the page number.

A header or footer can have up to three segments: a left-aligned segment, a centered segment, and a right-aligned segment. In Excel 4 and on there are three separate boxes for entering these segments. You simply click on and type in the box for the segment you want.

There are six tools above the three segment boxes. These are, from left to right, for adding formatting such as bold or italic, page number, total number of pages, date, time, and the worksheet filename. Before using these buttons, you need to select the segment in which you want the item. Clicking on one of the buttons places a code in the selected segment. For example, &P and &F are the codes for the page number and the filename, respectively. In versions of Excel prior to 4, you had to enter the codes manually. A complete list of these codes is supplied under the PAGE.SETUP entry in the Excel Dictionary section of this book.

Printing

The actual printing process is a bit anticlimactic after you've set up the page. You simply select Print from the File menu or from the Page Setup dialog box. When you do, the Print dialog box opens, as you can see here:

This dialog box is for the HP LaserJet III printer. The dialog box for your printer may be slightly different but should have most of the options shown here. You can specify the number of copies you want; print all or only selected pages; preview the output on your screen; and print just the worksheet, just the notes, or both.

If you select Preview and click on OK, an image of what the printed page will look like fills your screen. This lets you check the margins and heading without wasting time or paper. If necessary, you can go back to the Page Setup dialog box from the Preview screen. When the preview looks good, select Print and, assuming your printer is installed properly, you will get a printed copy of what you saw on the screen.

When you tell Excel to print, it creates a print job in memory that contains all of the information to be printed, and sends it to the Windows Print Manager. You can then go back to work while the Print Manager is printing in the background. You can have several print jobs in memory waiting to be printed. The Windows Print Manager enables you to cancel a job after it has left Excel and to rearrange the priority of the jobs waiting to be printed. For small worksheets and fast printers, the advantage of the Print Manager is not very evident, but with large jobs it offers a significant benefit.

Chapter 3

Creating Charts

Charts let you view information in pictorial form. Many people find worksheet information easier to understand when it is presented as a chart rather than as rows and columns of numbers. Excel's charting capabilities allow you to present information visually with 14 different types of charts. You can create each type of chart in as many as ten formats. You can also customize your charts by adding text, arrows, and legends.

This chapter explains how to create charts from worksheet information, describes the available chart types, and illustrates how to customize, format, and edit charts.

Preparing Information

You can create *embedded* charts, which are graphic elements of the worksheet and are saved with it; you can also create *chart documents*, which are separate from the worksheet and which you can view, edit, print, and save by themselves. Both embedded charts and chart documents are updated as you change the source information on the worksheet.

Creating a chart begins with selecting a range on the worksheet to provide the source information for the chart. Once you select the area of the worksheet that you want to chart, Excel offers three methods for creating, formatting, and editing charts: the ChartWizard, the Chart toolbar, and the chart menus. Each of these methods will be discussed later in this chapter.

Selecting Data

When selecting data to be transformed into a chart, you must follow certain guide-lines. Figure 3-1 contains a simple worksheet showing conference attendance in several locations for four years. An embedded Column chart of this information is placed below it on the worksheet. The range used to create the chart is highlighted, indicating it has been selected. We will use this worksheet and chart to show how to select information to chart.

Excel interprets the selected range of cells as a group of *data points*—one for each cell containing a number not formatted as a date. A row or column of related data points is a *data series*. In Figure 3-1, each number in the selected range—except the numbers in the top row, which are formatted as dates—is a data point. These are grouped into four data series, one for each city. In this example, each row is a data series. The data is also organized into *data categories*. A data category has one data point from each data series. In Figure 3-1, the column for each year (the category) is one data category that contains one data point (the attendance) from each data series (the city).

Excel creates a chart by plotting the data categories along the X axis, or *category axis,* and the values in the data series on the Y axis, or *value axis.* (Normally the X axis is horizontal and the Y axis is vertical.) The first data series begins with the first cell in the upper-left corner of the selected range containing a number not formatted as a date. The data series continues across the selected rows or columns. In Figure 3-1,

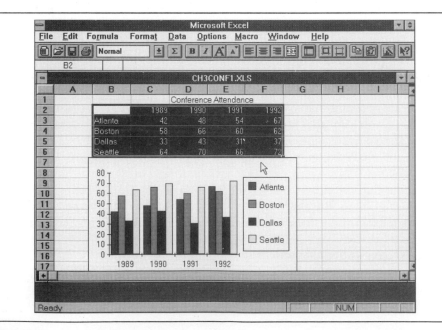

Figure 3-1.   *Data selected for a chart*

the first cell that meets the criteria for a data point is C3, making the first data series the row with the data for Atlanta. The first data point of the series is 42, the attendance for the first data category, 1989. As you can see in Figure 3-1, this is the first data point plotted. Next to it is the first data point for the second data series, the attendance for Boston in 1989.

Excel determines whether the data series are arranged *rowwise* (across rows) or *columnwise* (down columns) by whether more rows or more columns are selected. Since there are normally more data categories than data series, Excel assigns the data categories to the larger of the two. When you have an equal number of rows and columns selected, the data series are assumed to be rowwise. When there are more data series than data categories you will have to define the data series by using ChartWizard or the chart menus, as described later in this chapter.

Excel attempts to identify the chart's *category labels*, the text used to label the plot for each category, by looking at the upper-left cell in the selected range. If it is blank, or if the top row and/or leftmost column contain text or dates, the contents of the top row and/or leftmost column are used for the category labels. In Figure 3-1, the range B2:F6 has been selected. The upper-left cell (B2) is blank, and the data series are rowwise, so the top row (the conferences dates) becomes the category labels. The leftmost column becomes the *series names* (the conference locations). The rest of the selected range may contain text or numbers, but the text will be treated as zeros.

If a range is selected without text to be used for the category labels and series names (if the cell in the upper-left corner contains a data point, for example), you can add the labels and names with the chart menus. This topic will be covered later in the chapter.

On the Y or value axis, the numbers are in the same format as the numbers on the worksheet. If the data is formatted as currency, the value labels on the Y axis will also be formatted as currency. Excel scales the Y-axis range so that the largest data point to be plotted will be at or near the top edge of the displayed area of the chart. If the largest value to be plotted is 987, Excel will probably make 1,000 the largest value on the Y axis.

Multiple Selection

You can make a *multiple selection* to create a chart from several ranges that are not adjacent on the worksheet. When working with a multiple selection, Excel treats the selected ranges as a single rectangle. If the selected ranges cannot be combined into a single rectangle, the cells that won't fit in the rectangle will be ignored. Figure 3-2 shows a multiple selection; only the information for Atlanta and Seattle in the years 1990 and 1992 has been selected to be charted.

In Figure 3-3 the same ranges have been selected, with the exception of cell D6. When creating the chart in this case, Excel will ignore all the numbers from the Seattle data series because they cannot be combined with the other data to form a single rectangle.

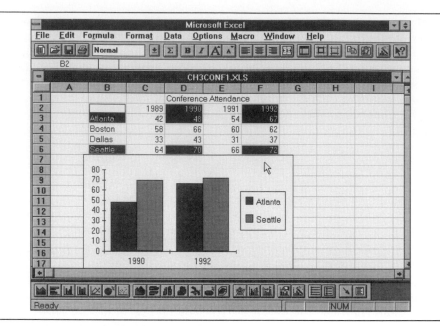

Figure 3-2.   *Multiple selections*

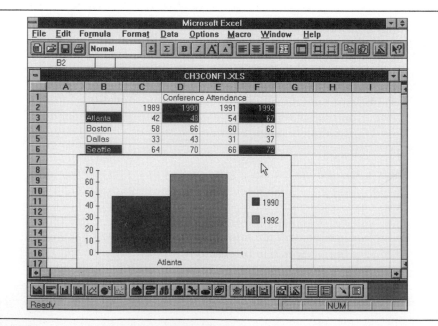

Figure 3-3.   *A non-rectangular multiple selection*

To make a multiple selection, select the first range as you would normally; then hold down the CTRL key as you select the additional ranges. You can also make multiple selections by selecting the first range, pressing SHIFT-F8 (Add Selection), and then selecting the other ranges.

Chart Types

Excel can create eight types of *two-dimensional* charts and six types of *three-dimensional* charts, with up to ten formats for each chart type. Two-dimensional (2-D) charts have two axes, the X or horizontal axis, and the Y or vertical axis. Three-dimensional (3-D) charts have a third axis, the Z axis, which is at a right angle to the X and Y axis and adds depth to the chart.

The Column chart is the default, or *preferred type* of chart. Excel will usually create this chart type unless you change the preferred type. Each chart type also has a default, or *preferred format*. This is the format the chart type will use when it is created. Changing the preferred type and preferred format settings will be covered later in this chapter.

Some chart formats control how the data will be plotted, while others add formatting, such as grid lines, labels, or legends to the chart. Most chart formats present the worksheet information as numerical values. Some chart formats, however, are used to show relative values—each data point is plotted as a percentage of the sum of a category. Area, Bar, Column, and Pie charts all have formats that plot the sum of a category as 100 percent, and express each number as a percentage of the total.

Each chart type and format will present the selected information in a different pictorial form. Which chart type will work best for a particular set of data depends on the information you are illustrating. The following sections discuss each chart type and its formats.

Area Charts

An area chart shows how the sum of several related values changes over time, and also shows the relative contribution of each individual value. For example, the chart in Figure 3-4 shows the sum of each year's attendance as well as the contribution of each city.

In the basic area chart, each data series is plotted above the previous data series. In this example, the first data point of the first data series (Atlanta, 1989) is 42, and the first data point of the second data series (Boston, 1989) is 58. In the column chart in Figure 3-1, the first point of the first series is plotted at 42 and the first point of the second series is plotted at 58. In the Area chart in Figure 3-4, the first point of the first data series is plotted at 42 and the first point of the second data series is plotted

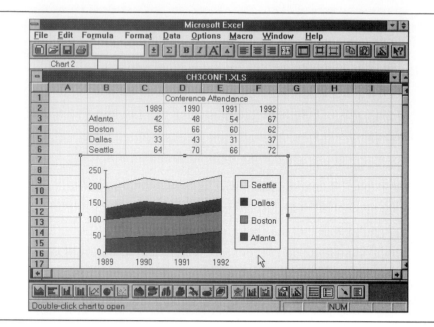

Figure 3-4. *An area chart*

at 100, the sum of the two data points. An Area chart is actually a stacked line chart, with the area between each line filled with color or shading.

There are five available formats for area charts:

- The basic area chart is the preferred format. It is also available from the Chart toolbar.

- The sum of the numbers from each data series in each category equals 100. Values are presented as a percentage of the sum of the data series.

- Drop lines are added along the chart's X axis.

- Grid lines are added to the chart.

- A legend showing the names of the data series is placed on the chart.

Three-Dimensional Area Charts

Three-dimensional area charts are similar to their two-dimensional counterparts, but a three-dimensional format allows Excel to plot each data series as a separate object placed behind the preceding one, as shown in Figure 3-5, as well as plotting all the series cumulatively. In other words, in a three-dimensional chart, the different data series can be plotted either parallel to each other or on top of each other.

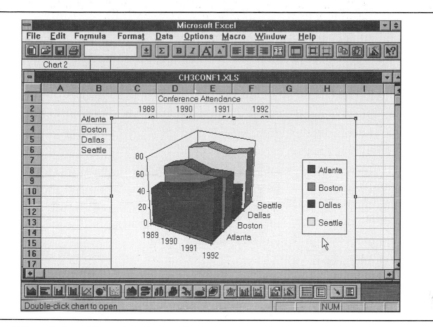

Figure 3-5.   *A three-dimensional area chart*

There are seven available formats for three-dimensional area charts:

- The basic three-dimensional area chart is the same as the basic two-dimensional area chart with a third dimension (depth) added.

- Value labels are added to the chart.

- Drop lines are added along the chart's X axis.

- Grid lines are added to the chart.

- The three-dimensional plot draws each data series as a separate object adjacent to the preceding data series. This is the preferred format. It is also available on the Chart toolbar.

- X-axis, Y-axis, and Z-axis grid lines are added to the three-dimensional plot.

- X-axis and Y-axis grid lines are added to the three-dimensional plot.

Bar Charts

Bar charts are useful when you need to place more emphasis on the individual values rather than the series. Each bar represents one number (data point) at one point in the series. As an example, Figure 3-6 shows the conference attendance for one city plotted as a bar chart.

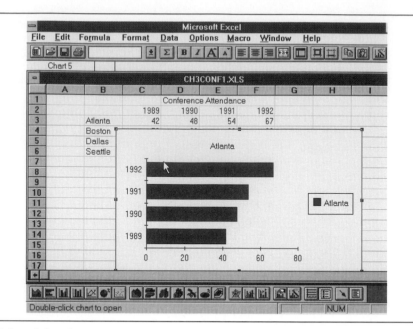

Figure 3-6.   *A bar chart*

There are ten available formats for bar charts:

- The basic bar chart plots each value as an individual bar and allows positive and negative values. This is the preferred format. It is also available on the Chart toolbar.

- Plots the numbers from a single data series, using varied patterns and/or colors for each bar.

- The stacked bar chart, like the area chart, stacks data points one on top of the other. The length of the bar is the sum of the numbers from each data series.

- Overlaps each data series over the previous data series. The percentage of overlap can be modified.

- In the 100% bar chart the sum of the numbers from each data series in each category equals 100 percent. Values are presented as a percentage of the sum of the data series.

- Vertical grid lines are added to the chart.

- Value labels are added to the chart.

- No space is left between each category.

- A stacked bar chart with lines connecting the numbers of each data series.

- A 100% bar chart with lines connecting the numbers of each data series.

3-D Bar Charts

Three-dimensional bar charts are very similar to two-dimensional bar charts, with an extra dimension (depth) added, as you can see in Figure 3-7. There are four formats of three-dimensional bar charts available:

- The basic three-dimensional bar chart plots each value as a three-dimensional bar. This is the preferred format. It is also available on the Chart toolbar.

- A stacked three-dimensional bar chart.

- A 100% three-dimensional bar chart.

- The basic three-dimensional bar chart with grid lines added.

Column Charts

Like bar charts, column charts use bars to show the data point values. However, while bar charts use horizontal bars, column charts use vertical bars. Column charts have

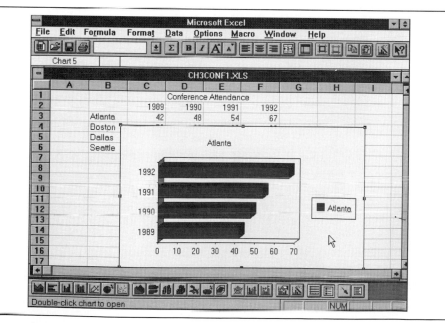

Figure 3-7. *A three-dimensional bar chart*

the same formats available as bar charts and represent numbers in the same way. Figure 3-8 shows the conference information as a two-dimensional column chart.

Three-Dimensional Column Charts

Three-dimensional column charts resemble their two-dimensional counterparts. As with three-dimensional bar charts, the principal difference is that they plot data series along an additional axis, as shown in Figure 3-9.

There are seven available three-dimensional column formats:

- The basic three-dimensional column chart plots each value as a three-dimensional column. It is the preferred format. It is also available on the Chart toolbar.

- A stacked three-dimensional column chart.

- A 100% three-dimensional column chart.

- Horizontal grid lines are added to the chart.

- The three-dimensional plot has each data point plotted as a separate column. This is the preferred format.

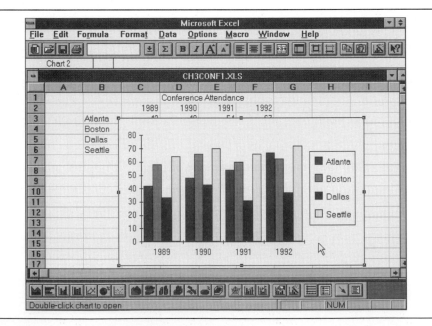

Figure 3-8.   *A column chart*

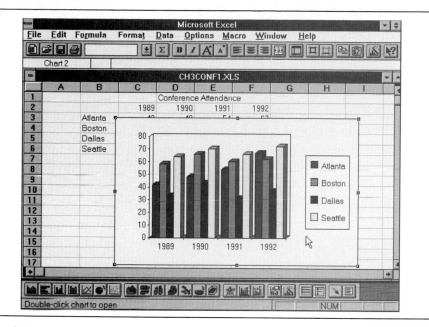

Figure 3-9.   *A three-dimensional column chart*

- A three-dimensional plot with X-, Y-, and Z-axis grid lines added.

- A three-dimensional plot with only X- and Y-axis grid lines added.

Combination Charts

A combination chart is one type of chart overlaid on another chart type. Combination charts are used to compare two types of related data, such as stock price and volume sold. Another example is the relationship of sales to advertising expenses that is shown in Figure 3-10. The sales are plotted as columns, with their value scale on the left vertical axis of the chart. The advertising expenses plotted as a line, with their value scale on the right vertical axis of the chart.

In a combination chart, the data series are always divided evenly between the two types of charts. If the number of data series is uneven, an extra series is placed on the base chart, giving the overlay one less data series.

Combination charts have six formats available:

- The basic combination chart is a column chart overlaid with a line chart. This is the preferred format. It is also available on the Chart toolbar.

- A column chart overlaid with a line chart but with a separate value scale on the right for the line chart.

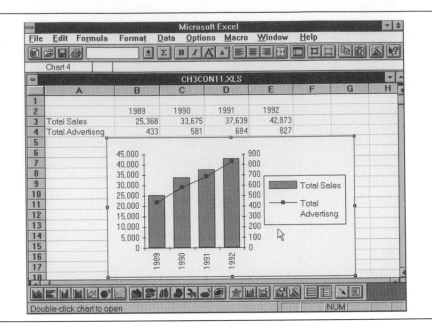

Figure 3-10. *A combination chart*

- A line chart overlaid with another line chart with a separate value scale for the overlaid line chart.

- An area chart overlaid by a column chart.

- A column chart overlaid by a hi-lo-close, or stock market, chart. Stock market charts are a type of line chart, and are described in a moment.

- A column chart overlaid by an open-hi-lo-close, or stock market chart.

Line Charts

Line charts emphasize changes over time. Like area charts, line charts allow projections into the future. Figure 3-11 shows the conference data plotted as a line chart. There are nine available formats for line charts:

- The basic line chart places a marker on each data point and the markers in each data series are connected with a line. This is the preferred format. It is also available on the Chart toolbar.

- Only the lines connecting each data point are shown.

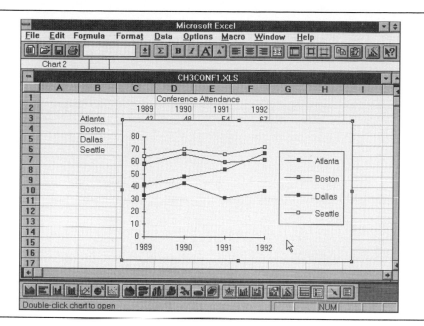

Figure 3-11. *A line chart*

- Only the markers on each data point are shown.

- Horizontal grid lines are added to the basic chart.

- Horizontal and vertical grid lines are added to the basic chart.

- The data series are plotted on a logarithmic scale with horizontal grid lines added to the chart.

- The markers on each data point are connected by a line between the high and low value in each category.

- The hi-lo-close stock market chart described next.

- The open-hi-lo-close stock market chart described next.

Stock Market Chart

The stock market or hi-lo-close chart is a special form of line chart that uses three data series to show a stock's high, low, and closing prices. This type of chart is also useful for commodity prices, currency exchange rates, and temperature and pressure measurements. An open-hi-lo-close chart, using four data series, is also available. Figure 3-12 shows a hi-lo-close chart. Both types of stock market charts are available as part of combination charts.

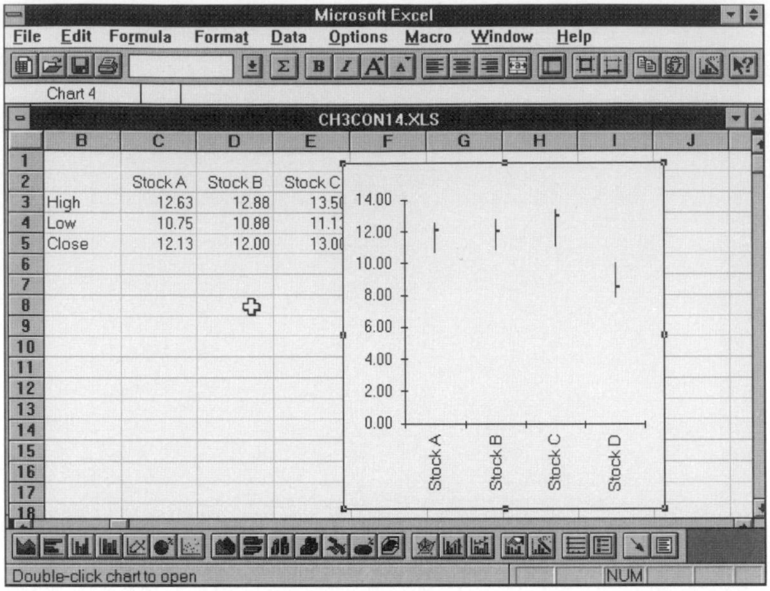

Figure 3-12.   *A hi-lo-close (or stock market) chart*

Three-Dimensional Line Charts

The lines in the three-dimensional line charts are drawn as two-dimensional ribbons, as shown in Figure 3-13. There are four formats available:

- The basic three-dimensional line chart. This is the preferred format. It is also available on the Chart toolbar.

- The basic three-dimensional line chart with X-, Y-, and Z-axis grid lines added.

- The basic three-dimensional line chart with X- and Y-axis grid lines added.

- The data series are plotted on a logarithmic scale with logarithmic grid lines added to the chart.

Pie Charts

The pie chart is used to show percentage distributions. The entire pie represents 100 percent of one data series. Each data point in the series becomes one wedge of the pie, representing its percentage of the total. A pie chart shows only one data series. If more than one data series is selected on the worksheet, only the first will be charted.

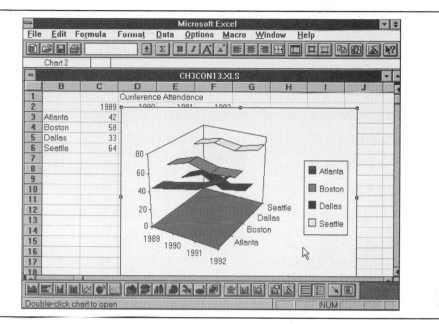

Figure 3-13.   *A three-dimensional line chart*

A pie chart representing the first data series from the conference worksheet is shown in Figure 3-14.

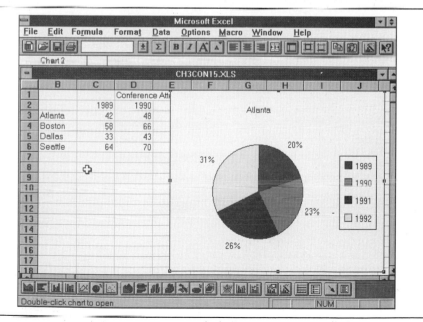

Figure 3-14.   *A pie chart*

There are seven available formats for pie charts:

- In the basic pie chart, each wedge has a different color or pattern. This is the preferred format.

- Each wedge has the same color or pattern but each category is labeled.

- The first wedge is separated (exploded) from the rest of the pie.

- All the wedges of the pie are separated from each other.

- The categories are labeled.

- Value labels are shown as percentages. It is also available on the Chart toolbar.

- Value labels are shown as percentages, and category labels are displayed.

Three-Dimensional Pie Charts

Three-dimensional pie charts show data series the same way that two-dimensional pie charts do, except with depth, as shown in Figure 3-15. The formats available duplicate the two-dimensional formats.

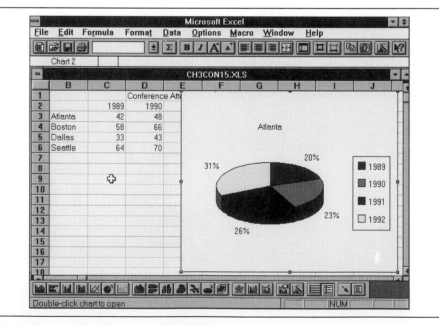

Figure 3-15. *A three-dimensional pie chart*

Radar Charts

Radar charts are new with Excel 4. A radar chart shows how numbers change in relation to a central point and to each other. The value (Y) axis of each category radiates from a central point. A radar chart is similar to a line chart, but a radar chart plots its information around a central point while a line chart plots it along a baseline.

Figure 3-16 shows the conference data plotted as a radar chart. With a radar chart, each data series creates an enclosed area. You can make visual comparisons of the relative areas between several data series.

There are five available formats for radar charts:

- The basic radar chart connects each data marker in a data series with a line. This is the preferred format. It is also available on the Chart toolbar.

- Only the lines, not the data markers, are shown.

- The lines are shown without any axes.

- Grid lines are added to the chart and the axes are shown.

- Logarithmic grid lincs are added to the chart and the axes are shown.

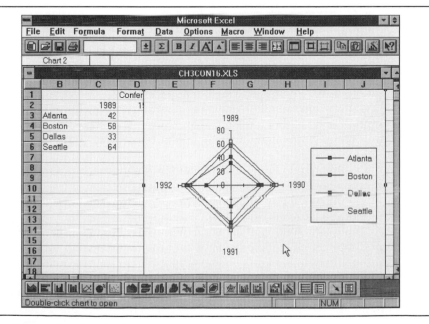

Figure 3-16.   *A radar chart*

Scatter Charts

Scatter or XY charts show the relationship between pairs of numbers and the trends they present. For each pair of numbers, one is plotted on the category (X) axis and the other is plotted on the value or Y axis. A symbol is placed on the chart at the point where the two meet. After a number of points have been plotted, a pattern may appear, as shown in Figure 3-17, a hypothetical correlation between hours of sleep on the X axis and units of production on the Y axis.

Unlike the other chart types, a scatter chart has a series of values in the first row for plotting on the X axis. When a selected range has values in the first row instead of text or dates, you will see this dialog box:

Excel needs to know if the first row is a data series to be plotted, X-axis labels, or X values for a scatter chart. If data for a scatter chart were plotted as a column chart

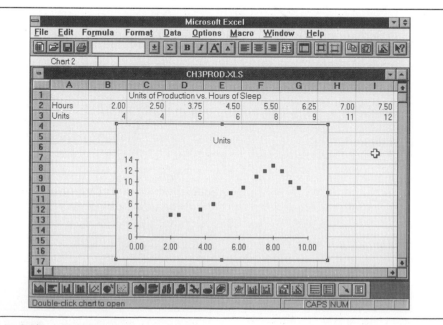

Figure 3-17.   *A scatter chart*

Drawing Toolbar

Toolbar 5	Tool Name	Number	Position
	Rotate Text Up	73	1
	Rotate Text Down	74	2
	Line	76	3
	Selection	81	4
	Reshape	82	5
	Rectangle	83	6
	Arc	85	7
	Polygon	86	8
	Filled Rectangle	88	9
	Freehand Polygon	87	10
	Filled Arc	90	11
	Arrow	77	12
	Text Box	79	13
	Button	80	14
	Filled Polygon	91	15
	Filled Freehand Polygon	92	16
	Group	93	17
	Ungroup	94	18
	Top Border	46	19

Excel 3.0 Toolbar

Toolbar 6	Tool Name	Number	Position
Normal	Style Box	70	1
	Promote	129	2
	Demote	130	3
	Show Outline Symbols	131	4
	Select Visible Cells	132	5
	AutoSum	39	6
	Bold	58	7
	Italic	59	8
	Left Align	63	9
	Center Align	64	10
	Right Align	65	11
	Selection	81	12
	Line	76	13
	Filled Rectangle	88	14
	Filled Oval	89	15
	Arc	85	16
	Preferred Chart	120	17
	Text Box	79	18
	Button	80	19
	Camera	125	20

Macro Toolbar

Toolbar 7	Tool Name	Number	Position
	New Macro Sheet	6	1
	Paste Function	40	2
	Paste Names	41	3
	Run Macro	100	4
	Step Macro	101	5
	Record Macro	98	6
	Resume Macro	102	7

Stop Recording Toolbar

Toolbar 8	Tool Name	Number	Position
	Resume Macro	102	1

Macro Paused Toolbar

Toolbar 9	Tool Name	Number	Position
	Stop Recording	99	1

Standard Toolbar

Toolbar 1	Tool Name	Number	Position
	New Worksheet	7	1
	Open File	1	2
	Save File	2	3
	Print	3	4
Normal	Style Box	70	5
	AutoSum	39	6
B	Bold	58	7
I	Italic	59	8
A	Increase Font Size	71	9
A	Decrease Font Size	72	10
	Left Align	63	11
	Center Align	64	12
	Right Align	65	13
	Center Across Columns	67	14
	AutoFormat	52	15
	Outline Border	43	16
	Bottom Border	47	17
	Copy	13	18
	Paste Formats	17	19
	ChartWizard	121	20
	Help	128	21

Formatting Toolbar

Toolbar 2	Tool Name	Number	Position
Normal	Style Box	70	1
MS Sans Serif	Font Name Box	68	2
10	Font Size Box	69	3
B	Bold	58	4
I	Italic	59	5
U	Underline	60	6
K	Strikeout	61	7
	Justify Align	66	8
$	Currency Style	53	9
%	Percent Style	54	10
,	Comma Style	55	11
	Increase Decimal	56	12
	Decrease Decimal	57	13
	Light Shading	50	14
	AutoFormat	52	15

Utility Toolbar

Toolbar 3	Tool Name	Number	Position
	Undo	10	1
	Repeat	11	2
	Copy	13	3
	Paste Values	18	4
	Paste Formats	17	5
	Zoom In	138	6
	Zoom Out	139	7
	Sort Ascending	134	8
	Sort Descending	135	9
	Lock Cell	136	10
	Promote	129	11
	Demote	130	12
	Show Outline Symbols	131	13
	Select Visible Cells	132	14
	Button	80	15
	Text Box	79	16
	Camera	125	17
	Check Spelling	127	18
	Set Print Area	5	19
	Calculate Now	126	20

Chart Toolbar

Toolbar 4	Tool Name	Number	Position
	Area Chart	103	1
	Bar Chart	104	2
	Column Chart	105	3
	Stacked Column Chart	106	4
	Line Chart	107	5
	Pie Chart	108	6
	Scatter Chart	115	7
	3-D Area Chart	109	8
	3-D Bar Chart	110	9
	3-D Column Chart	111	10
	3-D Perspective Column Chart	112	11
	3-D Line Chart	113	12
	3-D Pie Chart	114	13
	3-D Surface Chart	116	14
	Radar Chart	117	15
	Line/Column Combination Chart	118	16
	Volume/Hi-Lo-Close Combination Chart	119	17
	Preferred Chart	120	18
	ChartWizard	121	19
	Horizontal Gridlines	122	20
	Legend	124	21
	Arrow	77	22
	Text Box	79	23

THE EXCEL TOOLBARS

it would have two data series that would produce two sets of columns. A scatter chart instead needs a numeric X axis, against which the remaining data series are plotted. There are five available formats for scatter charts:

- The basic scatter chart has a marker placed on each pair of data points. It is also available on the Chart toolbar.

- Lines are added to connect the markers on the chart. This is the preferred format.

- Horizontal and vertical grid lines are added to the basic scatter chart.

- Semi-logarithmic horizontal grid lines are added to the basic scatter chart.

- Log-log grid lines are added to the basic scatter chart.

Logarithmic grid lines, either semi-log (horizontal axis only) or log-log (both horizontal and vertical axes), are useful when the data to be plotted produces a steep curve with the first values bunched together and with the subsequent values spread out. The data series 2, 4, 8, 16, 32, 64, 128 would produce such a curve. Plotting the data against logarithmic grid lines produces a straight line rather than a curve.

Three-Dimensional Surface Charts

Three-dimensional surface charts are new with Excel 4. Data series are plotted much as they are in a three-dimensional column chart, but instead of drawing columns Excel lays a flexible sheet over the plotted points, as shown in Figure 3-18. A range of values, not data series as in other charts, are marked with colors or patterns. Some correlations can be visualized more readily with this type of chart.

This type of chart is useful for finding the best combinations of two variables. For example, in the processing of photographic film there may be several combinations of time and developer strength that produce the desired result. By creating a 3-D surface chart from the processing data the best combinations of time and developer strength can be seen.

There are four available formats for three-dimensional surface charts:

- The basic three-dimensional surface chart. It is the preferred format. It is also available on the Chart toolbar. The basic three-dimensional surface chart uses colors or patterns to show value ranges, rather than showing data series as in other types of charts.

- The wireframe three-dimensional surface chart is the same as the basic three-dimensional surface chart except that the values are not colored.

- A two-dimensional surface chart that is a bird's-eye view of a three-dimensional surface chart.

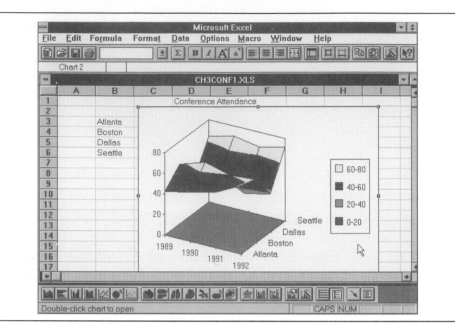

Figure 3-18.   *A three-dimensional surface chart*

- A two-dimensional wireframe surface chart that is a bird's-eye view of a three-dimensional wireframe surface chart.

Charting Methods

Excel offers an extensive array of charting options with the chart menus. All of these options are not always needed, so Excel provides two other methods that simplify the process of creating charts, the ChartWizard and the Chart toolbar. The ChartWizard and Chart toolbar each offer a subset of Excel's full charting options.

Using ChartWizard

The ChartWizard tool, pictured here, is located in both the Standard toolbar and the Chart toolbar, and offers the easiest way to create a customized embedded chart. The ChartWizard allows you to choose the type and format of the chart and to customize it using a series of dialog boxes.

To create a chart with ChartWizard, select a worksheet range to chart and click on the ChartWizard tool in either the Standard or Chart toolbar. Then select a location for the chart by dragging the mouse from the upper-left to the lower-right corner of the area for the chart. When you release the mouse button, the first of five ChartWizard dialog boxes will appear, as shown in Figure 3-19.

The command buttons across the bottom of the dialog box are common to each ChartWizard dialog box. The Help button, however, is not available from the first ChartWizard dialog box. The action performed by each button is described here:

Button	ChartWizard Action
Help	Opens Help window
Cancel	Cancels ChartWizard and returns to the worksheet
l<<	Returns to the first dialog box
<Back	Returns to the previous dialog box
Next>	Moves on to the next dialog box
>>	Creates a chart with the options chosen so far and exits ChartWizard

The first dialog box confirms that the selected range is the correct range to chart. If you want to change the range selection, either enter the changes directly into the

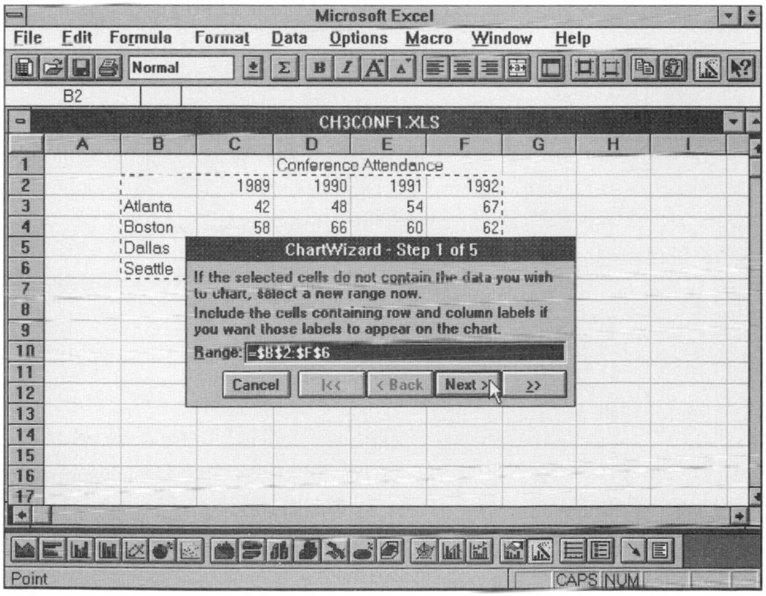

Figure 3-19.   *ChartWizard dialog box 1 of 5*

text box or use the mouse to select a new range. Once the range is correct, click on the Next button.

The second dialog box, shown in Figure 3-20, is a pictorial *gallery* of the 14 preferred chart types. The column chart is already highlighted because it is the preferred type of chart. Changing the preferred type of chart will be covered later in the chapter under "Editing and Formatting with the Chart Menus."

Choose the type of chart to create by double-clicking on the desired chart type or by clicking on the chart type once and then clicking on the Next button. You can select the preferred type simply by clicking on the Next button.

The third dialog box, shown in Figure 3-21, offers a gallery of the available chart formats for the type of chart you've selected. The highlighted format is the preferred format for the chart type. Choose the chart format the way you chose the chart type in the previous dialog box.

The fourth ChartWizard dialog box, shown in Figure 3-22, shows a preview of your chart and offers three options for changing the chart. The first option allows you to define whether the data series are in rows or in columns. Remember that Excel normally assumes there are more data points than data series to be charted. This option allows you to define the data series when there are more data series than data points to be charted.

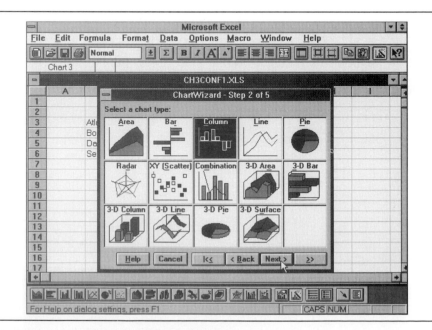

Figure 3-20.   *ChartWizard dialog box 2 of 5*

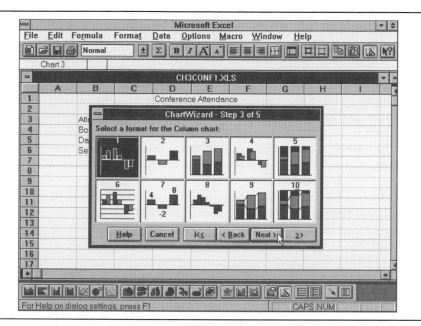

Figure 3-21.   *ChartWizard dialog box 3 of 5*

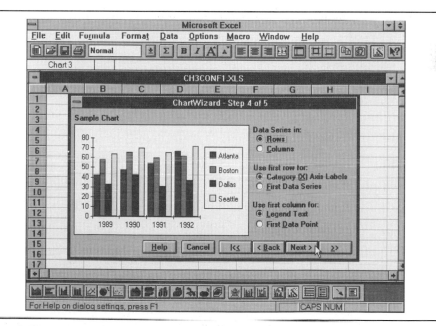

Figure 3-22.   *ChartWizard dialog box 4 of 5*

The second and third options define the first row and/or first column as either data or labels and text. To change a setting, click on the proper option button. You can use the Back command button to return to previous steps if you want to change the chart type or its format. Click on the Next button to bring up the final ChartWizard dialog box, which is shown in Figure 3-23.

The preview chart is still visible, and a series of text boxes have appeared for adding chart and axes titles. The chart title Conference Attendance has been added, and Year and Attendance have been added to the X and Y axis, respectively. If you were working with a Combination chart with a separate Y axis for the overlay chart, as shown in Figure 3-10, the Overlay text box would also be available so you could add a label for that axis.

You can also choose whether a legend will appear on the chart. The *chart legend* is a box on the chart that associates the name of each data series (the city names in the example) with its marker, line, or area on the chart. Since adding a legend is the default, clicking on the No option button would remove the legend box from the chart.

Clicking on OK creates an embedded chart on the worksheet corresponding to the ChartWizard settings you made and exits ChartWizard.

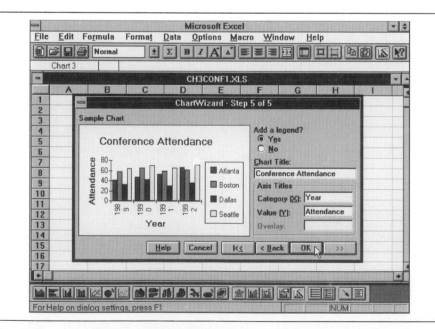

Figure 3-23.   *ChartWizard dialog box 5 of 5*

Editing Charts with ChartWizard

You can also use the ChartWizard tool to modify an existing chart. Two of the ChartWizard's dialog boxes are available—one to edit the selected range, the other to define the data series as rowwise or columnwise and to define the contents of the first row and/or column as data or labels. You cannot change the chart type, format, or title with ChartWizard; you must use the Chart toolbar or chart menus.

To edit a chart with ChartWizard, select the chart to be edited and then click on the ChartWizard tool in either toolbar. The first ChartWizard dialog box will appear (see Figure 3-19), allowing you to edit the worksheet range that the chart represents. Clicking on Next will bring up the ChartWizard dialog box shown in Figure 3-22. The button labeled Next in Figure 3-22 will change to an OK button. Clicking on OK will then close the dialog box and make the selected changes to the existing chart.

Using the Chart Toolbar

The Chart toolbar, shown here, provides tools for customizing charts and for creating embedded charts in several chart types.

The Chart toolbar is displayed at the bottom of the screen whenever a chart is selected. To display it if it is not already displayed, choose Toolbars from the Options menu, select Chart, and click on Show. For creating an embedded chart, the Chart toolbar is faster than ChartWizard but offers fewer formatting options.

The first set of tools on the Chart toolbar allow you to choose one of seven two-dimensional chart types: area, bar, column, stacked column, line, pie, and scatter. From the second set of tools you can choose from seven three-dimensional chart types: three-dimensional area, three-dimensional bar, three-dimensional column, three-dimensional perspective column, three-dimensional line, three-dimensional pie, and three-dimensional surface. The third set of tools lets you create three additional two-dimensional charts: radar, line/column combination, and column/hi-lo-close combination.

Creating or modifying a chart with one of these tools will create the chart in the preferred format for that chart type. You can change the preferred format with the chart menus.

The next two tools are the Preferred Type tool, which causes the selected chart to revert to the preferred chart type and format, and the ChartWizard tool. The remaining four tools are for adding or removing grid lines, a legend, an arrow, and a text box. The Text Box tool is used to place text anywhere on the chart.

The Chart toolbar offers a quick way to create a chart. Simply select the range you want to plot and then click on one of the chart tools on the Chart toolbar to select the type of chart that will be created. Select an area on the worksheet for the chart by dragging the mouse from the upper-left corner to the lower-right corner of the chart area. After you release the mouse button, an embedded chart of the selected type will appear in the defined area.

Figure 3-24 shows an area chart created from the conference data by choosing the Area tool in the Chart toolbar. You can change the chart type simply by clicking on the desired chart tool on the toolbar while the chart is selected. Clicking on the Preferred tool will set the chart to the preferred type and format.

You can customize charts with the Gridlines, Legend, Arrow, and Text Box tools. Clicking on the Gridlines tool will add or remove horizontal grid lines from the chart. The Legend tool will add or remove the chart's legend, as described in the ChartWizard section.

The Arrow tool creates arrows on the chart. Arrows are used to emphasize or point out information on a chart. Figure 3-25 shows the conference data as a column chart with grid lines and a legend added. The Arrow tool has been used to create an arrow pointing to the chart's legend and another is being drawn pointing to the grid lines. The Arrow tool is deselected each time an arrow is drawn, which means you must select it again if you need to draw another arrow.

You use the Text Box tool to add titles or names on the chart. The Text Box tool is also deselected after you create a text box. In Figure 3-26, the Text Box tool has

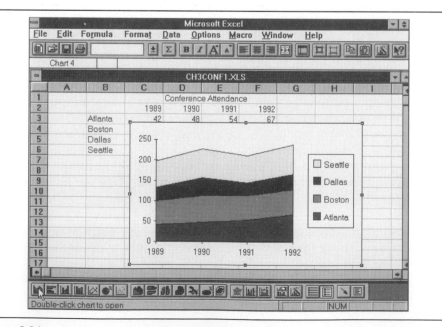

Figure 3-24. *An area chart created with the Chart toolbar*

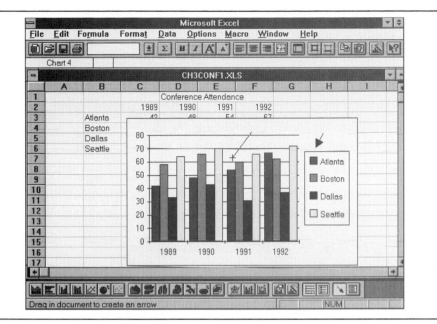

Figure 3-25.   *Adding an arrow*

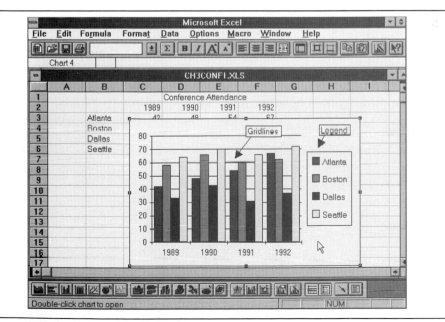

Figure 3-26.   *Text labels added to the arrows*

been used to add labels to the arrows. Editing arrows and other chart elements will be covered in the chart menus section.

Using the File Menu

You can create chart documents by using the New option in the File menu, or from an embedded chart. Double-clicking on an embedded chart will open the chart in its own window, where you can edit it with the chart menus, view it, print it, and save it as a separate chart document.

You create a chart document from the File menu by selecting the range to chart and choosing New from the File menu. The New dialog box will appear, as shown here:

Select Chart to create a chart document in a new window. The chart will be created in the current preferred type and preferred format.

Editing and Formatting with the Chart Menus

You use the Chart menus to format and edit charts. The Chart Menu bar replaces the Worksheet Menu bar when a Chart document is selected or an embedded chart is open in its own window. Of the eight menus, five—File, Edit, Macro, Window, and Help—are virtually the same as the Worksheet menus. The other three—Gallery, Chart, and Format—offer extensive options to create any chart type and format, and to customize or edit charts.

The Gallery Menu

The Gallery menu, shown here, provides access to all of Excel's chart types and formats. When you choose a chart type from the menu, a gallery (a pictorial dialog box) opens so you can choose the desired chart format, as shown here:

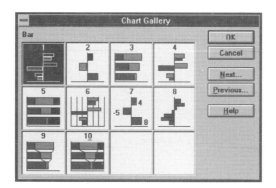

The preferred format for the chart type will be highlighted. On the right side of the gallery is the following set of command buttons:

Button	Gallery Command
OK	Closes the gallery and makes chosen changes to the chart
Cancel	Closes the gallery without making any changes to the chart
Next	Shows the chart formats for the next chart type
Previous	Shows the chart formats for the previous chart type
Help	Opens a Help window

Choosing the Preferred option from the Gallery menu will restore your chart to the preferred chart type and format. The Set Preferred option allows you to change the preferred chart type and format, but the setting will be lost when you leave Excel.

To change the preferred type or format:

- Use the Gallery menu to change the chart to the chart type and chart format that will be the new preferred type and format.

• Select Set Preferred from the Gallery menu.

The new settings will remain in use until you change them or exit Excel.

Chart Menu

The Chart menu, shown here, allows you to add text and chart objects such as arrows to your charts. Other options enable you to customize charts, protect charts with a password, change the color palette, recalculate the worksheet information, and spell check the chart.

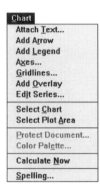

Adding Text   Chart text can be either *attached text* or *unattached text*. Attached text is linked to a part of the chart and cannot be moved from the attached object. Attached text is used for the chart title, for example. Unattached text can be moved around the chart as a separate chart object. You place unattached text on a chart with the Text Box tool, the Chart toolbar, or by typing in the edit area of the formula bar while the chart is selected.

The Attach Text option creates text linked to a chart object, rather than unattached text. Selecting the Attach Text option brings up the Attach Text dialog box:

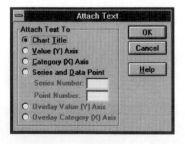

A series of option buttons allows you to select the chart object that the text will be attached to: the chart title, one of the axes, or a series or data point. If a combination chart is selected, you can also attach text to the overlying chart's axes.

You can modify both attached and unattached text with the formatting tools in the Standard toolbar, the Format menu, or the Shortcut menus. You can also link text to a worksheet so the text in a referenced cell appears on the chart. If you then make changes to the text on the worksheet, the text on the chart will automatically be updated. Linked text can be formatted on the chart like other chart text.

To link worksheet text to a chart:

1. Both the chart document and the worksheet must be open.

2. The text must be in a single cell, which can be a named cell.

3. If you want to replace existing chart text with linked text, first select the chart text. The text will then be in the formula bar.

4. Clear the text from the formula bar and type an equal sign.

5. To create new text, make sure no chart text is selected and the formula bar is clear when you type the equal sign.

6. Switch to the worksheet and click on the desired cell. A formula will appear in the formula bar linking the worksheet text to the chart. You can also edit the formula in the formula bar.

7. The formula must always begin with an equal sign, followed by the name of the worksheet, an exclamation point (!), and the cell reference. The cell reference can be an absolute reference or a name defined on the worksheet.

Adding Arrows   Arrows are used on charts to emphasize selected chart elements. To place an arrow on the chart, select Add Arrow from the Chart menu; Excel will draw an arrow on the chart. You can move the arrow by clicking the mouse on the arrow and dragging it. When the arrow is selected, handles at each end allow you to change its length, angle, and location. When an arrow is selected, the Add Arrow menu option changes to Delete Arrow. You can also delete arrows by selecting them and then pressing DEL. You can modify arrow elements with the Format menus, which will be covered later in this chapter.

Adding and Deleting Legends   A Chart Legend is a box on the chart that associates the name of each data series with its marker, line, or area on the chart. Chart legends are added and deleted with the Add Legend and Delete Legend option. The menu option toggles to reflect whether a legend is displayed (Delete Legend) or not (Add Legend). Simply select the option to add or delete the legend.

Adding Axes and Grid Lines   You can add or remove axes from the chart with the Axes option on the Chart menu. Selecting the Axes option brings up the Axes dialog box shown here:

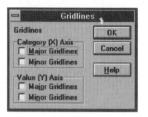

The Axes dialog box that appears depends on the chart type. Two-dimensional, three-dimensional, and combination charts all produce different dialog boxes. The check boxes in the Axes dialog box let you specify which axes will appear on the chart.

You can add or remove grid lines with the Gridlines option on the Chart menu. The Gridlines dialog box, shown here, is used in the same way as the Axes dialog box.

Adding an Overlaid Chart   You can create combination charts with the Add Overlay option. This method will preserve any custom formatting on the chart. When you select Add Overlay, Excel will plot the second half of the data series as a line chart overlaid on the base chart. Three-dimensional charts cannot have overlays and the other chart types can have only a single overlay. If an overlay chart exists, the Add Overlay option changes to Delete Overlay. You can modify the overlaid chart type using the Format menu.

Editing Series Formulas   Excel's charts are a visual representation of worksheet data. When a chart is created or modified, Excel creates a *series formula* that references the source worksheet data. You can edit series formulas and create new series formulas with the Edit Series option on the Chart menu. You can view a chart's series formulas in the edit area of the formula bar by selecting one of the chart's lines, columns, bars, or wedges.

Series formulas always begin with the SERIES function, which is written as =SERIES(. Up to four elements follow, separated by commas, and ending with a closing parenthesis. These are the four elements of a series formula:

- A reference to the cells containing the data series name or a reference to it

- The range containing the category names

- The range containing the data points in the data series

- The order in which the data series will be plotted

Figure 3-27 shows the conference data plotted as an area chart. The first data series, for Atlanta, is selected. The series formula for the Atlanta data series is displayed in the edit area of the formula bar. The first element of the series formula is CH3CHMU1.XLS!$B$3. This is an absolute reference to cell B3 on the worksheet CH3CHMU1.XLS. This cell contains the word Atlanta, the name of this data series. When a range is referenced from a chart or another worksheet, you must use the full worksheet name and extension (and path if it is stored in another directory), followed by an exclamation point (!), and the absolute reference or range name of the cells containing the data series. The second element is CH3CHMU1.XLS!$C$2:$F$2, a reference to the range containing the category names for the chart (1989 - 1992). The third element of the data series is CH3CHMU1.XLS!$C$3:$F$3, a reference to the range containing the data points to be plotted. The final element is the number 1, indicating this is the first data series to be plotted.

You can edit series formulas in the edit area of the formula bar, but the Edit Series option opens a dialog box, shown here, that simplifies the process.

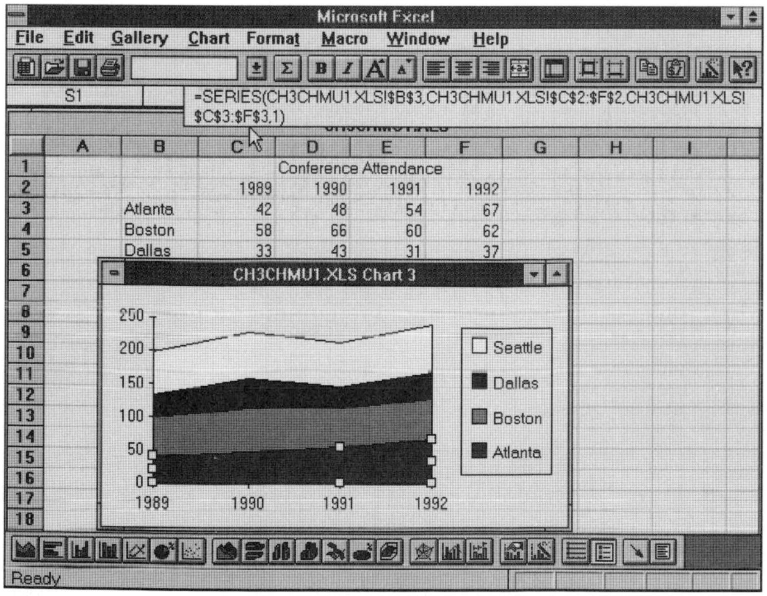

Figure 3-27.   *Area chart with the Atlanta series selected*

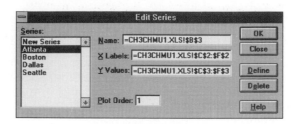

On the left side of the dialog box is a list box in which you can select which data series to edit. In the center are four text boxes for editing each element of the series formula. You can edit the series name in the Name text box by referencing a cell or by typing a literal name in quotes. On the right side of the dialog box are a series of command buttons, whose functions are listed next:

Button	Edit Series Function
OK	Applies changes to the chart and exits the dialog box
Close	Exits without changing the chart
Define	Applies changes to the chart without exiting the dialog box
Help	Opens the Help menus
Delete	Deletes the selected data series

Selecting Charts and Plot Areas   With the Select Chart and Select Plot Area options from the Chart menu, you can select either the entire chart, including text and other elements, or just the area of the plot.

Use Select Plot Area when you want to edit or format just the area with the actual data plot. Use Select Chart when you want to format the entire area within the chart window.

Password Protecting Your Charts   You can password protect your charts with the Protect Document option on the Chart menu. If an embedded chart is selected, this option will not be available in the Chart menu. To protect embedded charts, you must use the Protect Document option in the Options menu.

To protect a chart document, set the chart elements and window as you want them to be. Then select Protect Document from the Chart menu; the Protect Document dialog box will appear, as shown here:

This dialog box contains a text box in which you enter a password and two check boxes to set protection for either the chart, the window, or both. Passwords can be up to 15 characters in length; can contain any combination of letters, numbers, and symbols, and are case sensitive.

Coloring Your Charts   You set chart color palettes with the Color Palette option on the Chart menu. The Color Palette dialog box, shown in Figure 3-28, is the same dialog box that appears when you select Color Palette from the Option menu.

This dialog box consists of a series of color bars, representing the current color palette. Below the color bars is a drop-down list box for choosing the color palette from another chart. On the right side is a series of command buttons, which are explained here:

Button	Color Palette Action
OK	Applies changes to the color palette and exits the dialog box
Cancel	Exits without changing the color palette
Edit	Opens the Color Picker dialog box to edit the selected color
Default	Restores the default color palette
Help	Opens a Help window

The Color Picker dialog box, shown in Figure 3-29, is used to mix colors for the color palette. The Color Picker offers four methods of mixing and selecting colors. The large box contains possible color choices, and next to it is a column containing a range from light to dark of one color from the possible choices. You can choose colors by clicking on either color box. The narrow color box also has a slider; you can select the color tone by dragging this slider with the mouse. Below the large color

Figure 3-28.   *The Color Palette dialog box*

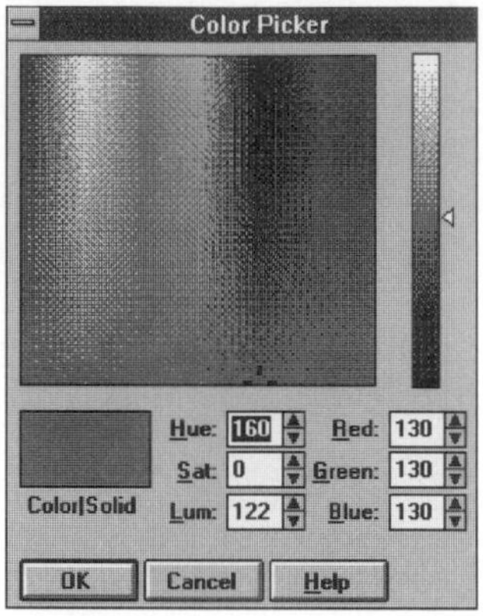

Figure 3-29.   *The Color Picker dialog box*

box is a smaller rectangle that previews the selected color as both a solid and shaded color. You can also select colors by specifying the Hue, Saturation, and Luminance values or the Red, Green, and Blue components.

Recalculating Your Charts   The Calculate Now option on the Chart menu recalculates all open worksheets, macro sheets, and redraws all charts. If the formula bar is active, the formula in it, or the selected part of the formula, will be replaced by the results of the calculation when you select this option.

Spell Checking Your Charts   The Spelling option on the Chart menu checks the spelling of the text on the selected chart. If Excel finds a word that is not in the selected dictionary, the Spelling dialog box shown here will appear.

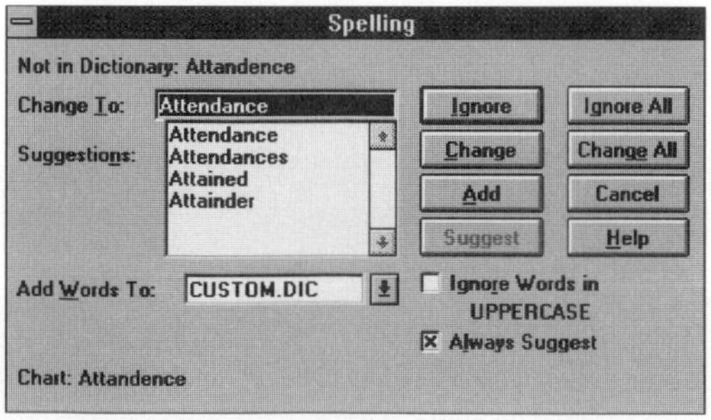

The word the spelling checker does not recognize is at the top of the dialog box. Below it is the Change To text box, which contains a suggested replacement word.

Below that is a list box containing other possible replacements words. On the right side of the dialog box are a series of command buttons:

Box	Spelling Action
Ignore	Accepts the current spelling and continues spell checking.
Ignore All	Accepts all occurrences of the word as spelled and continues spell checking.
Change	Changes the selected word to the suggested spelling.
Change All	Changes all occurrences of the selected word in the chart.
Add	Adds the selected word to the current dictionary.
Cancel/Close	Cancels the spell checking operation and exits the dialog box. If a word has been changed or added to the dictionary, the button changes to Close so the changes will be saved.
Suggest	When the Always Suggest check box is unselected, suggests replacement spellings for the selected word.
Help	Opens a Help window.

Below the command buttons are two check boxes, Ignore Words in UPPERCASE and Always Suggest. Ignore Words In UPPERCASE determines whether the spell checking operation will be case sensitive, and Always Suggest determines whether alternate spellings should be suggested for every selected word.

Using the Format Menu

The Format menu, shown here, allows you to change the patterns, font, color, shading, line width, size, and position of many chart elements.

```
Format
Patterns...
Font...
Text...
Scale...
Legend...

Main Chart...
Overlay...
3-D View...

Move
Size
```

Before you can apply any formatting, you must select the chart element you want to format. Chart elements include the titles and other text, either of the two scales, any of the data series, legends, the entire chart, and the plot area. You select most elements by clicking on them with the mouse—with the keyboard, press an arrow key to cycle through the elements.

When an element is selected, selection boxes appear around or on either end of the element. Attached text, such as titles and category labels, will have white or empty selection boxes. Unattached text and other movable elements will have black selection boxes that you can move and size with the mouse or keyboard.

Not every option in the Format menu is available for all elements. When an element is selected, only the applicable options will be selectable from the Format menu (the other options will be greyed). The Patterns, Font, and Text options apply to text elements such as titles. Patterns controls the border line width, style, and color, along with the foreground and background pattern and color. Font allows you to set the typeface, size, style, and color of the text. The Text option adjusts the alignment and position of the text.

The Scale option sets the type of scale as well as the minimum, maximum, major, and minor increments of the scale. The Legend option is used to position the legend. The Main Chart, Overlay, and 3-D View options determine the type of chart and some of its characteristics. Select the Move and Size options if you prefer to use the direction keys instead of the mouse to move and size elements.

Patterns   Selecting the pattern option will bring up the Patterns dialog box, which is shown here:

In the Patterns dialog box, you can control the formatting of the border and area of the selected elements by using several check boxes and drop-down list boxes to set the style, color, weight, and pattern. On the right side are a list of command buttons:

Box	Pattern Action
OK	Applies settings to selected objects and exits the dialog box
Cancel	Exits the dialog box without making any changes to the selected objects
Font	Calls up the Font dialog box
Text	Calls up the Text dialog box
Help	Opens a Help window

Font   Selecting the Font option either from the Format menu or another dialog box brings up the Font dialog box, shown in Figure 3-30, which controls the type attributes.

You can set the font, font style, and font size through a series of list boxes. Some type effects are also available through drop-down list boxes and option buttons. On the right side of the dialog box are a series of command buttons that are similar to those in the Patterns dialog box. (Selecting the Patterns command button will present the Patterns dialog box.)

Text   Selecting the Text option brings up the Text dialog box, pictured here:

The Text dialog box sets the vertical and horizontal alignment of the text with a series of option buttons. You can also alter the orientation of the text through this dialog box. On the right side are a series of command buttons that are similar to

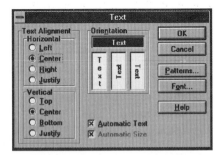

Figure 3-30.   *The Font dialog box*

those in the Patterns dialog box. Selecting the Patterns command button will present the Patterns dialog box. When the Automatic Text check box is selected, text that was created with the Attach Text option in the Chart menu, and then edited, will be restored. When the Automatic Size check box is selected, the text border is sized to fit exactly around the text.

Scale   The Scale option is active when one of the chart's axes has been selected. Choosing this option brings up the Axis Scale dialog box, shown here:

A series of check and text boxes are used to set the values and intervals for the tick marks on the selected axis. On the right side are a series of command buttons that are similar to those in the Patterns dialog box. Selecting the Patterns command button will present the Patterns dialog box. Selecting the Text command button will present the Text dialog box.

Legend   If you have placed a legend on the chart and selected it, you can modify it with the Legend option on the Format menu. The Legend dialog box looks like this:

You can position the legend in various places around the perimeter of the chart using a set of check boxes. This dialog box also includes the standard series of command buttons.

Main Chart   The Main Chart option on the Format menu offers a detailed selection of chart formatting choices. Selecting the Main Chart option brings up the Format Chart dialog box, which is shown in Figure 3-31.

At the top of the dialog box is a drop-down list box that lets you to select any of Excel's 14 chart types. The Data View boxes show several of the formats available for the selected chart type. You can format bar, column, pie, and three-dimensional charts with the options on the dialog box, and options for general formatting are also available.

The Bar/Column options allow you to set the spacing between bars or columns on the chart, and to add lines connecting each data point in each data series. The Format options allow you to add various lines connecting data points, and to add labels to your chart. The Angle of First Pie Slice sets the angle, in degrees clockwise from the vertical, at which the first pie slice will start. The 3-D options set the distance between each data series and the depth of the chart as a percentage of the width.

Overlay   The Overlay option also brings up the Format Chart dialog box just described. However, in this case the types of charts available reflect those usable with combination charts, rather than every chart type. You can also use the Format Chart dialog box to set the order in which the data series will be plotted.

3-D View   The 3-D View option allows you to rotate and scale three-dimensional charts, and to modify a chart's apparent viewpoint. The 3-D View dialog box, shown

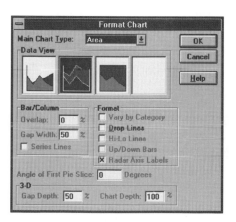

Figure 3-31.   *The Format Chart dialog box*

here, has settings for the apparent elevation of the observer, the rotation angle, and the perspective of the chart.

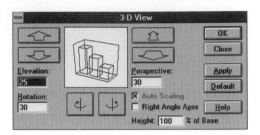

The Right Angle Axes option sets the axes at right angles regardless of the rotation angle or viewpoint. The Auto Scaling option is available when the Right Angle Axes option is selected. Sometimes when a two-dimensional chart is converted to a three-dimensional chart, the new chart is drawn smaller than the original. When auto scaling is active, the three-dimensional chart is scaled so that it will fit the available space. The Height option sets the height of the chart as a percentage of the width.

The 3-D View dialog box contains the following command buttons:

Button	3-D View Action
OK	Applies settings to selected objects and exits the dialog box
Close	Exits the dialog box without making any changes to the selected objects
Apply	Applies the changes to the selected chart without closing the dialog box
Default	Restores the default three-dimensional chart settings
Help	Opens a Help window

Move and Size   The Move and Size menu options are used to move and size various chart elements. You can also move chart elements with the mouse by placing the pointer on the selected element and dragging it to the new location. To size a chart element, point on one of the selection boxes and drag it until the element is the desired size.

Chapter 4

Using a Database

A *database* is an organized set of related information that has been structured to allow you to search for and retrieve the information it contains. In Excel, you can define one or more databases on a worksheet. Excel has commands you can then use to sort, locate, extract, and analyze the information. This chapter explains how to build and maintain an Excel database, as well as how to organize, manipulate, and analyze the information within it.

How an Excel Database Works

An Excel database is simply a range, a set of rows and columns on a worksheet that has been defined as a database. A database range is nothing more than a defined range, which you read about in Chapter 2. It's what you do with this range and the commands with which you manipulate it that make a database range significant.

Database Records and Fields

In a database, information is stored in *records*. For example, in a database containing customer information, a record is all the information for one customer. In an Excel database, each record is one row on a worksheet.

Each record is made up of a number of *fields*, which are simply the discrete elements of a record. For example, a customer's name, address, and phone number in a customer database are each considered fields. In Excel, each field is one column; in a single record, each field is one cell. A field can contain the same types of information as other cells: numbers, dates, text, functions, and formulas. You can organize and search for records based on the information in one or more fields.

Each field is identified by a *field name,* which is located in the first row of the database range. The field name applies to the information in its column in all the rows or records of the database range. Field names must conform to these rules:

- A field name must be formatted as text and must be unique; in the same database, no two field names can be the same.

- You cannot use numbers, logical values, error values, blank cells, or formulas as field names.

- A field name can be up to 255 characters long. However, when you use short field names, you can display more columns and still see the full name.

The maximum size of a database is 256 fields (columns) by 16,383 records (rows)—that is, the maximum size of an Excel worksheet, less one row for the field names. A database cannot be larger than the worksheet it's on, but a single worksheet may include several databases.

The Data Menu

You create and work with databases through the options in the Data menu, which is shown here:

```
Data
  Form...

  Find
  Extract...
  Delete
  Set Database
  Set Criteria
  Set Extract

  Sort...

  Series...
  Table...
  Parse...
  Consolidate...
  Crosstab...
```

In the Data menu, the Form option presents a dialog box, called a *Data Form,* that simplifies some database operations. You'll learn how to use a Data Form later in this chapter. The Find, Extract, and Delete options perform database searching and editing tasks. The Set options—Set Database, Set Criteria, and Set Extract—are used to define the worksheet ranges that will be used for database operations.

The Sort option is used to reorder information in a database. The remaining options—Series, Table, Parse, Consolidate, and Crosstab—are used for entering data, formatting, and analyzing database information. Each option will be covered in this chapter.

Building a Database

You build a database by selecting a range on a worksheet and defining it as a database. Figure 4-1 shows a worksheet with information for several sales offices selected. This range will be used to build a database. Each row in the selected range contains all the information for one sales office. When the database is defined, each row will become a database record. The labels in the first row will serve as field names.

When selecting a range for a database, include a blank row at the bottom of the database range for expansion. You can insert a record before the last row and the database range will expand to include it. Records added after the last row will be outside the database range; you will have to redefine the database range to include them.

Entering and defining the database involves the following straightforward steps:

1. Type a set of field names across a series of columns. These field names will define what you put in each column. The first row selected in Figure 4-1, B4:E4, contains the field names for that database.

2. Type the information on the worksheet that you want to be in the database. The information in a single row should pertain to one subject, such as a single customer or a single sales office. The information in a single column should

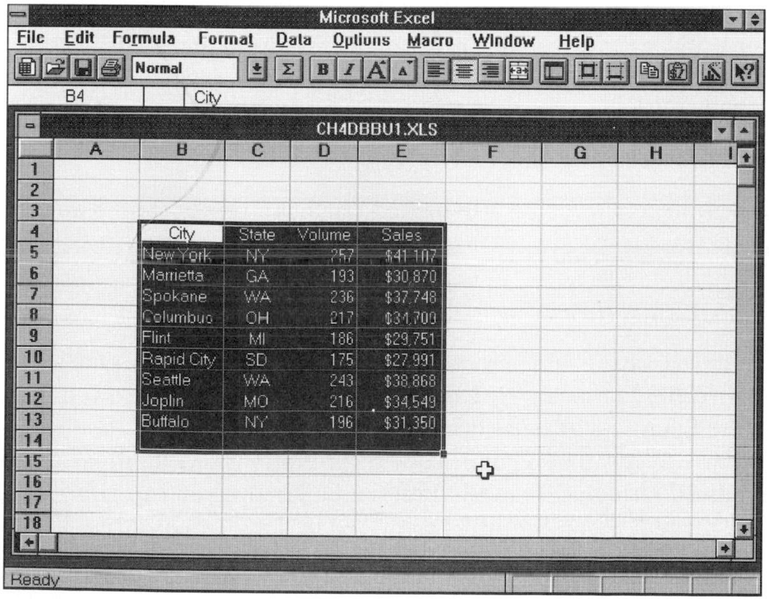

Figure 4-1.   *Worksheet range selected for a database*

all be alike and should relate to the field name. For example, one column might consist only of phone numbers or sales amounts.

3. Select the range on your worksheet that includes the field names, all of the data that you entered, and at least one empty row at the bottom for expansion. The range B4:E14 in Figure 4-1 is an example.

4. Choose Set Database from the Data menu. Excel automatically gives the selected range the name Database.

Even though you can define several databases on a worksheet, only one can be named Database; therefore, with the Data menu, you can only operate on a single database at a time. When you select one of the database options, it is applied to the range containing the active database.

In order to use the Data Menu commands, you will have to name each database on your worksheet something other than "Database." This is because some of the Data menu commands look for that range name to carry out their functions. Once you rename your databases, only the active database will be named Database. Follow these steps:

1. Select the range you want to use as one of the databases.

2. Use the Define Name option in the Formula menu to give the range a unique name other than Database. Repeat these first two steps until all the database ranges have been named.

3. Use the Goto option in the Formula menu, or press F5, and enter the range name of the database on which you want to operate.

4. Choose Set Database in the Data menu to define the selected range as the current database. The name Database will be given to the range in addition to the other name you assigned it.

5. To activate a new range, also named Database, repeat steps 3 and 4.

Adding Records to a Database

There are several ways to add new records to an existing database. One way is to insert a new row anywhere between the first and last rows of the database and then type the data into the fields in the usual manner. The new record is automatically included in the database. You can also cut or copy records and insert them into the database using the Insert Paste option in the Edit menu. Finally, you can add records with a Data Form. Using a Data Form will be covered in detail later in this chapter.

Sorting a Database

One of the uses of a database is to organize information in a specific order, such as by name or date. You can enter records into the database in any order, but you may want to use them in a specific sequence. In a customer database, for example, you may want to list the customers in alphabetical order by name, or in order by last invoice date, or by ZIP code. Using the Sort option in the Data menu lets you change the sequence of the records in a database. You can also use the Sort option to sort any worksheet range—the range needn't be defined as a database. As a matter of fact, when you sort a normal database range by rows, you do *not* want to include the row that includes field names because it probably would not end up as the first row after the sort.

When you select the Sort option from the Data menu, the Sort dialog box opens, as you can see here:

You can sort by rows or columns, as determined with the Sort By option buttons. Sorting by rows reorders the sequence of the rows—rows are moved while the columns stay in the same order. Sorting by columns will reorder the sequence of the columns in each row—columns are moved while the rows stay in the same order. For a column sort of a normal database, you *do* want to include the field names in the range to be sorted, otherwise the data will no longer match the field names.

Sorting is controlled by sort keys. A *sort key* is the column (for a row sort) or row (for a column sort) that is used to determine the sorted order. For example, if you want to sort the sales offices by city, you would select that column (B in Figure 4-1) as the sort key. You can use up to three consecutive sort keys in each sort, and each key can be sorted in ascending or descending order. A sort key can be identified by either a cell address or the defined name of a cell.

Sorting is performed in a specific sequence such that the last key sorted, which is always the 1st Key, is the primary determinant of the final sorted order. The 3rd Key is always the first key to be sorted and therefore has the least to say about the final order. If two records have different contents in the 1st Key field, the 1st Key will determine their final order. If the 1st Key fields are the same, the 2nd Key is used to determine the order. If the 2nd Key fields are the same, the 3rd Key is used. If you need to handle duplicates in the 3rd Key field, you can use multiple sorts. The last sort performed will take precedence, so multiple sorts should be performed in a lowest to highest priority order.

To see how this works, try sorting the example database with two sort keys, City and State, in ascending order (a to z). The sorted database will show the states in alphabetical order, with the cities within each state also in alphabetical order. To do this, you must first sort the database by City and then by State. Follow these general steps for sorting a database:

1. Select the range to be sorted; do not include the field names. In the Sales Office database (shown in Figure 4-1), B5:E13 should be the sort range.

2. Choose Sort from the Data menu.

3. Click on the Rows option button under Sort By if it is not already selected.

4. Set the 1st Key (the highest priority) by clicking on the 1st Key text box and then either clicking on any row in the column to be the primary sort key (column C in the example), or by typing in any address in that column.

4. Click on the Ascending option button below the text box for 1st Key if it is not already selected.

5. Repeat the last two steps for the 2nd key text. In the example, column B (the City) is selected as the second sort key. (The Sales Office database will be sorted on only two levels, so for this example you will not use the 3rd Key text box.)

6. Click on OK to perform the sort. The result of sorting the sample database is shown in Figure 4-2.

NOTE: You can undo the effect of a sort by choosing Undo Sort in the Edit menu immediately after the sort.

Determining the Sort Order

All the characters in each key field are used to determine the sorted order of the fields. Numbers in a field must be all numeric or all text values, since the numeric values will be sorted before the text values. Spaces will also affect sorting and searching operations.

Sorts can be ascending or descending, as set by the Ascending and Descending option buttons in the Sort dialog box. An ascending sort puts the information in a low to high order, such as 0 to 9 or "a" to "z". A descending sort puts the information in a high to low order, such as 9 to 0 or "z" to "a".

Excel uses preset rules to determine the sorted order. For an *ascending* sort, this is the sort order:

- Numbers entered as numbers are sorted from the largest negative to the largest positive number.

- Text, ignoring capitalization and including numbers entered as text, is sorted in this order:

  Space !" # $ % & ' ( ) * + , - . / : ; < = > ? @ [\ ] ^ _ ' { | } ~ 0 1 2 3 4 5 6 7 8 9 a b c d e f g h i j k l m n o p q r s t u v w x y z

- Logical values are sorted FALSE first and then TRUE.

- Error values are sorted in no particular order.

- Blank cells come last in the sort order.

The sequence of characters given in the preceding list is determined by the country selected in the International dialog box in the Windows Control Panel. The list represents the sequence in which characters will be sorted when the United States is the country selected. Descending sorts are done in the opposite order, with the exception of blank cells, which are always sorted last.

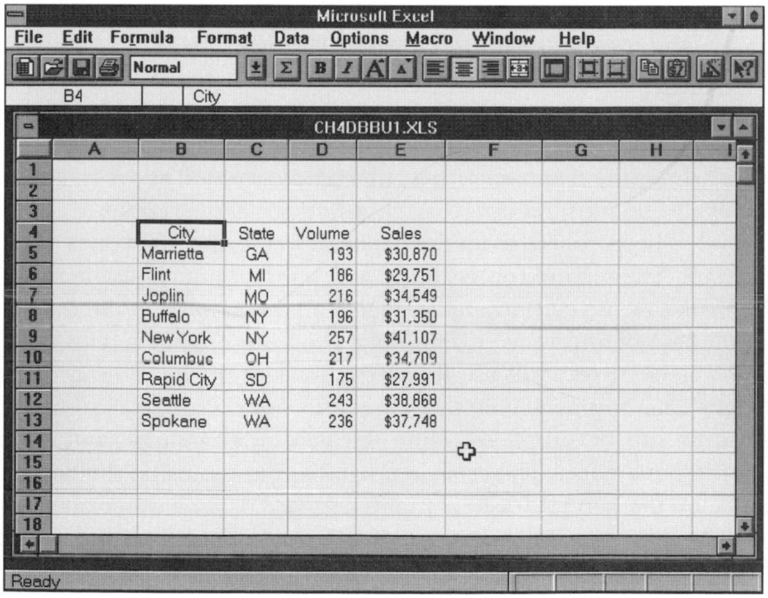

Figure 4-2. *The sorted database*

Building and Using Criteria

The purpose of a database is usually to find specific facts contained within a larger collection of information. This is done by comparing the information in a particular field in each database record against one or more values you define. These values are the *criteria* against which records can be compared and selections made. For example, if you wanted to select all the customers in a certain area, you could use the ZIP code for that area as the criteria. The value in the ZIP code field in each record would be compared against the ZIP code value in the criteria. Those records whose ZIP code matched the criteria would be selected.

Using criteria effectively is the key to using a database. A database can contain thousands of records. Of those thousands, you may need to find a dozen specific records. You can either look at each record to find the few that you need, or you can build a search criteria that will enable Excel to examine each record for you and select the few that meet your requirements.

Building a Criteria Range

You must enter criteria in a *criteria range* on a worksheet before you can use them with a database. A criteria range is similar to a database range, except that it contains the criteria that will be used to find, extract, or delete records in the database.

The first row of the criteria range contains the *criteria names*. These are the names of the database fields that the criteria will be compared against. The criteria for each field are entered in the rows below the criteria name. A criteria range must contain at least two rows and at least one column. The criteria range can be as large as needed.

Figure 4-3 shows the database with a criteria range added above it. You define the selected range as the criteria range by choosing Set Criteria from the Data menu. The first row has been copied from the database so the criteria names exactly match the field names. The second row is empty, which would match all the records in the database. Blank rows in a criteria range match all the records in the database.

Once you have defined the criteria range, you can change any of the names or values in the range. Excel will use the current values in the criteria range for the chosen operations. You may need to change the criteria range as you use different criteria. You do this by simply selecting the new criteria range and choosing Set Criteria in the Data menu. The criteria range has to be outside the database range and it can be on the same worksheet as the database or on a different worksheet.

Like a database range, only one criteria range can be active on a worksheet at a time. You can use the technique described earlier for keeping multiple databases on a worksheet to maintain several criteria ranges also.

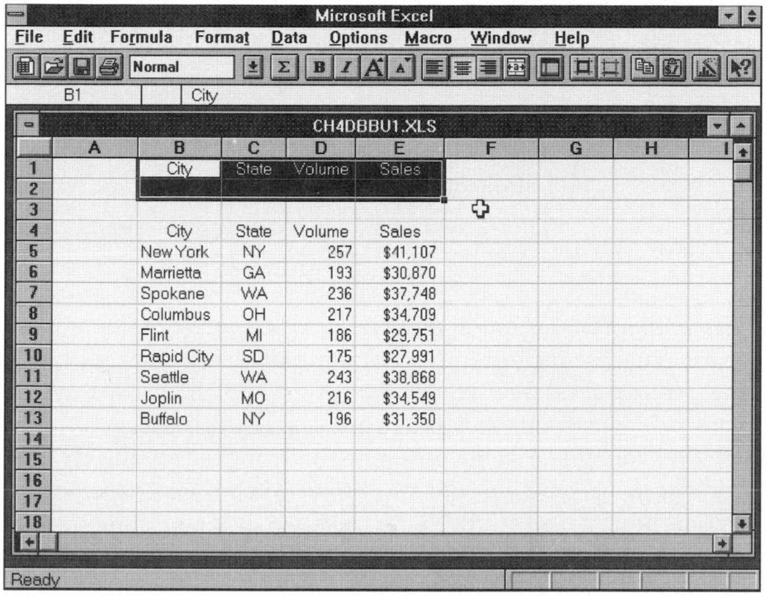

Figure 4-3. *The database with a criteria range added*

Entering Criteria

The criteria entered in the criteria range can have one or two elements: a mandatory *criteria entry* and an optional *comparison operator*. The criteria entry is the value that will be compared against the database records during the search of the database. All criteria have one or more criteria entries, which can be numbers, dates, text, functions, or formulas.

The comparison operator determines the relationship between the criteria entry and the values in each record. The default comparison operator is the equal sign (=). When a comparison operator is not included in the criteria the equal sign is assumed. All the records in the database that are equal to the criteria entry are selected in that case.

Other comparison operators allow you to search for records where the data has a different relationship to the criteria entry—for example, it could be larger or smaller. The comparison operators available in Excel are shown in the following table:

Operator	Meaning
=	The record's value must be equal to the criteria entry.
>	The record's value must be greater than the criteria entry.

Operator	Meaning
<	The record's value must be less than the criteria entry.
>=	The record's value must be greater than or equal to the criteria entry.
<=	The record's value must be less than or equal to the criteria entry.
<>	The record's value must be not be equal to the criteria entry.

Comparison operators also allow the criteria to be a range of values. For example, if the customer database includes a field with the date of the last payment made by the customer, you could define the criteria to find all the records where the last payment was made more than 30 days ago and less than 60 days ago.

Although you can create many different types of criteria with the comparison operators, they can be grouped into two broad categories: *comparison criteria* and *computed criteria*. Both types of criteria can be used alone or combined with other comparison or computed criteria to form multiple criteria.

Comparison criteria are the most common type of criteria. They are used to compare the values in database fields against the criteria you define. For you to use comparison criteria, a field in the database must contain the same type of information as the criteria entry. For example, if you wanted to find all the customers in a particular city, the database would need to have a field with each customer's city in it.

Unlike comparison criteria, computed criteria use information not contained in the database. Instead, the criteria is calculated from values in one or more existing fields which return a value for which there is not a field in the database. An example would be a sales database with a field containing the total for each sale, but without a field containing the sales commission on each sale. If you wanted to find selected records based on the sales commission paid, you could create a computed criteria. It would use the total for each sale and a known commission rate to calculate the commission paid and compare that value against the criteria entry.

The use of both comparison criteria and computed criteria will be covered in the following sections.

Comparison Criteria

For you to use comparison criteria, the criteria name (in the first row of the criteria range) must match a field name in the database. For example, if you wanted to locate the records for offices in one state, the criteria would be in a column with the criteria name STATE, and would be compared against the values in the STATE field of the database. The criteria range shown here has the criteria entry "wa" entered in the column below the criteria name STATE. This criteria range would select all the records with the letters "wa" (in uppercase or lowercase) in the STATE field. The case of text is ignored when the database is searched. Since a comparison operator is not included in the criteria, the equal sign is assumed, so a match with the criteria entry is needed for a record to be selected. This criteria would select the sales offices located in Washington.

B	C	D	E
City	State	Volume	Sales
	wa		

Multiple Criteria with AND   Often you will need to use more than one criteria to find records in a database. An example would be if you wanted to find the records for sales offices in one state with sales above a certain level. When you need to use values in more than one field, you build the criteria by combining two or more criteria in the criteria range. The previous example selected the records of all the offices in Washington. If you wanted to find only the offices in Washington that had sales greater than $38,000, you would use multiple criteria, as shown here, by adding another criteria to the criteria range.

B	C	D	E
City	State	Volume	Sales
	wa		>38000

In this example, the criteria >38000 has been added in the cell below the criteria name SALES. The comparison operator is the greater than sign (>), which means the value in the SALES field in the database must be larger than 38000 (the criteria entry) for the record to be selected. Because there are two criteria in the same row, records must meet *both* of the criteria to be selected. This type of criteria relationship is a logical AND relationship. This means that database records must meet both the first criteria and the second criteria. In this case, only one record in the database would meet the criteria in the criteria range: the office in Seattle, Washington, with $38,868 in sales.

This example used the criteria in two different fields, the STATE field and the SALES field, to select records. You can also use multiple criteria with a single field. This allows you to search the database for a range of values in a single field. For example, if you wanted to find all the offices in the database with sales between

$30,000 and $40,000, you would need two criteria in the SALES field. One criteria to set the low end of the range and the other to set the high end of the range. Selecting a range of values is another example of criteria with a logical AND relationship. The records selected will meet both the first criteria and the second criteria.

To build the criteria for a range of values in one field, you must use a separate column for each criteria but put them in the same row. The criteria need to be in the same row for the AND relationship to be established and you need two columns because you want to satisfy two criteria. To accomplish this, you must have two columns with the same criteria name SALES, one for each criteria. The criteria range will need to be redefined to include both SALES criteria. You redefine a criteria range as you defined it originally, by selecting the new range and choosing the Set Criteria option from the Data menu. The criteria range for a range of values is shown here:

B	C	D	E	F	G
City	State	Volume	Sales	Sales	
			>30000	<40000	

The first criteria, >30000, is entered in the cell below the first SALES criteria name. The second criteria, <40000, is entered in the cell below the second SALES criteria name. This criteria will match all the records in the database where the value in the SALES field is greater than $30,000 and less than $40,000.

The examples of multiple criteria shown so far have used a logical AND relationship. The rules for using a logical AND relationship with multiple criteria can be summarized as follows.

- When you use multiple criteria with several database fields, you should enter the criteria in the same row in different columns.

- When you use multiple criteria with one database field, you need to duplicate the criteria name for the field in the criteria range so that you can enter each criteria in a separate column in the same row.

Multiple Criteria with OR   Criteria ranges can also contain logical OR relationships. These are criteria where the record must meet only one of several criteria. For example, if you wanted to find only the offices in the database with sales less than $30,000 or greater than $40,000, but not between $30,000 and $40,000, you would need to establish a logical OR relationship in the criteria range.

Unlike the logical AND relationship, in a logical OR relationship you enter the criteria in separate rows. To find the offices with sales less than $30,000 or greater than $40,000, you would enter the criteria in the criteria range as shown here:

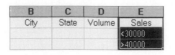

B	C	D	E
City	State	Volume	Sales
			<30000
			>40000

The two criteria are entered in the same column, SALES, in separate rows. The criteria range now needs to have three rows, so it will need to be redefined again to include all the rows with criteria. All the records that meet either criteria will be selected. You can also construct logical OR relationships with criteria in different fields. To do this, you enter the criteria for each field in a separate row in the criteria range. When the database is searched, all the records that meet either or both criteria are selected.

The criteria range shown here would select all the records for offices in Washington, using the criteria "wa" in the STATE field, along with all the offices with sales greater than $40,000, using the criteria >40000 in the SALES field.

This criteria range would select three sales offices, the two in Washington because they match the first criteria and the office in New York because it matches the second criteria. These three records match either one criteria or the other criteria.

The rules for using a logical OR relationship with multiple criteria can be summarized as follows.

- When you use a logical OR relationship with several fields in a criteria range, you must enter the criteria in separate rows.

- When you use multiple criteria with one field, you must enter the criteria in separate rows in the same column.

Combining the different comparison operators and criteria entries in logical AND or logical OR relationships gives you a great deal of flexibility in establishing criteria for database operations. You can obtain even more flexibility if you use computed criteria, as you'll see next.

Computed Criteria

The criteria examples given so far have selected records by comparing the values in existing database fields against the criteria in the criteria range. When you use computed criteria, you can select records by comparing values not in a database field against the criteria. Instead, the values used are calculated from existing database fields. For example, the sale office database lists the sales for each office, but not the commissions paid on those sales. With computed criteria, you could select records based on the amount of commission paid rather than the amount of sales, even though a field for commissions does not exist in the database.

To use computed criteria, you must enter a criteria name that is different from any field name in the first row of the criteria range. Any time a criteria name is the same as a field name, Excel assumes that comparison criteria are being used. In the cell below the new criteria name, you enter the computed criteria formula. The database field that will be used in the formula can be referred to by the field name or by a relative reference to its worksheet location. If you use an absolute reference (such as $B$5), only the record containing that cell will be compared against the criteria.

If a sales commission of 5 percent was paid on sales, the formula =SALES*0.05 would give the amount of commission paid on the sales for each office. If you wanted to select the records with sales commissions of more than $1,500 you would first type a criteria name, such as COMMISSION, in the first row of the criteria range and then enter the formula for the criteria in the row below the criteria name. In this case, the formula would be =SALES*0.05>1500 and the criteria range would appear as shown here:

B	C	D	E	F
City	State	Volume	Sales	Commission
				#NAME?

The criteria cell contains the error value #NAME? because the field name (SALES) was not defined before it was used in the formula. This will not affect the operation of the criteria, however. This criteria will select all records where the commission value, calculated from the SALES value, is greater than $1,500.

Wildcards

Sometimes you need a criteria entry that will match several database entries that are similar but not exactly alike. For example, say you want to select all the records with the name Johnson, Johnsen, and Johnston. You can construct a criteria using *wildcard characters*. Wildcard characters are used to match any character or group of characters. There are two wildcard characters, ? and *, that you can include in criteria. The question mark is used to match any single character and the asterisk is used to match any group of consecutive characters. For example, to select just Johnson and Johnsen, you would enter Johns?n. To expand the criteria to include Johnston, you would enter Johns*. As mentioned, you use the asterisk to match a varying number of characters.

To use an asterisk or question mark as a literal text character in a criterion, precede it with a tilde (~). This tells Excel to treat the next character as text rather than a wildcard. For example, *~? would match all character strings ending with a question mark.

When you use a criteria without a comparison operator, an asterisk wildcard is assumed to be the last character in the criteria entry. For example, a criteria of Port would match Porter, Portland, and Portsmouth. When an exact match is needed, you must include the equal sign. To match only Port you should use the formula ="=Port", including the quotation marks.

Searching the Database

Once you have defined a database range and a criteria range and established the search criteria, you find the records that meet the selection criteria by choosing Find from the Data menu.

Figure 4-4 shows both the database range and the criteria range on the worksheet. The criteria range contains one criteria, the text "wa" in the STATE criteria column. As you saw earlier, this criteria will match only the records beginning with the letters "wa" in the STATE field.

After you choose Find from the Data menu, the worksheet will appear as is shown in Figure 4-5. The upper-left cell of the database range will be in the upper-left corner of the worksheet window. The first record that meets the criteria in the criteria range will be highlighted and the scroll bars will have a striped pattern.

To view the selected records you can use the arrow keys or the scroll bars in the usual manner. However, Excel will scroll only to the records that match the criteria. You can end the search and restore normal scrolling by clicking on a cell outside the database, choosing another menu option, choosing Exit Find from the Data menu, or pressing ESC.

When you choose the Find option, Excel searches the database in sequence, from the beginning of the database range to the end of the range. If a cell within the

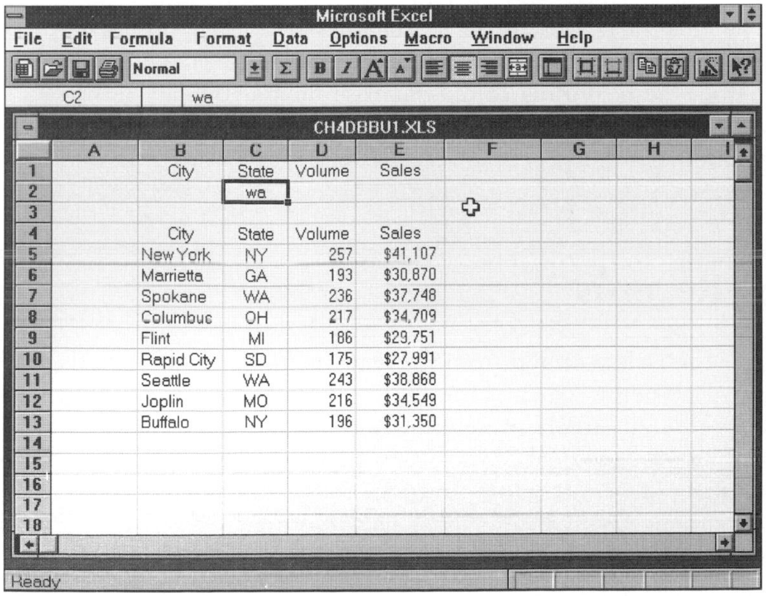

Figure 4-4.   *Criteria for database search*

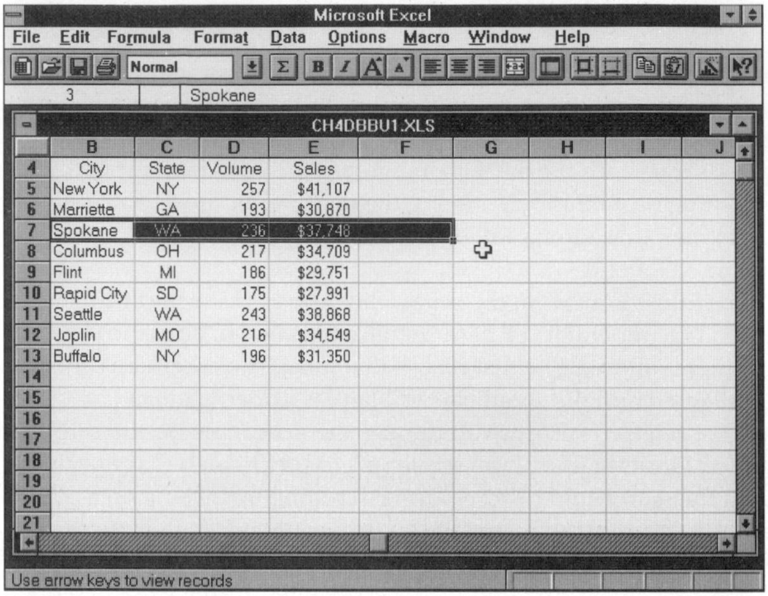

Figure 4-5. *Record selected by the search*

database range is the active cell, the search will start at that point and proceed to the end of the range. When Excel reaches the end of the database, the search will continue from the beginning of the database range. You can perform a search in reverse order, starting at the end of the database, by pressing SHIFT while choosing the Find option.

Deleting Records

You can use the Delete option from the Data menu to delete records that match a criteria range. When a match is found, the records are permanently deleted and cannot be recovered. Before using the Delete option, you should check the criteria range by using the Find option to confirm that the proper records will be selected. If the worksheet was saved before using the Delete option, you can recover deleted records by closing the changed worksheet without saving it and then opening the previously saved worksheet.

To delete selected records, follow these steps:

1. Save the worksheet.

2. Set the criteria range.

3. Choose Delete from the Data menu. Excel will warn you that the selected records will be permanently deleted.

4. Click on OK.

Extracting a Range

It is often useful to copy selected records from a database to use in reports, or to export to another application, such as a word processor. The Extract option on the Data menu allows you to copy selected records from a database to another range on the worksheet. You can extract entire records or partial records. The criteria in the criteria range are used to select the records that will be extracted.

To extract records, you must create an *extraction range* to which the extracted records will be copied. This range must be outside the database range, and the first row must contain the names of the fields that will be extracted. These can be some or all of the fields in the database, but only the fields included will be extracted. When the data is extracted, all the cells on the worksheet below the field names in the extract range will be cleared.

CAUTION: Extract operations cannot be undone; any data that was in the extract range prior to the extract will be lost.

The extraction range can contain just the one row with the field names, or a number of rows. If you define just one row as the extract range, all records meeting the criteria will be extracted. If you select a number of rows, records will be extracted only until that range is full. Specifying multiple rows allows you to prevent the extracted records from overwriting your existing data records. If there are more records than space available, you will receive an error message.

You create an extraction range much as you create a criteria range: you select the range and then choose Set Extract from the Data menu. Excel names the range Extract. To extract selected records, follow these steps:

1. Select the database, criteria, and extract ranges.

2. Choose Extract from the Data menu. The Extract dialog box will appear, as shown here:

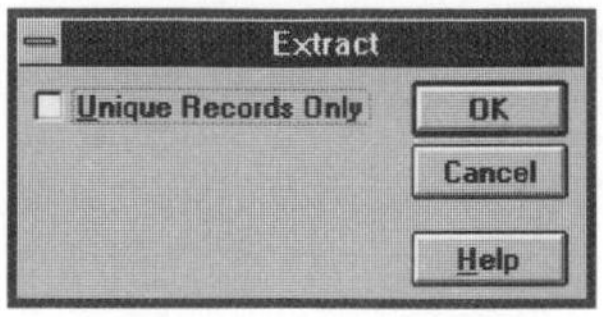

3. Click on the Unique Items Only check box if you only need one copy of duplicate records.

4. Click on OK. The data in the selected fields will be copied from the database to the extract range.

Using Data Forms

As mentioned earlier, a Data Form is a dialog box that you can use to perform different operations on the database. It offers a quick and simple way to add, find, edit, and delete records.

Figure 4-6 shows a Data Form, which appears when you choose Form from the Data menu. Only one record is shown in the Data Form, with the contents of each

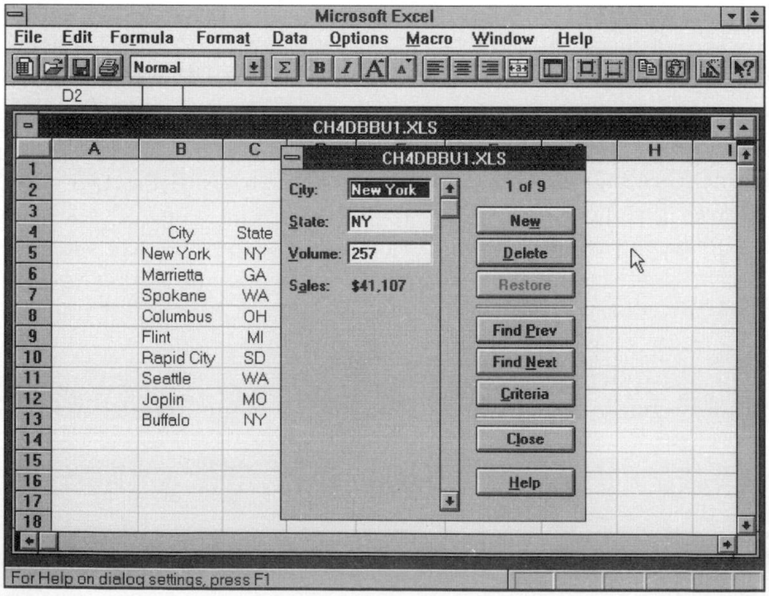

Figure 4-6.   *A standard Data Form*

field placed in a text box labeled with the field name. Fields that cannot be edited, such as computed or locked fields, are shown without text boxes. The Sales field in Figure 4-6 is an example of a computed field.

A Data Form includes a series of command buttons, each described in the following sections, for working with records. The function of several of the command buttons will change depending upon the operation being performed. Above the command buttons is the number of the record being displayed, along with the total number of records. You can use the scroll bar in the middle of the dialog box to browse through the database.

Adding Records with a Data Form

In a Data Form, you can add a new record with the New command button and enter the new information into the text boxes. The database range is automatically expanded to make room for the new record, which will include any computed fields in the database. To add records with a Data Form, follow these steps:

1. Click on the New command button, which will display a new, blank set of text boxes. The words New Record will appear in place of the number of records. (You can also enter New Record mode by using the scroll bar to scroll past the last record in the database.)

2. Enter the data for the new record in the proper text boxes, using TAB or the mouse to move to the next text box.

3. Click on New or press ENTER to add the new record to the database and display another set of blank text boxes.

4. Add additional records by repeating the last two steps.

5. If no more records are to be added, click on Close to add the last entered record to the database and close the Data Form.

Finding Records with a Data Form

Data Forms are also useful for searching a database for a specific record or group of records. You can search the database using comparison criteria, but you cannot use computed criteria and multiple criteria in one field (such as a range of values) with a Data Form.

To search a database using a Data Form, follow these steps:

1. Choose Form from the Data menu to open a Data Form.

2. Click on the Criteria command button. The Data Form will switch to Criteria mode, as shown in Figure 4-7. The word "Criteria" appears above the command

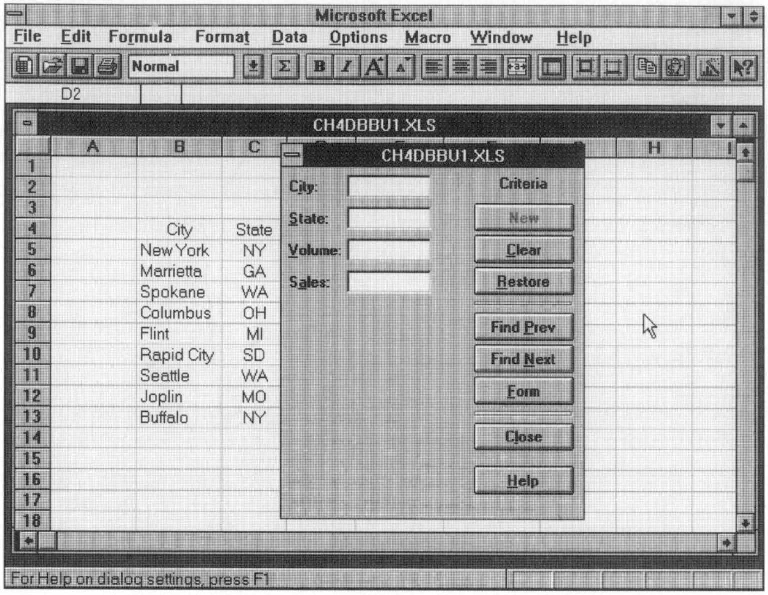

Figure 4-7.   *Data Form for entering criteria*

buttons, replacing the number of records, and a text box appears for each field, including computed and locked fields.

The Criteria command button is now labeled Form and can be used to switch back to the Form mode. The Delete command button is now labeled Clear, and you can use it to clear any criteria entered in the text boxes. The Restore command button becomes active; this button is used to restore the contents of the text boxes after they have been changed or cleared.

3. Now you can enter the search criteria into the text boxes; for example, to search for sales offices in Washington state with sales greater than $38,000, you would enter **WA** in the State text box and **$38,000** in the Sales text box.

4. Use the Find Prev and Find Next command buttons to find the records that meet the search criteria.

A blank text box acts like an asterisk wildcard: all fields are matched. If all the text boxes are blank, Find Prev and Find Next will display the previous and next records in sequence, without any selection.

Editing and Deleting Records with a Data Form

You can edit fields in a record with a Data Form simply by entering the new information in the appropriate text box and pressing ENTER or clicking on Close.

The Restore command button will become active when a field is edited. Clicking on Restore will undo any changes made to the record. Restore will only work if the edited record has not yet been replaced in the database.

You can delete records by clicking on the Delete command button. This deletes the record currently displayed in the Data Form.

CAUTION: Deleted records cannot be recovered. If you have saved the worksheet prior to deleting records, you can exit the worksheet file without saving it, then open the file again. The worksheet that appears will be the earlier, saved version, with your deleted records still intact.

Analyzing Database Information

In addition to organizing and locating information, databases are good for analyzing data. You can analyze information in Excel databases with database statistical functions, data tables, and cross tabulation (crosstab) tables.

Database Statistical Functions

Like the Sort option, the 12 database statistical functions Excel provides can be used with any selected range on the worksheet, not just a database. These functions are described here:

Function	Purpose
DAVERAGE	Averages selected numbers
DCOUNT	Counts selected numbers
DCOUNTA	Counts nonblank cells
DGET	Extracts a single value
DMAX	Finds the maximum value
DMIN	Finds the minimum value
DPRODUCT	Calculates the product of selected numbers
DSTDEV or DSTDEVP	Calculates the standard deviation
DSUM	Calculates the sum of selected numbers
DVAR or DVARP	Calculates the variance of selected numbers

Database statistical functions are similar to other worksheet statistical functions. The primary difference is that database functions operate only on cells within a range that meet specified criteria, while worksheet functions operate on all cells within the selected range.

The format for using database functions is

FUNCTION(*database,field,criteria*)

The *field* is the database field or column that will provide the data for the function, *database* is the range on the worksheet containing the field, and *criteria* is the criteria range that will be used to select the cells from the field.

You can enter the *database, field,* and *criteria* arguments as cell addresses, such as A1:F6, or as defined names of cells or ranges. If the function is to be used with the current database, you can use Database as the name of the database. If you have named a criteria range with Set Criteria, you can use Criteria as the name for the active criteria range.

How database statistical functions operate can be demonstrated with the worksheet in Figure 4-8. This worksheet lists the weekly sales for four sales offices. You can use database statistical functions to calculate the smallest and largest sales and the total sales for all the offices, and display these values on the worksheet. Using the criteria range, you can find the minimum, maximum, and total sales for all the weeks included in the database, or for just one week.

On the worksheet, the range A1:D22 has been named as the current database (not all the rows are visible in Figure 4-8), and the criteria range has been defined as F1:I2. The DMIN and DMAX functions have been used to find the minimum and

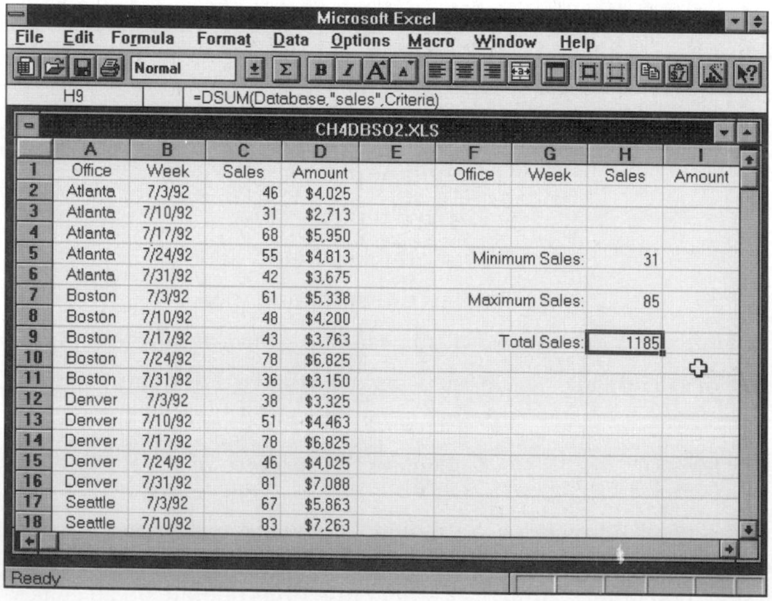

Figure 4-8.   *Minimum, maximum, and total sales by office*

maximum sales for the four offices and have placed the values in cells H5 and H7. The formula in H5 is =DMIN(Database,"sales",Criteria) and the formula in H7 is =DMAX(Database,"sales",Criteria). The names Database and Criteria are used in the formula because the active database and criteria ranges, which were defined with the Data menu Set commands, are being used by the function. Sales is the field containing the values the function will analyze.

The DSUM function has been used to find the total sales for all the offices and has placed the data in H9. The formula used to find the sum of the sales is visible in the edit area of the formula bar. As you can see, it is identical to the DMIN and DMAX formulas except for the function name. Since the criteria cells are blank, the criteria matches all the records, so the values returned by the functions represent the minimum, maximum, and total of all the sales.

In Figure 4-9, the week ending date 7/10/92 has been placed in the criteria field. The minimum, maximum, and total now represent the values for the week of July 10 only.

Each of the database statistical functions are explained in the Excel Dictionary portion of this book.

Data Tables

One of the more useful aspects of Excel is its ability to perform "what if" analyses of data. For example, "what if" the interest rate on a mortgage went up or down a

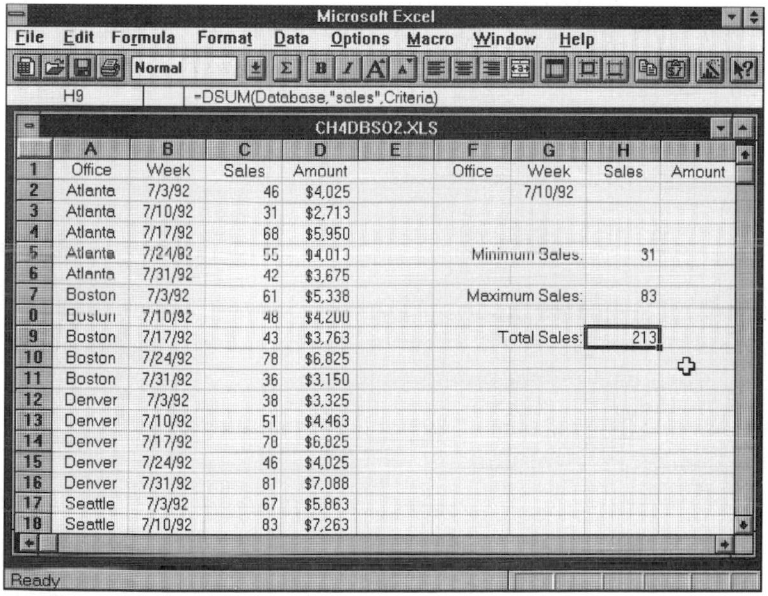

Figure 4-9. *Minimum, maximum, and total sales by office for one week*

percentage point or two? What would be the effect on monthly payments and the total interest paid? You accomplish this type of data analysis by substituting a range of values in one or two variables of a formula. The variable would be the interest rate in this example, and the objective would be to calculate what the mortgage payments and total interest would be with a number of different rates.

You can create a *data table* on a worksheet to perform this type of data analysis. A data table can be either a one-input or two-input data table. A *one-input* table can have multiple formulas, but only one variable. A *two-input* table has two variables, but only one formula.

Figure 4-10 is a two-input data table showing the relationship between commissions earned and the two variables: monthly sales and commission rates. In this table one variable, the commission rate, is in a row, and the other, the monthly sales, is in a column. There is a range of values for each of these variables. The formula is in the upper-left cell at the intersection of the first row and column.

Here are the steps involved in creating a two-input data table:

1. Enter the first variable—in this case the commission rate—in the first row of what will be the data table range, leaving the left cell empty for the formula.

2. Enter the second variable, monthly sales, in the first column of the data table range, again leaving the top cell empty for the formula.

3. Enter the formula, **=D1*G1** in this case, in the cell at the intersection of the first row and column of the data table range.

4. Select the data table range, A3:H10.

5. Choose Table from the Data menu. This brings up the Table dialog box, as shown here:

Table	
Row Input Cell: $D$1	OK
Column Input Cell: $G$1	Cancel
	Help

6. Enter **$D$1** in the Row Input Cell text box and **$G$1** in the Column Input Cell text box, or click on cell D1 when the Row Input Cell text box is selected and on G1 when the Column Input Cell text box is selected.

7. Click on OK. The balance of the table is then filled in by Excel, saving you a large number of calculations.

Crosstab Tables

A cross tabulation table, or *crosstab*, is used to summarize database information by showing the totals for columns on the bottom of the worksheet, the totals of the rows

	A	B	C	D	E	F	G	H	I
1		Commission Rate			Monthly Sales				
2									
3	0	3.0%	3.5%	4.0%	4.5%	5.0%	5.5%	6.0%	
4	40,000	1200	1400	1600	1800	2000	2200	2400	
5	50,000	1500	1750	2000	2250	2500	2750	3000	
6	60,000	1800	2100	2400	2700	3000	3300	3600	
7	70,000	2100	2450	2800	3150	3500	3850	4200	
8	80,000	2400	2800	3200	3600	4000	4400	4800	
9	90,000	2700	3150	3600	4050	4500	4950	5400	
10	100,000	3000	3500	4000	4500	5000	5500	6000	

Figure 4-10.   *A two-input data table*

on the right, and a grand total in the lower-right corner. You can use crosstabs when you need to compare summaries of database information to each other. The work-sheet in Figure 4-11, for example, shows the monthly sales of four sales offices over two months. In this form, it's easy to find the monthly sales of each office, but not the total sales for each month or for each office. A crosstab can quickly present this information, as shown in Figure 4-12.

You create crosstabs with the Crosstab ReportWizard, which is presented when you choose Crosstab from the Data menu. You can also use the Crosstab ReportWizard to recalculate or modify an existing crosstab. As with other database operations, you can use a criteria range to create the crosstab from only selected records in the database. The example in Figure 4-12 uses all the records in the database. The crosstab will be set up to show the data for each city in one row, with both the number of sales and the dollar amount of the sales shown.

To create a crosstab, follow these steps:

1. Choose Crosstab from the Data menu. Excel will display the Crosstab ChartWizard introductory screen shown in Figure 4-13.

2. Click on the Create a New Crosstab command button. Excel will present the Crosstab ReportWizard Row Categories screen, as shown in Figure 4-14. You

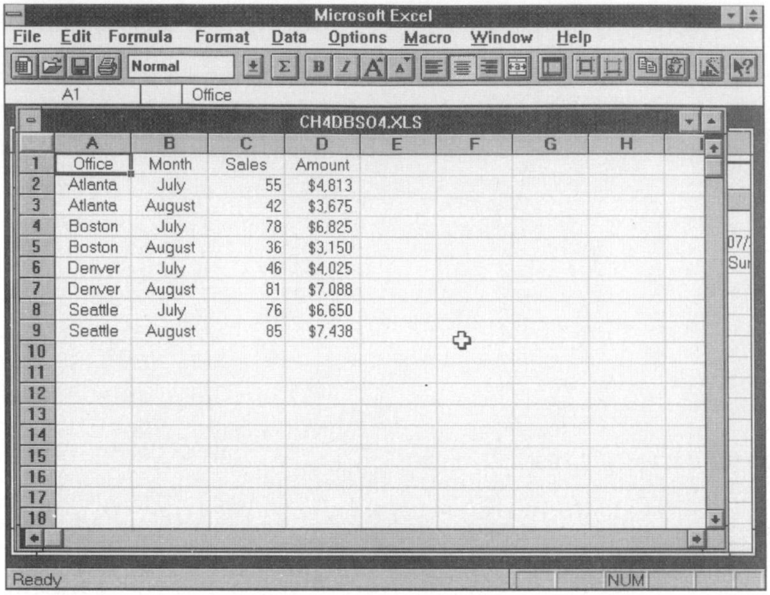

Figure 4-11.   Monthly sales by office

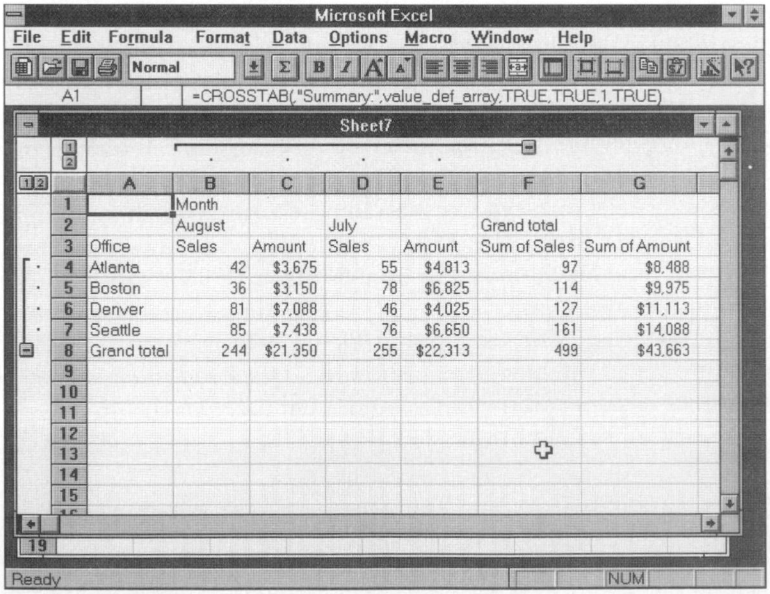

Figure 4-12.   A Crosstab sales summary

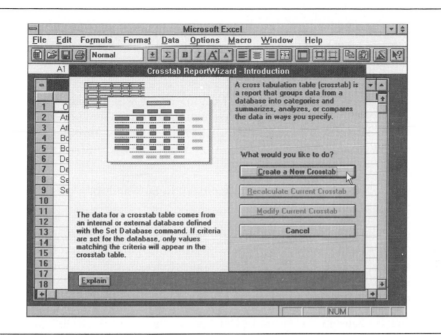

Figure 4-13.   *The Crosstab ReportWizard Introduction screen*

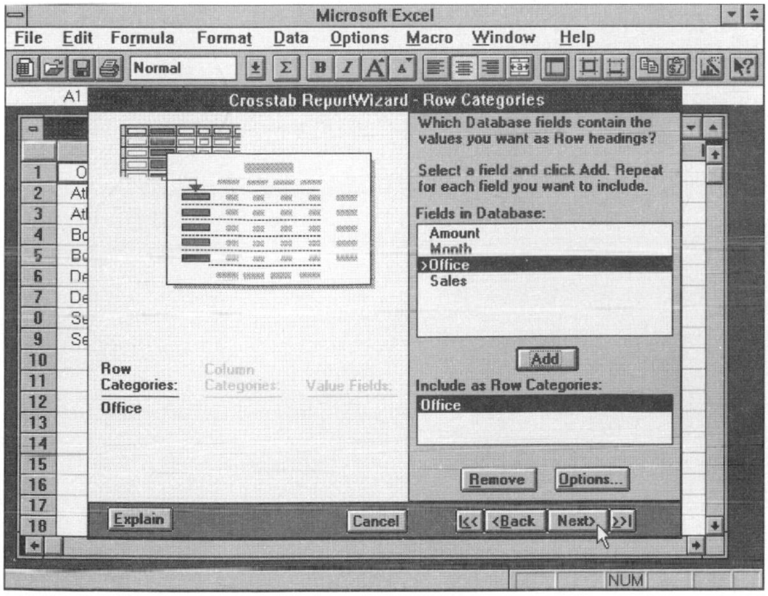

Figure 4-14.   *The Crosstab ReportWizard Row Categories screen*

use this screen to define which categories will be represented in each row. This example will use each row to show the data for one sales office.

3. Click on Office in the Fields in Database list box, and then click on the Add command button.

4. Click on the Next command button. Excel will display the Crosstab ReportWizard Column Categories screen, as shown in Figure 4-15. You use this screen to define which categories will be represented in the column headings. For this example, columns will be used to show the information for each month.

5. Click on Month in the Fields in Database list box, and then click on the Add command button.

6. Click on the Next command button. Excel will display the Crosstab ReportWizard Value Fields screen, as shown in Figure 4-16. You want both the number of sales and the dollar amount shown in this crosstab. Therefore, define both the Sales and Amount fields as the values to be displayed in the crosstab.

7. Click on Sales in the Fields in Database list box, and then click on the Add command button.

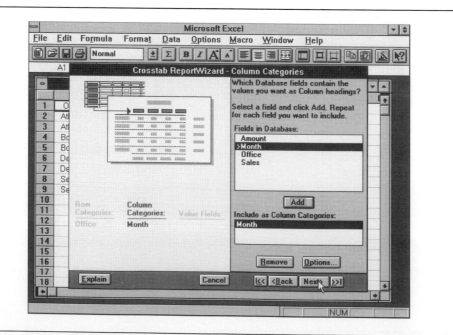

Figure 4-15. The Crosstab ReportWizard Column Categories screen

Chapter 4: Using a Database *151*

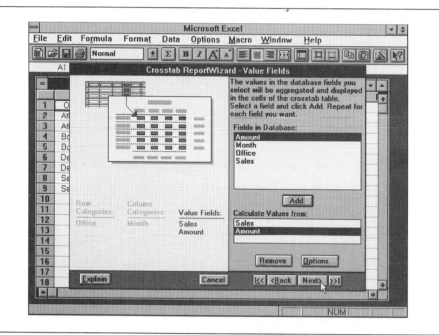

Figure 4-16. *The Crosstab ReportWizard Value Fields screen*

8. Click on Amount in the Fields in Database text box and again click on the Add command button.

9. Click on the Next command button. Excel will present the Crosstab ReportWizard Multiple Value Field Layout screen, as shown in Figure 4-17. Two values will be shown in the crosstab: Sales and Amount.

When multiple value fields are selected for either rows or columns, they can be formatted as either *inner* or *outer* rows or columns. An inner-column format, which was shown in Figure 4-11, places the Sales values and the Amount values for each week next to each other. An outer-column format would place all the Sales values in adjacent columns, and then all the Amount values in adjacent columns.

10. Click on the Inner Columns option button.

11. Click on Next. Excel will display the Crosstab ReportWizard Final screen, as shown in Figure 4-18. This screen includes two command buttons: Create It and Set Table Creation Options. The available options are listed here:

   - *Outline* determines whether the crosstab will be created in the outline format.

   - *New worksheet* determines whether the crosstab will be created on the current worksheet, or if a new worksheet will be created.

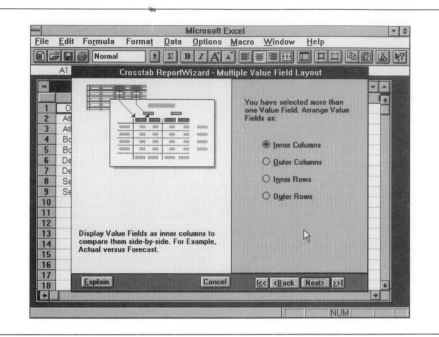

Figure 4-17. *The Crosstab ReportWizard Multiple Values screen*

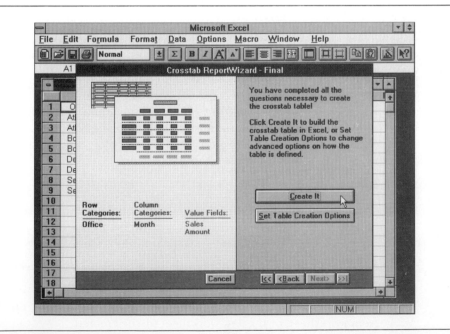

Figure 4-18. *The Crosstab ReportWizard Final screen*

- *Define names* allows you to refer to values by name rather than by cell reference.

- *Double click* to display source data, which allows you to view the source data for the crosstab by double-clicking on the crosstab with your mouse.

12. Create the crosstab by clicking on the Create It command button.

   The crosstab created will need to be formatted properly after it is created. Figure 4-12 showed the crosstab created in the inner-column format, as was explained in step 9. Figure 4-19 shows the same data created as an outer-column crosstab. Each type of crosstab presents the information with a different emphasis. An inner-column crosstab gives a better comparison of the total activities for each month, while the outer-column crosstab gives a better comparison of sales or amounts for each month.

Other Data Operations

   Several options on the Data menu have still not been discussed. These are other data operations that are not directly related to a database. They include generating a series of numbers, dividing or parsing a text string, and consolidating several worksheets.

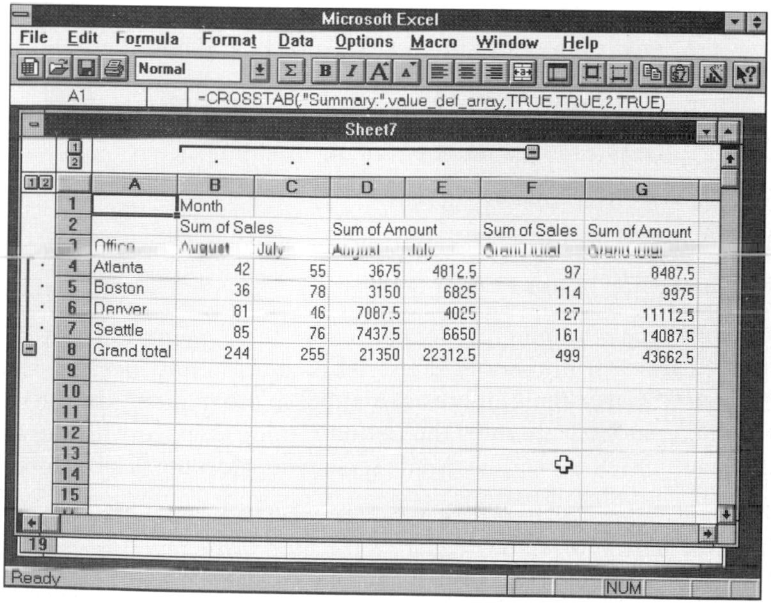

Figure 4-19.   An outer-column Crosstab

Entering Data Series

Whenever you need to enter a series of numbers or dates in a worksheet, you can automatically produce them using a data series. You can produce a data series in two ways: with the Series option in the Data menu and with the mouse. In both cases, you begin the series by entering a number or date in a cell, and then setting a pattern by extending the series either across a row or down a column.

Entering Series with the Series Option

Choosing Series from the Data menu presents the dialog box shown here:

You can define the series with the Series dialog box, or Excel will continue the pattern already entered on the worksheet with the AutoFill feature. With AutoFill, if the series started with 1, 3, 5, for example, Excel would continue with 7, 9, 11, and so on to fill the selected range. AutoFill will also extend patterns such as Product 1, with Product 2, Product 3, and so on.

To apply the Series option with the Series dialog box, follow these steps:

1. Click on the cell where the numbering sequence is to begin and type the starting value (it can be a number, a date, or a time).

2. Choose Series from the Data menu.

3. Select whether you want the series in rows or columns with the Rows and Columns option buttons under Series In.

4. Select the type of numbering sequence with the Type option buttons. Linear will increase each number in the series by the amount specified in the Step text box, Growth will multiply each number in the sequence by the step value, Date increases each value by the period of time selected with the Date Unit option buttons. If the series is a date series, you select the desired interval from the Date Unit option buttons.

5. Enter the maximum value needed in the Stop Value text box.

6. When the options have been set, click on OK.

Entering Series with the Mouse and the Fill Handle

Once the Series has been started, you can also extend the range by using the *fill handle* on the selected range. The fill handle is a small square located in the lower-right corner of the selection, as shown here:

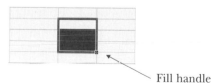

Fill handle

The mouse pointer changes to a small cross when you place it on the fill handle. You can then drag the range to the desired size and the series will be filled in.

Parsing

Excel can import data from a number of different sources, including text files from word processors and data from bulletin boards and from information services. Usually, Excel can place the imported data into the proper series of rows and columns. Some data, however, will be imported into only one column, because Excel sometimes cannot determine how data should be separated. The Parse option is used to separate the data into its components and place them into separate columns.

The Parse option is designed to work with imported data that uses spaces to fill out fields so that each field is the same length. To parse an imported file, follow these steps:

1. Select the range that contains the data to be parsed. The range can include as many rows as needed, but must include only one column.

2. Choose Parse from the Data menu. The Parse dialog box will open, as shown here:

Parse
Parse Line:
[Johnson][Tom][Louisville][KY]
Destination:
$A$16
OK   Cancel   Guess   Clear   Help

The first cell of the selected range is displayed in the Parse Line. Square brackets ([]) show where Excel will separate the data. The Clear command button will remove all brackets, and the Guess command button will restore Excel's placement of the brackets. You can adjust the brackets to change where the data will be divided into individual cells.

To separate the data and copy it to the new range, follow these steps:

1. If the displayed settings need to be adjusted, type or delete brackets until the data is separated properly.

2. Enter the address of the first cell where the parsed data will be placed. This will be the cell in the upper-left corner of the new range.

The new data will overwrite any data already on the worksheet in the selected range.

Consolidating

The Consolidate option in the Data menu allows you to summarize data from individual worksheets. You can use this technique to create summary worksheets containing data from several individual worksheets. For example, if the sales data from several offices is located on a separate worksheet for each office, you can consolidate totals for all the offices onto one worksheet. Figure 4-20 shows the consolidated worksheet that could be created from the individual worksheets for each sales office. As you can see, the sales data from each office is on a separate worksheet, these are the source worksheets. On the consolidated worksheet the sales and amount from each office have been added, giving the combined totals for each week. This is the destination worksheet.

You must define several elements to carry out a consolidation. These are: the type of mathematical function used, the type of source data, and the source and destination ranges to supply and receive the data. The following sections review each of these elements and then demonstrate the actual steps involved in performing the consolidation.

Consolidation Functions

The consolidated worksheet in Figure 4-20 summed the data from the individual worksheets. You can also use other functions to process the data on the source worksheets. There are 11 worksheet functions that you can use with the Consolidate option, as listed here:

Function	Purpose
AVERAGE	Averages selected numbers
COUNT	Counts selected numbers
COUNTA	Counts the nonblank cells
MAX	Finds the maximum value

Function	Purpose
MIN	Finds the minimum value
PRODUCT	Calculates the product of selected numbers
STDEV	Calculates the standard deviation of a sample of a group
STDEVP	Calculates the standard deviation of an entire group
SUM	Calculates the sum of selected numbers
VAR	Calculates the variance of a sample of a group
VARP	Calculates the variance of an entire group

Types of Source Data

You can consolidate individual worksheets by category or position. Consolidating by category selects the data from the source worksheets by category, regardless of its location on the source worksheets. Worksheet data is consolidated by position when the data is in the same relative position on each worksheet. You can establish links between the source worksheets and the consolidated worksheet so that changes in the source worksheets will be reflected in the consolidated worksheet.

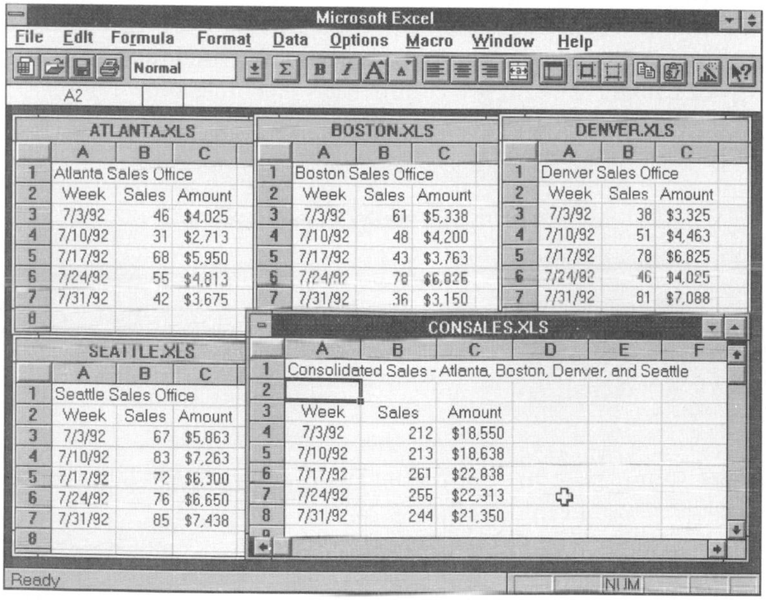

Figure 4-20. *The consolidated sales worksheet*

The Destination and Source Ranges

To consolidate the worksheet data, you must first specify a destination range on the destination worksheet. The range can be a single cell or a range of cells. If a single cell is selected Excel will use as many rows and columns as needed to contain the consolidated data. If a single row is selected, Excel will use as many rows as needed, but only as many columns as have been selected in the row. If a single column is selected, Excel will use as many columns as needed but only as many rows as are selected in the range. If a range of multiple rows and columns has been selected, Excel will use only the selected range for the consolidated data.

If you use a single cell as the destination range, all the data selected on the source worksheets can be consolidated onto the destination worksheet. If you select a larger range, not all the data may be consolidated, but data on the destination worksheet will not be overwritten by the consolidated data.

On the source worksheets, you must select a range to be consolidated. These source areas can be named ranges. Only values are consolidated from the source range; if a cell contains a formula, only the resulting value is copied to the destination range. The source worksheets do not have to be open for consolidation.

Performing a Consolidation

The following steps explain how to create the consolidated worksheet shown in Figure 4-20:

1. Select the destination range on the current worksheet. In this example, two columns are going to be consolidated onto the destination worksheet, so a range of a single row and two columns is selected, as shown here:

2. Choose Consolidate from the Data menu, the Consolidate dialog box will appear, as shown here:

3. Select the desired function from the Function drop-down list box. For this example, choose the SUM function to sum the consolidated data.

4. Select the Reference text box by clicking on it or by using TAB. Here you enter the ranges on the source worksheets to be consolidated.

5. If you are consolidating from an unopened worksheet, click on the Browse command button, which presents the Browse dialog box shown here:

6. Select the source worksheet in the file list text box and click on OK. The name of the worksheet will be entered in the Reference text box in the Consolidate dialog box. Enter the name or address of the source range after the worksheet name. Use an exclamation mark (!) to separate the worksheet name and the range name or address.

7. If consolidating from an open worksheet, you can enter the source area by selecting the range to be consolidated with the mouse. The selected range will be entered in the Reference text box.

8. Click on the Add command button in the Consolidate dialog box. The source range is entered in the All References list box. This contains the locations of all the data that will be consolidated on the destination worksheet.

9. Select additional worksheets and ranges for consolidation by repeating steps 5 to 8. The consolidated worksheet in Figure 4-20 used the data from four individual worksheets. After all the ranges had been entered in the Consolidate dialog box, this is what it looked like:

10. Click on OK to perform the consolidation.

Chapter *5*

Working with Macros

What Are Macros?

A *macro* is a shortcut, a way to carry out a series of worksheet operations by entering only a few keystrokes or by choosing a menu option. The menu choice or keystrokes tell Excel to execute the predefined series of instructions that the macro contains. Macros can be relatively simple, such as a macro to save the current worksheet, or much more elaborate—a macro to extract data and create a chart from it, for example. Macros simplify the use of worksheets for both experienced and novice users.

You can create a macro by *recording* a series of keystrokes or mouse actions. You do this by choosing Record from the Macro menu or by clicking on the Record Macro tool in the Macro toolbar, and then carrying out the operations that you want stored in the macro. The keystrokes or mouse actions are saved, or recorded, on a *macro sheet,* a type of worksheet used for storing macros. To end the macro recording, choose Stop Recorder in the Macro menu or click on the Stop Recording tool in the Macro toolbar. You use macros by *running* them, which you can do in one of several ways: you can choose Run in the Macro menu, click on Run Macro in the Macro toolbar, or use a shortcut key—a combination of the CTRL key and a letter.

You can also create macros by typing the macro operations directly on the macro sheet in much the same way as you enter information on a worksheet. You can also edit recorded macros on the macro sheet. This chapter will cover each of these methods for creating and running macros.

Recording a Macro

In the following sections, you'll learn how to record and run a macro by creating a simple macro that will save the current worksheet. When using a worksheet, you should save it several times an hour as a normal precaution to prevent data loss. To save the worksheet, you must either choose Save from the File menu using either the mouse or keyboard, click on the Save tool on the Standard toolbar, or press SHIFT-F12 or ALT-SHIFT-F2. This macro will save the current worksheet by simply pressing CTRL-S. This example illustrates how you can customize Excel for individual preferences with macros—in this case a keyboard shortcut that will save a worksheet.

You can record a macro by using either the Macro menu or the Macro toolbar. The same basic steps are used in either method, both of which are demonstrated in the next sections.

Recording with the Macro Menu

To record a macro you can use the Macro menu, which is shown here. To create this macro you must first have an active worksheet that has been saved at least once.

Follow these steps to record the macro:

1. Open the Macro menu and choose Record. While the macro is being recorded, the Record option in the Macro menu will change to Stop Recorder. The Record Macro dialog box appears, as shown here:

You next need to give the macro a name that will make the function of the macro clear and comply with Excel's rules for macro names. This name must start with a letter, cannot contain any spaces, can be up to 255 characters long, and can contain any combination of letters, numbers, periods, and underlines. Call this macro Save.Worksheet, using a period in place of a space.

2. Type **Save.Worksheet** in the Name text box and press TAB to move to the Key text box.

The Key text box is where you define the shortcut key that will be used with CTRL to run the macro. The shortcut key is case sensitive, meaning that if you enter an uppercase letter here you must use the SHIFT key when entering the shortcut key combination. CTRL-S (lowercase) is already the Excel shortcut for formatting worksheet cells with a style (a set of predefined formatting options), so the macro will use CTRL-SHIFT-S (uppercase). If CTRL-S were used for the macro, it would take precedence over the apply style shortcut. When selecting keys to use for shortcuts, take care to avoid conflicts with Excel's default shortcut keys. Excel will suggest a shortcut key that will not conflict with an existing shortcut key.

NOTE: You cannot use numbers and special characters for shortcut keys.

3. Type **S** in the Key text box.

You can record a macro on a regular macro sheet or the *global macro sheet*. The global macro sheet is a macro sheet that is opened automatically when Excel is started. The macros stored on this macro sheet are available for use with any open worksheet. In contrast, you must open other macro sheets before you can use the macros on them. Record this sample macro on the global macro sheet.

4. Click on the Global Macro Sheet option button.

5. Click on OK. Excel is now ready to record the macro. The Record Macro dialog box closes and the word Recording appears in the status bar at the bottom of the Excel window. All mouse actions and keystrokes will now become part of the Save.Worksheet macro.

6. Open the File menu and choose Save using either the mouse or keyboard.

7. Choose Stop Recorder from the Macro menu.

The macro Save.Worksheet has now been recorded on the global macro sheet. You can use it by pressing CTRL-SHIFT-S or by using the Macro menu or Macro toolbar, as explained in a moment. You'll also open the global macro sheet and look at the macro you just recorded. But first, you'll learn how to record a macro with the Macro toolbar.

Recording with the Macro Toolbar

The Macro toolbar provides another method to record and run macros. You open the Macro toolbar by choosing Toolbars from the Options menu and selecting Macro and then Show. The Macro toolbar looks like this:

The Macro toolbar tools are described here, from left to right:

	Tool	Purpose
	New Macro Sheet	Creates a new macro sheet
	Paste Function	Allows a function to be pasted into a macro
	Paste Names	Allows a name to be pasted into a macro
	Run Macro	Runs the selected macro
	Step Macro	Runs the selected macro one step at a time
	Record Macro	Records a macro
	Resume Macro	Resumes a macro that has been paused
	Stop Recording	Stops the recording of a macro

Recording a macro with the Macro toolbar involves the same steps as recording with the Macro menu. The only difference is that you start and stop the recording with the Macro toolbar instead of the Macro menu.

To record a macro using this method, click on the Record Macro tool (third from the right). Excel displays the Record Macro dialog box that you saw earlier. To end the recording, click on the Stop Recording tool.

Running a Macro

Shortcut keys provide a simple, quick way to run a macro and are well-suited to macros like Save.Worksheet, which is designed to be used often. In addition, you can run macros from the Macro menu and Macro toolbar.

Running a Macro with the Macro Menu

As the number of available macros and open macro sheets grows, choosing a macro to be run from a list has advantages. You may forget the shortcut key combination for an infrequently used macro or a macro may not have a shortcut key combination. There is a limit to the number of shortcut key combinations available and many of the combinations are already used by Excel. With the Macro menu you can run any macro simply by selecting it from a list. To use the Macro menu to run a macro, follow these steps:

1. Choose Run from the Macro menu. The Run Macro dialog box appears, as shown here:

The Run list box contains a list of the macros on the active macro sheets. Each entry consists of the shortcut key followed by the macro sheet name, an exclamation point (!) separator, and the macro name. Here, there is only one macro currently available: Save.Worksheet on the macro sheet GLOBAL.XLM, with the shortcut key CTRL-S.

2. Click on "S GLOBAL.XLM!Save.Worksheet" in the list box and click on OK. Excel runs the macro and saves the active worksheet.

Running a Macro with the Macro Toolbar

Running a macro from the Macro toolbar differs from using the Macro menu. When you choose the Run option from the Macro menu, Excel presents the Run Macro dialog box, allowing you to run any of the available macros. In contrast, with the

Macro toolbar, clicking on the Run Macro tool runs the single macro that has been assigned to the tool. To assign a macro to the Run Macro tool, follow these steps:

1. Display the Macro toolbar, if it is not currently displayed, by choosing Toolbars from the Options menu, selecting Macro, and clicking on Show.

2. Choose the Toolbars option in the Options menu.

3. Click on the Customize command button in the Toolbars dialog box. The Customize dialog box will appear, as shown in Figure 5-1.

4. Arrange the window so the Macro toolbar is visible.

5. Click on the Run Macro tool in the Macro toolbar.

6. Choose the Assign To Tool option in the Macro menu. Excel displays the Assign To Tool dialog box, which is shown here. (The Assign To Tool dialog box is similar to the Run Macro dialog box.)

7. Click on the name of the macro to be assigned to the Run Macro tool and click on OK to return to the Customize dialog box.

8. Click on the Close command button in the Customize dialog box.

The selected macro is now assigned to the Run Macro tool and can be run by clicking on the Run Macro tool. This method makes an often-used macro readily available.

Working with Macro Sheets

The Save.Worksheet macro was recorded on the global macro sheet. As mentioned, the global macro sheet is opened automatically when Excel is started. This is the only difference between the global macro sheet and regular macro sheets. Macro sheets are similar to normal worksheets and can be formatted, printed, and saved in the same way.

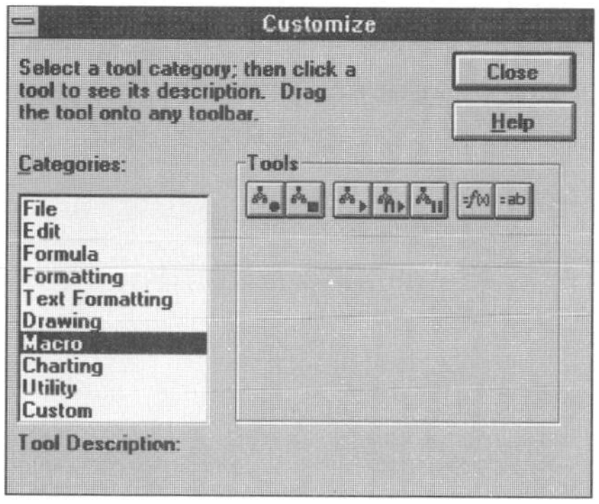

Figure 5-1.   *The Customize dialog box*

Opening a New Macro Sheet

You open a new macro sheet just as you open a new worksheet: by choosing New from the File menu. The New dialog box appears, as shown here. From this dialog box, select Macro Sheet and click on OK.

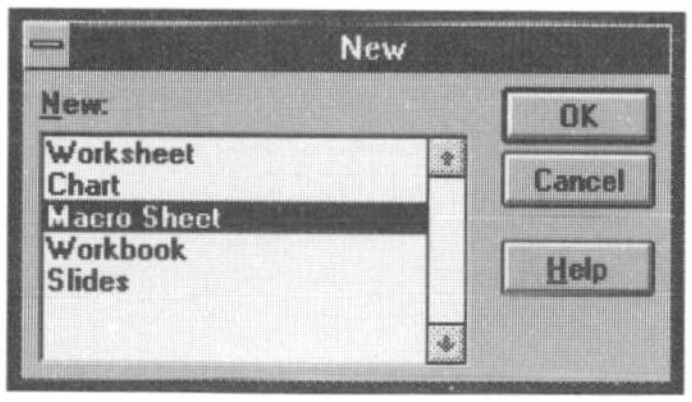

NOTE: You can also open a new macro sheet by clicking on the New Macro Sheet tool in the Macro toolbar.

Hidden Macro Sheets

Even though the global macro sheet is opened when Excel is started, it is not visible in the Excel application window. This is because it is a *hidden* document. Hidden documents are not visible in the Excel application window until you make them visible with the Unhide option on the Window menu. If no documents are visible, the Unhide option is on the File menu.

Macro sheets are usually kept hidden to avoid clutter in the Excel application window and to prevent accidental changes to the macros. As long as the macro sheet is open, the macros it contains are available whether or not the macro sheet is visible. If the Unhide option is greyed (not available), no macros have been placed on the global macro sheet. To see the Save.Worksheet macro on the global macro sheet, follow these steps:

1. Choose Unhide from the Window menu. The Unhide dialog box appears, as shown here:

The list box in the Unhide dialog box contains the filenames of all open documents that are hidden. GLOBAL.XLM is the filename of the global macro sheet.

2. Select GLOBAL.XLM and click on OK. The global macro sheet is now the active document. To hide the macro sheet choose Hide from the Window menu.

Macro Types

Save.Worksheet is a *command macro*. Command macros are used to automate a series of Excel commands and operations. A second type of macro is also available in Excel, the *function macro*. Function macros are custom functions that are used in the same way as Excel's built-in functions. Command macros always take some type of action, such as saving a worksheet. In contrast, function macros take no action; instead they return a result, such as the result of a calculation.

In addition, command macros are contained completely on a macro sheet and are run with one of the methods mentioned previously. Function macros are created on macro sheets, but are not run the same way as command macros. Instead, you use function macros the same way you use regular Excel functions: you enter the function macro name into the desired cell on the worksheet as a formula or part of a formula. The result is returned on the worksheet as the value of the cell in which it is entered.

Macro Functions

Macro functions are quite different from the function macros just described, and are the building blocks for macros. Each macro function is a single command or function that is one step in the process the macro will execute. Using macro functions, you can automate almost any worksheet operation, including menu selection, and worksheet functions and formulas. The Excel Dictionary section later in this book provides a complete list of macro functions.

The Save.Worksheet macro shows how macro functions are used to build a command macro. The Save.Worksheet macro is listed in the range A1:A3 on the global macro sheet, as shown in Figure 5-2.

Macros are listed in columns on the macro sheet; these columns are, by default, wider than the columns on a normal worksheet. The name of the macro is in the first cell of the range, A1, with the shortcut key in parentheses at the end of the name. This macro has two macro functions, located in cells A2 and A3.

Macro functions are formulas and must begin with an equal sign (=). The macro function in A2, =SAVE(), performs the same operation as choosing Save from the File menu. =SAVE() is a *macro command function,* a macro function that performs a worksheet action. The macro function in A3, =RETURN(), is a *macro control function.* Macro control functions are used to direct the execution of the macro—in this case,

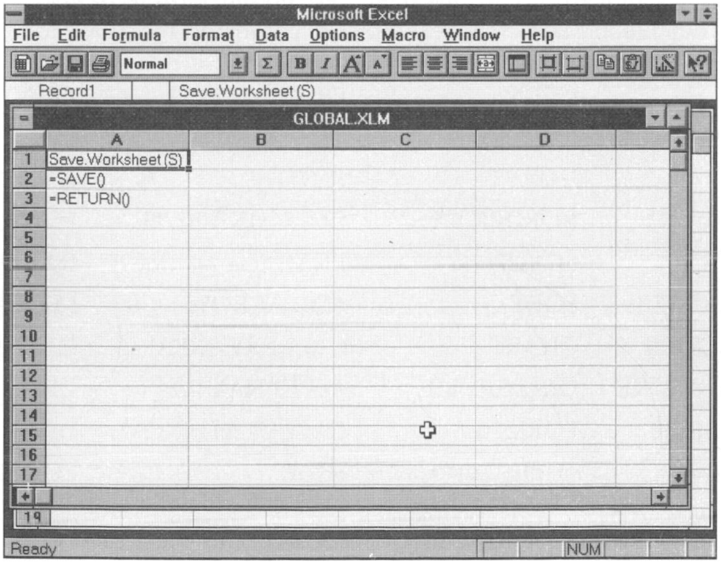

Figure 5-2.   *The Global macro sheet Save.Worksheet listing*

to end the macro and return to the active worksheet. Command and control macro functions are only two types of macro functions. Excel macro functions also include macro database, engineering, external, lookup and reference, statistical, and text functions. Any of Excel's regular functions can also be used in macros.

Again, don't confuse macro functions with function macros. A macro function is a single programming command that is combined with other commands to create a macro. A function macro is a series of functions that define a custom function used to process data and return a result. Also don't confuse command macros and macro commands. A command macro is a series of macro commands, while a macro command is a single step in the command macro. Command macros will be referred to as macros and function macros will be referred to as custom functions to avoid confusion.

Macro Command Functions

Command functions are used in macros to execute virtually any menu option. Each available menu option has a command function name that can be used in a macro. Command function names comply with the same rules as other Excel file names: they must start with a letter, cannot contain any spaces, can be up to 255 characters long, and can contain any combination of letters, numbers, periods, and underlines.

Command functions also manipulate the worksheet and its environment. For example, you can use command functions to scroll the active window both horizontally and vertically. You can also execute file operations, such as creating directories, by using macro command functions. There are literally dozens of macro command functions available in Excel. Some examples of command functions are listed here:

NEW	OPEN	QUIT	PRINT
SAVE	SAVE.AS	CLEAR	COPY
CUT	INSERT	PASTE	UNDO
ALIGNMENT	BORDER	COLUMN.WIDTH	FORMAT.FONT
PATTERNS	SCALE	EXTRACT	DATA.FIND
DATA.SERIES	SORT	ADD.ARROW	LEGEND
EDIT.SERIES	CHART	GALLERY.AREA	GALLERY.BAR
GALLERY.LINE	GALLERY.PIE	APPLY.NAMES	DEFINE.NAME
GOAL.SEEK	FORMULA	CALCULATE.NOW	DISPLAY
SPELLING	SHOW.INFO	HIDE	ZOOM

All of these command functions are described in the Excel Dictionary section of this book.

Macro Information Functions

When a macro needs to know something about the active worksheet or the worksheet environment, an information function is used to retrieve the information. For example, the information function ACTIVE.CELL is used to return to the macro the location or value of the active cell on the worksheet. Other information functions will return information about open documents, directories, and windows. There are 32 different macro information functions available, the most common or which are listed here:

CALLER	DIRECTORY	FILES	GET.BAR
GET.CELL	GET.DOCUMENT	GET.NAME	GET.NOTE
GET.TOOL	GET.WINDOW	LAST.ERROR	NAMES

Again, each of the information functions are described in the Excel Dictionary section of this book.

Macro Control Functions

Macro control functions are the operators that direct the execution of the macro. For example, every macro has to end with the control function RETURN or HALT. These control functions end the operation of the macro and return to the active worksheet. (For more details, see RETURN and HALT in the Excel Dictionary section of this book.) An error message is generated if one of these two control functions is not present. There are 21 different macro control functions available, some of which are listed here:

BREAK	ELSE	END.IF	FOR
GOTO	IF	NEXT	PAUSE
SET.NAME	STEP	WAIT	WHILE

Control functions also enable a macro to make a choice between two options in the macro. This is known as *branching*. Control functions can examine specific information on the worksheet, such as the value in a cell, and use that information to choose between two sets of macro actions.

The control function IF is commonly used in macros. IF uses a comparison test like A4>=B6 (which asks if cell A4 is greater than or equal to cell B6) to determine whether the statement is true or false. When the comparison test is true (namely A4 *is* greater than or equal to B6), IF returns a logical TRUE value; otherwise it returns a logical FALSE value. When the condition is TRUE, the macro will take one course of action, and when the condition is FALSE, the macro will take a different action.

Customizing Functions

You can employ macro customizing functions to create custom menus, toolbars, and dialog boxes for worksheets. To the user, these menus, toolbars, and dialog boxes will appear and function as if they were part of Excel's regular features.

You use these functions to build custom applications for Excel. In some situations, a worksheet application may be used by several people; an order entry system is one example. By creating a custom application for order entry, you can minimize the chances of mistakes. You can limit data entry to the proper data types and use macros to simplify complex operations. A single menu or toolbar command would replace a series of actions that would have to be executed in the proper sequence to avoid errors. Some examples of functions for customizing macros are listed here:

ADD.BAR	ADD.MENU	ADD.TOOL	ALERT
BEEP	DELETE.MENU	DELETE.TOOL	ECHO
ERROR	HELP	ON.TIME	SHOW.BAR

Using Macros

In most cases, you create macros by recording them, as you did with Save.Worksheet. This method is quick and efficient, and allows you to automate virtually any sequence of Excel operations. To use all of Excel's macro capabilities, however, you need to enter at least part of the macro directly on the macro sheet. Some macro control functions, such as IF, cannot be recorded and can only be used when typed on a macro sheet. Also, you can edit recorded macros or write an entire macro on the macro sheet.

The global macro sheet is the best place for macros that will be used with a number of different worksheets. Other macros that are tailored to a specific worksheet, such as a set of macros to produce financial reports, are best placed on their own macro sheet. You can then open and use this macro sheet only when the macros are needed.

Using Macro Ranges

When a macro is recorded on the global macro sheet, the macro name will be placed in the first row of the first empty column on a macro sheet. The macro functions, then, will be entered below the title, in the rows of that column. When the macro is recorded on a macro sheet, you must specify a range in which to place the macro. To select the range for the macro, follow these steps:

1. Make the macro sheet the active document by choosing it in the Windows menu or by creating a new macro sheet with the New option from the File menu.

2. Select the range on the macro sheet where the macro will be recorded.

If you select a single cell, the macro will be recorded in cells below the selected cell. All the cells below the selected cell should be blank. If the selected range has more than one column, the macro will be recorded in the first column of the range until the last cell in that column in the range, and will then continue in the first row of the next column. If the last cell in the range is reached before the macro is completed, an error message will be generated. The macro will not end with a RETURN function and will generate an error if it is run.

3. Choose Set Recorder from the Macro menu.

4. Make the desired worksheet the active document.

Now you can record the macro on a regular macro sheet. When the Record Macro dialog box is presented, the name of the macro sheet will appear by the Macro Sheet option button under Store Macro In, as shown here:

Writing a Macro

You write macros by typing the macro commands and functions directly on the macro sheet. In this section, you will write a simple macro that will also demonstrate how branching is used in a macro. The macro will examine the value in the active cell on the current worksheet and compare it against a value in the macro. If the value in the active cell is greater than the comparison value in the macro, the macro will take one action. If the value in the active cell is smaller than the comparison value in the macro, the macro will take a different action.

This macro shows one way worksheet data can be used by a macro, how comparisons are made by macro control functions, and how macros can return results to the active worksheet.

This macro will examine the numeric value in a cell and then place the text "TRUE" in the cell below the active cell if the number is greater than 10 (you could compare any value in the macro), or "FALSE" if the number is 10 or less. While this macro simply places text in a worksheet cell, you could use the same macro structure to branch to more involved operations. This macro, named IF.Example, is shown in Figure 5-3.

To create this macro on a regular macro sheet, follow these steps:

1. Open a new regular macro sheet with the New command on the File menu. The new macro sheet is automatically made the active document.

2. Click on the cell that will be the first cell of the macro.

There must be enough blank cells in the column below this cell to enter all the steps of the macro. If there aren't enough blank cells, the macro either will overwrite existing material or, if you've reached the end of the worksheet, will try to continue into the next column.

3. In the active cell, type the name of the macro, in this case type **IF.Example.**

4. Move down to the next cell in the column.

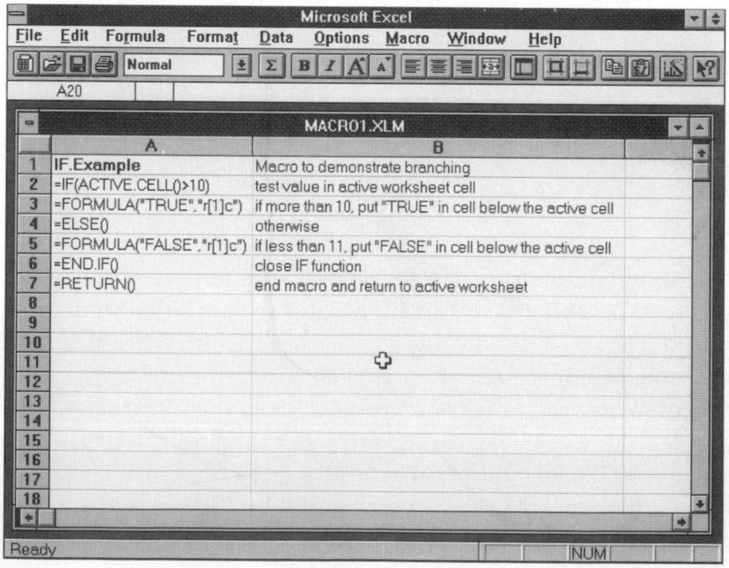

Figure 5-3.   *The IF.Example macro listing*

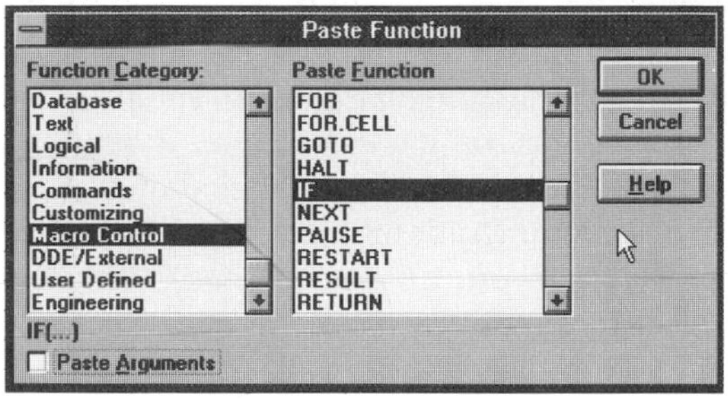

Figure 5-4.   *The Paste Function dialog box*

5. Enter the IF function by choosing Paste Function in the Formula menu or clicking on the Paste Function tool in the Macro toolbar (the second tool from the left). The Paste Function dialog box will appear, as shown in Figure 5-4.

6. In the Function Category list box, choose Macro Control.

7. In the Paste Function list box, choose IF. Then make sure the Paste Arguments check box is not checked and click on OK. The IF function is pasted into the active cell.

The arguments for the function need to be entered next. Since this macro will test the value of the active cell on the worksheet, the value of the active cell must be brought into the function. Using the information function ACTIVE.CELL, the IF function can compare the value in the active cell on the worksheet.

8. While the IF function is still in the Edit area with the insertion point between the parentheses, choose Paste Function from the Formula menu, choose Information from the Function Category list box, and choose ACTIVE.CELL from the Paste Function list box.

9. In the edit area of the formula bar, type **>10** for the comparison operator and comparison value in the formula, as shown here:

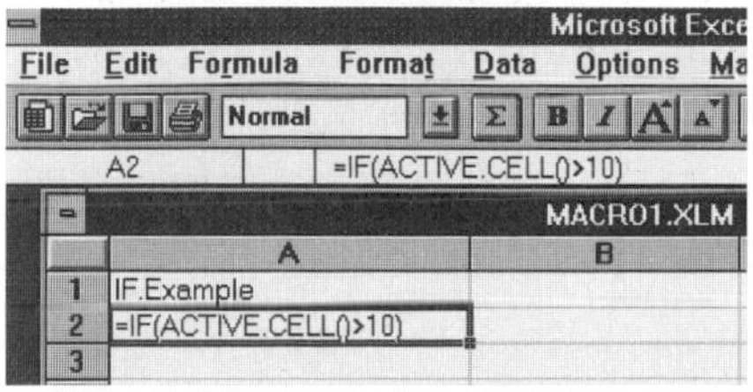

The > (greater than) symbol is the logical operator in the formula. (See the section "Logical Formulas" in Chapter 1). If the number in the active cell is greater than 10, the IF function will return a logical TRUE value.

You can also use the Paste Function dialog box to enter the other macro functions in this macro. When writing macros, it is often easier to use the Paste Function tool (second from the left) in the Macro toolbar to present the Paste Function dialog box than to use the Formula menu. (And, of course, both of these methods are easier than typing the macros directly on the macro sheet.) Click on the Paste Function tool in the Macro toolbar to present the Paste Function dialog box. Decide which of the two methods you'll use, and then use it while following these steps to display the Paste Function dialog box.

10. Move down to the next cell in the column and, from the Paste Function dialog box, choose Commands in the Function Category list box, choose Formula in the Paste Function list box, and click on OK.

You use the command function FORMULA to place a formula, reference, number, or text into a worksheet cell. It uses two arguments, the first is the value and the second is a reference to the cell where the value will be placed.

11. In the edit area of the formula bar type the arguments **"TRUE"** and **"r[1]c"** in the function, as shown here:

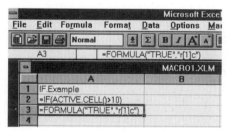

"TRUE" is the text value that will be placed in the cell "r[1]c" if the logical value returned by the IF function is TRUE. The cell reference "r[1]c" is a relative reference meaning one row down in the same column as the active cell. If the number in the active cell is greater than 10, the word "TRUE" will be placed in the cell one row below the active cell.

12. Using the Paste Function dialog box again, choose Macro Commands in the Function Category list box and ELSE in the Paste Function list box.

ELSE is a macro control function used with the IF function to direct the action that will be taken when the IF returns a logical FALSE value. In this case, the FORMULA function will be used again to place the word "FALSE" in the cell below the active cell when the number in the active cell is 10 or less.

13. Move to the next cell in the column and repeat steps 10 and 11. However, type the word **"FALSE"** instead of the word "TRUE" in the Formula function.

14. Move to the next cell in the column and, from the Paste Function dialog box, choose Macro Control in the Function Category list box and END.IF from the Paste Function list box.

The END.IF function is used to close the IF function. When END.IF is omitted an error message will be displayed.

15. To complete the macro, move to the next cell and, from the Paste Function dialog box, choose Macro Control from the Function Category list box and RETURN from the Paste Function list box.

When the IF function returns a logical TRUE, the subsequent steps in the macro are executed until the ELSE function is encountered; then all subsequent lines are ignored until the END.IF function is encountered. When a FALSE value is returned, the subsequent lines are ignored until the ELSE function is found. The lines following the ELSE function are then executed. The macro ends with RETURN, as described earlier.

Naming a Macro

For Excel to run a macro, it must know the name and the shortcut key you want to use. When you record a macro, you name it in the initial Record Macro dialog box you saw earlier. When you type the macro, you must use the Define Name option in the Formula menu. This opens the Define Name dialog box shown here:

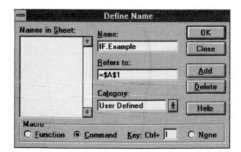

The steps to name a macro with the Formula Define Name dialog box are listed here:

1. Click on the first cell in the macro range, cell A1 in the IF.Example macro you just created.

2. Open the Formula menu and choose Define Names.

3. Click on the Command option button, type a capital I in the Key text box, and click on OK. The macro is named IF.Example and is given the shortcut key CTRL-SHIFT-I. You can now run the macro by selecting IF.Example from the list of macros in the Run Macro dialog box you saw earlier, or by pressing CTRL-SHIFT-I.

Testing a Macro

After building a macro you will of course want to see if it works. This means going to the regular worksheet, getting into the cell on which you want the macro to operate, and pressing the shortcut key. Since the macro may do something to the data on the worksheet and most importantly to the active cell, you should exercise caution when testing it.

CAUTION: Always save the worksheet and the macro sheet and move the active cell to a safe area on the worksheet before trying a new macro command.

Use the following instructions to test a macro:

1. Choose Save Workbook from the File menu. The Workbook Contents dialog box opens showing you that you have both a macro sheet and a regular worksheet identified.

2. Type a name for the workbook and click on OK.

3. Double-click on the workbook's Control-menu box to close it.

4. Move to a safe cell in the worksheet. Remember, the cell beneath the active cell will be written on in the IF.Example macro. Any existing data in that cell will be replaced.

5. To test the IF.Example macro, type **20**, press ENTER, and then press CTRL-SHIFT-I. If your macro is operating properly, the word TRUE should appear in the cell beneath the active cell—the one in which you entered 20. Try it again:

6. Move to the cell to the right of the one in which you entered 20, type 10, press Enter, and then press CTRL-SHIFT-I. The word FALSE should appear in the cell beneath the one in which you entered 10, as shown here:

	A	B	C
1	20	10	
2	TRUE	FALSE	
3			

Debugging a Macro

If your macro does not work, look at it very carefully and compare it against any listing you have that you know works. In this case compare your macro to the one shown in Figure 5-3. Look for obvious things like typos or misspellings. Check your procedure for running the macro. Are you sure you are pressing *and holding both* CTRL and SHIFT while typing I? Finally, review what happens when you run the macro, what messages you get, and what else appears on the screen.

If nothing else identifies the problem, try activating Step mode from the Run Macro dialog box. Use this procedure:

1. Choose Run from the Macro menu. The Run Macro dialog box will open.

2. Click on the name of the macro you want to test in the Run list box and click on the Step command button. The Single Step dialog box opens, as shown here:

```
┌─────────────────────────────────────────┐
│ ─          Single Step                   │
├─────────────────────────────────────────┤
│ Cell:  [BOOK1.XLW]Macro1!A1              │
│ Formula:                                 │
│ IF.Example                               │
│                                          │
│                                          │
│ ┌────────┐┌────────┐┌────────┐┌────────┐ │
│ │Step Into││Evaluate││  Halt  ││  Goto  │ │
│ └────────┘└────────┘└────────┘└────────┘ │
│ ┌────────┐┌────────┐┌────────┐┌────────┐ │
│ │Step Over││ Pause  ││Continue││  Help  │ │
│ └────────┘└────────┘└────────┘└────────┘ │
└─────────────────────────────────────────┘
```

The Single Step dialog box shows each step of the macro, one step at a time. Initially you see the macro name. If you press Step Into, you will go to the next cell in the macro. (In most instances the next cell is the one beneath the current cell.) By continuing to press Step Into, you can go through the entire macro, one step at a time.

3. Press Step Into to go to the next macro function and watch what is happening both on your worksheet and in the Single Step dialog box.

4. When you get to the IF function, slowly press Evaluate three times, looking at the substeps that show the function being evaluated and the resulting logical value. The Evaluate command button lets you look very carefully at formulas as they are evaluated.

5. Continue through your macro using either Step Into or Evaluate to go from macro function to macro function. When the macro is completed, the Single Step dialog box will disappear.

The other buttons in the Single Step dialog box are described in this table:

Command Button	Purpose
Step Into	Executes the next macro command
Evaluate	Evaluates each macro command and shows you the result prior to carrying out a command
Step Over	Skips the next macro command
Pause	Temporally suspends macro operation and displays the Macro Resume toolbar and tool
Continue	Resumes macro operation
Halt	Permanently stops the macro
Help	Opens the Help facility with specific information about the Single Step dialog box
Goto	Opens the macro sheet with the macro displayed

Documenting a Macro

You can readily determine the actions of simple macros, such as Save.Worksheet, by looking at the macro listing. When macros become more complex, the purpose of the macro, or each step of the macro, might not be as clear. The same problem exists if macros are seldom used or shared with others. Giving the macro an obvious name and shortcut key, such as Save.Worksheet and CTRL-SHIFT-S, helps make the purpose of the macro more clear.

For longer macros, and particularly with macros that use branching to direct the execution of the macro, documentation makes the macro more understandable. You can document macros in several ways. The macro name and shortcut key have been mentioned as one way. You can boldface the macro name on the macro sheet to make the listing easier to read. In addition, you can add cell notes, or comments, to a macro.

Adding comments to the macro operations is one of the best ways to document a macro. You can add comments in the column next to the column containing the macro. In Figure 5-3, for example, the IF.Example macro has been documented by formatting the macro name in bold type and by adding comments explaining the purpose of the macro and the functions it contains.

Using Custom Functions

Custom functions are generally calculations that need to be performed often on a worksheet. An example of a function macro would be a custom function that calculates sales tax on sales.

Like a built-in function, a custom function accepts values, performs a calculation with those values, and then returns the result of the calculation. Three special macro functions—RESULT, ARGUMENT, and RETURN—are used to create custom functions.

RESULT

The RESULT function is used when the data type returned by the custom function needs to be changed. When the RESULT function is not used, the result is assumed to be a number, text, or logical value. The data type is specified by a number, which is the argument used with the RESULT function. The format for using the RESULT function is RESULT(*data.type*). The possible data types are numbered as follows.

1	Number
2	Text
4	Logical
8	Reference
16	Error
64	Array

You can specify more than one data type by adding the data type numbers, except for reference and array types. For example, you can set number, text, and logical values (the default) by using a data type of 7 (1+2+4).

ARGUMENT

The arguments used by the custom function are the values the custom function will use for its calculations. The ARGUMENT function is used to define these values, or arguments. There must be one ARGUMENT function for each argument used in the custom function, and these functions must be in the same order as the values that will be used in the custom function. There can be a total of 13 arguments passed to the custom function. The ARGUMENT function uses either a name or a reference to define the argument for the custom function. A name will refer to the name of the argument or the name of the cell or cells containing the argument. A reference gives the location of the cell or cells which contain the argument. Only one of these two arguments is required, when one is specified the other is optional.

The third argument is the data type. Specifying a data type is optional, and you use the same data type numbers as for the RESULT function. If the data type is not specified, number, text, and logical values are accepted.

In a custom function used to calculate sales tax, there are two arguments: the sales tax rate and the amount to be taxed. Each is defined by a separate ARGUMENT function which includes either a name or reference for the value and the data type. The data type is 1 in this case since these would be number values. For example, the ARGUMENT function for the tax rate could be ARGUMENT("rate",1).

RETURN

As with other macros, custom functions must end with a RETURN function. The RETURN function returns the result of the custom function to the worksheet.

Writing Custom Functions

You must enter custom functions directly on the macro sheet; you cannot record them. To write a custom function to calculate sales tax, follow these steps:

1. Select the first cell on the macro sheet that will hold the custom function.

2. Type **Sales.Tax** in the cell and format it as bold. This is the name of the function.

3. Choose Define Name in the Formula menu. Click on Function and then click on OK.

4. Move to the next cell and choose Macro Control and Argument from the Paste Function dialog box.

5. In the edit area of the formula bar, type **"amount",1** as the arguments to the ARGUMENT function.

6. Repeat step 4, and in the edit area of the formula bar type **"rate",1** as arguments to the ARGUMENT function.

7. In the next cell, type **=amount*rate.**

8. Move to the next cell, and choose Macro Control and RETURN from the Paste Function dialog box.

9. In the edit area of the formula bar, type the address of the cell that holds the result of the calculation as the argument to the RETURN function. In this case, this is C4, as shown here:

	C
1	Sales.Tax
2	=ARGUMENT("amount",1)
3	=ARGUMENT("rate",1)
4	=amount*rate
5	=RETURN(C4)
6	

To use the Sales.Tax function, follow these steps:

1. Select the cell on the worksheet where the function will be pasted.

2. In the Paste Function dialog box, make sure the Paste Arguments option box is selected, and choose User Defined in the Function Category list box and MACRO1.XLM!Sales.Tax in the Paste Function list box.

The function name includes the name of the macro sheet and the defined name of the function separated with an exclamation point (!). The function is shown in the edit area of the formula bar. The argument names "amount" and "rate" are shown.

3. Delete the argument names and replace them with **150,7.8%.**Press ENTER. 150 is the amount that tax will be calculated on, and 7.8% is the tax rate.

The result of the function, 11.7 in this example, is displayed in the cell containing the function.

# Part II

The Excel Dictionary

A1.R1C1(X)

Macro Function

Specifies cell reference style. If X is TRUE the A1 style is used, and if X is FALSE the R1C1 style is used. Using this function is the same as using the Options Workspace menu command to specify how all cell references appear. The default style is the A1 reference style.

See Also

ADDRESSING	Explains addressing	Concept
OPTIONS WORKSPACE	Equivalent command	Menu Command

ABS(X)

Function

Returns the absolute value of X. The absolute value of a number is always a positive number.

Examples

ABS(−2400) returns the value 2400.
ABS(2400) returns the value 2400.

See Also

SIGN	Returns the sign of a number	Function

ABSREF(*offset,reference*)

Macro Function

Returns the absolute cell address for the reference modified by the *offset*. The *reference*, in A1 style, plus the *offset*, in R1C1 style, and given as a string (in quotes), produces a new A1 style reference. If the *reference* argument is a range, ABSREF returns a range in A1 style offset by the amount given in R1C1 style.

Examples

ABSREF("R[1]C[1]",A1) returns $B$2.
ABSREF("R[1]C[1]",A1:B2) returns $B$2:$C$3.

See Also

ADDRESSING	Explains types of addresses	Concept
OFFSET	Returns an offset from a cell	Macro Function
RELREF	Returns a relative reference	Macro Function

ACCRINT(*issue-date,interest-date,settlement-date,rate, par-value,nu-payments-code,basis-code*)

Function   New to Version 4.0

ACCRINT is an add-in function. The first time that you use it, you will see a #REF! error until Excel installs the add-in. Once ACCRINT is installed, the #REF! error will disappear, and the result of the function will appear.

ACCRINT returns the accrued interest for a security that pays interest periodically. The *issue-date* is the date that the security was issued, given as a serial number. The *interest-date* is the date that the security first pays interest, given as a serial number. The *settlement-date* is the security's maturity date, given as a serial number. The *rate* is the security's coupon rate, given as an annual percentage. The *par-value* is the security's par value. If *par-value* is not given, $1000 is the default value. The *nu-payments-code* represents the number of payments per year.

Nu-payments-code	Payment
1	Annual
2	Semi-annual
4	Quarterly

The *basis-code* is a code that represents the number of days per month and the number of days per year. If the *basis-code* argument is omitted, 0 is the default code.

Basis-code	Day Count
0	30/360
1	Actual/Actual
2	Actual/360
3	Actual/365

Example

ACCRINT(date(93,1,1),date(93,8,1),date(93,6,1),0.12, 1000,1,0) returns 50.

See Also

ACCRINTM	Similar function	Function
ADD-INS	Explains add-ins	Concept
ANALYSIS TOOLPAK	Explains the Analysis Toolpak	Concept
DATE	Returns the serial number of a date	Function

ACCRINTM(*issue-date,settlement-date,rate,par-value,basis-code*)

Function   **New to Version 4.0**

ACCRINTM is an add-in function. The first time that you use it, you will see a #REF! error until Excel installs the add-in. Once ACCRINTM is installed, the #REF! error will disappear, and the result of the function will appear.

ACCRINTM returns the accrued interest for a security that pays interest at maturity. The *issue-date* is the date that the security was issued, given as a serial number. The *settlement-date* is the security's maturity date, given as a serial number. The *rate* is the security's coupon rate, given as an annual percentage. The *par-value* is the security's par value. If *par-value* is not given, $1000 is the default value. The *basis-code* is a code that represents the number of days per month and the number of days per year. If *basis-code* is omitted, 0 is the default code.

Basis-code	Day Count
0	30/360
1	Actual/Actual
2	Actual/360
3	Actual/365

Example

ACCRINTM(date(1993,1,1), date(1993,8,1),0.12, 1000,1,0) returns 69.83607.

See Also

ACCRINT	Similar function	Function
ADD-INS	Explains add-ins	Concept
ANALYSIS TOOLPAK	Explains the analysis toolpak	Concept
DATE	Returns the serial number of a date	Function

ACOS(X)

Function

Returns the arccosine in radians of a value between –1 and 1 (radians times 180/PI() equals degrees).

Example

ACOS(.5) returns the arccosine of 0.5, which is 1.047 radians, or 60 degrees.

See Also

ASIN	Returns the arcsine in radians	Function
ATAN	Returns the arctangent in radians	Function
DEGREES	Returns degrees given radians	Function
RADIANS	Returns radians given degrees	Function

ACOSH(X)

Function

Returns the inverse hyperbolic cosine in radians of a value of 1 or greater.

Example

ACOSH(5) returns the inverse hyperbolic cosine of 5, which is 2.292432.

See Also

ASINH	Inverse hyperbolic sine	Function
COSH	Hyperbolic cosine	Function
DEGREES	Returns radians given degrees	Function
RADIANS	Returns degrees given radians	Function

ACTIVATE(*[window-name],[pane-number]*)

Macro Function

This macro function allows you to switch to another window or another pane. The *window-name* argument is the name of the window you want to activate. If this argument is omitted, the active window stays the same. The *pane-number* argument allows you to specify which pane you want activated if there is more than one pane in the window. If this argument is omitted, the active pane stays the same.

Pane-number	Pane
1	Upper-left
2	Upper-right
3	Lower-left
4	Lower-right

See Also

ACTIVATE.NEXT	Same as pressing CTRL-F6 keys	Macro Function
ACTIVATE.PREV	Same as pressing CTRL-SHIFT-F6 keys	Macro Function
WINDOWS	Returns a list of open windows	Macro Function
WINDOWS	Explains windows	Concept

ACTIVATE.NEXT(*[workbook-name]*)

Macro Function

Activates the next window. If *workbook-name* is omitted, ACTIVATE.NEXT works the same as pressing CTRL-F6. If *workbook-name* is included, ACTIVATE.NEXT works the same as pressing ALT-PGDN.

See Also

ACTIVATE	Switches to another window	Macro Function
ACTIVATE.PREV	Same as pressing CTRL-SHIFT-F6	Macro Function
WINDOWS	Explains windows	Concept

ACTIVATE.PREV(*[workbook-name]*)

Macro Function

Activates the previous window. If the *workbook-name* argument is omitted, ACTI-VATE.PREV works the same as pressing CTRL-SHIFT-F6. If the *workbook-name* argument is included, ACTIVATE.PREV works the same as pressing ALT-PGUP.

See Also

ACTIVATE	Switches to another window	Macro Function
ACTIVATE.NEXT	Same as pressing CTRL-F6	Macro Function
WINDOWS	Explains windows	Concept

ACTIVE CELL

Concept

The *active cell* is the cell that is currently in the Formula bar and is highlighted by the dark border on your worksheet. The cell address of the active cell is on the left of the Formula bar. If you have multiple cells selected, the active cell is the white cell in the block of selected cells, as shown in Figure A-1. Only one cell can be active at a time.

ACTIVE.CELL()

Macro Function

Returns the reference or address of the active cell in the current selection as an external cell reference, or the contents of the active cell if you use ACTIVE.CELL as an argument in another function. An external cell reference is a cell reference that includes the full path name, worksheet name, and cell reference.

Example

ACTIVE.CELL() returns the external reference of the active cell in the active window. For example, if the active cell is A1, and the worksheet is C:\WORK\JUNE.XLS, ACTIVE.CELL returns "C:\WORK\JUNE.XLS!$A$1".

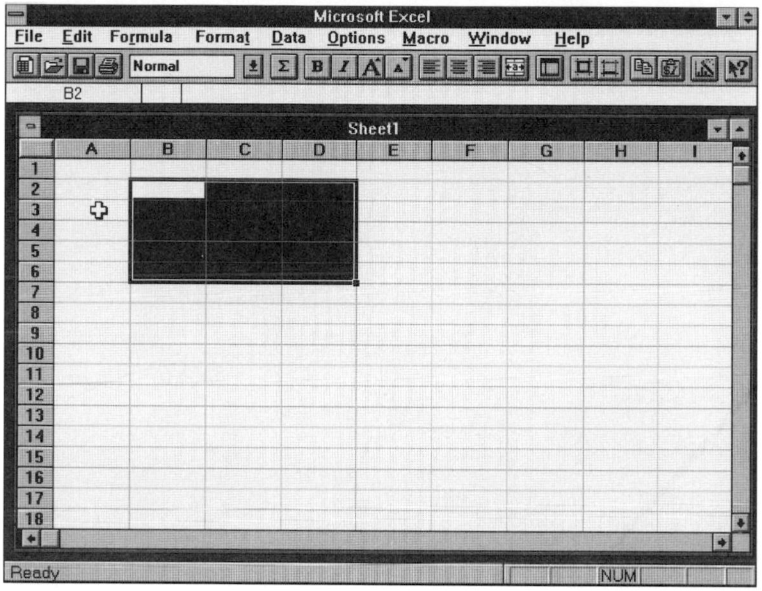

Figure A-1.   *The active cell is B2*

See Also

ACTIVE CELL	Defines active cell	Concept
REFTEXT	Turns a reference to text	Macro Function
SELECT	Selects a cell	Macro Function
TEXTREF	Turns text to a reference	Macro Function

ACTIVE WORKSHEET

Concept

The *active worksheet* is the worksheet in the window that has the darker border around it and has horizontal and vertical scroll bars. Only one window can be active at a time. All active windows—whether they are worksheets, macro sheets, or charts—are listed at the bottom of the Window menu. A checkmark indicates the currently active window, as you can see in Figure A-2.

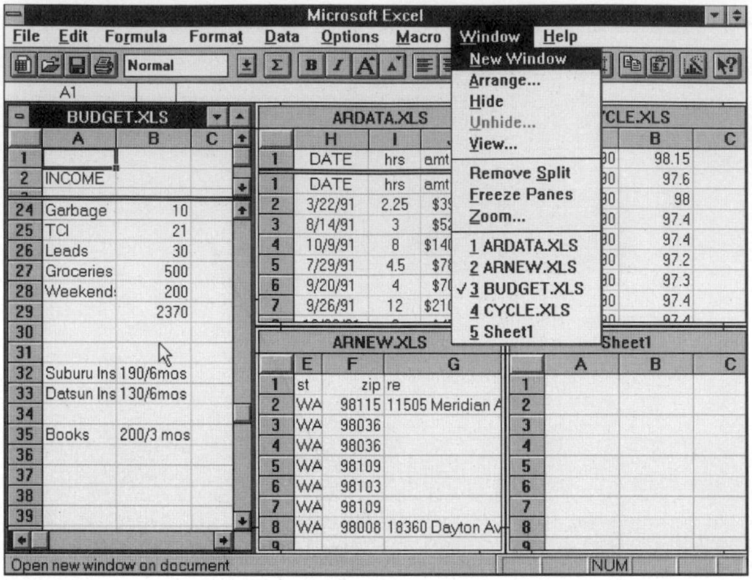

Figure A-2.   *BUDGET.XLS is the active worksheet*

ADD.ARROW()

Macro Function

The ADD.ARROW macro function adds an arrow to a chart, as shown in Figure A-3. The active window must be a chart, or you will receive an error message.

Using the ADD.ARROW macro function is the same as choosing the Chart Add Arrow menu command, or clicking on the Chart Arrow tool. Once you add the arrow, you can move, size, and format it with the functions listed in the following table.

See Also

CHART ADD ARROW	Equivalent command	Menu Command
CHARTS	Explains charting	Concept
DELETE.ARROW	Deletes arrows	Macro Function
FORMAT.MOVE	Moves an arrow	Macro Function
FORMAT.SIZE	Sizes an arrow	Macro Function
PATTERNS	Formats an arrow	Macro Function

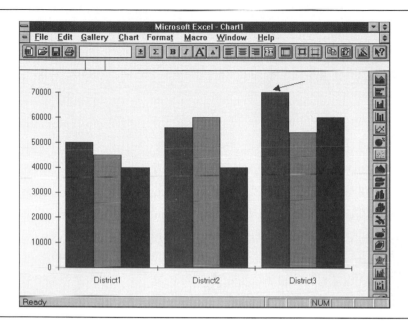

Figure A-3.   *A chart with an arrow*

ADD.BAR(*[number]*)

Macro Function

If the *number* argument is omitted, ADD.BAR adds a menu bar to the menu system and returns the menu bar's ID number. If there are already 15 menu bars, ADD.BAR returns the error #VALUE!. To display the bar that you have added, use SHOW.BAR.

If the *number* argument is included, an Excel built-in menu bar is restored. Use a number between 1 and 9 to restore one of the built-in menus, as shown in the following table. When you restore a built-in menu bar, custom menus will be deleted. If you want to restore a particular menu on a menu bar, but not the entire bar itself, use the ADD.MENU function. The ADD.COMMAND function restores individual functions on a menu.

Number	Menu Bar
1	Worksheet & macro (long)
2	Chart
3	Nothing open
4	Info
5	Worksheet & macro (short)
6	Chart (short)

Number	Menu Bar
7	Cell, toolbar, and workbook shortcut
8	Object shortcut
9	Chart shortcut

See Also

ADD.COMMAND	Adds a command to a menu	Macro Function
ADD.MENU	Adds a menu	Macro Function
DELETE.BAR	Deletes a menu bar	Macro Function
DELETE.COMMAND	Deletes a command	Macro Function
ENABLE.COMMAND	Enables a command	Macro Function
MENUS, CUSTOM	Explains custom menus	Concept
SHOW.BAR	Displays a menu bar	Macro Function

ADD.COMMAND(*number, menu, command-ref, [position]*)

Macro Function

The ADD.COMMAND macro function adds a command to a menu. The *number* argument is the number of the menu bar to which you want to add the command, as shown here:

Number	Menu Bar
1	Worksheet & macro (long)
2	Chart
3	Nothing open
4	Info
5	Worksheet & macro (short)
6	Chart (short)
7	Cell, toolbar and workbook shortcut
8	Object shortcut
9	Chart shortcut

The *menu* argument is the menu to which you want to add the command. The menu can be given as a name or the number of the menu.

The *command-ref* argument is a reference to a macro sheet where the new command is stored, if you are adding a custom command. *Command-ref* must refer to an area on the macro sheet that is four columns wide. The command name to be displayed in the menu should appear in the leftmost column of *command-ref*. The command macro name should be in the second column. The optional third and fourth columns in the reference can contain status bar messages and custom help references.

If you are restoring a command that you previously deleted, you should use the value returned by the DELETE.COMMAND function as the *command-ref* argument in the ADD.COMMAND function.

The optional *position* argument specifies where the command that you are adding will appear on the menu. If no *position* argument is given, the command will be placed at the bottom of the menu. The *position* argument can be given either as a number or a name of an existing command. If the *position* argument is a number, the number indicates the position on the menu, with 1 being the top position. If the *position* argument is a name, the command will be placed immediately before the named command.

See Also

DELETE.COMMAND	Deletes a command	Macro Function
ENABLE.COMMAND	Enables a command	Macro Function
MENUS, CUSTOM	Explains custom menus	Concept

ADD.MENU(*number, menu, [position]*)

Macro Function

The ADD.MENU macro function adds a menu to a menu bar, and returns the position of the new menu. You can use the ADD.MENU macro function to add a custom menu to a built-in menu bar, or you can use ADD.MENU to restore a previously deleted menu to a menu bar.

The *number* argument is the number of the menu bar to which you want to add a menu. The menu bars are numbered as follows.

Number	Menu Bar
1	Worksheet & macro (long)
2	Chart
3	Nothing open
4	Info
5	Worksheet & macro (short)
6	Chart (short)
7	Cell, toolbar, and workbook shortcut

Number	Menu Bar
8	Object shortcut
9	Chart shortcut

If you want to restore a built-in menu, the *menu* argument should be the name of the deleted menu.

If you want to add a custom menu, the *menu* argument is a reference to a macro sheet where the new menu is stored. The reference must be a minimum of two rows and two columns, and can be five columns wide. The first column contains the command names to be placed on the menu. The first cell in the first column contains the menu name. Use the & symbol immediately before the letter that you want to underline as a keyboard command. The second column contains the names of the macros that run the commands. The third column is not used, but needs to be included. (The third column is used in Excel for the Macintosh.) The fourth column contains the message that will appear in the status bar when that option is highlighted. The fifth column can be used for help topics.

The *position* argument indicates the location of the new menu. Positions are numbered starting with 1 from the left. *Position* can also be the name of the menu to the left of where you want the new menu to appear.

See the MENUS, CUSTOM entry for an example of a custom menu and the macros that display and restore the menu.

See Also

DELETE.MENU	Deletes a menu	Macro Function
MENUS, CUSTOM	Explains custom menus	Concept
SHOW.BAR	Displays a menu bar	Macro Function

ADD.OVERLAY()

Macro Function

The ADD.OVERLAY macro function adds an overlay to a chart. If there already is an overlay, this function does nothing but returns TRUE. Using this function is the same as choosing the Chart Add Overlay menu command.

See Also

| ADD.ARROW | Adds an arrow | Macro Function |
| CHART ADD OVERLAY | Equivalent command | Menu Command |

ADD.TOOL(*bar, position, tool*)

Macro Function   New to Version 4.0

The ADD.TOOL macro function adds a tool to a toolbar. The *bar* argument is either the number of a built-in toolbar or the name of a custom toolbar. The built-in toolbars are numbered as follows.

Bar	Toolbar
1	Standard
2	Formatting
3	Utility
4	Chart
5	Drawing
6	Excel 3.0
7	Macro
8	Macro stop recording
9	Macro paused

The *position* argument indicates the position on the toolbar at which the tool will appear. For example, the position 1 would be the leftmost or the upper tool.

The *tool* argument is the number of a built-in tool or a reference to custom tool definition. There are over 130 built-in tools in Microsoft Excel. Please see the TOOLBARS, CUSTOM entry for a list of all the available tools.

If you are adding a custom tool, the *tool* argument must be a reference to a range on the macro sheet that defines the tool. For an example of a custom tool macro, see TOOLBARS, CUSTOM.

See Also

DELETE.TOOL	Deletes a tool	Macro Function
TOOLBARS, CUSTOM	Explains custom toolbars	Concept

ADD.TOOLBAR(*bar, tools*)

Macro Function   New to Version 4.0

The ADD.TOOLBAR macro function adds a toolbar with the specified tools. The *bar* argument is the name of the bar that you are creating, given as a string. The *tools* argument is a reference to the tool or tools that you want to include on your toolbar.

The *tools* argument can be a tool number if you want to add a single built-in tool, or it can be a reference to an area on the worksheet that contains a custom tool definition or definitions. It can also be a reference to an array that contains the tool definitions. See the TOOLBARS, CUSTOM entry for a list of Excel's built-in tools.

See Also

DELETE.TOOLBAR	Deletes a toolbar	Macro Function
RESET.TOOLBAR	Resets a toolbar	Macro Function
TOOLBARS, CUSTOM	Explains custom toolbars	Concept

ADD-INS

Concept   New to Version 4.0

Add-ins are macros that become part of Excel for a session in which they are loaded. Add-ins provide additional functions and options. In order to save memory, Excel doesn't actually load an add-in macro until you try to use it. The first time you use a command or function that is an add-in macro, you will notice a delay until Excel loads the macro. There are many statistical, scientific, and financial functions that are add-in macros. Collectively, these functions are known as the Analysis Toolpak. The Analysis Toolpak is a set of add-ins that are used for data analysis. There are many other add-in macros packaged with Excel.

There are also several commands on Excel's menus that are actually add-in macros, including Data Crosstab, File Report Manager, Formula Scenario Manager, Formula Solver, and Window View.

The Add-Ins command on the Options menu will help you manage add-in macros. You can write your own add-in macros and use the Add-In manager to manage these new functions and commands.

ADDRESS(*row,column,[type],[style],[name]*)

Function

The ADDRESS function returns a cell address as a string. The *row* argument is the number of the row in the address. The *column* argument is the number of the column in the address. For example, 3 refers to column C. The *type* argument indicates the type of addressing to be used. If the *type* argument is omitted, 1 is the default type. The types of addresses are numbered as follows.

Type	Address Description
1	Absolute row, absolute column
2	Absolute row, relative column
3	Relative row, absolute column
4	Relative row, relative column

The *style* argument indicates A1 or R1C1 style. If the *style* argument is TRUE or omitted, A1 style is used. If the *style* argument is FALSE, R1C1 style is used.

The *name* argument is the name of the sheet. If this argument is included, the sheet name is used to create an external reference. If the *name* argument is omitted, the reference returned is an internal reference.

Examples

ADDRESS(2,2,1,TRUE,"FILENAME") returns "FILENAME!$B$2".
ADDRESS(1,1,4,FALSE) returns "R[1]C[1]".

See Also

ADDRESSING	Explains types of addresses	Concept
ACTIVE.CELL	Returns a cell reference	Macro Function
SELECTION	Returns a reference to a selection	Macro Function

ADDRESSING

Concept

There are four kinds of addresses in Excel: absolute addresses, relative addresses, and two kinds of mixed addresses. The type of address you specify depends on how you plan to use the reference.

Absolute addresses, like $A$1, are "locked in"; they do not change when copied. For example, if you have a formula that contains the address $A$1 and you copy that formula to another cell, the reference to cell $A$1 will not change.

Relative addresses, like A1, change relative to their position. For example, if you have a formula in cell A5 that contains a reference to cell A1, when you copy that formula to cell B5, the reference will change to B1.

Mixed addresses, like $A1 and A$1, have either the row or the column locked in. This is useful when you have formulas that you want to copy and you want only the row or the column to change depending on where you copy the formula. A dollar sign before the row number or the column letter indicates that the row or column is locked in.

If you place the cursor in or immediately after a cell reference in the edit bar, pressing the F4 key will cycle through the four types of addressing schemes.

See Also

| ADDRESS | Returns a cell address | Function |
| ACTIVE.CELL | Returns the address of the active cell | Macro Function |

ALERT(*message,[type],[help]*)

Macro Function

The ALERT macro function displays a dialog box with the *message* and returns a TRUE or FALSE value depending on the option taken. If OK is selected, TRUE is returned. If Cancel is selected, FALSE is returned.

The *type* argument controls the type of dialog box displayed. Type 1 displays a choice dialog box with OK and Cancel buttons. Type 2 displays an information dialog box with an OK button. Type 3 displays an error dialog box with an OK button. The default type is 1. The *help* argument allows you to specify custom help. If this argument is included, a Help button will appear in the dialog box.

Example

ALERT("Are you ready to continue?",1) displays a dialog box with the message "Are you ready to continue?", an OK button, and a Cancel button, as shown here:

See Also

| INPUT | Displays an input dialog box | Macro Function |

ALIGNMENT([*horizontal*],[*wrap*],[*vertical*],[*orientation*])
ALIGNMENT?([*horizontal*],[*wrap*],[*vertical*],[*orientation*])

Macro Function

The ALIGNMENT macro function aligns the current selection in accordance with the arguments. If the dialog box version is used (ALIGNMENT?), the arguments are used as default values.

The *horizontal* argument specifies the horizontal alignment. If this argument is not included, the horizontal alignment in the current selection remains the same.

Horizontal	Alignment
1	General
2	Left
3	Center
4	Right
5	Fill
6	Justify
7	Center across selection

The *wrap* argument is either TRUE or FALSE. If it is TRUE, the text is wrapped in the selected cells. If it is FALSE, the text is not wrapped. If the *wrap* argument is omitted, wrapping in the selected cells remains the same.

The *vertical* argument specifies the vertical alignment in the selected cells. If this argument is omitted, the vertical alignment in the selected cells remains the same.

Vertical	Alignment
1	Top
2	Center
3	Bottom

The *orientation* argument indicates the orientation of the text in the selected cells. If this argument is omitted, the orientation remains the same.

Orientation	Description
0	Horizontal
1	Vertical
2	Up
3	Down

Example

ALIGNMENT(2,TRUE,1,0) aligns the current selection left, wraps the text, vertically aligns it at the top, and gives it a horizontal orientation.

ANALYSIS TOOLPAK

Concept
New to Version 4.0

Excel version 4 provides a set of new functions, commands, and tools that will help you analyze your data. These features are not loaded into memory until you need them so that Excel can conserve the amount of memory being used.

Some functions and commands are loaded automatically. When you try to use a function that hasn't been loaded, you may see a #REF! error until Excel loads the function. Once the function is loaded, the result will appear in place of the error message. When you try to use a command that hasn't been loaded, there may be a slight delay while Excel loads it.

You need to load certain functions and commands before you can use them. To load an add-in that is part of the Analysis Toolpak, choose Add-Ins from the Options menu. Click on the Add button, select the add-in that you want, and click on Close.

AND($X1, X2,...$)

Function

The AND function returns TRUE if all arguments evaluate to logical TRUE values. If any argument evaluates to FALSE, it returns a FALSE value. This function can include up to 14 arguments. If any of the arguments are references, they should refer to cells or arrays that contain logical values. If no logical values are specified, AND returns the error message #VALUE.

Example

AND(E4>200) returns TRUE if the cell E4 contains a value greater than 200; otherwise it returns FALSE.

See Also

OR	Returns the logical OR	Function

ANOVA1(*input, output, [rc], [labels], [sig]*)

Macro Function
New to Version 4.0

The ANOVA1 add-in macro function is only available when you install the Analysis Toolpak. If you try to use it without having installed the Analysis Toolpak, you will

A,B

get a #NAME! error. To install this macro function, choose the Analysis Tools command from the Options menu.

ANOVA1 is a statistical function that tests whether means from several samples are equal. The *input* argument is a reference to the input range. The input range should include the labels if there are any.

The *output* argument is a reference to the output range. The *rc* argument is either R or C. If it is R, the input data is in rows. If it is C, the input data is in columns. If no *rc* argument is included, the default is C.

The *labels* argument is either TRUE or FALSE. If it is TRUE, the labels are included in the input range. The labels are either in the first row or first column of the input range, depending on the orientation of the input data. If it is FALSE, there are no labels. FALSE is the default *labels* value.

The *sig* argument is the significance to which the critical values are evaluated. If this argument is omitted, the default value is 0.05.

See Also

ADD-INS	Explains add-in macros	Concept
ANOVA2	Similar function	Macro Function
ANOVA3	Similar function	Macro Function

ANOVA2(*input, output, nu-rows, [sig]*)

Macro Functions   **New to Version 4.0**

The ANOVA2 add-in macro function is only available when you install the Analysis Toolpak. If you try to use this function without having installed the Analysis Toolpak, you will get a #NAME! error. To install this macro function, choose the Analysis Tools command from the Options menu.

ANOVA2 is an extension of ANOVA1. It performs two-factor analysis. Replication of input data is included. Replication of data means that more than one sample of data is used.

The *input* argument is a reference to the input range. The input range should include the labels in the first row and column, if there are any. The *output* argument is a reference to the upper-left cell in the output range. The *nu-rows* argument is the number of rows in each sample. The *sig* argument is the significance to which the critical values are evaluated. If this argument is omitted, the default value is 0.05.

See Also

ADD-INS	Explains add-in macros	Concept
ANOVA1	Similar function	Macro Function
ANOVA3	Similar function	Macro Function

ANOVA3(*input, output, [labels], [sig]*)

Macro Function   **New to Version 4.0**

The ANOVA3 add-in macro function is only available when you install the Analysis Toolpak. If you try to use this function without having installed the Analysis Toolpak, you will get a #NAME! error. To install this macro function, choose the Analysis Tools command from the Options menu.

ANOVA3 is an extension of ANOVA1. It performs two-factor analysis. Replication of input data is not included.

The *input* argument is a reference to the input range. The input range should include the labels if there are any. The *output* argument is a reference to the upper-left cell in the output range. The *nu-rows* argument is the number of rows in each sample. The *sig* argument is the significance to which the critical values are evaluated. If this argument is omitted, the default value is 0.05.

See Also

ADD-INS	Explains add-in macros	Concept
ANOVA2	Similar function	Macro Function
ANOVA3	Similar function	Macro Function

APP.ACTIVATE(*[title], [pause]*)

Macro Function

The APP.ACTIVATE macro function activates an application window. The *title* argument is the name of the application you want to activate. If *title* is omitted, the default *title* is Microsoft Excel. The *pause* argument must be a logical value. If *pause* is TRUE, APP.ACTIVATE waits until Excel is activated before activating the application window. If *pause* is FALSE or omitted, APP.ACTIVATE activates the application right away.

See Also

APP.MAXIMIZE	Maximizes application window	Macro Function
APP.MINIMIZE	Minimizes application window	Macro Function
APP.MOVE	Moves application window	Macro Function
APP.RESTORE	Restores application window	Macro Function
APP.SIZE	Sizes application window	Macro Function

APP.MAXIMIZE()

Macro Function

The APP.MAXIMIZE macro function performs the same action as the Control Maximize menu command. It maximizes the Excel application window.

See Also

APP.ACTIVATE	Activates application window	Macro Function
APP.MINIMIZE	Minimizes application window	Macro Function
APP.MOVE	Moves application window	Macro Function
APP.RESTORE	Restores application window	Macro Function
APP.SIZE	Sizes application window	Macro Function

APP.MINIMIZE()

Macro Function

The APP.MINIMIZE macro function performs the same action as the Control Minimize menu command. It minimizes the Excel application window to an icon.

See Also

APP.ACTIVATE	Activates application window	Macro Function
APP.MAXIMIZE	Maximizes application window	Macro Function
APP.MOVE	Moves application window	Macro Function
APP.RESTORE	Restores application window	Macro Function
APP.SIZE	Sizes application window	Macro Function

APP.MOVE(*horizontal, vertical*)
APP.MOVE?(*[horizontal], [vertical]*)

Macro Function

The APP.MOVE macro function performs the same action as the Control Move menu command. The optional arguments specify the starting horizontal and vertical coordinates of the window measured from the left and top of your screen. The APP.MOVE form allows you to specify horizontal and vertical coordinates of the window measured from the left and top of your screen in points, with approximately

6 points to the inch. The APP.MOVE? form of the function allows you to drag the window with the mouse or the keyboard.

See Also

APP.ACTIVATE	Activates application window	Macro Function
APP.MAXIMIZE	Maximizes application window	Macro Function
APP.MINIMIZE	Minimizes application window	Macro Function
APP.RESTORE	Restores application window	Macro Function
APP.SIZE	Sizes application window	Macro Function

APP.RESTORE()

Macro Function

The APP.RESTORE macro function performs the same action as the Control Restore menu command. It restores the Excel application window.

See Also

APP.MAXIMIZE	Maximizes application window	Macro Function
APP.MINIMIZE	Minimizes application window	Macro Function
APP.MOVE	Moves application window	Macro Function
APP.SIZE	Sizes application window	Macro Function

APP.SIZE(*width,height*)
APP.SIZE?(*[width]*,*[height]*)

Macro Function

The APP.SIZE macro function performs the same action as the Control Size menu command. The APP.SIZE form of the function allows you to specify the width and height of the window, measured in points. (There are approximately 6 points per inch.) The APP.SIZE? form allows you to drag the window with the mouse or the keyboard.

See Also

APP.MAXIMIZE	Maximizes application window	Macro Function
APP.MINIMIZE	Minimizes application window	Macro Function

| APP.MOVE | Moves application window | Macro Function |
| APP.RESTORE | Restores application window | Macro Function |

APP.TITLE(*[title]*)

Macro Function

The APP.TITLE function changes the title of the Excel application window to the *title* indicated by the argument. If no *title* argument is given, the title in the Excel application window is restored to Microsoft Excel.

Examples

APP.TITLE("Acme, Inc.") changes the application title for Excel to "Acme, Inc.," as you see in Figure A-4.
APP.TITLE() restores the application title to "Microsoft Excel."

See Also

| WINDOW.TITLE | Changes the window title | Macro Function |

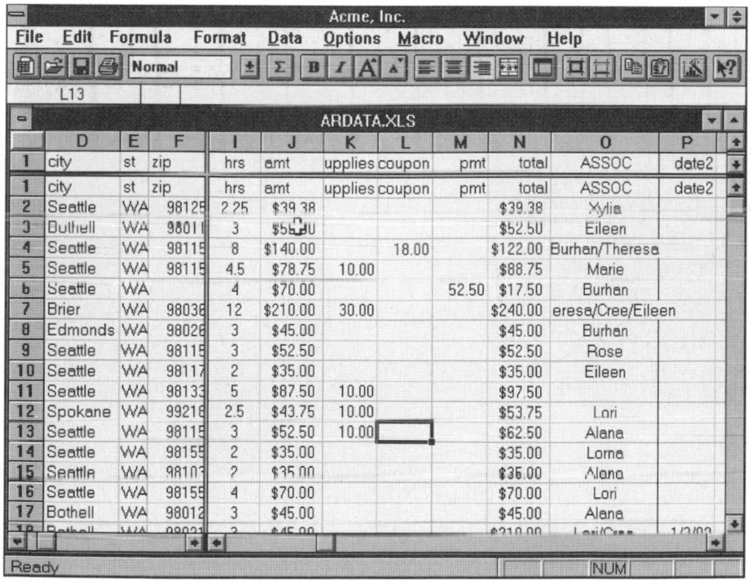

Figure A-4.   *Acme, Inc. is the new application title*

APPLY.NAMES(*name-array, ignore, row-col, omit-column, omit-row, order, append*)
APPLY.NAMES?(*[name-array], [ignore], [row-col], [omit-column], [omit-row], [order], [append]*)

Macro Function

The APPLY.NAMES macro function is the same as the Formula Apply Names menu command. APPLY.NAMES allows you to replace cell references with meaningful names in selected formulas on your worksheet. The *name-array* argument is the name or names to apply. The arguments *ignore, row-col, omit-column,* and *omit-row* correspond to check boxes in the Formula Apply Names dialog box, and are either TRUE or FALSE. The *ignore* argument indicates whether to ignore relative/absolute addressing. The *row-col* argument should be TRUE if you want to use the row and column names; otherwise, *row-col* should be FALSE. If *row-col* is TRUE, the *omit-column* and *omit-row* arguments indicate whether row and column names should be ignored. If *omit-column* is TRUE, the range is row-oriented. If *omit-row* is true, the range is column-oriented.

The *order* argument allows you to choose if the column name or row name comes first. If *order* is 1, row names come first. If *order* is 2, column names come first.

The *append* argument must be logical. If *append* is TRUE, APPLY.NAMES applies names to names defined by Formula Define Name or Formula Create Names. If *append* is FALSE, APPLY.NAMES applies names to names in the name array. In the dialog box version (with the question mark), all arguments are optional. If they are included, they are used as defaults for the dialog box that appears.

See Also

CREATE.NAMES	Creates new names	Macro Function
DEFINE.NAME	Defines a name	Macro Function
FORMULA APPLY NAMES	Equivalent command	Menu Command
LIST.NAMES	Lists existing names	Macro Function

APPLY.STYLE(*[style]*)
APPLY.STYLE?(*[style]*)

Macro Function

The APPLY.STYLE macro function performs the same task as the Format Style menu command. The *style* argument is the name of a previously defined style. If no *style* argument is given, the default style is Normal.

The question mark version of this function opens the dialog box. The arguments set the defaults in the dialog box. The version without the question mark does not open the dialog box, but performs the function with the settings that you pass as arguments.

See Also

DEFINE.STYLE	Defines a style	Macro Function
DELETE.STYLE	Deletes an existing style	Macro Function
FORMAT STYLE	Equivalent command	Menu Command

AREAS(*X*)

Function

The AREAS function returns the number of areas in the argument. An area is a single range. A multiple selection can be made up of many ranges. The argument *X* can be a reference to a single or multiple selection, or, more likely, a name referring to a single or multiple selection. You can use this function to find out how many ranges are in a named multiple selection.

Example

AREAS(Inventory) returns 2 if the name "Inventory" refers to the multiple selection A1:B200,F1:G200.

See Also

COLUMNS	Returns number of columns	Macro Function
ROWS	Returns number of rows	Macro Function

ARGUMENT(*name,[type]*)
ARGUMENT(*[name],[type],reference*)

Macro Function

ARGUMENT is used in a function macro to declare an argument. *Name* is the name of the argument. *Type* is the type of the argument, listed below. If you want to assign more than one type to an argument, sum the numbers associated with each type. If no *type* argument is given, 7 is the default value. *Reference* is the reference to the argument. The FUNCTION MACROS entry shows an example of the ARGUMENT macro function.

Type	Argument
1	Number
2	Text
4	Logical
8	Reference
16	Error
64	Array

See Also

FUNCTION MACROS   Explains function macros   Concept

ARRANGE.ALL (*[type]*, *[active]*, *[horizontal]*, *[vertical]*)
ARRANGE.ALL? (*[type]*, *[active]*, *[horizontal]*, *[vertical]*)

Macro Function

Like the Window Arrange All menu command, ARRANGE.ALL arranges all your windows on the screen. The *type* argument indicates how you want the windows arranged. If the *type* argument is omitted, 1 is the default value.

Type	Arrangement
1	Tiled
2	Horizontal
3	Vertical
4	None
5	Horizontal with respect to the active cell
6	Vertical with respect to the active cell

The *active* argument is either TRUE or FALSE. If it is TRUE, only the windows in the active document are arranged. Otherwise, all windows are arranged. FALSE is the default *active* value.

The *horizontal* argument is either TRUE or FALSE. If it is TRUE, Excel synchronizes horizontal scrolling. The *vertical* argument is also either TRUE or FALSE. If it is TRUE, Excel synchronizes vertical scrolling. These two arguments are only used when ACTIVE is TRUE. The default value for *horizontal* and *vertical* is FALSE.

See Also

ACTIVATE	Activates a window	Macro Function
WINDOW ARRANGE ALL	Equivalent command	Menu Command

ARRAYS

Concept

An *array* is a set of data. In Excel, an array is the same thing as a range. When a function asks for an array as an argument, the range should be enclosed in curly braces ({ }). When a function returns an array, it places the result in a range rather than in a single cell. You must specify the range in which you want the result returned. You also must let Excel know that it is working with an array by pressing the CTRL-SHIFT-ENTER keys instead of just pressing the ENTER key when you are done entering the formula.

Example

Highlight A1:C1, type **=column(a1:c3)** and press CTRL-SHIFT-ENTER. The result is shown in Figure A-5.

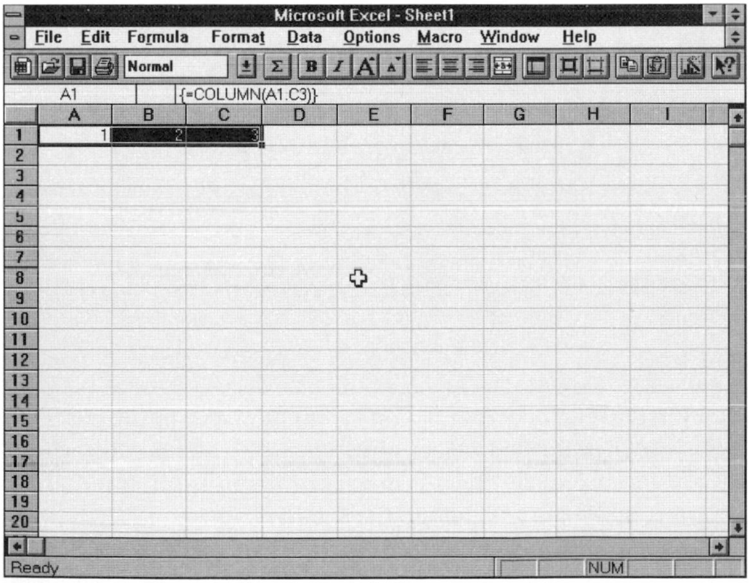

Figure A-5.   *The array is returned in cells A1:C1*

ASIN(X)

Function

The ASIN function returns the arcsine in radians of a value between −1 and 1 (radians times 180/PI() equals degrees).

Example

ASIN(.5) returns the arcsine of 0.5, which is 0.523599 radians, or 30 degrees.

See Also

ACOS	Returns arccosine	Function
ATAN	Returns arctangent	Function

ASINH(X)

Function

The ASINH function returns the inverse hyperbolic sine in radians of a value (radians times 180/PI() equals degrees).

Example

ASINH(5) returns the inverse hyperbolic sine of 5, which is 2.312438.

See Also

ACOSH	Returns inverse hyperbolic cosine	Function
ATANH	Returns inverse hyperbolic tangent	Function

ASSIGN.TO.OBJECT($[ref]$) ASSIGN.TO.OBJECT?($[ref]$)

Macro Function

The ASSIGN.TO.OBJECT macro function assigns a macro to the currently selected object. When you click on that object with a mouse, the macro is started. The *ref* argument is a reference to the macro. If this argument is not given, the previously assigned macro is no longer assigned to the selected object.

The question mark version of this function opens the dialog box. The arguments set the defaults in the dialog box. The version without the question mark does not open the dialog box, but performs the function with the settings that you pass as arguments.

See Also

MACRO ASSIGN TO OBJECT	Assigns a macro to an object	Menu Command

ASSIGN.TO.TOOL(*bar,position,[ref]*)

Macro Function   **New to Version 4.0**

Using the macro function ASSIGN.TO.TOOL is the same as using the Toolbars command from the Options menu to assign a macro to a tool on a toolbar. The *bar* argument is the bar number of the toolbar to which you want to assign a macro, as shown here:

Bar	Toolbar
1	Standard
2	Formatting
3	Utility
4	Chart
5	Drawing
6	Excel 3.0
7	Macro
8	Macro stop recording
9	Macro paused

The *position* argument is the position at which you want the tool to appear, starting at 1 from the top or left, depending on whether the toolbar is horizontal or vertical.

The *ref* argument is a reference to the macro that you want to run when the tool is clicked on. It can be a range or a name of a macro. If the *ref* argument is not included, the macro that was previously assigned to the tool is no longer assigned to that tool.

See Also

ADD.TOOL	Adds a tool to a toolbar	Macro Function
OPTIONS TOOLBARS	Related command	Menu Command
TOOLBARS, CUSTOM	Explains custom toolbars	Concept

ATAN(*X*)

Function

The ATAN function returns the arctangent in radians of a value (radians times 180/PI() equals degrees).

Example

ATAN(.5) returns the arctangent of 0.5, which is 0.464 radians, or 26.6 degrees.

See Also

ACOS	Returns arccosine	Function
ASIN	Returns arcsine	Function

ATAN2(*x-coordinate-of-an-angle,y-coordinate-of-an-angle*)

Function

The ATAN2 function returns the four-quadrant arctangent in radians of an angle, given the x and y coordinates of the angle (radians times 180/PI() equals degrees).

Example

ATAN2(–.5,.5) returns the four-quadrant arctangent of the angle whose x and y coordinates are –0.5 and 0.5, respectively—2.356 radians, or 135 degrees.

See Also

ATAN	Returns arctangent	Function
TAN	Returns tangent	Function

ATANH(*X*)

Function

The ATANH function returns the inverse hyperbolic tangent in radians of a value. The argument *X* must be between –1 and 1 (radians times 180/PI() equals degrees).

Example

ATANH(.5) returns the inverse hyperbolic tangent of 0.5, which is 0.549306.

See Also

ACOSH	Returns inverse hyperbolic cosine	Function
ASINH	Returns inverse hyperbolic sine	Function

ATTACH.TEXT(*attach*,*[series]*,*[point]*)
ATTACH.TEXT?(*[attach]*,*[series]*,*[point]*)

Macro Function

ATTACH.TEXT is the same as the Chart Attach Text menu command. The *attach* argument allows you to define where you want to attach the text. If the chart is two-dimensional, the following table gives the possible values for the *attach* argument.

Attach	Location
1	Title
2	Y (Value axis)
3	X (Category axis)
4	Series or data point
5	Y (Overlay axis)
6	X (Overlay axis)

If the chart is three-dimensional, the following table gives the possible values for the *attach* argument.

Attach	Location
1	Title
2	Z (Value axis)
3	Y (Series axis)
4	X (Category axis)
5	Series or data point

The *series* argument indicates the series to which to attach the text. If the *series* argument is not included, the macro halts. If the *series* number is given, the number of the data *point* must also be given.

See Also

CHART ATTACH TEXT	Equivalent command	Menu Command

AUTOSUM

Tool

The AutoSum tool is a very useful shortcut. It performs the same task as typing the formula =SUM(range). It guesses which range you want to sum, and often guesses correctly. If the range is not the one you want, simply type in your range reference. Figure A-6 shows the result of clicking on the AutoSum tool.

See Also

SUM   Equivalent Function   Function

AVEDEV(*X1,X2,X3...*)

Function   New to Version 4.0

AVEDEV is the average absolute deviation of the input. This function can take up to 30 arguments. Alternatively, you can use a reference to an array that contains the values rather than the individual numbers.

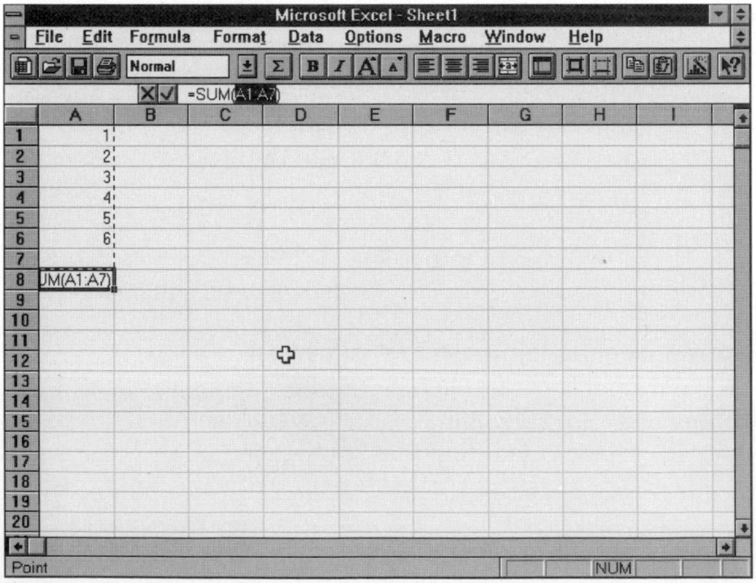

Figure A-6.   Summing a column of numbers using the AutoSum tool

See Also

STDEV   Returns standard deviation   Function

AVERAGE(*range1,range2,...*)

Function

Returns the average of all the values in the listed ranges. There is a limit of 30 arguments. The arguments can be numbers, ranges, arrays, or names that refer to numbers, ranges, or arrays.

Example

AVERAGE(H15:H35) returns the average of the values in cells H15 through H35.

See Also

DAVERAGE   Returns average from a database   Function

AXES(*[main-category], [main-value], [main-z] [overlay-category],* *[overlay-value], [overlay-z]*)
AXES?(*[main-category], [main-value], [main-z],* *[overlay-category], [overlay-value], [overlay-z]*)

Macro Function

The AXES macro function is the same as the Chart Axes menu command. AXES causes axes on your chart to be displayed or not displayed. When an argument is TRUE, that axis is displayed. If an argument is FALSE, that axis is not displayed. If an argument is omitted, the axis will not change. The arguments correspond to the check boxes in the Axes dialog box, and represent the different axes on the chart. In the dialog box version (with the question mark), if the arguments are included, they are the defaults for the dialog box that appears, as shown here:

See Also

CHART AXES   Equivalent command   Menu Command

B

BASE(*X,base,[digits]*)

Function   **New to Version 4.0**

Converts *X*, a base-10 number, to a number in another *base. Digits* is an optional argument that specifies the number of digits to the right of the decimal point. If *digits* is not given, the default is 0.

   BASE is an add-in function. If you get a #NAME? error when you try to use this function, you need to install it by using the Add-Ins command from the Options menu. If Add-In Functions does not appear in the list box, click on the Add button, choose addinfns.xla from the list box, and click on OK. If the #NAME? error still does not disappear, press the F2 key and then press ENTER.

Example

BASE(35,5,2) converts 35 to base 5, which is 120.

See Also

BIN2DEC	Converts binary to decimal	Function
DEC2BIN	Converts decimal to binary	Function
DEC2HEX	Converts decimal to hexadecimal	Function
HEX2DEC	Converts hexadecimal to decimal	Function

BEEP(*[tone]*)

Macro Function

The BEEP macro function sounds a tone on the computer. The *tone* argument, which is a number between 1 and 4, can optionally be used to vary the tone. If *tone* is absent, the number 1 is used as a default. There may be little or no difference between tone numbers on most computers.

Example

BEEP(2) BEEP(4) makes a sound twice using different tones.

BESSELI(X,N)

Function   **New to Version 4.0**

The BESSELI function returns the Bessel function $I_n(x)$ for imaginary numbers. N must be 0 or greater, and both X and N must be numeric.

BESSELI is an add-in function that loads automatically. When you try to use this function for the first time in a session, you may see a #REF! error while Excel loads the function. Once the function is loaded, there will be no delay the next time you use it.

Example

BESSELI(5,1) returns 24.33564.

See Also

BESSELJ	Bessel function $J_n(x)$	Function
BESSELK	Modified Bessel function $K_n(x)$	Function
BESSELY	Bessel function $Y_n(x)$	Function

BESSELJ(X,N)

Function   **New to Version 4.0**

BESSELJ returns the Bessel function $J_n(x)$. N must be 0 or greater, and both X and N must be numeric.

BESSELJ is an add-in function that loads automatically. When you try to use this function for the first time in a session, you may see a #REF! error while Excel loads the function. Once the function is loaded, there will be no delay the next time you use it.

Example

BESSELJ(5,1) returns –0.32758.

See Also

BESSELI	Bessel function $I_n(x)$ of an imaginary number	Function
BESSELK	Modified Bessel function $K_n(x)$	Function
BESSELY	Bessel function $Y_n(x)$	Function

BESSELK(X,N)

Function   **New to Version 4.0**

BESSELK returns the modified Bessel function $K_n(x)$. N must be 0 or greater, and both X and N must be numeric.

BESSELK is an add-in function that loads automatically. When you try to use this function for the first time in a session, you may see a #REF! error while Excel loads the function. Once the function is loaded, there will be no delay the next time you use it.

Example

BESSELK(5,1) returns 0.004045.

See Also

BESSELI	Bessel function $I_n(x)$ of an imaginary number	Function
BESSELJ	Bessel function $J_n(x)$	Function
BESSELY	Bessel function $Y_n(x)$	Function

BESSELY(X,N)

Function   **New to Version 4.0**

BESSELY returns the Bessel function $Y_n(x)$. N must be 0 or greater, and both X and N must be numeric.

BESSELY is an add-in function that loads automatically. When you try to use this function for the first time in a session, you may see a #REF! error while Excel loads the function. Once the function is loaded, there will be no delay the next time you use it.

Example

BESSELY(5,1) returns 0.147863.

See Also

BESSELI	Bessel function $I_n(x)$ of an imaginary number	Function
BESSELJ	Bessel function $J_n(x)$	Function
BESSELK	Modified Bessel function $K_n(x)$	Function

BETADIST(*X, alpha, beta, [lower], [upper]*)

Function   **New to Version 4.0**

BETADIST evaluates the cumulative beta probability density. *X* is the value to evaluate, *alpha* and *beta* are parameters to the distribution, and *upper* and *lower* are bounds of *X*.

Example

BETADIST(3,9,15,1,5) returns 0.89498.

See Also

BETAINV	Related function	Function

BETAINV(*X, alpha, beta, [lower], [upper]*)

Function   **New to Version 4.0**

BETAINV evaluates the inverse cumulative beta probability density. *X* is the value to evaluate, *alpha* and *beta* are parameters to the distribution, and *upper* and *lower* are bounds of *X*.

Example

BETAINV(0.89498,9,15,1,5) returns 3.

See Also

BETADIST	Related function	Function

BIN2DEC(*X*)

Function   **New to Version 4.0**

BIN2DEC converts a number *X* from binary to decimal.

Example

BIN2DEC(0110) returns 6.

See Also

DEC2BIN	Converts decimal to binary	Function
HEX2BIN	Converts hexadecimal to binary	Function
OCT2BIN	Converts octal to binary	Function

BIN2HEX(*X,characters*)

Function   **New to Version 4.0**

BIN2HEX converts a number *X* from binary to hexadecimal, and returns the result in *characters* number of places. For example, if *characters* is 8, there will always be eight *characters* in the result, which will be padded with 0's if necessary.

Example

BIN2HEX(0110,8) returns 00000006.

See Also

DEC2BIN	Converts decimal to binary	Function
HEX2BIN	Converts hexadecimal to binary	Function
OCT2BIN	Converts octal to binary	Function

BIN2OCT(*X,characters*)

Function   **New to Version 4.0**

BIN2OCT converts a number *X* from binary to octal, and returns the result in *characters* number of places. For example, if *characters* is 8, there will always be eight *characters* in the result, which will be padded with 0's if necessary.

Example

BIN2OCT(0110,8) returns 00000006.

See Also

DEC2BIN	Converts decimal to binary	Function
HEX2BIN	Converts hexadecimal to binary	Function
OCT2BIN	Converts octal to binary	Function

BINOMDIST(*successes, trials, probability, cumulative*)

Function   **New to Version 4.0**

BINOMDIST provides the binomial distribution probability for an individual term, where *successes* is the number of successes in *trials,* the number of independent trials each of which has *probability* probability of success. To use the cumulative distribution function, *cumulative* must be TRUE. If *cumulative* is FALSE, the probability mass function is used.

See Also

COMBIN	Related function	Function
CRITBINOM	Related function	Function
NEGBINOMDIST	Returns the negative binomial distribution	Function

BORDER(*outline, left, right, top, bottom, shade, outline-color, left-color, right-color, top-color, bottom-color*)
BORDER?(*[outline], [left], [right], [top], [bottom], [shade], [outline-color], [left-color], [right-color], [top-color], [bottom-color]*)

Macro Function

The BORDER macro function is the same as the Format Border menu command. The arguments correspond to the options that appear in the Border dialog box. In the dialog box version (with the question mark), if the arguments are included, they are used as defaults for the dialog box options.

   BORDER places a border around cells in the current selection. You can also shade the cells, and change the color of the borders if desired. If you want a border around the entire selection, use the *outline* and *outline-color* arguments. If you want a border around each cell in the selection, use the *top, bottom, right, left, top-color, bottom-color, right-color,* and *left-color* arguments.

The *outline, top, bottom, right,* and *left* arguments are line style values, corresponding to the line styles in the dialog box. The possible values for these arguments are listed here:

Line Style	Description
0	None
1	Thin
2	Medium
3	Dashed
4	Dotted
5	Thick
6	Double
7	Hairline

The *shade* argument is TRUE or FALSE, indicating whether or not you want the cells in the selection shaded.

The *outline-color, left-color, right-color, top-color,* and *bottom-color* arguments are color codes from 0 to 16:

Color Code	Description
0	Automatic
1	Black
2	White
3	Red
4	Green
5	Blue
6	Yellow
7	Magenta
8	Cyan
9	Maroon
10	Forest green
11	Navy blue
12	Avocado green
13	Purple
14	Grey green
15	Light grey
16	Dark grey

A,B

See Also

FORMAT BORDER	Equivalent Command	Menu Command
PATTERNS	Related Function	Macro Function

BREAK()

Macro Function

The BREAK macro function causes a break in a loop. Execution continues with the code following the loop code. The LOOPING concept shows an example of a loop with BREAK.

See Also

LOOPING	Explains looping	Concept

BRING.TO.FRONT()

Macro Function   **New to Version 4.0**

BRING.TO.FRONT performs the same action as the Bring To Front command from the Format menu: It brings the currently selected objects to the front. If there isn't an object selected, a #VALUE! error is returned.

See Also

FORMAT BRING TO FRONT	Equivalent command	Menu Command

BUTTONS

Concept

Buttons are objects on the screen that you click on to perform various actions. For example, most dialog boxes include an OK button and a Cancel button. The OK button will carry out the task defined in the dialog box. The Cancel button will abort the task. You can see these buttons in the dialog box shown here:

Zoom

Magnification
○ 200%
● 100%
○ 75%
○ 50%
○ 25%
○ Fit Selection
○ Custom: 100 %

OK

Cancel

Help

See Also

TOOLS, CUSTOM   Explains custom tools   Concept

CALCULATE.DOCUMENT()

Macro Function

The CALCULATE.DOCUMENT macro function causes the active document to be calculated. (See the CALCULATION entry later in this section for an explanation of how calculation and recalculation work.) Using the CALCULATE.DOCUMENT macro function is the same as using the Options Calculation menu command and then choosing the Calc Document button.

See Also

CALCULATE.NOW	Calculates all open documents	Macro Function
CALCULATION	Controls calculation	Macro Function
CALCULATION	Explains calculation	Concept
OPTIONS CALCULATE DOCUMENT	Equivalent command	Menu Command

CALCULATE.NOW()

Macro Function

The CALCULATE.NOW macro function causes all open documents to be calculated. (See the CALCULATION entry for an explanation of how calculation and recalculation work.) Using the CALCULATE.NOW macro function is the same as choosing the Options Calculation menu command and then choosing the Calc Now button.

See Also

CALCULATE.DOCUMENT	Calculates the active document	Macro Function
CALCULATION	Controls calculation	Macro Function
CALCULATION	Explains calculation	Concept
OPTIONS CALCULATE NOW	Equivalent command	Menu Command

CALCULATION

Concept

Calculation in Excel is performed automatically unless you change the default settings to manual calculation. Automatic calculation means that when you change a value or a formula, all the cells affected by that change are automatically updated. While a worksheet is being calculated, you can still perform some operations; the calculation activity will pause.

If you are working on a large spreadsheet, or a spreadsheet with external links, it may take too long to recalculate every time you enter a formula or value. If so, you can switch calculation from automatic to manual by using the Options Calculation command. This command opens the Calculation Options dialog box, shown here, which allows you to control many aspects of calculating formulas in Excel. The Calculation buttons in the upper-left section of the dialog box allow you to switch between manual and automatic calculation.

Whenever you change a formula or a value that affects your worksheet, you'll see this message indicating that calculation needs to be performed:

Ready   Calculate

When you want to recalculate your active document, choose the Options Calculate Document menu option. (You must hold down the SHIFT key while choosing the Options menu to display this option.) To recalculate all open documents, choose the Options Calculate Now option. If your active document is a chart, the Options Calculate Now option will be located on the Chart menu.

See Also

CALCULATE.DOCUMENT	Calculates the active document	Macro Function
CALCULATE.NOW	Calculates all open documents	Macro Function
CALCULATION	Controls calculation	Macro Function
OPTIONS CALCULATION	Controls calculation	Menu Command

CALCULATION(*type, iteration, max-iterations, max-change, remote-ref, precision, date-system, save, links, lotus-exp, lotus-form*)
CALCULATION?(*[type], [iteration], [max-iterations], [max-change], [remote-ref], [precision], [date-(1) system], [save], [links], [lotus-exp], [lotus-form]*)

Macro Function

The CALCULATION function performs the same operation as the Options Calculation menu command. The arguments correspond to the options in the Calculation Options dialog box, shown under the CALCULATION entry earlier in this section.

The question mark version of this function opens the dialog box, and the arguments set the dialog box defaults. The version without the question mark does not open the dialog box, but performs the function with the settings that you pass as arguments.

The CALCULATION arguments are detailed here:

Argument	Corresponds To	Default
type	(See the Type values below)	1
iteration	Iteration Check Box	FALSE
max-iterations	Maximum Iterations	100
max-change	Maximum Change	0.001
remote-ref	Update Remote References	TRUE
precision	Precision as Displayed	FALSE
date-system	1904 Date System	FALSE
save	Recalculate Before Save	TRUE
links	Save External Link Values	TRUE
lotus-exp	Alternate Expression Evaluation	FALSE
lotus-form	Alternate Formula Entry	FALSE

The possible values for the *type* argument are listed here:

Type	Description
1	Automatic calculation
2	Automatic calculation except for tables
3	Manual calculation

Normally, a worksheet or a set of documents is calculated only once each time the Options Calculation command or equivalent macro function is given. If you have a series of formulas that refer to each other, forming a chain or *circular reference,* you must calculate the worksheet multiple times to get the correct result. If the *iteration* argument is set to TRUE, the calculation is repeated either until the number of iterations exceeds *max-iterations,* or until *max-change* is greater than the maximum change in any cell.

The *lotus-exp* argument, which corresponds to the Alternate Expression Evaluation check box, determines if Lotus' rules for calculation will apply when evaluating expressions. The *lotus-form* argument, which corresponds to the Alternate Formula Entry check box, should be set to TRUE if formulas on the spreadsheet were entered in Lotus 1-2-3 style.

See Also

CALCULATE.DOCUMENT	Calculates the active document	Macro Function
CALCULATE.NOW	Calculates all open documents	Macro Function
CALCULATION	Explains calculation	Concept
OPTIONS CALCULATION	Equivalent command	Menu Command

CALL(*reg-result,[argument-list]*)

Macro Function

CALL activates a procedure from the Windows Dynamic Link Library (DLL). CALL requires that you do a REGISTER macro first to establish the procedure to be called. The *reg-result* argument references the result of the macro, and the argument list is passed to the procedure.

CAUTION: You should only use CALL if you are an accomplished programmer. Used incorrectly, CALL can cause errors in your system, and may result in the loss of data.

See Also

REGISTER	Registers a DLL procedure	Macro function

CALLER()

Macro Function

CALLER returns a reference to the function macro that called the function macro currently running, as shown in the following table. If the currently running macro is a command macro rather than a function macro, CALLER returns the error #REF!.

Called By	Reference Returned
Function in a cell	Cell address
Function in an array	Range address
AUTO_OPEN	Calling sheet name
AUTO_ACTIVATE	Calling sheet name
AUTO_DEACTIVATE	Calling sheet name
AUTO_CLOSE	Calling sheet name

Called By	Reference Returned
Menu	Array (option #, menu#, bar#)
Object	Object identifier
Toolbar tool	Array (position #, toolbar #)
ON.DOUBLECLICK	Chart object ID/Cell address
ON.ENTRY	Chart object ID/Cell address
Anything else	#REF!

CANCEL.COPY()

Macro Function

When you copy a range, a marquee appears around the selection that you are copying, as shown in Figure C-1. This marquee remains until you press the ESC key. CANCEL.COPY is the equivalent macro command.

See Also

COPY	Copies the selection	Macro Function
COPYING	Explains copying in Excel	Concept
EDIT COPY	Related command	Menu Command

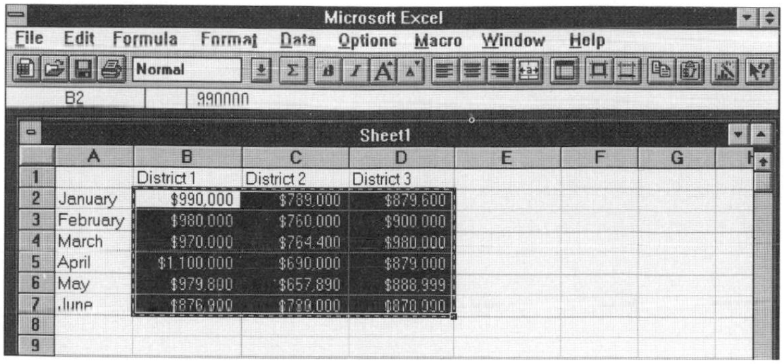

Figure C-1.   *A selection surrounded by the copy marquee*

CANCEL.KEY (*escape, [macro-reference]*)

Macro Function

CANCEL.KEY disables the ESC key if the *escape* argument is FALSE. If the *escape* argument is TRUE, the ESC key is enabled. If the *escape* argument is TRUE and a *macro-reference* is included, the macro referred to by *macro-reference* is started when the ESC key is pressed.

Examples

If CANCEL.KEY(FALSE) is included in a macro, pressing ESC will not halt the macro. If =CANCEL.KEY(TRUE,test_macro()) is included in a macro, pressing ESC will start a macro named test_macro.

CEILING (*X, sig*)

Function   New to Version 4.0

CEILING rounds the number *X* to the nearest multiple of *sig*. If *sig* divides *X* perfectly, CEILING returns *X*. If *sig* does not divide *X* perfectly, it is rounded to the next highest multiple of *sig*. *X* and *sig* must have the same sign, or CEILING returns #NUM!.

Examples

=CEILING (3.1,1) returns 4.
=CEILING(–3.1,1) returns –4.

See Also

FLOOR	Rounds a number down	Function
ROUND	Rounds to a specified number of digits	Function
TRUNC	Truncates a number	Function

CELL

Concept

The *cell* is the basic unit of a worksheet. A worksheet is made up of rows and columns, the intersection of which is a cell. Each cell has an address consisting of its column letter and row number. The address of the *active cell* (the one in which you are working) appears on the left side of the formula bar. When you type text, values, or a formula, it is entered into the active cell. If you enter more information into a cell than can be displayed, Excel displays as much as possible on your worksheet. The cell will contain everything that you entered up to the maximum of 255 characters, but the entire contents of the cell may not be displayed.

Notice in Figure C-2 that the entire contents of the active cell B1 is shown in the formula bar, but it doesn't all fit in the worksheet cell. Cell D1 contains a similar label, but since there is nothing in cell E1, Excel displays the entire label by using the adjacent cell.

You can change the display area of a cell and format its contents. You can change the display area by changing the width of the column and the height of the row that the cell occupies. Formatting a cell's contents includes changing number formats, fonts, or alignment, and adding borders and shading.

You can remove or clear a cell's contents by pressing the DEL key. You can also choose the Edit Clear menu command; this brings up the Clear dialog box, shown here, which allows you to remove the cell's formulas or content, its formats, notes, or all of these. When you want to remove the contents only, click on the Formulas button.

You can copy or move a cell's contents to another cell with the Edit Copy, Edit Cut, and Edit Paste commands or with the Drag and Drop mouse operations. You can also delete a cell, as a part of the worksheet, with the Edit Delete option. This causes other cells to move and take its place. (See the entry, CLEARING CELLS VERSUS DELETING CELLS.)

	A	B	C	D	E	F	G
1		District 1 - North	District 2 - South	District 3 - Eastern Region			
2	January	$990,000	$789,000	$879,600			
3	February	$980,000	$760,000	$900,000			
4	March	$970,000	$764,400	$980,000			
5	April	$1,100,000	$690,000	$879,000			
6	May	$979,800	$657,890	$888,999			
7	June	$876,900	$789,000	$878,990			
8							

Figure C-2.   The entire contents of the cell may not be displayed

See Also

ADDRESSING   Explains addressing in Excel   Concept

CELL(*attribute,[range]*)

Function

CELL examines the first cell in a range and returns information depending on the attribute specified. If the *range* argument is omitted, the current selection is considered to be the range. You can use the following attributes:

Attribute	Returns
"address"	The absolute cell address
"col"	The column number
"color"	1 if color for negative values
"contents"	The contents of the cell
"filename"	Full path of the filename
"format"	The format of the cell
"parentheses"	1 if formatted with parentheses
"prefix"	The alignment prefix
"protect"	1 if the cell is locked
"row"	The row number of the cell
"type"	The type of data the cell contains
"width"	The width of the cell in characters

If the attribute that you want returned is the format, the CELL function will return the following format codes to indicate the type of formatting associated with the cell:

Cell	Format Codes
,0	Comma, 0 digits to right of decimal point
,2	Comma, 2 digits to right of decimal point
C0	Currency, 0 digits to right of decimal point
C0–	Currency, 0 digits to right of decimal point, red negative values
C2	Currency, 2 digits to right of decimal point
C2–	Currency, 2 digits to right of decimal point, red negative values
F0	Fixed, 0 digits to right of decimal point

Cell	Format Codes
F2	Fixed, 2 digits to right of decimal point
G	General, a label or a blank cell
P0	Percent, 0 digits to right of decimal point
P2	Percent, 2 digits to right of decimal point
S2	Scientific, 2 digits to right of decimal point
D1	Date in D-MMM-YY format
D2	Date in D-MMM format
D3	Date in MMM-YY format
D4	Date in M/D/YY or M/D/YY H:MM or MM/DD/YY format
D5	Date in MM/DD format
D6	Time in H:MM:SS AM/PM format
D7	Time H:MM AM/PM format
D8	Time in H:MM:SS format
D9	Time in H:MM format

If you use "prefix" as the attribute argument, the following prefix codes will be returned to indicate the kind of alignment associated with the cell:

Prefix Code	Cell Alignment
'	Left-aligned label
"	Right-aligned label
^	Centered label
\	Fill-aligned label
Blank	Empty or a value

If you want to know what type of information is in the cell, use the "type" attribute. One of the following type codes will be returned:

Type Code	Information in Cell
b	Blank
v	Value or formula
l	Label

Example

=(CELL("format",G25) returns D1 if cell G25 is formatted with the *M/DDD/YY* date format.

See Also

ADDRESSING	Explains addressing in Excel	Concept
RANGE	Explains ranges	Concept

CELL.PROTECTION(*[locked]*, *[hidden]* **)**
CELL.PROTECTION?(*[locked]*, *[hidden]* **)**

Macro Function

Like the Format Cell Protection menu option, the CELL.PROTECTION function controls whether the current selection is protected and/or hidden. The optional arguments are either TRUE or FALSE; FALSE is the default.

The question mark version of this function opens the dialog box. The arguments set the defaults in the dialog box. The version without the question mark does not open the dialog box, but performs the function with the settings that you pass as arguments.

Examples

=CELL.PROTECTION(TRUE) protects the current selection.
=CELL.PROTECTION(TRUE,TRUE) protects and hides the current selection.

See Also

CELL	Returns attributes of a cell	Function
FORMAT CELL PROTECTION	Equivalent command	Menu Command
PROTECT.DOCUMENT	Protects the active document	Macro Function

CELL REFERENCE

Concept

A *cell reference,* also called the *cell address,* generally consists of the cell's column letter followed by its row number. This is known as the A1 style of cell reference. However, at times it is useful to refer to a cell by a row number and a column number. This is known as R1C1 style of cell reference. For example, cell B2 can also be called R2C2. With either style of cell reference, the address of the active cell appears on the left side of the formula bar.

See Also

ADDRESSING	Explains addressing	Concept
CELL	Explains cells	Concept
CELL	Returns attributes of a cell	Function

CHANGE.LINK(*old-link-doc-name, new-link-doc-name, [type]* **)**
CHANGE.LINK?(*[old-link-doc-name], [new-link-doc-name], [type]* **)**

Macro Function

CHANGE.LINK allows you to change a link to the active document from one document to another document. The optional *type* argument allows you to specify whether the link is an Excel link or a DDE link. The default for *type* is 1.

Type	Description
1	Excel link
2	DDE link

The question mark version of this function opens the dialog box. The arguments set the defaults in the dialog box. The version without the question mark does not open the dialog box, but performs the function with the settings that you pass as arguments.

See Also

FILE LINKS	Equivalent command	Menu Command
OPEN.LINKS	Opens linked documents	Macro Function
UPDATE.LINK	Updates a link	Macro Function

CHAR(*ASCII-code* **)**

Function

CHAR returns the character matching the ASCII (American Standard Code for Information Interchange) code.

Example

=CHAR(100) produces the character d.

The ASCII codes and the standard U.S. Windows characters they produce are shown in Appendix B.

CHART

Menu

The Chart menu only appears on the menu bar if the active document is a chart. The Chart menu contains options that allow you to change the appearance of your chart, as shown in Figure C-3. Each of these options is explained in the entries that follow.

CHART ADD ARROW

Menu Command

The Chart Add Arrow option allows you to add an arrow to your chart, as shown in Figure C-4. Once you add the arrow, you can move and size it with the Format Move or Format Size options or with the mouse. You also can change its appearance with the Format Patterns option.

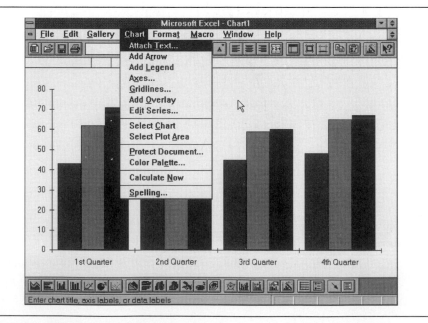

Figure C-3.   *The Chart menu*

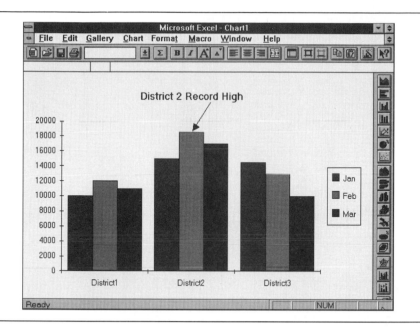

Figure C-4. *A chart with an arrow*

See Also

ADD.ARROW   Equivalent function   Macro Function

CHART ADD LEGEND

Menu Command

The Chart Add Legend menu command allows you to add a legend to your chart similar to the one shown in Figure C-5. If you included the series names when you selected the area to be charted on your worksheet, the series names will automatically be used for the legend. Once you have added a legend by choosing the Chart Add Legend option, you can format the legend using the Format Patterns, Font, and Legend options. Once you choose the Add Legend option, the Delete Legend option appears in its place on the Chart menu, as you can see in the figure.

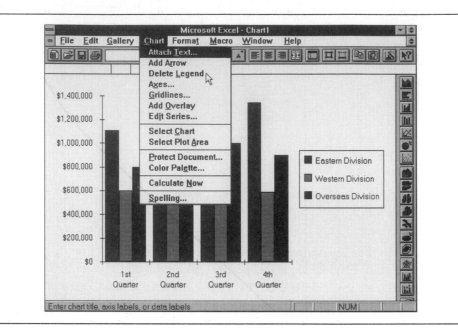

Figure C-5.   *A chart with a legend showing regional divisions*

CHART ADD OVERLAY

Menu Command

The Add Overlay menu option allows you to create an overlay chart for an existing chart. Figure C-6 shows such an overlay chart. In versions of Excel prior to 4, the Chart Add Overlay menu option only appears on the Chart menu if Full Menus is activated. If there are an odd number of series when the overlay is added, there will be one more series on the main chart than on the overlay. If there are an even number of series, there will be the same number of series on the main chart and on the overlay. If you want to control this default distribution of series, see the Format Overlay option. The overlay chart will be created as a line chart. To change it to another type of chart, use the Format Overlay option.

See Also

ADD.OVERLAY   Equivalent function   Macro Function

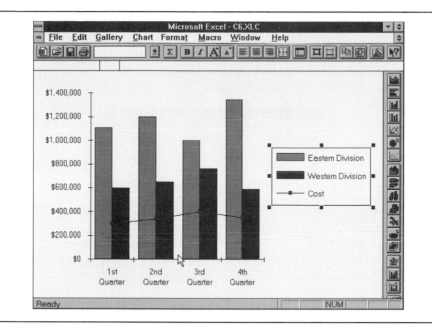

Figure C-6.   *A chart with an overlay*

CHART ATTACH TEXT

Menu Command

The Chart Attach Text menu option allows you to attach text such as titles to the chart, the value (Y) axis, the category (X) axis, a series, or a data point. Once you choose the Chart Attach Text option, you will see the Attach Text dialog box, shown here, which permits you to choose where you want the text attached.

Attach Text

Attach Text To
- ● Chart Title
- ○ Value (Y) Axis
- ○ Category (X) Axis
- ○ Series and Data Point
  - Series Number:
  - Point Number:
- ○ Overlay Value (Y) Axis
- ○ Overlay Category (X) Axis

OK
Cancel
Help

Once you choose where you want your title and press ENTER or click on OK, you can type a title. For example, if you choose Title and then click on OK, you will see the word "Title" in the middle of your chart, surrounded by squares (called *handles*) indicating that the "Title" text is selected, as shown here. Once you've typed in your title and pressed ENTER, your title will replace the word "Title" on the chart.

You can also use text on any worksheet you can link to as a chart title. Simply type a formula that references a cell on the worksheet in place of the word "Title." For example, if you replaced the word "Title" with "=DATA.XLS!$C$7", the text in cell C7 of the DATA.XLS worksheet would be used as the chart title.

See Also

ATTACH TEXT   Equivalent function   Macro Function

CHART AXES

Menu Command

The Chart Axes menu option allows you to display or hide the axes on your chart. Once you choose the Chart Axes option, you will see the Axes dialog box shown here. This dialog box allows you to turn on or off the category (X) axis and/or the value (Y) axis for both the main chart and the overlay chart.

See Also

AXES   Equivalent function   Macro Function

CHART CALCULATE NOW

Menu Command

➤   *Shortcut Key:* F9

The Chart Calculate Now menu option recalculates all open documents and redraws all open charts according to the options that you set in the Calculation Options dialog box shown here:

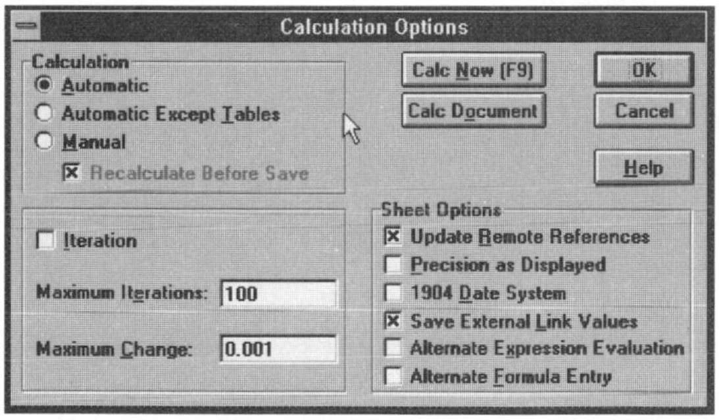

The Options Calculation option appears on the Options menu, which appears on the menu bar when the active document is a worksheet. You would use the Chart Calculate Now option if you had set the calculation to manual in the Calculation Options dialog box, and you want to recalculate and redraw your chart.

See Also

CALCULATION	Explains calculation	Concept
CALCULATE.DOCUMENT	Calculates active document	Macro Function
CALCULATE.NOW	Equivalent function	Macro Function

CHART, CUSTOMIZING

Concept

Once you have created a chart with either the File New Chart option or the ChartWizard, there are many ways of changing the appearance of your chart. First, you can use the Gallery menu or the Chart toolbar to change the type of chart; there are 14 different chart types from which to choose. When you choose a chart type from the Gallery menu or the Chart toolbar, you will see a dialog box similar to the Gallery dialog box shown here. This chart gallery will provide up to eight alternatives for the selected chart type, as well as a Previous button and a Next button. You can use the Previous and Next buttons to cycle through the built-in chart types.

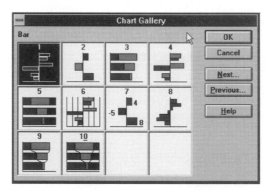

Once you have selected the type of chart that you want, you can modify it using the options on the Chart menu. You can add text, an arrow, a legend, grid lines, and an overlay. You can also modify the series or the axes with the Chart menu.

Using the Chart toolbar, you can add or delete grid lines, a legend, arrows, or unattached text. You can make further changes by selecting chart items and using the options on the Format menu to change the patterns, fonts, color, shading, line width, size, and position of chart items.

For example, you can use the Chart Attach Text option to attach titles to the chart, axes, and series. You can use the Format Patterns, Format Font, and Format Text options to change selected items on your chart. Before formatting anything, you must select it by clicking on it. Handles will appear on or around the selection to indicate that it is selected. Once a chart element has been selected, only menu options that are appropriate for that chart element are available. The unavailable options will appear grayed. The legend in Figure C-7 is selected.

When the legend is selected, you can use the Format Font option to change its appearance. You can use this same method to change the appearance of any item on your chart.

You can change the color or pattern of a series by clicking on any item in the series and then choosing the Format Patterns option. The Patterns dialog box opens, as shown here, allowing you to choose the color and pattern for that series:

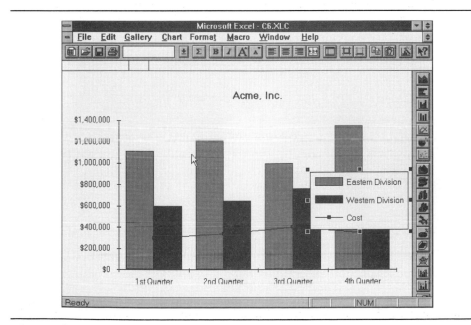

CHART DELETE ARROW

Menu Command

The Chart Delete Arrow menu command allows you to remove a selected arrow from your chart. This option only appears if you have an arrow selected. Otherwise, the Chart Add Arrow option appears on the Chart menu in its place.

Figure C-7.   *A chart with the legend selected*

See Also

CHART ADD ARROW   Adds an arrow to a chart   Menu Command

CHART DELETE LEGEND

Menu Command

The Chart Delete Legend menu option removes the legend from your chart. This option only appears on the Chart menu if your chart contains a legend. If not, the Chart Add Legend option appears on the Chart menu instead.

See Also

CHART ADD LEGEND   Adds a legend to a chart   Menu Command

CHART DELETE OVERLAY

Menu Command

The Chart Delete Overlay menu option deletes an overlay chart, putting all the series from the overlay chart onto the main chart. This option only appears on the Chart menu if you have an overlay chart on your active chart. If not, the option Chart Add Overlay appears on the menu instead. In versions of Excel prior to 4, the Chart Delete Overlay option only appeared on the Chart menu if the Full Menus option was activated.

See Also

CHART ADD OVERLAY   Adds an overlay to a chart   Menu Command

CHART FULL MENUS

Menu Command   **Prior to Version 4.0 Only**

The Chart Full Menus option allows you to turn on the Full Menus option, so that all menus appear with all their options. The Chart Full Menus option only appears on the Chart menu in versions prior to 4 if the Short Menus option is activated. If you have full menus, the option appears as Chart Short Menus instead. (This option does not appear in Excel versions 4.0 and later.)

See Also

CHART SHORT MENUS   Turns on short menus   Menu Command

CHART GRIDLINES

Menu Command

The Chart Gridlines option allows you to display or hide the grid lines on your chart. When you choose this option, the Gridlines dialog box appears, as shown here. This dialog box enables you to turn on or off major and minor grid lines for both the value axis and the category axis. The default setting has grid lines turned off.

Figure C-8 shows a chart with the major grid lines turned on.

See Also

CHART, CUSTOMIZING   Explains formatting a chart   Concept

CHART PROTECT DOCUMENT

Menu Command

The Chart Protect Document menu option allows you to protect your chart from modifications. When you choose the Chart Protect Document option, Excel displays the Protect Document dialog box, which allows you to enter a password and choose whether you want the chart contents, the window, or both protected. The contents refers to the all aspects of the chart—series, formatting, and so forth. The windows refers to the window in which the chart appears. If you protect the window, you won't be able to move, size, or hide the window. Once you choose OK in the Protect Document dialog box, you cannot change what you have protected unless you supply the password. If you want to unprotect the chart using the Chart Unprotect Document option, you must have the password you typed here.

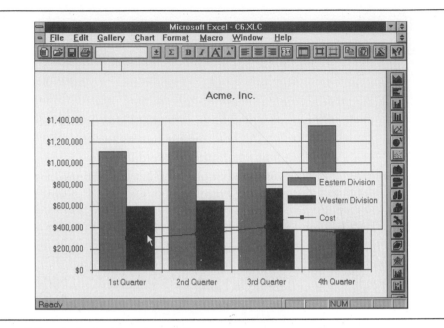

Figure C-8. *A chart with major grid lines*

See Also

CHART UNPROTECT DOCUMENT	Related command	Menu Command

CHART SELECT CHART

Menu Command

The Chart Select Chart menu option selects the entire active chart. Once you have selected the chart, you can use other options to change the chart, including the options listed here:

Edit Clear	Clear the formats and/or data series
Edit Copy	Copy the formats and/or data series
Format Overlay	Change the overlay type and formats
Format Font	Change the font used for the text for the entire chart
Format Main Chart	Change the chart type and formats
Format Patterns	Change the borders, background, or foreground

CHART SELECT PLOT AREA

Menu Command

The Chart Select Plot Area menu command selects the area within the axes on your chart so you can format it using the Format Patterns option.

See Also

FORMAT PATTERNS   Changes patterns on the chart   Menu Command

CHART SHORT MENUS

Menu Command   Prior to Version 4.0 Only

The Chart Short Menus option allows you to shorten all menus so that only the most frequently used menu options appear. The Chart Short Menus option only appears on the Chart menu in versions of Excel prior to 4, and then only if the Full Menus option is activated. If you have short menus, this option is replaced by Chart Full Menus. (This option does not appear in Excel version 4.0.)

See Also

CHART FULL MENUS   Turns on full menus   Menu Command

CHART UNPROTECT DOCUMENT

Menu Command

The Chart Unprotect Document option only appears on the Chart menu if the Full Menus option is activated. The Chart Unprotect Document option allows you to unprotect a document that you protected with the Chart Protect Document option. You must remember the password you used to protect the document; otherwise, you won't be able to unprotect it. When you choose the Chart Unprotect Document option, you will see a dialog box into which you must type the password and choose OK. Once you unprotect the document, the option Chart Protect Document appears on the Chart menu in place of Chart Unprotect Document.

See Also

CHART PROTECT DOCUMENT   Related command   Menu Command

CHARTS

Concept

Charts present your data in a visual format. Seeing numbers on a worksheet often doesn't give you a clear understanding of the relationship between different sets of data. Charts are a good way of creating presentations and summary reports.

There are two types of charts in Excel, embedded charts and separate charts. An embedded chart is part of the worksheet from which it is created. A separate chart is an independent document. The easiest way to create an embedded chart is using the ChartWizard tool. Simply select the values to be charted, click on the ChartWizard tool, and the ChartWizard will lead you through the steps of creating an embedded chart. The ChartWizard tool is the second tool from the right in the Standard toolbar, which is shown here:

Once you have created the chart, you can double-click on the chart to open a window for the embedded chart. The Chart menu bar appears, and all of Excel's formatting features are available for formatting the embedded chart.

It is also easy to create a separate chart in Excel. Select the values that you would like to chart, choose the File New menu option, and select the Chart file type. A new chart will be created with default settings. Once your chart is created, you can use the Chart, Format, and Gallery menus to format it.

All the numbers that you want charted needn't be located contiguously on the worksheet. You can chart a multiple selection. The following example demonstrates how to create a chart from the worksheet shown in Figure C-9. For an example of creating an embedded chart using the ChartWizard, see the CHARTWIZARD entry.

Example

1. Select the ranges A1:G1, A6:G6, and A12:G12, as shown in Figure C-10. (To select multiple cells, hold down the CTRL key while selecting with the mouse or press SHIFT-F8 and use the arrow keys for selection.)

2. Click on the File menu and choose the New option. A chart like the one shown in Figure C-11 will be created.

3. Click on the Gallery menu and the 3-D Column option. The Chart Gallery dialog box opens with the 3-D Column options.

4. Click on option 6 and then choose OK.

5. Click on the Chart menu and the Add Legend option.
   The chart should now look like Figure C-12.

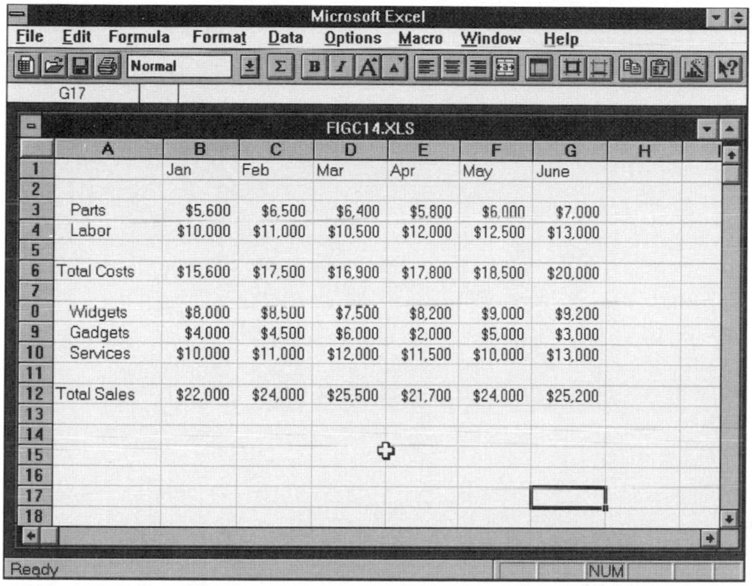

Figure C-9. *A worksheet with data to be charted from a multiple selection*

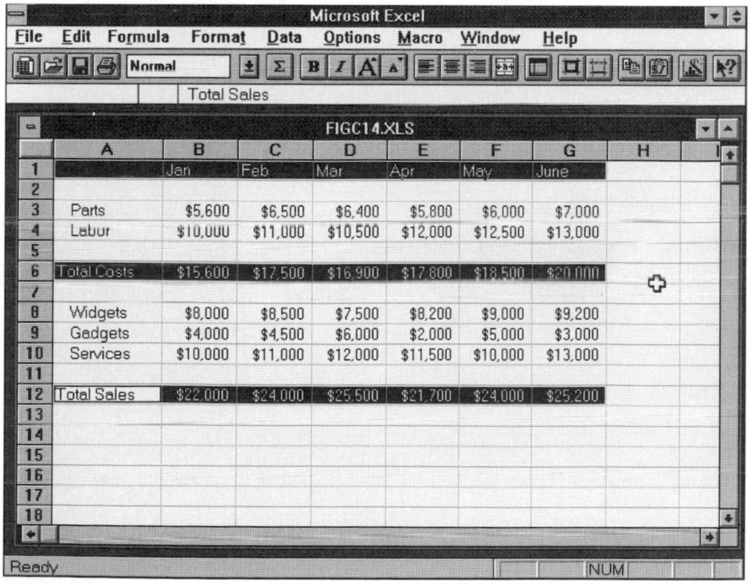

Figure C-10. *Selecting discontiguous cells*

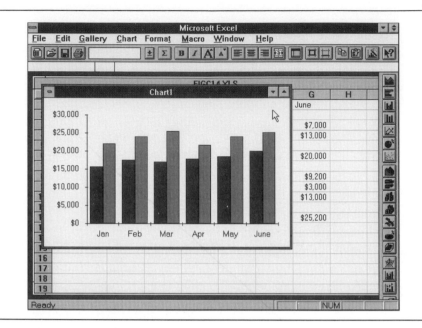

Figure C-11. *The chart created with File New*

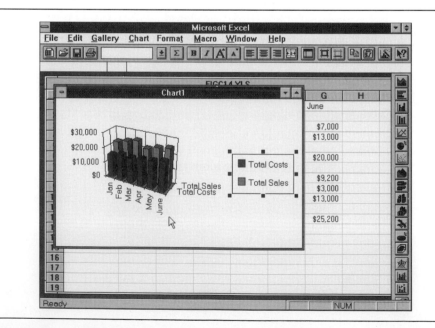

Figure C-12. *A three-dimensional column chart with a legend*

You can use the options on the Gallery, Chart, and Format menus to further customize your chart. You can also use the tools on the Chart toolbar to select different chart types rather than going through the Gallery menu, and to add grid lines, legends, arrows, and unattached text instead of using the Chart menu.

See Also

CHART, CUSTOMIZING	Explains customizing charts	Concept
CHARTS, EMBEDDED VS SEPARATE	Explains chart types	Concept
CHARTWIZARD	How to use the ChartWizard	Concept

CHARTS, EMBEDDED VS SEPARATE

Concept

There are two types of charts in Excel, embedded and separate. An *embedded chart* is part of the document in which it is created. A *separate chart* is a separate document. When you save a separate chart, it is saved in its own file, which has an .XLC extension. An embedded chart is saved with the worksheet in which it is created.

The easiest way to create an embedded chart is to use the ChartWizard tool. Simply select the values to be plotted and click on the ChartWizard tool—the second tool from the right on the Standard toolbar, as shown here. The ChartWizard will then lead you through the steps of creating an embedded chart.

Once you have created an embedded chart, you can double-click on it to open a window and place a separate copy of the chart in it. The Chart menu bar and Chart toolbar then appear, and all the formatting features available in Excel are available for formatting the chart.

It is also easy to create a separate chart in Excel. Select the values that you want to chart, choose the File New menu option, and select the Chart file type. Excel will create a new chart with default settings in a separate window. You can then use the Chart, Format, and Gallery menus and the Chart toolbar to change and format the chart.

See Also

CHART, CUSTOMIZING	Explains formatting a chart	Concept
CHARTS	Explains creating a chart	Concept
CHARTWIZARD	Explains the ChartWizard	Concept

CHARTWIZARD

Tool   **New to Version 4.0**

The ChartWizard tool is the second tool from the right on the Standard toolbar. It provides the easiest way to create an embedded chart, since it guides you through the process. The following example shows how to use ChartWizard to create an embedded chart for the worksheet shown in Figure C-13.

Example

1. Create a worksheet like the one shown in Figure C-13.

2. Select the area A1:D5.

3. Click on the ChartWizard tool from the Standard toolbar.

4. The cursor icon turns into a crosshair. Drag it from the upper-left corner to the lower-right corner of the area where you want the chart to appear, as shown in Figure C-14.

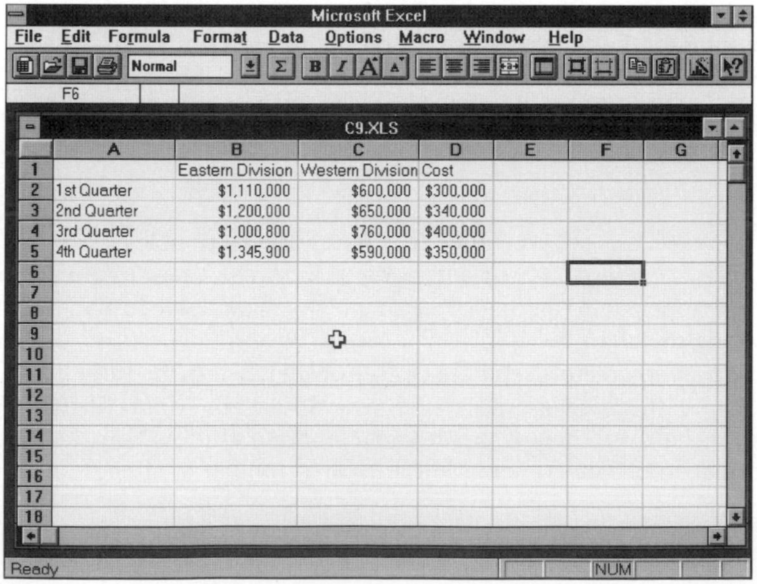

	A	B	C	D
1		Eastern Division	Western Division	Cost
2	1st Quarter	$1,110,000	$600,000	$300,000
3	2nd Quarter	$1,200,000	$650,000	$340,000
4	3rd Quarter	$1,000,800	$760,000	$400,000
5	4th Quarter	$1,345,900	$590,000	$350,000

Figure C-13.   *The worksheet to be charted*

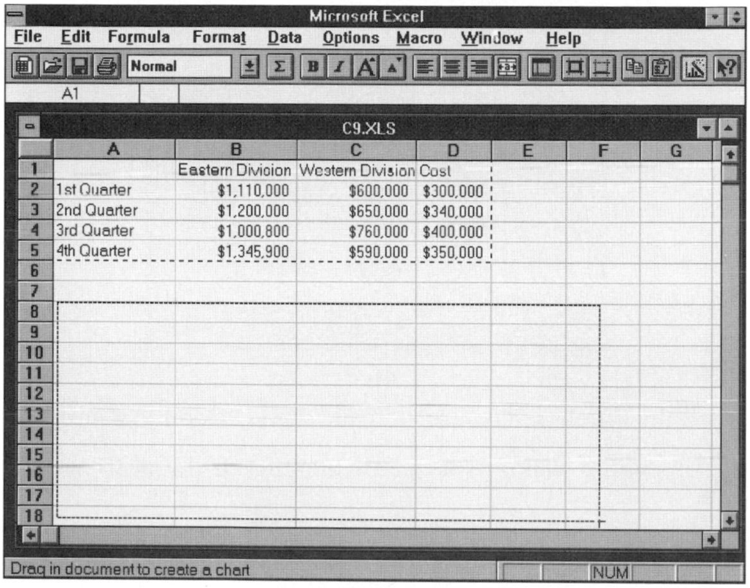

Figure C-14.   *To define the chart area, drag the crosshair within the worksheet*

5. Once you have defined an area on your worksheet for the chart, you'll see the dialog box shown here, which asks you to confirm whether the current selection is what you want to chart.

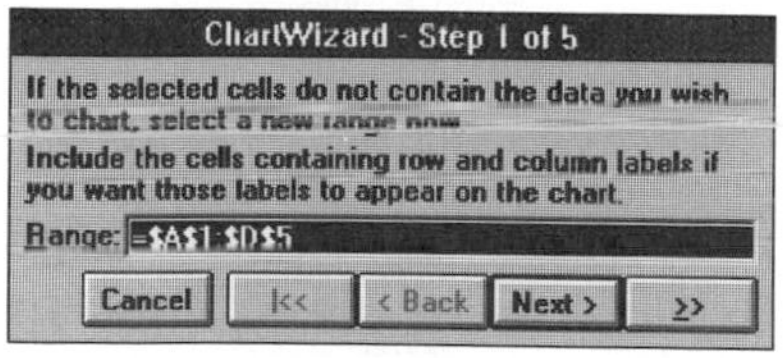

6. Since the selection is correct, press ENTER.

7. Finally, choose the type of chart you want from the dialog box shown here:

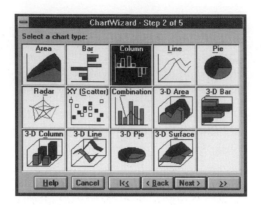

8. Click on the Combination selection and then click on the Next button.

9. Next, the Step 3 dialog box opens, showing all the possible Combination charts:

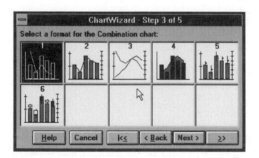

10. Choose type 2 and click on the Next button.

11. Next, the Step 4 dialog box opens, displaying a sample chart like the one shown here:

12. Click on the Next button.

13. You will see the Step 5 dialog box, as shown here:

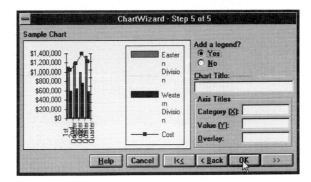

14. Click on the OK button.

15. The chart shown in Figure C-15 appears. In order to edit or format this chart further, double-click on it to open it in its own window, as you see in Figure C-16.

Once you have created the chart and double-clicked on it to put it in its own window, you can edit and format the chart using all the options available on the chart menus and all of the tools available on the Chart toolbar. You can also size and move the window as desired.

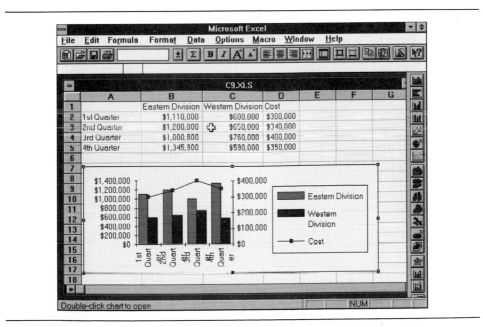

Figure C-15.   *The embedded chart created by ChartWizard*

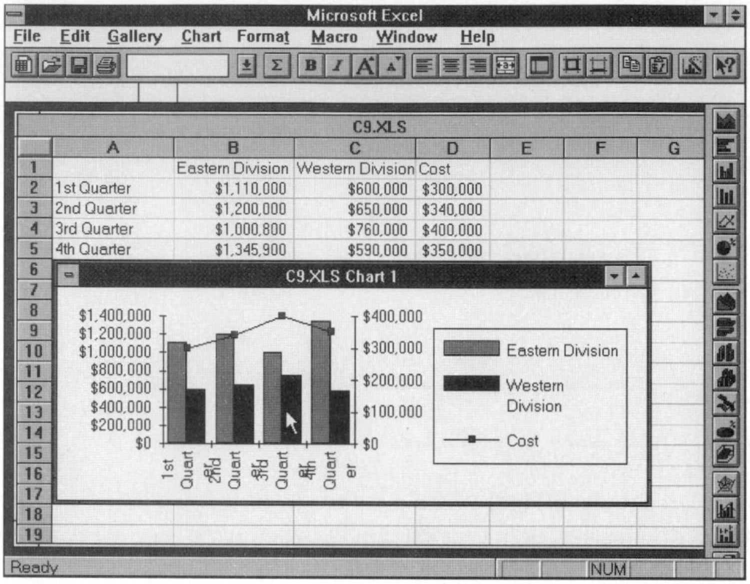

Figure C-16.   *The embedded chart in its own window*

See Also

CHARTS	Description of Excel Charts	Concept
CHARTS, EMBEDDED VS SEPARATE	Explains chart types	Concept

CHECK.COMMAND (*bar, menu, option, check*)

Macro Function

CHECK.COMMAND adds or removes a check mark from beside a menu option. The *bar* argument represents the number of the menu bar, *menu* is the name or number of the menu, and *option* is the name or number of the menu option where you want to place or remove a check mark. If *check* is TRUE, a check mark is placed beside the option. If *check* is FALSE, a check mark is removed from beside the option.

Bar	Menu Bar
1	Worksheet & macro (long)
2	Chart
3	Nothing open

Bar	Menu Bar
4	Info
5	Worksheet & macro (short)
6	Chart (short)
7	Cell, toolbar, and workbook shortcut
8	Object shortcut
9	Chart shortcut

See Also

ADD.COMMAND	Adds a command to a menu	Macro Function
ADD.MENU	Adds a menu to a menu	Macro Function

CHIDIST(*X,freedom*)

Function   **New to Version 4.0**

CHIDIST returns the one-tailed probability of the chi-squared distribution of X, with *freedom* degrees of freedom. The *freedom* argument must be between 1 and 10_{10} or CHIDIST will return a #NUM! error.

Example

=CHIDIST(7.908,5) returns 0.161379.

See Also

CHIINV	Similar function	Function
CHITEST	Similar function	Function

CHIINV

Function   **New to Version 4.0**

CHIINV returns the inverse of the one-tailed probability of the chi-squared distribution of X, with *freedom* degrees of freedom. The *freedom* argument must be between 1 and 10_{10} or CHIDIST will return a #NUM! error.

Example

=CHIINV(0.161379,5) returns 7.908001.

See Also

CHIDIST	Similar function	Function
CHITEST	Similar function	Function

CHITEST(*actual-data,expected-data*)

Function   New to Version 4.0

CHITEST determines the chi-squared distribution to test if a set of *expected-data* is proven by a set of *actual-data*.

See Also

CHIDIST	Similar function	Function
CHIINV	Similar function	Function

CHOOSE(*offset,list*)

Function

CHOOSE returns an entry from the *list* whose position in *list* is given by *offset*. The *offset* argument can be any value from 1 to the number of items in *list*. A 1 will retrieve the contents of the first item, and *n*, where *n* is the number of items in the list, will retrieve the contents of the last item. The list can be up to 29 items long.

Example

=CHOOSE(3,"Jan","Feb","Mar","Apr","May") returns the string value "Mar".

See Also

INDEX	Returns the index of an element in an array	Function

CLEAN(*range*)

Function

CLEAN returns the contents of *range* with all nonprintable characters removed.

Example

=CLEAN(A1) returns the contents of cell A1 with all nonprintable characters removed.

See Also

TRIM   Removes spaces from a string   Function

CLEAR(*[X]*)
CLEAR?(*[X]*)

Macro Function

Using the CLEAR function is the same as choosing the Clear option from the Edit menu or pressing the DEL key. You can use CLEAR to erase the contents, formats, notes, or everything from the cells in the current selection.

X	Information Erased
1	All
2	Formats
3	Formulas or contents
4	Notes

The default value for *X* is 3. The question mark version of this function opens the Clear dialog box, shown here, in which the defaults are established by the arguments. (The version without the question mark does not open the dialog box, but performs the function with the settings that you pass as arguments.)

See Also

TRIM   Removes spaces from a string   Function

CLEARING CELLS VS DELETING CELLS

Concept

Clearing cells removes the contents, formats, or notes contained in cells but doesn't delete the cell itself. Deleting cells removes the cells themselves from the worksheet.

In this case, all the cells to the right of or below the cells being deleted move to fill in the empty space. When deleting cells, it is always a good idea to save your worksheet beforehand. Because cells are moved during the process of deleting, formulas that are dependent on cells that have been deleted may no longer be valid.

When you want to clear the contents of a cell but leave the formatting and location of other cells intact, use Edit Clear or the DEL key, and when the Clear dialog box appears, choose the Formulas option (the default option).

When you want to delete cells rather than just their contents, choose the Edit Delete option. The delete dialog box will ask if you want to move cells up or move cells to the left, as shown here:

```
┌─────────────── Delete ───────────────┐
│ ┌─Delete───────────┐   ┌──────────┐  │
│ │ ◉ Shift Cells Left│   │   OK     │  │
│ │ ○ Shift Cells Up  │   └──────────┘  │
│ │                   │   ┌──────────┐  │
│ │ ○ Entire Row      │   │  Cancel  │  │
│ │ ○ Entire Column   │   └──────────┘  │
│ │                   │   ┌──────────┐  │
│ │                   │   │   Help   │  │
│ └───────────────────┘   └──────────┘  │
└───────────────────────────────────────┘
```

See Also

CLEAR	Erases contents, formats, or notes from cells	Macro Function
DATA.DELETE	Eliminates cells	
EDIT CLEAR	Erases contents, formats, or notes from cells	Menu Command
EDIT DELETE	Eliminates cells	Menu Command

CLOSE(*[X]*)

Macro Function

CLOSE performs the same action as the File Close menu option. The argument X is a logical value that tells CLOSE what to do with unsaved changes. If X is TRUE, the changes are saved. If X is FALSE, the changes are not saved. If X is omitted, a dialog box allows you to choose whether you want to save your changes.

See Also

FILE CLOSE	Equivalent command	Menu Command

CLOSE.ALL()

Macro Function

CLOSE.ALL performs the same action as the File Close All menu option. All open files are closed, and if there are changes in any of the open files, a dialog box asks if you want to save the changes in each file.

See Also

FILE CLOSE ALL   Equivalent command   Menu Command

CODE(*string*)

Function

CODE returns the ASCII (American Standard Code for Information Interchange) code for the first character in *string*. The *string* argument can be a literal text string, a formula or a function that evaluates to a string, or a reference to a cell containing a string. The ASCII codes and the standard U.S. Windows characters they produce are shown in Appendix B.

Example

=CODE("abc") returns the value 97, which corresponds to the lowercase letter *a*.

See Also

CHAR   Returns the character given the code   Function

COLOR.PALETTE(*filename*)

Macro Function

COLOR.PALETTE copies to the active document the color palette from *filename*, which must be an open document. Using this function is the same as choosing the Color Palette option from the Options menu and clicking on a filename in the Copy Colors From box in the Color Palette dialog box shown here:

See Also

OPTIONS COLOR PALETTE   Equivalent command   Menu Command

COLUMN(*range*)

Function

Returns the column numbers (*not* the number of columns) in a range. If you press ENTER after entry, you get the column number of the first column in the range; if you press CTRL-SHIFT-ENTER after entry, you get a horizontal array of all of the columns in the range.

Example

=COLUMN(A2:D3) returns 1 if you press ENTER. If you select a range four cells wide, type =**COLUMN(A2:D3)**, and press CTRL-SHIFT-ENTER, the array {1,2,3,4} is entered into the range.

See Also

COLUMNS   Returns the number of columns in a range   Function

COLUMN WIDTH

Concept

Changing the width of a column is one of the most common ways of formatting the data form. You can change the width of a column in a data form by using either the Format Column Width menu option or the mouse. You can change the width of many columns at once, even if they are not contiguous. For example, consider the worksheet shown in Figure C-17.

Example

Follow these steps to change column widths in Figure C-17.

1. Click on the column headings for columns C, E, and G while holding down the CTRL key. This will select the entire columns C, E, and G.

2. Place your mouse icon between the column headings for columns C and D. The icon changes to a plus sign with arrows, as shown in Figure C-18.

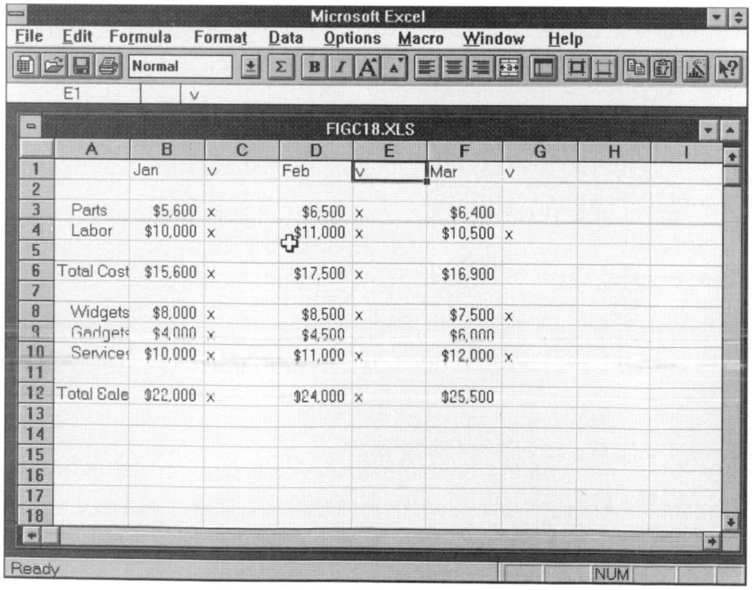

Figure C-17.   *The worksheet before changes to column width*

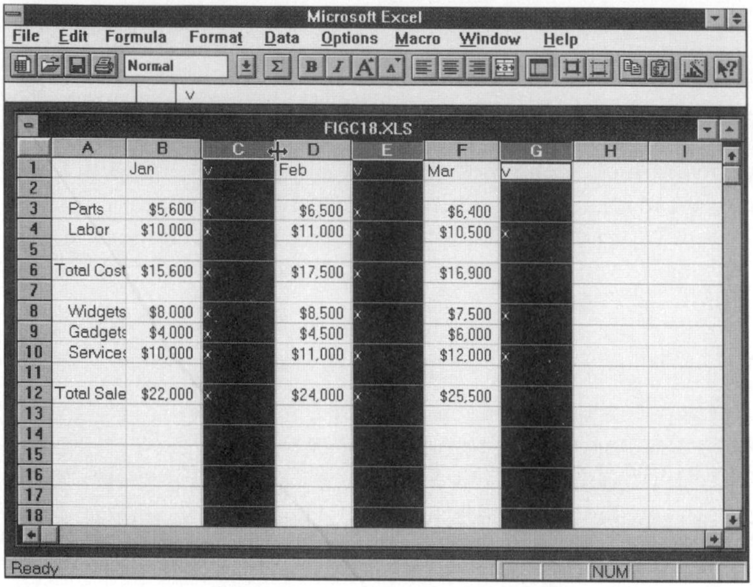

Figure C-18. *Selecting columns C, E, and G and placing the column width mouse icon between columns C and D*

3. Drag column C to the right or left until it's the desired width, and then release the mouse. Notice that the column width appears on the left side of the formula bar and changes as you move the mouse.

Your worksheet should look roughly like the worksheet shown in Figure C-19. You can size rows with the same technique.

See Also

COLUMN.WIDTH	Related function	Macro Function
FORMAT COLUMN WIDTH	Related command	Menu Command

COLUMN.WIDTH(*width,*[*cols*]*,*[*standard*]*,*[*type*]*,*[*standard-width*])
COLUMN.WIDTH?(*[width]*,*[cols]*,*[standard]*,*[type]*,*[standard-width]*)

Macro Function

The COLUMN.WIDTH function performs the same action as the Format Column Width menu option. The *width* argument is given as a number. The unit of *width* is the width of one character of the primary font for the current document. The primary font is the font that appears first in the Format Font dialog box.

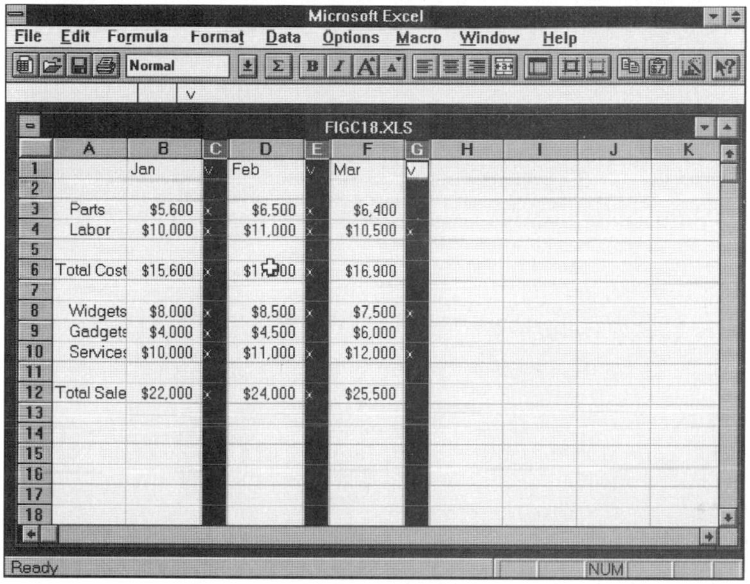

Figure C-19.   *The worksheet after columns C, E, and G have been sized*

Specify which columns you want to change with the *cols* argument. *Cols* is assumed to be the current selection if it is omitted. *Standard* is either TRUE or FALSE. If it is TRUE, the columns referred to by *cols* are set to the standard width. The *action* argument is one of the following codes that indicate some action to be taken:

Action	Description
1	Sets the column width to 0
2	Restores a hidden column
3	Sets a column to the best fit width (as wide as the widest cell in the selection)

Standard-width allows you to change the default standard width for columns to the number you specify.

The question mark version of this function opens the dialog box. The arguments set the defaults in the dialog box. The version without the question mark does not open the dialog box, but performs the function with the settings that you pass as arguments.

See Also

FORMAT COLUMN WIDTH   Equivalent command   Menu Command

| ROW.HEIGHT | Returns the height of a row | Macro Function |

COLUMNS(*range*)

Function

COLUMNS returns the number of columns in an array or a range.

Example

=COLUMNS(A1:B20) returns 2.

See Also

| COLUMN | Returns the column number of a selection | Function |

COLUMNS, DELETING

Concept

To delete a column, select any cell or cells in the column that you want to delete and choose the Edit Delete menu option. The Delete dialog box opens, as shown here. Choose the Entire Column option and click on OK.

You can also select the entire column by clicking on the column heading, and then choose the Edit Delete menu option. If you use this method, no dialog box opens, since Excel knows that you want to delete the entire column.

When you delete a column, the column to the right takes its place. If you delete column B, column C moves to the left and becomes a new column B.

See Also

| CLEARING CELLS VS DELETING CELLS | Explains clearing and deleting | Concept |
| EDIT DELETE | Related command | Menu Command |

COMBIN(*objects,group-size*)

Function

COMBIN determines how many groups of *group-size* can be formed from the number of *objects*.

Example

=COMBIN(4,2) returns 6. If you have a group of four objects, A, B, C, and D, you can have six possible combinations of two: AB, CD, AD, BC, AC, and BD.

COMBINATION(*altern*)
COMBINATION?(*altern*)

Macro Function

The COMBINATION function changes the current chart to a combination chart. This function is the same as choosing the Gallery Combination menu option. The *altern* argument must be a number corresponding to one of the alternatives in the Chart Gallery dialog box, shown in Figure C-20. If there are an equal number of

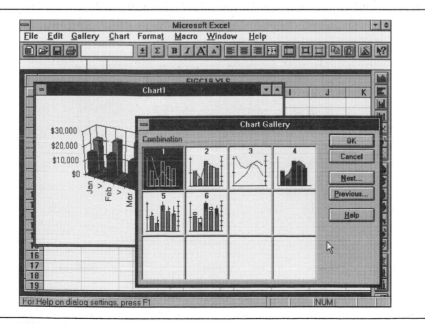

Figure C-20.   *The Chart Gallery dialog box*

series, half of them go on the primary chart and half on the overlay. If there are an odd number of series, the extra series goes on the primary chart.

The question mark version of this function opens the dialog box and the arguments set its defaults. The version without the question mark does not open the dialog box, but performs the function with the settings that you pass as arguments.

See Also

GALLERY COMBINATION   Equivalent command   Menu Command

COMMAND MACROS

Concept

A *command macro* is a program that runs in Excel and automates one or more tasks. Command macros can perform simple tasks like repetitive formatting or can be as sophisticated as a full accounting system.

The easiest way to create a command macro is to record it. The following simple example shows how to record a command macro that performs some formatting tasks. Before you start, open a new worksheet.

Example

1. Choose the Record option from the Macro menu. The Record Macro dialog box opens, as shown here:

2. Type **format** in the Name box, and **f** for the shortcut key, click on the Macro Sheet option to store the macro on a regular macro sheet, and then click on the OK button. Every keystroke that you enter from this point on will be recorded.

You can either choose to have the command macro stored on the global macro sheet, or a regular macro sheet. If you want to have access to the macro at all times and don't want to have to open a special macro sheet in order to run it, store it on the global macro sheet. Otherwise, store it on a regular macro sheet. You will need to save and name the macro sheet just like any other document. When you want to run the macro, you will have to open the macro sheet in which the macro is stored.

3. Select columns B, C, and D, then open the Format menu and select the Number option. Click on Currency, and choose $#,##0_),($#,##0) format.

4. Make column A about twice its current width.

5. Assign the 0.00% format to column E.

6. Choose Stop Recorder from the Macro menu.

You have now created a simple command macro that performs some formatting tasks for you. To play back the macro, press CTRL-F (the shortcut key). To look at the macro code, activate the macro sheet. You should have a macro that looks something like the one shown in Figure C-21. You will have to widen column A to see all of the code.

Another way to create a command macro is to type the code by hand, and then declare the code as a command macro using the Formula Define Name menu option. Type in the following code on your macro sheet to see how this works.

Example

1. Open a new macro sheet by choosing New from the File menu, then choosing Macro as the file type.

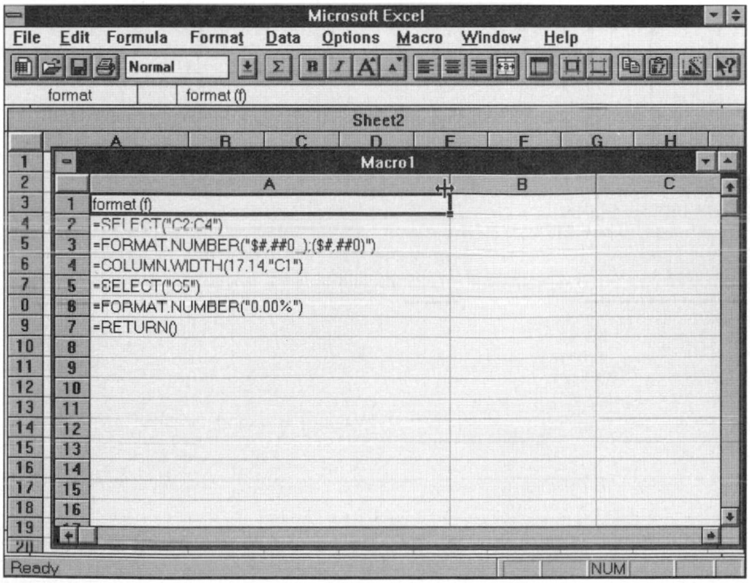

Figure C-21.   *The macro created by the recording example*

2. Type in the code that appears in Figure C-22.

3. Select cells A1:A3.

4. Choose the Define Name option from the Formula menu. You will see the Define Name dialog box, as shown here.

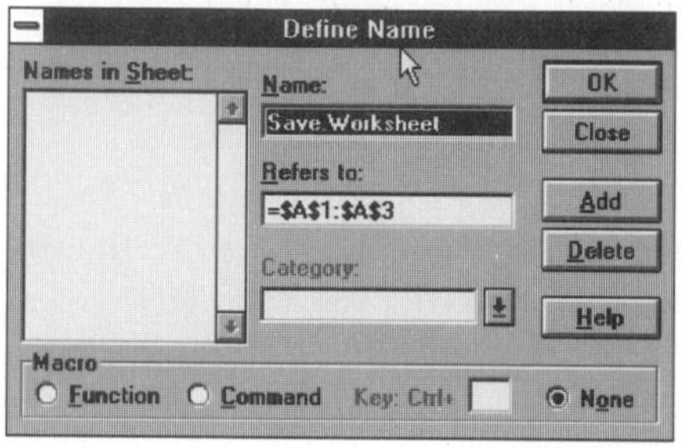

5. Click on the Command option button to select it, and type **S** (uppercase) as the name of the shortcut key.

You have now written a macro that will save the active document when you press CTRL-SHIFT-S. This simple example illustrates a technique that is useful when you want to create macros that are too complex to record.

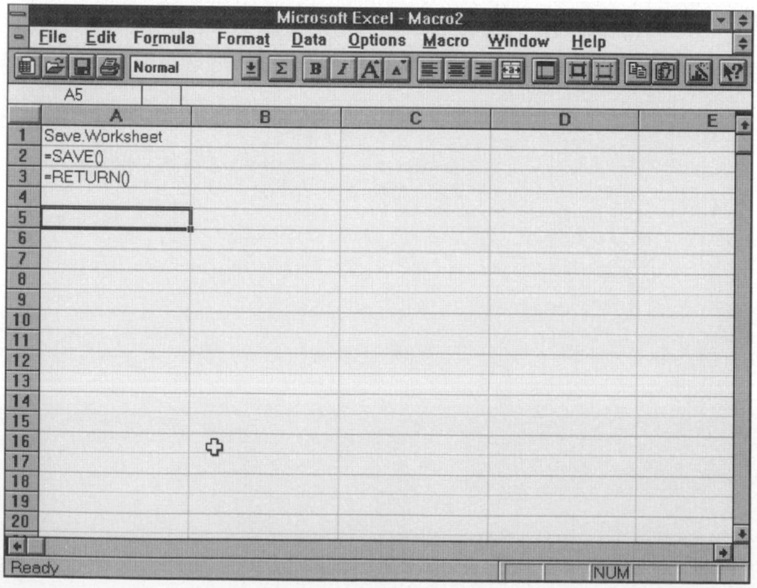

Figure C-22.   *Example of a command macro*

See Also

FORMULA DEFINE NAME	Defines a name and a shortcut key	Menu Command
MACRO RECORD	Records Excel macros	Menu Command

COMMANDS

Concept

Excel menus consist of sets of commands. Commands appear on a menu, and are referred to by their menu name followed by their command name. For example, Data Form is a menu command. To choose a command from a menu using the mouse, click on the menu name to open the menu, and then click on the command that you want.

You can also select a menu command using the keyboard. Hold down the ALT key and press the underlined letter in the desired menu name. The menu will open. If you didn't pull down the right menu, you can use the RIGHT ARROW and LEFT ARROW keys to cycle through the different menus. To choose a command from the menu, press the underlined letter in the command name.

See Also

MENU COMMANDS	Explains Excel menus	Concept

COMPLEX(*X, Y, [i-or-j]*)

Function   **New to Version 4.0**

COMPLEX returns a complex number in the form $X + Yi$ or $X + Yj$. If the *i-or-j* argument is not included, the default is *i*. The *i-or-j* argument must either be *i* or *j*, in lowercase and in quotation marks.

Examples

=COMPLEX(6,7) returns 6 + 7i.
=COMPLEX(2,3,"j") returns 2 + 3j.

See Also

IMAGINARY	Returns the coefficient of an imaginary number	Function

CONFIDENCE(*sig, st-dev, size*)

Function **New to Version 4.0**

CONFIDENCE returns the confidence level of a population mean given the significance level, standard deviation, and size of the sample. *Sig*, or significance level, must be a number greater than 0 and less than 1. *St-dev* can be determined by using the STDEV function.

Example

Suppose that a group of 100 athletes run a race with an average time of 120 minutes, and a standard deviation of 3.1. Assume a significance level of 5%.

=CONFIDENCE(0.05,3.1,100) returns 0.607588.

You can be 95% confident (100 – *sig*) that the mean is between 120 + 0.607588 and 120 – 0.607588.

See Also

STDEV	Returns the standard deviation	Function

CONSOLIDATE(*source, [function], [top-row], [left-col], [links]*)

Macro Function **New to Version 4.0**

The CONSOLIDATE function performs the same action as the Consolidate command in the Data menu. It consolidates data from multiple ranges by performing the indicated *function*.

Source is an array of external references for the ranges that you want to consolidate. Each reference should be given as a string in quotation marks, and should include the entire path.

The following table gives the possible *function* codes. If no *function* argument is given, the default is 9.

Function	Description
1	AVERAGE
2	COUNT
3	COUNTA
4	MAX
5	MIN

Function	Description
6	PRODUCT
7	STDEV
8	STDEVP
9	SUM
10	VAR
11	VARP

The *top-row* and *left-col* are logical arguments that correspond to the Top Row and Left Column check box in the Consolidate dialog box that is shown here. If you want to consolidate the data by category, you must indicate whether the category labels are located in the top row, the left column, or both. The default for both these arguments is FALSE.

The *links* argument corresponds to the Create Links To Source Data check box in the dialog box. If you want to create links, *links* should be TRUE. Otherwise, it should be FALSE, which is the default.

Example

The following macro function consolidates named range DISTRICT1 on worksheet JANUARY.XLS and a named range DISTRICT2 on worksheet FEBRUARY.XLS by summing them:

    =CONSOLIDATE({"C:\MYWORK\JANUARY.XLS!DISTRICT1","C:\MYWORK\
    FEBRUARY.XLS!DISTRICT2",9})

See Also

CHANGE.LINK	Changes a link to a different worksheet	Macro Function
DATA CONSOLIDATE	Equivalent command	Menu Command

LINKS	Returns a list of linked document names	Macro Function
OPEN.LINKS	Opens linked documents	Macro Function
UPDATE.LINK	Updates a link	Macro Function

CONSTRAIN.NUMERIC(*[on]*)

Macro Function   **New to Version 4.0**

CONSTRAIN.NUMERIC is only available when you are using Microsoft Windows for Pen Computing. If *on* is TRUE, handwriting recognition is constrained to these numbers and symbols:

0 1 2 3 4 5 6 7 8 9
@ # $ % ( ) - + = { } : < > , . ? |

If the *on* argument is FALSE, all characters are recognized. If *on* is omitted, CONSTRAIN.NUMERIC toggles TRUE to FALSE or FALSE to TRUE.

CONTROL MENU

Concept

The Control menu allows you to move, size, or close the window, or switch to or run utilities such as the Control Panel or other applications. (The Control menu is a Windows feature, universal to all Windows applications.) There is a Control menu for each document window and a Control menu for the application window. To open the Control menu, press ALT-SPACEBAR or click on the Control-menu box in the upper-left corner of the window. The Control menu looks like this:

CONVERT(*X,from,to*)

Function   **New to Version 4.0**

CONVERT converts *X* from one unit of measure to another unit of the same type. The following table lists all the units available by type. *From* and *to* should be unit codes of the same type.

Unit	Code	Type
Angstrom	ang	Distance
Foot	ft	Distance
Inch	in	Distance
Meter	m	Distance
Nautical mile	Nmi	Distance
Statute mile	mi	Distance
Yard	yd	Distance
Ampere	A	Electricity
Colomb	C	Electricity
Volt	V	Electricity
BTU	btu	Energy
Calorie	cal	Energy
Electron volt	ev	Energy
Erg	e	Energy
Foot-pound	flb	Energy
Horsepwr-hr	hh	Energy
Joule	J	Energy
Thermo calorie	c	Energy
Watt-hour	wh	Energy
Dyne	dy	Force
Newton	N	Force
Pound force	lbf	Force
Cup	cup	Liquid measure
Fluid ounce	oz	Liquid measure
Gallon	gal	Liquid measure
Liter	lt	Liquid measure
Pint	pt	Liquid measure

Unit	Code	Type
Quart	qt	Liquid measure
Teaspoon	tsp	Liquid measure
Tablespoon	tbs	Liquid measure
Gauss	ga	Magnetism
Tesla	T	Magnetism
atto	a	Metric prefix—1E–18
centi	c	Metric prefix—1E–2
deci	d	Metric prefix—1E–1
deka	e	Metric prefix—1E+1
exa	E	Metric prefix—1E+18
femto	f	Metric prefix—1E–15
giga	G	Metric prefix—1E+9
kilo	k	Metric prefix—1E+3
mega	M	Metric prefix—1E+6
micro	u	Metric prefix—1E–6
milli	m	Metric prefix—1E–3
nano	n	Metric prefix—1E–9
peta	P	Metric prefix—1E+15
pico	p	Metric prefix—1E–12
tera	T	Metric prefix—1E+12
Horsepower	h	Power
Watt	w	Power
Pascal	p	Pressure
Atmosphere	at	Pressure
Celsius	cel	Temperature
Fahrenheit	fah	Temperature
Kelvin	kel	Temperature
Day	day	Time
Hour	hr	Time
Minute	mn	Time
Second	sec	Time
Year	yr	Time
Gram	g	Weight/Mass
Ounce mass	ozm	Weight/Mass

Unit	Code	Type
Pound	lbm	Weight/Mass
Slug	sg	Weight/Mass
U (atomic)	u	Weight/Mass

Example

=CONVERT(60,"mn","hr") returns 1.

COPY([*from*],[*to*])

Macro Function

COPY copies the range specified with *from* to the location specified by *to*. *From* and *to* should both be cell reference ranges. If these arguments are not included, COPY performs the same action as the Edit Copy menu command: it captures the current selection so it can be pasted to another location. if *from* and *to* are included, *to* must be one of three references: the upper-left cell of the range that you want to copy to, a range the same size as *from*, or a range that is a multiple of *from*. If *to* is a range that is a multiple of *from*, multiple copies of *from* are pasted to the *to* range.

Example

=COPY(Sheet1!$A$1:$B$2,Sheet1!$C$1:$D$8) copies four copies of the range A1:B2 to C1:D8 on Sheet1.

See Also

EDIT COPY	Related command	Menu Command
EDIT PASTE	Related command	Menu Command

COPY.PICTURE(*appearance,size,type*)
COPY.PICTURE?(*appearance,size,type*)

Macro Function

COPY.PICTURE copies the currently selected chart or worksheet range as a graphic image to the Windows Clipboard. This is the same as choosing the Edit Copy Picture menu command. The Edit Copy Picture command only appears on the Edit menu if you hold down the SHIFT key when you activate the menu. The *appearance* and *size* arguments must be either 1 or 2. If the argument is 1, the picture is copied as it appears on the screen. If the argument is 2, the picture is copied as it appears when it is printed. *Type* indicates the format type of the picture that you are copying. If *type* is 1, the format is the Excel Picture format. If *type* is 2, the format is the Windows Bitmap format.

The question mark version of this function opens the dialog box. The arguments set the defaults in the dialog box. The version without the question mark does not open the dialog box, but performs the function with the settings that you pass as arguments.

See Also

EDIT COPY PICTURE   Equivalent command   Menu Command

COPY.TOOL(*bar,position*)

Macro Function   **New to Version 4.0**

COPY.TOOL copies a tool face to the Clipboard. A tool face is a graphical image that, when clicked on, activates the corresponding tool. COPY.TOOL performs the same action as the Edit Copy Tool Face command. *Bar* is the bar number or name that contains the tool face that you want to copy, as shown here:

Bar	Toolbar
1	Standard
2	Formatting
3	Utility
4	Chart
5	Drawing
6	Excel 3.0
7	Macro
8	Macro stop recording
9	Macro paused

The *position* argument represents the tool's position in the toolbar, beginning with 1 at the left or at the top, depending on whether the toolbar is horizontal or vertical.

Example

COPY.TOOL(1,2) copies the Open File tool face to the Clipboard.

See Also

ADD.TOOL	Adds a tool to a toolbar	Macro Function
TOOLBARS, CUSTOM	Explains custom toolbars	Concept

COPYING

Concept

Copying using the menu commands is a simple task. Select the range that you want to copy and choose the Edit Copy command. A marquee appears around the range to be copied. Select the upper-left cell of the range that you want to copy to and press ENTER. Make sure that you have enough room below and to the right of the cell you choose as the upper-left cell of the destination range. When the cells are copied to the new location, anything that was there previously will be overwritten.

You can also copy cells using the Fill Down and Fill Right commands from the Edit menu. Select the cell you want to copy from, and as many adjacent cells below or to the right of the source cell that you want to copy to. Choose Edit Fill Down, or Edit Fill Right, and the contents of the source cell is copied to all of the selected destination cells. Excel 4 has Fill Down and Fill Right tools, shown below, that you can place on a convenient toolbar if you use these commands often.

Still another method of copying involves using the mouse. This method is only available in version 4, and then only if Options Workspace Cell Drag and Drop is turned on. Select the cells you want to copy, and then place the mouse on the border around the cells. The mouse pointer will change to an arrow. Hold down the CTRL key and drag the box to the location where you want to copy the cells; then release the mouse button. You will see an outline that indicates the new location for the cells you are copying. Figure C-23 shows a Drag and Drop maneuver in progress.

See Also

COPY	Copies a selection	Macro Function
EDIT COPY	Defines selection to be copied	Menu Command
EDIT PASTE	Pastes defined selection	Menu Command

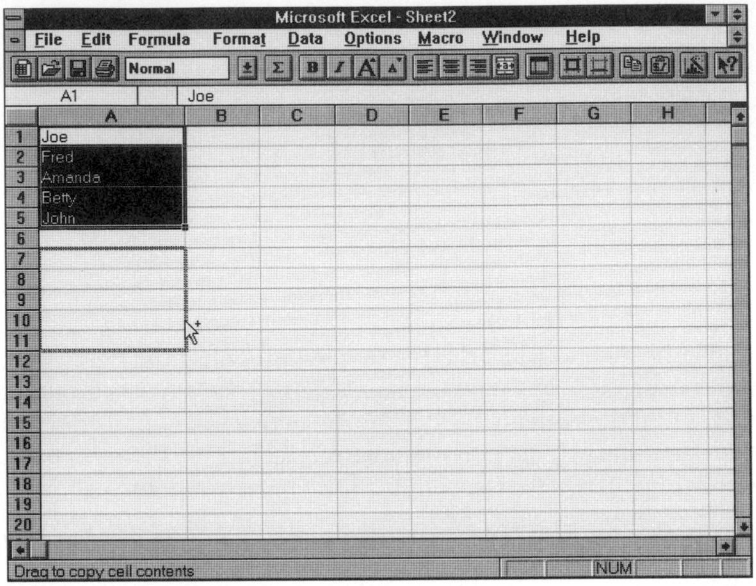

Figure C-23.   *Copying cells by using the mouse to drag and drop*

CORREL(*array-1, array-2*)

Function   **New to Version 4.0**

CORREL returns the correlation coefficient of *array-1* and *array-2*. The correlation coefficient specifies the relationship between two arrays. *Array-1* and *array-2* must be the same size.

Example

=CORREL({1,2,3},{4,5,6}) returns 1.

See Also

COVAR	Returns the covariance	Function
FISHER	Returns the Fisher transformation	Function
MCORREL	Returns a matrix representing the correlation coefficient	Function

COS(*X*)

Function

COS returns the cosine of the angle *X* measured in radians. (Degrees times PI()/180 equals radians.)

Example

=COS(H15) returns the cosine of the angle, measured in radians, contained in H15.

See Also

SIN	Returns the sine of an angle	Function
TAN	Returns the tangent of an angle	Function

COSH(*X*)

Function

COSH returns the hyperbolic cosine in radians of the value *X*.

Example

=COSH(3) returns 10.067662.

See Also

ACOSII	Returns the inverse hyperbolic cosine	Function
COS	Returns the cosine of an angle	Function

COUNT(*range1,range2,...*)

Function

COUNT returns the number of cells containing numbers in the ranges listed. Cells containing text, logical values, empty cells, or error values are ignored.

Example

=COUNT(H15:H27) counts the number of cells containing numbers in the range H15 to H27.

See Also

| COUNTA | Counts nonblank values | Function |
| DCOUNT | Counts cells containing numbers using criteria | Function |

COUNTA(*range1,range2,...*)

Function

COUNTA returns the number of nonblank cells in the ranges listed. Cells containing text, values (including 0), or errors are considered nonblank.

See Also

| COUNT | Returns number of numbers | Function |
| DCOUNTA | Returns number of nonblank cells in a database | Function |

Example

=COUNTA(H15:H27) counts the number of nonblank cells in the range H15 to H27.

COUPDAYBS(*set-date,mat-date,payments,[basis-code]*)

Function   New to Version 4.0

COUPDAYBS returns the number of days between the start of the coupon period and *set-date.* You have to load the Analysis ToolPak add-in if this function is not available. *Set-date* is the settlement date of the security, given as a date serial number. *Mat-date* is the maturity date of the security, given as a date serial number. *Payments* is the number of payments per year, as shown in this table:

Payments	Frequency
1	Annual
2	Semi-annual
4	Quarterly

Basis-code is a code that indicates the day count basis for months and years. If *basis-code* is omitted, the default value is 0.

Basis-Code	Day Count
0	30/360
1	Actual/Actual
2	Actual/360
3	Actual/365

Example

=COUPDAYBS(date(92,1,1),date(93,6,1),2,2) returns 31.

See Also

COUPDAYS	Returns the number of days in the period containing the settlement date	Function
COUPDAYSNC	Returns the number of days between settlement date and next coupon	Function
COUPNCD	Returns the date of next coupon after settlement date	Function
COUPNUM	Returns the number of coupons from settlement to maturity	Function
COUPPCD	Returns the date of last coupon before settlement date	Function
DATE	Returns the serial number of a date	Function

COUPDAYS(*set-date, mat-date, payments, [basis-code]*)

Function   **New to Version 4.0**

COUPDAYS returns the number of days until the next settlement date in the current coupon period. You have to load the Analysis ToolPak add-in if this function is not available. *Set-date* is the settlement date of the security, given as a date serial number. *Mat-date* is the maturity date of the security, given as a date serial number. *Payments* is the number of payments per year, as shown in this table:

Payments	Frequency
1	Annual
2	Semi-annual
4	Quarterly

Basis-code is a code that indicates the day count basis of months and years. If *basis-code* is omitted, the default value is 0.

Basis-Code	Day Count
0	30/360
1	Actual/Actual
2	Actual/360
3	Actual/365

Example

=COUPDAYS(date(92,1,1),date(93,6,1),2,2) returns 183.

See Also

COUPDAYBS	Returns the number of days between beginning and settlement dates	Function
COUPDAYSNC	Returns the number of days between settlement date and next coupon	Function
COUPNCD	Returns the date of next coupon after settlement date	Function
COUPNUM	Returns the number of coupons from settlement to maturity	Function
COUPPCD	Returns the date of last coupon before settlement date	Function
DATE	Returns the serial number of a date	Function

COUPDAYSNC(*set-date, mat-date, payments, [basis-code]*)

Function   **New to Version 4.0**

COUPDAYSNC returns the days between the settlement date and the next coupon. You have to load the Analysis ToolPak add-in if this function is not available. *Set-date* is the settlement date of the security, given as a date serial number. *Mat-date* is the maturity date of the security, given as a date serial number. *Payments* is the number of payments per year, as shown in this table:

Payments	Frequency
1	Annual
2	Semi-annual
4	Quarterly

Basis-code is a code that indicates the day count basis for months and years. If *basis-code* is omitted, the default value is 0.

Basis-Code	Day Count
0	30/360
1	Actual/Actual
2	Actual/360
3	Actual/365

Example

=COUPDAYSNC(date(92,1,1),date(93,6,1),2,2) returns 152.

See Also

COUPDAYBS	Returns the number of days between beginning and settlement dates	Function
COUPDAYS	Returns the number of days in the period containing the settlement date	Function
COUPNCD	Returns the date of next coupon after settlement date	Function
COUPNUM	Returns the number of coupons from settlement to maturity	Function
COUPPCD	Returns the date of last coupon before settlement date	Function
DATE	Returns the serial number of a date	Function

COUPNCD(*set-date, mat-date, payments, [basis-code]*)

Function   **New to Version 4.0**

COUPNCD returns the date of the next coupon after *set-date*. You have to load the Analysis ToolPak add-in if this function is not available. *Set-date* is the settlement date of the security, given as a date serial number. *Mat-date* is the maturity date of the security, given as a date serial number. *Payments* is the number of payments per year, as shown in this table:

Payments	Frequency
1	Annual
2	Semi-annual
4	Quarterly

Basis-code is a code that indicates the day count basis for months and years. If *basis-code* is omitted, the default value is 0.

Basis-Code	Day Count
0	30/360
1	Actual/Actual
2	Actual/360
3	Actual/365

Example

=COUPNCD(date(92,1,1),date(93,6,1),2,2) returns 6/1/92.

See Also

COUPDAYBS	Returns the number of days between beginning and settlement dates	Function
COUPDAYS	Returns the number of days in the period containing the settlement date	Function
COUPDAYSNC	Returns the number of days between settlement date and next coupon	Function
COUPNCD	Returns the date of next coupon after settlement date	Function
COUPNUM	Returns the number of coupons from settlement to maturity	Function
COUPPCD	Returns the date of last coupon before settlement date	Function
DATE	Returns the serial number of a date	Function

COUPNUM(*set-date, mat-date, payments, [basis-code]*)

Function   **New to Version 4.0**

COUPNUM returns the number of coupons between *set-date* and *mat-date*. You have to load the Analysis ToolPak add-in if this function is not available. *Set-date* is the settlement date of the security, given as a date serial number. *Mat-date* is the maturity date of the security, given as a date serial number. *Payments* is the number of payments per year, as shown in this table:

Payments	Frequency
1	Annual
2	Semi-annual
4	Quarterly

Basis-code is a code that indicates the day count basis for months and years. If *basis-code* is omitted, the default value is 0.

Basis-Code	Day Count
0	30/360
1	Actual/Actual
2	Actual/360
3	Actual/365

Example

=COUPNUM(date(92,1,1),date(93,6,1),2,2) returns 3.

See Also

COUPDAYBS	Returns the number of days between beginning and settlement dates	Function
COUPDAYS	Returns the number of days in the period containing the settlement date	Function
COUPDAYSNC	Returns the number of days between settlement date and next coupon	Function
COUPNCD	Returns the date of next coupon after settlement date	Function
COUPPCD	Returns the date of last coupon before settlement date	Function
DATE	Returns the serial number of a date	Function

COUPPCD(*set-date, mat-date, payments, [basis-code]*)

Function

COUPPC returns the date of the previous coupon before *set-date*. You have to load the Analysis ToolPak add-in if this function is not available. *Set date* is the settlement date of the security, given as a date serial number. *Mat-date* is the maturity date of the security, given as a date serial number. *Payments* is the number of payments per year:

Payments	Frequency
1	Annual
2	Semi-annual
4	Quarterly

Basis-code is a code that indicates the day count basis for months and years. If *basis-code* is omitted, the default value is 0.

Basis-Code	Day Count
0	30/360
1	Actual/Actual
2	Actual/360
3	Actual/365

Example

=COUPPCD(date(92,1,1),date(93,6,1),2,2) returns 12/1/91.

See Also

COUPDAYBS	Returns the number of days between beginning and settlement dates	Function
COUPDAYS	Returns the number of days in the period containing the settlement date	Function
COUPDAYSNC	Returns the number of days between settlement date and next coupon	Function
COUPNCD	Returns the date of next coupon after settlement date	Function
COUPNUM	Returns the number of coupons from settlement to maturity	Function
DATE	Returns the serial number of a date	Function

COVAR(*array-1, array-2*)

Function   **New to Version 4.0**

COVAR returns the covariance between two data sets, *array-1* and *array-2*. *Array-1* and *array-2* must contain the same number of values.

Example

=COVAR({1,2,3,4},{3,4,5,6}) returns 1.25.

See Also

CORREL	Returns the correlation coefficient	Function
FISHER	Returns the Fisher transformation	Function
MCORREL	Returns a matrix representing the correlation coefficient	Function

---

CREATE.DIRECTORY(*directory*)

Macro Function   **New to Version 4.0**

CREATE.DIRECTORY is an add-in macro. If it isn't available, you have to open FILEFNS.XLA from the Excel Library directory. *Directory* can be either a directory name, which will create a subdirectory in the current directory, or a full path name.

Example

=CREATE.DIRECTORY("data") creates a subdirectory called "data" in the current directory.

See Also

| ADD-INS | Explains add-in macros | Concept |
| DELETE.DIRECTORY | Deletes a directory | Macro Function |

CREATE.NAMES(*top-row, left-col, bottom-row, right-col*)
CREATE.NAMES?(*[top-row], [left-col], [bottom-row], [right-col]*)

Macro Function

CREATE.NAMES performs the same action as the Formula Create Names menu command. This function allows you to define many names at once. You must select a range of cells with names included on one edge of the range. The arguments are either TRUE or FALSE and indicate on which edge of the range the names appear. *Top-row* should be TRUE if the names are in the top row. Each cell in the top row names the cell below it. If *left-col* is TRUE, the names are in the left column of the range, and each cell in the left column names the cell to its right. If *bottom-row* is TRUE, the names are in the bottom row, and each cell in the bottom row names the cell above it. If *right-col* is TRUE, the names are in the right column, and each cell in the right column names the cell to its left.

The question mark version of this function opens the dialog box. The arguments set the defaults in the dialog box. The version without the question mark does not open the dialog box, but performs the function with the settings that you pass as arguments.

See Also

FORMULA CREATE   Creates ranges of names   Menu Command
  NAMES

CREATE.OBJECT(*object, upper-l, horz-1, vert-1, lower-r, horz-2, vert-2, text, fill*)
CREATE.OBJECT(*object, upper-l, horz-1, vert-1, lower-r, horz-2, vert-2, array, fill*)
CREATE.OBJECT(*object, upper-l, horz-1, vert-1, lower-r, horz-2, vert-2, series, fill, gallery, type*)

Macro Function

The first version of the CREATE.OBJECT function creates arcs, buttons, lines, ovals, pictures, rectangles, and text boxes. The second version creates polygons, and the third version creates embedded charts.

Object is the type of object you want to create. The possible values for the *object* argument are listed here:

Object	Description
1	Line
2	Rectangle
3	Oval
4	Arc
5	Embedded chart
6	Text box
7	Button
8	Picture created with camera
9	Closed polygon
10	Open polygon

Upper-l is the upper-left cell closest to the object. *Horz-1* is the horizontal distance in points from the upper-left cell (*upper-l*) to the upper-left corner of the object. *Vert-1* is the vertical distance in points from the upper-left cell (*upper-l*) to the upper-left corner of the object. *Lower-r* is the lower-right cell closest to the object. *Horz-2* is the horizontal distance in points from the lower-right cell (*lower-r*) to the lower-right corner of the object. *Vert-2* is the vertical distance in points from the lower-right cell (*lower-r*) and the lower-right corner of the object. *Text* is the text that appears in a text box or a button object. *Fill* is either TRUE or FALSE, indicating whether an object is filled. The *array* argument is used when you are defining a polygon. It is a 2 by *n* array specifying the vertices of the polygon. *Series* is used when you are defining a chart, and indicates how the data appears, as shown here:

Series	Description
0	Displays a dialog box
1	First row or column is the first series (default)
2	First row or column is the categories
3	First row or column contains the x values

Gallery indicates the type of chart that you want to create.

Gallery	Chart
1	Area
2	Bar
3	Column
4	Line
5	Pie
6	Radar
7	XY scatter
8	Combination
9	3-D area
10	3-D bar
11	3-D column
12	3-D line
13	3-D pie
14	3-D surface

Type is a number that corresponds to the specific type of chart that you want to create. Each general type has several different options. If you open the Gallery dialog box, you can see these different options. The *type* argument is a number corresponding to the number on the dialog box.

See Also

FORMAT.MOVE	Moves an object	Macro Function
FORMAT.SIZE	Sizes an object	Macro Function
GET.OBJECT	Returns information about an object	Macro Function
TEXT.BOX	Puts characters in a text box	Macro Function

CRITBINOM(*trials,probability,criteria*)

Function

CRITBINOM returns the smallest integer for which the cumulative binomial distribution is greater than or equal to *criteria*. *Trials* is the number of Bernoulli trials and *probability* is the probability of success in each.

Example

=CRITBINOM(100,0.5,0.8) returns 54.

See Also

BINOMDIST	Returns the binomial distribution	Function
NEGBINOMDIST	Returns the negative binomial distribution	Function

CROSSTAB(*label,headings*)
CROSSTAB(*label, "columns:",columns*)
CROSSTAB(*label, "rows:",rows*)
CROSSTAB(*label, "summary:",values,outline,names,summaries, drilldown*)

Function   New to Version 4.0

CROSSTAB defines a *crosstab table*—one in which the rows are summed on the right and the columns are summed on the bottom. You may have to load the Crosstab add-in if this function is not available. You should use the Crosstab Wizard to create a crosstab and not this function. Once the Crosstab Wizard has built a crosstab table, you can edit the formulas as needed.

The first version of CROSSTAB is used to produce the row and column headings of a crosstab table. *Label* is the label for the cell containing the *headings* formula. *Headings* is some expression that is used to define the row and column headings in a crosstab table. The remaining versions of CROSSTAB define the rows, columns, and summaries in a crosstab table. To use these versions of CROSSTAB, you must enter the second argument in quotation marks.

Rows is an array that specifies the fields that appear in the rows of the crosstab table. *Columns* is an array that specifies the fields that appear in the columns of the crosstab table. *Values* is an array that specifies the value fields. The *rows, columns,* and *values* arrays have defined layouts that are described under CROSSTAB.CREATE. *Outline* is TRUE if you want an outline around your crosstab table. *Names* is TRUE if you want names for the values. *Summaries* specifies where to place multiple summaries, as follows.

Summaries	Placement
1	Inner columns
2	Outer columns
3	Inner rows
4	Outer rows

Drilldown should be TRUE if you want drilldown formulas to specify the records that are summarized in a cell.

See Also

CROSSTAB.CREATE   Creates a crosstab table   Macro Function

CROSSTAB.CREATE(*rows, columns, values, outline, names, summaries, drilldown, new*)
CROSSTAB.CREATE?()

Macro Function   **New to Version 4.0**

CROSSTAB.CREATE creates a crosstab table—one in which the rows are summed on the right and the columns are summed on the bottom. You may have to load the Crosstab add-in if this function is not available. You should create this macro function by using the macro recorder and the Crosstab Wizard.

Rows is an array that specifies the fields that appear in the rows of the crosstab table and *columns* is an array that specifies the fields that appear in the columns of the crosstab table. Both of these arrays have a structure that is best shown by this example, where the range C7:G7 is a valid *rows* or *columns* array:

	B	C	D	E	F	G
4						
5		Name	Type	Start	End	Function
6						
7		Office	0	Auto	Auto	NNNNNNN
8						
9						
10						

In the *rows* and *columns* arrays, *Name* is the name to be used as the row or column heading. It can be a literal name or a reference to a cell containing the name. *Type* is the type of grouping to be applied. The types values and their types of grouping are listed here:

Type	Grouping
0	Text or no grouping
1	By days
2	By week
3	By month
4	By 30-day period
5	By quarters
6	By years
Size	Other numeric values

Start and *End* are the starting and ending values to be used. These may be numeric values, text strings, or date serial numbers or literal dates for numeric, text, or date fields, respectively. "Auto" specifies all values in a field.

Function is a seven-character string where each character represents a type of function. You can turn on a function by placing a Y in its position, and turn it off with an N. The functions and their position are as follows.

Position	Function
1	SUM
2	COUNT
3	AVERAGE
4	MINIMUM
5	MAXIMUM
6	STANDARD DEVIATION
7	VARIANCE

Values is an array that specifies the values that appear in the row and column intersections of the crosstab table. This array has a structure that is best shown by this example, where the range C7:G7 is a valid *values* array:

	B	C	D	E	F	G
			Sheet1			
4						
5		Label	Expression	Display	All	
6						
7		Amount	SUM(Amount)	YNNNN	FALSE	
8						
9						
10						

In the *values* array, *Label* is the label to be used as the heading for the summary. It can be either a literal name or a reference to a cell containing the name. *Expression* is the formula to be used for the summary expressed as a text string. *Display* is a five-character string where each character represents a type of display. You turn on a display type by placing a Y in its position and turn it off with an N. The display types and their positions are as follows.

Position	Display
1	Values
2	Row Percent
3	Column Percent
4	Total Percent
5	Index

All specifies whether to use all values, even those outside the Start and End range, when calculating crosstab summaries or only those values that are in the crosstab table. If *All* is TRUE, all values are used. If *All* is FALSE, only crosstab values are used.

Outline is TRUE if you want an outline around your crosstab table. *Names* is TRUE if you want names for the values. *Summaries* specifies where to place multiple summaries, as follows.

Summaries	Placement
1	Inner columns
2	Outer columns
3	Inner rows
4	Outer rows

Drilldown should be TRUE if you want drilldown formulas to specify the records that are summarized in a cell. *New* should be TRUE if you want your crosstab table on a new sheet, or FALSE if you want it on the active sheet.

The question mark version of this function opens the dialog box. The version without the question mark does not open the dialog box, but performs the function with the settings that you pass as arguments.

Example

If the database in Figure C-24 is used to produce a crosstab and the process is recorded with the macro recorder, the resulting CROSSTAB.CREATE macro function looks like this:

```
=CROSSTAB.CREATE({"Office",0,"Auto","Auto","NNNNNNN"},
{"Week",0,"Auto","Auto","NNNNNNN"},{"Amount","SUM(Amount)",
"YNNNN",FALSE},TRUE,TRUE,1,TRUE,TRUE)
```

See Also

DATA CROSSTAB	Equivalent command	Menu Command

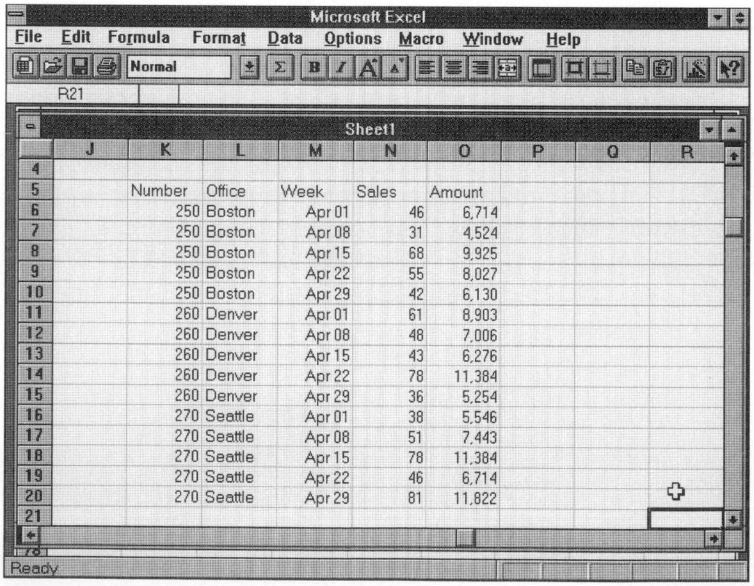

Number	Office	Week	Sales	Amount
250	Boston	Apr 01	46	6,714
250	Boston	Apr 08	31	4,524
250	Boston	Apr 15	68	9,925
250	Boston	Apr 22	55	8,027
250	Boston	Apr 29	42	6,130
260	Denver	Apr 01	61	8,903
260	Denver	Apr 08	48	7,006
260	Denver	Apr 15	43	6,276
260	Denver	Apr 22	78	11,384
260	Denver	Apr 29	36	5,254
270	Seattle	Apr 01	38	5,546
270	Seattle	Apr 08	51	7,443
270	Seattle	Apr 15	78	11,384
270	Seattle	Apr 22	46	6,714
270	Seattle	Apr 29	81	11,822

Figure C-24. Database for a crosstab table

CROSSTAB.DRILLDOWN

Macro Function   **New to Version 4.0**

CROSSTAB.DRILLDOWN retrieves the records that are summarized in the active cell. This macro function performs the same action as double-clicking on a summary cell in a crosstab table. (Remember, a crosstable table is one in which the rows are summed on the right and the columns are summed on the bottom. You may have to load the Crosstab add-in if this function is not available.)

See Also

| ADD-INS | Explains add-in macros | Concept |
| CROSSTAB.CREATE | Creates a crosstab table | Macro Function |

CROSSTAB.RECALC(*[recalc]*)

Macro Function   **New to Version 4.0**

CROSSTAB.RECALC performs the same action as the Data Recalculate Existing Crosstab menu command. You may have to load the Crosstab add-in if this function is not available. *Recalc* is either TRUE or FALSE. If it is TRUE, the crosstab table is recreated. If it is FALSE, the table is recalculated as is.

See Also

| ADD-INS | Explains add-in macros | Concept |
| CROSSTAB.CREATE | Creates a crosstab table | Macro Function |

CUMIPMT(*rate, periods, pv, start, end, type*)

Function   **New to Version 4.0**

CUMIPMT returns the cumulative interest paid between *start* and *end*. The result is normally negative, representing a cash outflow. *Rate* is the interest rate. *Periods* is the total number of periods during the life of the loan. *Pv* is the present value. *Start* is the first period and *end* is the last period, inclusive, for which you want to know the interest paid. *Type* is either 0 if the payments are made at the end of the period or 1 if the payments are made at the beginning of the period. The time basis for the rate and the number of periods needs to be the same. If the periods are months, the rate needs to be per month.

Example

If you have a 10-year (120 month) loan with an interest rate of 12%, or .01 per month, and a present value of $10,000, then =CUMIPMT(.01,120,10000,1,12,0) returns –1170.33. The cumulative interest paid in the first year (between periods 1 and 12 inclusive) is $1,170.33.

See Also

CUMPRINC   Returns the cumulative principal   Function

CUMPRINC(*rate, periods, pv, start, end, type*)

Function   **New to Version 4.0**

CUMPRINC returns the cumulative principal paid between *start* and *end*. The result is normally negative, representing a cash outflow. *Rate* is the interest rate. *Periods* is the total number of periods during the life of the loan. *Pv* is the present value. *Start* is the first period and *end* is the last period, inclusive, for which you want to know the principal paid. *Type* is either 0 if payments are made at the end of the period or 1 if payments are made at the beginning of the period. The time basis for the rate and the number of periods needs to be the same. If the periods are months, the rate needs to be per month.

Example

If you have a 10-year (120 month) loan with an interest rate of 12%, or .01 per month, and a present value of $10,000, then =CUMPRINC(.01,120,10000,1,12,0) returns –551.32. The cumulative principal paid in the first year (between periods 1 and 12 inclusive) is $551.32.

See Also

CUMIPMT   Returns the cumulative interest   Function

CUSTOM.REPEAT(*[macro], [repeat], [record]*)

Macro Function

CUSTOM.REPEAT enables you to repeat custom commands using the Repeat tool or the Edit Repeat command. *Macro* is the name or reference of the macro you want to run. *Repeat* is the text that you want to appear on the Edit menu. *Record* is the name of the macro that you wish to record.

See Also

CUSTOM.UNDO	Undoes a custom command	Macro Function
EDIT REPEAT	Related command	Menu Command

CUSTOM.UNDO(*macro, undo*)

Macro Function

CUSTOM.UNDO replaces the Edit Undo command and Undo tool with custom commands. *Macro* is the name of or reference (in R1C1 format) to a macro that you want to run when Undo is chosen. *Undo* is text that appears on the Edit menu.

See Also

CUSTOM.REPEAT	Repeats custom commands	Macro Function
EDIT UNDO	Related command	Menu Command

CUSTOMIZE.TOOLBAR?(*category*)

Macro Function   **New to Version 4.0**

CUSTOMIZE.TOOLBAR causes the Customize Tools dialog box to be displayed. Using this macro function is the same as choosing the Options Toolbars menu command and clicking on the Customize button. *Category* is the category of tools that you want to appear in the dialog box.

Category	Tools
1	File
2	Edit
3	Formula
4	Formatting, nontext
5	Formatting, text
6	Drawing
7	Macro

Category	Tools
8	Charting
9	Utility
10	Custom

Example

=CUSTOMIZE.TOOLBAR?(8) displays the Customize Tools dialog box, as shown in Figure C-25.

See Also

ADD.TOOLBAR	Makes a new toolbar	Macro Function
OPTIONS TOOLBARS	Equivalent command	Menu Command
SHOW.TOOLBAR	Displays a previously created toolbar	Macro Function

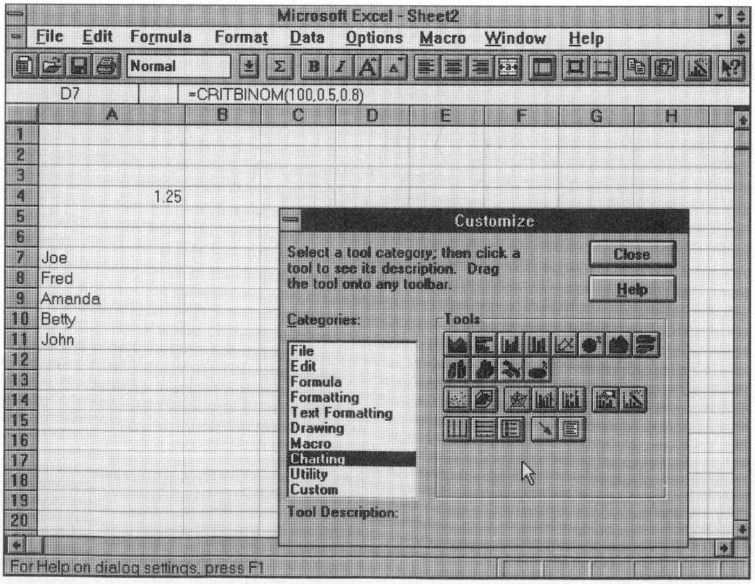

Figure C-25. *The Customize Tools dialog box*

CUT(*[from]*, *[to]*)

Macro Function

CUT performs the same action as the Edit Cut menu command. *From* is the range that you want to cut. If *from* is omitted, the current selection is cut. *To* Is the range into which you want to place the cut cells. It has to be the same size as the range specified by *from,* or one cell. If *to* is one cell, the *from* cells are pasted from the *to* cell down and to the right. If no *to* argument is given, you can use the PASTE or PASTE.SPECIAL function to paste the cells.

See Also

COPY	Selects objects for copying	Macro Function
PASTE	Pastes object previously selected	Macro Function
PASTE.SPECIAL	Same as Edit Paste Special	Macro Function

DATA

Menu

The Data menu contains options for setting up and manipulating a database. Included are options to define a database; to identify selection criteria; to find, extract, or delete selected records based on the criteria; to view and maintain database records as a form instead of a table; and to sort database records. Other options will fill a range of cells with a series of numbers or dates, create a table, and divide a text string into individual cells (Parse). Finally, the Data menu contains an option that consolidates data from multiple locations using a chosen summation function and another option that allows you to summarize a database into a crosstab table that is totaled on the right and at the bottom.

The Data menu is shown here:

See Also

DATABASE	Explains databases	Concept

DATA CONSOLIDATE

Menu Command

Data Consolidate allows you to consolidate data from several ranges or documents into one range or document. The ranges to be consolidated can come from multiple locations on multiple worksheets. The data is combined with some designated function, such as =SUM, and the resulting data is placed in a range designated by the active cell. When you choose the Consolidate option from the Data menu, the following dialog box appears.

For example, imagine that you want to average the monthly sales for your various products for the first half of the year. If the sales data is stored on two quarterly worksheets, as shown in Figures D-1 and D-2, you can determine the average monthly sales for each product with the following procedure:

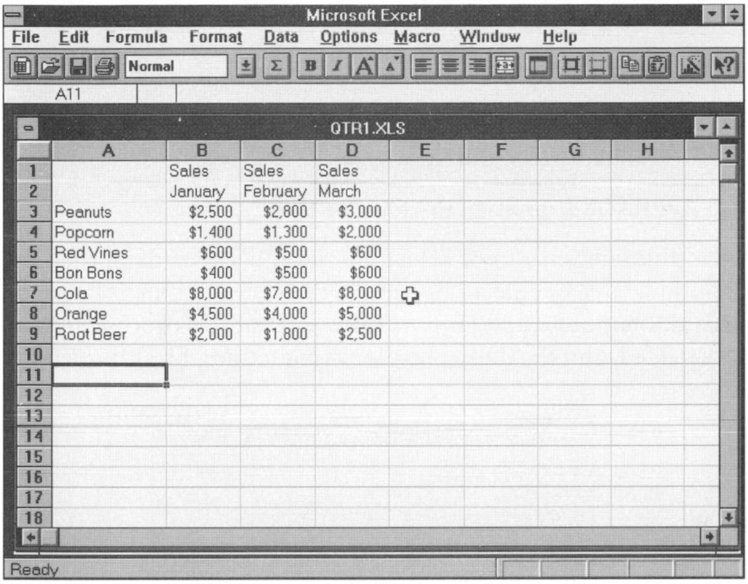

Figure D-1.   *First quarterly worksheet of sales data*

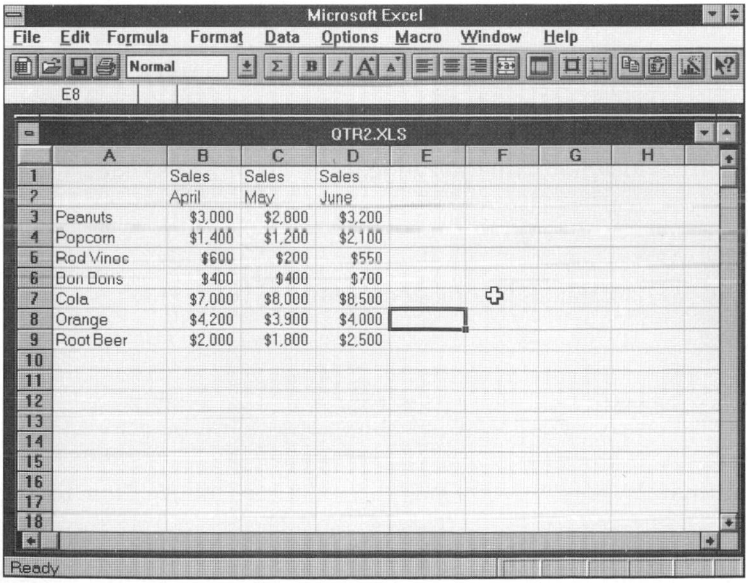

Figure D-2.   *Second quarterly worksheet of sales data*

Example

1. Activate the receiving worksheet and select the upper-left cell in the range in which you want to place the results. In this example, activate cell A1.

2. Select Consolidate from the Data menu.

3. Select AVERAGE from the Function list box.

4. Type in the reference to or select one month's sales data; then click on the Add button. For example, select cells B3:B9 (or enter that cell range) and click on the add button to add January sales. Repeat this process until all data has been selected, and the dialog box looks something like this:

5. Click on the OK button. The result of averaging the sales data is placed in the range including and below the active cell, as you can see in Figure D-3.

You can consolidate data by location or by category. If you want to consolidate by category, make sure to include the labels in your ranges. The Consolidate option is particularly useful for combining large amounts of data from several different worksheets. It is much faster than creating formulas with external cell references.

See Also

LINKING   Explains linking documents   Concept

DATA CROSSTAB

Menu Command   **New to Version 4.0**

Data Crosstab creates a crosstab table—one in which the rows are summed on the right and the columns are summed on the bottom. Before you can create a crosstab table, the database must be defined with the Data Set Database option. When you

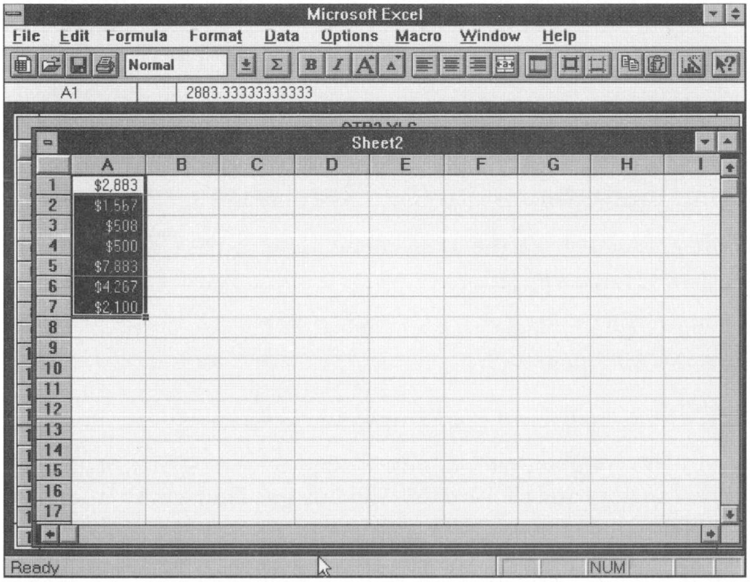

Figure D-3.   *The consolidated average sales*

choose the Crosstab option from the Data menu, the Crosstab ReportWizard Introduction window opens, as shown in Figure D-4.

This is the first of a series of dialog boxes that demonstrate how to create a cross tabulation table. If you need further assistance at any step, click on the Explain button in the lower-left corner of the dialog box. As an example, if you start with a database

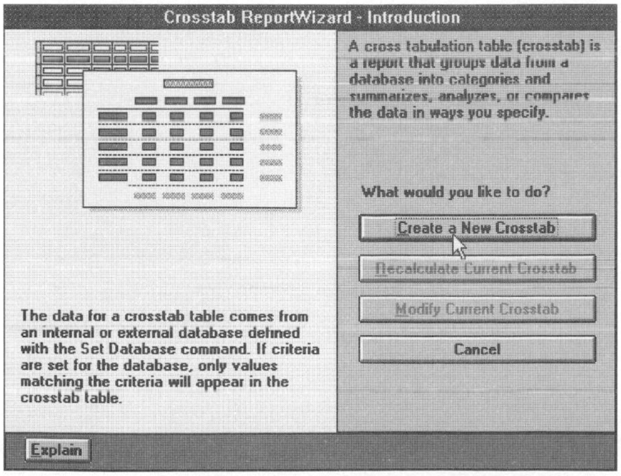

Figure D-4.   *The Crosstab ReportWizard Introduction window*

of weekly sales data by office, as shown in Figure D-5, you can create a crosstab table with these steps:

Example

1. Highlight the database, B2:F17, and choose Set Database from the Data menu to define the database.

2. Choose Crosstab from the Data menu. The initial Crosstab dialog box will open. (See Figure D-4.)

3. Click on Create a New Crosstab. The Row Categories dialog box shown in Figure D-6 will open.

4. Select Office as the row category and click on the Add button.

5. Click on Next to open the Column Categories dialog box. Select Week for the column category and click on the Add button. Then click on Next to open the Value Fields dialog box.

6. Amount should already be selected for the Value Field so just click on Add, as has been done in Figure D-7.

7. Click on Next to go to the Final Crosstab dialog box and then click on Create it to create the crosstab table. You'll see a number of messages in the status bar and then the crosstab table will appear on a new worksheet, as shown in Figure D-8.

	Number	Office	Week	Sales	Amount
	250	Boston	4/1/92	46	6,714
	250	Boston	4/8/92	31	4,524
	250	Boston	4/15/92	68	9,925
	250	Boston	4/22/92	55	8,027
	250	Boston	4/29/92	42	6,130
	260	Denver	4/1/92	61	8,903
	260	Denver	4/8/92	48	7,006
	260	Denver	4/15/92	43	6,276
	260	Denver	4/22/92	78	11,384
	260	Denver	4/29/92	36	5,254
	270	Seattle	4/1/92	38	5,546
	270	Seattle	4/8/92	51	7,443
	270	Seattle	4/15/92	78	11,384
	270	Seattle	4/22/92	46	6,714
	270	Seattle	4/29/92	81	11,822

Figure D-5. *Database used to create a crosstab table*

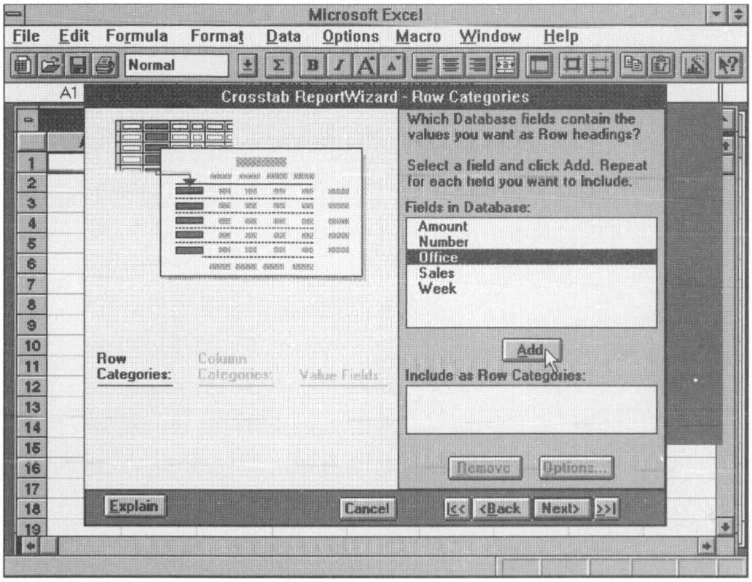

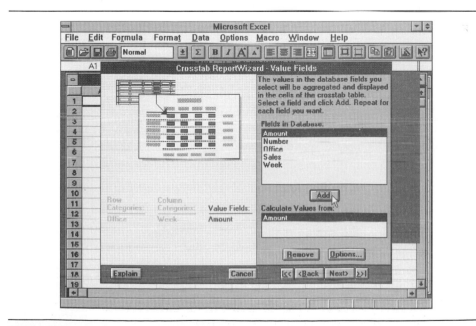

Figure D-6. *Crosstab Row Categories dialog box with Office selected*

Figure D-7. *Crosstab Value Fields dialog box with Amount added*

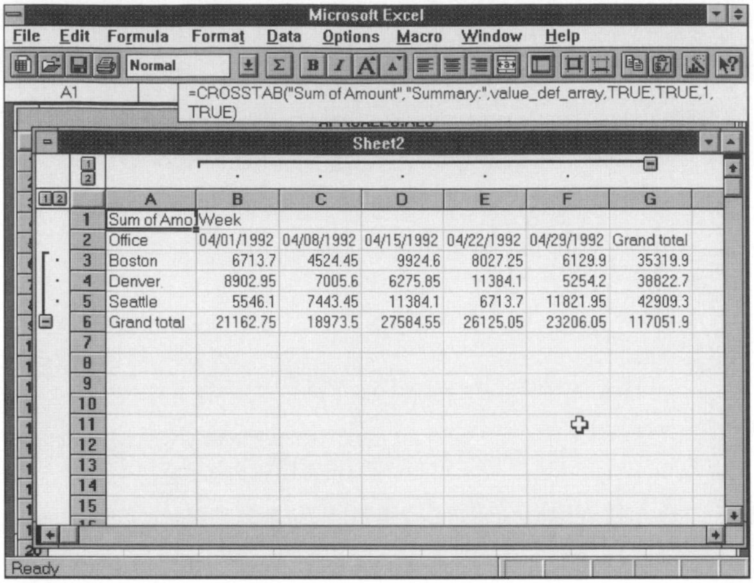

Figure D-8. *Initial crosstab table*

8. You can now format the table to create the image you want. Among other things, you can turn off the Outline symbols in the Options Display dialog box, format the numbers, replace the dates (they are functions that cannot be formatted), and add, delete, and center titles as necessary. One possible resulting image is shown in Figure D-9.

See Also

CROSSTAB.CREATE	Equivalent function	Macro Function
DATA SET DATABASE	Declares the current selection as a database	Command

DATA DELETE

Menu Command

The Delete command in the Data menu will permanently delete any records in the database that match the criteria you set. To delete records from the database, you must first define the criteria using the Set Criteria option.

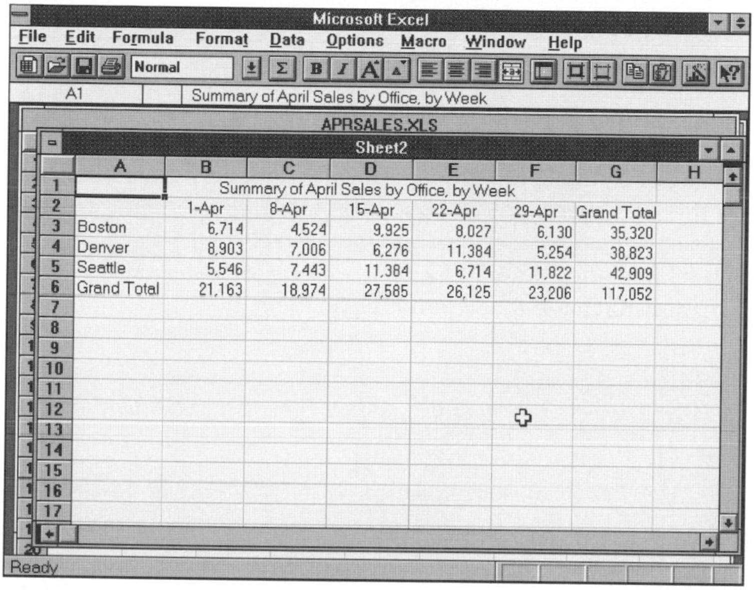

```
┌────────────────────────────────────────────────────────────────┐
│ ▄                    Microsoft Excel                      ▼│▲│  │
│ File  Edit  Formula  Format  Data  Options  Macro  Window  Help │
│ ┌──┬──┬──┬──┐┌──────┐ ±│Σ│B│I│A│A│ ═│═│═│═│ □│□│□│ ▣│▣│▣│▨│�W?│  │
│ └──┴──┴──┴──┘ Normal                                            │
│     A1              │ Summary of April Sales by Office, by Week │
│ ┌──────────────────────────APRSALES.XLS─────────────────────┐  │
│ │ ▭                      Sheet2                      ▼│▲ │     │
│ │     A       B      C       D       E      F       G      H  │▲ │
│ │ 1       Summary of April Sales by Office, by Week           │ │
│ │ 2         1-Apr   8-Apr  15-Apr  22-Apr  29-Apr  Grand Total│ │
│ │ 3 Boston  6,714   4,524   9,925   8,027   6,130   35,320    │ │
│ │ 4 Denver  8,903   7,006   6,276  11,384   5,254   38,823    │ │
│ │ 5 Seattle 5,546   7,443  11,384   6,714  11,822   42,909    │ │
│ │ 6 Grand Total 21,163 18,974 27,585 26,125 23,206 117,052    │ │
│ │ 7                                                           │ │
│ │ 8                                                           │ │
│ │ 9                                                           │ │
│ │10                                                           │ │
│ │11                                                           │ │
│ │12                                    ⊹                      │ │
│ │13                                                           │ │
│ │14                                                           │ │
│ │15                                                           │ │
│ │16                                                           │ │
│ │17                                                           │ │
│ │◀                                                          ▶ │▼│
│ Ready                                                          │  │
└────────────────────────────────────────────────────────────────┘
```

Figure D-9.   *Final formatted crosstab table*

The criteria range must contain some or all of the field names in your database in the first row. The rows underneath the first row contain the criteria that will be the basis of your selection. (See the DATA SET CRITERIA entry for an example.)

Once you have set your criteria, the database records that match the criteria will be deleted permanently from the database when you choose the Delete command from the Data menu.

CAUTION: You can't undo Data Delete with the Edit Undo option. Make sure you want to delete the records before selecting Delete from the Data menu. It is a good idea to save the worksheet immediately before choosing Data Delete, so you can recover it if you make an error. Also, don't include blank rows in the criteria range unless you want to delete all records in the database.

See Also

DATA.DELETE	Related function	Macro Function
DATA SET CRITERIA	Define records to delete	Menu command

DATA.DELETE()
DATA.DELETE?()

Macro Function

The DATA.DELETE macro function performs the same action as the Delete command from the Data menu. DATA.DELETE permanently deletes records from the active database that match the criteria you have established with SET.CRITERIA. The dialog box version of the DATA.DELETE function (with the question mark) displays a dialog box warning that the deletion is permanent.

 CAUTION: The version without the question mark does not display the warning.

See Also

DATA DELETE	Equivalent command	Menu Command
DATA SET CRITERIA	Related command	Menu Command
SET.CRITERIA	Related function	Macro Function

DATA EXIT FIND

Menu Command

➤   *Shortcut Key:* ESC

You can choose the Data Exit Find option to exit from the Data Find option. Exit Find only appears on the Data menu after you have chosen the Find option. You can also exit from Data Find by choosing another option, editing a cell, or selecting (clicking on) a cell outside the database. Once you choose the Exit Find option from the Data menu, the Find option once again appears on the Data menu. If you choose the Data Find option again, Excel will find the next occurrence of a database record that matches the criteria defined with the Set Criteria option. (For more information, see DATA FIND.)

See Also

DATA FIND	Finds the next match in the database	Menu Command
DATA SET CRITERIA	Establishes criteria for finding records	Menu Command
SET.CRITERIA	Related function	Macro Function

DATA EXTRACT

Menu Command

The Extract option in the Data menu copies database records that match the criteria specified with the Set Criteria option, and places them in the extract range. Before you choose the Extract option from the Data menu, you must select the extract range. It's easiest to select a range that contains only the field names of the data you will extract. Then when you choose the Data Extract option, Excel will put the extracted data in the cells immediately below the field names and clear all the cells below the extracted data to the bottom of the worksheet. You can also select an extract range that contains field names and cells that will contain the extracted data. All the cells in the extract range will be replaced with extracted data. If your extract range is too small, Excel will warn you, allow you to redefine the extract range, and choose the Data Extract option again.

After you choose the Data Extract option, you'll see the following dialog box:

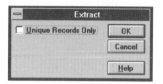

The Extract dialog box lets you decide if you want to exclude duplicate records. If you do, click on the Unique Records Only check box.

Figure D-10 shows a database with a criteria range defined and an extract range declared. When you choose the Extract option from the Data menu, Excel finds the records that match the criteria specified in the criteria range, and places the data from those records in the cells beneath the appropriate field names in the extract range.

CAUTION: You can't undo a Data Extract with the Edit Undo option. Also, if an extract range is defined by field names alone, all of the cells beneath the field names are cleared all the way to the bottom of the worksheet. In addition, if a cell in a record you are extracting contains a formula, the extracted record will contain the value of the cell, not the formula.

See Also

DATA DELETE	Deletes records from a database	Menu Command
DATA SET CRITERIA	Establishes criteria for extracting records	Menu Command

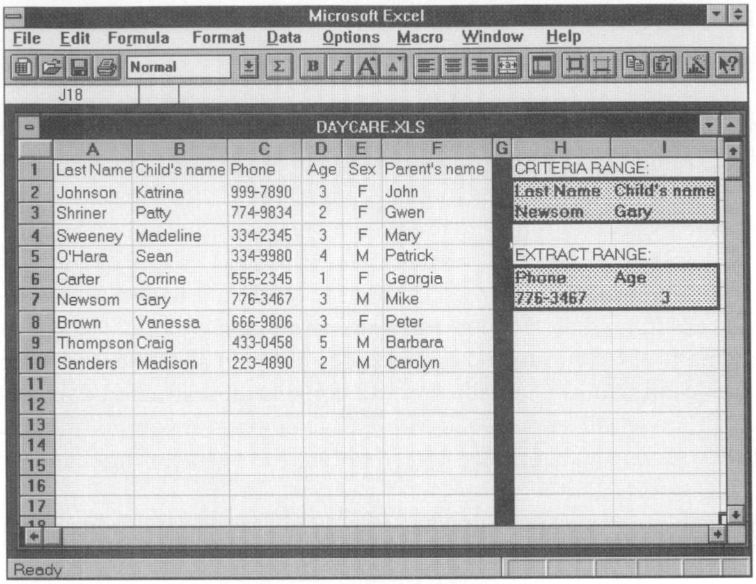

Figure D-10. *A database with criteria and extract ranges*

DATA FIND

Menu Command

Data Find selects (highlights) the first record in the database that matches the criteria defined using the Set Criteria option. The scroll bars in the dialog box become striped. If you click on the down arrow in the scroll bar, Excel selects the next record that matches the defined criteria. If you click on the scroll bar below the scroll box, Excel selects a record that matches the criteria, approximately one screen height down from your current location.

To exit from Data Find, choose the Exit Find option from the Data menu. This option only appears after you have chosen the Data Find option. You can also exit from Data Find by choosing another menu option, editing a cell, selecting a cell outside the database, or pressing the ESC key. Once you choose the Data Exit Find option, or exit in another way from Data Find, the Data Find option once again appears on the menu.

If you want to search backward through the database rather than forward, hold down the SHIFT key when you choose the Data Find option.

See Also

DATA EXIT FIND	Exits from Data Find	Menu Command
DATA SET CRITERIA	Establishes criteria for finding records	Menu Command

---

DATA.FIND(X)

Macro Function

Using DATA.FIND is the same action as choosing the Find option from the Data menu if X is TRUE and the Exit Find option if X is FALSE. DATA.FIND selects the first record in the database that matches the criteria defined using the SET.CRITERIA macro function.

See Also

DATA FIND	Equivalent Command	Menu Command
DATA.FIND.NEXT	Finds the next matching record	Macro Function
DATA.FIND.PREV	Finds the previous matching record	Macro Function
DATA SET CRITERIA	Establishes criteria for finding records	Menu Command
SET.CRITERIA	Establishes criteria for finding records	Macro Function

---

DATA.FIND.NEXT()

Macro Function

Using DATA.FIND.NEXT is the same as pressing the DOWN ARROW key after choosing the Data Find menu command. DATA.FIND.NEXT finds the next record in the database that matches the criteria established with the SET.CRITERIA macro function. If no matching record is found, DATA.FIND.NEXT returns FALSE.

See Also

DATA FIND	Equivalent Command	Menu Command
DATA.FIND	Finds the first matching record	Macro Function
DATA.FIND.PREV	Finds the previous matching record	Macro Function

| DATA SET CRITERIA | Establishes criteria for finding records | Menu Command |
| SET.CRITERIA | Establishes criteria for finding records | Macro Function |

DATA.FIND.PREV()

Macro Function

Using DATA.FIND.PREV is the same as pressing the UP ARROW key after choosing the Data Find menu command. DATA.FIND.PREV finds the previous record in the database that matches the criteria established with the SET.CRITERIA macro function. If no matching record is found, DATA.FIND.PREV returns FALSE.

See Also

DATA FIND	Equivalent Command	Menu Command
DATA.FIND	Finds the first matching record	Macro Function
DATA.FIND.NEXT	Finds the next matching record	Macro Function
DATA SET CRITERIA	Establishes criteria for finding records	Menu Command
SET.CRITERIA	Establishes criteria for finding records	Macro Function

DATA FORM

Menu Command

The Form option in the Data menu displays the currently defined database as a form in a dialog box. Each of the field names in your database appears on the left side of the dialog box, next to its own field. Figure D-11 shows a database on a worksheet, and Figure D-12 shows the Data Form for the database in Figure D-11.

On the right side of the dialog box are the options New, Delete, Restore, Find Prev, Find Next, Criteria, and Close. You can add new records to your database by choosing the New option and then filling in the blank fields. You can find records by setting the criteria with the Criteria option, and then choosing the Find option. These options are *not* the same as the Set Criteria, Data Find, Data Delete, and Data Extract options. Setting your criteria using the Criteria option in the dialog box will not change the criteria you defined using the Set Criteria option.

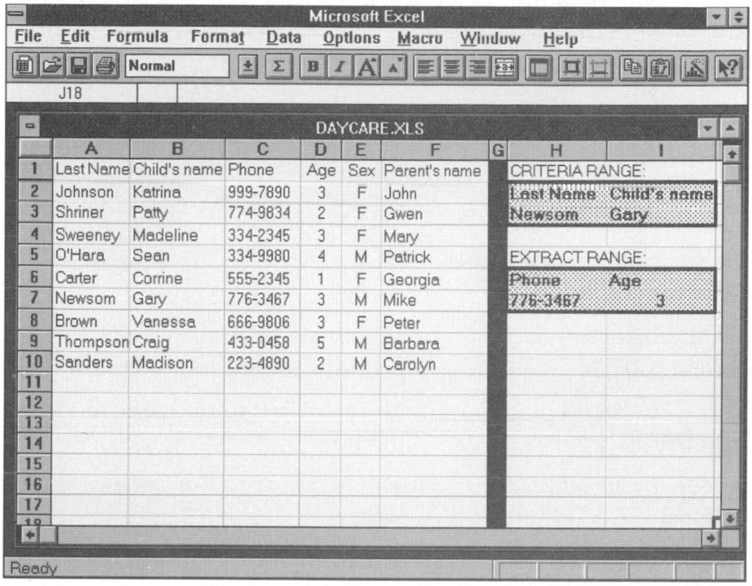

Figure D-11.   *A sample database*

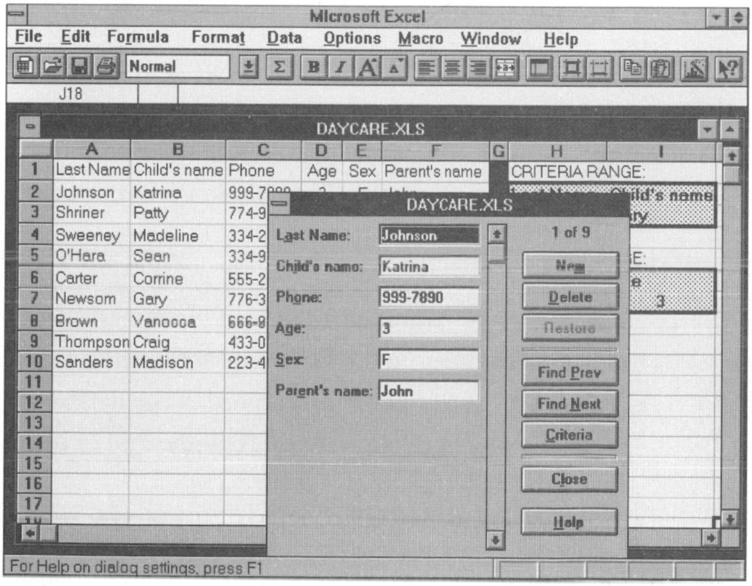

Figure D-12.   *The Data Form for the database in Figure D-11*

The Data Form also contains a scroll bar that allows you to move up and down through the database with your mouse. The following two lists summarize how to move around the dialog box with your mouse and with your keyboard.

Navigating in the Data Form with the Mouse	
Mouse Action	*Result*
Click in a field	Selects a field
Click on the down arrow at the bottom of the scroll bar	Moves cursor to the same field in the next record
Click on the up arrow at the top of the scroll bar	Moves cursor to the same field in the previous record
Click below the scroll box on the scroll bar	Moves cursor to the same field ten records forward
Click above the scroll box on the scroll bar	Moves cursor to the same field ten records back
Drag the scroll box to the bottom of the scroll bar	Moves cursor to a new record at the end of the database
Drag the scroll box to the top of the scroll bar	Moves cursor to the first record in the database

Navigating in the Data Form with the Keyboard	
Keypress	*Result*
TAB	Moves cursor to the next field in the current record
ENTER	Moves cursor to the first field in the next record
SHIFT-TAB	Moves cursor to the previous field in the current record
SHIFT-ENTER	Moves cursor to the first field in the previous record
UP ARROW	Moves cursor to the same field in the previous record
DOWN ARROW	Moves cursor to the same field in the next record
PGUP	Moves cursor to the same field ten records back
PGDN	Moves cursor to the same field ten records forward
CTRL-PGUP	Moves cursor to the first record in the database
CTRL-PGDN	Moves cursor to a new record at the end of the database

The other items in the Data Form are described here:

- The record indicator in the upper-right corner of the Data Form indicates which record of the database you are in. For example, if the record indicator displays "2 of 15," you are in the second record of a database 15 records long. The total number of records indicates how many nonblank records there are in the database.

- The Delete button deletes the record currently displayed in the Data Form, moving subsequent records up to fill in the space.

- The Criteria button is not the same as the Data Set Criteria option. Instead, it allows you to define criteria to be used to find records within the Data Form environment.

- The Close button takes you out of the Data Form.

- The Find Next button finds the next instance in the database that matches the criteria you set using the Criteria option in the Data Form (*not* the Data Set Criteria option).

- The Find Prev button finds the previous instance in the database that matches the criteria you set using the Criteria option in the Data Form (*not* the Data Set Criteria option).

- The Form button only appears in the Data Form after you choose the Criteria option. Choosing this Form button returns you to the regular Data Form.

- The Restore button allows you to undo changes that you made to a record. To undo such edits, you must choose the Restore option before you go on to a new record.

DATA.FORM()

Macro Function

The DATA.FORM macro function performs the same action as the Form option on the Data menu. DATA.FORM opens a dialog box where you can enter new records, delete records, and move around the database. (See the DATA FORM menu command entry for more information.) You can replace the normal Data Form by designing a custom dialog box with the Dialog Editor and then naming the dialog box definition table "Data_form" on the worksheet with the database. Excel provides both the Close and OK buttons, so you needn't include them in your custom dialog box.

See Also

DATA FORM	Equivalent command	Menu Command

DATA PARSE

Menu Command

You generally use the Data Parse menu option after you import data into Excel from another application. Sometimes, each record of the imported data is placed into one cell. You then need to spread the data from the single cell to many cells, so each field appears in its own cell. You accomplish this using Data Parse.

After you import the data, select the parse range. The range can only be one column wide, but can include as many rows as you want. Then select the Data Parse option. A dialog box appears with a Parse Line text box and the options Guess and Clear. The Parse Line text box displays the contents of the first cell in your parse range with Excel's best guess about where to parse your data indicated by square brackets. You can add or delete square brackets in the box to indicate where you want the cell divisions to occur. The Guess option tells Excel to guess again where the cell divisions should occur. The Clear option clears previously set brackets so you can try again. It may take several tries to get the data parsed the way you want it.

DATA SERIES

Menu Command

The Data Series menu option fills in the selected range with incremental values. The first cell in the range must contain the starting value. For example, if you select part of a column and the first cell in the selection contains 10, you can use Data Series to fill in the rest of the selection with either 11, 12, and 13 or 20, 30, and 40.

After you choose the Data Series option, this dialog box appears.

The Series In options allow you to decide whether you want the series filled in by row or by column. If you choose Rows, Excel will fill in the series starting at the upper-left corner of the selection and fill across row by row. If you choose Columns, Excel will fill in the series starting at the upper-left corner of the selection and fill down column by column.

The Type options in the Series dialog box allows you to decide how the series is incremented. Here are the choices and their descriptions:

Series Type	Description
Linear	Adds the step value to the value in each cell to get the value of the next cell
Growth	Multiplies the value in each cell by the step value to get the value of the next cell
Date	Uses date calculations to determine the incremental values
AutoFill	Automatically extends a value in its logical sequence

The Date Unit options are only accessible if you have set the Type to Date. Here you can select whether the date will be incremented by day, weekday, month, or year.

The Step Value is the amount by which you want to increment each value in the series. If you want to decrement the series, use a negative number.

The Stop Value is the value that you want to be the last value in the series. Data Series will stop filling in values when it gets to the end of the selected range or the stop value.

Selecting the Trend check box causes the range to be filled with values based on a linear or exponential trend. The step values are calculated from the values located to the top or left of the range.

DATA.SERIES(*row-col, series, date, step, stop, trend*)
DATA.SERIES?(*[row-col], [series], [date], [step], [stop], [trend]*)

Macro Function

The DATA.SERIES macro function performs the same action as the Data Series menu option. The *row-col* argument must be either 1 (for rows) or 2 (for columns). The *series* argument must be 1, 2, 3, or 4. If *series* is 1, it is a linear type series. If *series* is 2, it is a growth type series. If *series* is 3, it is a date type series. If *series* is 4, it is an AutoFill series. The *date* argument must be 1 (day), 2 (weekday), 3 (month), or 4 (year). The *step* value is the amount by which each number in the series is increased or decreased to get the next number in the series. The default *step* value is 1. The *stop* value indicates where to stop the series. If this argument is omitted, the series will fill the current active range. The *trend* argument, which corresponds to the Trend check box is either TRUE or FALSE. If *trend* is TRUE, the series is generated as a linear or exponential trend. If *trend* is FALSE or omitted, the series is generated as a standard data series. In the dialog box version (with the question mark), the arguments, if included, are used as default values for the dialog box that appears.

See Also

DATA SERIES	Equivalent command	Menu Command

DATA SET CRITERIA

Menu Command

The Data Set Criteria option sets the criteria range. The criteria set in this range is used to select records using the Data Find, Data Extract, and Data Delete options.

The criteria range is usually on the same worksheet as the database but outside the database range. Since you could use it often, place the criteria range in a convenient location (to the side or above the database). The first row of the criteria range must consist of field names that match one or more of the field names in the database. You must have one or more rows beneath the first row in which to place the criteria. Once you have set up and selected your criteria range, choose the Data Set Criteria option.

After you have defined your criteria range using the Data Set Criteria option, you can change the criteria as much as you want. You don't have to redefine the range every time you change the criteria. Figure D-13 shows an example of a small database with the criteria range in cells H2:I3.

Excel creates the name "Criteria" for the criteria range. You can access, change, and delete the name and range using the Formula Define Names option. Here is the Define Names dialog box; notice the criteria range:

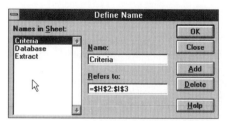

You can set the criteria range to include more than one restriction. Use relational operators such as less than (<), greater than (>), equal to (=), not equal to (<>), greater than or equal to (>=), and less than or equal to (<=). Wildcard characters (* and ?) allow you to set criteria for text strings that don't exactly match. For example, "a*" would select all text strings that begin with the letter *a*. The string "a?" would select all text strings that begin with *a* and are exactly two characters long.

If you put criteria in multiple columns but a single row (as shown in Figure D-13), it is as if there were a logical AND between the fields: both fields must be matched for the record to be selected. If you put criteria in multiple rows, it is as if there were a logical OR between the fields: matching either of the rows will select a record. If you have a blank row in your criteria range, all records will be selected.

See Also

DATA DELETE	Deletes records from a database	Menu Command
DATA EXTRACT	Extracts records from a database	Menu Command
DATA FIND	Finds a record in a database	Menu Command

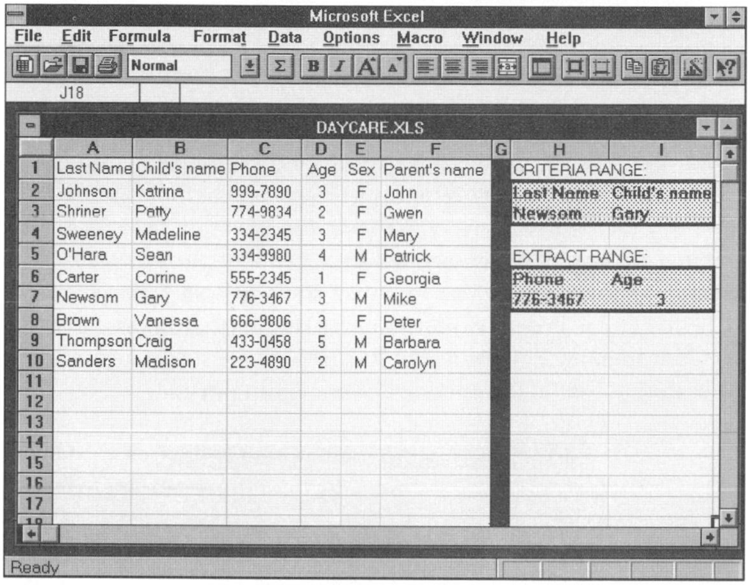

Figure D-13. *The criteria range is in cells H2:I3*

DATA SET DATABASE

Menu Command

The Data Set Database option allows you to define a range as a database. The first row in your range must contain field names, and the rows beneath them must contain data. You can use the Data Set Database option on an existing worksheet with data already filled in, or before you enter any data. Be sure to include a few blank lines at the bottom of the database range to allow for expansion. That way you can insert new records and automatically expand the range definition. If you don't include several blank rows and add a new record at the bottom of the database, the new record will be outside of the database definition. When you choose Data Set Database, Excel creates the name "Database" for the database. You can access, change, and delete the name and range using the Formula Define Names menu option.

See Also

DATA SET CRITERIA	Related command	Menu Command
DATABASE	Explains databases	Concept

DATA SORT

Menu Command

The Data Sort option sorts the data in the selected range. Selecting the range to be sorted and choosing the Data Sort option brings up the Sort dialog box, which is shown below. The dialog box allows you to sort the selection by rows or columns, and allows you to define sort keys. *Sort keys* tell Excel which column you want to sort by if you are sorting by rows, and which row you want to sort by if you are sorting by columns. The 1st Key is the predominant sort key; sorting takes place according to the 3rd key, then the 2nd Key, and then the 1st Key. Each sort key box allows you to decide if you want to sort in Ascending or Descending order.

Here is the sequence in which Excel sorts when you select the Ascending option:

1. Numbers entered as values from the largest negative number to the largest positive number

2. Text, ignoring capitalization, and including numbers entered as text, in this sequence: SPACE ! " # $ % & ' ( ) *+, − . / : ; < = > ? @ [\ ] ^ _ ' { | } ~ ¢ ¥ (and all other special characters) 0 1 2 3 4 5 6 7 8 9 a b c d e f g h i j k l m n o p q r s t u v w x y z

3. Logical values, FALSE first and then TRUE

4. Error values (all with equal value)

5. Blank cells

The descending order is the reverse of the order just shown, but blank cells are always sorted last.

See Also

SORT   Equivalent function   Macro Function

D

DATA TYPES

Concept

Data types in Excel include numbers, text, error values, logical values, references, and dates. Sometimes you will need to convert one type to another to use something as an argument for a function. Numbers are simply any kind of numeric values. Text is strings of characters, including numbers and symbols. Text that looks like a number can be converted to a number with the VALUE function. Errors are returned by functions and can be converted to text with the TEXT function, which can also convert numbers to text. Logical values are TRUE and FALSE. Logical values can be converted to text with the TEXT function. References can be converted to text with the REFTEXT function, and text can be converted to references with the TEXTREF function. Text dates can be converted to a number with the DATEVALUE function, and numeric dates can be converted to text with the TEXT function.

See Also

DATEVALUE	Converts text to a date	Function
REFTEXT	Converts references to text	Function
TEXT	Converts other types to text	Function
TEXTREF	Converts text to references	Function
VALUE	Converts text to a number	Function

DATABASE

Concept

A *database* is a set of records all of which have a common set of fields. A *record* is a single row or set of data. A *field* is a single item in the record. For example, a record might contain a name field, an address field, and a phone number field. Excel has a natural structure for a database, with records contained in rows and fields contained in columns. A database has a set of field names in the first row and records containing actual data in the rows beneath. Once you build a database, you can sort it, extract records, find records, delete records, and add records. You can also perform several types of analysis on the data.

A database must be contained on a single worksheet. To declare a database, select the range containing the field names and all of the data records beneath. Include at least one blank row at the end of the database to allow for expansion. Your database will automatically increase when you insert rows above the last record in the database.

If you add a record beneath the last record, however, it will not be in the database. Choose the Set Database option from the Data menu to define a range as a database. Figure D-14 shows a database. The entire database, plus extra rows at the end, has been selected.

The Data Form menu option provides easy access to your database. It opens a dialog box that allows you to add, delete, or find specific records. Figure D-15 shows the Data Form for the database in Figure D-14.

To extract, delete, or find records from the Data menu, you must first set a criteria range with the Data Set Criteria option. Use Data Delete to delete records that satisfy the criteria. Use Data Find to find records that match the criteria. You can extract records with the Data Extract command. The Extract command requires not only a criteria range, but also an extract range. Use the Set Extract command to declare a range in which the extracted range can be placed. The first row of the extract range should contain field names of the fields that you want to extract.

See Also

DATA SET DATABASE	Declares a database	Menu Command
DATABASE FUNCTIONS	Explains database functions	Concept

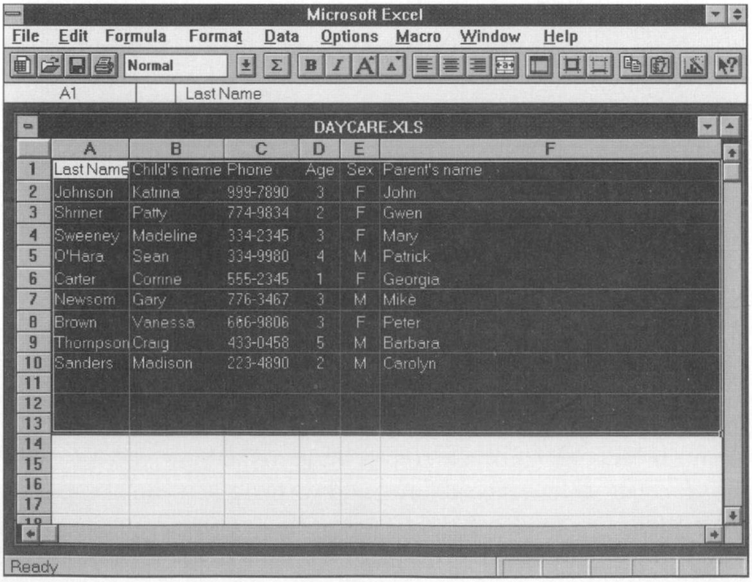

Figure D-14.   *A sample database*

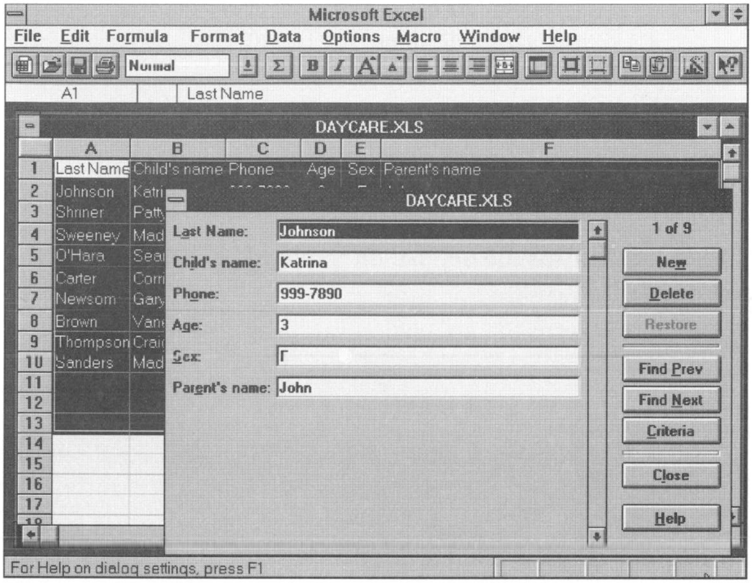

Figure D-15.   *The Data Form for the database in Figure D-14*

DATABASE FUNCTIONS

Concept

Database functions allow you to do certain calculations on a database. Each of these functions take three arguments: *input-range, field,* and *criteria-range.* The *input-range* argument is the database range or range name. When you use the Data Set Database command, Excel names the selected database with the name "Database."

The *field* argument is the field in the database on which you want to perform the function. If you give the name of the field as text, you should enclose it within quotation marks. The field argument may also be a number, where the leftmost or uppermost field is numbered 1, the next field is numbered 2, and so on.

The *criteria-range* argument is a range or range name where the criteria is stored. If you define the criteria using the Data Set Criteria command, the criteria range will be named "Criteria." If you want to perform a function on all records in a database, make sure you have a blank line below the field names in the criteria range.

See Also

DAVERAGE	Averages values from chosen fields and records	Function
DCOUNT	Counts the cells that contain numbers	Function
DCOUNTA	Counts the nonblank cells	Function
DGET	Extracts a single value	Function
DMAX	Returns the maximum	Function
DMIN	Returns the minimum	Function
DPRODUCT	Returns the product of the values	Function
DSUM	Sums the chosen fields and records	Function
DSTDEV	Returns the standard deviation	Function
DSTDEVP	Returns the population standard deviation	Function
DVAR	Returns the variance	Function
DVARP	Returns the population variance	Function

DATE(*year, month, day*)

Function

DATE returns the date serial number for a given year, month, and day value. The date serial number (a number between 1 and 65380) is by default formatted as a date from 1/1/1900 through 12/31/2078. Several alternative formats may be applied.

DATE is useful when another function asks for a date serial number as an argument.

Example

=DATE(93,4,5) returns the value 34064, which can be formatted as 4/5/1992.

See Also

DATES	Explains dates	Concept
DATEVALUE	Converts a string to a date	Function
NOW	Returns the current date and time	Function
TODAY	Returns the current date	Function

DATES

Concept

In Excel, dates are stored as date serial numbers. Each date has a number associated with it, beginning with January 1, 1900 (which equals 1) and ending with December 31, 2078 (which equals 65380). You can use these serial numbers to perform certain calculations involving dates. Even though dates are stored as serial numbers, you can format them in many different ways to display the dates as normal calendar dates. Use the Format Number option to format dates.

See Also

DATE	Returns a serial number for a date	Function
DATEVALUE	Converts a string to a date	Function
DAY	Returns the day of the month (1-31)	Function
FORMAT NUMBER	Formats dates	Menu Command
NOW	Returns the current date and time	Function
TODAY	Returns the current date	Function

D

DATEVALUE(*string*)

Function

DATEVALUE returns the date serial number for a string of characters that look like a date. This is used to convert dates entered as text, or dates from other applications, into date serial numbers that Excel can use in calculations. By default, date serial numbers are formatted to look like normal dates.

Example

=DATEVALUE("6/7/93") returns the value 34127.

See Also

DATE	Returns a serial number for a date	Function
DATES	Explains dates	Concept
DAY	Returns the day of the month (1-31)	Function
FORMAT NUMBER	Formats dates	Menu Command
NOW	Returns the current date and time	Function
TODAY	Returns the current date	Function

DAVERAGE(*input-range,field,criteria-range*)

Function

Based on criteria contained in criteria range, DAVERAGE searches an input range for all records matching the criteria. When it finds matching records, it averages the values contained in the designated field of those records.

The *input-range* argument is the range or range name containing the database. When the database is defined with the Data Set Database command, it is named "Database."

The *field* argument is the field in the database on which you want to perform the averaging. If you give the field name as text, you should enclose it within quotation marks. The field argument may also be a number, where the leftmost or uppermost field is numbered 1, the next field is numbered 2, and so on.

The *criteria-range* argument is a range or range name where the criteria is stored. If you defined the criteria using the Data Set Criteria command, the criteria range is named "Criteria." If you want to perform a function on all records in a database, make sure there is a blank line below the field names in the criteria range.

Example

=DAVERAGE(INPUT,"DOLLARS",CRIT-RANGE), based on the criteria in CRIT-RANGE, searches the INPUT database for selected customers and returns an average of the values in the DOLLARS field of matching records.

See Also

DATABASE FUNCTIONS	Explains database functions	Concept

DAY(*date-serial-number*)

Function

DAY returns a value from 1 to 31 representing the day of the month based on the *date-serial-number*, which can be either a literal serial number or a formatted date as a text string in quotation marks.

Example

=DAY(33699) or =DAY("4/5/93") returns 5.

See Also

DATE	Returns a serial number for a date	Function
DATES	Explains dates	Concept
FORMAT NUMBER	Formats dates	Menu Command
NOW	Returns the current date and time	Function
TODAY	Returns the current date	Function

DAYS360(*begin,end*)

Function

DAYS360 returns the number of days between *begin* and *end*, assuming twelve 30-day months for a 360-day year. *Begin* and *end* can be either text dates in quotation marks or date serial numbers.

Examples

=DAYS360("1/1/92","12/31/94") returns 1080.
="12/31/94"−"1/1/92" returns 1095.

See Also

DATE	Returns the serial number of a date	Function
DATES	Explains dates	Concept
TODAY	Returns the current date	Function

D

DB(*cost,salvage,life,period,[month]*)

Function   New to Version 4.0

DB returns the depreciation for a specific period using the fixed-declining balance method of depreciation. *Cost* is the cost of the asset. *Salvage* is the salvage value of the asset. The *life* of the asset is the number of periods for which it is being depreciated. *Period* is the period for which you want to determine the depreciation and *month* is the number of months in the first year. If *month* is omitted, the default value is 12.

Example

=DB(57000,12000,5,2) returns a depreciation of $11,182.03 for the second year of an asset that cost $57,000, has a salvage value of $12,000, and has a 5-year life.

See Also

| DDB | Related function | Function |

DCOUNT(*input-range,[field],criteria-range*)

Function

DCOUNT searches the input range for a match to the criteria that is contained in the criteria range, returning the number of cells that contain numbers in the named field. If no *field* argument is included, DCOUNT returns the number of records that match the criteria as contained in the criteria range.

The *input-range* argument is a range or range name that contains the database. When you use the Data Set Database command, Excel names the selected database "Database."

The *field* argument is the field in the database on which you want to perform the function. If you give the field name as text, you should enclose it in quotation marks. The field argument may also be a number, where the leftmost or uppermost field is numbered 1, the next field is numbered 2, and so on.

The *criteria* argument is a range or range name that contains the criteria. If the criteria was defined using the Data Set Criteria command, the criteria range will be named "Criteria." If you want to perform a function on all records in a database, make sure you have a blank line below the field names in the criteria range.

Example

=DCOUNT(INPUT,"DOLLARS",CRIT-RANGE) searches the INPUT database for selected customers, as defined in CRIT-RANGE, and returns a count of customers that contain numbers in the DOLLARS field.

See Also

| DATABASE | Explains databases | Concept |
| DCOUNTA | Counts the cells that are not blank | Function |

DCOUNTA(*input-range, [field], criteria-range*)

Function

DCOUNTA searches the input range for a match to the criteria as contained in a criteria range, and then returns the number of nonblank cells in the named field. If no *field* argument is included, DCOUNTA returns the number of records that match the criteria contained in a criteria range. Without a *field* argument, DCOUNT and DCOUNTA return the same results.

The *input-range* argument is a range or range name that contains the database. If the database is defined with the Data Set Database command, it is named "Database."

The *field* argument is the field in the database on which you want to perform the function. If you supply the field name as text, you should enclose it within quotation marks. The *field* argument may also be a number, where the leftmost or uppermost field is numbered 1, the next field is numbered 2, and so on.

The *criteria-range* argument is a range or range name that contains the criteria. If the criteria is defined using the Data Set Criteria command, the criteria range is named "Criteria." If you want to perform a function on all records in a database, make sure you have a blank line below the field names in the criteria range.

D

Example

=DCOUNTA(INPUT,"DOLLARS",CRIT-RANGE) searches the INPUT database for selected customers, as defined in CRIT-RANGE, and returns a count of customers that contain nonblank cells in the DOLLARS field.

See Also

| DATABASE | Explains databases | Concept |
| DCOUNT | Counts the cells that contain numbers | Function |

DDB(*cost, salvage, life, period, [factor]*)

Function

DDB returns the depreciation for a specific period using the double-declining balance method of depreciation. *Cost* is the cost of the asset. *Salvage* is the salvage value of the asset. The *life* of the asset is the number of periods for which it is being depreciated. *Period* is the period for which you want to determine the depreciation. *Factor* is the declining rate; if *factor* is omitted, the double-declining rate of 2 is assumed. The *factor* for 150% declining balance would be 1.5.

Example

=DDB(57000,12000,5,2) returns the depreciation of $13,680 for the second year of an asset that cost $57,000, has a salvage value of $12,000, and has a 5-year life.

See Also

| DB | Related function | Function |

DEC2BIN(*X, [characters]*)

Function   New to Version 4.0

DEC2BIN converts the decimal integer *X* to binary. *X* must be between −512 and 511. *Characters* is the optional number of characters or places in the result and is used to add leading zeros. *Characters* is ignored if *X* is negative and a ten-character binary number is returned. The most significant bit is the sign bit and the remaining 9 bits are the magnitude. Two's-complement notation is used for negative numbers.

DEC2BIN is an add-in function. The first time you use it, you may see a #REF! error briefly while Excel loads the macro that runs the function.

Example

=DEC2BIN(6,4) returns 0110.

See Also

BIN2DEC	Converts binary to decimal	Function
DEC2HEX	Converts decimal to hexadecimal	Function
HEX2BIN	Converts hexadecimal to binary	Function

DEC2HEX(X, *[characters]*)

Function   **New to Version 4.0**

DEC2HEX converts the decimal integer X to hexadecimal. X must be between –549,755,813,888 and 549,755,813,887. *Characters* is the optional number of characters or places in the result; this argument is useful for adding leading zeros. *Characters* is ignored if X is negative and a ten-character or 40-bit hexadecimal number is returned. The most significant bit is the sign bit and the remaining 39 bits are the magnitude. Two's-complement notation is used for negative numbers.

DEC2HEX is an add-in function. The first time you use it, you may see a #REF! error briefly while Excel loads the macro that runs the function.

Example

=DEC2HEX(16,4) returns 0010.

See Also

BIN2DEC	Converts binary to decimal	Function
DEC2BIN	Converts decimal to binary	Function
HEX2BIN	Converts hexadecimal to binary	Function

DEC2OCT(X, *[characters]*)

Function   **New to Version 4.0**

DEC2OCT converts the decimal integer X to octal. X must be between –536,870,912 and 536,870,911. *Characters* is the optional number of characters or places in the result and is useful for adding leading zeros. *Characters* is ignored if X is negative and a ten-character or 30-bit octal number is returned. The most significant bit is the sign bit and the remaining 29 bits are the magnitude. Two's-complement notation is used for negative numbers.

DEC2OCT is an add-in function. The first time you use it, you may see a #REF! error briefly while Excel loads the macro that runs the function.

Example

=DEC2OCT(16,4) returns 0020.

See Also

DEC2BIN	Converts decimal to binary	Function
OCT2BIN	Converts octal to binary	Function
OCT2DEC	Converts octal to decimal	Function

DEFINE.NAME(*name,[reference],[type],[shortcut], [hidden],[category]*)
DEFINE.NAME?(*[name],[reference],[type],[shortcut],
[hidden],[category]*)

D

Macro Function

DEFINE.NAME performs the same action as the Formula Define Name menu option. The *name* argument is the name that you want to assign to the *reference*. The *reference* is assumed to be the current selection if it is omitted. If included, the reference can be text, a value, a formula, a cell reference, or a range. The *type* and *shortcut* arguments are used only if the item being named is a macro. If *type* is 1, the macro is a function macro. If *type* is 2, the macro is a command macro. If *type* is 3, the item is not a macro. The default value for *type* is 3. The *shortcut* argument specifies the shortcut key for a macro. *Hidden* is either TRUE or FALSE and determines if the name is hidden (TRUE) or not (FALSE or omitted). *Category* is the category of the function. *Category* can be either text or a number representing the existing categories in the Function Category list box, shown here within the Paste Function dialog box:

Categories are numbered starting with 1. If *category* is given as text it must exactly match the name in the Function Category list box; otherwise Excel will create a new custom category.

The question mark version of this function opens the dialog box. The arguments set the defaults in the dialog box. The version without the question mark does not open the dialog box, but performs the function with the settings that you pass as arguments.

See Also

DELETE.NAME	Deletes a defined name	Macro Function

FORMULA DEFINE NAME	Equivalent command	Menu Command
NAMES	Returns defined names	Macro Function

DEFINE.STYLE(*style,[number],[font],[alignment],[border],[pattern], [protection]*)

DEFINE.STYLE?(*[style],[number],[font],[alignment],[border],[pattern], [protection]*)

Macro Function

Using DEFINE.STYLE is the same as selecting Style from the Format menu, then clicking on the Define button in the Style dialog box. There are six other versions of this function. Each version defines a different style attribute. This particular version of DEFINE.STYLE allows you to define a style based on the formatting of the active cell. *Style* is the name of the style that you are defining. The remaining arguments correspond to the check boxes in the Style dialog box, which is shown here:

The check box arguments are either TRUE or FALSE. If TRUE, that attribute of the active cell is assigned to the style you are defining. If FALSE, that aspect of the cell's formatting is not assigned to the style.

The question mark version of this function opens the dialog box and the arguments set the dialog box defaults. The version without the question mark does not open the dialog box, but performs the function with the settings that you pass as arguments.

See Also

APPLY.STYLE	Applies a style	Macro Function
DELETE.STYLE	Deletes a style	Macro Function
FORMAT STYLE	Related command	Menu Command
MERGE.STYLE	Merges a style from another document	Macro Function

DEFINE.STYLE(*style, attribute, number-format*)

Macro Function

Using DEFINE.STYLE is the same as selecting Style from the Format menu, then clicking on the Define button in the Style dialog box. There are six other versions of this function. Each version defines a different style attribute. This version defines the number format and performs the same action as clicking on the Number button. The *style* argument is the name of the style that you are defining. The *attribute* argument must be 2. The *number-format* argument is the format given as a text string. The Style dialog box is shown here:

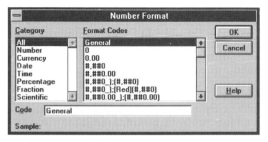

See Also

APPLY.STYLE	Applies a style	Macro Function
DELETE.STYLE	Deletes a style	Macro Function
FORMAT STYLE	Related command	Menu Command
MERGE.STYLE	Merges a style from another document	Macro Function

DEFINE.STYLE(*style, attribute, font, size, bold, italic, underline, strikethrough, color, outline, shadow*)

Macro Function

Using DEFINE.STYLE is the same as selecting Style from the Format menu, then clicking on the Define button in the Style dialog box. There are six other versions of this function. Each version defines a different style attribute. This version defines the font and is the same as clicking on the Font button. The *style* argument is the name of the style that you are defining. The *attribute* argument must be 3. The *font* argument is the name of the font given as a text string. The Font dialog box is shown here:

The *size* argument determines the size of the font, in points. The *bold, italic, underline,* and *strikethrough* arguments are either TRUE or FALSE and indicate whether the corresponding attribute is assigned to the style. The *color* argument indicates the color of the font. This table lists the possible values for *color:*

Color	Description
0	Automatic
1	Black
2	White
3	Red
4	Green
5	Blue
6	Yellow
7	Magenta
8	Cyan
9	Dark Red
10	Dark Green
11	Dark Blue
12	Light Brown
13	Purple
14	Dark Cyan
15	Light Grey
16	Grey

See Also

APPLY.STYLE	Applies a style	Macro Function
DELETE.STYLE	Deletes a style	Macro Function
FORMAT STYLE	Related command	Menu Command
MERGE.STYLE	Merges a style from another document	Macro Function

D

DEFINE.STYLE(*style, attribute, horizontal-alignment, wrap, vertical-alignment, orientation*)

Macro Function

Using DEFINE.STYLE is the same as selecting Style from the Format menu, then clicking on the Define button in the Style dialog box. There are six other versions of this function. Each version defines a different style attribute. This version defines the alignment and performs the same action as clicking on the Alignment button. The *style* argument is the name of the style that you are defining. The *attribute* argument must be 4. The Alignment dialog box is shown here:

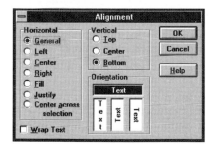

The *horizontal-alignment* argument is a number corresponding to the following alignment alternatives:

Number	Horizontal Alignment
1	General
2	Left
3	Center
4	Right
5	Fill
6	Justify
7	Center across selection

The *wrap* argument is either TRUE or FALSE. If *wrap* is TRUE, the text is wrapped within the cell. Otherwise, the text is not wrapped.

The *vertical-alignment* argument is a number corresponding to the following alignment alternatives:

Number	Vertical Alignment
1	Top
2	Center
3	Bottom

The *orientation* argument is a number that determines the orientation of the text. The following alternatives are available:

Number	Orientation
0	Horizontal
1	Vertical
2	Read from the right
3	Read from the left

See Also

APPLY.STYLE	Applies a style	Macro Function
DELETE.STYLE	Deletes a style	Macro Function
FORMAT STYLE	Related command	Menu Command
MERGE.STYLE	Merges a style from another document	Macro Function

DEFINE.STYLE(*style, attribute, left, right, top, bottom, left-color, right-color, top-color, bottom-color*)

Macro Function

Using DEFINE.STYLE is the same as selecting Style from the Format menu, then clicking on the Define button in the Style dialog box. There are six other versions of this function. Each version defines a different style attribute. This version defines the border and performs the same action as clicking on the Border button. The *style* argument is the name of the style that you are defining. The *attribute* argument must be 5. The Border dialog box is shown here:

D

The *left, right, top,* and *bottom* arguments are numbers that indicate the type of line for that part of a border. The following table lists the possible alternatives for these arguments:

Number	Type of Line
0	None
1	Thin line
2	Medium line
3	Dashed line
4	Dotted line
5	Thick line
6	Double line
7	Hairline

The *left-color, right-color, top-color,* and *bottom-color* arguments are numbers that indicate the color of the border. The possible values for these arguments are listed here:

Number	Color
0	Automatic
1	Black
2	White
3	Red
4	Green
5	Blue
6	Yellow
7	Magenta
8	Cyan

Number	Color
9	Dark Red
10	Dark Green
11	Dark Blue
12	Light Brown
13	Purple
14	Dark Cyan
15	Light Grey
16	Grey

See Also

APPLY.STYLE	Applies a style	Macro Function
DELETE.STYLE	Deletes a style	Macro Function
FORMAT STYLE	Related command	Menu Command
MERGE.STYLE	Merges a style from another document	Macro Function

DEFINE.STYLE(*style, attribute, pattern, foreground, background*)

Macro Function

Using DEFINE.STYLE is the same as selecting Style from the Format menu, then clicking on the Define button in the Style dialog box. There are six other versions of this function. Each version defines a different style attribute. This version defines the pattern used and performs the same action as clicking on the Patterns button. The *style* argument is the name of the style that you are defining. The *attribute* argument must be 6.

The *pattern* argument is a value that indicates the pattern style. The possible values for pattern are numbers from 0 to 18, and correspond to the patterns in the Patterns dialog box (shown in Figure D-16) that appears when you select Patterns from the Format menu.

The *foreground* and *background* arguments are numbers that indicate the color used for the foreground and background. *Foreground* is the color of the fill pattern. If the foreground pattern is solid, the fill will be the color indicated by *foreground*. If the pattern is not solid, the fill pattern uses both the foreground and background colors. The possible values for these arguments are shown here:

Number	Color
0	Automatic
1	Black
2	White
3	Red
4	Green
5	Blue
6	Yellow
7	Magenta
8	Cyan
9	Dark Red
10	Dark Green
11	Dark Blue
12	Light Brown
13	Purple
14	Dark Cyan
15	Light Grey
16	Grey

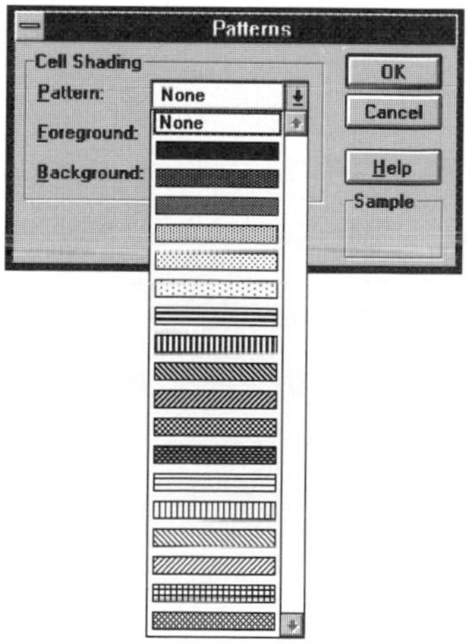

D

Figure D-16.   *The Patterns dialog box*

See Also

APPLY.STYLE	Applies a style	Macro Function
DELETE.STYLE	Deletes a style	Macro Function
FORMAT STYLE	Related command	Menu Command
MERGE.STYLE	Merges a style from another document	Macro Function

DEFINE.STYLE(*style, attribute, locked, hidden*)

Macro Function

Using DEFINE.STYLE is the same as selecting Style from the Format menu, then clicking on the Define button in the Style dialog box. There are six other versions of this function. Each version defines a different style attribute. This version defines the protection status and performs the same action as clicking on the Protection button. *Style* argument is the name of the style that you are defining. *Attribute* must be 7. The Cell Protection dialog box is shown here:

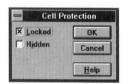

The *locked* and *hidden* arguments are either TRUE or FALSE and indicate whether the cells affected by the style are locked or hidden.

See Also

APPLY.STYLE	Applies a style	Macro Function
DELETE.STYLE	Deletes a style	Macro Function
FORMAT STYLE	Related command	Menu Command
MERGE.STYLE	Merges a style from another document	Macro Function

DEGREES(*X*)

Function   New to Version 4.0

DEGREES converts *X* from radians to degrees. Since it is an add-in function, the first time you use it you may briefly see a #REF! error while Excel loads the macro that runs the function.

Example

=DEGREES(1) returns 57.29578 degrees.

See Also

RADIANS Converts degrees to radians Function

DELETE.ARROW()

Macro Function

DELETE.ARROW deletes an arrow from a chart and performs the same action as choosing the Chart Delete Arrow menu option. The arrow must be selected in order for DELETE.ARROW to work. If no arrow is selected, DELETE.ARROW returns a #VALUE! error.

See Also

ADD.ARROW Adds an arrow to a chart Macro Function

DELETE.BAR(X)

Macro Function

DELETE.BAR deletes the menu bar specified by X. The menu bar must have previously been added with the ADD.BAR function. X is the number of the menu bar returned by ADD.BAR.

See Also

ADD.BAR Adds a menu bar Macro Function
SHOW.BAR Displays a menu bar Macro Function

DELETE.COMMAND(*bar-number, menu, command*)

Macro Function

DELETE.COMMAND deletes a command from a menu. *Bar-number* is the number of the menu bar from which you want to delete the command. *Menu* is the menu that you want to delete the command from; it can be a name or the number of the menu. Menus are numbered starting with 1 on the left. *Command* is the name or number of the command that you want to delete. Commands are numbered starting with 1 at the top.

See Also

ADD.COMMAND	Adds a command to a menu	Macro Function

DELETE.DIRECTORY(*path*)

Function   **New to Version 4.0**

DELETE.DIRECTORY deletes the directory specified by *path*. The directory in *path* must be empty, should be given as a string in quotation marks, and can be a full path. It can also be a directory name without the full path if the directory is a subdirectory of the current directory.

DELETE.DIRECTORY is an add-in function. The first time you use it within an Excel session, you will have to load FILEFNS.XLA from your \EXCEL\LIBRARY\ subdirectory. Do this with File Open, change to the \EXCEL\LIBRARY\subdirectory, and double-click on FILEFNS.XLA. If you use DELETE.DIRECTORY and FILEFNS.XLA is not loaded, you will get a #NAME? error.

When DELETE.DIRECTORY successfully deletes a directory, it returns a TRUE.

Example

=DELETE.DIRECTORY("C:\DATA\TEMP") deletes the DATA\TEMP directory from drive C.

See Also

CREATE.DIRECTORY	Creates a new directory	Macro Function
FILE.DELETE	Deletes a file	Macro Function

DELETE.FORMAT(*string*)

Macro Function

DELETE.FORMAT deletes a custom format and produces the same result as choosing the Format Number option, selecting a custom format, and clicking on the Delete button. *String* is the custom format that you want to delete. It should be enclosed in quotation marks. All cells formatted with the custom format that you delete are reformatted with the General format.

Example

=DELETE.FORMAT("0.0%") deletes the custom format 0.0% and applies the General format to all cells that were formatted with 0.0%.

See Also

FORMAT NUMBER	Related command	Menu Command
FORMAT.NUMBER	Related function	Macro Function

D

DELETE.MENU(*bar-number, menu*)

Macro Function

DELETE.MENU deletes a menu from a menu bar. The *bar-number* is the number of the menu bar from which you want to delete the menu. The *menu* argument is the name or number of the menu you want to delete. After you delete the menu, all the menus to its right are shifted one position to the left, so that their numbers are decreased by 1.

See Also

ADD.MENU	Adds a menu	Macro Function

DELETE.NAME(*name*)

Macro Function

DELETE.NAME deletes a previously defined range name. This is the same as choosing Formula Define Name, selecting a name, and clicking on the Delete button. The *name* argument is the name that you want to delete, enclosed within quotation marks.

Example

=DELETE.NAME("Sales") deletes the name "Sales" from the active document.

See Also

DEFINE.NAME	Defines a name	Macro Function
FORMULA DEFINE NAME	Related command	Menu Command

DELETE.OVERLAY()

Macro Function

The DELETE.OVERLAY macro function deletes the overlay chart in the active chart window, placing all the series from the overlay chart onto the main chart. This is the same as choosing the Chart Delete Overlay menu option.

See Also

ADD.OVERLAY	Adds an overlay to a chart	Macro Function
CHART DELETE OVERLAY	Equivalent command	Menu Command

DELETE.STYLE(*style*)

Macro Function

DELETE.STYLE deletes a style from the active document, and applying the Normal style to all cells formatted with the style you are deleting. The *style* argument is the name of the style, given as a text string in quotation marks.

See Also

DEFINE.STYLE	Defines a style	Macro Function
FORMAT STYLE	Related command	Menu Command

DELETE.TOOL(*bar,position*)

Macro Function   **New to Version 4.0**

DELETE.TOOL deletes a tool from a toolbar. This is the same as dragging a tool off a toolbar. The *bar* argument is either the number of a built-in toolbar, or the name of a custom toolbar enclosed within quotation marks. The built-in toolbars are numbered as follows.

Bar	Toolbar
1	Standard
2	Formatting
3	Utility
4	Chart
5	Drawing
6	Excel 3.0

Bar	Toolbar
7	Macro
8	Macro stop recording
9	Macro paused

The *position* argument indicates the tool's position on the toolbar. Position 1 is the leftmost or the top tool.

See Also

ADD.TOOL	Adds a tool to a bar	Macro Function

DELETE.TOOLBAR(*bar*)

Macro Function   **New to Version 4.0**

DELETE.TOOLBAR deletes the toolbar specified by *bar*. The *bar* argument is either the number of a built-in toolbar, or the name of a custom toolbar enclosed within quotation marks. The built-in toolbars are numbered as follows.

Bar	Toolbar
1	Standard
2	Formatting
3	Utility
4	Chart
5	Drawing
6	Excel 3.0
7	Macro
8	Macro stop recording
9	Macro paused

See Also

ADD.TOOLBAR	Adds a toolbar	Macro Function

DELTA(*X,[Y]*)

Function   **New to Version 4.0**

DELTA checks whether *X* and *Y* are equal. If they are, DELTA returns 1; otherwise, it returns 0. If *Y* is not given, the default value is 0.

DELTA is an add-in function. The first time you use it, you may see a #REF! error briefly while Excel loads the macro that runs the function.

Example

=DELTA(7,8) returns 0.

DEMOTE(*[rc]*)
DEMOTE?(*[rc]*)

Macro Function

DEMOTE demotes the currently selected rows or columns of an outline. If *rc* is 1, rows are demoted. If *rc* is 2, columns are demoted. If *rc* is omitted, 1 (rows) is the default value.

The question mark version of this function opens the dialog box. The arguments set the dialog box defaults. The version without the question mark does not open the dialog box, but performs the function according to the settings that you pass as arguments.

DEREF(*reference*)

Macro Function

DEREF returns the value of the cell or range of cells referred to by *reference*. If *reference* refers to a range, the value returned is an array.

DESCR(*input, output, [rc], [labels], [statistics], [large], [small], [confidence]*)

Macro Function   **New to Version 4.0**

DESCR returns descriptive statistics for the *input* range. *Output* should be the cell in the upper-left corner of the range in which you want to place the statistics. *Rc* indicates whether the data is in rows or columns. If the data is in rows, *rc* should be "R". If the data is in columns, *rc* should be "C". If *rc* is omitted, the default value is "C".

The *labels* argument is either TRUE or FALSE. If *labels* is TRUE, the labels are located in the first row or column of the input range, depending on how the data is structured. If *labels* is FALSE, no labels are included. The default value for *labels* is FALSE.

Statistics is either TRUE or FALSE. If *statistics* is TRUE, summary statistics are returned. If *statistics* is FALSE or not present, summary statistics are not returned.

Large is a number X. If the *large* argument is present, then DESCR returns the Xth largest data point. If *large* is not given, this information is not returned.

Small is a number X. If the *small* argument is present, then DESCR returns the Xth smallest data point. If *small* is not given, this information is not returned.

Confidence is the confidence level of the mean and has a default value of 95%. The *confidence* argument causes the confidence interval to be returned.

DESCR is an add-in function. The first time you use it, you may see a #REF! error briefly while Excel loads the macro that runs the function.

See Also

AVERAGE	Returns the average	Function
MAX	Returns the maximum value	Function
MEDIAN	Returns the median	Function
MIN	Returns the minimum value	Function

DEVSQ(*X1, X2,...*)

Function   New to Version 4.0

DEVSQ returns the sum of the squares of deviations of the set of numbers (X1, X2, ...) from the sample mean of those numbers. You can include up to 30 numbers. Instead of using a list of numbers, you can also use an array or a reference to an array as the argument for this function.

Example

=DEVSQ(1,2,3,6,7,9) returns 49.3333.

See Also

AVEDEV	Returns the average deviation	Function
STDEV	Returns the standard deviation	Function
VAR	Returns the variance	Function

DGET(*input-range, field, criteria*)

Function

DGET extracts a single value from the field specified in a database based on the *criteria*. If there is more than one match to *criteria*, the error value #NUM! is returned. If there is no match to the *criteria*, #VALUE! is returned.

The *input-range* argument is a range or range name that contains the database. If the database is defined with the Data Set Database command, the database is named "Database."

The *field* argument is the field in the database on which you want to perform the function. If you give the field name as text, you should enclose it within quotation marks. The *field* argument may also be a number, where the leftmost or top field is numbered 1, the next field is numbered 2, and so on.

The *criteria-range* argument is a range or range name that contains the criteria. If the criteria is defined using the Data Set Criteria command, the criteria range is named "Criteria." If you want to perform a function on all records in a database, make sure there is a blank line below the field names in the criteria range.

See Also

DATABASE FUNCTIONS	Explains database functions	Concept

DIALOG.BOX(*reference*)

Macro Function

DIALOG.BOX displays the dialog box described in the area of a macro sheet given by the *reference* argument. If the *reference* is invalid, DIALOG.BOX returns the error #VALUE!. The *reference* area must a minimum of two rows high and must be seven columns wide. The seven columns include the following:

Column	Contents
1	Item number
2	Horizontal position
3	Vertical position
4	Width
5	Height
6	Text
7	Result or default value

The first row contains the specifications for the dialog box itself. Column 1 of the first row is usually blank but can contain a reference for the Help button. Column 6 of the first row contains the name of the dialog box and column 7 can contain the position number of the default item. The remaining rows of the *reference* area contain the specifications for the items in the dialog box such as buttons, text boxes, list boxes, and check boxes. Many rows are paired, with one being a text label for the other. For example, a pair of rows could be a text box and its label.

You can have the following types of items in a dialog box:

Item Number	Type of Item
1	Default OK button
2	Cancel button
3	OK button
4	Default Cancel button
5	Text
6	Text edit box
7	Integer edit box
8	Number edit box
9	Formula edit box
10	Reference edit box
11	Option button group
12	Option button
13	Check box
14	Group box
15	List box
16	Linked list box
17	Icon
18	Linked file list box
19	Linked drive and directory list box
20	Directory text box
21	Drop-down list box
22	Drop-down exit/list box
23	Picture button
24	Help button

If an item number has 100 added to it and the associated item is selected, control is returned to the calling macro, but the dialog box is still displayed. This allows you to change the dialog box or display a message. Edit boxes, Help buttons, text, icons, and group boxes cannot have 100 added to their item numbers. If an item number has 200 added to it, the associated item is dimmed and cannot be selected.

The easiest way to build a *reference* area is to use the Excel Dialog Editor.

See Also

ALERT	Displays a message in a dialog box	Macro Function
INPUT	Displays an input dialog box	Macro Function

DIRECTORIES(*[path]*)

Macro Function   **New to Version 4.0**

DIRECTORIES returns a list of subdirectories of the directory specified by *path,* or a list of subdirectories of the current directory if the *path* argument is omitted. The list of directories is presented as a horizontal array.

  DIRECTORIES is an add-in function. The first time you use it within an Excel session, you will have to load FILEFNS.XLA from your \EXCEL\LIBRARY\subdirectory. Do this with File Open, change to the \EXCEL\LIBRARY\ subdirectory, and double-click on FILEFNS.XLA. If you try to use DIRECTORIES and FILEFNS.XLA is not loaded, you will get a #NAME? error.

Example

=DIRECTORIES() returns an array containing all the subdirectories of the current directory.

See Also

CREATE.DIRECTORY	Creates a directory	Macro Function
DELETE.DIRECTORY	Deletes a directory	Macro Function
DIRECTORY	Sets the current directory	Macro Function

DIRECTORY(*[path]*)

Macro Function

DIRECTORY causes the current drive and directory to be set to the drive and directory specified by *path* and returns that name as text. The current drive and directory is returned if *path* is omitted.

Example

DIRECTORY("C:\data") sets the current directory to C:\DATA.

See Also

CREATE.DIRECTORY	Creates a directory	Macro Function
DELETE.DIRECTORY	Deletes a directory	Macro Function
DIRECTORIES	Returns the names of the subdirectories	Macro Function

DISABLE.INPUT(*test*)

Macro Function

DISABLE.INPUT disables all input from the keyboard and mouse if *test* is TRUE. If *test* is FALSE, input is enabled again. Your macro must have both forms of this function or you cannot regain control without restarting your computer.

See Also

CANCEL.KEY   Prevents macro interruption   Macro Function

D

DISC(*settlement-date, maturity-date, price, redemption, basis-code*)

Function   New to Version 4.0

DISC returns a security's discount rate. *Settlement-date* is a date serial number for the security's settlement date. *Maturity-date* is a date serial number for the maturity date of the security. *Price* is the price per $100 value. *Redemption* is the redemption per $100 value. *Basis code* is a number identifying the days-per-month and days-per-year. If *basis-code* is omitted, the default is 0. The possible basis codes and their meanings are listed here:

Basis-Code	Day Count
0	30/360
1	Actual/Actual
2	Actual/360
3	Actual/365

DISC is an add in function. The first time you use it, you may see a #REF! error briefly while Excel loads the macro that runs the function.

Example

=DISC(DATE(93,1,1),DATE(93,6,1),95,100,3) returns .120861 or 12%.

See Also

PRICEDISC   Returns the price   Function
                   discount

YIELDDISC   Returns the yield   Function
                   discount

DISPLAY(*[formulas],[gridlines],[headings],[zeros],[color],[reserved],*
[outline],[page-breaks],[objects])
DISPLAY?(*[formulas],[gridlines],[headings],[zeros],[color],[reserved],*
[outline],[page-breaks],[objects])

Macro Function

DISPLAY controls what the screen displays. There are two versions of this function. The first version, described here, performs the same action as the Options Display menu option. The arguments correspond to the items on the Display Options dialog box shown in Figure D-17.

Formulas, gridlines, headings, zeros, outline, and *page-breaks* are all either TRUE or FALSE. A screen element is displayed if the associated argument is TRUE and not displayed if the argument is FALSE. *Formulas* and *page-breaks* have a default of FALSE; the others have a default of TRUE. If an argument is omitted, its status is unchanged. The *color* argument is a number from 0 to 16; the default is 0. The description of each color number is as follows.

Color	Description
0	Automatic
1	Black
2	White
3	Red
4	Green
5	Blue
6	Yellow
7	Magenta
8	Cyan
9	Dark Red
10	Dark Green
11	Dark Blue
12	Light Brown
13	Purple
14	Dark Cyan
15	Light Grey
16	Grey

Figure D-17.   *The Display Options dialog box*

The *reserved* argument is not used in the United States. The *objects* argument is one of the following codes for displaying objects:

Code	Meaning
1 (the default)	Show all
2	Show placeholders
3	Hide all

The question mark version of this function opens the dialog box. The arguments set the dialog box defaults. The version without the question mark does not open the dialog box, but performs the function according to the settings that you pass as arguments.

See Also

OPTIONS DISPLAY   Equivalent command   Menu Command

DISPLAY(*[cell]*,*[formula]*,*[value]*,*[format]*,*[protection]*,*[names]*, *[precedents]*,*[dependents]*,*[note]*)

Macro Function

DISPLAY controls the screen display. There are two versions of this function. The second version, described here, performs the same action as the Info menu. Each argument corresponds to an option on the Info menu. If you omit an argument, its status is unchanged. All arguments except *precedents* and *dependents* must be either TRUE, FALSE, or omitted. Supplying an argument that is TRUE is the same as enabling that option on the Info menu. The *precedents* and *dependents* arguments can be either 0, 1, or 2. If the argument is 0, no levels are listed. If the argument is 1, direct references are listed. If the argument is 2, all reference levels are listed.

DMAX(*input-range,field,criteria-range*)

Function

DMAX searches the input range for all matches to the criteria as defined in the criteria range, and then returns the largest value in the named field.

The *input-range* argument is a range or range name that contains the database. If the database is defined with the Data Set Database command, it is named "Database."

The *field* argument is the field in the database on which you want to perform the function. If you give the field name as text, you should enclose it within quotation marks. The *field* argument may also be a number, where the leftmost or top field is numbered 1, the next field is numbered 2, and so on.

The *criteria-range* argument is a range or range name that contains the criteria. If the criteria is defined using the Data Set Criteria command, it is named "Criteria." If you want to perform a function on all records in a database, make sure to include a blank line below the field names in the *criteria range*.

Example

=DMAX(INPUT,"COST",CRIT-RANGE) searches the INPUT database for the matching records defined in CRIT-RANGE. Then it returns the largest value in the COST field.

See Also

DATABASE FUNCTIONS	Explains database functions	Concept
DMIN	Related function	Function

DMIN(*input-range, field, criteria-range*)

Function

DMIN searches the input range for all matches to the criteria defined in the criteria range and then returns the smallest value found in the named field.

The input-range argument is a range or range name that contains the database. If the database is defined with the Data Set Database command, it is named "Database."

The *field* argument is the field in the database on which you want to perform the function. The name of the field, if given as text, should be enclosed in quotation marks. The *field* argument may also be a number, where the leftmost or top field is numbered 1, the next field is numbered 2, and so on.

The *criteria-range* argument is a range or range name that contains the criteria. If the criteria is defined using the Data Set Criteria command, the *criteria range* is named "Criteria." If you want to perform a function on all records in a database, make sure to include a blank line below the field names in the criteria range.

Example

=DMIN(INPUT,"COST",CRIT-RANGE) searches INPUT for the matching records defined in CRIT-RANGE, and then returns the smallest value found in the COST field.

See Also

DATABASE FUNCTIONS	Explains database functions	Concept
DMAX	Related function	Function

DOCUMENTS(*[add-ins], [names]*)

Macro Function

DOCUMENTS returns a horizontal array containing the names of all open documents in alphabetical order. *Add-ins* is a number that determines whether add-in documents are included. The possible values for *add-ins* are as follows.

Number	Meaning
1 (the default)	All but add-ins are returned
2	Add-ins only are returned
3	All including add-ins are returned

Names is a list of documents names that are to be returned. This argument can include the standard wildcard characters of ? to replace any single character and * to replace any number of characters. If *names* is omitted, all document names are returned.

See Also

FILES	Returns all the filenames	Macro Function
GET.DOCUMENT	Returns document information	Macro Function

DOLLAR(*number,[digits]*)

Function

DOLLAR rounds *number* off to the number of digits to the right of the decimal point specified by *digits,* and then converts the rounded number to text in the currency format $#,##0.00;($#,##0.00). If you omit the *digits* argument, the default value is 2.

Example

=DOLLAR(5.00234,2) returns the string "$5.00".

See Also

FIXED	Converts a number to text	Function
FORMAT NUMBER	Related command	Menu Command

DOLLARDE(*fraction,denominator*)

Function   New to Version 4.0

DOLLARDE converts a fractional dollar amount, such as you might have in stock prices, to a decimal amount. *Fraction* is the amount in fraction form and *denominator* is the denominator of the fraction.

DOLLARDE is an add-in function. The first time you use it, you may see a #REF! error briefly while Excel loads the macro that runs the function.

Example

=DOLLARDE(3.4,5) returns 3.8.

See Also

DOLLAR	Converts a number to currency	Function
DOLLARFR	Converts decimal currency to fraction currency	Function

---

DOLLARFR(*decimal, denominator*)

Function   **New to Version 4.0**

DOLLARFR converts a decimal dollar amount to a fraction that might be used in a stock price. *Decimal* is the amount in decimal form and *denominator* is the number to use in the denominator of the fraction.

DOLLARFR is an add-in function. The first time you use it, you may see a #REF! error briefly while Excel loads the macro that runs the function.

Example

=DOLLARFR(3.4,5) returns 3.2.

See Also

DOLLAR	Converts a number to currency	Function
DOLLARDE	Converts fraction currency to decimal currency	Function

---

DPRODUCT(*input-range, field, criteria-range*)

Function

DPRODUCT searches the input range for all matches to the criteria defined in *criteria range* and then returns the product of the values found in the named field.

Input-range is a range or range name that contains the database. If the database is defined with the Data Set Database command, it is named "Database."

The *field* argument is the field in the database on which you want to perform the function. If you give the field name as text, you should enclose it within quotation marks. The *field* argument may also be a number, where the leftmost or top field is numbered 1, the next field is numbered 2, and so on.

The *criteria-range* argument is a range or range name that contains the criteria. If the criteria is defined using the Data Set Criteria command, the *criteria range* is named "Criteria." If you want to perform a function on all records in a database, make sure to include a blank line below the field names in the criteria range.

Example

=DPRODUCT(INPUT,"COST",CRIT-RANGE) searches the INPUT database for matching records as defined in CRIT-RANGE. Then it multiplies the values in the COST field and returns the product.

See Also

DATABASE FUNCTIONS	Explains database functions	Concept

DSTDEV(*input-range, field, criteria-range*)

Function

DSTDEV searches the input range for all matches to the criteria defined in the criteria range and then calculates the sample standard deviation of values in the named field. With a small database, DSTDEV is more accurate than DSTDEVP.

The *input-range* argument is a range or range name that contains the database. If the database is defined with the Data Set Database command, it is named "Database."

The *field* argument is the field in the database on which you want to perform the function. If you give the field name as text, you should enclose it within quotation marks. The *field* argument may also be a number, where the leftmost or top field is numbered 1, the next field is numbered 2, and so on.

The *criteria-range* argument is a range or range name that contains the criteria. If the criteria is defined using the Data Set Criteria command, the criteria range is named "Criteria." If you want to perform a function on all records in a database, make sure to include a blank line below the field names in the criteria range.

Example

=DSTDEVP(INPUT,"INCOME",CRIT-RANGE) searches the INPUT database for matching records as defined in CRIT-RANGE. Then it calculates the estimated standard deviation of a sample of values in the INCOME field.

See Also

DATABASE FUNCTIONS	Explains database functions	Concept
DSTDEVP	Related function	Function

DSTDEVP(*input-range, field, criteria-range*)

Function

DSTDEVP searches the input range for all matches to the criteria defined in the criteria range and then calculates the population standard deviation of all the values in the named field. With a large database, DSTDEVP is more accurate than DSTDEV.

The *input-range* argument is a range or range name that contains the database. If the database is defined with the Data Set Database command, it is named "Database."

The *field* argument is the field in the database on which you want to perform the function. If you give the field name as text, you should enclose it within quotation marks. The *field* argument may also be a number, where the leftmost or top field is numbered 1, the next field is numbered 2, and so on.

The *criteria-range* argument is a range or range name that contains the criteria. If the criteria is defined using the Data Set Criteria command, the criteria range is named "Criteria." If you want to perform a function on all records in a database, make sure to include a blank line below the field names in the criteria range.

Example

=DSTDEVP(INPUT,"INCOME",CRIT-RANGE) searches the INPUT database for matching records as defined in CRIT-RANGE and then calculates the population standard deviation of all of the values in the INCOME field.

See Also

DATABASE FUNCTIONS	Explains database functions	Concept
DSTDEV	Related function	Function

DSUM(*input-range, field, criteria-range*)

Function

DSUM searches the input range for all values matching the criteria defined in the criteria range and then sums the values in the named field.

The input-range argument is a range or range name that contains the database. If the database is defined with the Data Set Database command, it is named "Database."

The *field* argument is the field in the database on which you want to perform the function. If you give the field name as text, you should enclose it within quotation marks. The *field* argument may also be a number, where the leftmost or top field is numbered 1, the next field is numbered 2, and so on.

The *criteria-range* argument is a range or range name that contains the criteria. If the criteria is defined using the Data Set Criteria command, the criteria range is named "Criteria." If you want to perform a function on all records in a database, make sure to include a blank line below the field names in the criteria range.

Example

=DSUM(INPUT,"SALESAMT",CRIT-RANGE) searches the INPUT database for records matching the one defined in CRIT-RANGE. Then it adds the values in the SALESAMT field to calculate the total.

See Also

DATABASE FUNCTIONS	Explains database functions	Concept

DUPLICATE()

Macro Function

DUPLICATE duplicates the selected object.

See Also

COPY	Selects for copying	Macro Function
PASTE	Pastes active selection	Macro Function

DURATION(*settlement-date, maturity-date, rate, yield, payments, [basis-code]*)

Function   **New to Version 4.0**

DURATION returns the Macauley duration, the weighted average of the present value of the cash flow. The *settlement-date* is a date serial number for the security's settlement date. *Maturity-date* is a date serial number for the security's maturity date. *Rate* is the annual coupon rate. *Yield* is the annual yield. *Payments* is a number indicating the number of payments per year:

Number	Payment Cycle
1	Annual
2	Semi-annual
4	Quarterly

The *basis-code* indicates the number of days per month and per year, as shown in this table:

Basis-Code	Day Count
0 (the default)	30/360
1	Actual/Actual
2	Actual/360
3	Actual/365

D

DVAR(*input-range, field, criteria-range*)

Function

DVAR searches the input range for values matching those defined in the criteria range and then returns the estimated variance of a sample of values in the named field. With small databases, the results are more accurate than DVARP.

The *input-range* argument is a range or range name that contains the database. If the database is defined with the Data Set Database command, it is named "Database."

The *field* argument is the field in the database on which you want to perform the function. If you give the field name as text, you should enclose it within quotation marks. The *field* argument may also be a number, where the leftmost or top field is numbered 1, the next field is numbered 2, and so on.

The *criteria-range* argument is a range or range name that contains the criteria. If the criteria is defined using the Data Set Criteria command, the criteria range is named "Criteria." If you want to perform a function on all records in a database, make sure to include a blank line below the field names in the criteria range.

Example

=DVAR(INPUT,"POP",CRIT-RANGE) searches the INPUT database for the values defined in CRIT-RANGE. When matches are found, it calculates the variance of a sample of the POP field.

See Also

DATABASE FUNCTIONS	Explains database functions	Concept
DVARP	Related function	Function

DVARP(*input-range, field, criteria-range*)

Function

DVARP searches the input range for values matching those defined in the criteria range and then returns the population variance of all the values in the named field. With large databases, the results are more accurate with DVARP than they are with DVAR.

The *input-range* argument is a range or range name that contains the database. If the database is defined with the Data Set Database command, it is named "Database."

The *field* argument is the field in the database on which you want to perform the function. If you give the field name as text, you should enclose it within quotation marks. The *field* argument may also be a number, where the leftmost or top field is numbered 1, the next field is numbered 2, and so on.

The *criteria-range* argument is a range or range name that contains the criteria. If the criteria is defined using the Data Set Criteria command, the criteria range is named "Criteria." If you want to perform a function on all of the records in a database, make sure that you include a blank line below the field names in the criteria range.

Example

=DVARP(INPUT,"POP",CRIT-RANGE) searches the INPUT database for the values defined in CRIT-RANGE. When matches are found, it calculates the variance for the entire POP field.

See Also

DATABASE FUNCTIONS	Explains Excel database functions	Concept
DATA SET CRITERIA	Defines the selected range as the criteria range	Menu Command
DVAR	Related function	Function

E

ECHO(*[X]*)

Macro Function

ECHO disables screen updating while the macro is running if *X* is FALSE. It enables screen updating if *X* is TRUE. If *X* is omitted, screen updating is switched to the opposite state. Once the macro is done, screen updating is automatically turned on.

EDATE(*start-date,nu-months*)

Function

EDATE returns a date serial number that is determined by adding *nu-months* to the *start-date*. *Nu-months* can be positive or negative. EDATE is an add-in function. The first time that you use it, you may see a #REF! error while Excel loads the function.

Example

=EDATE(date(92,6,1),5) returns 33909, which is the serial number for 11/1/92.

See Also

EOMONTH	Returns the last day of a specified month	Function
NOW	Returns today's date serial number	Function
NETWORKDAYS	Returns the number of work days between two dates	Function
WORKDAY	Returns the date *X* work days before or after a given date	Function

EDIT

Menu

The Edit menu contains options that enable you to edit your document. You use the Edit menu to copy, move, and clear the contents of a cell or range of cells; to undo or repeat your last action; to duplicate a cell's entry across a row or up or down a column; and to insert and delete rows and columns. You can also use the Edit menu to copy certain attributes of a cell or range of cells, to insert graphic objects into a document, and to link documents. The Edit menu is shown here:

EDIT.COLOR(*color,[red],[green],[blue]*)
EDIT.COLOR?(*color,[red],[green],[blue]*)

Macro Function

Using EDIT.COLOR is the same as choosing the Options Color Palette menu option and then clicking on the Edit button. Excel's color palette contains 16 colors. If your system supports more than 16 colors, you can use EDIT.COLOR to replace one of the existing colors with a custom color. Anything formatted with the color you are replacing will be formatted with the new color.

The arguments *red, green,* and *blue* are all numbers from 0 to 255 that determine how much of each of these colors is in the new color. If *red, green,* and *blue* are all 0, the color will be black. If *red, green,* and *blue* are all 255, the color will be white.

The *color* argument is a number from 1 to 16. It represents the color on the color palette that you will be replacing with the new color.

The dialog box version of EDIT.COLOR displays your system's color dialog box.

See Also

COLOR.PALETTE	Allows a palette to be shared	Macro Function
OPTIONS COLOR PALETTE	Related command	Menu Command

EDIT COPY

Menu Command

➤   *Shortcut Key:* CTRL-INS

The Edit Copy menu option defines your selection so that you can paste it with either the Edit Paste or the Edit Paste Special option. You can use Edit Copy followed by Edit Paste or Edit Paste Special to copy text, numbers, and formulas from one location in a file to another location on a worksheet in memory. You can copy a single cell, a range in the current worksheet, a range in another worksheet, or characters from the formula bar.

To copy cells, you must first select the range—a rectangular area—that you want to copy. Then choose Edit Copy. Excel outlines the selection with a marquee. After selecting the cells to be copied, you need to paste them into their new location. To do this, move to the upper-left cell of the range that you want to copy to and press the ENTER key. Alternatively, you can use the Edit Paste or Edit Paste Special menu options. (For additional information, see the EDIT PASTE and EDIT PASTE SPECIAL entries later in this section).

You can copy characters to a chart from another chart or from the formula bar. First you must activate the chart you want to copy from. Choose the Edit Copy option. Activate the chart you want to copy to, and then choose Edit Paste or Edit Paste Special. (For more information, see EDIT PASTE and EDIT PASTE SPECIAL.)

See Also

COPYING	Explains copying	Concept
EDIT PASTE	Related command	Menu Command
EDIT PASTE SPECIAL	Related command	Menu Command

E

EDIT COPY PICTURE

Menu Command

The Edit Copy Picture menu option allows you to copy a pictorial representation of your current selection into the Windows Clipboard. This option only appears on the Edit menu if you hold down the SHIFT key as you select the menu. The Edit Copy Picture option appears instead of the Edit Copy option, as shown here:

Once you have the pictorial representation of part of a worksheet or a chart on the Clipboard, you can paste it into a document that was created using a word processor.

EDIT CUT

Menu Command

➤   *Shortcut Key:* SHIFT-DEL

The Edit Cut menu option allows you to define your selection so that you can move it with the Edit Paste or Edit Paste Special option. You can use Edit Cut followed by Edit Paste or Edit Paste Special to move text, numbers, and formulas from one location in a file to another location on a worksheet in memory. You can cut a single cell, a range in the current worksheet, a range in another worksheet, or characters from the formula bar.

To cut cells, you must first select the range—a rectangular area—you want to cut. Then choose Edit Cut. After defining the cells to be moved, you need to paste them into their new location. (For additional information, see EDIT PASTE and EDIT PASTE SPECIAL.)

When your active document is a chart, the Edit Cut option only works on characters in the formula bar.

See Also

EDIT PASTE	Related command	Menu Command
EDIT PASTE SPECIAL	Related command	Menu Command

EDIT DELETE

Menu Command

➤   *Shortcut Key:* CTRL-MINUS (–)

The Edit Delete menu option allows you to remove the cells in your selection from the worksheet. (In contrast, the Edit Clear command deletes cell contents without deleting the cells themselves.) The cells adjacent to the area selected for deletion will move over to fill in the space. If you delete one or more entire rows, Excel moves up the cells below the deleted area. If you delete one or more an entire columns, the cells to the right of the deleted area are moved to the left. If you delete a partial row or column, Excel asks you if you want to shift the remaining cells up or to the left.

NOTE: If you want to clear cells without actually deleting them—and without moving the cells located below them or to their right—use the Edit Clear option instead of Edit Delete.

See Also

CLEARING CELLS VS DELETING CELLS	Explains the difference	Concept
EDIT.DELETE	Equivalent function	Macro Function

EDIT.DELETE
EDIT.DELETE?(*X*)

Macro Function

EDIT.DELETE removes selected cells from the active worksheet. It is the same as the Edit Delete menu option. If *X* is 1, cells are shifted to the left. If *X* is 2, cells are shifted up. If *X* is 3, the entire row is deleted. If *X* is 4, the entire column is deleted. In the dialog box version (with the question mark), if the argument *X* is included, its value is used as the default for the dialog box that appears.

See Also

| CLEARING CELLS VS DELETING CELLS | Explains the difference | Concept |
| EDIT DELETE | Equivalent command | Menu Command |

EDIT FILL DOWN

Menu Command

➤   *Shortcut Key:* CTRL-D

The Edit Fill Down menu option allows you to copy the contents and formats from the top row (or rows) in a selection to the remaining cells in the selection below it. If there is existing data or formatting in the selection, it will be replaced by the formatting and data from the top row.

To fill down, select the cells that you want to fill, including the cell (or range of cells) at the top that contains the data you want to enter in the other selected cells. (See Figure E-1.) Choose the Edit Fill Down menu option, and the cell contents will be copied from the top cell or cells to all the remaining cells in the selection.

You can use the mouse to achieve the same effect if Cell Drag and Drop is turned on. Simply press CTRL and drag the fill handle in the lower-right corner of the cell

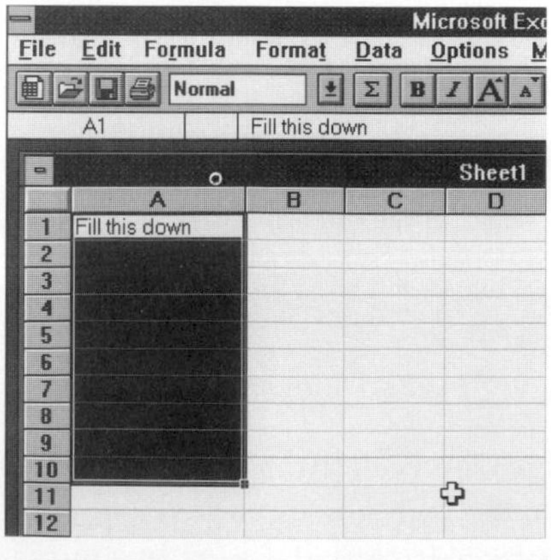

Figure E-1.   *Cells selected for Fill Down*

border. (You can activate Drag and Drop by choosing the Workspace option from the options menu, then checking the Drag and Drop check box.)

See Also

EDIT FILL LEFT	Fills left in the selection	Menu Command
EDIT FILL RIGHT	Fills right in the selection	Menu Command
EDIT FILL UP	Fills up in the selection	Menu Command

EDIT FILL GROUP

Menu Command

Edit Fill Group copies the current selection to all worksheets in the group declared by the Options Group Edit menu command. Edit Fill Group only appears on the Edit menu if you have previously defined a group. The cells are copied from the current selection to the same location in every worksheet in the group. When you choose the Edit Fill Group menu option, you'll see a dialog box that allows you to fill all information, just formulas, or just formats.

See Also

EDIT FILL DOWN	Fills down the selection	Menu Command
EDIT FILL LEFT	Fills left in the selection	Menu Command
EDIT FILL RIGHT	Fills right in the selection	Menu Command
EDIT FILL UP	Fills up in the selection	Menu Command

EDIT FILL LEFT

Menu Command

The Edit Fill Left menu option only appears on the Edit menu if you hold down the SHIFT key when you activate the menu. Edit Fill Left allows you to copy the contents and formats from the right row in a selection to the cells in the selection to the left of it. If there is data or formatting in the selection already, it will be replaced by the data and formatting from the rightmost row in the selection.

To fill left, select the cells that you want to fill, including the cell at the right containing the entry that you want to fill left, as shown in Figure E-2. Choose the Edit Fill Left menu option, and the entry will be copied from the right cell in the selection

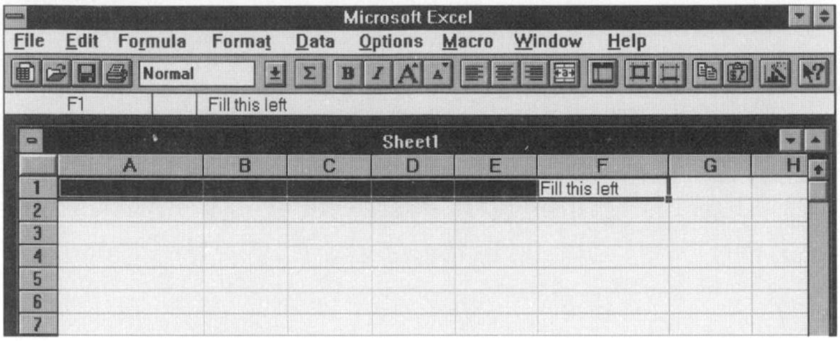

Figure E-2.   *Cells selected for Fill Left*

to all the cells in the selection. Remember to hold down the SHIFT key when activating the Edit menu.

Fill Left can also be accomplished with the mouse if Cell Drag and Drop is turned on in Options Workspace, by pressing CTRL and dragging the fill handle in the lower-right corner of the cell border.

See Also

EDIT FILL DOWN	Fills down the selection	Menu Command
EDIT FILL RIGHT	Fills right in the selection	Menu Command
EDIT FILL UP	Fills up the selection	Menu Command

EDIT FILL RIGHT

Menu Command

➤   *Shortcut Key:* CTRL-R

The Edit Fill Right menu option allows you to copy the contents and formats from the left row in a selection to the cells to its right in the selection. If there is existing data or formatting in the selection, it will be replaced by the data and formatting from the leftmost row in the selection.

To fill right, select the cells that you want to fill, including the cell at the left containing the entry that you want to duplicate in the cells to the right, as shown in Figure E-3. Choose the Edit Fill Right menu option, and the entry will be copied from the left cell in the selection to all the cells in the selection.

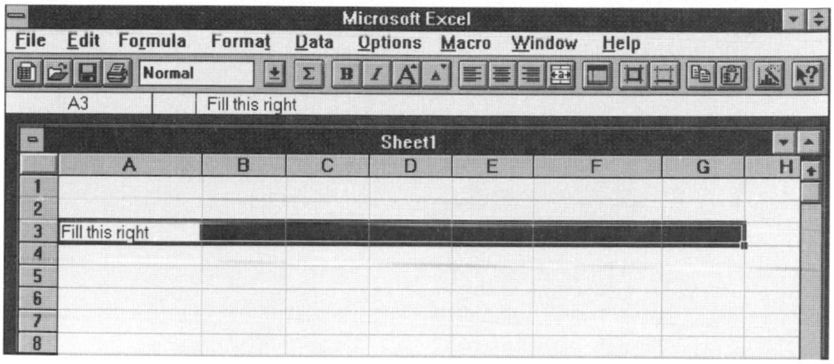

Figure E-3. *Cells selected for Fill Right*

You can accomplish the same thing with the mouse if Cell Drag and Drop is turned on in Options Workspace. Simply press CTRL and drag the fill handle in the lower-right corner of the cell border.

See Also

EDIT FILL DOWN	Fills down the selection	Menu Command
EDIT FILL LEFT	Fills left in the selection	Menu Command
EDIT FILL UP	Fills up in the selection	Menu Command

EDIT FILL UP

Menu Command

The Edit Fill Up menu option only appears on the Edit menu if you hold down the SHIFT key when you activate the menu. This option allows you to copy the contents and formats from the bottom row in a selection to the cells above it in the selection. If there is data or formatting in the selection already, it will be replaced by the data and formatting from the bottom row.

To fill up, select the cells that you want to fill, including the cell at the bottom containing the entry that you want to duplicate in the cells above, as shown in Figure E-4. Choose the Edit Fill Up menu option, and the entry will be copied from the bottom cell in the selection to all the cells in the selection. Remember to hold down the SHIFT key when activating the Edit menu.

You can achieve the same effect with the mouse if Cell Drag and Drop is turned on in Options Workspace. Simply press CTRL and drag the fill handle in the lower-right corner of the cell border.

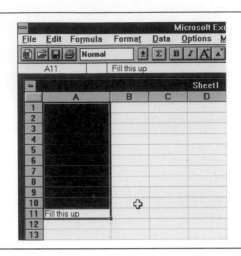

Figure E-4.   *Cells selected for Fill Up*

See Also

EDIT FILL DOWN	Fills down in the selection	Menu Command
EDIT FILL LEFT	Fills left in the selection	Menu Command
EDIT FILL RIGHT	Fills right in the selection	Menu Command

EDIT INSERT

Menu Command

➤   *Shortcut Key:* CTRL-PLUS (+)

The Edit Insert menu option allows you to insert a blank cell or range of cells into the selected area. The selected cells are shifted to accommodate the new cells. If whole rows are selected, Excel automatically moves the rows beneath those inserted to make room for the new rows. Similarly, if whole columns are selected, Excel automatically moves the columns to the right of the inserted columns to make room for the new columns. If a range smaller than whole rows or columns is selected, Excel asks whether you want to shift the affected cells down or to the right.

See Also

EDIT DELETE	Related command	Menu Command

CLEARING CELLS VS DELETING CELLS	Related concept	Concept

EDIT.OBJECT(*[verb]*)

Macro Function   **New to Version 4.0**

EDIT.OBJECT performs the same action as the Edit Object shortcut menu command. EDIT.OBJECT starts the application represented by the selected object and performs some action on the object. The action performed depends on the *verb* specified. *Verb* is a number defined by the object's source application. If *verb* is omitted, the default value is 1, which often means "edit."

See Also

INSERT.OBJECT	Inserts an object	Macro Function

EDIT PASTE

Menu Command

➤   *Shortcut Key:* SHIFT-INS

The Edit Paste menu option allows you to copy or relocate a cell or group of cells that you have selected using Edit Cut or Edit Copy. Edit Paste inserts all cell properties. If you want to paste only certain cell properties—for example, contents or formatting—use Edit Paste Special. You can also use Edit Paste to place characters cut from the formula bar.

Once you have selected the cells and activated the marquee with Edit Cut or Edit Copy, you need to determine where to move the group of cells. You can simply go to the upper-left cell of the new location, then choose Edit Paste (or press SHIFT-INS). Excel fills down and right to match the size of the cut or copied region. Alternatively, you can select a region that is exactly the same size as the region that you defined using Edit Cut or Edit Copy.

CAUTION: Edit Paste will overwrite existing data, formulas, and formatting on the worksheet. If you don't want this to happen, be sure that the area you are pasting to includes enough blank space for all the cells you have cut or copied.

If you defined your region using Edit Copy, you can make multiple copies. There are two ways to do this. If you want to make multiple copies simultaneously, choose all the areas that you want to paste to using a multiple selection. To make a multiple selection, use SHIFT-F8, or hold down the CTRL key while selecting with the mouse. You can also create multiple copies just by continuing to select paste areas and choose the Edit Paste option until you have copied the cells everywhere you want them. You don't need to redefine the source area each time you use Edit Copy.

NOTE: You can't make multiple copies of a region defined with Edit Cut.

The Edit Paste option allows you to copy from a worksheet to a chart, or from a chart to another chart. When the copied area is from a worksheet, Excel creates a data series out of the cells and pastes them into the active chart. You can also paste copied or cut characters from the formula bar.

When you are copying from one chart to another chart, Excel adds the data series to any data series already on the active chart, but replaces the formatting with the formatting from the copied chart. If you only want to paste certain attributes of the chart, use the Edit Paste Special option.

See Also

EDIT CUT	Cuts selected cells	Menu Command
EDIT PASTE SPECIAL	Pastes specified attributes of the selection	Menu Command

EDIT PASTE LINK

Menu Command

The Edit Paste Link option allows you to copy data into the cells in the current selection and establish a link with the origin of the data. When this link is in place, your worksheet changes when the source data changes. The source of the data can be an Excel worksheet or another application.

In order to use Edit Paste Link, you must first select and copy the source data. Then select the cell or cells that you want to paste to, and choose Edit Paste Link. If your copy area is more than one cell and your paste selection is one cell, Excel will fill down and to the right to match the size of the copy area. Any data and formatting in that area will be lost, so make sure you have enough room to paste the entire selection.

See Also

LINKING	Explains linking	Concept

EDIT PASTE SPECIAL

Menu Command

The Edit Paste Special option allows you to paste certain attributes from a copied selection to your current selection. You can paste formatting without pasting any data, for example. You can also combine (for example, add) values from the paste area with values from the copy area.

In order to use Edit Paste Special, you first must use Edit Copy to copy a selection of cells. Then select where you want to paste the cells and choose Edit Paste Special. You will see a dialog box that allows you to choose which attributes of the copied cells you want to paste into the new area. You can also choose a mathematical function which combines the values of the cells from the copied area with the values in the paste area (assuming that there is data in the paste area).

To paste from another chart, select and copy the chart using Edit Copy, activate or create a chart, and choose Edit Paste Special. You will see a dialog box from which you can choose the attributes of the copied chart that you want to place in the active chart.

To paste from a worksheet, select and copy the cells using Edit Copy, activate or create a chart, and choose Edit Paste Special. A dialog box allows you to choose how you want to add the data from the worksheet to the chart.

See Also

EDIT COPY	Selects active range for copying	Menu Command
EDIT PASTE	Pastes selection	Menu Command

EDIT REPEAT

Menu Command

➤   *Shortcut Key:* ALT-ENTER

The Edit Repeat menu option allows you to repeat the last menu option you selected (including dialog box selections) if possible. You can use this option to repeat formatting in different groups of cells.

See Also

EDIT.REPEAT	Equivalent function	Macro Function

EDIT.REPEAT()

Macro Function

EDIT.REPEAT performs the same action as the Edit Repeat menu command. It repeats the last action, including options, if possible.

See Also

EDIT REPEAT   Equivalent command   Menu Command

EDIT.SERIES(*[series-num]*,*[series-name]*,*[X]*,*[Y]*,*[Z]*,*[order]*)
EDIT.SERIES?(*[series-num]*,*[series-name]*,*[X]*,*[Y]*,*[Z]*,*[order]*)

Macro Function

EDIT.SERIES performs the same action as the Chart Edit Series menu command. It allows you to change an existing series or create a new series. *Series-num* is the number of the series that you want to change. If this argument is omitted, a new series is created.

Series-name is the name of the series and is used for the legend. It can be a string or an external reference to a cell containing a name. *X* is an external reference to the cells containing the category labels, or the x-coordinate data for scatter charts. *Y* is an external reference to the cells containing the values, or the y-coordinate data for scatter charts. *Z* is an external reference to the cells containing values for x-coordinate data for three-dimensional charts.

Order is the plot order of the series. All series have unique plot orders. If the plot order given by *order* has already been taken, the series given by *series-num* is given the plot order, and the series previously plotted in that order is increased by 1. All series with plot orders greater than *order* are also increased by 1.

Example

=EDIT.SERIES(3, "March Costs", MARCH.XLS!$A$3:$A$6, MARCH.XLS!$B$3:$B$6,,1) defines the third data series in the active chart to have the name "March Costs," its labels in cells A3:A6, its values in cells B3:B6, and its plot order is 1.

See Also

CHART EDIT SERIES   Equivalent Command   Menu Command

EDIT UNDO

Menu Command

➤ *Shortcut Key:* ALT-BACKSPACE
Shortcut Key: CTRL-Z

The Edit Undo option allows you to reverse your last action, if possible. You can only undo the last option you selected, the last cell entry you typed, or the last undo.

EDITING

Concept

When you enter data into a cell, you are in Enter mode; the word "Enter" appears on the left of the status bar as a mode indicator. In Enter mode you can do only limited editing, using the BACKSPACE key to remove several characters and then retyping them or using ESC to remove the entire entry. You remain in Enter mode until you either press ENTER, or move to another cell by using one of the arrow keys or by clicking with the mouse.

If you want to do more extensive editing without retyping the entry, you must go into Edit mode by pressing the F2 key or by clicking your mouse in the formula bar. While you're in Edit mode, the word "Edit" appears in the status bar, as shown here:

You remain in Edit mode until you either press ENTER, click on another cell, or click on the check mark in the formula bar. However, you cannot use the arrow keys to exit from Edit mode. When you are in Edit mode, many menu commands will appear grayed because they are not available.

If you decide to modify data that you have entered into a cell, you can simply retype the contents of the cell. Alternatively, you can press the F2 key or click on the formula bar. This places you in Edit mode, and you can now use the direction keys or your mouse to place the cursor wherever you want. You can use the DEL or

BACKSPACE key to erase characters to the right or left, respectively. You can control whether you are in insert or overtype mode by pressing the INS key. (When you are in insert mode, Excel adds all the characters you type to the data in a cell without replacing any of the existing characters. When you are in overtype mode, Excel replaces the existing characters with new characters that you type.) While in Edit mode a number of keys have the following special uses:

Keypress	Result
CTRL-'	Copies the formula from the cell above
CTRL-"	Copies the value from the cell above
CTRL-ENTER	Fills selected range with the selected formula
CTRL-;	Inserts the current date
CTRL-:	Inserts the current time
ALT-ENTER	Inserts a line break
arrow key	Moves cursor one character in the direction of the key
CTRL-arrow key	Moves cursor one word in the direction of the key
END	Moves cursor to the right end of the current entry
HOME	Moves cursor to the left end of the current entry

See Also

EDIT UNDO	Reverses last action	Menu Command

EDITION.OPTIONS(*type, name, ref, option, [appearance], [size], [format]*)

Macro Function

EDITION.OPTIONS allows Excel for Windows users to change or cancel publisher or subscriber options created in Excel for the Macintosh. (Publisher and subscriber are Macintosh features that allow Excel to share information with other applications.) A publisher is the source of data or graphics. The data or graphics are selected, then placed in an edition file. Subscribing applications can then access the data or graphics by importing the edition file. When the publishing application modifies the published information, the edition file is updated. The applications that subscribe to the edition file then pick up the changes, as defined by the options.

Type specifies the type of edition. If *type* is 1, Excel is a publisher. If *type* is 2, Excel is a subscriber. Either *name* or *ref* is required. *Name* is the name of the edition that you want to change; *ref* is a reference to the edition that you want to change.

The *option* argument is a number that specifies the option that you want to set. *Option* values are different depending on whether *type* is 1 (publisher) or 2 (subscriber). The following tables specify the possible values:

Type 1—Publisher	
Option	*Description*
1	Cancels the publisher
2	Immediately sends the edition
3	Selects data or object for publishing to the specified edition
4	Updates the edition file upon saving the document
5	Updates the edition file upon request
6	Changes the edition file as specified by appearance, size, and format

Type 2—Subscriber	
Option	*Description*
1	Cancels the subscriber
2	Gets the edition file
3	Opens the publisher document
4	Updates automatically when the edition file changes
5	Updates upon request

The *appearance* argument should be 1 if you want the selection to be stored as shown on the screen, or 2 if you want the selection stored as shown when printed. The default for *appearance* is 2 if the selection is a chart; otherwise the default is 1.

The *size* argument is only applicable if the selection is a chart. If *size* is 1, the chart is sized as shown on the screen. If *size* is 2, the chart is sized as shown when printed. The default value for *size* is 1.

The *format* argument specifies the file format as follows.

Format	Description
1	PICT
2	BIFF
4	RTF
8	VALU

You can combine the formats by adding the numbers. A *format* value of 3 indicates PICT and BIFF formats. The default value for *format* is 1.

EFFECT(*rate,periods*)

Function   **New to Version 4.0**

EFFECT returns the effective annual interest rate. *Rate* is the nominal annual interest rate. *Periods* is the number of compounding periods per year.

   EFFECT is an add-in function. The first time that you use it, you may see a #REF! error while Excel loads the function.

Example

=EFFECT(6%,12) returns 0.061678 or 6.17%.

See Also

NOMINAL	Returns the nominal interest rate	Macro Function

ELSE()

Macro Function

ELSE is used with an IF function to identify which instructions are to be performed if logical tests defined with the IF function and any ELSE.IF functions are FALSE. (For an example, see the IF entry later in this section.)

See Also

ELSE.IF	ELSE IF control statement	Macro Function
END.IF	Ends an IF block	Macro Function
IF	IF control statement	Macro Function

ELSE.IF(*test*)

Macro Function

ELSE.IF is used with an IF function to identify which instructions are to be performed if logical *tests* defined with an IF function or other ELSE.IF functions are FALSE. (See the IF entry for an example.)

See Also

ELSE	ELSE control statement	Macro Function

END.IF	Ends an IF block	Macro Function
IF	IF control statement	Macro Function

EMBED(*type, [item]*)

EMBED is the formula that is automatically created and displayed when an object is embedded in an Excel worksheet and linked to the application that created it. *Type* is the type of the object. For example, ExcelChart is a chart created with Excel. *Item* is the object to be embedded. If *item* is not present, the default is the entire document. You cannot use EMBED on either a macro or a worksheet.

ENABLE.COMMAND(*bar, menu, command, enable*)

Macro Function

ENABLE.COMMAND enables a menu command if the *enable* argument is TRUE. It disables a menu command if the *enable* argument is FALSE. *Bar* is the number of the menu bar on which you want to enable or disable the command.

Bar	Menu Bar
1	Worksheet and macro sheet
2	Chart
3	Nothing open
4	Information
5	Worksheet and macro sheet
6	Chart (short)
7	Cell
8	Object shortcut
9	Chart shortcut

The *menu* argument is the menu on which you want to enable or disable the command. This argument can be given as a name or as the number of the menu. Menus are numbered starting with 1 on the left. *Command* is the name or the number of the command you want to enable or disable. Commands are numbered starting with 1 at the top.

See Also

ADD.COMMAND	Adds a command to a menu	Macro Function

DELETE.COMMAND　　Removes a command from a　　Macro Function
　　　　　　　　　　　menu

ENABLE.TOOL(*bar,position,enable*)

Macro Function　　　　　　　　　　　　　　　**New to Version 4.0**

The ENABLE.TOOL macro function enables or disables a tool. The *bar* argument is either the number of a built-in toolbar or the name of a custom toolbar. The built-in toolbars are numbered as follows.

Bar	Toolbar
1	Standard
2	Formatting
3	Utility
4	Chart
5	Drawing
6	Excel 3.0
7	Macro
8	Stop recording
9	Macro paused

The *position* argument indicates the tool's position on the toolbar. Position 1 is the leftmost or the top tool.

Enable is TRUE if you want to enable the tool, or FALSE if you want to disable the tool. The default value for *enable* is TRUE.

END.IF()

Macro Function

END.IF ends an IF macro function. An IF function controls which instructions are to be performed based on logical tests. (See the IF entry for an example.)

See Also

ELSE	ELSE control statement	Macro Function
ELSE.IF	ELSE IF control statement	Macro Function
IF	IF control statement	Macro Function

ENTER.DATA(*test*)

Macro Function   **New to Version 4.0**

ENTER.DATA turns data entry mode on or off, depending on the result of *test*. *Test* is some expression that evaluates to TRUE or FALSE. If *test* evaluates to TRUE, data entry mode is turned on; if it evaluates to FALSE, data entry mode is turned off. *Test* can also be the number 2, which turns on data entry mode and prevents the ESC key from turning it off. If *test* is omitted, data entry mode is a toggle.

In data entry mode, you can only enter data into the unlocked cells of the current selection. You can use the arrow keys and the TAB key to move from one cell to the next within the data entry area (the current selection).

EOMONTH(*start-date, nu-months*)

Function   **New to Version 4.0**

EOMONTH returns a date serial number of the last day of the month, which is determined by adding *nu-months* to the *start-date*.

EOMONTH is an add-in function. The first time that you use it, you may see a #REF! error while Excel loads the function.

Example

=EOMONTH(date(92,6,1),5) returns 33938, which is the serial number for 11/30/92.

ERF(*A,[B]*)

Function   **New to Version 4.0**

ERF returns the error function integral calculated between the *A* and *B* limits. If *B* is not given, the integral is calculated between 0 and *A*.

ERF is an add-in function. The first time that you use it, you may see a #REF! error while Excel loads the function.

Example

=ERF(1,2) returns 0.152622.

See Also

ERFC   Calculates the complementary error integral   Function

ERFC(*A*)

Function   **New to Version 4.0**

ERFC returns the complementary error function integral calculated between *A* and infinity. This is the same as 1–ERF(*A*).

   ERFC is an add-in function. The first time that you use it, you may see a #REF! error while Excel loads the function.

Example

=ERFC(2) returns 0.004678.

ERROR(*enable, [macro]*)

Macro Function

ERROR turns error checking on if *enable* is TRUE, and turns error checking off is *enable* is FALSE. If *enable* is TRUE and a macro reference is included, control is given to the macro specified by the *macro* argument if an error occurs. This allows you to customize error handling.

See Also

CANCEL.KEY	Causes macro interruption to be disabled	Macro Function
LAST.ERROR	Returns a reference to the last error	Macro Function

ERROR.TYPE(*error*)

Function   **New to Version 4.0**

ERROR.TYPE evaluates the argument *error* and returns the error type. *Error* can be an error value, a formula, or a reference to a cell containing a formula. Here is a table of the possible values ERROR.TYPE can return, and their associated errors:

Returns	Error
1	#NULL!
2	#DIV/0!
3	#VALUE!
4	#REF!

Returns	Error
5	#NAME?
6	#NUM!
7	#N/A
#N/A	Other

Example

=ERROR.TYPE(A3) returns 6, if cell A3 contains the formula =ERFC(−1).
=ERFC(−1) returns a #NUM! error.

See Also

ERRORS	Explains Excel's errors	Concept
ISERR	Checks for all errors except #N/A	Function
ISERROR	Checks for errors	Function

E

ERRORS

Concept

Formulas and functions may return error values if they cannot be evaluated. The errors returned by Excel may help you to determine the problem. The following list includes the possible errors and their meanings:

Error	Description
#DIV/0!	Divide by zero error.
#N/A	Not available.
#NAME?	There is an unrecognized name in your formula or function.
#NULL!	Two ranges you expected to intersect do not intersect.
#NUM!	There is a problem with a number.
#REF!	There is a problem with a reference.
#VALUE!	One of the arguments is the wrong type.

See Also

ISERR	Checks for all errors except #N/A	Function
ISERROR	Checks for errors	Function

EVALUATE(*formula-text*)

Macro Function   **New to Version 4.0**

EVALUATE evaluates a formula that is given as text in the argument *formula-text*.

EVEN(*X*)

Function   **New to Version 4.0**

EVEN returns X rounded to the next highest even number, if X is positive, or the next lowest even number, if X is negative.

Examples

=EVEN(5) returns 6.
=EVEN(–3) returns –4.

See Also

INT	Rounds down to the nearest integer	Function
ODD	Rounds to the next odd number	Function

EXACT(*string1,string2*)

Function

EXACT returns TRUE if *string1* and *string2* are exactly the same; otherwise it returns FALSE. The strings can be literal strings, formulas that evaluate to strings, or references to cells containing strings.

Example

=EXACT(A5,"April") compares the contents of A5 with the string "April" and returns TRUE or FALSE depending on the match. If A5 contained APRIL or april, EXACT would return FALSE.

EXEC(*name,[window]*)

Macro Function

EXEC starts the program named in the *name* argument. The *window* argument must be 1, 2, or 3. If the argument is 1, the program is started in a normal window. If the argument is 2, the program is started in a minimized window. If the argument is 3, the program is started in a maximized window. The default value for *window* is 2. If the EXEC function cannot start the program, an error value of #VALUE! is returned. If EXEC is successful, the ID number of the started program is returned.

Example

=EXEC("C:\WINWORD\WINWORD.EXE C:\DOC\TEXT.DOC") starts Microsoft Word for Windows and opens the document TEXT.DOC.

See Also

APP.ACTIVATE	Activates an external application	Macro Function
EXECUTE	Executes commands in an external program	Macro Function
SEND.KEYS	Sends keystrokes to an external application	Macro Function

EXECUTE(*channel,string*)

Macro Function

EXECUTE executes the command or commands specified by the *string* argument in the application connected to the given *channel*. If the *channel* number is not valid, EXECUTE returns a #VALUE! error. If the application connected to the given *channel* is unavailable, EXECUTE returns an #N/A! error. If the ESC key is pressed before the application has a chance to answer, EXECUTE returns a #DIV/0! error. If the request is refused by the application, EXECUTE returns a #REF! error. When an application is initiated with the INITIATE macro function, INITIATE returns the channel number.

Example

=EXEC(10,"1") sends the number 1 to the application associated with channel 10.

See Also

INITIATE	Initiates a channel to another application	Macro Function
TERMINATE	Terminates a channel to another application	Macro Function

EXIT

Concept

You can exit from Excel by choosing either the File Exit menu command or the Control Close menu command. Either way, you will be prompted to save changes in any open documents that haven't been saved yet. If you want to save the changes, choose Yes.

See Also

FILE EXIT	Exits from Excel	Menu Command

$\mathbf{EXP}(X)$

Function

EXP returns the value e (approximately 2.718282) raised to the power of *X*.

Example

=EXP(2)raises the value of e to the second power. This equals 7.389.

See Also

LN	Returns the natural log of a number	Function
LOG	Returns the log of a number	Function

$\mathbf{EXPON}(input, output, [damping\text{-}factor], [standard], [chart])$

Macro Function   New to Version 4.0

The EXPON macro function returns a value that represents a prediction based on the prior period adjusted for error. EXPON performs the same function as the Analysis Tool called Exponential Smoothing.

Input is a reference to the *input* range. *Output* is a reference to the upper-left corner of the output range. The *damping-factor* is the exponential smoothing constant. The default value for *damping-factor* is 0.3. *Standard* should be TRUE if you want standard error values included in the output. If you don't want standard error values returned, *standard* should be FALSE. If *chart* is TRUE, Excel generates a chart from the actual and forecasted values. If *chart* is FALSE, no chart is generated.

EXPON is an add-in function. The first time that you use it, you may see a #REF! error while Excel loads the function.

See Also

FORECAST	Linear trend forecast	Macro Function
GROWTH	Exponential trend forecast	Macro Function

EXPONDIST($X, parameter, cum$)

Function   **New to Version 4.0**

EXPONDIST returns the exponential distribution. X must be 0 or greater. *Parameter* is the parameter value of the function, and must be greater than 0. *Cum* should be TRUE if you want to use the cumulative distribution function. It should be FALSE if you want to use the probability density function.

Example

=EXPONDIST(0.5,5,TRUE) returns 0.917915.

See Also

GAMMADIST	Returns the gamma distribution	Function
POISSON	Returns the Poisson probability	Function

EXTEND.POLYGON(*array*)

Macro Function   **New to Version 4.0**

EXTEND.POLYGON extends a polygon created with the CREATE.OBJECT function by adding one or more vertices to it. *Array* is an array of values representing the vertices of the polygon. *Array* can also be a reference to cells containing the values.

It is easier to record creating a polygon using the macro recorder and the freehand polygon tool on the Drawing toolbar. You can then modify the recorded macro if necessary.

See Also

CREATE.OBJECT	Creates a graphic object	Macro Function
FORMAT.SHAPE	Changes the size, shape, and position of a polygon	Macro Function

EXTERNAL REFERENCE

Concept

An *external reference* is a reference to a range outside the current worksheet. An external reference includes the entire path and document name, an exclamation point as a separator, and an absolute range.

Example

C:\DATA\JULY.XLS!$A$1:$B$5 is a reference to the range A1:B5 on the worksheet JULY.XLS in the DATA directory on drive C.

EXTRACT(*unique*)
EXTRACT?(*[unique]*)

Macro Function

EXTRACT performs the same action as the Data Extract menu option. Database records are extracted according to the criteria set with the SET.CRITERIA macro function. The extracted records are placed in the extract range defined by the SET.EXTRACT macro function. If *unique* is TRUE, only unique records are extracted. If *unique* is FALSE, all records matching the criteria are extracted. If the *unique* argument is included in the dialog box version (with the question mark), the value is used as a default for the dialog box that appears.

See Also

DATA SET CRITERIA	Defines the criteria range	Menu Command
DATA SET DATABASE	Defines the database	Menu Command
SET.CRITERIA	Defines the criteria range	Macro Function
SET.DATABASE	Defines the database	Macro Function
SET.EXTRACT	Defines the extract range	Macro Function

FACT(*X*)

Function

FACT returns the factorial of the argument *X*. The formula for the factorial of *X* is

$$FACT(X) = X * (X - 1) * (X - 2) * \ldots * 1$$

Examples

=FACT(4) = 4 * 3 * 2 * 1 = 24.
=FACT(3.2) = 3 * 2 * 1 = 6 (nonintegers are truncated).

See Also

FACTDOUBLE	Returns the double factorial	Function
PRODUCT	Returns the product of the arguments	Function

FACTDOUBLE(X)

Type

FACTDOUBLE returns the double factorial of the argument X. The formula for the double factorial, if X is even, is

$$X!! = X(X-2)(X-4) \dots (4)(2)$$

The formula for the double factorial if X is odd is

$$X!! = X(X-2)(X-4) \dots (3)(1)$$

FACTDOUBLE is an add-in function. The first time that you use it, you may see a #REF! error while Excel loads the function.

Example

=FACTDOUBLE(8) returns 384.

See Also

FACT	Returns the factorial	Function

FALSE()

Function

FALSE returns the logical FALSE value.

Example

=IF(B6=FALSE,.15,0) tests cell B6 for a false condition. If B6 is blank or zero, the value .15 is returned; otherwise, 0 is returned.

See Also

TRUE	Returns logical TRUE	Function

FASTMATCH(*value, range, [type]*)

Function   **New to Version 4.0**

FASTMATCH returns the first number in the range or array given by *range* that matches *value*.

Type controls how *value* is matched to an element in the *range*. The following table lists possible values for *type*, how *range* is assumed to be ordered, and which element will be returned.

FASTMATCH is an add-in function. The first time that you use it, you may see a #REF! error while Excel loads the function.

Type	Order of Range	Number Returned
−1	Descending	Smallest value >= *value*
0	Any order	First value = *value*
1	Ascending	Largest value <= *value*

If *type* is omitted, the default value is 1.

Example

=FASTMATCH(3,A1:A5,1) returns 3 if the range A1:A5 contains the values 1, 2, 3, 4, and 5.

See Also

MATCH	Used for smaller arrays	Function

FCLOSE(*X*)

Macro Function

FCLOSE closes a file opened with the FOPEN function. The argument *X* is the file number returned by FOPEN. If *X* is not a valid file number, FCLOSE returns the error #VALUE!.

See Also

CLOSE	Closes the active window	Macro Function
FILE.CLOSE	Closes the active document	Macro Function
FOPEN	Opens a file	Macro Function

FDIST(*X, num, denom*)

Function   New to Version 4.0

FDIST returns the F-probability distribution of *X*. *Num* is the numerator degrees of freedom, and *denom* is the denominator degrees of freedom.

Example

=FDIST(12.34567,5,3) returns 0.032477.

See Also

FINV	Returns the inverse F-probability	Function
FTEST	Returns the F-test result	Function

FILE

Menu

The File menu enables you to create new worksheets, charts, and macro sheets; open existing worksheets, charts, and macro sheets stored on disk; and close, save, and delete worksheets, charts, and macro sheets. The File menu also allows you to set up the page you will print, set up your printer, print a worksheet or chart, and exit Excel.

FILE CLOSE

Menu Command

The File Close menu option allows you to close the active document. If the document contains changes that have not been saved, Excel displays the following dialog box:

If you click on the Yes button, the file is saved if it has previously been named. If the file has never been saved before and doesn't have a name, the Save As dialog box opens, as shown here:

See Also

| FILE.CLOSE | Equivalent function | Macro Function |

FILE.CLOSE(*[X]*)

Macro Function

The FILE.CLOSE macro function allows you to close the active document. *X* should be a logical value. If *X* is TRUE, the file is saved before being closed. If *X* is FALSE, the file is not saved before being closed. If *X* is omitted and if you've made changes to the file, a dialog box gives you a chance to save the file.

See Also

| CLOSE | Closes the active window | Macro Function |
| CLOSE.ALL | Closes all open windows | Macro Function |

FILE CLOSE ALL

Menu Command

The File Close All menu option only appears on the File menu if you hold down the SHIFT key when you activate the menu. Close All closes all of the windows on your screen. If any of the open documents have unsaved changes, Excel displays the following dialog box:

If you click on the Yes button and the file has not been saved previously, the Save As dialog box appears.

See Also

FILE CLOSE	Closes the active document	Menu Command
FILE SAVE	Saves the active document	Menu Command
FILE SAVE AS	Saves and names the active document	Menu Command

FILE DELETE

Menu Command

The File Delete menu option deletes a file on disk from the current directory. When you choose the File Delete option, you see the Delete Document dialog box:

Select the file you want to delete from the File Name box, and then click on OK. Before finally deleting a file, Excel confirms whether you really want to do so. Answering No cancels the deletion; answering Yes completes the deletion. Repeat these steps to delete more files. The entry in the File Name box determines which files are listed in the Files box. For example *.* shows all files in the directory. *.XLM shows all files with the .XLM extension. If the current directory is not the directory you want, type in the desired directory in the File Name box—for example, C:\DATA*.XLS.

CAUTION: Make absolutely sure you want to delete a file before you go ahead with the deletion. Once you delete a file, it is gone for good.

See Also

FILE.DELETE   Equivalent function   Macro Function

F

FILE.DELETE(*name*)
FILE.DELETE?(*[name]*)

Macro Function

FILE.DELETE performs the same action as the File Delete menu option. The *name* argument is a string that is the name of the document you want to delete. In the version without the question mark, FILE.DELETE displays a dialog box asking for a valid filename if the name is invalid. In the dialog box version (with the question mark), you can use wildcards in the name argument to show only certain files in the dialog box that appears.

See Also

FILE DELETE   Equivalent command   Menu Command

FILE.EXISTS(*path*)

Macro Function   **New to Version 4.0**

FILE.EXISTS returns TRUE if the file or directory given by *path* exists. The *path* argument should be given as a string, and must either be in the current directory or be given as a full path.

Example

=FILE.EXISTS("C:\DATA\OCTOBER.XLS") returns a value of TRUE if the file OCTOBER.XLS exists in the directory C:\DATA.

FILE EXIT

Menu Command

If you choose the File Exit menu command, you exit from Microsoft Excel. If you have any open documents containing unsaved changes, Excel asks if you want to save the changes. You can choose Yes to save, No to ignore changes, or Cancel to cancel the File Exit option.

See Also

    FILE CLOSE   Closes the active document   Menu Command

FILE LINKS

Menu Command

The File Links menu option causes Excel to open all supporting documents to the active document. If the active document has no supporting documents, the option will appear greyed on the menu. The Links dialog box, shown here, also allows you to mark the linked files Read Only or to change document links.

FILE NEW

Menu Command

➤   *Shortcut Keys:* SHIFT-F11 *(worksheet)*, F11 *(chart)*, CTRL-F11 *(macro)*

The File New menu option opens a new document in a new window. Choosing the File New option opens the dialog box shown here:

Excel asks whether you want to open a new worksheet, chart, macro sheet, workbook, or slide. If you want to create a new chart, you must select the cells you want to chart on a worksheet, choose New from the File menu, and choose Chart from the dialog box; Excel will automatically plot the contents of the selected cells onto the new chart.

FILE OPEN

Menu Command

The File Open menu option allows you to open an existing document from disk. When you choose this option, the following dialog box appears.

Select the file you want to open from the File Name box, and then click on OK. The entry in the File Name box determines which files are listed in the Files box. For example *.* shows all files in the directory and *.XLM shows all files with the .XLM extension. If the current directory is not the directory you want, type in the desired directory in the File Name box—for example, C:\DATA*.XLS. You can set files to Read Only by checking the Read Only option in the dialog box.

See Also

FILE NEW   Opens a new document   Menu Command

FILE PAGE SETUP

Menu Command

The File Page Setup menu command allows you to change the appearance of the printed document. When you choose the Page Setup option from the File menu, the Page Setup dialog box appears, as shown in Figure F-1.

This dialog box allows you to set the header, footer, margins, orientation, and scaling of a worksheet. (Assigning page setup options for a chart will be discussed shortly.) It also permits you to add gridlines or row and column headings to the document. Here is a table of codes that control how the headers and footers look on the printed page:

Code	Action
&B	Prints the left, center, or right part of the header or footer in boldface
&C	Centers the text that follows
&D	Prints the current date
&F	Prints the name of the document
&I	Prints the left, center, or right part of the header or footer in italic
&L	Left-justifies the text that follows
&P	Prints the page numbers
&P+*number*	Adds the *number* to the page number and prints it
&P−*number*	Subtracts the *number* from the page number and prints it
&R	Right-justifies the characters that follow
&T	Prints the current time
&&	Prints an ampersand

If you are in a chart when you choose File Page Setup, a different dialog box appears, as shown in Figure F-2.

This Page Setup dialog box allows you to determine the printed size of the current chart. You can print it the same size as the screen, fit it on the page while retaining the same proportions as the screen, or print it to use the entire page.

See Also

| OPTIONS SET PRINT AREA | Defines a custom print area | Menu Command |

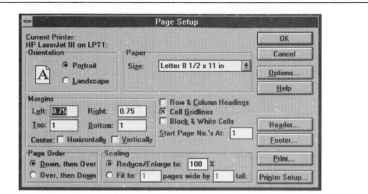

Figure F-1.   *The Page Setup dialog box for worksheets*

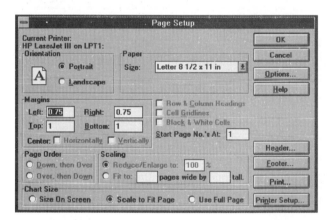

Figure F-2.   *The Page Setup dialog box for charts*

FILE PRINT

Menu Command

➤   *Shortcut Key:* SHIFT-F12

The File Print menu command prints the active document. The Page Setup options associated with the document are used to format the output. (See FILE PAGE

SETUP.) File Print prints the entire worksheet unless you set a different print area with the Options Set Print Area option. Choosing Print from the File menu displays the following dialog box, in which you can specify which pages you want printed and how many copies you need, and choose options such as Draft Quality and Preview.

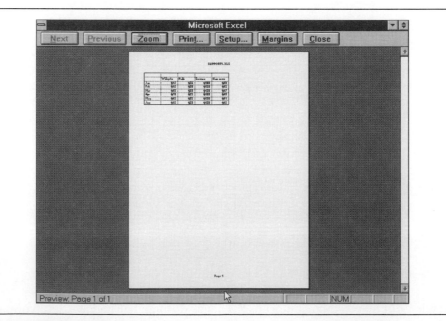

The Preview option allows you to look at the document on the screen the way it will appear on paper. If you select the Preview check box, Excel generates a print preview screen, as shown in Figure F-3.

Figure F-3. *The preview screen*

The size of the printout, like its other characteristics, is determined by the File Page Setup dialog box settings.

See Also

FILE PAGE SETUP   Sets print options   Menu Command

FILE PRINTER SETUP

Menu Command   **Prior to Version 4.0**

The File Printer Setup menu command allows you to tell Excel which printer you will be using. You should choose the File Printer Setup option the first time you use a printer, whenever you change printers, and whenever you want to change the settings of your printer. If you want to install a new printer or change the printer port, you must use the Windows Control Panel.

FILE SAVE

Menu Command

➤   *Shortcut Key:* SHIFT-F12

The File Save menu command saves the current document to a disk. If the active document is a worksheet, it is saved in worksheet format with an .XLS extension, unless you designate another extension. If the active document is a chart, it is saved with an .XLC extension. Macros are saved with an .XLM extension. The first time you save a file, Excel asks you for a filename by displaying the Save As dialog box shown here:

Every subsequent time that you choose File Save, you cannot enter another filename. Excel simply saves an updated version of the file using the current filename. If you want to save the file under a different name, you must use the File Save As option.

See Also

FILE CLOSE	Closes the active document	Menu Command
FILE SAVE AS	Saves and names the active document	Menu Command

FILE SAVE AS

Menu Command

➤   *Shortcut Key:* F12

The File Save As menu command allows you to save a new document, or to save an existing document under a different name. If the document already has a name, the name appears in the dialog box. You can leave the name unchanged by choosing the OK button. If you want to save the document under another name, type the name in the Save As dialog box. You needn't type the extension (for example .XLS). You can choose the Options option from the dialog box to select the file format, create a password for the file, or create a backup file.

FILE SAVE WORKBOOK

Menu Command

The File Save Workbook menu option saves a group of windows and documents under one name. Typically, you use this command to save all open documents and windows. It is useful when you are working on a project that uses a number of files at once. Before you end your Excel session, you can use the File Save Workspace command. For your work session, you can open the workbook file to open all the files you had open when you saved the workspace. Workbook files have an .XLW extension.

 CAUTION: The workbook file contains a list of the documents that were open when you chose the Save Workbook option. It does not contain the actual documents. Do not delete the individual files just because you saved them with the Save Workbook option.

See Also

FILE CLOSE	Closes the active document	Menu Command
FILE SAVE	Saves the active document	Menu Command
FILE SAVE AS	Saves and names the active window	Menu Command

FILE UNHIDE WINDOW

Menu Command   **Prior to Version 4.0**

The File Unhide Window menu option only appears on the File menu when there are open, hidden windows in the workspace. When you choose the Unhide Window option, Excel displays a dialog box listing the windows you have previously hidden. Choose the file you want to unhide, and then click on the OK button. If the hidden file is password protected, you will be asked for the password before the window is revealed. You can cancel the option by clicking on the Cancel button.

FILES(*[directory]*)

Macro Function

FILES returns an array containing the filenames of the files in the *directory* given. If the *directory* argument is omitted, Excel searches the current directory. You can use wildcard characters and filenames to restrict the filenames that are returned.

Example

=FILES("C:\DATA\JUNE*.XL?") returns an array containing all filenames that begin with the characters "JUNE" and have a three-character extension beginning with the letters "XL."

FILL.AUTO(*ref,[copy]*)

Macro Function   **New to Version 4.0**

FILL.AUTO performs the same action as the AutoFill feature. FILL.AUTO copies the current selection in the range indicated by *ref* if *copy* is TRUE. If *copy* is FALSE, FILL.AUTO fills the cells in *ref* with the data in the cells at the top, left, right, or bottom edge of *ref*.

F

Example

The macro shown here performs AutoFill:

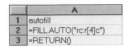

	A
1	autofill
2	=FILL.AUTO("rc:r[4]c")
3	=RETURN()

If cell A1 is active and contains the number 1, running this macro will place the number 1 in all cells in the range A1:A5.

If cell A1 contains the number 1 and cell A2 contains the number 2, and cells A1:A2 are selected, running this macro will produce the following result: A1:A5 will contain the numbers 1, 2, 3, 4, and 5.

See Also

FILL.DOWN	Fills down a selection	Macro Function
FILL.GROUP	Fills from one sheet to another	Macro Function
FORMULA.FILL	Fills a formula in a range	Macro Function

FILL.DOWN()

Macro Function

FILL.DOWN performs the same action as the Edit Fill Down menu option. It allows you to copy the contents and formats from the top row in the current selection to the remaining cells below it. If there is already data or formatting in the selection, it will be replaced by the formatting and data from the top row.

See Also

EDIT FILL DOWN	Equivalent command	Menu Command
FILL.LEFT	Fills left in a selection	Macro Function
FILL.RIGHT	Fills right in a selection	Macro Function
FILL.UP	Fills up in a selection	Macro Function

FILL.GROUP(*type*)
FILL.GROUP?(*[type]*)

Macro Function   New to Version 4.0

FILL.GROUP copies the current selection to all worksheets in the group. The cells are copied to the same location on all the worksheets. Worksheets are grouped together using the WORKGROUP function. The *type* argument refers to the three choices available in the Fill Workgroup dialog box:

Type	Information Copied
1	All
2	Formulas
3	Formats

The question mark version of this function displays a dialog box. The *type* argument, if given, is used as a default setting.

See Also

WORKGROUP	Creates a workgroup	Macro Function

FILL.LEFT()

Macro Function

FILL.LEFT performs the same action as the Edit Fill Left menu option. It allows you to copy the contents and formats from the right cell in the current selection to the remaining cells to its left. If there is already data or formatting in the selection, it will be replaced by the formatting and data from the right cell.

See Also

EDIT FILL LEFT	Equivalent command	Menu Command
FILL.DOWN	Fills down in a selection	Macro Function
FILL.RIGHT	Fills right in a selection	Macro Function
FILL.UP	Fills up in a selection	Macro Function

FILL.RIGHT()

Macro Function

FILL.RIGHT performs the same action as choosing the Edit Fill Right menu option. FILL.RIGHT allows you to copy the contents and formats from the left cell in the current selection to the remaining cells to its right. If there is already data or formatting in the selection, it will be replaced by the formatting and data from the left cell.

See Also

EDIT FILL RIGHT	Equivalent command	Menu Command
FILL.DOWN	Fills down in a selection	Macro Function
FILL.LEFT	Fills left in a selection	Macro Function
FILL.UP	Fills up in a selection	Macro Function

FILL.UP( )

Macro Function

FILL.UP performs the same action as the Edit Fill Up menu option. It allows you to copy the contents and formats from the bottom cell in the current selection to the remaining cells above it. If there is already data or formatting in the selection, it will be replaced by the formatting and data from the bottom cell.

See Also

EDIT FILL UP	Equivalent command	Menu Command
FILL.DOWN	Fills down in a selection	Macro Function
FILL.LEFT	Fills left in a selection	Macro Function
FILL.RIGHT	Fills right in a selection	Macro Function

FIND(*search-string,string,[start-position]*)

Function

Beginning at the *start-position* of a string, FIND searches the string for a match to the *search-string* argument and returns the position where the match is found. The *search-string* and *string* arguments can be literals, formulas that evaluate to strings, or references to cells containing strings. The search is case-sensitive and will not find letters when the case is not identical. If the *start-position* argument is omitted, the default value is 1.

Example

=FIND("x","Excel") would result in a value of 2.

FINV(*X,num,denom*)

Function   **New to Version 4.0**

FINV returns the inverse of the F-probability distribution of *X*. *Num* is the numerator degrees of freedom, and *denom* is the denominator degrees of freedom.

Example

=FINV(.1234567,5,3) returns 4.480782.

See Also

| FDIST | Returns the F-probability distribution | Function |
| FTEST | Returns the F-test result | Function |

FISHER(*X*)

Function   **New to Version 4.0**

FISHER returns the Fisher transformation of *X*. The Fisher transformation formula is

$$\text{FISHER}(X) = \frac{1}{2} \ln \frac{(1 + X)}{(1 - X)}$$

Example

=FISHER(0.5) returns 0.549306.

See Also

CORREL	Returns the correlation coefficient	Function
COVAR	Returns the covariance	Function
FISHERINV	Returns the inverse Fisher transformation	Function

FISHERINV(*X*)

Function   **New to Version 4.0**

FISHERINV returns the inverse Fisher transformation of *X*. The inverse Fisher transformation formula is

$$\text{FISHERINV}(X) = \frac{e^{2X} - 1}{e^{2X} + 1}$$

Example

=FISHERINV(0.549306) returns 0.5.

See Also

CORREL	Returns the correlation coefficient	Function
COVAR	Returns the covariance	Function
FISHERINV	Returns the inverse Fisher transformation	Function

FIXED(*number, [digits], [comma]*)

Function

FIXED returns the *number* as text, rounded to the number of digits to the right of the decimal point given by the *digits* argument, if *digits* is positive. If *digits* is a negative number, the number will be rounded to the left of the decimal point. The *digits* argument is optional; if you omit it, the default value for digits is 2. The *comma* argument is also optional; if TRUE, commas are excluded from the returned text; if FALSE or omitted, commas are included.

Examples

=FIXED(456.76834,2) returns "456.77".
=FIXED(456325.76,−2) returns "456,300".

See Also

DOLLAR	Returns a currency formatted string	Function
ROUND	Rounds a number	Function
TEXT	Converts a number to text	Function

FLOOR(*X, round*)

Function   **New to Version 4.0**

FLOOR rounds *X* down to the nearest multiple of *round*.

Examples

=FLOOR(3.45,1) returns 3.
=FLOOR(−3.45,−1) returns −3.

See Also

CEILING	Rounds a number up	Function
EVEN	Rounds to the nearest even integer	Function
INT	Rounds down to nearest integer	Function
ODD	Rounds to the nearest odd integer	Function
ROUND	Rounds to a certain number of digits	Function

FOPEN(*name-string,[access-type]*)

Macro Function

FOPEN opens the file specified by *name-string* and returns an ID number. If *name-string* is not a valid filename, FOPEN returns an #N/A error. The *access-type* argument must be 1, 2, or 3. If the access type is 1, the file is given a Read/Write status. If the access type is 2, the file is given a Read Only status. If the access type is 3, a new file is opened and given Read/Write status. If *access-type* is omitted, the default value is 1.

See Also

FCLOSE	Closes a file	Macro Function
FREAD	Reads from a file	Macro Function
FWRITE	Writes to a file	Macro Function
OPEN	Opens a document	Macro Function

FOR(*counter,start,end,[step]*)

Macro Function

FOR begins a FOR-NEXT loop. FOR loops until the *counter* reaches the *end* value, or until the ESC key is pressed. The *counter* argument is the name of the counter as text. The *counter* controls how many times that the FOR-NEXT loop is executed. *Start* is the value to which counter is initially set. The FOR-NEXT loop will stop when *counter* equals the *end* value. *Step* is the amount by which *counter* is incremented each time the loop is executed. If *step* is omitted, it is assumed to be 1. There must be a NEXT statement in your macro somewhere below the FOR statement. All statements between the FOR and the NEXT statement are part of the loop.

Example

=FOR("Counter",1,10,1) executes the statements between the FOR statement and the NEXT statement ten times.

See Also

BREAK	Breaks a loop	Macro Function
NEXT	Ends a FOR-NEXT loop	Macro Function
WHILE	Starts a WHILE-NEXT loop	Macro Function

FOR.CELL(*name,[area],[skip-blanks]*)

Macro Function

FOR.CELL begins a FOR.CELL-NEXT loop. A FOR.CELL-NEXT loop executes all the instructions between the FOR.CELL statement and the NEXT statement over a range of cells. The *name* argument is the name given to the cell that is currently being operated on; *name* is a text string. The *area* is the range that you want to operate on; *area* can be a multiple selection. If *area* is omitted, FOR.CELL operates on the current selection. If *skip-blanks* is TRUE, cells in the area that are blank are skipped over. If *skip-blanks* is FALSE, blank cells are treated the same as any other cell.

Example

=FOR.CELL("Cell",A1:A5,TRUE) causes all instructions between this FOR.CELL statement and a subsequent NEXT statement to be executed one time for every nonblank cell in the range A1:A5.

See Also

BREAK	Breaks a loop	Macro Function
NEXT	Ends a FOR-NEXT loop	Macro Function
WHILE	Starts a WHILE-NEXT loop	Macro Function

FORECAST(*X,dependent,independent*)

Function   New to Version 4.0

FORECAST predicts a linear regression value for *X* based on *dependent* and *independent* data. *Dependent* is a range or array that contains the dependent data. *Independent* is a range or array that contains the independent data.

Example

=FORECAST(90,{1,2,4,6,8},{6,8,9,10,20}) returns 41.10235.

See Also

EXPON	Predicts a value based on the prior period	Function
GROWTH	Returns an exponential trend	Function
MOVEAVG	Returns a moving average trend	Function
TREND	Returns a linear trend	Function

FORMAT

Menu

The Format menu allows you to determine how a cell entry looks. If it contains a number, you can format it as a dollar amount, a percentage, or with or without commas; you can also set the number of decimal places. You can left-align, right-align, or center both text entries and numbers, in individual cells or in a range of cells. You can place borders around cells, shade them, and protect them from being overwritten. Finally, you can specify a cell's width and height. In Chart mode, you can format various parts of either the main chart or the overlay chart.

FORMAT ALIGNMENT

Menu Command

The Format Alignment menu option aligns selected cells. Choosing the Format Alignment option displays the dialog box shown here:

The Alignment dialog box allows you to choose the alignment you want: General, Left, Center, Right, Fill, Justify, or Center Across Selection.

The Center Across Selection option allows you to center text that is contained in one cell across a group of cells. This is useful for centering titles on a worksheet.

The Fill option fills the entire cell with the contents of the cell. For example, if the cell contains an asterisk and you choose the Format Alignment Fill option, the entire cell will be filled with asterisks.

The General option right-aligns numbers, left-aligns text, and centers errors and logical values. This is the Excel default alignment.

The Alignment dialog box also allows you to change the orientation and vertical alignment for the current selection. In addition, the Wrap Text check box allows text to wrap inside a cell.

The standard toolbar contains three alignment tools that are used more frequently than the Format Alignment menu command. The three tools shown here are used to left-align, center, and right-align text:

See Also

ALIGNMENT   Equivalent function   Macro Function

FORMAT.AUTO(*[format],[number],[font],[alignment], [border], [pattern],[width]* **)**
FORMAT.AUTO?(*[format], [number],[font], [alignment], [border], [pattern], [width]* **)**

Macro Function   **New to Version 4.0**

FORMAT.AUTO performs the same action as the AutoFormat option from the Format menu. It applies a built-in format to the selected cells. All the arguments except *format* correspond to the check boxes that appear in the AutoFormat dialog box, which is shown here. You must click on the Options button to see the check boxes.

The *format* argument is a number that represents the format you want to use from the Table Format list box. The first format listed is number 1, the next is number 2, and so on. The default value for format is 1.

Number, font, alignment, border, pattern, and *width* are TRUE or FALSE depending on whether you want to apply that particular characteristic of the formatting to your selection. If the argument is TRUE, that formatting characteristic is applied. If it is FALSE, the characteristic is not applied. The default value for all of these arguments is TRUE.

The FORMAT.AUTO? version of this function displays the dialog box, and the arguments are used as default values.

See Also

ALIGNMENT	Aligns cell entries	Macro Function
BORDER	Places borders around cells	Macro Function
FORMAT AUTOFORMAT	Equivalent command	Menu Command
FORMAT.FONT	Formats fonts	Macro Function
FORMAT.NUMBER	Formats number entries	Macro Function
FORMAT.TEXT	Formats text entries	Macro Function

FORMAT AUTOFORMAT

Menu Command   **New to Version 4.0**

The Format AutoFormat menu command applies a built-in format to the selection. When you choose the AutoFormat option from the Format menu, the AutoFormat dialog box appears.

To apply a built-in format, select the format that you want in the Table Format list box. A sample of the format appears in the Sample window. Then choose the attributes of the format that you want to use by selecting the desired check boxes.

See Also

FORMAT ALIGNMENT	Aligns cell contents	Menu Command
FORMAT.AUTO	Equivalent function	Macro Function
FORMAT BORDER	Places borders around cells	Menu Command
FORMAT FONT	Formats fonts in a selection	Menu Command
FORMAT NUMBER	Formats numbers in a selection	Menu Command

F

FORMAT BORDER

Menu Command

The Format Border menu option places a border around selected cells, shades the selection, or both. Choosing Format Border brings up the following dialog box:

The Border dialog box allows you to choose the options Outline, Left, Right, Top, Bottom, and Shade.

If you want to put a border around every cell in the selection, choose the Left, Right, Top, and Bottom option. If you want to put a border around the entire selection, choose the Outline option.

There are several different border styles from which to choose. There are different colors, weights, and varieties of lines. Pick one of these line styles for your border.

See Also

BORDER   Equivalent function   Macro Function

FORMAT BRING TO FRONT

Menu Command

The Format Bring To Front menu command brings the selected graphic objects to the front of other objects.

FORMAT CELL PROTECTION

Menu Command

The Format Cell Protection menu option allows you to protect the cells in the current selection. You can use this menu option to select cells that you want to prevent from being edited. You can also use the Format Cell Protection option to hide the formulas that cells contain.

Format Cell Protection is the first of a two-part protection scheme built into Excel. The second part is Options Protect Document. First you need to identify the cells to be locked or unlocked with Format Cell Protection. Then, with Options Protect Document, you turn on or off total document protection. If a cell is locked, it cannot be written to after you use Options Protect document. All cells are locked by default. Therefore, you need to unlock cells that you want to be able to write to.

When you choose Format Cell Protection, the following dialog box appears.

Locked

The Locked option unlocks the selected range, if the current status is "Locked," or relocks it if the status is "Not Locked." Cells are locked by default.

Hidden

The Hidden option hides the formulas within the range if they are currently not hidden, and unhides them if they are currently hidden. By default formulas are not hidden.

See Also

OPTIONS PROTECT DOCUMENT	Related command	Menu Command

FORMAT COLUMN WIDTH

Menu Command

The Format Column Width menu option sets the width of the selected column or columns. You only need to select one cell in the column to set the width for the entire column. The default column width for Excel is 8.43 standard characters.

You can also change the column width using the mouse. First select all the columns you want to widen. Then point to the line between the column headings to the right of one of the columns you want to format. The mouse pointer will change into a cross with horizontal arrows, as shown in Figure F-4. Click the mouse and drag to the width you want; then release the mouse. All selected columns will be set to the new width. If you are changing the width of a single column with the mouse, you needn't select anything. Just drag the edge of the column to the desired width with the mouse. As you drag the column-width pointer, you can see the width in the cell reference area change.

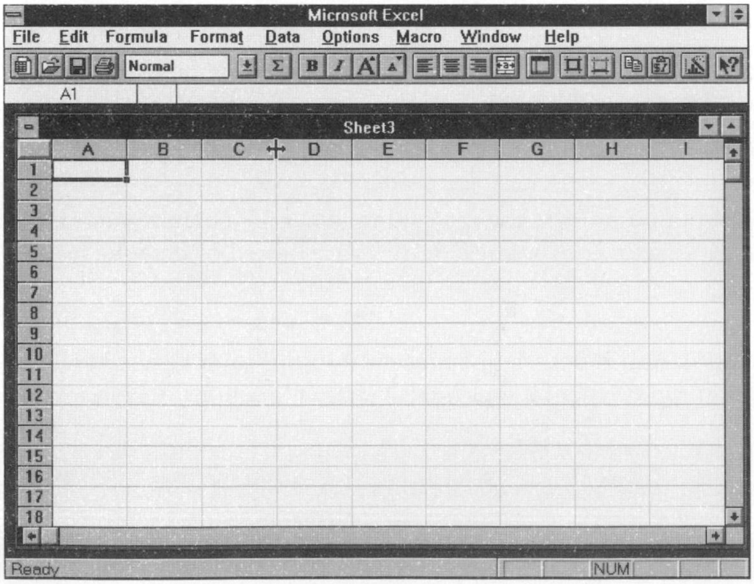

Figure F-4. *The column-width pointer is between columns C and D*

FORMAT FONT

Menu Command

The Format Font menu option allows you to choose the fonts for your document. When you select Format Font, the dialog box that appears is determined by whether you are working on a worksheet or a chart.

Font Options for Worksheets

The Font dialog box for worksheets is shown in Figure F-5.

The Format Font option changes the font for the selected cells. You can also change the font for the entire worksheet by selecting the entire worksheet before choosing the Format Font menu option. Choosing the Format Font option displays a dialog box with many font selections. When you select a font, your row height may adjust to accommodate the new font if necessary.

The Font list box in the upper-left corner of the dialog box lists all available fonts. If your printer will print the font, a small printer icon appears next to the font name.

The Font dialog box also includes the following options: Font Style, Size, Effects, Color, and Normal Font.

Font Style   You can choose one or several of the styles for your font. You can choose from the styles Regular, Bold, Italic, or Bold and Italic.

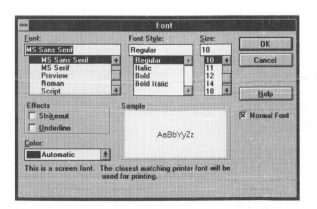

Figure F-5.   *The Font dialog box for worksheets*

Size   The sizes available for the selected font appear in the Size box. You can choose any of these sizes for your font.

Effects   You can turn on or off the Strikeout and Underline effects.

Color   The color drop-down list box allows you to choose a color for your font.

Normal Font   The Normal Font check box allows you to return to the default font.

Font Options for Charts

To change fonts on your chart, select the text you want to format with a new font and choose the Format Font option. If you want to change the font for the entire chart, choose the Select Chart option from the Chart menu, and then choose the Format Font option. If you haven't selected the text to be formatted, the Format Font option is greyed on the Format menu. Once you choose the Format Font option, the Font dialog box appears, as shown in Figure F-6.

The options in this dialog box are nearly the same as the ones in the dialog box that appears when a worksheet is the active document. However, the Background options do not appear on the worksheet version.

Background   The Background options control the background behind the text. The options are Automatic, Transparent, and Opaque.

Automatic	Automatically sets the background
Transparent	Sets the background area to transparent, so you can see what is behind the text
Opaque	Sets the background area to whatever background color or pattern you are using in your chart

Patterns   The Patterns command button opens the Patterns dialog box. Any changes you made in the Font dialog box are carried out, and the Patterns dialog box is displayed. (For more information, see the FORMAT PATTERNS entry later in this section.)

See Also

ALIGNMENT	Aligns cell entries	Macro Function
FORMAT FONT	Equivalent command	Menu Command
FORMAT.NUMBER	Formats values in cells	Macro Function
FORMAT.TEXT	Formats text in cells	Macro Function

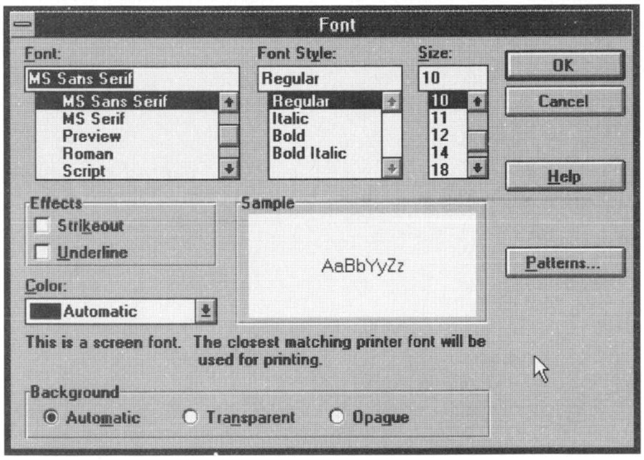

Figure F-6.   *The Font dialog box for charts*

FORMAT.FONT(*[name]*,*[size]*,*[bold]*,*[italic]*,*[underline]*,*[strikeout]*, *[color]*,*[outline]*,*[shadow]*)
FORMAT.FONT?(*[name]*,*[size]*,*[bold]*,*[italic]*,*[underline]*,*[strikeout]*, *[color]*,*[outline]*,*[shadow]*)

FORMAT.FONT(*[name]*,*[size]*, *[bold]*, *[italic]*, *[underline]*, *[strikeout]*,*[color]*,*[outline]*,*[shadow]*,*[object]*,*[start]*,*[char]*)
FORMAT.FONT?(*[name]*,*[size]*,*[bold]*,*[italic]*,*[underline]*,*[strikeout]*, *[color]*,*[outline]*,*[shadow]*,*[object]*,*[start]*,*[char]*)

FORMAT.FONT(*[color]*,*[background]*,*[apply]*,*[name]*,*[size]*,*[bold]*, *[italic]*,*[underline]*,*[strikeout]*,*[outline]*,*[shadow]*)
FORMAT.FONT?(*[color]*,*[background]*,*[apply]*,*[name]*,*[size]*,*[bold]*, *[italic]*,*[underline]*,*[strikeout]*,*[outline]*,*[shadow]*)

Macro Function

FORMAT.FONT performs the same action as choosing the Format Font menu option. There are three argument profiles for this function. The one you use will be determined by the type of text you select for formatting.

Argument Profile 1 - Worksheets and Macro Sheets   The arguments in the first set of functions correspond to the options in the Font dialog box for worksheets, which is shown in Figure F-5.

The *name* argument is the name of the font as it appears in the Fonts list box. *Name* should be given as a string.

Size is the size of the font in points. *Bold, italic, underline,* and *strikeout* are TRUE to turn the option on, and FALSE to turn the option off.

Color is a number from 0 to 16, representing one of the 17 colors available. The following table summarizes the different *color* options:

Color	Description
0	Automatic
1	Black
2	White
3	Red
4	Lime green
5	Royal blue
6	Yellow
7	Pink
8	Aqua
9	Maroon
10	Forest green
11	Navy blue
12	Avocado green
13	Purple
14	Grey green
15	Light grey
16	Dark grey

Outline and *shadow* are arguments that are included for macro compatibility with Excel for the Macintosh. They correspond to check boxes in the Macintosh version of the Font dialog box.

In the dialog box version (with the question mark), if the argument(s) are included, they are used as the default values for the dialog box that appears.

Argument Profile 2 - Text Boxes and Buttons   The second set of functions includes the *object, start,* and *char* arguments, which are used to format text boxes and buttons on worksheets and macro sheets.

Object is the object name of the object that you want to format. If *object* is omitted, then the currently selected object is formatted.

Start and *char* are numbers that indicate which characters should be formatted. *Start* is the first character in the string you want formatted, and *char* is the number of characters you want formatted. If *start* is omitted, the value is assumed to be 1. If *char* is omitted, the default value is all the characters in the string.

Argument Profile 3 - Charts   The third version of FORMAT.FONT uses a different syntax than the worksheet version. This set of functions, used to format text on charts, includes the *background* and *apply* arguments.

Background can be either 1 (automatic), 2 (transparent), or 3 (opaque). *Apply* is either TRUE or FALSE. If *apply* is TRUE, the fonts are applied to all data labels.

In the dialog box version (with the question mark), any arguments included are used as the default values for the dialog box that appears.

See Also

ALIGNMENT	Aligns cell entries	Macro Function
FORMAT FONT	Equivalent command	Menu Command
FORMAT.NUMBER	Formats values in cells	Macro Function
FORMAT.TEXT	Formats text in cells	Macro Function

FORMAT JUSTIFY

Menu Command

The Format Justify menu option justifies the text in the leftmost column of a selection. The left column in the selection must contain text only. The text in the left column is treated as a single string, and is distributed from the top cell in the column so that each successive cell is filled with text. Any blank cells in the column are interpreted as paragraph separators. Every paragraph is justified separately.

To justify text, select the cells that contain the text and then choose the Format Justify option. If justifying the text will cause overflow into the cells below, a dialog box gives you the opportunity to abort the operation.

Figure F-7 shows some cells containing text before a Format Justify operation. Figure F-8 shows the result of selecting the cells A2:A8 in Figure F-7 and choosing the Format Justify menu option.

See Also

FORMAT ALIGNMENT	Aligns cell entries	Menu Command
FORMAT FONT	Formats fonts for cell entries	Menu Command
JUSTIFY	Equivalent function	Macro Function

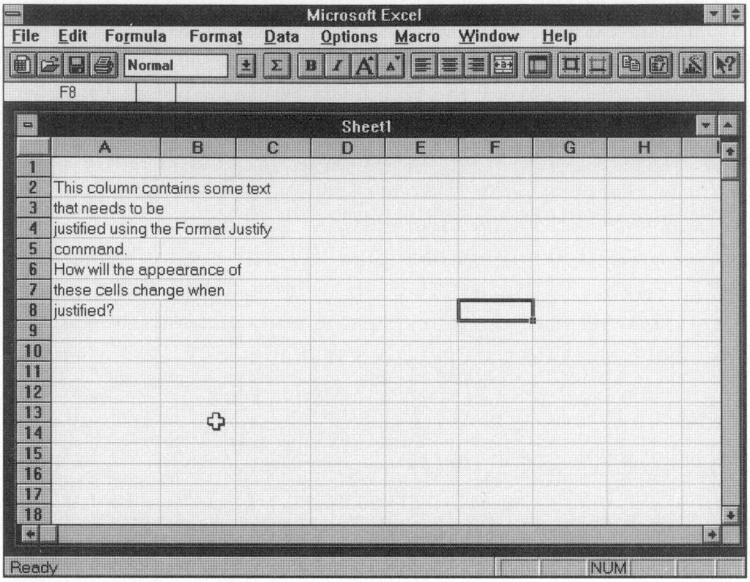

Figure F-7. *Some text before a Format Justify command*

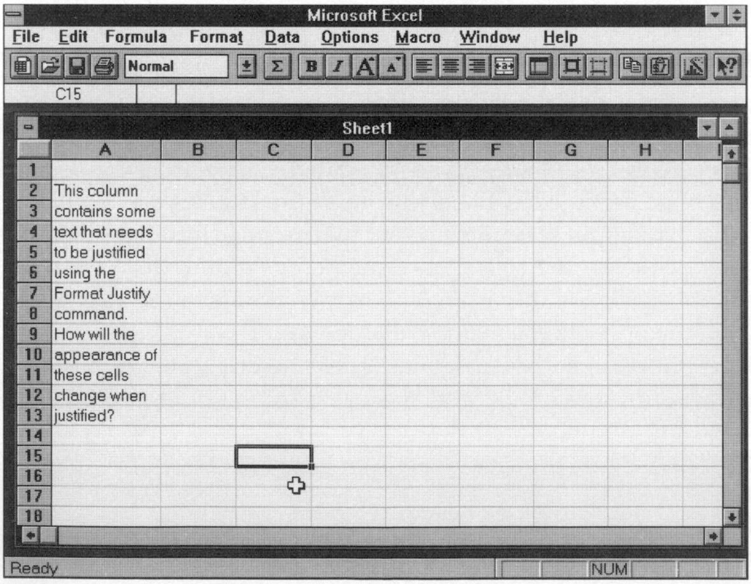

Figure F-8. *The same text after a Format Justify command*

FORMAT LEGEND

Menu Command

The Format Legend menu option appears on the Format menu only when the active document is a chart. The Format Legend option allows you to choose where the legend will appear on your chart. To add a legend, you must use the Chart Add Legend option. To format a legend, you must select the legend; otherwise the Legend option will be greyed on the Format menu. When you choose the Format Legend option, the following dialog box appears.

The Legend dialog box includes a Type box and the Patterns and Font command buttons.

Type   The options in the Type box allow you to choose the location of the legend. The following table summarizes the possible locations:

Bottom	Places the legend horizontally at the bottom of the chart.
Corner	Places the legend vertically in the upper-right corner of the chart.
Top	Places the legend horizontally at the top of the chart.
Right	Places the legend vertically on the right side of the chart
Left	Places the legend vertically on the left side of the chart

Font   If you click on the Font button, any changes you make in the Format Legend box are carried out, and the Font dialog box shown in Figure F-6 appears. (For more information, see FORMAT FONT.)

Patterns   If you click on the Patterns button, any changes you made in the Format Legend box are carried out, and the Patterns dialog box is displayed, as shown here:

For more information, see FORMAT PATTERNS.

See Also

CHART ADD LEGEND	Adds a legend to a chart	Menu Command
FORMAT FONT	Formats selected text with a font	Menu Command
FORMAT PATTERNS	Formats selected object with a pattern	Menu Command

FORMAT.LEGEND(*position*)
FORMAT.LEGEND?(*position*)

Macro Function

FORMAT.LEGEND performs the same action as the Format Legend menu option. It changes the position of the legend, returning a TRUE value if it does so successfully. If the legend on the active chart is not selected, FALSE is returned. The *position* argument can be any of the following numbers:

Position	Description
1	Bottom
2	Corner
3	Top
4	Right
5	Left

In the dialog box version (with the question mark), the position argument, if included, is used as a default value for the dialog box that appears.

See Also

FORMAT.FONT	Formats selected text with a font	Macro Function
LEGEND	Adds or deletes a legend or a chart	Macro Function
PATTERNS	Formats a selection with patterns or colors	Macro Function

---

FORMAT.MAIN(*type, [view],[overlap],[gap],[vary],[drop],[hilo], [angle],[gap-depth],[chart-depth],[up-down],[series-lines],[labels]*)
FORMAT.MAIN?(*[type],[view],[overlap],[gap],[vary],[drop],[hilo], [angle],[gap-depth],[chart-depth],[up-down],[series-lines],[labels]*)

Macro Function

FORMAT.MAIN performs the same action as the Format Main Chart menu command. It formats the main chart. The arguments correspond to the arguments in the Format Main Chart dialog box. (For more information, see the FORMAT MAIN CHART entry.)

Type is the type of chart. Each type of chart has a number associated with it:

Type	Chart
1	Area
2	Bar
3	Column
4	Line
5	Pie
6	XY Scatter
7	3-D Area
8	3-D Column
9	3-D Line
10	3-D Pie
11	Radar
12	3-D Bar
13	3 D Surface

The *view* argument is a number that corresponds to one of the views in the Format Main Chart dialog box. The value for *view* depends on the type of chart. The views change as different chart types are selected. A value of 1 would be the leftmost view in the dialog box. (See FORMAT MAIN CHART for more information.)

The *overlap* argument corresponds to the Overlap option in the Format Main Chart dialog box. The *overlap* argument allows you to choose the percentage of the width of a column or bar that the different bars or columns within a cluster overlap. This argument is used only if the chart type is bar or column. The default value for *overlap* is 0.

The *gap* argument corresponds to the Gap Width option in the Format Main Chart dialog box. The *gap* argument allows you to determine the gap between clusters as a percentage of the width of a column or bar. The default *gap* value is 50, or whatever was previously set.

The *vary* argument corresponds to the Vary By Categories option in the Format Main Chart dialog box. This argument is only used if there is a single series on the chart, and is either TRUE or FALSE. Excel gives each data point a different pattern or color. If the *vary* argument is omitted, *vary* is unchanged.

The *drop* argument corresponds to the Drop Lines option in the Format Main Chart dialog box. This argument, if TRUE, causes Excel to put lines on the chart from the highest value in each category to the category axis. If the *drop* argument is omitted, *drop* is unchanged.

The *hilo* argument corresponds to the Hi-Lo Lines option in the Format Main Chart dialog box. This argument causes Excel to extend lines from the highest to the lowest point in each category. *Hilo* is either TRUE or FALSE, turning the Hi-Lo Lines option on or off. If this argument is omitted, *hilo* is unchanged.

The *angle* argument corresponds to the Angle Of First Pie Slice option in the Format Main Chart dialog box. The *angle* argument is only relevant for pie charts. It allows you to choose the angle of the first edge of the first slice. The angle is measured clockwise from the Y axis (vertical axis). If *angle* is omitted, the default value is 0.

The *gap-depth* and *chart-depth* arguments are percentages that control the third dimension attributes of a 3-D chart. The default value for *gap-depth* is 50, or unchanged if it was previously set. The default value for *chart-depth* is 100, or whatever was previously set.

The *up-down* argument corresponds to the Up/Down Bars option in the Format Main Chart dialog box. This argument is only relevant for line charts. If *up-down* is TRUE, a bar is placed between lines for each series. The default value for *up-down* is FALSE.

The *series-lines* argument corresponds to the Series Lines check box in the Format Main Chart dialog box. *Series-lines* is either TRUE or FALSE, and turns series lines on or off for either stacked bar or column charts. The default value for *series-lines* is FALSE, or whatever was previously set.

The *labels* argument corresponds to the Radar Axis Labels check box. If *labels* is TRUE, this argument places axis labels on the chart if it is a radar chart. The default value for *labels* is FALSE, or whatever was previously set.

In the dialog box version of FORMAT.MAIN, the arguments are used as default values for the dialog box that appears.

See Also

FORMAT MAIN CHART	Equivalent command	Menu Command
FORMAT.OVERLAY	Formats an overlay chart	Macro Function

FORMAT MAIN CHART

Menu Command

The Format Main Chart menu option only appears if the active document is a chart.

The Format Main Chart option allows you to set the main chart's formats and type. When you select this option, the Format Chart dialog box shown in Figure F-9 appears.

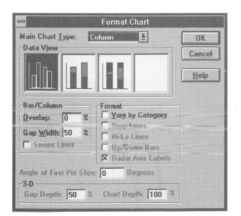

Figure F-9. *The Format Chart dialog box*

All available options appear in the dialog box. Options that aren't currently relevant are greyed.

Type   The Main Chart Type drop-down list box allows you to choose the type of chart you want.

Area	Causes the main chart to be an area chart
Bar	Causes the main chart to be a bar chart
Column	Causes the main chart to be a column chart
Line	Causes the main chart to be a line chart
Pie	Causes the main chart to be a pie chart
XY-Scatter	Causes the main chart to be a scatter chart
Radar	Causes the main chart to be a radar chart
3-D Area	Causes the main chart to be a 3-D area chart
3-D Bar	Causes the main chart to be a 3-D bar chart
3-D Column	Causes the main chart to be a 3-D column chart
3-D Line	Causes the main chart to be a 3-D line chart
3-D Pie	Causes the main chart to be a 3-D pie chart
3-D Surface	Causes the main chart to be a 3-D surface chart

Data View   The Data View box gives pictorial choices. Each picture represents a different view for the type of chart that you have selected in the Main Chart Type box. For example, if you've selected a column chart, Data View shows and allows you to select various types of column charts that are available.

Bar/Column   The Bar/Column section of the dialog box allows you to control overlap, gaps, and series lines for bar and column charts.

Overlap	Allows you to choose the percentage of the width of a column or bar by which the bars or columns within a cluster overlap, if the Overlapped option is selected. If the Overlapped option is not selected, the Overlap option sets the distance between bars or columns within a cluster.
Gap Width	Allows you to determine the gap between clusters. The percentage is the percentage of the width of a column or bar.
Series Lines	Turns series lines on or off.

Format The Format box allows you to set the formatting options for the main chart that are applicable to the main chart type that you have selected.

Vary By Category	Only relevant if there is a single series on the chart. Excel gives each data point a different pattern or color.
Drop Lines	Causes Excel to put lines on the chart from the highest value in each category to the category axis.
Hi-Lo Lines	Causes Excel to extend lines from the highest to the lowest point in each category.
Up/Down Bars	Only relevant for line charts. Places a bar between lines for each series.
Radar Axis Labels	Places axis labels on the radar charts.

Angle Of First Pie Slice The Angle Of First Pie Slice option is only relevant for pie charts. It allows you to choose the angle of the first edge of the first slice. The angle is measured clockwise from the Y axis (vertical axis).

3-D The Gap Depth and the Chart Depth options are percentages that control the three-dimensional attributes of a 3-D chart.

See Also

FORMAT FONT	Formats selected text with a font	Menu Command
FORMAT OVERLAY	Formats the overlay	Menu Command
FORMAT PATTERNS	Formats selected object with a pattern	Menu Command

FORMAT MOVE

Menu Command

The Format Move menu option only appears on the Format menu if the active document is a Chart.

This option allows you to move a selected chart object with the keyboard. After you select the object, choose the Format Move option, use the direction keys to move the object to the desired location, and then press ENTER.

F

See Also

FORMAT.MOVE	Equivalent function	Macro Function
FORMAT SIZE	Sizes the selected object	Menu Command

FORMAT.MOVE(X, Y)
FORMAT.MOVE?($[X], [Y]$)

Macro Function

FORMAT.MOVE performs the same action as the Format Move menu option. The units for the arguments X and Y are points. (A point is 1/72 of an inch.) X and Y are measured from the lower-left corner of the window. In the dialog box version (with the question mark), the arguments, if included, are used as default values for the dialog box that appears.

See Also

CREATE.OBJECT	Creates an object	Macro Function
FORMAT MOVE	Equivalent command	Menu Command
FORMAT.SIZE	Sizes a selected object	Macro Function

FORMAT NUMBER

Menu Command

The Format Number menu option allows you to format the numbers in selected cells. After selecting the cells you want to format, choose the Format Numbers option and the Number Format dialog box, shown here, will appear.

This dialog box allows you to choose from Excel's built-in number formats in the Format Codes box, or to create your own format in the Code box. You can also delete formats that you previously created from the Format Codes box.

The Category box allows you to find the format that you are looking for more easily. When a category is selected in the Category box, only formats in that category are displayed in the Format Codes box. If you want to see all available formats, choose the All category.

The Format Codes box is where Excel displays all the built-in number formats, as well as any custom formats you have created. The default format is General. The following table shows how the built-in formats will display a number or a date. The formats appear in the same order as they do in the dialog box when the category All is selected.

Format	Resulting Displays for Entries of		
	8000	**–8**	**.8**
General	8000	–8	0.8
0	8000	–8	1
0.00	8000.00	–8.00	0.80
#,##0	8,000	–8	1
#,##0.00	8,000.00	–8.00	0.80
#,##0_);(#,##0)	8,000	(8)	1
#,##0_); [RED](#,##0)	8,000	(8)*	1
#,##0.00_); (#,##0.00)	8,000.00	(8.00)	0.80
#,##0.00_); [RED](#,##0.00)	8,000.00	(8.00)*	0.80
$#,##0;($#,##0)	$8,000	($8)	$1
$#,##0; [RED]($#,##0)	$8,000	($8)*	$1
$#,##0.00; ($#,##0.00)	$8,000.00	$(8.00)	$0.80
$#,##0.00; [RED]($#,##0.00)	$8,000.00	($8.00)**	$0.80
0%	800000%	–800%	80%
0.00%	800000.00%	–800.00%	80.00%
0.00E+00	8.00E+03	–8.00E+00	8.00E–01

Format	Resulting Display for Entry of 1 3/4
# ?/?	1 3/4
# ??/??	1 3/4

Format	Resulting Display for Entry of 7/6/93
m/d/yy	7/6/93
d-mmm-yy	6-Jul-93
d-mmm	6-Jul
mmm-yy	Jul-93

Format	Resulting Display for Entry of 7:45:36 PM
h:mm AM/PM	7:45 PM
h:mm:ss AM/PM	7:45:36 PM
h:mm	19:45
h:mm:ss	19:45:36

Format	Resulting Display for Entry of 7/6/93 7:45 PM
m/d/yy h:mm	7/6/93 19:45

The Code box is where you can create custom formats. A format consists of up to four parts, separated by semicolons. The first part is for positive numbers, the second for negative numbers, the third part for zero values, and the fourth part for text. If you want to exclude certain types of numbers from being displayed, don't put any formatting between the semicolons. For example, if you don't want negative numbers displayed, you could have a format such as #,##0;;0.00, which will display positive numbers in one format, will not display negative numbers, and will display zero numbers in a different format. Here is a list of formatting symbols you can use when creating your own formats:

Symbol	Use
0	Specifies the number of decimal places to the right of the decimal point and the minimum digits to the left of the decimal point. For example, the built-in format 0.00 says you will always have two decimal places to the right of the decimal point and at least one digit to the left of the decimal point. With the 0.00 format, the following numbers are formatted as shown here:

Symbol	Use

		Entry	Display
		.456	0.46
		45	45.00

Specifies the number of optional digits on either side of the decimal point. For example, in the built-in format #,##0, the # provides the optional digits surrounding the comma that is used as a thousands separator. These will be blank if there are not enough digits to fill the number of places. The first place should be a 0 and not a # so that a 0 prints if you have a fraction too small to round to 1. With the #,##0 format, the following entries are formatted as shown here:

Entry	Display
46.67	47
12345	12,345

. Specifies the location of the decimal point.

, Specifies that the thousands separator is a comma if a comma is surrounded by 0's or #'s.

; Separates sections of a format. There can be up to four sections. The first, or leftmost, specifies how to format positive numbers. The second section specifies how to format negative numbers. The third specifies how to format zero, and the fourth sections specifies how to handle text. All numbers are handled the same if there is only one section. With two sections, positive and zero values are formatted with the first, and negative numbers are formatted with the second. Text is not given special treatment with only three sections. An example of using a semicolon is shown with the next set of symbols.

$ + – ( ) :
space Specifies a literal character to be displayed. For example, the built-in format $#,##0 ;($#,##0) says that you will have a dollar sign to the left of the leftmost number and parentheses around negative numbers. With the $#,##0 ;($#,##0) format, the following numbers are formatted as shown here:

Entry	Display
–45.67	($46)
1234	$1,234

Symbol	Use
()	If parentheses are specified for negative numbers, positive numbers are shifted one position to the left so that negative numbers will line up.
"text"	Specifies that whatever is between the quotation marks is to be displayed. For example, $#,##0"DB" ;$#,##0"CR" ;0 says the a DB will be placed after positive numbers, a CR will be placed after negative numbers, and a 0 will appear for zero values.
\	Specifies that the character following the backslash is to be displayed. This is the same as enclosing a single character in quotation marks.
@	Specifies where any text in a cell is placed in a format. For example, 0.00 ;@ says that all numbers should be formatted with 0.00 and that any text appearing in the cell should also be displayed. (0.00 by itself says the same thing.)
*	Specifies that the following character is to be repeated to fill any unused space in the cell. For example, $**#,##0 says that a dollar sign should be placed in the leftmost position in a cell, that any intervening space should be filled with asterisks, and that the number should be right-aligned in the cell as usual. With the $**#,##0 format, the following numbers will be formatted as shown here:

Entry	Display
45	$*******45
1234	$***1,234

Symbol	Use
%	Specifies that a number should be multiplied by 100 and a % placed to its right. For example, the built-in format 0.00% says multiply the number by a 100 and place a % after it. With the 0.00% format, the following numbers will be formatted as shown here:

Entry	Display
.07	7.00%
.4575	45.75%
−0.067	−6.70%

Symbol	Use
E+ E– e+ e–	Specifies that the scientific format should be used with either E or e. If a – is specified, only negative numbers have a sign. With +, both positive and negative numbers have a sign. For example, the built-in format 0.00E+00 says that the scientific format should be used with a capital E and both plus and minus signs. With the 0.00E+00 format, the following numbers will be formatted as shown here:

Entry	Display
4567	4.57E+03
–12345	–1.23E+04
.0045	4.50E–03

Symbol	Use
m mm mmm mmmm	Specifies that a month should be displayed as a number without a leading zero (m) or with a leading zero (mm), as a three-letter abbreviation (Apr or Sep), or as a full name. If m or mm follows h or hh, it specifies minutes rather than a month.
d dd ddd dddd	Specifies that a day should be displayed as a number without a leading zero (d) or with a leading zero (dd), as a three-letter abbreviation (Tue or Thu), or as a full name.
yy yyyy	Specifies that a year should be displayed as either a two- (93) or four-digit number (1993).
h hh	Specifies that an hour should be displayed as either a number without a leading zero (4) or a number with a leading zero (04).
m mm	Specifies that a minute should be displayed as either a number without a leading zero (5) or a number with a leading zero (05). If the m or mm do not appear after an h or hh, the month will be displayed.
s ss	Specifies that a second should be displayed as either a number without a leading zero (6) or a number with a leading zero (06).
AM/PM am/pm A/P a/p	Specifies that time should be displayed using a 12-hour clock with AM, am, A, or a before noon and PM, pm, P, or p from noon to midnight.

F

Symbol	Use
[color]	Specifies that the characters in the cell should be displayed in a color. The available colors are black, white, red, green, blue, yellow, magenta, and cyan.

When you have a fixed number of decimal places, the decimal digits are rounded to fit the format. Also, having blank format sections (semicolons with nothing between them) tells Excel not to display that type of number. For example 0.00;;;@ says display and format positive numbers and text, but do not display negative numbers and zero values.

See Also

FORMAT FONT	Formats fonts in a selection	Menu Command
FORMAT.NUMBER	Equivalent function	Macro Function

FORMAT.NUMBER(*string*)
FORMAT.NUMBER?(*[string]*)

Macro Function

FORMAT.NUMBER performs the same action as the Format Number menu option. It formats the current selection. The argument *string* is the format for the number given as a string. In the dialog box version (with the question mark), if the argument is given, it is used as a default for the dialog box that appears.

Excel's built-in number formats are listed here:

Format	Resulting Display for Entries of		
	8000	**–8**	**.8**
General	8000	–8	0.8
0	8000	–8	1
0.00	8000.00	–8.00	0.80
#,##0	8,000	–8	1
#,##0.00	8,000.00	–8.00	0.80
#,##0_);(#,##0)	8,000	(8)	1
#,##0_);[RED] (#,##0)	8,000	(8)*	1
#,##0.00_); (#,##0.00)	8,000.00	(8.00)	0.80

Format	Resulting Display for Entries of		
	8000	–8	.8
#,##0.00_); 　[RED](#,##0.00)	8,000.00	(8.00)*	0.80
$#,##0;($#,##0)	$8,000	($8)	$1
$#,##0; 　[RED]($#,##0)	$8,000	($8)*	$1
$#,##0.00; 　($#,##0.00)	$8,000.00	$(8.00)	$0.80
$#,##0.00; 　[RED]($#,##0.00)	$8,000.00	($8.00)*	$0.80
0%	800000%	–800%	80%
0.00%	800000.00%	–800.00%	80.00%
0.00E+00	8.00E+03	–8.00E+00	8.00E–01

Format	Resulting Display for Entry of 1 3/4
# ?/?	1 3/4
# ??/??	1 3/4

Format	Resulting Display for Entry of 7/6/93
m/d/yy	7/6/93
d-mmm-yy	6-Jul-93
d-mmm	6-Jul
mmm-yy	Jul-93

Format	Resulting Display for Entry of 7:45:36 PM
h:mm AM/PM	7:45 PM
h:mm:ss AM/PM	7:45:36 PM
h:mm	19:45
h:mm:ss	19:45:36

Format	Resulting Display for Entry of 7/6/93 7:45 PM
m/d/yy h:mm	7/6/93 19:45

You can also create a custom format. A format consists of up to four parts, separated by semicolons. The first part is for positive numbers, the second part is for negative numbers, the third part is for zero values, and the fourth part is for text. If you want to exclude certain types of numbers from being displayed, don't put any formatting between the semicolons. For example, if you don't want negative numbers displayed, you could have a format such as #,##0;;0.00, which will display positive numbers in one format, will not display negative numbers, and will display zero numbers in a different format. Here is a list of formatting symbols you can use when creating your own formats:

Symbol	Use
0	Specifies the number of decimal places to the right of the decimal point and the minimum digits to the left of the decimal point. For example, the built-in format 0.00 says you will always have two decimal places to the right of the decimal point and at least one digit to the left of the decimal point. With the 0.00 format, the following numbers are formatted as shown here:

Entry	*Display*
.456	0.46
45	45.00

Symbol	Use
#	Specifies the number of optional digits on either side of the decimal point. For example, in the built-in format #,##0, the # provides the optional digits surrounding the comma that is used as a thousands' separator. These will be blank if there are not enough digits to fill the number of places. You want the first place to be a 0 and not a # so you will get at least a 0 printed if you have a fraction too small to round to 1. With the #,##0 format, the following entries are formatted as shown here:

Entry	*Display*
46.67	47
12345	12,345

Specifies the location of the decimal point.

Symbol	Use
,	Specifies that the thousands' separator is a comma if a comma is surrounded by 0's or #'s.
;	Separates sections of a format. There can be up to four sections. The first, or leftmost, specifies how to format positive numbers. The second section specifies how to format negative numbers. The third specifies how to format zero, and the fourth section specifies how to handle text. All numbers are handled the same if there is only one section. With two sections, positive and zero values are formatted with the first, and negative numbers are formatted with the second. Text is not given special treatment with only three sections. An example of using a semicolon is shown with the next set of symbols.
$ + − () : space	Specifies a literal character to be displayed. For example, the built-in format $#,##0 ;($#,##0) says that you will have a dollar sign to the left of the leftmost number and parentheses around negative numbers. With the $#,##0 ;($#,##0) format, the following numbers are formatted as shown here:

Entry	*Display*
−45.67	($46)
1234	$1,234

Symbol	Use
()	If parentheses are specified for negative numbers, positive numbers are shifted one position to the left so that negative numbers will line up.
"text"	Specifies that whatever is between the quotation marks is to be displayed. For example, $#,##0"DB" ;$#,##0"CR";0 says that a DB will be placed after positive numbers, that a CR will be placed after negative numbers, and that a 0 will appear for zero values.
\	Specifies that the following character is to be displayed. Using the backslash is the same as enclosing a single character within quotation marks.
@	Specifies where any text in a cell is placed in a format. For example, 0.00 ;@ says that all numbers should be formatted with 0.00 and any text appearing in the cell should also be displayed. (0.00 by itself says the same thing.)

Symbol	Use
*	Specifies that the following character is to be repeated to fill any unused space in the cell. For example, $**#,##0 says that a dollar sign should be placed in the leftmost position in a cell, that any intervening space should be filled with asterisks, and that the number be right-aligned in the cell as usual. With the $**#,##0 format, the following numbers will be formatted as shown here:

Entry	Display
45	$*******45
1234	$***1,234

Symbol	Use
%	Specifies that a number should be multiplied by 100 and a percent sign placed to its right. For example, the built-in format 0.00% says multiply the number by 100 and place a percent sign after it. With the 0.00% format, the following numbers will be formatted as shown here:

Entry	Display
.07	7.00%
.4575	45.75%
−0.067	−6.70%

Symbol	Use
E+ E− e+ e−	Specifies that the scientific format should be used with either E or e. If a − is specified, only negative numbers have a sign. With +, both positive and negative numbers have a sign. For example, the built-in format 0.00E+00 says that the scientific format should be used with a capital E and both plus and minus signs. With the 0.00E+00 format, the following numbers will be formatted as shown here:

Entry	Display
4567	4.57E+03
−12345	−1.23E+04
.0045	4.50E-03

Symbol	Use
m mm mmm mmmm	Specifies that a month should be displayed as a number without a leading zero (m) or with a leading zero (mm), as a three-letter abbreviation (Apr or Sep), or as a full name. If m or mm follows h or hh, it specifies minutes rather than a month.
d dd ddd dddd	Specifies that a day should be displayed as a number without a leading zero (d) or with a leading zero (dd), as a three-letter abbreviation (Tue or Thu), or as a full name.
yy yyyy	Specifies that a year should be displayed as either a two- (93) or four-digit number (1993).
h hh	Specifies that an hour should be displayed as either a number without a leading zero (4) or a number with a leading zero (04).
m mm	Specifies that a minute should be displayed as either a number without a leading zero (5) or a number with a leading zero (05). If the m or mm do not appear after an h or hh, the month will be displayed.
s ss	Specifies that a second should be displayed as either a number without a leading zero (6) or a number with a leading zero (06).
AM/PM am/pm A/P a/p	Specifies that time should be displayed using a 12-hour clock with AM, am, A, or a before noon and PM, pm, P, or p from noon to midnight.
[color]	Specifies that the characters in the cell should be displayed in a color. The available colors are black, white, red, green, blue, yellow, magenta, and cyan.

Example

=FORMAT.NUMBER("#,##0") formats the current selection with the #,##0 number format.

See Also

DELETE.FORMAT	Deletes a format	Macro Function
FORMAT.FONT	Formats a selection with a font	Macro Function
FORMAT.NUMBER	Equivalent command	Menu Command
FORMAT.TEXT	Formats selected text	Macro Function

FORMAT OVERLAY

Menu Command

The Format Overlay menu option only appears on the Format menu if the active document is a chart.

The Format Overlay option allows you to format overlays you have created with Chart Add Overlay. The Overlay option is greyed on the Format menu until you add the overlay with Chart Add Overlay. Choosing the Format Overlay option brings up the Format Chart dialog box, which is shown in Figure F-10.

All available options appear in the dialog box. Options that aren't currently relevant are greyed.

Type   The Overlay Chart Type drop-down list box allows you to choose the type of chart you want.

Area	Causes the main chart to be an area chart
Bar	Causes the main chart to be a bar chart
Column	Causes the main chart to be a column chart
Line	Causes the main chart to be a line chart
Pie	Causes the main chart to be a pie chart
Scatter	Causes the main chart to be a scatter chart
Radar	Causes the main chart to be a radar chart.

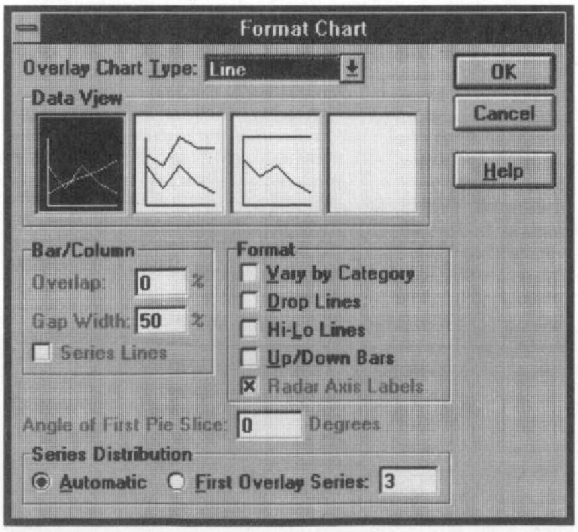

Figure F-10.   *The Format Chart dialog box*

Data View   The Data View box gives pictorial choices. Each picture represents a different view for the type of chart selected in the Overlay Chart Type box. For example, if you've selected a column chart, Data View shows you the various types of column charts available and allows you to select from them.

Bar/Column   The Bar/Column section of the dialog box allows you to control overlap, gaps, and series lines for bar and column charts.

Overlap	Allows you to choose the percentage of the width of a column or bar that the different bars or columns within a cluster overlap, if the Overlapped option is selected. If the Overlapped option is not selected, the Overlap option sets the distance between bars or columns within a cluster.
Gap Width	Allows you to determine the gap between clusters. The percentage is the percentage of the width of a column or bar.
Series Lines	Turns series lines on or off.

Format   The Format box allows you to set the formatting options for the main chart that are applicable to the selected main chart type.

Vary By Categories	Only relevant if there is a single series on the chart. Excel gives each data point a different pattern or color.
Drop Lines	Causes Excel to put lines on the chart from the highest value in each category to the category axis.
Hi-Lo Lines	Causes Excel to extend lines from the highest to the lowest point in each category.
Up/Down Bars	Only relevant for line charts. A bar is placed between the line for each series.
Radar Axis Labels	Places axis labels on radar charts.

Angle Of First Pie Slice   The Angle Of First Pie Slice option is only relevant for pie charts. It allows you to choose the angle of the first edge of the first slice. The angle is measured clockwise from the Y axis (vertical axis).

Series Distribution   Series distribution is either automatic or manual. If the Automatic option button is selected, Excel automatically distributes the series between the main chart and the overlay chart.

If you want to control the series that is overlayed, use the First Overlay Series box. The number you put in this box tells Excel which series you want plotted on the overlay chart. If you have four series and you put a 2 in the First Overlay Series box, the first series will appear on the main chart, and series 2, 3, and 4 will appear on the overlay chart.

See Also

FORMAT FONT	Formats selected text with a font	Menu Command
FORMAT MAIN CHART	Formats the main chart	Menu Command
FORMAT PATTERNS	Formats selected object with a pattern or color	Menu Command

FORMAT.OVERLAY(*type,[view],[overlap],[gap],[vary],[drop],[hilo], [angle],[distribution],[first-series],[up-down],[series-lines],[labels]*)
FORMAT.OVERLAY?(*[type],[view],[overlap],[gap],[vary],[drop],[hilo], [angle],[distribution],[first-series],[up-down],[series-lines],[labels]*)

Macro Function

FORMAT.OVERLAY performs the same action as the Format Overlay menu command. It formats the overlay chart. The arguments correspond to the arguments in the Format Overlay dialog box. (For more information, see the FORMAT OVERLAY menu command entry.)

Type is the type of chart. Each chart type has a number associated with it. Here is a list of the possible values for *type*:

Type	Chart Format
1	Area
2	Bar
3	Column
4	Line
5	Pie
6	XY Scatter
11	Radar

The *view* argument is a number that corresponds to one of the views in the Format Chart dialog box. The value for *view* depends on the chart type. The views change as different chart types are selected. A value of 1 would be the leftmost view in the dialog box. (See the FORMAT MAIN CHART entry for more information.)

The *overlap* argument corresponds to the Overlap option in the Format Chart dialog box. The *overlap* argument allows you to choose the percentage of the width of a column or bar that the different bars or columns within a cluster overlap. The *overlap* argument is used only if the chart type is bar or column. The default value for *overlap* is 0.

The *gap* argument corresponds to the Gap Width option in the Format Chart dialog box. The *gap* argument allows you to determine the gap between clusters as a percentage of the width of a column or bar. The default *gap* value is 50, or whatever was previously set.

The *vary* argument corresponds to the Vary By Categories option in the Format Chart dialog box. This argument is only used if there is a single series on the chart, and is either TRUE or FALSE. Excel gives each data point a different pattern or color. If the *vary* argument is omitted, *vary* is unchanged.

The *drop* argument corresponds to the Drop Lines option in the Format Chart dialog box. This argument, if TRUE, causes Excel to put lines on the chart from the highest value in each category to the category axis. If the *drop* argument is omitted, *drop* is unchanged.

The *hilo* argument corresponds to the Hi-Lo Lines option in the Format Chart dialog box. This argument causes Excel to extend lines from the highest to the lowest point in each category. *Hilo* is either TRUE or FALSE, turning the Hi-Lo Lines option on or off. If the *hilo* argument is omitted, *hilo* is unchanged.

The *angle* argument corresponds to the Angle Of First Pie Slice option in the Format Chart dialog box. This argument is only relevant for pie charts. It allows you to choose the angle of the first edge of the first slice. The angle is measured clockwise from the Y axis (vertical axis). If *angle* is omitted, the default value is 0.

The *distribution* argument is 1 if you want automatic series distribution, or 2 if you want manual series distribution. The default value for *distribution* is 1. If *distribution* is 2, the *first-series* argument should be the number of the series that is the first overlay series.

The *up-down* argument corresponds to the Up/Down Bars option in the Format Chart dialog box. This argument is only relevant for line charts. If *up-down* is TRUE, a bar is placed between lines for each series. The default value for *up-down* is FALSE.

The *series-lines* argument corresponds to the Series Lines check box in the Format Chart dialog box. *Series-lines* is either TRUE or FALSE and turns series lines on or off for either stacked bar or column charts. The default value for *series-lines* is FALSE, or whatever was previously set.

The *labels* argument corresponds to the Radar Axis Labels check box. This argument places axis labels on radar charts if *labels* is TRUE. The default value for *labels* is FALSE, or whatever was previously set.

In the dialog box version of FORMAT.OVERLAY, the arguments are used as default values for the dialog box that appears.

See Also

FORMAT.MAIN	Formats a main chart	Macro Function
FORMAT OVERLAY	Equivalent command	Menu Command

FORMAT PATTERNS

Menu Command

The Format Patterns menu option only appears on the Format menu if the active document is a chart.

The Format Patterns option allows you to change the pattern of an object or objects selected on your chart. For example, if your chart is a bar chart, you can select a series and use Format Patterns to make the bars appear striped, checked, dotted, and so on. When you select an object and choose the Format Patterns option, you'll see the Patterns dialog box:

There are two main sections in the dialog box: Border and Area. Each of these sections contains three option buttons: Automatic, None, and Custom. The Custom option button for borders allows you to pick a style, color, and weight for the border. The Custom option button for Area allows you to pick a pattern, foreground color, and background color. The Invert If Negative box should be turned on if you want the pattern inverted for negative numbers.

In addition, if you select the Apply To All check box, Excel applies the choices you make to all data points on the chart.

Depending on the object that you have selected, some of these options may not appear in your dialog box. Only options relevant to the selected object will appear.

See Also

FORMAT BORDER	Places a border around a selection	Menu Command
FORMAT FONT	Formats selected text with a font	Menu Command
FORMAT PATTERNS	Formats a selection with a pattern or color	Menu Command

FORMAT ROW HEIGHT

Menu Command

The Format Row Height menu option sets the height of the selected row or rows. Only one cell in the row needs to be selected for you to set the height for the entire row. The default row height for Excel is 12.75 points.

You can also change the row height using the mouse. First select all the rows you want to format. The selection can be a multiple selection, meaning that you select more than one range at once.

Point to the line between the row headings at the bottom of one of the rows you want to format. The mouse pointer will change into a cross with vertical arrows, as shown here. (This example shows a multiple selection of rows 5 and 7; both these rows would be sized simultaneously.)

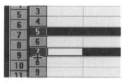

Click the mouse and drag the row height pointer until the row above it is the desired height. Then release the mouse. All selected rows will be set to the new height.

See Also

FORMAT COLUMN WIDTH	Changes the width of selected columns	Menu Command
ROW.HEIGHT	Equivalent function	Macro Function

FORMAT SCALE

Menu Command

The Format Scale menu option only appears on the Format menu if the active document is a chart.

The Format Scale option allows you to control the appearance of the axes on your chart. You must select an axis to format before you select the Format Scale option.

Different dialog boxes appear if you select the category axis or the value axis. If you select the category axis before choosing the Format Scale option, the Category Axis Scale dialog box, shown here, will appear.

```
┌─────────────────────────────────────────────┐
│ ▬            Axis Scale                       │
├─────────────────────────────────────────────┤
│ Category (X) Axis Scale          ┌─────────┐ │
│                                  │   OK    │ │
│                                  └─────────┘ │
│ Value (Y) Axis Crosses           ┌─────────┐ │
│ at Category Number:  [1    ]     │ Cancel  │ │
│ Number of Categories             └─────────┘ │
│ Between Tick Labels: [1    ]     ┌─────────┐ │
│                                  │Patterns.│ │
│ Number of Categories             └─────────┘ │
│ Between Tick Marks:  [1    ]     ┌─────────┐ │
│                                  │  Font.. │ │
│                                  └─────────┘ │
│                                  ┌─────────┐ │
│                                  │  Text.. │ │
│                                  └─────────┘ │
│                                  ┌─────────┐ │
│                                  │  Help   │ │
│ [X] Value (Y) Axis Crosses Between Categories│
│ [ ] Categories in Reverse Order              │
│ [ ] Value (Y) Axis Crosses at Maximum Category│
└─────────────────────────────────────────────┘
```

Here is a list of options that appear in the Category Axis Scale dialog box:

Value Axis Crosses At Category Number	Allows you to select the value on the category axis where you want the value axis to cross. The default value for this option is 1.
Number of Categories Between Tick Labels	Allows you to decide how many categories you want between tick labels. The default value for this option is 1, which puts a tick label at every category. If you want tick labels at every other category, enter 2 in this box.
Number of Categories Between Tick Marks	Allows you to decide how many categories you want between tick marks. The default value is 1, which puts a tick mark at every category. If you want tick marks every other category type 2 in this box.
Value Axis Crosses Between Categories	If this option is turned on, Excel crosses the axis between categories.
Categories In Reverse Order	If this option is turned on, the categories are shown right-to-left rather than left-to-right.
Value Axis Crosses At Maximum Category	If this option is turned on, the value axis crosses the category axis at the maximum category.
Patterns	Any changes you made in the Format Scale box are carried out, and the Patterns dialog box is displayed. (For more information, see Format Patterns.)

| Font | Any changes you made in the Format Scale box are carried out, and the Font dialog box is displayed. (For more information, see Format Font.) |
| Text | Any changes you made in the Format Scale box are carried out, and the Text dialog box is displayed. (For more information, see Format Text.) |

If you select the value axis before you choose the Format Scale option, the Value Axis Scale dialog box, shown here, will appear.

Here are the options that appear in the Value Format Scale dialog box:

Minimum	When the Automatic box is turned on, the lowest value in any series in the chart is included. If it is not turned on, you can type a value in the box on the right side to tell Excel what you want the minimum value on your chart to be.
Maximum	When the Automatic box is turned on, the highest value in any series in the chart is included. If it is not turned on, you can type a value in the box on the right side to tell Excel what you want the maximum value on your chart to be.
Major Unit	The Automatic box tells Excel to determine the distance between the major tick marks. If you don't have the Automatic box turned on, you can type a number in the box on the right to tell Excel the distance you want between major tick marks.

F

Minor Unit	The Automatic box tells Excel to determine the distance between the minor tick marks. If you don't have the Automatic box turned on, you can type a number in the box on the right to tell Excel the distance you want between minor tick marks.
Category Axis Crosses At	The Automatic box tells Excel to cross the value axis at zero. If you want the category axis to cross the value axis at some other value, type the value in the box to the right, and turn off the Automatic box.
Logarithmic Scale	Tells Excel you want to use a logarithmic scale for your chart.
Values In Reverse Order	If turned on, this option tells Excel to display values in ascending order from top to bottom.
Category Axis Crosses At Maximum Value	If this option is turned on, Excel crosses the category axis and the value axis at the maximum value on the value axis.
Value Axis Crosses At Maximum Category	If this option is turned on, the value axis will cross the category axis at the maximum category. This option is only relevant for scatter charts.
Patterns	Any changes you made in the Format Scale box are carried out, and the Patterns dialog box is displayed.
Font	Any changes you made in the Format Scale box are carried out, and the Format Font dialog box is displayed.
Text	Any changes you made in the Format Scale box are carried out, and the Format Text dialog box is displayed.

See Also

FORMAT FONT	Formats font of selected text	Menu Command
FORMAT PATTERNS	Formats a selection with a pattern or color	Menu Command
FORMAT TEXT	Formats selected text	Menu Command

FORMAT SEND TO BACK

Menu Command

The Format Send To Back menu command places the selected graphic objects behind other objects.

FORMAT.SHAPE(*vertex, insert, [ref], [X], [Y]*)

Macro Function

FORMAT.SHAPE allows you to shape an existing polygon by inserting, deleting, or moving a vertex. This macro function performs the same action as clicking on the drawing toolbar's Reshape tool.

Vertex is the number of the vertex that you want to insert, delete, or move. *Insert* is either TRUE or FALSE. If *insert* is TRUE, the vertex is inserted according to the specifications given. If *insert* is FALSE, the vertex is either moved or deleted. If the arguments *ref*, *X*, and *Y* are given, the vertex is moved to the location specified by those arguments. If *ref*, *X*, and *Y* are not given, the vertex is deleted.

Ref is the location from which the *X* and *Y* offsets are calculated. *X* and *Y* are horizontal and vertical distances from *ref* that determine the location of the vertex. *X* and *Y* are measured in points (1/72 of an inch).

See Also

CREATE.OBJECT	Creates a polygon	Macro Function
EXTEND.POLYGON	Adds a vertex to a polygon	Macro Function

FORMAT SIZE

Menu Command

The Format Size menu option only appears on the Format menu if the active document is a chart. This option allows you to resize a selected chart object using the keyboard. After selecting the chart object and choosing the Format Size option, use the direction keys to size the object and then press ENTER.

See Also

FORMAT MOVE	Moves a selected object	Menu Command
FORMAT.SIZE	Equivalent function	Macro Function
SIZE	Changes window size	Macro Function

FORMAT.SIZE(*width, height, [reference]*)
FORMAT.SIZE?(*[width], [height], [reference]*)

Macro Function

FORMAT.SIZE is equivalent to the Format Size menu option. *Width* and *height* are numbers whose units are points. In the dialog box version (with the question mark), the arguments, if included, are used as default values for the dialog box that appears.

The *reference* argument is the reference for the *width* and *height* offsets. This argument is only used if you are sizing worksheet objects. It is easier to record this function for your macro.

Example

=FORMAT.SIZE(100,100) sizes the currently selected object to 100 points by 100 points.

See Also

FORMAT.MOVE	Moves a selected object	Macro Function
FORMAT SIZE	Equivalent command	Menu Command
SIZE	Changes window size	Macro Function

FORMAT STYLE

Menu Command

The Format Style menu command allows you do define a combination of cell formats as a style. You can format the cell or cells with the desired attributes and then choose the Format Style menu command to name the style. Alternatively, you can choose the Format Style menu command, then click on the Define button. The dialog box expands to show the Number, Font, Alignment, Border, Patterns, and Protection buttons. Clicking on one of these buttons opens the corresponding dialog box, allowing you to define the cell attributes as desired.

See Also

FORMAT ALIGNMENT	Aligns contents of selected cells	Menu Command
FORMAT BORDER	Places borders around selected cells	Menu Command
FORMAT FONT	Formats text fonts in a selection	Menu Command
FORMAT NUMBER	Formats numbers in selected cells	Menu Command
FORMAT PATTERNS	Formats pattern or color of selected object	Menu Command

FORMAT TEXT

Menu Command

The Format Text option only appears on the Format menu if the active document is a chart. This option allows you to format selected text. Once you select the text you want to format and choose the Format Text option, you'll see this dialog box:

Here is a list of the options that appear in the Text dialog box. (Your dialog box may show different options depending on the selected text.)

Text Alignment	Allows you to decide if you want Horizontal text aligned to the Left, Center, Right, or Justified, and if you want Vertical text aligned to the Top, Center, Bottom, or Justified.
Orientation	Allows you to choose one of four different orientations.
Automatic Text	If the Automatic Text box is turned on, Excel restores any edited text to the text originally created with Attach Text.
Automatic Size	If Text border sizes have been changed, turning this box on restores the box to its original size.
Patterns	Any changes you made in the Format Text box are carried out, and the Patterns dialog box appears.
Font	Any changes you made in the Format Text box are carried out, and the Font dialog box appears.

See Also

FORMAT FONT	Formats selected text with a font	Menu Command
FORMAT PATTERNS	Formats a selection with a pattern or color	Menu Command
FORMAT.TEXT	Equivalent function	Macro Function

FORMAT.TEXT(*horizontal-alignment, vertical-alignment, orientation, automatic-text, automatic-size, show-key, show-value*)
FORMAT.TEXT?(*horizontal-alignment, vertical-alignment, orientation, automatic-text, automatic-size, show-key, show-value*)

Macro Function

FORMAT.TEXT performs the same action as the Format Text menu option. *Horizontal-alignment* can be 1 (left), 2 (center), 3 (right), or 4 (justified). *Vertical-alignment* can be 1 (top), 2 (center), 3 (bottom), or 4 (justified).

The *orientation* argument can be 1 (horizontal), 2 (vertical), 3 (upward), or 4 (downward). *Automatic-text, automatic-size, show-key,* and *show-value* correspond to check boxes with the same names in the Text dialog box. A value of TRUE turns on the check box. A value of FALSE turns off the check box. In the dialog box version (with the question mark), the arguments, if included, are used as default values for the dialog box that appears.

FORMULA

Menu

The Formula menu is used to build and maintain formulas on the worksheet. This includes creating, using, and deleting range names, adding functions, and switching between absolute and relative references. You can also use the Formula menu to add notes to cells, go to a particular cell, select cells based on their contents or type, search for and replace text. Finally, the Formula menu provides access to Excel's Outline, Goal Seek, Solver, and Scenario Manager commands.

FORMULA(*formula-string, [reference]*)

Macro Function

If the current document is a worksheet, FORMULA causes the formula given in the *formula-string* argument to be entered into the cell designated by the *reference* argument. *Formula-string* can be a formula, a value, a reference, or text. References must be given in R1C1 style. If *reference* is omitted, *formula-string* is entered in the active cell.

If the current document is a chart, *formula-string* is entered in the current selection and the *reference* argument is omitted. The current selection determines how *formula-string* is treated in a chart. Normally, this function would be used to enter a new text label or change an existing text label. If you want to change an existing text label, select the label first. You can also use FORMULA to add or change a series, but the EDIT.SERIES function is more commonly used for this purpose.

Examples

=FORMULA("January") enters the label "January" into the active cell.
=FORMULA("January Sales") enters the label "January Sales" as the chart title, if the chart title is selected.

See Also

    EDIT.SERIES   Adds or changes a chart series   Macro Function

F

FORMULA APPLY NAMES

Menu Command

The Formula Apply Names menu option allows you to replace cell references with meaningful names in selected formulas on your worksheet. First, you must define names using the Formula Define Name menu option. Then you must select a region in which you want to apply names to your formulas. If you choose the Formula Apply Names option and only one cell is selected, names will be applied to all formulas on the worksheet.

Selecting the Formula Apply Names option brings up the following dialog box:

This dialog box allows you to select which of the names that you have defined using the Formula Define Name option you want applied to the formulas in your selected range. The items available in the dialog box are described here:

Apply Names	Allows you to select the names that you want to apply to the formulas in the selected range. You can select as many names as you want. Use the direction keys while holding down the CTRL key and pressing the SPACEBAR to select or remove a name. Alternatively, hold down the SHIFT key while clicking the mouse on the names you want.

Ignore Relative/Absolute	With this box turned off, Excel replaces only absolute cell references with absolute names, relative cell references with relative names, and mixed cell references with mixed names. If the box is turned on, Excel replaces cell references with names despite their type.
Use Row And Column Names	With this box turned off, Excel only replaces cell references with names if an exact match can be found. If this box is turned on, Excel tries to replace the cell references with exact names, but if it cannot find a match, it will look for a name defined for the range that contains the cell in question and use the name it finds in the formula.

If you click on the Options button, three more options appear in the dialog box: Omit Column Name if Same Column, Omit Row Name if Same Row, and Name Order.

Omit Column Name If Same Column	If this box is turned on and if the cell in question is in a row-oriented named range, Excel uses the row-oriented named range even if there is a column-oriented name for the same cell. If this box is turned off, Excel replaces cell references with both the column and row name, if both names are defined.
Omit Row Name If Same Row	If this box is turned on and if the cell in question is in a column-oriented named range, Excel uses the column-oriented named range even if there is a row-oriented name for the same cell. If this box is turned off, Excel replaces cell references with both the row and column name, if both names are defined.
Name Order	Allows you to choose which name you want to come first if the cell is in both a row-oriented named range and a column-oriented named range.

F

See Also

FORMULA CREATE NAMES	Creates named ranges	Menu Command
FORMULA DEFINE NAME	Defines and deletes names	Menu Command

FORMULA.ARRAY(*formula-string, [reference]*)

Macro Function

Using FORMULA.ARRAY is the same as entering an array formula while pressing the CTRL-SHIFT-ENTER keys. *Formula-string* is text that you want entered into the array. *Reference* is optional, and refers to the location where you want *formula-string* entered. If no *reference* argument is given, *formula-string* is entered into the active cell.

See Also

FORMULA	Enters a formula into a cell	Macro Function
FORMULA.FILL	Enters a formula into a range	Macro Function

FORMULA.CONVERT(*formula, input-a1, [output-a1], [output-type], [ref]*)

Macro Function

FORMULA.CONVERT converts the style of references and addressing contained in a formula. *Formula* is a text string. *Input-a1* should be TRUE if the references in the formula are given in A1 style. *Input-a1* should be FALSE if the references in *formula* are given in R1C1 style. *Output-a1* is either TRUE or FALSE, and indicates the reference style of the output. *Output-a1* should be TRUE if you want the references in the output in A1 style, and FALSE if you want the references in the output in R1C1 style. If *output-a1* is omitted, the reference style of the output is the same as the input. *Output-type* indicates the reference type of the output. Here is a list of possible values for *output-type:*

Output-type	Reference
1	Absolute
2	Absolute row, relative column
3	Relative row, absolute column
4	Relative

If the *output-type* argument is not given, the output reference type is the same as the input reference type. *Ref* is an absolute cell reference to use for relative addresses. In other words, all relative addresses are relative to *ref*.

Example

=FORMULA.CONVERT("=SUM(R1C1:R10C1)",FALSE,TRUE,1) returns "=SUM($A$1:$A$10)".

See Also

ABSREF	Converts to absolute references	Macro Function
RELREF	Converts to relative references	Macro Function

FORMULA CREATE NAMES

Menu Command

➤   *Shortcut Key:*   CTRL-SHIFT-F3

The Formula Create Names menu option allows you to define several names at once. You need to select a range of cells with names included on one edge of the range. Then choose the Formula Create Names option. This displays the following dialog box, which allows you to tell Excel where the names are in your selection:

You can put the names along more than one edge in your selection.

Top Row	The names are in the top row. Each cell in the top row names the column below it.
Left Column	The names are in the left column. Each cell in the left column names the row to its right.
Bottom Row	The names are in the bottom row. Each cell in the bottom row names the column above it.
Right Column	The names are in the right column. Each cell in the right column names the row to its left.

See Also

FORMULA APPLY NAMES	Applies names to formulas in a selection	Menu Command
FORMULA DEFINE NAME	Defines or deletes names	Menu Command

FORMULA DEFINE NAME

Menu Command

➤   *Shortcut Key:* CTRL-F3

The Formula Define Name menu option allows you to create a name for a cell or for a range of cells, a multiple selection, a value, or a formula. You can also delete names that Excel creates automatically while executing other options. For example, if you create a print area with the Set Print Area option, Excel creates a named print range. You can delete that print range using the Formula Define Name option.

Worksheet

If you select a range before you choose the Formula Define Name option, the selected range will automatically appear in the Refers To text box located in the dialog box, as shown here:

If you don't select a range before you choose the Formula Define Name option, you can type in a range or formula in the Refers To box. There are five objects in the Define Name dialog box: the Names in Sheet list box, the Name and Refers To text boxes, and the Add and Delete buttons.

Names In Sheet	Lists all the names defined for the worksheet. If you want to delete a name, or change the name it refers to, you can select the name with the mouse and delete or modify it.

Name	Excel will, if possible, propose a name for the range that you selected before choosing the Formula Define Name command. If the active cell in the active range contains a name, it will propose that name as the name for the selected range. If you didn't select a range or Excel can't find a name to propose, you can type a name in here. Or, you can select a name from the Names in Sheet box and it will appear in the Name box.
Refers To	Contains the selected range if you selected a range before choosing the Formula Define Name command. If you didn't select a range, you can type in a range, a formula, a value, or another name. The name in the Name box is the name for what appears or what you put in the Refers To box.
Add	Adds the name in the Name box and associates it with the range that appears in the Refers To box.
Delete	Deletes the selected name from the Names in Sheet box. If you delete a name that appears in formulas on your worksheet, the #NAME? error appears in the formula.

F

Macro Sheet

If you select the Formula Define Name option when the active document is a macro sheet, all the options described for the worksheet will appear, plus an additional option, Macro, which is described here:

Macro	Allows you to define the type of macro on your macro sheet. There are three options: Function, Command, and None. If you choose the Command option, you can also type a shortcut key, which can be any alphabetic character. To run a macro using the shortcut key, hold down the CTRL key and press the shortcut key.
Category	Allows you to assign a function or a command macro to a category.

See Also

FORMULA APPLY NAMES	Applies names to formulas in a selection	Menu Command
FORMULA CREATE NAMES	Creates named ranges	Menu Command

FORMULA.FILL(*formula-string, [reference]*)

Macro Function

Using FORMULA.FILL is the same as entering a formula while pressing the CTRL key. The formula in the *formula-string* argument is entered into the cell or cells specified by the *reference* argument. If the *reference* argument is omitted, the formula is entered into the cells in the current selection.

Example

=FORMULA.FILL("=SUM(R[-2]C:R[−1]C)") enters the formula =SUM(B8:B9) in cell B10, =SUM(C8:C9) in cell C10, and =SUM(D8:D9) in cell D10 if the current selection is B10:D10.

See Also

DATA.SERIES	Enters a series into a range	Macro Function
FORMULA	Enters a formula into a cell	Macro Function
FORMULA.ARRAY	Enters an array into a reference	Macro Function

FORMULA FIND

Menu Command

➤   *Shortcut Key:* F7

The Formula Find menu option allows you to search the current selection or the entire worksheet for occurrences of text or numbers. If you select cells before you choose the Formula Find option, Excel will search only the selected cells. If you don't select a range before choosing the Formula Find option, Excel will search the entire worksheet. Selecting the Formula Find option brings up the following dialog box:

This dialog box includes the options Find What, Look In, Look At, Look By, and Match Case.

Find What	Allows you to enter the string of characters you want to search for. You can type in #REF! and #NAME? to find error messages.
Look In	Allows you to choose which cells you want to search in the worksheet. You can choose Formulas, Values, or Notes.
Look At	Allows you to specify whether Excel should search only for cells whose contents match the character string in the Find What box exactly, or also locate cells in which the string appears as part of the cell contents.
Look By	Allows you to specify whether Excel should carry out the search by rows or by columns.
Match Case	Turning this box on tells Excel to match uppercase and lowercase characters.

See Also

FORMULA.FIND(*string, in, at, by, dir*)
FORMULA.FIND?(*[string], [in], [at], [by], [dir]*)

Macro Function

FORMULA.FIND performs the same action as the Formula Find menu option. *String* specifies the search string. The arguments *in, at, by,* and *dir* are defined as follows.

IN		
	1	Formulas
	2	Values
	3	Notes
AT		
	1	Whole
	2	Part
BY		
	1	Rows
	2	Columns

DIR	
1	Next
2	Previous

In the dialog box version (with the question mark), if the arguments are included, they are used as default values for the dialog box that appears.

Example

=FORMULA.FIND("Total",1,2,1,1) searches by rows for the string "Total".

See Also

DATA.FIND	Searches a database	Macro Function
FORMULA.FIND.NEXT	Finds the next match	Macro Function
FORMULA.FIND.PREV	Finds the previous match	Macro Function

FORMULA.FIND.NEXT()

Macro Function

Using FORMULA.FIND.NEXT is the same as pressing the F7 key. The function finds the next match for the string originally searched for with FORMULA.FIND. If a match is found, FORMULA.FIND.NEXT returns TRUE. If a match is not found, it returns FALSE.

See Also

DATA.FIND	Searches a database	Macro Function
FORMULA.FIND	Finds a match	Macro Function
FORMULA.FIND.PREV	Finds the next previous match	Macro Function

FORMULA.FIND.PREV()

Macro Function

Using FORMULA.FIND.PREV is the same as pressing SHIFT-F7. The function searches backwards through the document and finds the next preceding match for the string originally searched for with FORMULA.FIND. If a match is found, FORMULA.FIND.PREV returns TRUE. If a match is not found, it returns FALSE.

See Also

DATA.FIND	Searches a database	Macro Function
FORMULA.FIND	Finds a match	Macro Function
FORMULA.FIND.NEXT	Finds the next match	Macro Function

FORMULA GOAL SEEK

Menu Command   **New to Version 4.0**

Formula Goal Seek is one of Excel's new analysis tools. It allows you search for a value that causes a formula to equal a given value. The dialog box that appears when you choose Formula Goal Seek asks for Set Cell, To Value, and By Changing Cell. Put the reference of the cell for which you want to set the value in the Set Cell box. This cell must contain a formula. Put the value you want the formula to equal in the To Value box. Put the cell on which the formula is dependent and that you want to vary in the By Changing Cell box. When you click on OK, Excel will vary that cell until the desired value is achieved.

Goal Seek is normally used when you want a solution for a function by changing one variable. Use Formula Solver to find a solution for a function by changing more than one variable.

See Also

FORMULA SCENARIO MANAGER	Keeps track of analysis scenarios	Menu Command
FORMULA SOLVER	Multiple variable solver	Menu Command
GOAL.SEEK	Equivalent function	Macro Function

FORMULA GOTO

Menu Command

➤   *Shortcut Key:* F5

The Formula Goto menu option allows you to quickly select a named area or cell. Choosing this option brings up the following dialog box:

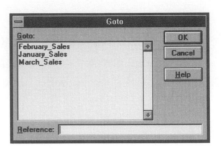

After you click on OK, Excel remembers where you were before. If you choose Formula Goto again, your previous selection appears in the Reference box automatically. This makes it easy to go back and forth between two parts of your worksheet.

Goto	Lists all of the defined names on your worksheet. If you select one of these names and click on OK, the area associated with the defined name will be selected on your worksheet.
Reference	Typing a cell reference or a name in this box and choosing OK takes you to the specified area or cell.

See Also

FORMULA.GOTO   Equivalent function   Macro Function

FORMULA.GOTO(*reference,[corner]*)
FORMULA.GOTO?(*[reference],[corner]*)

Macro Function

FORMULA.GOTO performs the same action as the Formula Goto menu option. *Reference* is the reference to the cell or cells where you want to go; it can be in either A1 style or R1C1 style. The dialog box version (with the question mark) of the FORMULA.GOTO function has an optional reference. If *reference* is omitted, FORMULA.GOTO? goes to the cells that were active before the FORMULA.GOTO? function was executed.

Corner is either TRUE or FALSE, and indicates how Excel scrolls. If *corner* is TRUE, Excel scrolls the worksheet so that *reference* is the upper-left cell in the window. If *corner* is FALSE, Excel scrolls normally. If no *corner* argument is given, the default value is FALSE.

In the dialog box version of FORMULA.GOTO, the arguments, if given, are used for default values in the dialog box that appears.

Examples

=FORMULA.GOTO("SALES.XLS!R1C1:R2C2") goes to A1:B2 on the worksheet SALES.XLS.
=FORMULA.GOTO(SALES.XLS!$A$1:$B$2) goes to A1:B2 on the worksheet SALES.XLS.

See Also

HSCROLL	Horizontally scrolls the document	Macro Function
SELECT	Selects a cell, range, or object	Macro Function
VSCROLL	Vertically scrolls the document	Macro Function

FORMULA NOTE

Menu Command

➤ *Shortcut Key:* SHIFT-F2

The Formula Note menu option allows you to attach a note to a cell. The note doesn't actually appear on the worksheet, but you can print the notes with the worksheets or you can look at notes with the Window Show Info option. The Formula Note option lets you document your worksheet. Choosing the Formula Note option displays the Cell Note dialog box:

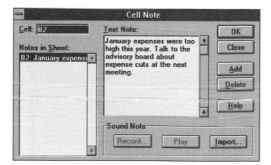

The items in the dialog box are described here:

Cell	Allows you to type in a cell reference that you want to enter a note for. If you want to modify or delete an existing note, you can select a note from the Notes in Sheet box, and the cell reference will automatically appear in the Cell box.

Notes In Sheet	Allows you to select existing notes so that you can modify or delete them.
Note	Allows you to enter new notes, or displays existing notes.
Add	Adds the text in the note box to the cell in the Cell box.
Delete	Deletes the note selected in the Notes in Sheet box.
Sound Note	Allows you to record sound that will play back whenever you double-click on the cell. To use this feature, you must have recording hardware installed in your computer.

See Also

NOTE   Equivalent function   Macro Function

FORMULA OUTLINE

Menu Command   **New to Version 4.0**

The Formula Outline menu option allows you to create an outline for your worksheet. Outlining provides a way of creating up to eight levels of information. To create an outline, simply select the range that you want to outline and choose the Formula Outline menu command. A dialog box appears, from which you can choose manual or automatic outline creation. If you are creating a manual outline, you can set the summary information to be below or to the right of the detail information. Once you have set all the options in the dialog box, click on the Create button. Now that you have created an outline, you can select levels in the outline for hiding, moving, or copying. The Outline dialog box is shown here:

See Also

OUTLINE   Equivalent function   Macro Function

FORMULA PASTE FUNCTION

Menu Command

➤   *Shortcut Key:* SHIFT-F3

The Formula Paste Function option allows you to paste a built-in Excel function into the formula bar. If the formula bar is already active when you choose the option, the function is pasted in at the insertion point. If the formula bar is not active, Excel activates the formula bar and pastes the function into the formula bar. Choosing the Paste Function option displays a dialog box, shown here, that contains three items: Function Category, Paste Function, and Paste Arguments.

Function Category	Allows you to select a category of functions. When you select a category, only functions that belong to that category appear in the Paste Function box. If you want to list all the functions, choose All.
Paste Function	Lists all of Excel's built-in functions in the category selected in the Function Category box. Also lists any function macros that you have created on any open macro sheets. To choose a function, select it and then click on the OK button.
Paste Arguments	If you turn this check box on, descriptions of the arguments will be pasted with the function. If the function has more than one argument profile, another dialog box will appear where you can choose which profile you want.

FORMULA PASTE NAME

Menu Command

Worksheet

➤   *Shortcut Key:* F3

The Formula Paste Name menu option allows you to paste any names that you have previously defined with the Formula Define Name or the Formula Create Names option into the formula bar. You can also paste a list of all defined names onto your worksheet. Choosing the Formula Paste Name option displays this dialog box:

This dialog box contains a Paste Name list box and a Paste List command button.

Paste Name	Lists all defined names for your worksheet. You can choose which name to paste by selecting it and then clicking on the OK button.
Paste List	Tells Excel that you want to paste all defined names and what they refer to on your worksheet. The paste region will be two columns wide, and will start from the active cell. Any data in the paste region will be overwritten. If you make a mistake, choose the Edit Undo command immediately.

Macro Sheet

If the active document is a macro sheet, the Paste List command button behaves differently. Everything else works exactly the same.

Paste List	Tells Excel you want to paste all defined names and what they refer to on your worksheet. The paste region will be five columns wide, and will start from the active cell. Any data in the paste region will be overwritten. If you make a mistake, choose the Edit Undo command immediately. The first column contains the name; the second contains what the name refers to; the third column contains a 1 if the name is for a function macro, and a 2 if the name is for a command macro; the fourth column contains the shortcut key if there is one; and the last column contains a number relating to the category.

See Also

FORMULA DEFINE NAME   Defines names in a   Menu Command
                             worksheet

F

FORMULA REPLACE

Menu Command

The Formula Replace menu option allows you to replace characters with new characters. If you have selected a range, Excel replaces within that range. If you haven't selected a range, Excel replaces the whole worksheet. Choosing the Formula Replace option displays the following dialog box:

The items in the dialog box are described here:

Find What	Allows you to enter the string of characters you want to replace. If you have performed a search using Formula Find, Excel automatically places the string you searched for in this box. You can choose to accept the characters that Excel suggests, or you can type in other characters. You can use the Excel wildcard symbols ? and * in the Find What box.
Replace With	Allows you to enter the characters you want to use as a replacement string.
Look At	Allows you to specify whether Excel should search only for cells whose contents match the character string in the Find What box exactly, or also locate cells in which the string appears as part of the cell contents.
Look By	Allows you to specify whether Excel should carry out the search by rows or by columns.
Replace All	Tells Excel to replace all occurrences of the character string in the Find What box with the characters in the Replace With box.
Find Next	Tells Excel to find the next occurrence of the character string in the Find What box. If you want to find the previous occurrence, hold down the SHIFT key while you click on Find Next.
Replace	Tells Excel to replace the characters in the Find What box with the characters in the Replace With box if the current cell contains the characters in the Find What box. Excel will then search for the next occurrence of the characters in the Find What box.
Match Case	Turning this box on tells Excel to match uppercase and lowercase characters.

See Also

FORMULA FIND	Finds the string given	Menu Command
FORMULA.REPLACE	Equivalent function	Macro Function

FORMULA.REPLACE(*search-string,replace-string,[at],[by],
[which-cells], [match-case]*)
FORMULA.REPLACE?(*[search-string],[replace-string],[at],[by],
[which-cells],[match-case]*)

Macro Function

FORMULA.REPLACE performs the same action as the Formula Replace menu option. The string specified by *search-string* is replaced with *replace-string*. *At* indicates whether *search-string* is all or part of the string being searched for. *By* indicates the order of the search. The arguments *at* and *by* are defined here:

At	
1	Whole
2	Part
By	
1	Rows
2	Columns

The *which-cells* argument is a logical value that is TRUE if you want to replace only the current cell. *Which-cells* is FALSE if you want to replace the whole selection or the whole document (if the current selection is a cell). *Match-case* is a logical value that is TRUE if you want to match upper- and lowercase, and FALSE otherwise. In the dialog box version (with the question mark), the arguments, if included, are used as default values for the dialog box that appears.

See Also

| FORMULA.FIND | Finds a specified string | Macro Function |
| FORMULA REPLACE | Equivalent command | Menu Command |

FORMULA SCENARIO MANAGER

Menu Command   **New to Version 4.0**

FORMULA SCENARIO MANAGER is an analysis tool new to Version 4. Scenario Manager keeps track of different sets of values, or *scenarios,* for you. You can access the Scenario Manager through the menu directly, or through other analysis tools. You can use Goal Seek or the Solver to set up a scenario, and the Scenario Manager to store the solution. Each set of values, or scenario, can be stored with a meaningful name. In this way, you can organize your solutions to a problem. Once you have stored your scenarios, you can create a report to compare the various alternatives.

See Also

FORMULA GOAL SEEK	Solves a one-variable problem	Menu Command
FORMULA SOLVER	Solves a multiple-variable problem	Menu Command

FORMULA SELECT SPECIAL

Menu Command

The Formula Select Special menu option allows you to select cells with particular characteristics. You define the characteristics by which you want to select in the dialog box that appears when you choose the Formula Select Special option, as shown here:

If you selected a range before choosing the Formula Select Special option, Excel selects only within that range. If only one cell was selected before the option was chosen, Excel selects from the entire worksheet. The options in the dialog box are described here:

Notes	Causes Excel to make a multiple selection of all the cells that have a note attached.
Constants	Causes Excel to make a multiple selection of all the cells that contain a constant. You use the four check boxes under the Formulas option to choose the kinds of constants to select.

Formulas	Causes Excel to make a multiple selection of all the cells that contain a formula. You use the four boxes under the Formulas option to choose the kinds of formulas to select.
Numbers	Selects cells that have formulas that evaluate to numbers.
Text	Selects cells that have formulas that evaluate to text.
Logicals	Selects cells that have formulas that evaluate to TRUE or FALSE.
Errors	Selects cells that have formulas that produce errors.
Blanks	Causes Excel to make a multiple selection of all the cells that contain a blank.
Current Region	Causes Excel to make a selection around the active cell.
Current Array	If the active cell belongs to an array, causes the entire array to be selected.
Row Differences	Causes Excel to compare the cell in the same column as the active cell with all the other cells in its row, selecting cells that are different from the comparison cell.
Column Differences	Causes Excel to compare the cell in the same row as the active cell with all the other cells in its column, selecting cells that are different from the comparison cell.
Precedents	Causes Excel to make a multiple selection of all the cells that the formulas in the original selection refer to.
Dependents	Causes Excel to make a multiple selection of all the cells that are referred to by formulas in the original selection.
Direct Only	Supplemental to the Precedents and Dependents options. Causes Excel to make a multiple selection of all the cells that the formulas in the original selection refer to directly if the Precedents option is on. Causes Excel to make a multiple selection of all the cells that are referred to directly by formulas in the original selection if the Dependents option is on.
All Levels	Supplemental to the Precedents and Dependents options. Causes Excel to make a multiple selection of all the cells that the formulas in the original selection refer to directly or indirectly if the Precedents option is on. Causes Excel to make a multiple selection of all the cells that are referred to directly or indirectly by formulas in the original selection if the Dependents option is on.
Last Cell	Causes Excel to select the last cell in the selection.

F

Visible Cells Only	Causes Excel to select only those cells that are currently visible.
Objects	Causes Excel to make a multiple selection of all objects.

See Also

SELECT.SPECIAL   Equivalent function   Macro Function

FORMULA SOLVER

Menu Command   **New to Version 4.0**

Formula Solver is one of Excel's new analysis tools. The Solver allows you to find a solution to a formula that has multiple variables. Solver allows you to define up to 200 variables, and up to 100 constraints on those variables. A *constraint* limits the values that a variable is allowed to take on. For example, you could constrain a variable to be an integer, to be greater than zero, or to be no larger than a certain value. Solver tries to solve the formula to equal the value you specify by trying different values for the variables you defined within the constraints. In addition, you can indicate that you want the formula to be a maximum or minimum value. When you choose Formula Solver, the Solver Parameters dialog box appears, as shown here:

The Solver Parameters dialog box contains the following items:

Set Cell	Allows you to enter the address of the cell that contains the formula you want to solve.
Equal To	Allows you to ask for a maximum, minimum, or specific value for the formula.
By Changing Cells	Allows you to enter the addresses of the cells that you want to change. This can be a multiple selection.

| Subject to the Constraints | Lets you use comparative operators, such as <, >, and =, to constrain the cells you want to change. You can use the Add, Change, Delete, and Reset All buttons to control constraint settings. |

See Also

| FORMULA GOAL SEEK | Solves a single-variable problem | Menu Command |
| SOLVER.ADD | Equivalent function | Macro Function |

FOURIER(*input, output, [inverse]*)

Macro Function

FOURIER performs a Fourier transformation on the *input* range. The number of cells in the *input* range must be a power of 2. The result is placed in the output range. *Output* is the upper-left cell of the output range. *Inverse* is either TRUE or FALSE. If *inverse* is TRUE, an inverse Fourier transformation is performed. If *inverse* is FALSE, a regular Fourier transformation is performed. The default value for *inverse* is FALSE.

See Also

| SAMPLE | Sample the input data | Macro Function |

FPOS(*file, [position]*)

Macro Function

FPOS positions the file opened with the FOPEN function, specified by the *file* number given by the FOPEN function. To position a file means to set the *position* of where characters are read to and written from when FREAD, FREADLN, FWRITE, and FWRITELN are used. If the *position* argument is not given, it is assumed to be the current position.

See Also

FCLOSE	Closes a file	Macro Function
FOPEN	Opens a file	Macro Function
FREAD	Reads a character from a file	Macro Function

FREADLN	Reads a line from a file	Macro Function
FWRITE	Writes a character to a file	Macro Function
FWRITELN	Writes a line to a file	Macro Function

FREAD(*file, number-of-characters*)

Macro Function

FREAD reads *number-of-characters* from *file*. The file must have previously been opened with FOPEN. The *file* argument must be the file number returned by FOPEN. If the file number is not valid, FREAD returns a #VALUE! error. If FREAD can't read the specified value, FREAD returns an #N/A error.

See Also

FCLOSE	Closes a file	Macro Function
FOPEN	Opens a file	Macro Function
FPOS	Positions read/write point in a file	Macro Function
FREADLN	Reads a line from a file	Macro Function
FWRITE	Writes a character to a file	Macro Function
FWRITELN	Writes a line to a file	Macro Function

FREADLN(*file*)

Macro Function

FREADLN reads from the current position to the end of the line from the *file*. *File* must be a file opened with the FOPEN function and specified by the file number returned by FOPEN. If the file number is not valid, FREADLN returns a #VALUE! error. If FREAD can't read the specified value, FREADLN returns an #N/A error.

See Also

FCLOSE	Closes a file	Macro Function
FOPEN	Opens a file	Macro Function
FPOS	Positions read/write point in a file	Macro Function
FREAD	Reads a character from a file	Macro Function

FREADLN	Reads a line from a file	Macro Function
FWRITE	Writes a character to a file	Macro Function
FWRITELN	Writes a line to a file	Macro Function

FREEZE.PANES(*X,col,row*)

Macro Function

FREEZE.PANES creates panes and freezes or unfreezes existing panes. If *X* is TRUE, FREEZE.PANES performs the same action as the Options Freeze Panes menu option. If *X* is FALSE, FREEZE.PANES performs the same action as the Options Unfreeze Panes option. FREEZE.PANES creates new panes if *X* is omitted and if no panes exist. If panes exist and *X* is omitted, panes are unfrozen if they are currently frozen, and frozen if they are currently unfrozen. *Col* and *row* identify where the window should be split. *Row* is measured in number of rows from the top, and *col* is measured in number of columns from the left.

See Also

| OPTIONS FREEZE PANES | Freezes, unfreezes, and creates panes | Menu Command |
| SPLIT | Splits a window | Macro Function |

FREQUENCY(*data,intervals*)

Function   **New to Version 4.0**

FREQUENCY returns a frequency distribution of the data. *Data* and *intervals* are arrays or ranges containing values. *Data* contains the values, and *intervals* specifies the intervals over which you want to know the frequency of occurrence.

Example

=FREQUENCY(A1:A5,B1:B2) returns {0;4;1} if cells A1:A5 contain the values 25, 30, 35, 35, and 40 and cells B1:B2 contain the values 15 and 35. There are no values between 0 and 15, there are four values between 16 and 35, and there is 1 value greater than 35.

See Also

COUNT	Counts the number of values in a list	Function
DCOUNT	Counts the number of values in a database	Function

FSIZE(*file*)

Macro Function

FSIZE returns the size of the file, measured in number of characters. The file must have been opened with the FOPEN function. *File* must be specified with the number that FOPEN returns. If the file number is not valid, FSIZE returns a #VALUE! error.

See Also

FCLOSE	Closes a file	Macro Function
FOPEN	Opens a file	Macro Function
FPOS	Positions read/write point in a file	Macro Function
FREAD	Reads a character from a file	Macro Function
FREADLN	Reads a line from a file	Macro Function
FWRITE	Writes a character to a file	Macro Function
FWRITELN	Writes a line to a file	Macro Function

FTEST(*array1, array2*)

Macro Function   New to Version 4.0

FTEST performs an F-test, or a one-tailed probability calculation on *array1* and *array2*. FTEST will determine if *array1* and *array2* have different variances.

See Also

FDIST	Returns the F-probability	Macro Function
FINV	Returns the inverse F-probability	Macro Function
FTESTV	Performs a two-sample F-test	Macro Function

FTESTV(*input1, input2, output, [labels]*)

Macro Function   **New to Version 4.0**

FTESTV performs a two-sample F-test. *Input1* and *input2* are input ranges, and *output* is a reference to the upper-left cell in the *output* range. *Labels* is a logical value. If *labels* is TRUE, there are *labels* in the first row or column of the input ranges. If *labels* is FALSE, there are no input labels. The default value for *labels* is FALSE.

See Also

FDIST	Returns the F-probability	Macro Function
FINV	Returns the inverse F-probability	Macro Function
FTEST	Performs an F-test	Macro Function

FULL(*X*)

Macro Function

If *X* is TRUE, FULL performs the same action as maximizing the active window by pressing CTRL-F10; the window is changed to full size. If *X* is FALSE, FULL performs the same action as restoring the active window by pressing CTRL-F5; the window is restored to its previous size.

FUNCTION MACROS

Concept

Function macros are custom functions that you create on a macro sheet and then use on a worksheet to return a value or other result. You can distinguish function macros from command macros in two ways. First, command macros take some action such as formatting, copying, or saving. In contrast, function macros take no action, but rather produce a result, like you might get from a calculation. Second, a command macro is wholly contained on the macro sheet and is executed with either the shortcut key or the Run option on the Macro menu. A function macro is created on a macro sheet, but to use it you must enter the resulting function on a worksheet.

Function macros are generally calculations that you have to perform repeatedly. They have arguments through which you supply values and they use formulas and regular functions to calculate a result based on the values you supply. When you build a function macro, you must use three special macro functions that handle the arguments and the result. These functions, in the order in which they must be used, are as follows.

RESULT

The RESULT function is used only if you need to change the data type of the result. This function has one argument, the data type number. If you have not used a RESULT function to change it, the result is assumed to be a number, text, or a logical value. The possible data type numbers are listed here:

Number	Data Type
1	Number
2	Text
4	Logical
8	Reference
16	Error
64	Array

You can add data type numbers except for the reference and array types. For example, the default of number, text, or logical is a type 7 (1+2+4).

ARGUMENT

You must have one ARGUMENT function for each argument in the function macro you are building, and the arguments must be in the order in which they are presented in the function macro. The ARGUMENT function can have up to three arguments: a name, a data type, and a reference. You must have either a name or a reference. Whichever you specify, the other is optional. The data type is always optional. The name must be a legitimate Excel name and becomes defined by the ARGUMENT function. It can then be used by the formulas and regular functions that follow. If you do not specify the data type, Excel assumes it to be a number, text, or logical value. If the value received by the ARGUMENT function is not a default type and you have not used the data type argument to change that, you will get a #VALUE! error. The reference argument is a cell or range reference on the macro sheet where the value received by the ARGUMENT function is placed. If you use both a name and a reference, the reference is given the name and can be referred to by it.

RETURN

All function macros must end with the RETURN function. The RETURN function has one argument in a function macro: the cell on the macro sheet that contains the result.

The formulas and regular functions to be used in a function macro must be placed after the last ARGUMENT and before the RETURN function.

Example

The following is a function macro that calculates tax. The macro starts at cell A1.

	A
1	Tax
2	=ARGUMENT("amount",1)
3	=ARGUMENT("rate",1)
4	=amount*rate
5	=RETURN(A4)
6	

See Also

ARGUMENT	Defines arguments	Macro Function
RESULT	Controls type	Macro Function
RETURN	Ends a function macro	Macro Function

FV(*interest, number-of-periods, payment, [present-value], [type]*)

Function

FV returns the future value of an investment consisting of a series of equal payments made for a term (*number-of-periods*) at a fixed interest rate. *Interest* is the interest rate, and *payment* must be on the same basis. For example, if *interest* represents a monthly interest rate, *payment* should be a monthly payment. If the optional arguments *present-value* and *type* are omitted, the default value for both arguments is 0. A *type* of 0 means that the payment is due at the end of the period, and a *type* of 1 means that the payment is due at the beginning of the period.

Example

=FV(.1,15,1500) calculates the future value of a series of $1,500 annual payments invested at 10% per year for 15 years. The result is $22,658.18.

See Also

IPMT	Returns the interest payment	Function
NPER	Returns the number of periods	Function
PMT	Returns the payment	Function
PPMT	Returns the principle payment	Function

FVSCHEDULE(*pv,schedule*)

Function   New to Version 4.0

FVSCHEDULE returns the future value given the present value and a series of compound interest rates. *Pv* is the present value, and *schedule* is an array of interest rates.

FVSCHEDULE is an add-in function. You may see a REF! error the first time you use it. If FVSCHEDULE is not available, you must install the Analysis Toolpak.

Example

=FVSCHEDULE(10,{0.10,0.11,0.12}) returns 13.6752.

See Also

FV　　　　Returns the future value　　　　Function

FWRITE(*file,string*)

Macro Function

FWRITE causes *string* to be written into the *file* at the current position. *File* must be a file opened with the FOPEN function and specified by the number returned by FOPEN. If the file number is not valid, FWRITE returns a #VALUE! error. If FWRITE is unable to write to the file, the function returns an #N/A error.

See Also

FCLOSE	Closes a file	Macro Function
FOPEN	Opens a file	Macro Function
FPOS	Positions read/write point in a file	Macro Function
FREAD	Reads a character from a file	Macro Function
FREADLN	Reads a line from a file	Macro Function
FWRITELN	Writes a line to a file	Macro Function

FWRITELN(*file,string*)

Macro Function

FWRITELN causes *string*, followed by a carriage return and line feed, to be written into *file* at the current position. *File* must be a file opened with the FOPEN function, and specified by the number returned by FOPEN. If the file number is not valid, FWRITELN returns a #VALUE! error. If FWRITELN cannot write to the file, it returns an #N/A error.

See Also

FCLOSE	Closes a file	Macro Function
FOPEN	Opens a file	Macro Function
FPOS	Positions read/write point in a file	Macro Function
FREAD	Reads a character from a file	Macro Function
FREADLN	Reads a line from a file	Macro Function
FWRITE	Writes a character to a file	Macro Function

GALLERY

Menu

The Gallery menu only appears on the menu bar if the active document is a chart. The Gallery menu allows you to choose the format of the active chart. The options on this menu (with the exception of Preferred and Set Preferred) display dialog boxes containing pictorial representations of each option for that type of chart. Next and Previous buttons allow you to display the gallery dialog box for the next or previous options on the Gallery menu. To choose a chart type, click on its picture and then click on OK, or double-click on the picture. If you have an overlay chart, hold down the SHIFT key while choosing the OK button to preserve the overlay. The Gallery menu is shown here:

GALLERY 3-D AREA

Menu Command   **New to Version 4.0**

➤   *Shortcut: 3-D Area Chart tool*

The Gallery menu only appears on the menu bar if the active document is a chart. The 3-D Area option on the Gallery menu allows you to format the active chart as a three-dimensional area chart. When you choose the 3-D Area option from the Gallery menu, Excel displays the following Chart Gallery dialog box:

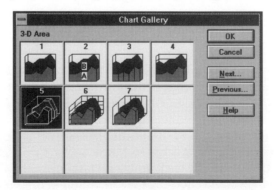

This dialog box contains pictorial representations of all available three-dimensional area charts. To set your format, choose one of the available options and then click on OK, or double-click on the picture. If you have an overlay chart and want to preserve the overlay, hold down the SHIFT key while you click on OK. The choices in the Chart Gallery dialog box for three-dimensional area charts are as follows.

3-D Area	1 (Stacked area chart with 3-D markers)
	2 (Stacked 3-D areas and labels)
	3 (Stacked 3-D areas and drop lines)
	4 (Stacked 3-D areas and grid lines)
	5 (3-D areas, series plotted separately)
	6 (3-D areas, series plotted separately, with X-axis, Y-axis, and Z-axis grid lines)
	7 (3-D areas, series plotted separately, with X-axis and Y-axis grid lines)
Next	Allows you to display the dialog box for the next chart type on the Gallery menu
Previous	Allows you to display the dialog box for the previous chart type on the Gallery menu

The 3-D Area tool is a shortcut that formats your chart using type 5 listed in the preceding table.

See Also

GALLERY	Description of the menu	Menu
GALLERY.3D.AREA	Equivalent function	Macro Function

GALLERY.3D.AREA(*format*)
GALLERY.3D.AREA?(*[format]*)

Macro Function **New to Version 4.0**

GALLERY.3D.AREA performs the same action as the Gallery 3-D Area menu option. That is, it formats the active chart as a three-dimensional area chart. *Format* is the number of the format, corresponding to the number in the Chart Gallery dialog box. The choices for *format* are as follows.

3-D Area	1 (Stacked area chart with 3-D markers)
	2 (Stacked 3-D areas and labels)
	3 (Stacked 3-D areas and drop lines)
	4 (Stacked 3-D areas and grid lines)
	5 (3-D areas, series plotted separately)
	6 (3-D areas, series plotted separately, with grid lines)
	7 (3-D areas, series plotted separately, with X-axis and Y-axis grid lines)

In the dialog box version (with the question mark), if the argument is included, its value is used as the default for the dialog box that appears.

See Also

GALLERY	Description of the menu	Menu
GALLERY 3-D AREA	Equivalent command	Menu Command

GALLERY 3-D BAR

Menu Command   **New to Version 4.0**

➤   *Shortcut: 3-D Bar Chart tool*

The Gallery menu only appears on the menu bar when the active document is a chart. The 3-D Bar option on the Gallery menu allows you to format the active chart as a three-dimensional bar chart. When you choose the 3-D Bar option from the Gallery menu, the following dialog box appears.

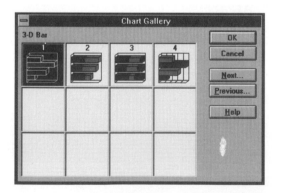

This Chart Gallery dialog box contains pictorial representations of the available three-dimensional bar charts. To set your format, choose one of the options and then click on OK, or double-click on the picture representing the chart type of your choice. If you have an overlay chart and want to preserve the overlay, hold down the SHIFT key while you click on OK. The choices shown in the Chart Gallery dialog box for three-dimensional bar charts are as follows.

3-D Bar	1 (Simple bar chart with 3-D markers) 2 (Stacked 3-D bars) 3 (Stacked 100% 3-D bars) 4 (3-D bars with grid lines)
Next	Allows you to display the dialog box for the next chart type on the Gallery menu
Previous	Allows you to display the dialog box for the previous chart type on the Gallery menu

The 3-D bar tool is a shortcut that formats your chart using type 1 listed in the preceding table.

See Also

GALLERY	Description of the menu	Menu
GALLERY.3D.BAR	Equivalent function	Macro Function

GALLERY.3D.BAR(*format*)
GALLERY.3D.BAR?(*[format]*)

Macro Function   **New to Version 4.0**

GALLERY.3D.BAR performs the same action as the Gallery 3-D Bar menu option. It formats the active chart as a three-dimensional bar chart. *Format* is the number of the format, corresponding to the number in the Chart Gallery dialog box.

The choices for *format* are as follows.

3-D Bar	1 (Simple bar chart with 3-D markers) 2 (Stacked 3-D bars) 3 (Stacked 100% 3-D bars) 4 (3-D bars with X-axis and Y-axis grid lines)

In the dialog box version (with the question mark), if the argument is included, its value is used as the default for the dialog box that appears.

See Also

GALLERY	Description of the menu	Menu
GALLERY 3-D BAR	Equivalent command	Menu Command

GALLERY 3-D COLUMN

Menu Command   **New to Version 4.0**

➤   *Shortcut: 3-D Column Chart tool*

➤   *Shortcut: Perspective 3-D Column Chart tool*

The Gallery menu only appears on the menu bar when the active document is a chart. The 3-D Column option on the Gallery menu allows you to format the active chart as a three-dimensional column chart. When you choose the 3-D Column option from the Gallery menu, the following dialog box appears.

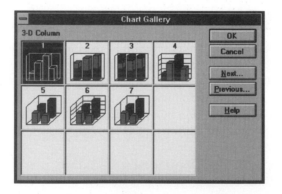

This Chart Gallery dialog box contains pictorial representations of all available three-dimensional column charts. To set your format, choose one of the options and then click on OK, or double-click on the picture. If you have an overlay chart and want to preserve the overlay, hold down the SHIFT key while clicking on the OK button. The choices in the Chart Gallery dialog box for three-dimensional column charts are as follows.

3-D Column	1 (Simple column chart with 3-D markers)
	2 (Stacked 3-D columns)
	3 (Stacked 100% 3-D columns)
	4 (3-D columns with Z-axis grid lines)
	5 (3-D columns, series plotted separately)
	6 (3-D columns, series plotted separately, with grid lines)
	7 (3-D columns, series plotted separately, with X-axis and Y-axis grid lines)
Next	Allows you to display the dialog box for the next chart type on the Gallery menu
Previous	Allows you to display the dialog box for the previous chart type on the Gallery menu

There are two three-dimensional column tools. The 3-D Column Chart tool formats your chart with type 1. The Perspective 3-D Column Chart tool formats your chart with type 5.

See Also

GALLERY	Description of the menu	Menu
GALLERY.3D.COLUMN	Equivalent function	Macro Function

GALLERY.3D.COLUMN(*format*)
GALLERY.3D.COLUMN?(*[format]*)

Macro Function   **New to Version 4.0**

GALLERY.3D.COLUMN performs the same action as the Gallery 3-D Column menu option. It formats the active chart as a three-dimensional column chart. *Format* is the number of the format, corresponding to the number in the Chart Gallery dialog box.

The choices for *format* are as follows.

3-D Column	1 (Simple column chart with 3-D markers)
	2 (Stacked 3-D columns)
	3 (Stacked 100% 3-D columns)
	4 (3-D columns with Z-axis grid lines)
	5 (3-D columns, series plotted separately)
	6 (3-D columns, series plotted separately, with grid lines)
	7 (3-D columns, series plotted separately, with X-axis and Y-axis grid lines)

In the dialog box version (with the question mark), if the argument is included, its value is used as the default for the dialog box that appears.

See Also

GALLERY	Description of the menu	Menu
GALLERY 3-D COLUMN	Equivalent command	Menu Command

GALLERY 3-D LINE

Menu Command   **New to Version 4.0**

➤   *Shortcut: 3-D Line Chart tool*

The Gallery menu only appears on the menu bar when the active document is a chart. The 3-D Line option on the Gallery menu allows you to format the active chart as a three-dimensional line chart. When you choose the 3-D Line option from the Gallery menu, the following dialog box appears.

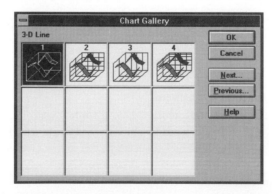

This Chart Gallery dialog box contains pictorial representations of all available three-dimensional line charts. To set your format, choose one of the chart options and then click on OK, or double-click on the picture representing the chart type of your choice. If you have an overlay chart and want to preserve the overlay, hold down the SHIFT key while you click on the OK button. The choices in the Chart Gallery dialog box for three-dimensional line charts are as follows.

3-D Line	1 (3-D line chart) 2 (3-D line chart with grid lines) 3 (3-D line chart with X-axis and Y-axis grid lines) 4 (3-D line chart with logarithmic Z-axis and grid lines)
Next	Allows you to display the dialog box for the next chart type on the Gallery menu
Previous	Allows you to display the dialog box for the previous chart type on the Gallery menu

The 3-D Line Chart tool is a shortcut that formats your chart using type 1 listed in the preceding table.

See Also

GALLERY	Description of the menu	Menu
GALLERY.3D.LINE	Equivalent function	Macro Function

GALLERY.3D.LINE(*format*)
GALLERY.3D.LINE?(*[format]*)

Macro Function **New to Version 4.0**

GALLERY.3D.LINE performs the same action as the Gallery 3-D Line menu option. It formats the active chart as a three-dimensional line chart. *Format* is the number of the format, corresponding to the number in the Chart Gallery dialog box.

The choices for *format* are as follows.

3-D Line	1 (3-D line chart) 2 (3-D line chart with grid lines) 3 (3-D line chart with X-axis and Y-axis grid lines) 4 (3-D line chart with logarithmic Z-axis and grid lines)

In the dialog box version (with the question mark), if the argument is included, its value is used as the default for the dialog box that appears.

See Also

GALLERY	Description of the menu	Menu
GALLERY 3-D LINE	Equivalent command	Menu Command

GALLERY 3-D PIE

Menu Command   **New to Version 4.0**

➤   *Shortcut: 3-D Pie Chart tool*

The Gallery menu only appears on the menu bar when the active document is a chart. The 3-D Pie option on the Gallery menu allows you to format the active chart as a 3-D pie chart. When you choose the 3-D Pie option from the Gallery menu, the following dialog box appears.

This Chart Gallery dialog box contains pictorial representations of the available 3-D pie charts. To set your format, choose one of the chart options and then choose OK, or double-click on the picture. If you have an overlay chart and want to preserve the overlay, hold down the SHIFT key while you click on the OK button. The choices in the Chart Gallery dialog box for three-dimensional pie charts are as follows.

3-D Pie	1 (Each slice colored or patterned differently)
	2 (All slices colored and patterned the same; has category labels)
	3 (First slice exploded)
	4 (All slices exploded)
	5 (Has category labels)
	6 (Value labels are percentages)
	7 (Has category labels; value labels are percentages)

Next	Allows you to display the dialog box for the next chart type on the Gallery menu
Previous	Allows you to display the dialog box for the previous chart type on the Gallery menu

The 3-D Pie Chart tool is a shortcut that formats your chart using type 6 listed in the preceding table.

See Also

GALLERY	Description of the menu	Menu
GALLERY.3D.PIE	Equivalent function	Macro Function

GALLERY.3D.PIE(*format*)
GALLERY.3D.PIE?(*[format]*)

Macro Function   **New to Version 4.0**

GALLERY.3D.PIE performs the same action as the 3-D Pie option on the Gallery menu. It formats the active chart as a three-dimensional pie chart. *Format* is the number of the format, corresponding to the number in the Chart Gallery dialog box.

The choices for *format* are as follows.

3-D Pie	1 (Each slice colored or patterned differently)
	2 (All slices colored and patterned the same; has category labels)
	3 (First slice exploded)
	4 (All slices exploded)
	5 (Has category labels)
	6 (Value labels are percentages)
	7 (Has category labels; value labels are percentages)

In the dialog box version (with the question mark), if the argument is included, its value is used as the default for the dialog box that appears.

See Also

GALLERY	Description of the menu	Menu
GALLERY 3-D PIE	Equivalent command	Menu Command

GALLERY 3-D SURFACE

Menu Command   **New to Version 4.0**

➤   *Shortcut: 3-D Surface Chart tool*

The Gallery menu only appears on the menu bar when the active document is a chart. The 3-D Surface option on the Gallery menu allows you to format the active chart as a three-dimensional surface chart. When you choose the 3-D Surface option from the Gallery menu, the following dialog box appears.

This Chart Gallery dialog box contains pictorial representations of all the different kinds of 3-D surface charts available. To set your format, choose one of the chart options and then click on OK, or double-click on the picture representing the chart type of your choice. If you have an overlay chart and want to preserve the overlay, hold down the SHIFT key while you click on the OK button. The choices in the Chart Gallery dialog box for three-dimensional surface charts are as follows.

3-D Surface	1 (3-D surface chart)
	2 (3-D wireframe chart)
	3 (3-D contour surface chart)
	4 (3-D contour wireframe chart)
Next	Allows you to display the dialog box for the next chart type on the Gallery menu
Previous	Allows you to display the dialog box for the previous chart type on the Gallery menu

The 3-D Surface Chart tool is a shortcut that formats your chart using type 1 listed in the preceding table.

See Also

| GALLERY | Description of the menu | Menu |
| GALLERY.3D.SURFACE | Equivalent function | Macro Function |

GALLERY.3D.SURFACE(*format*)
GALLERY.3D.SURFACE?(*[format]*)

Macro Function   **New to Version 4.0**

GALLERY.3D.SURFACE performs the same action as the 3D Surface option on the Gallery menu. It formats the active chart as a three-dimensional surface chart. *Format* is the number of the format, corresponding to the number in the Chart Gallery dialog box.

The choices for *format* are as follows.

3-D Surface	1 (3-D surface chart)
	2 (3-D wireframe chart)
	3 (3-D contour surface chart)
	4 (3-D contour wireframe chart)

In the dialog box version (with the question mark), if the argument is included, its value is used as the default for the dialog box that appears.

See Also

| GALLERY | Description of the menu | Menu |
| GALLERY 3-D SURFACE | Equivalent command | Menu Command |

GALLERY AREA

Menu Command

➤   *Shortcut: Area Chart tool*

The Gallery menu only appears on the menu bar when the active document is a chart. The Area option on the Gallery menu allows you to format the active chart as an area chart. When you choose the Area option from the Gallery menu, the following dialog box appears.

This Chart Gallery dialog box contains pictorial representations of the available area charts. To set your format, choose one of the chart options and then click on OK, or double-click on the picture representing the chart type of your choice. If you have an overlay chart and want to preserve the overlay, hold down the SHIFT key while you click on the OK button. The choices in the Chart Gallery dialog box for Area charts are as follows.

Area	1 (Simple area chart) 2 (100% area chart) 3 (Area chart with drop lines) 4 (Area chart with grid lines) 5 (Area chart with area labels)
Next	Allows you to display the dialog box for the next chart type on the Gallery menu
Previous	Allows you to display the dialog box for the previous chart type on the Gallery menu

The Area Chart tool is a shortcut that formats your chart using type 1 listed in the preceding table.

See Also

GALLERY	Description of the menu	Menu
GALLERY.AREA	Equivalent function	Macro Function

GALLERY.AREA(*format,[cancel-overlay]*)
GALLERY.AREA?(*[format],[cancel-overlay]*)

Macro Function

GALLERY.AREA performs the same action as the Gallery Area menu option. *Format* is the number of the format in the gallery.

If *cancel-overlay* is TRUE, the overlay chart is deleted. If *cancel-overlay* is FALSE, the format is applied to whichever chart contains the current selection. The default value for *cancel-overlay* is FALSE. In the dialog box version (with the question mark), the arguments, if included, are used as default values for the dialog box that appears.

See Also

GALLERY	Description of the menu	Menu
GALLERY AREA	Equivalent command	Menu Command

GALLERY BAR

Menu Command

➤   *Shortcut: Bar Chart tool*

The Gallery menu only appears on the menu bar when the active document is a chart. The Bar option on the Gallery menu allows you to format the active chart as a bar chart. When you choose the Bar option from the Gallery menu, the following dialog box appears.

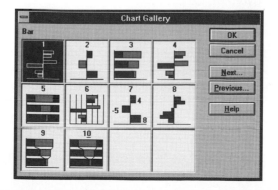

This Chart Gallery dialog box contains pictorial representations of the available bar charts. To set your format, choose one of the chart options and then click on OK, or double-click on the picture representing the chart type of your choice. If you have an overlay chart and want to preserve the overlay, hold down the SHIFT key while you click on the OK button. The choices in the Chart Gallery dialog box for bar charts are as follows.

Bar	1 (Simple bar chart)
	2 (Bar chart for a single series with varied patterns or colors)
	3 (Stacked bar chart)
	4 (Overlapped bar chart)
	5 (100% stacked bar chart)
	6 (Bar chart with vertical grid lines)
	7 (Bar chart with value labels)
	8 (Bar chart with no space between bars)
	9 (Stacked bar chart with series lines)
	10 (Stacked 100% bar chart with series lines)
Next	Allows you to display the dialog box for the next chart type on the Gallery menu
Previous	Allows you to display the dialog box for the previous chart type on the Gallery menu

The Bar Chart tool is a shortcut that formats your chart using type 1 listed in the preceding table.

See Also

GALLERY	Description of the menu	Menu
GALLERY.BAR	Equivalent function	Macro Function

GALLERY.BAR(*format,[cancel-overlay]*)
GALLERY.BAR?(*[format],[cancel-overlay]*)

Macro Function

GALLERY.BAR performs the same action as the Gallery Bar menu option. *Format* is the number of the format in the gallery.

If *cancel-overlay* is TRUE, the overlay chart is deleted. If *cancel-overlay* is FALSE, the format is applied to whichever chart contains the current selection. The default value for *cancel-overlay* is FALSE. In the dialog box version (with the question mark), the arguments, if included, are used as default values for the dialog box that appears.

See Also

GALLERY	Description of the menu	Menu
GALLERY BAR	Equivalent command	Menu Command

GALLERY COLUMN

Menu Command

➤ *Shortcut: Column Chart tool*

➤ *Shortcut: Stacked Column Chart tool*

The Gallery menu only appears on the menu bar when the active document is a chart. The Column option on the Gallery menu allows you to format the active chart as a column chart. When you choose the Column option from the Gallery menu, the following dialog box appears.

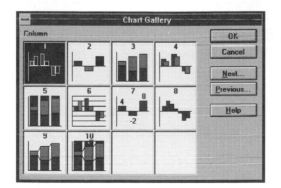

This Chart Gallery dialog box contains pictorial representations of the available column charts. To set your format, choose one of the chart options and then click on OK, or double-click on the picture representing the chart type of your choice. If you have an overlay chart and want to preserve the overlay, hold down the SHIFT key while you click on the OK button. The choices in the Chart Gallery dialog box for column charts are as follows.

Column	1 (Simple column chart)
	2 (Column chart for a single series with varied patterns)
	3 (Stacked column chart)
	4 (Overlapped column chart)
	5 (100% stacked column chart)
	6 (Column chart with horizontal grid lines)
	7 (Column chart with value labels)
	8 (Column chart with no space between columns)
	9 (Stacked column chart with series lines)
	10 (Stacked 100% column chart with series lines)
Next	Allows you to display the dialog box for the next chart type on the Gallery menu
Previous	Allows you to display the dialog box for the previous chart type on the Gallery menu

The Column Chart tool is a shortcut that formats your chart using type 1 listed in the preceding table. The Stacked Column Chart tool is a shortcut that formats your chart using type 3 listed in the preceding table.

See Also

GALLERY	Description of the menu	Menu
GALLERY.COLUMN	Equivalent function	Macro Function

GALLERY.COLUMN(*format,[cancel-overlay]*)
GALLERY.COLUMN?(*[format],[cancel-overlay]*)

Macro Function

GALLERY.COLUMN performs the same action as the Gallery Column menu option. *Format* is the number of the format in the gallery.

If *cancel-overlay* is TRUE, the overlay chart is deleted. If *cancel-overlay* is FALSE, the format is applied to whichever chart contains the current selection. The default value for *cancel-overlay* is FALSE. In the dialog box version (with the question mark), the arguments, if included, are used as default values for the dialog box that appears.

See Also

GALLERY	Description of the menu	Menu
GALLERY COLUMN	Equivalent command	Menu Command

GALLERY COMBINATION

Menu Command

➤ *Shortcut: Line/Column Chart tool*

➤ *Shortcut: Volume/Hi-Lo-Close Chart tool*

The Gallery menu only appears on the menu bar when the active document is a chart. The Combination option on the Gallery menu allows you to format the active chart as a combination chart. The Combination option allows you to create an overlay chart. If there are an odd number of series, there will be one more series in the main chart than the overlay chart. If there are an even number of series, there will be the same number of series in the main chart and the overlay chart. If you want to control this default distribution of series, use the Format Overlay option. When you choose the Combination option from the Gallery menu, the following dialog box appears.

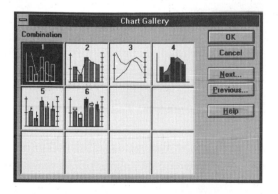

This Chart Gallery dialog box contains pictorial representations of the available combination charts. To set your format, choose one of the chart options and then click on OK, or double-click on the picture representing the chart type of your choice. If you have an overlay chart and want to preserve the overlay, hold down the SHIFT key while you click on the OK button. The choices in the Chart Gallery dialog box for combination charts are as follows.

Combination	1 (Column main chart and line overlay chart)
	2 (Column main chart and line overlay chart with separate scales)
	3 (Line main chart and line overlay chart with separate scales)
	4 (Area main chart and column overlay chart)
	5 (Column main chart and line overlay chart with high, low, and closing series for use with stock market applications)
	6 (Column main chart and open-hi-lo-close overlay chart)
Next	Allows you to display the dialog box for the next chart type on the Gallery menu
Previous	Allows you to display the dialog box for the previous chart type on the Gallery menu

The Line/Column Chart tool is a shortcut that formats your chart using type 1 listed in the preceding table. The Volume/Hi-Lo-Close Chart tool is a shortcut that formats your chart using type 5 listed in the preceding table.

See Also

GALLERY   Description of the menu   Menu

GALLERY LINE

Menu Command

➤   *Shortcut: Line Chart tool*

The Gallery menu only appears on the menu bar when the active document is a chart. The Gallery Line option allows you to format the active chart as a line chart.

When you choose the Line option from the Gallery menu, the following dialog box appears.

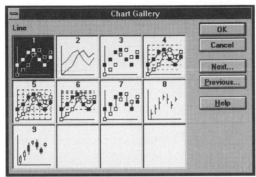

This Chart Gallery dialog box contains pictorial representations of all the available line charts. To set your format, choose one of the chart options and then click on OK, or double-click on the picture representing the chart type of your choice. If you have a overlay chart and want to preserve the overlay, hold down the SHIFT key while you click on the OK button. The choices in the Chart Gallery dialog box for line charts are as follows.

Line	1 (Chart with lines and markers)
	2 (Chart with lines only)
	3 (Chart with markers only)
	4 (Chart with lines, markers, and horizontal grid lines)
	5 (Chart with lines, markers, and horizontal and vertical grid lines)
	6 (Chart with lines, markers, and logarithmic scaled grid lines)
	7 (Hi-lo chart with markers and hi-lo lines)
	8 (Chart for stock quotes with hi-lo lines and close markers)
	9 (Chart for stock quotes with hi-lo lines and open and close markers)
Next	Allows you to display the dialog box for the next chart type on the Gallery menu
Previous	Allows you to display the dialog box for the previous chart type on the Gallery menu

The Line Chart tool is a shortcut that formats your chart using type 1 listed in the preceding table.

See Also

GALLERY	Description of the menu	Menu
GALLERY.LINE	Equivalent function	Macro Function

GALLERY.LINE(*format,[cancel-overlay]*)
GALLERY.LINE?(*[format], [cancel-overlay]*)

Macro Function

GALLERY.LINE performs the same action as the Gallery Line menu option. *Format* is the number of the format in the gallery.

If *cancel-overlay* is TRUE, the overlay chart is deleted. If *cancel-overlay* is FALSE, the format is applied to whichever chart contains the current selection. The default value for *cancel-overlay* is FALSE. In the dialog box version (with the question mark), the arguments, if included, are used as default values for the dialog box that appears.

See Also

GALLERY	Description of the menu	Menu
GALLERY LINE	Equivalent command	Menu Command

GALLERY PIE

Menu Command

➤   *Shortcut: Pie Chart tool*

The Gallery menu only appears on the menu bar when the active document is a chart. The Pie option on the Gallery menu allows you to format the active chart as a pie chart. When you choose the Pie option from the Gallery menu, the following dialog box appears.

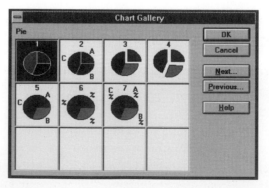

This Chart Gallery dialog box contains pictorial representations of all available pie charts. To set your format, choose one of the chart options and then click on OK, or double-click on the picture representing the pie chart of your choice. If you have an overlay chart and want to preserve the overlay, hold down the SHIFT key while you click on the OK button. The choices in the Chart Gallery dialog box for pie charts are as follows.

Pie	1 (Simple pie chart)
	2 (Pie chart with the same pattern on every slice and category labels for each slice)
	3 (Pie chart with first slice exploded)
	4 (Pie chart with all slices exploded)
	5 (Pie chart with category labels)
	6 (Pie chart with value labels as percentages)
	7 (Pie chart with category labels and value labels as percentages)
Next	Allows you to display the dialog box for the next chart type on the Gallery menu
Previous	Allows you to display the dialog box for the previous chart type on the Gallery menu

The Pie Chart tool is a shortcut that formats your chart using type 6 listed in the preceding table.

See Also

GALLERY	Description of the menu	Menu
GALLERY.LINE	Equivalent function	Macro Function

GALLERY.PIE(*format,[cancel-overlay]*)
GALLERY.PIE?(*[format],[cancel-overlay]*)

Macro Function

GALLERY.PIE performs the same action as the Pie option from the Gallery menu. *Format* is the number of the format in the gallery.

If *cancel-overlay* is TRUE, the overlay chart is deleted. If *cancel-overlay* is FALSE, the format is applied to whichever chart contains the current selection. The default value for *cancel-overlay* is FALSE. In the dialog box version (with the question mark), the arguments, if included, are used as default values for the dialog box that appears.

See Also

GALLERY	Description of the menu	Menu
GALLERY PIE	Equivalent command	Menu Command

GALLERY PREFERRED

Menu Command

The Preferred option on the Gallery menu allows you to set the active chart format to the format you set with the Set Preferred option on the Gallery menu. Excel's default preferred format is format 1 of Gallery Column.

See Also

GALLERY	Description of the menu	Menu
GALLERY SET PREFERRED	Sets the preferred chart type	Menu Command

GALLERY SCATTER

Menu Command

➤ *Shortcut: Scatter Chart tool*

The Gallery menu only appears on the menu bar when the active document is a chart. The Scatter option on the Gallery menu allows you to format the active chart as a scatter chart. When you choose the Scatter option from the Gallery menu, the following dialog box appears.

This Chart Gallery dialog box contains pictorial representations of all available scatter charts. To set your format, choose one of the chart options and then click on OK, or double-click on the picture representing the chart type of your choice. If you have an overlay chart and want to preserve the overlay, hold down the SHIFT key while you click on the OK button. The choices in the Chart Type dialog box for scatter charts are as follows.

Scatter	1 (Scatter chart with markers only)
	2 (Scatter chart with markers connected by lines)
	3 (Scatter chart with markers and both horizontal and vertical grid lines)
	4 (Scatter chart with markers and horizontal logarithmic grid lines)
	5 (Scatter chart with markers and horizontal and vertical logarithmic grid lines)
Next	Allows you to display the dialog box for the next chart type on the Gallery menu
Previous	Allows you to display the dialog box for the previous chart type on the Gallery menu

The Scatter Chart tool is a shortcut that formats your chart using type 1 listed in the preceding table.

See Also

GALLERY	Description of the menu	Menu
GALLERY.SCATTER	Equivalent function	Macro Function

GALLERY.SCATTER(*format, [cancel-overlay]*)
GALLERY.SCATTER?(*[format], [cancel-overlay]*)

Macro Function

GALLERY.SCATTER performs the same action as the Gallery Scatter menu option. *Format* is the number of the format in the gallery.

If *cancel-overlay* is TRUE, the overlay chart is deleted. If *cancel-overlay* is FALSE, the format is applied to whichever chart contains the current selection. The default value for *cancel-overlay* is FALSE. In the dialog box version (with the question mark), the arguments, if included, are used as default values for the dialog box that appears.

See Also

GALLERY	Description of the menu	Menu

GALLERY SCATTER   Equivalent command   Menu Command

GALLERY SET PREFERRED

Menu Command

The Set Preferred option in the Gallery menu allows you to change the default chart format that Excel uses when you choose the New Chart option from the File menu. To change the preferred chart format, change the active chart to the format you want as the default and then choose the Set Preferred option from the Gallery menu. The next time you open a new chart or choose the Preferred option from the Gallery menu, the chart will automatically take on the format you set using the Set Preferred options.

If you want your preferred chart formatting preserved, you can use the Save Workspace option from the File menu. The next time you use Excel, you can open the workspace file and your preferred chart formatting will be restored to its previous setting.

See Also

PREFERRED   Formats the active chart   Menu Command

GAMMADIST(*X, alpha, beta, cum*)

Function   **New to Version 4.0**

GAMMADIST returns the gamma (Erlang) distribution or probability mass for *X*, where *alpha* and *beta* are parameters. *Cum* is either TRUE or FALSE. If *cum* is TRUE, the cumulative distribution function is used. If *cum* is FALSE, the probability mass function is used.

The gamma distribution equation is as follows.

$$f(x; \alpha, \beta) = \frac{1}{\beta^{\alpha}\Gamma(\alpha)}\ x^{\alpha-1}e^{-\frac{x}{\beta}}$$

Examples

=GAMMADIST(15,5,1,TRUE) returns 0.999143.
=GAMMADIST(15,5,1,FALSE) returns 0.000645.

See Also

CHIDIST	Returns the one-tailed probability of the chi distribution	Function
EXPONDIST	Returns the exponential distribution	Function
GAMMAINV	Returns the inverse gamma distribution	Function

GAMMAINV(*prob, alpha, beta*)

Function   **New to Version 4.0**

GAMMAINV returns the inverse gamma distribution. *Prob* is the probability of the gamma distribution. *Alpha* and *beta* are parameters of the gamma distribution.

Example

=GAMMAINV(0.999143,5,1) returns 14.99953.

See Also

GAMMADIST	Returns the gamma distribution	Function

GAMMALN(*X*)

Function   **New to Version 4.0**

GAMMALN returns the natural log of the gamma function of *X*.

Example

=GAMMALN(10) returns 12.80183.

See Also

FACT	Returns the factorial	Function

GCD(*X1, X2,...*)

Function   **New to Version 4.0**

GCD returns the greatest common divisor of a list of up to 29 numbers.

GCD is an add-in function. The first time you use it, you may see a #REF! error while Excel loads the function.

Example

=GCD(9,3,12) returns 3.

See Also

LCM   Returns the least common multiple   Function

GEOMEAN($X1,X2,...$)

Function   **New to Version 4.0**

GEOMEAN returns the geometric mean of a list of up to 30 numbers. The list can be a list of numbers, an array containing numbers, or a range containing numbers.

Example

=GEOMEAN(1,4,7,9,15) returns 5.193957.

See Also

AVERAGE	Returns the average of a list of numbers	Function
HARMEAN	Returns the harmonic mean	Function
MEDIAN	Returns the median	Function

GESTEP($X,step$)

Function   **New to Version 4.0**

GESTEP compares X to *step*, returning 1 if X is greater than or equal to *step*, and returning 0 if X is less than *step*.

GESTEP is an add-in function. The first time that you use it, you may see a #REF! error while Excel loads the function.

Examples

=GESTEP(8,1) returns 1.
=GESTEP(1,8) returns 0.

See Also

DELTA   Returns 1 if two numbers are equal   Function

GET.BAR(*[bar],[menu],[command]*)

Macro Function

GET.BAR returns the number representing the current menu bar, or returns information about a menu or command. If no arguments are given, GET.BAR returns the number of the current menu bar. If arguments are given, the position of a menu or a command is returned. *Bar* is the number or the menu bar. *Menu* is the menu you are interested in; it can be either a name or a number. Menus are numbered starting with 1 on the left or top. *Command* is the command that you are interested in; it can be either a name or a number. Commands are numbered starting with 1 at the top.

Example

=GET.BAR() returns the number of the current menu bar.

See Also

ADD.BAR	Adds a menu	Macro Function
SHOW.BAR	Displays a menu	Macro Function

GET.CELL(*type,[reference]*)

Macro Function

GET.CELL returns information about a cell. The cell is given as a cell reference. If the reference is a range, information about the upper-left cell in the range is returned. The *type* argument allows you to specify the type of information you want returned about the cell. Here are the possible values for *type*:

Type	Information Returned
1	Absolute reference of the upper-left cell, as text.
2	Top row.
3	Left column.
4	Type of the cell.
5	Contents of the cell.
6	Formula in the cell, as text.
7	Number format of the cell, as text.

Type	Information Returned
8	A number representing the alignment of the cell:
	1 General
	2 Left
	3 Center
	4 Right
	5 Fill
	6 Justify
	7 Center across cells
9	A number representing the left border style of a cell:
	0 None
	1 Thin
	2 Medium
	3 Dashed
	4 Dotted
	5 Thick
	6 Double
	7 Hairline
10	A number representing the right border style of a cell:
	0 None
	1 Thin
	2 Medium
	3 Dashed
	4 Dotted
	5 Thick
	6 Double
	7 Hairline
11	A number representing the top border style of a cell:
	0 None
	1 Thin
	2 Medium
	3 Dashed
	4 Dotted
	5 Thick
	6 Double
	7 Hairline

Type	Information Returned
12	A number representing the bottom border style of a cell:
	0 None
	1 Thin
	2 Medium
	3 Dashed
	4 Dotted
	5 Thick
	6 Double
	7 Hairline
13	A number representing the pattern associated with the cell. (The number is a number from 0 to 18, corresponding to the patterns in the drop-down list in the Patterns dialog box.)
14	TRUE if the cell is locked; otherwise FALSE.
15	TRUE if the cell is hidden; otherwise FALSE.
16	Width of the cell, in characters.
17	Height of the cell, in points.
18	Name of the font used in the cell, as text.
19	Font size, in points.
20	TRUE if the cell is bold; otherwise FALSE.
21	TRUE if the cell is italic; otherwise FALSE.
22	TRUE if the cell is underlined; otherwise FALSE.
23	TRUE if the cell is overstruck; otherwise FALSE.
24	A number indicating the color of the font. The number is a number from 0 to 16, corresponding to the colors in the drop down list in the Patterns dialog box. 0 is automatic.
25	TRUE if the cell is outlined; otherwise FALSE (Macintosh only).
26	TRUE if the cell is shadowed; otherwise FALSE (Macintosh only).
27	A number representing the page break associated with the cell:
	0 None
	1 Row
	2 Column
	3 Row and column
28	Row level outline.
29	Column level outline.

G

Type	Information Returned
30	TRUE if the cell is in a summary row; otherwise FALSE.
31	TRUE if the cell is in a summary column; otherwise FALSE.
32	Name of the document.
33	TRUE if the cell is formatted with text wrap; otherwise FALSE.
34	A number indicating the color of the left border. The number is a number from 0 to 16, corresponding to the colors in the Color drop-down box in the Border dialog box. 0 is automatic.
35	A number indicating the color of the right border. The number is a number from 0 to 16, corresponding to the colors in the Color drop-down box in the Border dialog box. 0 is automatic.
36	A number indicating the color of the top border. The number is a number from 0 to 16, corresponding to the colors in the Color drop-down box in the Border dialog box. 0 is automatic.
37	A number indicating the color of the bottom border. The number is a number from 0 to 16, corresponding to the colors in the Color drop-down box in the Border dialog box. 0 is automatic.
38	A number indicating the color of the foreground. The number is a number from 0 to 16, corresponding to the colors in the Color drop-down box in the Border dialog box. 0 is automatic.
39	A number indicating the color of the background. The number is a number from 0 to 16, corresponding to the colors in the Color drop-down box in the Border dialog box. 0 is automatic.
40	Style of the cell.
41	Nontranslated formula in the cell.
42	Distance from the left edge of the window to the left edge of the cell in points.
43	Distance from the top of the active window to the top edge of the cell in points.
44	Distance from the left edge of the active window to the right edge of the cell in points.
45	Distance from the top edge of the active window to the bottom edge of the cell in points.
46	TRUE if the cell contains a note; otherwise FALSE.
47	TRUE if the cell contains a sound note; otherwise FALSE.
48	TRUE if the cell contains a formula; otherwise FALSE.
49	TRUE if the cell is part of an array; otherwise FALSE.

Type	Information Returned
50	A number representing the cell's vertical alignment:
	1 Top
	2 Center
	3 Bottom
51	A number representing the cell's vertical orientation:
	0 Horizontal
	1 Vertical
	2 Upward
	3 Downward
52	Alignment prefix character, or "" if there is none.
53	Cell contents as is.

Example

=GET.CELL(17) returns the height of the active cell in points.

See Also

ACTIVE.CELL	Returns the reference of the active cell	Macro Function
GET.FORMULA	Returns the contents of a cell	Macro Function

GET.CHART.ITEM(*horizontal-vertical,[point],[item]*)

Macro Function

GET.CHART.ITEM returns the position of a chart item. If you want the horizontal position, set the *horizontal-vertical* argument to 1. If you want the vertical position, set the *horizontal-vertical* argument to 2. The *point* argument defines the section of the item whose position you want. If the *item* is a point, set the *point* argument to 1.

If the *item* is a nondata line, set the *point* argument to 1 for lower-left and 2 for upper-right.

If the *item* is an arrow, set the *point* argument to 1 for the base of the arrow, and 2 for the head of the arrow.

If the *item* is an area, use the following values for the *point* argument.

Point	Section
1	Upper-left
2	Upper-middle
3	Upper-right

Point	Section
4	Middle-right
5	Lower-right
6	Lower-middle
7	Lower-left
8	Middle-left

If the *item* is a pie section, use the following values for the *point* argument.

Point	Section
1	Outer counterclockwise point
2	Outer center point
3	Outer clockwise point
4	Mid-clockwise point
5	Center point
6	Mid-counterclockwise point

The *item* argument allows you to select an item. If the argument is omitted, the current item is assumed to be selected. Here are the possible codes for *item*:

Item	Description
"Chart"	Whole chart
"Plot"	Plot area
"Legend"	Legend
"Axis 1"	Main chart value axis
"Axis 2"	Main chart category axis
"Axis 3"	Overlay chart value or three-dimensional series axis
"Axis 4"	Overlay chart category axis
"Title"	Chart title
"Text Axis 1"	Main chart value axis label
"Text Axis 2"	Main chart category axis label
"Text Axis 3"	Main chart series axis label
"Text n"	nth floating text item
"Arrow n"	nth arrow
"Gridline 1"	Value axis major grid lines
"Gridline 2"	Value axis minor grid lines
"Gridline 3"	Category axis major grid lines

Item	Description
"Gridline 4"	Category axis minor grid lines
"Gridline 5"	Series axis major grid lines
"Gridline 6"	Series axis minor grid lines
"Dropline 1"	Main chart drop lines
"Dropline 2"	Overlay chart drop lines
"Hiloline 1"	Main chart hi-lo lines
"Hiloline 2"	Overlay chart hi-lo lines
"Up Bar 1"	Main chart up bar
"Up Bar 2"	Overlay chart up bar
"Down Bar 1"	Main chart down bar
"Down Bar 2"	Overlay chart down bar
"Series line 1"	Main chart series line
"Series line 2"	Overlay chart series line
"Sn"	Entire series
"SnPm"	Point m in series n data
"Text SnPm"	Point m in series n attached text
"Text Sn"	Series title of series n of an area chart
"Floor"	Base of a three-dimensional chart
"Walls"	Back of a three-dimensional chart
"Corners"	Corners of a three-dimensional chart

See Also

FORMAT.MOVE   Moves a chart item   Macro Function

GET.DEF(*definition-string,[document],[type]*)

Macro Function

GET.DEF returns a name that is defined for the *definition-string* in the document. If *definition-string* is a cell reference, it should be given in R1C1 style. If more than one name is defined for the definition string, the first name is returned.

    Document is the name of the document that contains *definition-string*. If no document name is given, the default is the active document.

    Type is the type of name to be returned. 1 is normal names, 2 is hidden names, and 3 is all names. The default value for *type* is 1.

Example

=GET.DEF("R1C1:R2C2") returns "Interest-Rates" if the cells A1:B2 on the active sheet are named "Interest-Rates."

See Also

GET.CELL	Gets information about a cell	Macro Function
GET.NAME	Gets the definition of a name	Macro Function
NAMES	Returns defined names for a document	Macro Function

GET.DOCUMENT(*type,[name]*)

Macro Function

GET.DOCUMENT returns information about a document. The *type* argument controls what information is returned. The following table lists and describes the possible values for *type*. The meaning of a *type* value may change depending on the type of document you are working with. *Name* is the name of the document. If no document name is given, the default is the active document.

Type	Information Returned
1	Document name as text.
2	Path of the document as text. If the document is unsaved, GET.DOCUMENT returns an #N/A error.
3	A number representing the document type:
	1 Worksheet
	2 Chart
	3 Macro
	4 Info
	5 Workbook
4	TRUE if there are unsaved changes in the document; otherwise FALSE.
5	TRUE if the document is read only; otherwise FALSE.
6	TRUE if the document is protected; otherwise FALSE.
7	TRUE if the document contents are protected; otherwise FALSE.
8	TRUE if the document windows are protected; otherwise FALSE.

Type	Information Returned
9	If the document is a chart, a number representing the chart type:
	1 Area
	2 Bar
	3 Column
	4 Line
	5 Pie
	6 Scatter
	7 3D Area
	8 3D Column
	9 3D Line
	10 3D Pie
	11 Radar
	12 3D Bar
	13 3D Surface
9	The number of the first nonempty row, if the document is a worksheet or a macro.
10	If the document is a chart, #N/A if there is no overlay chart; otherwise, a number representing the overlay chart type:
	1 Area
	2 Bar
	3 Column
	4 Line
	5 Pie
	6 Scatter
	11 Radar
10	The number of the last nonempty row, if the document is a worksheet or a macro.
11	The number of series there are in the main chart, if the document is a chart.
11	The number of the first nonempty column, if the document is a worksheet or a macro.
12	The number of series there are in the overlay chart, if the document is a chart.

Type	Information Returned
12	The number of the last nonempty column, if the document is a worksheet or a macro.
13	The number of windows there are for the document.
14	A number representing the calculation type: 1 Automatic 2 Automatic, except tables 3 Manual
15	TRUE if iteration is turned on; otherwise FALSE.
16	The maximum number of iterations.
17	The maximum change between iterations.
18	TRUE if remote reference updating is turned on; otherwise FALSE.
19	TRUE if document is set to Precision As Displayed; otherwise FALSE.
20	TRUE if 1904 date system is enabled; otherwise FALSE.
21	The four fonts for the document in an array (prior to version 4).
22	The sizes of the four fonts for the document in an array (prior to version 4).
23	A logical array indicating which of the four fonts are bold (prior to version 4).
24	A logical array indicating which of the four fonts are italic (prior to version 4).
25	A logical array indicating which of the four fonts are underlined (prior to version 4).
26	A logical array indicating which of the four fonts are overstruck (prior to version 4).
27-29	Provided for macro compatibility with earlier versions of Excel.
30	A horizontal array containing consolidation references, or #N/A if there are none.
31	A number representing the consolidation function: 1 AVERAGE 2 COUNT 3 COUNTA 4 MAX

Type	Information Returned
31 (*cont.*)	5 MIN
	6 PRODUCT
	7 STDEV
	8 DTDEVP
	9 SUM
	10 VAR
	11 VARP
32	An array of three logical values. The logical values correspond to the check boxes in the Data Consolidate dialog box. The first item is the Top Row check box, the second is the Left Column check box, and the third is the Create Links to Source Data check box.
33	TRUE if the Recalculate Before Save check box is on in the Calculation dialog box; otherwise FALSE.
34	TRUE if the document is read-only recommended; otherwise FALSE.
35	TRUE if the document is write-reserved; otherwise FALSE.
36	The user name that has write permission for the document.
37	A number representing the file type of the document:
	1 Normal
	2 SYLK
	3 Text
	4 WKS
	5 WK1
	6 CSV
	7 DBF2
	8 DBF3
	9 DIF
	10 Reserved
	11 DBF4
	15 WK3
	16 Excel 2.*x*
	17 Template

G

Type	Information Returned
37 (*cont.*)	18 Add-in macro
	19 Macintosh text
	20 Windows text
	21 MS-DOS text
	22 Macintosh CSV
	23 Windows CSV
	24 MS-DOS CSV
	25 International macro
	26 International add-in macro
	29 Excel 3.0
38	TRUE if the Summary Rows Below Detail check box is on in the Outline dialog box; otherwise FALSE.
39	TRUE if the Summary Columns To Right of Detail check box is on the Outline dialog box; otherwise FALSE.
40	TRUE if the Create Backup File check box is on in the Save As dialog box; otherwise FALSE.
41	A number representing which objects are displayed:
	1 All objects displayed
	2 Placeholders for charts and pictures
	3 All objects hidden
42	An array of all objects in the document, or #N/A if there are no objects.
43	TRUE if the Save External Link Values check box is turned on in the Calculation dialog box; otherwise FALSE.
44	TRUE if the objects in the document or documents in the workbook are protected; otherwise FALSE.
45	A number representing window synchronization:
	0 Not synchronized
	1 Synchronized horizontally
	2 Synchronized vertically
	3 Synchronized horizontally and vertically
46	An array of print settings that can be set by LINE.PRINT:
	1 Setup text

Type	Information Returned
	2 Left margin
	3 Right margin
	4 Top margin
	5 Bottom margin
	6 Page length
	7 TRUE (formatted) or FALSE (unformatted)
47	TRUE if the Alternate Expression Evaluation check box in the Calculation dialog box is turned on; otherwise FALSE.
48	The standard column width.
49	The starting page number.
50	The number of printed pages.
51	The number of printed pages of notes if the document is not a chart; otherwise #N/A.
52	An array containing the left, right, top, and bottom margin settings.
53	Returns 1 if the orientation is portrait, and returns 2 if the orientation is landscape.
54	The header, including formatting codes.
55	The footer, including formatting codes.
56	An array containing two logical values indicating horizontal and vertical centering.
57	TRUE if row and column headings will be printed; otherwise FALSE.
58	TRUE if grid lines will be printed; otherwise FALSE.
59	TRUE if cell colors will be printed; otherwise FALSE.
60	A number representing the printed size:
	1 Size on screen
	2 Scale to fit page
	3 Full page
61	A number representing the pagination method:
	1 Down, then over
	2 Over, then down

G

Type	Information Returned
62	A percentage indicating the reduction or enlargement, or #N/A if the document is a chart or if the printer doesn't allow reduction or enlargement.
63	An array containing two items: the first is the number of pages the document is scaled to fit vertically (height), and the second is the number of pages the document is scaled to fit horizontally (width). If no scaling is set or if the document is a chart, #N/A is returned.
64	An array containing all the row numbers of rows below page breaks.
65	An array containing all the column numbers of columns to the right of page breaks.
66	TRUE if the Alternate Formula Entry check box is turned on in the Calculation dialog box; otherwise FALSE.
67	TRUE if the workbook document is bound; otherwise FALSE, or #N/A if the document is not part of a workbook.
68	The name of the workbook that the document belongs to, or an array of names of workbooks if the document belongs to multiple workbooks, or #N/A if the document is not part of a workbook.

Example

=GET.DOCUMENT(50) returns the total number of printed pages for the current document.

See Also

GET.CELL	Returns information about a cell	Macro Function
GET.WINDOW	Returns information about a window	Macro Function
GET.WORKSPACE	Returns information about a workspace	Macro Function

GET.FORMULA(*reference*)

Macro Function

GET.FORMULA returns the contents of the cell, as text, referred to by *reference*, as it appears in the formula bar. If *reference* is a range, GET.FORMULA returns as text the contents of the upper-left cell of the range.

Example

=GET.FORMULA(ACTIVE.CELL()) returns the contents of the active cell, as it appears in the formula bar.

See Also

| GET.CELL | Returns information about a cell | Macro Function |
| GET.NAME | Returns the definition of a name | Macro Function |

GET.LINK.INFO(*link,type,doc-type,ref*)

Macro Function **New to Version 4.0**

GET.LINK.INFO returns information about a link. *Link* is the path as displayed in the File Links dialog box, given as a string. *Type* is the type of information you want returned, as indicated here:

Type	Information Returned
1	1 if the link is automatically updated; 2 if the link is not automatically updated.
2	Date of the latest update if the document is a publisher or a subscriber; otherwise #N/A (Macintosh only).

Doc-type is a number that indicates the link document type, as listed here:

Doc-Type	Link
1	Not applicable
2	DDE link
3	Not applicable
4	Not applicable (Macintosh only)
5	Publisher (Macintosh only)
6	Subscriber (Macintosh only)

Ref is a reference in R1C1 style that specifies the range in the linked document that you want information about.

Example

=GET.LINK.INFO("WordDocument|C:\WORK\COLLECT.DOC!DDE_LINK1",1,2) returns information about a DDE linked Word for Windows document called COLLECT.DOC.

See Also

UPDATE.LINK   Updates a link   Macro Function

GET.NAME(*name*)

Macro Function

GET.NAME returns what *name* refers to. If *name* is given as a reference, it should be a R1C1 style reference.

Example

=GET.NAME("Total") returns "=A30" if cell A30 is defined as the name "Total."

See Also

DEFINE.NAME	Defines a name	Macro Function
NAMES	Returns all defined names	Macro Function
SET.NAME	Defines a name as a value	Macro Function

GET.NOTE(*reference, [start], [length]*)

Macro Function

GET.NOTE returns the note attached to the cell referred to by *reference*, starting at the *start*, and of the length given by the argument *length*. If *start* is omitted, the default value is 1. If *length* is omitted, the default value is the length of the note, or 255, whichever is less.

Example

=GET.NOTE(!$A$1,1,100) returns the first 100 characters in the note attached to cell A1 on the active worksheet.

See Also

GET.CELL	Returns information about a cell	Macro Function
NOTE	Creates or modifies a text note	Macro Function
SOUND.NOTE	Creates or modifies a sound note	Macro Function

GET.OBJECT(*type,[object],[start],[count]*)

Macro Function   **New to Version 4.0**

GET.OBJECT returns information about an object. *Type* is the type of information that you want returned, as indicated here:

Type	Information Returned
1	A number representing the type of the object:
	1 Line
	2 Rectangle
	3 Oval
	4 Arc
	5 Embedded chart
	6 Text box
	7 Button
	8 Picture
	9 Closed polygon
	10 Open polygon
2	TRUE if the object is locked; otherwise FALSE.
3	The z-order position of the object.
4	The cell reference of the cell under the upper-left corner of the object in R1C1 style, or the start point if the object is a line or arc.
5	The horizontal offset from the cell under the upper-left corner of the object in points measured from the upper-left corner of the cell.
6	The vertical offset in points from the upper-left corner of the cell under the upper-left corner of the object.
7	The cell reference of the cell under the lower-right corner of the object in R1C1 style, or the end point if the object is a line or arc.
8	The horizontal offset from the cell under the lower-right corner of the object in points measured from the upper-left corner of the cell.
9	The vertical offset in points from the upper-left corner of the cell under the lower-right corner of the object.

G

Type	Information Returned
10	The name of the macro assigned to the object, or FALSE if there is no macro assigned.
11	A number representing how the object moves and sizes:
	1 Object moves and sizes with cells
	2 Object moves with cells
	3 Object is fixed

Types 12 through 25 apply only to text boxes and buttons, and
will return a #VALUE! or #N/A error if another type of object is selected.

Type	Information Returned
12	A text string starting at *start* and *count* characters long.
13	The font name of the text starting at *start* and *count* characters long, if there is only one font; otherwise #N/A.
14	The font size of the text starting at *start* and *count* characters long, if there is only one font size; otherwise #N/A.
15	TRUE if all the text starting at *start* and *count* characters long is bold; otherwise #N/A.
16	TRUE if all the text starting at *start* and *count* characters long is italic; otherwise #N/A.
17	TRUE if all the text starting at *start* and *count* characters long is underlined; otherwise #N/A.
18	TRUE if all the text starting at *start* and *count* characters long is overstruck; otherwise #N/A.
19	Always returns FALSE.
20	Always returns FALSE.
21	A number indicating the color of the text starting at *start* and *count* characters long:
	0 Automatic
	1 Black
	2 White
	3 Red
	4 Lime green
	5 Royal blue
	6 Yellow
	7 Pink
	8 Aqua

Type	Information Returned
21 (*cont.*)	9 Maroon
	10 Forest green
	11 Navy blue
	12 Avocado green
	13 Purple
	14 Grey green
	15 Light grey
	16 Dark grey
22	A number representing the horizontal alignment:
	1 Left
	2 Center
	3 Right
	4 Justified
23	A number representing the vertical alignment:
	1 Top
	2 Center
	3 Bottom
	4 Justified
24	A number representing the orientation:
	0 Horizontal
	1 Vertical
	2 Upward
	3 Downward
25	TRUE if the button or text box is set for automatic sizing; otherwise FALSE.
26	TRUE if the object is visible; otherwise FALSE.
27	A number representing the border type:
	0 Custom
	1 Automatic
	2 None
28	A number representing the border style:
	0 None
	1 Solid line
	2 Dashed line

G

Type	Information Returned
28 (*cont.*)	3 Dotted line
	4 Dashed dotted line
	5 Dashed dotted double line
	6 50% grey line
	7 75% grey line
	8 25% grey line
29	A number representing the color of the border or line:
	0 Automatic
	1 Black
	2 White
	3 Red
	4 Lime green
	5 Royal blue
	6 Yellow
	7 Pink
	8 Aqua
	9 Maroon
	10 Forest green
	11 Navy blue
	12 Avocado green
	13 Purple
	14 Grey green
	15 Light grey
	16 Dark grey
30	A number representing the weight of the border or line:
	1 Hairline
	2 Thin
	3 Medium
	4 Thick
31	A number representing the fill type:
	0 Custom
	1 Automatic
	2 None

Type	Information Returned
32	A number from 1 to 18, indicating the fill pattern, and corresponding to one of the patterns shown in the Patterns dialog box.
33	#N/A if the object is a line; otherwise, a number representing the foreground color of the fill pattern:

    0 Automatic

    1 Black

    2 White

    3 Red

    4 Lime green

    5 Royal blue

    6 Yellow

    7 Pink

    8 Aqua

    9 Maroon

    10 Forest green

    11 Navy blue

    12 Avocado green

    13 Purple

    14 Grey green

    15 Light grey

    16 Dark grey

Type	Information Returned
34	#N/A if the object is a line; otherwise, a number representing the background color of the fill pattern:

    0 Automatic

    1 Black

    2 White

    3 Red

    4 Lime green

    5 Royal blue

    6 Yellow

    7 Pink

    8 Aqua

    9 Maroon

    10 Forest green

G

Type	Information Returned
34 (*cont.*)	11 Navy blue
	12 Avocado green
	13 Purple
	14 Grey green
	15 Light grey
	16 Dark grey
35	#N/A if the object is a line; otherwise, a number representing the arrowhead width:
	1 Narrow
	2 Medium
	3 Wide
36	#N/A if the object is a line; otherwise, a number representing the arrowhead length:
	1 Short
	2 Medium
	3 Long
37	#N/A if the object is a line; otherwise, a number representing the arrowhead style:
	1 No arrowhead
	2 Open arrowhead
	3 Closed arrowhead
38	TRUE if the border has round corners, FALSE if the border has square corners, and #N/A if the object is a line.
39	TRUE if the border has a shadow, FALSE if the border has no shadow, and #N/A if the object is a line.
40	TRUE if the Lock Text check box is turned on in the Object Protection dialog box; otherwise FALSE.
41	TRUE if the objects are to be printed; otherwise FALSE.
42	The horizontal distance in points from the left edge of the window to the left edge of the object.
43	The vertical distance in points from the top edge of the window to the top edge of the object.
44	The horizontal distance in points from the left edge of the window to the right edge of the object.
45	The vertical distance in points from the top edge of the window to the bottom edge of the object.

Type	Information Returned
46	The number of vertices of a polygon if the object is a polygon; otherwise #N/A.
47	A two-dimensional array containing coordinates of *count* number of vertices starting at *start*.

Object is the object you want information about, referred to by the string as it appears in the reference area when the object is selected. If *object* is omitted, the default is the currently selected object.

Start is the starting character in text objects, or the first vertex in a polygon. If *start* is omitted, the default is 1.

Count is the number of characters or vertices. The default value is 255.

Example

=GET.OBJECT(1) returns 2 if the selected object is a rectangle.

See Also

CREATE.OBJECT	Creates an object	Macro Function
OBJECT.PROTECTION	Protects or unprotects an object	Macro Function

GET.TOOL(*type, bar, position*)

Macro Function   **New to Version 4.0**

GET.TOOL returns information about a tool. *Type* is the type of information that you want returned, as indicated here:

Type	Information Returned
1	The tool ID number.
2	The reference to the macro assigned to the tool, if one is assigned, 0 if the tool is built in, or #N/A.
3	TRUE if the tool button is down; otherwise FALSE.
4	TRUE if the tool is enabled; otherwise FALSE.
5	TRUE if the tool face is a bitmap; otherwise FALSE.
6	The help text associated with the tool, or #N/A if the tool is built in.
7	The balloon text associated with the tool, or #N/A if the tool is built in.

Bar is the name or the number of the toolbar that the tool is on. Toolbar numbers are listed here:

Bar	Toolbar
1	Standard
2	Formatting
3	Utility
4	Chart
5	Drawing
6	Excel 3.0
7	Macro
8	Macro recording
9	Macro paused

Position is the position of the tool on the toolbar. Positions start with 1 from the top or left, depending on the orientation of the toolbar.

Example

=GET.TOOL(1,"Standard",1) returns the tool ID number of the first tool on the standard toolbar.

See Also

ADD.TOOL	Adds a tool to a toolbar	Macro Function
DELETE.TOOL	Deletes a tool from a toolbar	Macro Function
ENABLE.TOOL	Enables or disables a tool	Macro Function
GET.TOOLBAR	Returns information about a toolbar	Macro Function

GET.TOOLBAR(*type, [bar]*)

Macro Function   **New to Version 4.0**

GET.TOOLBAR returns information about a toolbar or toolbars. *Type* specifies the type of information that you want returned. Types 8 and 9 return information about all toolbars that are currently active. Types 1 through 7 return information about specific toolbars, and the bar argument is necessary.

Type	Information Returned
1	An array of tool IDs on the toolbar, with gaps represented by zeros.
2	The horizontal position of the toolbar.
3	The vertical position of the toolbar.
4	The width of the toolbar in points.
5	The height of the toolbar in points.
6	A number representing the location of the toolbar:
	1 Top dock
	2 Left dock
	3 Right dock
	4 Bottom dock
	5 Floating
7	TRUE if the toolbar is visible; otherwise FALSE.
8	An array of all toolbar IDs.
9	An array of toolbar IDs for all visible toolbars.

Bar is the name or the number of the toolbar. Bar numbers are listed here:

Bar	Toolbar
1	Standard
2	Formatting
3	Utility
4	Chart
5	Drawing
6	Excel 3.0
7	Macro
8	Macro recording
9	Macro paused

Example

=GET.TOOLBAR(8) returns an array containing all toolbar IDs.

See Also

ADD.TOOLBAR	Creates a new toolbar	Macro Function

| DELETE.TOOLBAR | Deletes a custom toolbar | Macro Function |
| GET.TOOL | Returns information about a tool | Macro Function |

GET.WINDOW(*type, [window-name]*)

Macro Function

GET.WINDOW returns information about the window referred to by *window-name*. *Window-name* is a string that is the name exactly as it appears in the title of the window. The *type* argument allows you to determine the type of information that is returned. Types 1 through 7 are general information, types 8 through 12 apply to worksheets and macros, and types 13 through 16 return horizontal arrays, as shown in the following table:

Type	Information Returned
1	Name of the document in the window, as text.
2	Number of the window.
3	Horizontal position measured in points from the left edge of the screen.
4	Vertical position measured in points from the top of the screen.
5	Width of the window, in points.
6	Height of the window, in points.
7	TRUE if the window is hidden; otherwise FALSE.
8	TRUE if formulas are displayed; otherwise FALSE.
9	TRUE if grid lines are displayed; otherwise FALSE.
10	TRUE if row and column headings are displayed; otherwise FALSE.
11	TRUE if zeros are displayed; otherwise FALSE.
12	Color of the grid lines and headings as a number from 0 through 8, as shown in the Options Display dialog box. (0 is Automatic.)
13	Left column of every window pane as a horizontal array.
14	Top row of every window pane as a horizontal array.
15	Number of columns in every window pane as a horizontal array.
16	Number of rows in every window pane as a horizontal array.
17	Number of the active pane. (1 is upper-left or upper, 2 is upper-right or right, 3 is lower-left or lower, 4 is lower-right.)
18	Logical value TRUE if the window is split vertically.
19	Logical value TRUE if the window is split horizontally.
20	TRUE if the window is maximized; otherwise FALSE.

Type	Information Returned
22	TRUE if the Outline Symbols check box is on in the Display Options dialog box; otherwise FALSE.
23	A number representing the size of the window:
	1 Restored
	2 Minimized
	3 Maximized
24	TRUE if the panes are frozen; otherwise FALSE.
25	Percentage of magnification as set in the Zoom dialog box, if one is set; otherwise 100.

See Also

GET.DOCUMENT	Returns information about a document	Macro Function
GET.WORKSPACE	Returns information about the workspace	Macro Function

GET.WORKBOOK(*type,[name]*)

Macro Function

GET.WORKBOOK returns information about a workbook. *Type* is the type of information that you want, and *name* is the name of the workbook. If *name* is omitted, the default is the active workbook. The possible values for *type* are listed here:

Type	Information Returned
1	Array of all document names in the workbook
2	Active document name
3	Array of all selected documents in the workbook
4	Number of documents in the workbook

Example

=GET.WORKBOOK(4) returns the number of documents in the active workbook.

See Also

GET.DOCUMENT	Returns information about a document	Macro Function

| WORKBOOK.SELECT | Selects documents in a workbook | Macro Function |

GET.WORKSPACE(*type*)

Macro Function

GET.WORKSPACE returns information about the workspace, where *type* controls the information that is returned.

Type	Information Returned
1	The name of the environment, as text.
2	Version of Microsoft Excel that you are running.
3	Number of decimals if auto-decimal is turned on; otherwise 0.
4	TRUE if the workspace is in R1C1 mode; otherwise FALSE.
5	TRUE if the scroll bars are displayed; otherwise FALSE.
6	TRUE if the status bar is displayed; otherwise FALSE.
7	TRUE if the formula bar is displayed; otherwise FALSE.
8	TRUE if remote DDE requests are allowed; otherwise FALSE.
9	Either the alternate menu key, or if there is no alternate menu key set, #N/A.
10	A number representing the mode of the workspace: 0 No mode 1 Data find mode 2 Copy mode 3 Cut mode 4 Data entry 5 Unused 6 Copy and data entry 7 Cut and data entry
11	Horizontal position of the Excel window measured from the left edge of the screen to the left edge of the window, in points.
12	Vertical position of the Excel window measured from the top edge of the screen to the top edge of the window, in points.
13	Width of the workspace, in points.
14	Height of the workspace, in points.

Type	Information Returned
15	A number representing the status of the Excel workspace: 1 Regular 2 Minimized 3 Maximized
16	Amount of free memory in kilobytes.
17	Total amount of memory available in kilobytes.
18	TRUE if you have a math coprocessor; otherwise FALSE.
19	TRUE if you have a mouse; otherwise FALSE.
20	Array of documents in the group, if the document is part of a group; otherwise #N/A.
21	TRUE if the Excel 3.0 toolbar is displayed; otherwise FALSE.
22	DDE application-specific error code.
23	Path of the default startup directory.
24	Path of the alternate startup directory if there is one; otherwise #N/A.
25	TRUE if relative recording is set, and FALSE if absolute recording is set.
26	Name of the user.
27	Name of the organization.
28	1 if the alternate menu or help key switches to Excel menus, and 2 if it switches to Lotus 1-2-3 Help.
29	TRUE if alternate navigation keys are turned on; otherwise FALSE.
30	Horizontal array containing default print settings: 1 Setup text 2 Left margin 3 Right margin 4 Top margin 5 Bottom margin 6 Page length 7 TRUE (wait after each page) or FALSE (continuous form feed) 8 TRUE (automatic line feed) or FALSE (requires line feed characters) 9 The printer port number
31	TRUE if a macro is running in step mode; otherwise FALSE.
32	Full path of the Excel directory.

G

Type	Information Returned
33	Array of file names in the File New list, in the same order as they appear.
34	An array of paths and names of all custom template files in the File New list, and #N/A for all built-in document types.
35	TRUE if a macro is paused; otherwise FALSE.
36	TRUE if the Cell Drag and Drop check box is turned on in the Options Workspace dialog box; otherwise FALSE.
37	An array of 45 entries of country versions and settings. The INDEX function can be used to access a single item in the array:

    1 Country version of Excel, as a number

    2 Country setting in the Windows Control Panel, as a number

    3 Decimal separator

    4 Zero separator (1000s)

    5 List separator

    6 Row character in R1C1 references

    7 Column character in R1C1 references

    8 Lowercase row character in R1C1 references

    9 Lowercase column character in R1C1 references

    10 Character used instead of [in R1C1 references

    11 Character used instead of] in R1C1 references

    12 Character used instead of { in arrays

    13 Character used instead of } in arrays

    14 Column separator used in arrays

    15 Row separator used in arrays

    16 Alternate item separator in arrays

    17 Date separator in format code

    18 Time separator in format code

    19 Year symbol in format code

    20 Month symbol in format code

    21 Day symbol in format code

    22 Hour symbol in format code

    23 Minute symbol in format code

    24 Second symbol in format code

    25 Currency symbol in format code

    26 General symbol in format code

Type	Information Returned
37 (*cont.*)	27 Number of decimal digits in currency formats
	28 A number representing the negative currency format
	0 ($currency) or (currency$)
	1 –$currency or –currency$
	2 $–currency or currency–$
	3 $currency– or currency$–
	29 Number of decimal digits in noncurrency formats
	30 Number of characters to use in months
	31 Number of characters to use in weekdays
	32 A number representing the date order:
	0 M-D-Y
	1 D-M-Y
	2 Y-M-D
	33 TRUE (24-hour time) or FALSE (12-hour time)
	34 TRUE (functions displayed not in English) or FALSE (otherwise)
	35 TRUE (using the metric system) or FALSE (otherwise)
	36 TRUE (space before currency symbol) or FALSE (otherwise)
	37 TRUE (currency symbol before value) or FALSE (currency symbol after value)
	38 TRUE (minus sign for negative numbers) or FALSE (parentheses for negative numbers)
	39 TRUE (trailing zeros are displayed for zero currency values) or FALSE (otherwise)
	40 TRUE (leading zeros are displayed for zero currency values) or FALSE (otherwise)
	41 TRUE (leading zeros are displayed for months) or FALSE (otherwise)
	42 TRUE (leading zeros are displayed for days) or FALSE (otherwise)
	43 TRUE (using four-digit years) or FALSE (using two-digit years)
	44 TRUE (M-D-Y date order for long form) or FALSE (otherwise)
	45 TRUE (leading zero is displayed in time) or FALSE (otherwise)
38	A number indicating the type of error checking set with the ERROR function.
39	A reference to the current error-handling macro, if one is set; otherwise returns #N/A.

G

Type	Information Returned
40	TRUE if screen updating is on (set by ECHO); otherwise FALSE.
41	An array containing the references to the cells selected the last time the FORMULA.GOTO function was executed.
42	TRUE if your computer can play sound; otherwise FALSE.
43	TRUE if your computer can record sound; otherwise FALSE.
44	An array three columns wide containing all DLL registered procedures, with the first column containing names of the DLLs, the second column containing names of the procedures, and the third column containing a text string specifying the returned data types, and the input arguments and types.
45	TRUE if Microsoft Windows for Pen Computing is running; otherwise FALSE.
46	TRUE if the Move After Enter check box is turned on in the Options Workspace dialog box.

Examples

=GET.WORKSPACE(29) returns TRUE if the alternate navigation keys are turned on.

=INDEX(GET.WORKSPACE(37),38) returns FALSE if parentheses are used for negative numbers.

See Also

GET.DOCUMENT	Returns information about a document	Macro Function
GET.WINDOW	Returns information about a window	Macro Function

GOAL.SEEK(*target-cell, value, variable*)

Macro Function   **New to Version 4.0**

GOAL.SEEK performs the same action as the Goal Seek option from the Formula menu. Goal Seek is one of Excel's new analysis tools. It allows you to search for a value that causes a formula to equal a given value. The arguments *target-cell, value,* and *variable* correspond to the Set Cell, To Value, and By Changing Cell text boxes in the Goal Seek dialog box shown here:

Target-cell is the reference of the cell for which you want to set the value. This cell must contain a formula. *Value* is the value you want the formula to equal. *Variable* is the cell that the formula is dependent on and that you want to vary. Excel will vary that cell until the desired value is achieved.

Goal Seek is normally used when you want to find a solution for a function by changing one variable. Use Formula Solver to find a solution for a function by changing more than one variable.

See Also

FORMULA GOAL SEEK	Equivalent command	Menu Command
FORMULA SCENARIO MANAGER	Keeps track of analysis scenarios	Menu Command
FORMULA SOLVER	Multiple variable solver	Menu Command

GOTO(*reference*)

Macro Function

GOTO moves the current cell to the cell referred to by *reference*. Usually, *reference* is a cell; if it is a range, however, the current cell is the upper-left cell in the range. GOTO is used to control the execution flow of a macro.

Example

=GOTO($A$5) causes the macro to jump to cell A5 on the macro sheet.

See Also

FORMULA.GOTO	Selects a range	Macro Function

GRIDLINES

Concept

Grid lines are horizontal and vertical lines on worksheets, macro sheets, and charts. On worksheets and macro sheets, grid lines are displayed by default. To turn off grid lines, choose the Options Display menu option and unselect the Gridlines check box. Options Display controls your screen display and your printed document. To add or delete grid lines on your printed document, use the File Page Setup menu command.

Charts can be formatted with or without grid lines. Some charts in the gallery have grid lines, and others do not. Once you have formatted your chart, you can always add or delete grid lines using the Gridlines option on the Chart menu. Printed charts will have the same formatting as displayed charts.

See Also

CHART GRIDLINES	Turns grid lines on or off	Menu Command
FILE PAGE SETUP	Controls printed display options	Menu Command
OPTIONS DISPLAY	Controls display options	Menu Command

GRIDLINES(*x-major, x-minor, y-major, y-minor, z-major, z-minor*)
GRIDLINES?(*[x-major], [x-minor], [y-major], [y-minor], [z-major], [z-minor]*)

Macro Function

GRIDLINES performs the same action as the Gridlines option on the Chart menu. GRIDLINES allows you to control whether the grid lines on your chart are visible or invisible. The arguments correspond to check boxes in the dialog box shown here:

If the arguments are included, they are used as default settings for the dialog box.

GROUP()

Macro Function   **New to Version 4.0**

GROUP performs the same action as the Group command from the Format menu. It groups selected objects to create a single object.

See Also

UNGROUP   Separates objects   Macro Function

GROWTH(*y-array*, *[x-array]*, *[new-x-array]*, *[constant]*)

Function

GROWTH returns an array that describes an exponential curve fit to the data stored in the *y-array,* and optionally, the *x-array*. If the *x-array* argument is omitted, it is assumed that the *x-array* is {1, 2, :.}. If the *new-x-array* argument is omitted, it is assumed to be the same as the *x-array* argument. *Constant* is either TRUE or FALSE. If it is FALSE, the constant b (in the relationship $y = b * m^x$) is forced to be 1; otherwise, GROWTH is calculated normally. GROWTH must be entered as an array formula, by pressing CTRL-SHIFT-ENTER, or pressing CTRL-SHIFT and then clicking the mouse. Before entering the function, you must highlight the number of cells in the resulting array. The array returned by GROWTH describes the exponential curve with co-ordinates. If you want an exponential curve array described by a y-intercept and a slope, use LOGEST.

Example

Given the following worksheet:

	A	B
1	MON	300
2	TUE	310
3	WED	340
4	THU	350
5	FRI	380

–GROWTH(B1:B5) returns the array {297.3, 315.5, 334.8, 355.3, 377.0} if you highlight C1:G1 prior to entering the function and press CTRL-SHIFT-ENTER after typing it.

See Also

LINEST   Fits data to a line   Function
LOGEST   Calculates a regressive curve   Function

HALT(*[cancel-close]*)

Macro Function

HALT causes all macros to stop execution. If the currently running macro was called by another macro, both macros will be halted.

Cancel-close controls whether a document is closed if the macro is an Auto_Close macro. If *cancel-close* is TRUE, the document is not closed. If *cancel-close* is FALSE, the document is closed. The default value for *cancel-close* is FALSE.

See Also

BREAK	Interrupts a loop	Macro Function
RETURN	Halts the running macro	Macro Function

HARMEAN(*X1,[X2],...*)

Function

HARMEAN returns the harmonic mean of a list of up to 30 numbers. Alternatively, you can give the numbers in an array, or a reference to an array.

Example

=HARMEAN(1,3,4,7,5,6,23) returns 3.276639.

See Also

AVERAGE	Returns the average of a list of numbers	Function
GEOMEAN	Returns the geometric mean	Function
MEDIAN	Returns the median of a list of numbers	Function

HELP

Menu

The Help menu provides access to the Help system. This can begin with a search of Help topics, information about product support, or Lotus 1-2-3 or Multiplan equivalent commands. The Help menu also provides access to a Microsoft Excel tutorial and an introduction to the product. Finally the Help menu provides information about the version of Excel you are using and the amount of memory available. The Help menu is shown here:

HELP(*[topic]*)

Macro Function

HELP displays help on the *topic* given. The *topic* is a reference to a range in a custom help file. If no *topic* argument is given, HELP displays the help index. Once you have activated help in your macro, you can use APP.ACTIVATE() to return to Excel.

Example

=HELP("C:\EXCEL\CUSTHELP.DOC!50") displays the 50th help topic in the file CUSTHELP.DOC.

See Also

APP.ACTIVATE   Activates Excel   Macro Function

HELP ABOUT MICROSOFT EXCEL

Menu Command

The Help About Microsoft Excel option provides information about Excel and hardware resources, including how much memory you have available, whether you

H-I

have a math coprocessor, and which version of Excel you are running. The About Microsoft Excel dialog box is shown here:

HELP CONTENTS

Menu Command   **New to Version 4.0**

➤   *Shortcut Key: F1*

The Contents command on the Help menu displays a list of Help topics, as shown in Figure H-1.

Figure H-1.   *Microsoft Excel Help topics*

To find out about a topic, place the grabber hand mouse pointer over the desired item and click to display more specific information. You can also search for a specific Help topic by clicking on the Search button. You can go back to a previous topic by clicking on the Back button. Help about how to use Help is available through the Help option within the Help window.

See Also

HELP INDEX   Equivalent command in older versions   Menu Command

HELP FEATURE GUIDE

Menu Command   **Prior to Version 4.0**

The Help Feature Guide menu option allows you to start the Excel Feature Guide. The Feature Guide is an online reference that explains various features of Excel, and lets you practice using the features in a guided environment. There are seven parts to the Feature Guide, as listed here:

What's In The Feature Guide	Explains how to move around the Feature Guide.
Basic Mechanics	Gives descriptions of and opportunities to practice basic Excel skills, such as moving around, using menus, editing, copying, saving, and printing.
Multiple Windows	Describes how to use multiple windows, including splitting and freezing. There are opportunities for guided practice of these options.
Worksheet Formatting	Instructs you how to do formatting, and includes guided practice exercises.
Charts	Demonstrates how to create and customize charts, letting you practice these options in a guided environment.
Macros	Teaches you how to use Excel's macro capabilities. Guided practice sessions can help you learn how to record, use, write, and edit macros.
Auditing And Documenting	Teaches you how to define and apply names to your worksheet, also shows you how to use notes. Guided practice sessions are available.

H-I

HELP INDEX

Menu Command   **Prior to Version 4.0**

The Help Index option tells Excel to display the Excel Help Index. You can use the Index to find help on any option or function. If you want to get help on any topic listed in the Help Index, simply select that topic and press the ENTER key.

See Also

HELP CONTENTS   Equivalent command for version 4   Menu Command

HELP INTRODUCING MICROSOFT EXCEL

Menu Command   **New to Version 4.0**

The Introducing Microsoft Excel option of the Help menu starts a tutorial program that explains the basics of Excel, introduces the new features of version 4, and provides help for Lotus 1-2-3 users. The screen that appears after you choose the Introducing Microsoft Excel option from the Help menu is shown in Figure H-2.

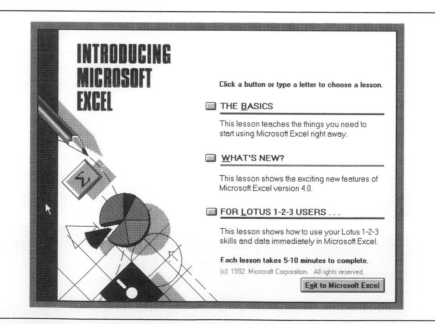

Figure H-2.   Introducing Microsoft Excel

See Also

HELP LEARNING MICROSOFT EXCEL	Accesses tutorials	Menu Command

---

HELP KEYBOARD

Menu Command   **Prior to Version 4.0**

The Help Keyboard option displays help on the different keys you can use when working in Excel. If Help is already open, the Help window is activated and keyboard help is displayed in the window. If Help is not open, Excel opens a Help window and displays keyboard help in that window.

HELP LEARNING MICROSOFT EXCEL

Menu Command   **New to Version 4.0**

The Learning Microsoft Excel option on the Help menu provides access to tutorials. The screen that appears when you choose the Learning Microsoft Excel option from the Help menu is shown in Figure H-3. An introduction to Excel will help you get

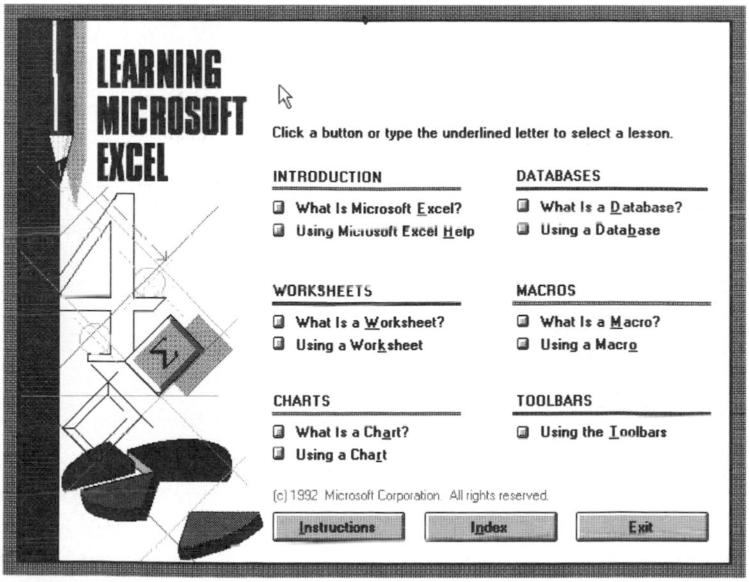

H-I

Figure H-3. *Learning Microsoft Excel*

started quickly. Tutorials on worksheets, charts, databases, macros, and toolbars are also included. Choose the Instructions button to find out how to use the tutorials. Choose the Index button to find a tutorial on a specific topic.

See Also

HELP INTRODUCING MICROSOFT EXCEL	Introduces Excel version 4	Menu Command

HELP LOTUS 1-2-3

Menu Command

The Lotus 1-2-3 option on the Help menu provides help to Lotus 1-2-3 users. You can learn the equivalent Excel commands, or view a demo. The dialog box that is displayed when you choose Lotus 1-2-3 from the Help menu is shown here:

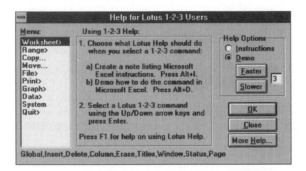

See Also

HELP MULTIPLAN	Help for Multiplan users	Menu Command

HELP MULTIPLAN

Menu Command

The Multiplan option on the Help menu allows you to type a Multiplan command into a dialog box and have Excel tell you the equivalent Excel option, if any. The Multiplan Help dialog box is shown here:

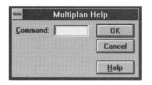

See Also

HELP LOTUS 1-2-3   Help for Lotus 1-2-3 users   Menu Command

HELP PRODUCT SUPPORT

Menu Command   **New to Version 4.0**

The Product Support option on the Help menu provides access to Excel product support information, which includes answers to commonly asked questions and instructions on how to use and find help. When you choose the Product Support option from the Help menu, the screen in Figure H-4 appears.

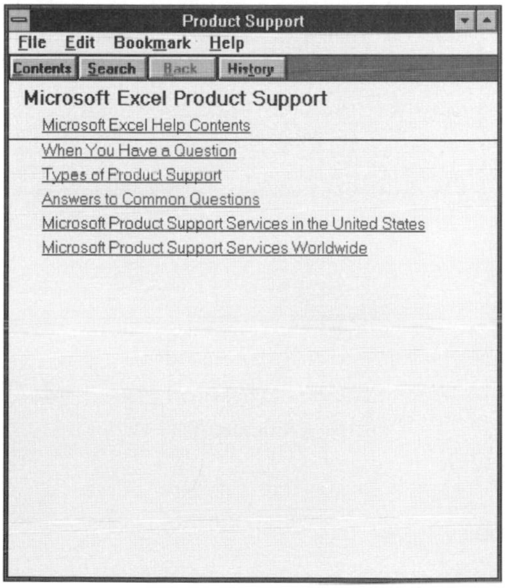

H-I

Figure H-4.   *The Microsoft Excel Product Support screen*

See Also

HELP LEARNING MICROSOFT EXCEL	Accesses tutorials	Menu Command
HELP SEARCH	Finds help on a topic	Menu Command

HELP SEARCH

Menu Command   **New to Version 4.0**

The Search option on the Help menu searches for help on a particular topic. Find the topic that you want help on and then click on the Go To button. When you choose Search from the Help menu, the following dialog box appears.

See Also

HELP LEARNING MICROSOFT EXCEL	Accesses tutorials	Menu Command
HELP PRODUCT SUPPORT	Provides access to help on product support	Menu Command

HELP TUTORIAL

Menu Command   **Prior to Version 4.0**

The Help Tutorial option starts the Excel tutorial. This tutorial gives you an overview of Excel and a chance to practice using Excel in a guided environment. If you have documents open when you start the tutorial, Excel saves them and restores your workspace when you exit the tutorial. You can start and stop at any time; you don't need to go through the complete the tutorial. There are six modules in the tutorial, as described here:

How To Use This Tutorial	Explains how to use the Excel tutorial.
Introduction	Explains the key features of Excel, and how to use online help.
Worksheets	Helps you learn how to create, format, edit, print, and save worksheets; also teaches you how to use functions.
Charts	Introduces Excel charts, and shows you how to create, format, edit, print, and save charts.
Databases	Introduces Excel databases, and illustrates how to set up and use a database.
Macros	Explains Excel macro basics, showing you how to record, run, and edit macros.

HEX2BIN(X, [characters])

Function   **New to Version 4.0**

HEX2BIN converts a number X from hexadecimal to binary, and returns the result in *characters* number of places. For example, if *characters* is 8, there will always be eight characters in the result, which will be padded with 0's if necessary.

HEX2BIN is an add-in function. The first time you use it, you may see a #REF! error while Excel loads the function.

Example

=HEX2BIN(4,8) returns 00000100.

See Also

BIN2HEX	Converts binary to hexadecimal	Function
HEX2DEC	Converts hexadecimal to decimal	Function
HEX2OCT	Converts hexadecimal to octal	Function

HEX2DEC(X)

Function   **New to Version 4.0**

HEX2DEC converts a number X from hexadecimal to decimal.

HEX2DEC is an add-in function. The first time that you use it, you may see a #REF! error while Excel loads the function.

Example

=HEX2DEC(11) returns 17.

See Also

BIN2HEX	Converts binary to hexadecimal	Function
HEX2BIN	Converts hexadecimal to binary	Function
HEX2OCT	Converts hexadecimal to octal	Function

HEX2OCT(X, [characters])

Function   **New to Version 4.0**

HEX2OCT converts a number X from hexadecimal to octal, and returns the result in *characters* number of places. For example, if *characters* is 8, there will always be eight characters in the result, which will be padded with 0's if necessary.

HEX2OCT is an add-in function. The first time that you use it, you may see a #REF! error while Excel loads the function.

Example

=HEX2OCT(10,8) returns 00000020.

See Also

BIN2HEX	Converts binary to hexadecimal	Function
HEX2BIN	Converts hexadecimal to binary	Function
HEX2DEC	Converts hexadecimal to decimal	Function

HIDE()

Macro Function

HIDE performs the same action as the Hide option on the Window menu. HIDE hides the active window.

See Also

UNHIDE	Unhides a hidden window	Macro Function

HIDE.OBJECT(*[object],[hide]*)

Macro Function   **New to Version 4.0**

HIDE.OBJECT hides or displays the object specified by the argument *object*. If no *object* argument is given, the default is the currently selected object or objects. *Object* should be given as the text string that appears in the formula bar when the object is selected. *Hide* should be TRUE if you want to hide the specified or selected object, or FALSE if you want to display the object. The default value for *hide* is TRUE.

See Also

CREATE.OBJECT	Creates a new object	Macro Function
DISPLAY	Controls how an object appears	Macro Function

HISTOGRAM(*input,output,[bins],[presentation],[cum-chart],[chart]*)

Macro Function

HISTOGRAM returns an output table with the result of calculating individual and cumulative percentages of the input range. The output table is placed in a range with *output* as the upper-left corner. *Bins* is a set of numbers, given in descending order, that define bin ranges.

If *presentation* is TRUE, the output table is given in both ascending-bin and descending-frequency order. If *presentation* is FALSE, the output table is given in ascending-bin order. If *presentation* is omitted, the default value is FALSE.

If *cum-chart* is TRUE, cumulative percentages are included in the output table. If *cum-chart* is FALSE, cumulative percentages are not included. If *cum-chart* is omitted, the default value is FALSE.

If *chart* is TRUE, a histogram chart is returned in addition to the output table. If *chart* is FALSE, a chart is not returned. If *chart* is omitted, the default value is FALSE.

HLINE(*number-of-columns*)

Macro Function

HLINE performs the same action as scrolling by column. The *number-of-columns* argument controls how many columns to scroll past. Positive numbers scroll to the right; negative numbers scroll to the left.

H-1

Example

=HLINE(5) scrolls five columns to the right.

See Also

HPAGE	Scrolls horizontally by page	Macro Function
HSCROLL	Scrolls horizontally by page or percent	Macro Function
VLINE	Scrolls vertically by line	Macro Function

HLOOKUP(*X,range,row*)

Function

HLOOKUP returns an entry from a two-dimensional horizontal lookup table. Excel searches the top row of a range for the largest value that is less than or equal to *X* and then in that column, retrieves the contents of a second cell, which is in the specified row. A *horizontal lookup table* is a range of cells in which the ascending overall values are in a row. Here is an example of a horizontal lookup table:

EMPLOYEES	1985	1990	1995
Smith	20,000	30,000	40,000
Jones	18,000	36,000	54,000

If the value of *X* is not exactly equal to a value in the top row of the lookup range, HLOOKUP finds the closest value that is not larger than *X*. *Row* is the number of the row from which the value is to be retrieved. The first (top) row is 1.

Example

=HLOOKUP(1990,SALARIES,2) would search for 1990 in the first row of the SALARIES range (SALARIES is the previous table) and return the value that is in row 2. This is 30,000.

See Also

LOOKUP	Lookup function for an array or range	Macro Function
VLOOKUP	Vertical lookup function	Macro Function

HOUR(*time-serial-number*)

Function

HOUR returns the hour from a *time-serial-number.* The hour can be a number from 0 (midnight) to 23 (11:00 P.M.).

Examples

=HOUR(NOW()) returns the current hour.
=HOUR(.5) returns 12 (noon).

See Also

NOW	Returns the current date and time	Function

HPAGE(*number-of-windows*)

Macro Function

HPAGE performs the same action as scrolling by window. The *number-of-windows* argument controls how many windows to scroll past. Positive numbers scroll to the right; negative numbers scroll to the left.

Example

=HPAGE(4) scrolls four windows to the right.

See Also

HLINE	Scrolls horizontally by column	Macro Function
HSCROLL	Scrolls horizontally	Macro Function
VLINE	Scrolls vertically by line	Macro Function
VPAGE	Scrolls vertically by window	Macro Function
VSCROLL	Scrolls vertically	Macro Function

HSCROLL(*scroll-to, [logical]*)

Macro Function

HSCROLL scrolls horizontally. If the *logical* argument is TRUE, HSCROLL scrolls to the column given as the *scroll-to* argument. If the *logical* argument is FALSE, the *scroll-to* argument should be given as a fraction between 0 and 1. If *scroll-to* is 0, HSCROLL scrolls to the left edge. If *scroll-to* is 1, HSCROLL scrolls to the right edge. Any fraction between 0 and 1 causes HSCROLL to scroll to the appropriate column.

See Also

HPAGE	Scrolls horizontally by page	Macro Function
LINE	Scrolls horizontally by column	Macro Function
VPAGE	Scrolls vertically by window	Macro Function

HYPGEOMDIST(*successes-in-sample, sample-size, successes-in-pop, pop-size*)

Function   **New to Version 4.0**

HYPGEOMDIST calculates the hypergeometric distribution. The equation for the hypergeometric distribution is as follows.

$$p(X = x) = h(x; s, y, N) = \frac{\binom{y}{x} \binom{N-y}{s-x}}{\binom{N}{s}}$$

x	*successes-in-sample*
y	*successes-in-pop*
s	*sample-size*
p	*pop-size*

Successes-in-sample is the number of successes in the sample, and *successes-in-pop* is the number of successes in the population. *Sample-size* is the size of the sample, and *pop-size* is the size of the population.

Example

=HYPGEOMDIST(1,8,16,35) returns 0.034255.

See Also

BINOMDIST	Returns the binomial distribution	Function
NEGBINOMDIST	Returns the negative binomial distribution	Function

I

IF(*condition, true-value, [false-value]*)
IF(*condition*)

Function and Macro Function

The first form of the IF function (with three arguments) evaluates a *condition* or equation for TRUE or FALSE and returns one value for a TRUE condition and another value for a FALSE condition. The *false-value* argument is optional.

The second form of the IF function (with one argument) is used in macros to control the flow of execution. If the *condition* evaluates to TRUE, the macro executes the instructions immediately following the IF function until it reaches the next IF, ELSE, ELSE.IF, or END.IF function. If the *condition* evaluates to FALSE, the macro skips the instructions immediately following the IF function and jumps to the next ELSE, ELSE.IF, or END.IF function.

H-I

Example

IF(PMT>5000,.05,.025) determines whether PMT is greater than 5000. If the condition is TRUE (PMT is greater than 5000), the value 5% is returned. Otherwise, a value of 2.5% is returned.

Figure I-1 shows an example of a macro that prompts the user to answer the question, "Do you want to create a chart?" If the user responds with **Y**, a chart is created. If the user responds with anything other than **Y**, the macro stops executing and no chart is created.

See Also

ELSE	Changes the execution flow	Macro Function
ELSE.IF	Changes the execution flow	Macro Function
END.IF	Ends an IF block	Macro Function

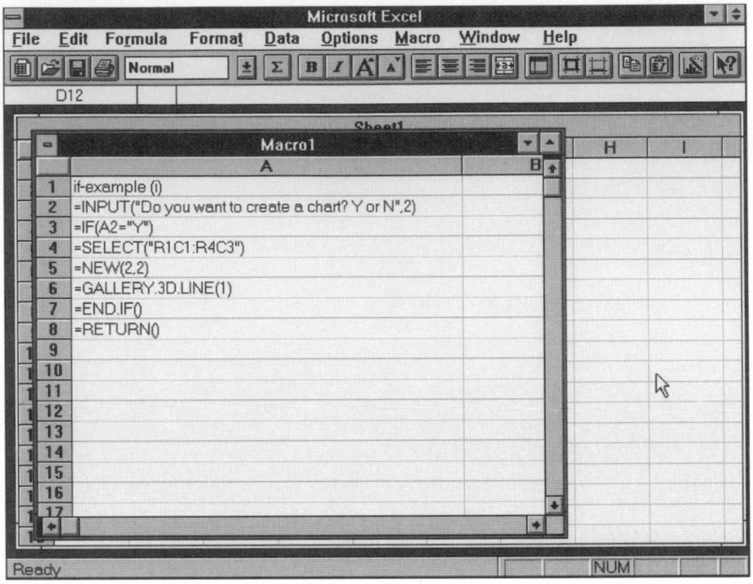

Figure I-1.   *Using IF in a macro*

IMABS(*number*)

Function   New to Version 4.0

IMABS returns the absolute value of an imaginary number given in the form $X + Y$i
or $X + Y$j. The absolute value of the imaginary number is equal to the square root of
the sum of the squares of X and Y.

IMABS is an add-in function. The first time that you use it, you may see a #REF!
error while Excel loads the function.

Example

=IMABS("3+4i") returns 5.

See Also

Other imaginary functions:

IMAGINARY	Returns the imaginary coefficient	Function
IMARGUMENT	Returns the argument	Function
IMCONJUGATE	Returns the conjugate	Function
IMCOS	Returns the cosine	Function

IMDIV	Returns the quotient of two complex numbers	Function
IMEXP	Returns the exponential	Function
IMLN	Returns the natural log	Function
IMLOG2	Returns the base 2 log	Function
IMLOG10	Returns the base 10 log	Function
IMPOWER	Raises a complex number to a power	Function
IMPRODUCT	Returns the product of two complex numbers	Function
IMREAL	Returns the real coefficient	Function
IMSIN	Returns the sine	Function
IMSQRT	Returns the square root	Function
IMSUB	Subtracts one complex number from another	Function
IMSUM	Sums complex numbers	Function

IMAGINARY(*number*)

Function   **New to Version 4.0**

IMAGINARY returns the imaginary coefficient of a complex number, where *number* is given as a text string in the format $X + Y$i or $X + Y$j.

IMAGINARY is an add-in function. The first time that you use it, you may see a #REF! error while Excel loads the function.

Example

=IMAGINARY("3+5i") returns 5.

See Also

Other imaginary functions:

IMABS	Returns the absolute value	Function
IMARGUMENT	Returns the argument	Function
IMCONJUGATE	Returns the conjugate	Function
IMCOS	Returns the cosine	Function
IMDIV	Returns the quotient of two complex numbers	Function
IMEXP	Returns the exponential	Function
IMLN	Returns the natural log	Function
IMLOG2	Returns the base 2 log	Function

IMLOG10	Returns the base 10 log	Function
IMPOWER	Raises a complex number to a power	Function
IMPRODUCT	Returns the product of two complex numbers	Function
IMREAL	Returns the real coefficient	Function
IMSIN	Returns the sine	Function
IMSQRT	Returns the square root	Function
IMSUB	Subtracts one complex number from another	Function
IMSUM	Sums complex numbers	Function

IMARGUMENT(*number*)

Function   **New to Version 4.0**

IMARGUMENT returns the argument $\tilde{\theta}$ given a complex number, given as a text string in the format $X + Y\text{i}$ or $X + Y\text{j}$, such that:

$$X + Y\text{i} = |X + Y\text{i}|(\cos\tilde{\theta} + i\sin\tilde{\theta})$$

The result is returned in radians.

IMARGUMENT is an add-in function. The first time that you use it, you may see a #REF! error while Excel loads the function.

Example

=IMARGUMENT("3+5i") returns 1.030377.

See Also

Other imaginary functions:

IMABS	Returns the absolute value	Function
IMAGINARY	Returns the imaginary coefficient	Function
IMCONJUGATE	Returns the conjugate	Function
IMCOS	Returns the cosine	Function
IMDIV	Returns the quotient of two complex numbers	Function
IMEXP	Returns the exponential	Function
IMLN	Returns the natural log	Function
IMLOG2	Returns the base 2 log	Function
IMLOG10	Returns the base 10 log	Function
IMPOWER	Raises a complex number to a power	Function

IMPRODUCT	Returns the product of two complex numbers	Function
IMREAL	Returns the real coefficient	Function
IMSIN	Returns the sine	Function
IMSQRT	Returns the square root	Function
IMSUB	Subtracts one complex number from another	Function
IMSUM	Sums complex numbers	Function

IMCONJUGATE(*number*)

Function   **New to Version 4.0**

IMCONJUGATE returns the complex conjugate of a complex number, where *number* is given as a text string in the format $X + Y$i or $X + Y$j.

IMCONJUGATE is an add-in function. The first time that you use it, you may see a #REF! error while Excel loads the function.

Example

=IMCONJUGATE("3+5i") returns 3–5i.

See Also

Other imaginary functions:

IMABS	Returns the absolute value	Function
IMAGINARY	Returns the imaginary coefficient	Function
IMARGUMENT	Returns the argument	Function
IMCOS	Returns the cosine	Function
IMDIV	Returns the quotient of two complex numbers	Function
IMEXP	Returns the exponential	Function
IMLN	Returns the natural log	Function
IMLOG2	Returns the base 2 log	Function
IMLOG10	Returns the base 10 log	Function
IMPOWER	Raises a complex number to a power	Function
IMPRODUCT	Returns the product of two complex numbers	Function
IMREAL	Returns the real coefficient	Function
IMSIN	Returns the sine	Function
IMSQRT	Returns the square root	Function
IMSUB	Subtracts one complex number from another	Function
IMSUM	Sums complex numbers	Function

H-I

IMCOS(*number*)

Function   New to Version 4.0

IMCOS returns the cosine of a complex number, where *number* is given as a text string in the format $X + Yi$ or $X + Yj$.

IMCOS is an add-in function. The first time that you use it, you may see a #REF! error while Excel loads the function.

Example

=IMCOS("0.5+i") returns 1.354180657–0.563421465i.

See Also

Other imaginary functions:

IMABS	Returns the absolute value	Function
IMAGINARY	Returns the imaginary coefficient	Function
IMARGUMENT	Returns the argument	Function
IMCONJUGATE	Returns the conjugate	Function
IMDIV	Returns the quotient of two complex numbers	Function
IMEXP	Returns the exponential	Function
IMLN	Returns the natural log	Function
IMLOG2	Returns the base 2 log	Function
IMLOG10	Returns the base 10 log	Function
IMPOWER	Raises a complex number to a power	Function
IMPRODUCT	Returns the product of two complex numbers	Function
IMREAL	Returns the real coefficient	Function
IMSIN	Returns the sine	Function
IMSQRT	Returns the square root	Function
IMSUB	Subtracts one complex number from another	Function
IMSUM	Sums complex numbers	Function

IMDIV(*number1, number2*)

Function   New to Version 4.0

IMDIV returns the quotient of two complex numbers, where *number1* and *number2* are given as text strings in the format $X + Yi$ or $X + Yj$.

IMDIV is an add-in function. The first time that you use it, you may see a #REF! error while Excel loads the function.

Example

=IMDIV("3+5i","4+6i") returns 0.807692308+0.038461538i.

See Also

Other imaginary functions:

IMABS	Returns the absolute value	Function
IMAGINARY	Returns the imaginary coefficient	Function
IMARGUMENT	Returns the argument	Function
IMCONJUGATE	Returns the conjugate	Function
IMCOS	Returns the cosine	Function
IMEXP	Returns the exponential	Function
IMLN	Returns the natural log	Function
IMLOG2	Returns the base 2 log	Function
IMLOG10	Returns the base 10 log	Function
IMPOWER	Raises a complex number to a power	Function
IMPRODUCT	Returns the product of two complex numbers	Function
IMREAL	Returns the real coefficient	Function
IMSIN	Returns the sine	Function
IMSQRT	Returns the square root	Function
IMSUB	Subtracts one complex number from another	Function
IMSUM	Sums complex numbers	Function

IMEXP(*number*)

Function   **New to Version 4.0**

IMEXP returns the exponential of a complex number, where *number* is given as a text string in the format $X + Yi$ or $X + Yj$.

IMEXP is an add-in function. The first time that you use it, you may see a #REF! error while Excel loads the function.

Example

=IMEXP("3+5i") returns 5.6975073–19.26050893i.

See Also

Other imaginary functions:

IMABS	Returns the absolute value	Function
IMAGINARY	Returns the imaginary coefficient	Function
IMARGUMENT	Returns the argument	Function
IMCONJUGATE	Returns the conjugate	Function
IMCOS	Returns the cosine	Function
IMDIV	Returns the quotient of two complex numbers	Function
IMLN	Returns the natural log	Function
IMLOG2	Returns the base 2 log	Function
IMLOG10	Returns the base 10 log	Function
IMPOWER	Raises a complex number to a power	Function
IMPRODUCT	Returns the product of two complex numbers	Function
IMREAL	Returns the real coefficient	Function
IMSIN	Returns the sine	Function
IMSQRT	Returns the square root	Function
IMSUB	Subtracts one complex number from another	Function
IMSUM	Sums complex numbers	Function

IMLN(*number*)

Function   **New to Version 4.0**

IMLN returns the natural logarithm of a complex number, where *number* is given as a text string in the format $X + Yi$ or $X + Yj$.

IMLN is an add-in function. The first time that you use it, you may see a #REF! error while Excel loads the function.

Example

=IMLN("3+5i") returns 1.763180262–1030376827i.

See Also

Other imaginary functions:

IMABS	Returns the absolute value	Function
IMAGINARY	Returns the imaginary coefficient	Function
IMARGUMENT	Returns the argument	Function

IMCONJUGATE	Returns the conjugate	Function
IMCOS	Returns the cosine	Function
IMDIV	Returns the quotient of two complex numbers	Function
IMEXP	Returns the exponential	Function
IMLOG2	Returns the base 2 log	Function
IMLOG10	Returns the base 10 log	Function
IMPOWER	Raises a complex number to a power	Function
IMPRODUCT	Returns the product of two complex numbers	Function
IMREAL	Returns the real coefficient	Function
IMSIN	Returns the sine	Function
IMSQRT	Returns the square root	Function
IMSUB	Subtracts one complex number from another	Function
IMSUM	Sums complex numbers	Function

IMLOG2(*number*)

Function   **New to Version 4.0**

IMLOG2 returns the base 2 logarithm of a complex number, where *number* is given as a text string in the format $X + Yi$ or $X + Yj$.

   IMLOG2 is an add-in function. The first time that you use it, you may see a #REF! error while Excel loads the function.

Example

=IMLOG2("3+5i") returns 2.543731421+1.486519538i.

See Also

Other imaginary functions:

IMABS	Returns the absolute value	Function
IMAGINARY	Returns the imaginary coefficient	Function
IMARGUMENT	Returns the argument	Function
IMCONJUGATE	Returns the conjugate	Function
IMCOS	Returns the cosine	Function
IMDIV	Returns the quotient of two complex numbers	Function
IMEXP	Returns the exponential	Function
IMLN	Returns the natural log	Function

H-I

IMLOG10	Returns the base 10 log	Function
IMPOWER	Raises a complex number to a power	Function
IMPRODUCT	Returns the product of two complex numbers	Function
IMREAL	Returns the real coefficient	Function
IMSIN	Returns the sine	Function
IMSQRT	Returns the square root	Function
IMSUB	Subtracts one complex number from another	Function
IMSUM	Sums complex numbers	Function

IMLOG10(*number*)

Function   **New to Version 4.0**

IMLOG10 returns the base 10 logarithm of a complex number, where *number* is given as a text string in the format $X + Yi$ or $X + Yj$.

    IMLOG10 is an add-in function. The first time that you use it, you may see a #REF! error while Excel loads the function.

Example

=IMLOG10("3+5i") returns 0.765739459+0.44748697i.

See Also

Other imaginary functions:

IMABS	Returns the absolute value	Function
IMAGINARY	Returns the imaginary coefficient	Function
IMARGUMENT	Returns the argument	Function
IMCONJUGATE	Returns the conjugate	Function
IMCOS	Returns the cosine	Function
IMDIV	Returns the quotient of two complex numbers	Function
IMEXP	Returns the exponential	Function
IMLN	Returns the natural log	Function
IMLOG2	Returns the base 2 log	Function
IMPOWER	Raises a complex number to a power	Function
IMPRODUCT	Returns the product of two complex numbers	Function
IMREAL	Returns the real coefficient	Function

IMSIN	Returns the sine	Function
IMSQRT	Returns the square root	Function
IMSUB	Subtracts one complex number from another	Function
IMSUM	Sums complex numbers	Function

IMPOWER(*number, power*)

Function   **New to Version 4.0**

IMPOWER raises a complex number to a power, where *number* is given as a text string in the format $X + Yi$ or $X + Yj$.

IMPOWER is an add-in function. The first time that you use it, you may see a #REF! error while Excel loads the function.

Example

=IMPOWER("3+5i",2) returns $-16+30i$.

See Also

Other imaginary functions:

IMABS	Returns the absolute value	Function
IMAGINARY	Returns the imaginary coefficient	Function
IMARGUMENT	Returns the argument	Function
IMCONJUGATE	Returns the conjugate	Function
IMCOS	Returns the cosine	Function
IMDIV	Returns the quotient of two complex numbers	Function
IMEXP	Returns the exponential	Function
IMLN	Returns the natural log	Function
IMLOG2	Returns the base 2 log	Function
IMLOG10	Returns the base 10 log	Function
IMPRODUCT	Returns the product of two complex numbers	Function
IMREAL	Returns the real coefficient	Function
IMSIN	Returns the sine	Function
IMSQRT	Returns the square root	Function
IMSUB	Subtracts one complex number from another	Function
IMSUM	Sums complex numbers	Function

H-I

IMPRODUCT(*number1,number2*)

Function   **New to Version 4.0**

IMPRODUCT returns the product of two complex numbers, where *number1* and *number2* are given as text strings in the format $X+Yi$ or $X+Yj$.

   IMPRODUCT is an add-in function. The first time that you use it, you may see a #REF! error while Excel loads the function.

Example

=IMPRODUCT("3+5i","4+6i") returns −18+38i.

See Also

Other imaginary functions:

IMABS	Returns the absolute value	Function
IMAGINARY	Returns the imaginary coefficient	Function
IMARGUMENT	Returns the argument	Function
IMCONJUGATE	Returns the conjugate	Function
IMCOS	Returns the cosine	Function
IMDIV	Returns the quotient of two complex numbers	Function
IMEXP	Returns the exponential	Function
IMLN	Returns the natural log	Function
IMLOG2	Returns the base 2 log	Function
IMLOG10	Returns the base 10 log	Function
IMPOWER	Raises a complex number to a power	Function
IMREAL	Returns the real coefficient	Function
IMSIN	Returns the sine	Function
IMSQRT	Returns the square root	Function
IMSUB	Subtracts one complex number from another	Function
IMSUM	Sums complex numbers	Function

IMREAL(*number*)

Function   **New to Version 4.0**

IMREAL returns the real coefficient of a complex number, where *number* is given as a text string in the format $X+Yi$ or $X+Yj$.

IMREAL is an add-in function. The first time that you use it, you may see a #REF! error while Excel loads the function.

Example

=IMREAL("3+5i") returns 3.

See Also

Other imaginary functions:

IMABS	Returns the absolute value	Function
IMAGINARY	Returns the imaginary coefficient	Function
IMARGUMENT	Returns the argument	Function
IMCONJUGATE	Returns the conjugate	Function
IMCOS	Returns the cosine	Function
IMDIV	Returns the quotient of two complex numbers	Function
IMEXP	Returns the exponential	Function
IMLN	Returns the natural log	Function
IMLOG2	Returns the base 2 log	Function
IMLOG10	Returns the base 10 log	Function
IMPOWER	Raises a complex number to a power	Function
IMPRODUCT	Returns the product of two complex numbers	Function
IMSIN	Returns the sine	Function
IMSQRT	Returns the square root	Function
IMSUB	Subtracts one complex number from another	Function
IMSUM	Sums complex numbers	Function

IMSIN(*number*)

Function   **New to Version 4.0**

IMSIN returns the sine of a complex number, where *number* is given as a text string in the format $X + Y$i or $X + Y$j.

IMSIN is an add-in function. The first time that you use it, you may see a #REF! error while Excel loads the function.

Example

=IMSIN("0.5+i") returns 0.739792264+1.031336074i.

See Also

Other imaginary functions:

IMABS	Returns the absolute value	Function
IMAGINARY	Returns the imaginary coefficient	Function
IMARGUMENT	Returns the argument	Function
IMCONJUGATE	Returns the conjugate	Function
IMCOS	Returns the cosine	Function
IMDIV	Returns the quotient of two complex numbers	Function
IMEXP	Returns the exponential	Function
IMLN	Returns the natural log	Function
IMLOG2	Returns the base 2 log	Function
IMLOG10	Returns the base 10 log	Function
IMPOWER	Raises a complex number to a power	Function
IMPRODUCT	Returns the product of two complex numbers	Function
IMREAL	Returns the real coefficient	Function
IMSQRT	Returns the square root	Function
IMSUB	Subtracts one complex number from another	Function
IMSUM	Sums complex numbers	Function

IMSQRT(*number*)

Function   **New to Version 4.0**

IMSQRT returns the square root of a complex number, where *number* is given as a text string in the format $X + Yi$ or $X + Yj$.

IMSQRT is an add-in function. The first time that you use it, you may see a #REF! error while Excel loads the function.

Example

=IMSQRT("3+5i") returns 2.101303393+1.189737764i.

See Also

Other imaginary functions:

IMABS	Returns the absolute value	Function
IMAGINARY	Returns the imaginary coefficient	Function
IMARGUMENT	Returns the argument	Function

IMCONJUGATE	Returns the conjugate	Function
IMCOS	Returns the cosine	Function
IMDIV	Returns the quotient of two complex numbers	Function
IMEXP	Returns the exponential	Function
IMLN	Returns the natural log	Function
IMLOG2	Returns the base 2 log	Function
IMLOG10	Returns the base 10 log	Function
IMPOWER	Raises a complex number to a power	Function
IMPRODUCT	Returns the product of two complex numbers	Function
IMREAL	Returns the real coefficient	Function
IMSIN	Returns the sine	Function
IMSUB	Subtracts one complex number from another	Function
IMSUM	Sums complex numbers	Function

IMSUB(*number1, number2*)

Function   **New to Version 4.0**

IMSUB returns the difference between two complex numbers, where *number1* and *number2* are given as text strings in the format $X + Yi$ or $X + Yj$.

IMSUB is an add-in function. The first time that you use it, you may see a #REF! error while Excel loads the function.

Example

=IMSUB("3+5i","4+6i") returns –1–i.

See Also

Other imaginary functions:

IMABS	Returns the absolute value	Function
IMAGINARY	Returns the imaginary coefficient	Function
IMARGUMENT	Returns the argument	Function
IMCONJUGATE	Returns the conjugate	Function
IMCOS	Returns the cosine	Function
IMDIV	Returns the quotient of two complex numbers	Function
IMEXP	Returns the exponential	Function
IMLN	Returns the natural log	Function

H-I

IMLOG2	Returns the base 2 log	Function
IMLOG10	Returns the base 10 log	Function
IMPOWER	Raises a complex number to a power	Function
IMPRODUCT	Returns the product of two complex numbers	Function
IMREAL	Returns the real coefficient	Function
IMSIN	Returns the sine	Function
IMSQRT	Returns the square root	Function
IMSUM	Sums complex numbers	Function

IMSUM(*number1,number2,[number3],...*)

Function   New to Version 4.0

IMSUM returns the sum of complex numbers, where *number1, number2, number3,* and so on are given as text strings in the format $X + Yi$ or $X + Yj$.

IMSUM is an add-in function. The first time that you use it, you may see a #REF! error while Excel loads the function.

Example

=IMSUM("3+5i","4+6i") returns 7+11i.

See Also

Other imaginary functions:

IMABS	Returns the absolute value	Function
IMAGINARY	Returns the imaginary coefficient	Function
IMARGUMENT	Returns the argument	Function
IMCONJUGATE	Returns the conjugate	Function
IMCOS	Returns the cosine	Function
IMDIV	Returns the quotient of two complex numbers	Function
IMEXP	Returns the exponential	Function
IMLN	Returns the natural log	Function
IMLOG2	Returns the base 2 log	Function
IMLOG10	Returns the base 10 log	Function
IMPOWER	Raises a complex number to a power	Function
IMPRODUCT	Returns the product of two complex numbers	Function
IMREAL	Returns the real coefficient	Function

IMSIN	Returns the sine	Function
IMSQRT	Returns the square root	Function
IMSUB	Subtracts one complex number from another	Function

INDEX(*range(s),[row],[column],[area]*)
INDEX(*array, [row],[column]*)

Function

The first form of INDEX, with four arguments, searches a specified *range* or *ranges* and returns the value that is in the specified *row* and *column*. The first row is row 1 and the first column is column 1. If you have multiple ranges (C1:D5,E8:G9,F4:H8, for example), *area* specifies which range to use. In the example, area 1 would be C1:D5 and area 3 would be F4:H8. Use INDEX instead of HLOOKUP or VLOOKUP when you want to search for a value according to its placement in a range, instead of looking for another value associated with it. If *row* and *column* arguments are not given, the range specified by *area* is returned. If the *area* argument is omitted, the default value is 1.

Example

=INDEX((A1:F18,A20:F38),13,4,2) will return the value from the range of cells A20:F38, in cell D33 (13th row, 4th column, and second area or range).

The second form of INDEX, with three arguments, looks up a value in an array by row and column number. The *row* and *column* arguments are optional if you have a one-dimensional array. If you have a horizontal array, the *row* argument is not used. If you have a vertical array, the *column* argument is not used.

Example

=INDEX({1,3,5;2,4,6},1,3) returns 5.

See Also

HLOOKUP	Horizontal lookup function	Function
LOOKUP	Looks up a value in a table	Function
VLOOKUP	Vertical lookup function	Function

INDIRECT(*cell-reference,[reference-type]*)

Function

INDIRECT returns the contents of the cell that *cell-reference* refers to. If *cell-reference* is not valid, Excel returns the error value #REF!. If *reference-type* is omitted, *cell-reference* is assumed to be in the A1 format. If *reference-type* is included, it is expected to be either TRUE or FALSE. If it is TRUE, the *cell-reference* is assumed to be in the A1 format. If it is FALSE, the *cell-reference* is assumed to be in R1C1 format.

Example

=INDIRECT(E3) returns 5 if E3 contains the cell reference B3 as a text entry and the cell B3 contains the number 5.

See Also

OFFSET	Returns a reference offset	Function
TEXTREF	Converts text to a reference	Function

INFO

Menu

The Info menu appears as part of a new menu bar if you choose Workspace from the Options menu and select the Info Window check box. The Info menu lets you turn on or off ("toggle") nine types of information that can be displayed in the Info window. These nine types of information are the options on the menu, as listed here:

Cell	Displays the address of the active cell, which is the cell being displayed in the Info window. The default setting is on.
Dependents	Displays the list of cells whose formulas refer to the active cell. The default is off.
Format	Displays the format characteristics of the active cell, including alignment, borders, font, numeric format, and shading. The default is off.
Formula	Displays the contents of the active cell as it is displayed in the Edit area of the Formula bar. The default is on.
Precedents	Displays the list of cells referred to by formulas in the active cell. The default is off.
Protection	Displays the protection status of the active cell, telling you if the cell is locked or the formula is hidden. The default is off.
Names	Displays the list of range names that include the active cell. The default is off.

Note	Displays the contents of a note attached to the active cell. The default is on.
Value	Displays the contents of the active cell as it is displayed in the cell itself. The default is off.

INFO(*type*)

Function

INFO returns information about the operating system. *Type* is a text string describing the information that you want. Here are possible values for *type*:

Type	Description
"directory"	Returns the path of the current directory.
"memavail"	Returns the amount of memory available.
"memused"	Returns the amount of memory used.
"numfile"	Returns the number of files open.
"origin"	Returns the absolute A1 style reference of the active cell preceded with an $A: for Lotus 1-2-3 version 3.*x* compatibility.
"osversion"	Returns the version of the operating system as text.
"recalc"	Returns "Automatic" or "Manual" calculation mode.
"release"	Returns the version number of Microsoft Excel as text.
"system"	Returns "mac" if the system is a Macintosh, or "pcdos" if the system is a DOS system.
"totmem"	Returns the total amount of memory available.

Example

=INFO("origin") returns $A:$A$1.

See Also

INFO	Describes the Info menu	Menu

INITIATE(*application, topic*)

Macro Function

INITIATE opens a DDE (Dynamic Data Exchange) channel between Excel and the specified application and returns the channel number. The *topic* can be something specific to the application, the name of a document, or simply "System". To use INITIATE you must have the full version of Windows (version 2.0 or later).

See Also

POKE	Sends data to an external application	Macro Function
RETURN	Gets data from an external application	Macro Function
TERMINATE	Closes a DDE channel	Macro Function

INPUT(*prompt, type, [name], [default], [horizontal], [vertical]*)

Macro Function

INPUT causes an input dialog box to be displayed. The *prompt, name,* and *default* arguments are strings. The *name* argument is the title of the dialog box. The *default* argument is the text that appears in the edit box. The *horizontal* and *vertical* arguments specify the location of the box in points, measured from the edge of the screen. The *type* argument can be one of the following numbers:

Type	Description
1	Formula
2	Number
3	Text
4	Logical
8	Reference
16	Error
64	Array

INSERT(*[direction]*)
INSERT?(*[direction]*)

Macro Function

INSERT performs the same action as the Insert option on the Edit menu. It shifts cells in the worksheet and inserts new cells. The *direction* argument specifies in which direction existing cells are shifted, and can be one of the following values:

Direction	Shifts
1	Right
2	Down

Direction	Shifts
3	Entire Row
4	Entire Column

If *direction* is omitted, the cells are shifted in the direction that makes the most sense based on the current selection.

See Also

COPY	Selects objects or cells for copying	Macro Function
CUT	Selects objects or cells for moving	Macro Function
EDIT.DELETE	Deletes cells	Macro Function
PASTE	Pastes objects or cells	Macro Function

INSERT.OBJECT(*type*)
INSERT.OBJECT?(*[type]*)

Macro Function   **New to Version 4.0**

INSERT.OBJECT performs the same action as the Insert Object option from the Edit menu. It inserts an embedded object created with a different application, and, if appropriate, starts the application for the type of object that you want to insert. The *type* argument specifies the type of object that you want to embed, and is given as a string. The possible values for *type* are the Object Types as they appear in the Insert Object dialog box, as shown here:

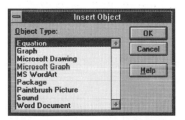

The possible object types depend on the applications that you have installed on your computer. In the dialog box version (with the question mark), the argument (if included) is used as a default in the dialog box that appears.

See Also

EDIT.OBJECT	Edits an object	Macro Function

INT(X)

Function

INT returns X rounded down to the nearest integer.

Example

=INT(5.357) returns the value 5.

See Also

CEILING	Rounds a number up to an integer	Function
FLOOR	Rounds a number down to an integer	Function
ROUND	Rounds to a given number of digits	Function

INTERCEPT(*dependent,independent*)

Function   **New to Version 4.0**

INTERCEPT returns the interception of the linear regression line through the dependent and independent data. The interception is the point on the Y axis where the regression line intersects.

The equation for the interception of the regression line is as follows,

$$a = \overline{Y} - b\overline{X}$$

where

$$b = \frac{n\Sigma xy - (\Sigma x)(\Sigma y)}{n\Sigma x^2 - (\Sigma x)^2}$$

Example

=INTERCEPT({1,2,5,7,9},{3,4,6,8,12}) returns −1.20703.

See Also

GROWTH	Exponential trend function	Function
SLOPE	Returns the slope of the linear regression	Function
TREND	Returns values on linear trend	Function

INTRATE(*settlement, maturity, investment, redemption, [basis-code]*)

Function   **New to Version 4.0**

INTRATE returns the interest rate for a security that is fully vested. *Settlement* is the issue date for the security, given as a serial number. *Maturity* is the maturity date of the security, given as a serial number. *Investment* is the amount invested. *Redemption* is the redemption value of the security. *Basis-code* is the day count basis. The possible values for *basis-code* are as follows.

Basis-Code	Day Count
0	30/360
1	Actual/Actual
2	Actual/360
3	Actual/365

INTRATE is an add-in function. The first time that you use it, you may see a #REF! error while Excel loads the function.

Example

=INTRATE(DATE(93,1,1),DATE(93,4,1),200000,205000,2) returns 10%, which is the interest rate for a $200,000 investment issued on January 1, 1993, maturing on April 1, 1993 with a value of $205,000 and a day count basis of Actual/360.

See Also

DATE   Returns the serial number of a date   Function

IPMT(*interest, period, number-of-periods, present-value, [future-value], [type]*)

Function

IPMT returns the interest payment amount for a loan given the interest and the loan terms. *Period* is the period for which you want to find the interest payment, and *number-of-periods* is the total number of payments. *Present-value* is the present value of the loan. *Future-value* is an optional argument. If this argument is omitted, the future value of a loan is assumed to be $0. If this argument is included, it is the balance that you wish to obtain after the last payment is made. *Type* is also an optional argument. A *type* of 1 means that payments are due at the beginning of the period; a *type* of 0 means that payments are due at the end of the period. If the *type* argument is omitted, it is assumed to be of type 0.

Example

=IPMT(0.12,4,4,9000) returns –$317.48, the interest payment in the fourth period for a $9,000 loan at 12 percent interest and four periods.

See Also

INTRATE	Returns the interest rate	Function
PMT	Returns the periodic payment	Function
PPMT	Returns the principal payment	Function
RATE	Returns the rate per period	Function

IRR(*range, [estimated-rate-of-return]*)

Function

IRR returns the internal rate of return for a series of cash flows contained in the range. The *estimated-rate-of-return,* if omitted, is assumed to be 10 percent. The *estimated-rate-of-return* is not usually necessary, as the default argument is sufficient. If you get a #NUM! error, you may need to use or modify your *estimated-rate-of-return*. The first cell usually contains a negative number for the initial investment or outflow of cash; positive numbers are inflows. The internal rate of return is the interest rate that gives a series of cash flows a net present value of zero.

Example

=IRR(A2:A10,0.08) estimates the internal rate of return for the cash flows that are contained in cells A2 to A10. It uses 8 percent as the beginning estimated rate of return.

See Also

MIRR	Related function	Function
NPV	Returns the net present value	Function
RATE	Returns the interest rate	Function

ISBLANK(*X*)

Function

ISBLANK evaluates a location *X* for a blank cell and returns TRUE if it contains a blank cell, or returns FALSE if it does not contain a blank cell.

Example

=ISBLANK(B3) evaluates the contents of B3 for a blank cell. If a blank cell is found, TRUE is returned; otherwise, FALSE is returned.

See Also

ISERR	Determines if *X* is an error, except #N/A	Function
ISERROR	Determines if *X* is an error	Function
ISLOGICAL	Determines whether *X* is TRUE or FALSE	Function
ISNA	Determines if *X* is #N/A	Function
ISNONTEXT	Determines if *X* is not text	Function
ISNUMBER	Determines if *X* is a number	Function
ISREF	Determines if *X* is a reference	Function
ISTEXT	Determines if *X* is text	Function

ISERR(X)

Function

ISERR returns TRUE if *X* contains an Excel error value except #N/A, or FALSE for an error value of #N/A or anything other than an Excel error value.

Example

=IF(ISERR(B15),0,B26) checks B15 for an error condition. If an error condition other than #N/A exists, ISERR returns a TRUE and IF returns 0. Otherwise, the formula returns the value in B26.

See Also

ISBLANK	Determines if a cell is blank	Function
ISERROR	Determines if *X* is an error	Function
ISLOGICAL	Determines whether *X* is TRUE or FALSE	Function
ISNA	Determines if *X* is #N/A	Function
ISNONTEXT	Determines if *X* is not text	Function
ISNUMBER	Determines if *X* is a number	Function
ISREF	Determines if *X* is a reference	Function
ISTEXT	Determines if *X* is text	Function

ISERROR(*X*)

Function

ISERROR returns TRUE if *X* contains an Excel error value or FALSE for anything other than an Excel error value.

Example

=IF(ISERROR(B15/B25),0,B15/B25) checks a division of B15 by B25 for any Excel error condition. If an error condition exists (possibly indicating division by 0), the calculation returns 0. Otherwise, the formula returns the result of the division.

See Also

ISBLANK	Determines if a cell is blank	Function
ISERR	Determines if *X* is an error, other than #N/A	Function
ISLOGICAL	Determines if *X* is TRUE or FALSE	Function
ISNA	Determines if *X* is #N/A	Function
ISNONTEXT	Determines if *X* is not text	Function
ISNUMBER	Determines if *X* is a number	Function
ISREF	Determines if *X* is a reference	Function
ISTEXT	Determines if *X* is text	Function

ISEVEN(*X*)

Function

ISEVEN returns TRUE if *X* is an even number, and returns FALSE if X is an odd number.

ISEVEN is an add-in function. The first time you use it, you may see a #REF! error while Excel loads the function.

Example

=ISEVEN(5) returns FALSE.

See Also

ISODD	Returns TRUE if a number is odd	Function

ISLOGICAL(*X*)

Function

ISLOGICAL evaluates *X*, which can be a location, string, condition, or value for a logical value (TRUE or FALSE), returning TRUE if a cell contains a logical value or FALSE if the cell does not contain a logical value.

Example

=ISLOGICAL(B6) returns TRUE if B6 contains a logical value and returns FALSE for any other values.

See Also

ISBLANK	Determines if a cell is blank	Function
ISERR	Determines if *X* is an error, other than #N/A	Function
ISERROR	Determines if *X* is an error	Function
ISNA	Determines if *X* is #N/A	Function
ISNONTEXT	Determines if *X* is not text	Function
ISNUMBER	Determines if *X* is a number	Function
ISREF	Determines if *X* is a reference	Function
ISTEXT	Determines if *X* is text	Function

ISNA(*X*)

Function

ISNA returns TRUE if *X* is an #N/A value and returns FALSE for anything else.

Example

=ISNA(F2) returns TRUE if F2 contains #N/A; otherwise it returns FALSE.

See Also

ISBLANK	Determines if a cell is blank	Function
ISERR	Determines if *X* is an error, other than #N/A	Function
ISERROR	Determines if *X* is an error	Function

ISLOGICAL	Determines whether X is TRUE or FALSE	Function
ISNONTEXT	Determines if X is not text	Function
ISNUMBER	Determines if X is a number	Function
ISREF	Determines if X is a reference	Function
ISTEXT	Determines if X is text	Function

ISNONTEXT(X)

Function

ISNONTEXT evaluates X, which can be a location, string, value, or condition for a text string, returning TRUE if it is not a text string or FALSE if it is a text string.

Example

=ISNONTEXT(NAME) evaluates the contents of NAME for a text string. If a text string is found, FALSE is returned; otherwise, TRUE is returned.

See Also

ISBLANK	Determines if a cell is blank	Function
ISERR	Determines if X is an error, other than #N/A	Function
ISERROR	Determines if X is an error	Function
ISLOGICAL	Determines whether X is TRUE or FALSE	Function
ISNA	Determines if X is #N/A	Function
ISNUMBER	Determines if X is a number	Function
ISREF	Determines if X is a reference	Function
ISTEXT	Determines if X is text	Function

ISNUMBER(X)

Function

ISNUMBER evaluates X, which can be a location, string, condition, or numeric value. ISNUMBER returns TRUE if X is a number or is blank, and returns FALSE if it is anything else.

Example

=ISNUMBER(B6) returns TRUE if B6 contains a number or blanks and returns FALSE for any other values.

See Also

ISBLANK	Determines if a cell is blank	Function
ISERR	Determines if X is an error, other than #N/A	Function
ISERROR	Determines if X is error	Function
ISLOGICAL	Determines whether X is TRUE or FALSE	Function
ISNA	Determines if X is #N/A	Function
ISNONTEXT	Determines if X is not text	Function
ISREF	Determines if X is a reference	Function
ISTEXT	Determines if X is text	Function

ISODD(X)

Function

ISODD returns TRUE if X is an odd number and FALSE if X is an even number.
    ISODD is an add-in function. The first time that you use it, you may see a #REF! error while Excel loads the function.

Example

=ISODD(5) returns TRUE.

See Also

ISEVEN	Returns TRUE if a number is even	Function

ISREF(X)

Function

ISREF evaluates X, which can be a location, string, value, or condition for a reference, returning TRUE if it is a reference or FALSE if it is not a reference.

Example

=ISREF(NAME) evaluates NAME to see if it is a range name. If it is a range name, TRUE is returned; otherwise, FALSE is returned.

See Also

ISBLANK	Determines if a cell is blank	Function
ISERR	Determines if X is an error, other than #N/A	Function
ISERROR	Determines if X is error	Function
ISLOGICAL	Determines whether X is TRUE or FALSE	Function
ISNA	Determines if X is #N/A	Function
ISNONTEXT	Determines if X is not text	Function
ISNUMBER	Determines if X is a number	Function
ISTEXT	Determines if X is text	Function

ISTEXT(X)

Function

ISTEXT evaluates X, which can be a location, string, value, or condition for a text string, returning TRUE if it is (or contains) a text string, or FALSE if it is not (or does not contain) a text string.

Example

=ISTEXT(NAME) evaluates the contents of NAME for a text string. If a text string is found, TRUE is returned; otherwise, FALSE is returned.

See Also

ISBLANK	Determines if a cell is blank	Function
ISERR	Determines if X is an error, other than #N/A	Function
ISERROR	Determines if X is an error	Function
ISLOGICAL	Determines whether X is TRUE or FALSE	Function
ISNA	Determines if X is #N/A	Function
ISNONTEXT	Determines if X is not text	Function
ISNUMBER	Determines if X is a number	Function
ISREF	Determines if X is a reference	Function

JUSTIFY()

Macro Function

JUSTIFY performs the same action as the Justify option from the Format menu. It evenly fills text in a range. For example, if there is a long text string in cell A1, JUSTIFY will evenly distribute that text so that it fills the active range.

See Also

FORMAT JUSTIFY   Equivalent command   Menu Command

KURT(*X1,[X2],...*)

Function

KURT returns the kurtosis of the numbers *X1, X2,* and so on. There can be up to 30 numbers, names, arrays, or references. KURT compares the normal distribution with the distribution of the data.

See Also

SKEW	Returns the skew of a distribution	Function
STDEV	Returns the standard deviation	Function
VAR	Returns the estimated variance	Function

LARGE(*array, n*)

Function   **New to Version 4.0**

LARGE returns the *n*th largest value in an array. *Array* can be either an array or a reference to a range that contains the values.

Example

=LARGE({1,2,3,4,5,6,7},2) returns the second largest value in the array, which is 6.

See Also

SMALL	Returns the *n*th smallest value	Function

LAST.ERROR()

Macro Function   **New to Version 4.0**

LAST.ERROR returns the cell address of the location where the last error on the macro occurred, if there was an error. If no error was encountered, #N/A is returned.

See Also

ERROR	Enables or disables error checking	Macro Function

LCM(*[X1],[X2],[X3],...*)

Function   **New to Version 4.0**

LCM returns the least common multiple of a list of numbers *X1, X2, X3,* and so on. LCM is an add-in function. The first time you use it, you may see a #REF! error while Excel loads the function.

Example

=LCM(2,3) returns 6.

See Also

| GCD | Returns the greatest common divisor | Function |

LEFT(*string,[X]*)

Function

LEFT returns the leftmost number of characters specified by *X* that are contained in the *string* argument. The string can be a literal, a reference to a cell containing a label, or a formula that evaluates to a string. The *X* argument is optional. If it is omitted, the default value is 1.

Example

=LEFT(G8,10) returns the first ten characters in the string contained in G8.

See Also

| MID | Returns a section of a string | Function |
| RIGHT | Returns the right end of a string | Function |

LEGEND(*[logical]*)

Macro Function

If the logical argument is TRUE, LEGEND performs the same action as the Add Legend option on the Chart menu. If the logical argument is FALSE, LEGEND performs the same action as choosing the Delete Legend option on the Chart menu. LEGEND adds or deletes a legend. If the logical argument is not given, the default value is TRUE.

J-L

See Also

CHART ADD LEGEND	Equivalent command	Menu Command
FORMAT.LEGEND	Formats the legend	Macro Function

LEN(*string*)

Function

LEN returns the number of characters in the specified string. The string can be a literal, a reference to a cell containing a label, or a formula that evaluates to a string.

Example

=LEN(B8&C8) returns the number of characters in cells B8 and C8.

See Also

EXACT	Determines if two strings are equal	Function
SEARCH	Searches for a substring within a string	Function

LINE.PRINT(*command*, *[file]*, *[append]*)
LINE.PRINT(*command*, *[setup]*, *[left]*, *[right]*, *[top]*, *[bottom]*, *[length]*, *[formatted]*)
LINE.PRINT(*command*, *[setup]*, *[left]*, *[right]*, *[top]*, *[bottom]*, *[length]*, *[wait]*, *[line-feed]*, *[port]*, *[update]*)

Macro Function   **New to Version 4.0**

LINE.PRINT prints the active document. LINE.PRINT is Lotus 1-2-3 compatible. You should use the PRINT function to print documents, unless you need the Lotus 1-2-3 compatibility provided by LINE.PRINT.

Command is the command that you want to perform. The following table lists all possible values of *command*:

Command	Description
1	Go
2	Line
3	Page
4	Align
5	Document settings

Command	Description
6	Global settings
7	Reset to global settings

The first version of LINE.PRINT is used for commands 1, 2, 3, 4, and 7. The second version of LINE.PRINT is used for command 5, document settings. The third version of LINE.PRINT is used for command 6, global settings.

File is the name of the file to which you want to print. If you want to print to the printer instead of to a file, omit the *file* argument. The *append* argument is used only if you are printing to a file. If *append* is TRUE, the printed file is appended to the end of *file*. If *append* is FALSE, the printed file overwrites whatever is currently contained in *file*.

Setup is a string that contains printer control codes for your printer. This argument is optional.

Left, right, top, and *bottom* are margin sizes. Margins are measured in characters from the left side of the page, or lines from the top or bottom of the page. The default values for the margins are shown here:

Margin	Default
Left	4 characters from the left side of the page
Right	76 characters from the left side of the page
Top	2 lines from the top of the page
Bottom	2 lines from the bottom of the page

Length is the length of the page in lines. The default value for *length* is 66 lines. If you are using a Hewlett-Packard LaserJet, set *length* to 60 lines.

Formatted should be TRUE if you want the output formatted, or FALSE otherwise. The default value for *formatted* is TRUE.

Wait should be TRUE if you want the printer to pause after each page, or FALSE otherwise. The default value for *wait* is FALSE.

Line-feed should be TRUE if your printer has automatic line feeding, or FALSE otherwise. The default value for *line-feed* is FALSE.

Port is the port you want to print to. The possible values for *port* are listed here:

Port	Description
1	LPT1
2	COM1
3	LPT2
4	COM2
5	LPT1

J-L

Port	Description
6	LPT2
7	LPT3
8	LPT4

The default value for *port* is 1.

Update should be TRUE if you want to update the global print settings, or FALSE otherwise.

See Also

PRINT   Prints the active document   Macro Function

LINEST(*y-array*, *[x-array]*, *[constant]*, *[statistics]*)

Function

LINEST returns an array that describes a straight line fit to the data stored in *y-array* and, optionally, in *x-array*. If the *x-array* argument is omitted, it is assumed that *x-array* is {1, 2, :.}. The formula for LINEST is as follows.

$$y = m1x1 + m2x2 + ... + b \text{ or } y = mx + b$$

Constant should be TRUE if you want the constant b to be forced to 0, or FALSE otherwise. The *constant* b is the y-intercept of the line. The default value for *constant* is TRUE.

Statistics should be TRUE if you want the regression statistics returned, or FALSE otherwise. The default value for *statistics* is FALSE.

You must enter LINEST as an array formula, by pressing CTRL-SHIFT-ENTER (or pressing CTRL-SHIFT and clicking the mouse). The array returned by LINEST describes the straight line fit with a y-intercept and a slope. If you want a straight line array described by coordinates, use TREND.

Example

Figure L-1 shows a worksheet with a table. =LINEST(B1:B5) returns the array {20, 276}, where 20 is the slope of the line, and 276 is the y-intercept.

See Also

LOGEST   Fits data to an exponential curve   Function
TREND   Fits data to a line and returns y values   Function

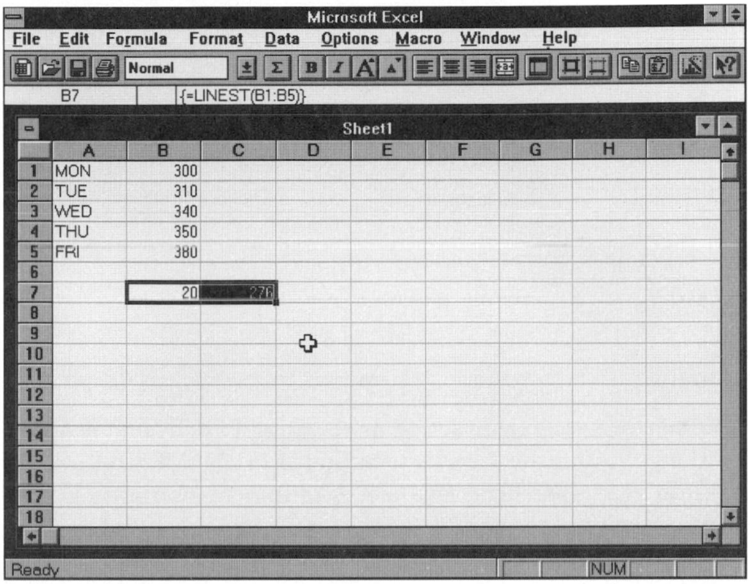

Figure L-1.   *An example of LINEST*

LINKS([*name*], [*type*])

Macro Function

LINKS returns an array of names of all external links to the document named by the argument *name*. If *name* is not given, it is assumed to be the active document. *Type* is the type of linked documents to return in the array. Here are all the possible values for *type*:

Type	Description
1	Microsoft Excel link
2	DDE link
5	Publisher
6	Subscriber

If there are no external references, LINKS returns an #N/A error.

Example

=LINKS() returns all the Excel links for the current document in an array.

See Also

CHANGE.LINK	Changes a link	Macro Function
GET.LINK.INFO	Returns information about a link	Macro Function
OPEN.LINK	Opens linked document(s)	Macro Function
UPDATE.LINK	Updates a link	Macro Function

LIST.NAMES()

Macro Function

LIST.NAMES performs the same action as choosing Paste Name from the Formula menu, and then clicking the Paste List button. LIST.NAMES returns information about names on your worksheet. Five pieces of information are supplied for each name. The information is returned in a range on your worksheet beginning with the active cell in the upper-left corner. If you only want some of the information returned, select a range fewer then five columns wide. If you want all the information returned, select one cell only, or a range at least five columns wide.

   LIST.NAMES lists all the names defined on your worksheet, unless the names are hidden, in the first column. The second column contains the cells to which the name refers. The third column contains 1 if the name refers to a custom function, 2 if the name refers to a custom macro, or 0 for anything else. The fourth column contains the shortcut key if there is one. The last column contains the function category if appropriate.

Example

=LIST.NAMES() returns all the names on the active document.

See Also

GET.DEF	Returns the name of a specified definition	Macro Function
GET.NAME	Returns the definition of a specified name	Macro Function
NAMES	Returns a list of names	Macro Function

LN(X)

Function

LN returns the natural logarithm to the base e of a value X.

Example

=LN(B9) returns the natural logarithm of the number contained in B9.

See Also

EXP	Returns e raised to X	Function
LOG	Returns the log base X of a number	Function
LOG10	Returns the log base 10 of a number	Function

LOG(*X, [base]*)

Function

LOG returns the logarithm of X to the optionally given *base* of a value. If the *base* argument is omitted, the default value is 10.

Example

=LOG(H15,8) returns the base 8 logarithm of the value contained in H15.

See Also

EXP	Returns e raised to X	Function
LN	Returns the natural log of a number	Function
LOG10	Returns the log base 10 of a number	Function

J-L

LOG10(*X*)

Function

LOG10 returns the common (base 10) logarithm of a value.

Example

=LOG10(H15) returns the common logarithm of the value contained in H15.

See Also

EXP	Returns e raised to X	Function
LN	Returns the natural log of a number	Function
LOG	Returns the log base X of a number	Function

LOGEST(*y-array*, *[x-array]*, *[constant]*, *[statistics]*)

Function

LOGEST returns an array that describes an exponential curve fit to the data stored in the y-array and, optionally, the x-array. If the *x-array* argument is omitted, it is assumed that the x-array is {1, 2, :.}. The formula for LOGEST is as follows.

$$y = (b(m1^{\wedge}x1)(m2^{\wedge}x2)...) \text{ or } y = bm^{\wedge}x$$

Constant should be TRUE if you want the constant b to be forced to 1, or FALSE otherwise. The *constant* b is the y-intercept of the line. The default value for *constant* is TRUE.

Statistics should be TRUE if you want the regression statistics returned, or FALSE otherwise. The default value for *statistics* is FALSE.

You must enter LOGEST as an array formula, by first highlighting two empty cells where you want the results, typing the function, and then pressing CTRL-SHIFT-ENTER (or pressing CTRL-SHIFT and clicking the mouse). The array returned by LOGEST describes the exponential curve fit as a y-intercept and a slope. If you want a straight line array described by coordinates, use GROWTH.

Example

Figure L-2 shows a worksheet with a table. =LOGEST(B1:B5) returns the array {1.061214, 280.126}.

See Also

GROWTH	Calculates an exponential curve	Function
LINEST	Fits data to a line	Function
TREND	Fits data to a line	Function

LOGINV(*probability*, *mean*, *sd*)

Function   New to Version 4.0

LOGINV returns the inverse lognormal cumulative distribution. LOGINV is the inverse function of LOGNORMDIST. *Probability* is the probability of the lognormal distribution. *Mean* is the mean of the lognormal distribution. *Sd* is the standard deviation of the lognormal distribution.

Example

=LOGINV(0.169479,4,2.5) returns 4.999975.

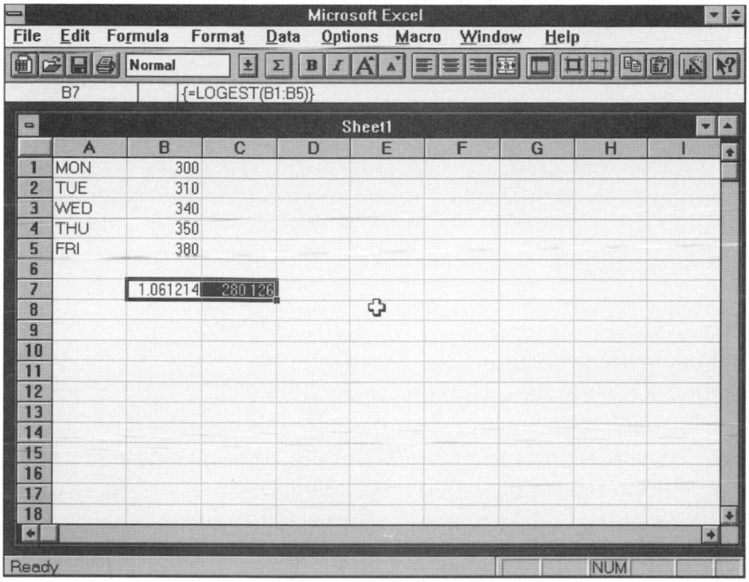

Figure L-2.   An example of LOGEST

See Also

LN	Returns the natural log of a number	Function
LOG	Returns the log base *X* of a number	Function
LOGNORMDIST	Inverse function of LOGINV	Function

LOGNORMDIST(*X,mean,sd*)

Function   **New to Version 4.0**

LOGNORMDIST returns the lognormal cumulative distribution of *X*, given the mean and the standard deviation (*sd*) of the natural log of *X*.

Example

=LOGNORMDIST(5,4,2.5) returns 0.169479.

See Also

LN	Returns the natural log of a number	Function
LOG	Returns the log base *X* of a number	Function
LOGINV	Inverse function of LOGNORMDIST	Function

LOOKUP(*X, lookup-range, return-range*)
LOOKUP(*X, array*)

Function

The first form of LOOKUP returns an entry from a range. Excel searches through the first column or row of the lookup range and looks for the value *X*. If the value of *X* is not exactly equal to a value in the top row or column of the lookup range, LOOKUP finds the closest value that is not larger than *X*. *Lookup-range* should contain values in ascending order. *Return-range* is where the result is placed, and should be the same size as the *lookup-range*, but containing only one row or column.

If your lookup range is more than one column or row, Excel determines the orientation of the lookup range by comparing the width to the height of the lookup range. If the lookup range is wider than it is tall, or is square, LOOKUP searches for *X* in the top row and returns the contents of the corresponding cell in the bottom row. If the lookup range is taller than it is wide, LOOKUP searches for *X* in the left column and returns the contents of the corresponding cell in the rightmost column.

The second form of LOOKUP searches for an entry matching *X* in an array. This form of the function is included for compatibility with other spreadsheet programs. The orientation of the array is determined in the same way that the orientation of lookup range is determined.

Examples

Figure L-3 shows a table used in this example.
=LOOKUP(28,A2:A6,B2:B6) returns "Excelerator."
=LOOKUP(28,A2:B6) also returns "Excelerator." Notice that you can use either method in this case because the example array only has a lookup column and a return column.

See Also

HLOOKUP	Horizontal lookup function	Function
MATCH	Looks up a value in an array	Function
VLOOKUP	Vertical lookup function	Function

LOOPING

Concept

Looping is a technique used to control the flow of execution of a macro. Loops allow you to repeat certain instructions until a condition is met. For example, Figure L-4 shows a macro that prompts the user for input until the counter reaches 5, or until

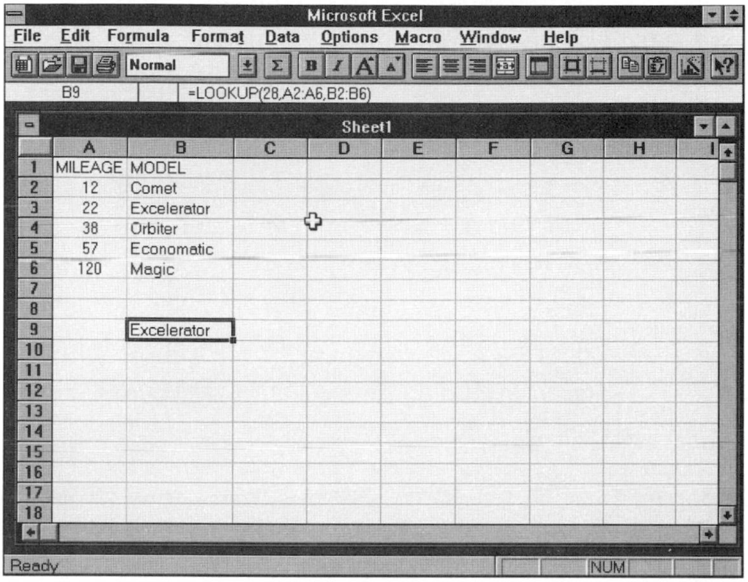

Figure L-3. *An example of LOOKUP*

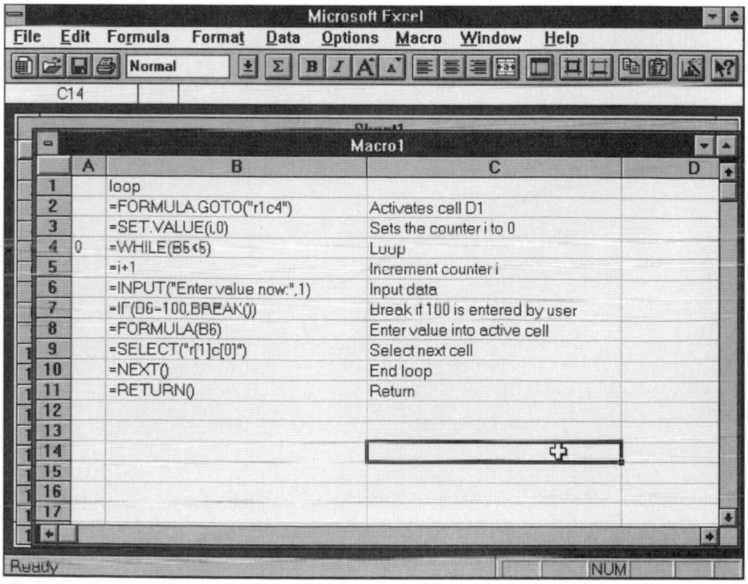

J-L

Figure L-4. *A WHILE loop with a BREAK statement*

the user enters the value 100. There are several different kinds of loops. FOR and FOR.CELL functions loop for a certain number of iterations. The WHILE function loops until a condition has been met. (See the entries for these functions for more information.)

See Also

BREAK	Breaks out of a loop	Macro Function
FOR	Starts a FOR loop	Macro Function
FOR.CELL	Starts a FOR.CELL loop	Macro Function
NEXT	Ends a loop	Macro Function
WHILE	Starts a WHILE loop	Macro Function

LOWER(*string*)

Function

LOWER converts all characters in the specified string to lowercase letters.

Example

=LOWER("STANDARD") will be converted to "standard."

MACRO

Menu

The Macro menu allows you to record functions on the macro sheet as you carry out commands on a regular worksheet, to run macros once they have been recorded or written, and to set several options for recording macros.

See Also

MACRO ABSOLUTE RECORD	Sets recorder to use absolute addressing	Menu Command
MACRO ASSIGN TO OBJECT	Assigns a macro to an object	Menu Command
MACRO RUN	Runs macros	Menu Command
MACRO RECORD	Records macros	Menu Command
MACRO RELATIVE RECORD	Sets recorder to use relative addressing	Menu Command
MACRO RESUME	Resumes a macro	Menu Command
MACRO SET RECORDER	Sets the location of a macro	Menu Command
MACRO START RECORDER	Starts recording a macro	Menu Command
MACRO STOP RECORDER	Stops recording a macro	Menu Command

MACRO ABSOLUTE RECORD

Menu Command

The Absolute Record option on the Macro menu lets you tell Excel to record your macro using absolute cell references. After choosing this option, you can go ahead and record your macro. This option will change to Relative Record as soon as you choose Absolute Record from the Macro menu.

MACRO ASSIGN TO OBJECT

Menu Command   New to Version 4.0

The Assign To Object command on the Macro menu assigns a command macro to an existing graphic object. Once a macro is assigned to an object, you can click on the object to run the macro. Assigning a macro to an object makes your macro easily accessible.

Use the graphics tools to create a graphic object. For example, Figure M-1 shows a rectangle that has a macro assigned to it. The rectangle was created with the rectangle tool on the Drawing toolbar. You can create any kind of a graphic object—such as a circle, button, or polygon—and assign your macro to it.

M-N

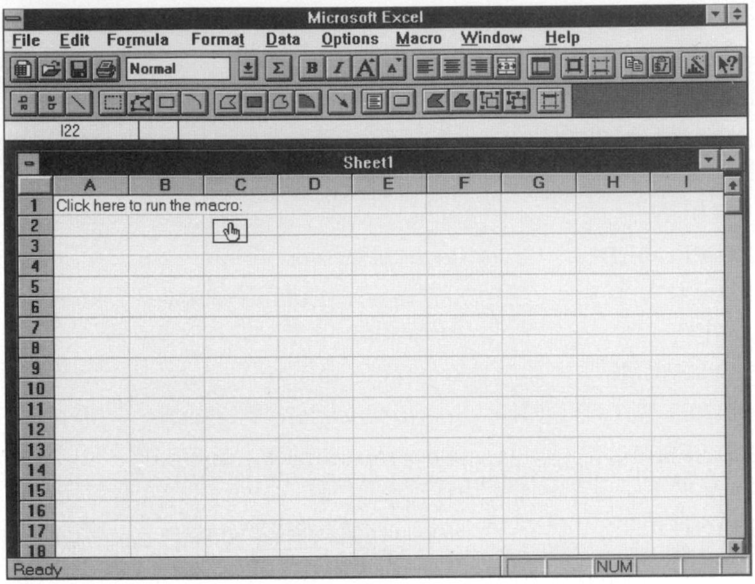

Figure M-1. *A macro assigned to a rectangle*

Once you create the graphic object, choose Assign To Object from the Macro menu. All open macros are listed in the dialog box. Choose the macro you want to assign to the object by clicking on it, then clicking on OK. Now clicking on the object will run the macro. The dialog box is shown here:

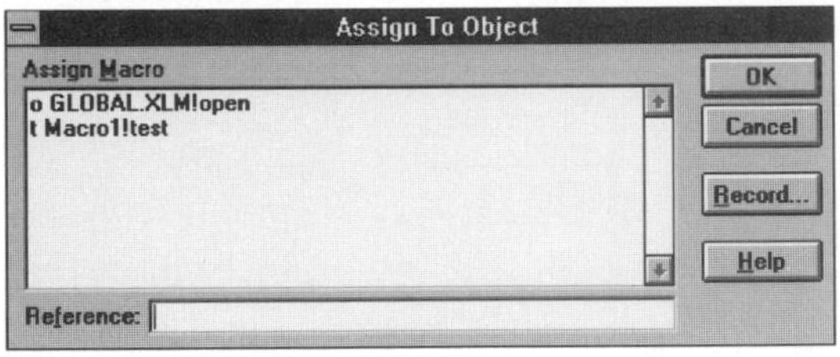

See Also

OPTIONS TOOLBARS   Creates a custom tool   Menu Command

MACRO RECORD

Menu Command

The Record option on the Macro menu turns on the macro recorder, which records your subsequent actions so you can repeat them later. Your actions are recorded on a macro sheet. If no macro sheet is open, Excel opens one for you. The Excel macro recording function works like a tape recorder. You turn on the recorder, perform the actions that you want to record, turn off the recorder, and play back the macro with the Run option on the Macro menu. When you choose the Record option, you'll see this dialog box, in which you can name the macro and choose a control key for the macro.

Name	Allows you to type in a name for your macro. If you don't, Excel names the macro for you.
Key	Allows you to define the shortcut key, which can be any uppercase or lowercase letter. You can start the macro by holding down the control key and pushing the shortcut key.
Global Macro Sheet	Stores the macro in the global macro sheet. It will be available to you anytime you are in Excel.
Macro Sheet	Stores the macro in a normal macro sheet that you will have to open when you want to run the macro.

After you type in the name and the shortcut key, click on OK. Now everything you do will be recorded. When you want to stop recording, choose Stop Recorder from the Macro menu; this command only appears on the menu after you have chosen the Macro Record option.

M-N

MACRO RELATIVE RECORD

Menu Command

The Relative Record option on the Macro menu allows you to record your macro using relative cell references. After choosing this option, you can go ahead and record. This option will change to Absolute Record as soon as you choose Relative Record from the Macro menu.

MACRO RESUME

Menu Command

The Resume option on the Macro menu resumes a macro that has been paused. To pause a macro, choose the Run option from the Macro menu to run a macro, click on the Step button in the Run Macro dialog box, and then click on the Pause button in the Single Step dialog box. The Resume option in the Macro menu appears greyed on the menu unless a macro is currently paused.

MACRO RUN

Menu Command

The Run option on the Macro menu allows you to run a macro from any open macro sheet. Choosing the Run option brings up the following dialog box.

The dialog box options are described here:

Run	Lists all the available macros. Macros are available if they are on open macro sheets and are named. Each named macro appears in the Run box. Select the macro you want to run and then click on OK.

Reference	Allows you to type the name of the macro you want to run yourself. If you chose a macro from the Run box, its name appears automatically in the Reference box.

MACRO SET RECORDER

Menu Command

The Set Recorder option on the Macro menu lets you tell Excel where to record your next macro. If you select a range before you choose the Set Recorder option, Excel uses the range to record your macro by starting in the upper-left corner, going down to the end of the column, going to the top of the next column, and so on. If you select only a cell, Excel uses that cell as the start cell, and records the macro down in the same column.

MACRO START RECORDER

Menu Command

The Start Recorder option on the Macro menu allows you to record your subsequent actions on a macro sheet. You must first use the Set Recorder option on the Macro menu to set the macro range (or you must have used the Record option previously). Once you have chosen the Start Recorder option from the Macro menu, the Stop Recorder option takes its place. You can use the Stop Recorder and Start Recorder options on the Macro menu to pause while you are recording a macro, then resume recording.

M-N

MACRO STOP RECORDER

Menu Command

The Stop Recorder option on the Macro menu stops a macro recording that you started with either Macro Record or Macro Start Record. On the Macro menu, the Stop Recorder option appears in place of the Macro Start Recorder option after you start recording a macro.

MAIN.CHART(*type,[stacked],[100%],[vary-by-cat],[overlapped],
[drop-lines],[hi-lo-lines],[overlap%],[cluster%],[pie-angle]*)
MAIN.CHART?(*[type],[stacked],[100%],[vary-by-cat],[overlapped],
[drop-lines],[hi-lo-lines],[overlap%],[cluster%],[pie-angle]*)

Macro Function

MAIN.CHART performs the same action as the Main Chart option on the Formula menu in Excel versions 2.2 or earlier. (This function is included for compatibility with earlier versions of Excel.) To format a chart for Excel 3 or higher, use the FORMAT.MAIN macro function. The *type* argument can have the following values:

Type	Value
1	Area
2	Bar
3	Column
4	Line
5	Pie
6	Scatter

The *stacked, 100%, vary-by-cat, overlapped, drop-lines,* and *hi-lo-lines* arguments correspond to check boxes in the dialog box. If the argument is TRUE, the check box is checked. The *overlap%, cluster%,* and *pie-angle* arguments are numbers indicating the percentage of overlap, cluster, and the angle of the first pie slice. If an argument does not apply to a type of chart, it is ignored. In the dialog box version (with the question mark), the arguments, if included, are used as default values for the dialog box that appears.

See Also

FORMULA MAIN CHART   Equivalent command   Menu Command

MATCH(*X,range,[type]*)

Function

MATCH returns the relative position of an entry in the *range* that matches *X* according to the *type*. The following table summarizes the possible types:

Type	Returns Relative Position for	Order of Range Array
1	Largest value <= *X*	Ascending order

Type	Returns Relative Position for	Order of Range Array
–1	Smallest value >= X	Descending order
0	Value = X	Any order

Examples

Figure M-2 shows a table used in the following example. Notice that the array is in ascending order.

=MATCH(20,A2:A7,1) would return 3, the relative position of the largest value <= 20, which is 18 in cell A4.

Figure M-3 shows a table used in the next two examples. Notice that the array is in descending order.

=MATCH(20,A2:A7,–1) would return 2, the relative position of the smallest value >= 20, which is 27 in cell A3.

=MATCH("mon*",B2:B7,0) would return 3, the relative position of Monkey in cell B4.

*NOTE: MATCH is not case-sensitive, and it allows the use of Excel wildcards. (Wildcards are used to represent unknown characters. The * wildcard character represents any number of characters, while ? represents a single character.)*

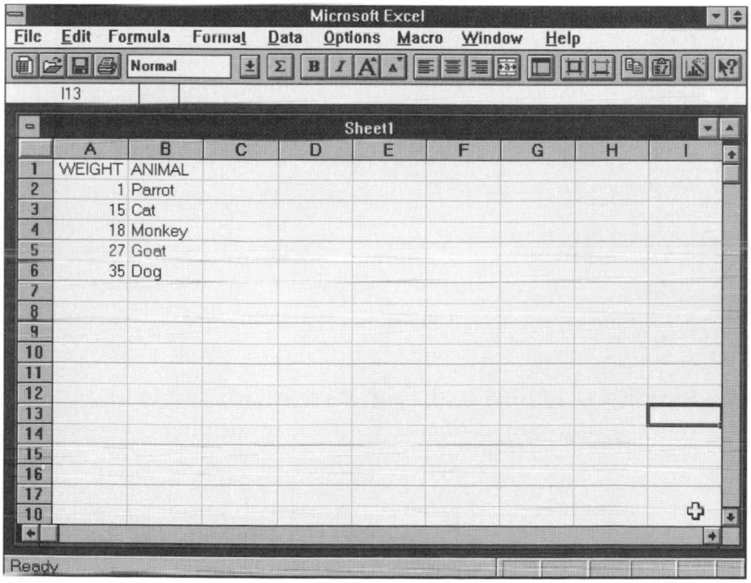

M-N

Figure M-2. *A table of ascending values used for an example of MATCH*

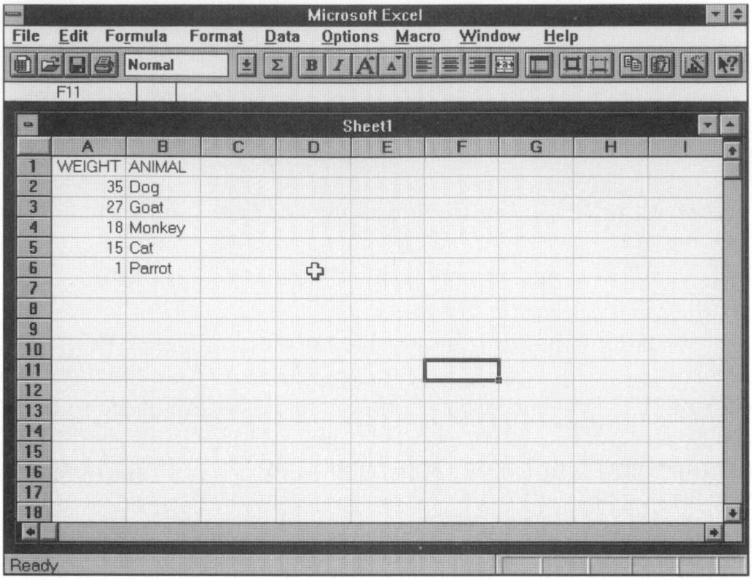

Figure M-3. *A table of descending values used for examples of MATCH*

See Also

HLOOKUP	Horizontal lookup function	Function
INDEX	Returns an item from a range or array	Function
LOOKUP	Lookup function	Function
VLOOKUP	Vertical lookup function	Function

MAX(*list*)

Function

MAX returns the largest number in the specified list, which can be a list of numbers, formulas, or references to ranges of cells containing numbers or formulas.

Example

=MAX(87,A8,B9:B11) returns the largest number between the number 87 and the numbers contained in A8 or the range B9 to B11.

See Also

| DMAX | Database MAX function | Function |
| MIN | Returns the minimum from a list | Function |

MCORREL(*input, output, [row-col], [labels]*)

Macro Function   **New to Version 4.0**

MCORREL returns a matrix that expresses the correlation between independently scaled data sets. *Input* is the input range, and *output* is a reference to the upper-left cell in the output range. *Row-col* is either C or R. If *row-col* is C, the input range is organized by column. If *row-col* is R, the input range is organized by row. If *row-col* is omitted, the default value is C. *Labels* is either TRUE or FALSE. If *labels* is TRUE, there are labels in the first row or column of the input range, depending on how the data is organized. If *labels* if FALSE, there are no labels. The default value for labels is FALSE.

MCORREL is an add-in function. The first time that you use it, you may see a #REF! error while Excel loads the function.

See Also

| CORREL | Returns the correlation coefficient | Macro Function |

MCOVAR(*input, output, [grouped], [labels]*)

Macro Function

MCOVAR returns a matrix that represents the covariance between data sets. *Input* is the input range. *Output* is a reference to the upper-left corner of the output range. *Grouped* is either C or R. If *grouped* is C, the data is organized in columns. If *grouped* is R, the data is organized by rows. If no grouped argument is given, the default value is C. *Labels* is a logical value that indicates whether or not labels are present. If *labels* is TRUE, labels are present in the range either in the first row or first column, depending on how the data is organized. If *labels* is FALSE, there are no labels.

MCOVAR is an add-in function. The first time that you use it, you may see a #REF! error while Excel loads the function.

See Also

| CORREL | Returns the correlation coefficient | Macro Function |
| COVAR | Returns the covariance | Macro Function |

M-N

MDETERM(*numeric-square-array*)

Function

MDETERM return the matrix determinant of the *numeric-square-array*. If the array is not square, does not contain numbers, or is empty, MDETERM return an error #VALUE!.

Example

Shown here is a table that is used in the following example:

=MDETERM(A1:C3) returns 12.

See Also

MINVERSE	Returns the matrix inverse	Function
MMULT	Returns the product of two matrices	Function
TRANSPOSE	Transposes an array	Function

MEDIAN(*X1,[X2],...*)

Macro Function

MEDIAN returns the median for a list of values. The median is the middle number in a list of numbers, if the number of values in the list is an odd number. If the number of values in the list of values is an even number, the average of the two middle numbers is returned.

Example

=MEDIAN(1,2,4,5,6,9,10) returns 5.

See Also

AVERAGE	Returns the average of a list of values	Function
SUM	Returns the sum of a list of values	Function

MENU COMMANDS

Concept

The primary way of telling Excel what you want to do is through a menu. To make a choice from a menu, you first select the menu and then choose the option that meets your needs. The second bar from the top of the Excel window is the menu bar. To select a menu, you can click on it with the mouse or use one of several keyboard techniques. With the keyboard, you can either press ALT, press / (slash), or press F10. Then you can pull down a menu by typing the underlined letter in the menu name or by using the direction keys to highlight the menu name and pressing ENTER.

Once you have opened a menu, you can choose an option from it in one of three ways: you can click on the option with the mouse, you can type the underlined letter in the option name, or you can use the direction keys to move the highlight to the option and press ENTER. If an option is already highlighted, as is New in the File menu, you can select it simply by pressing ENTER. (When you first open a menu, its top option is highlighted by default.)

The status bar at the bottom of the screen indicates what action the highlighted menu option will perform.

The menu bar that appears depends on the active document. If the active document is a chart, menus pertaining to charts will appear in the menu bar. If the active document is a worksheet, menus pertaining to worksheets will appear in the menu bar.

MENUS, CUSTOM

M-N

Concept

Custom menus make macros that you have created easily accessible to users. You can add menus to existing menu bars, or you can create a unique menu bar for your application.

To create a custom menu, you need to create the menu specifications, write a macro to activate the menu, and write a macro to restore normal Excel menus. Figure M-4 shows sample specifications, and the associated macros, for a custom menu.

In this example, the range A12:E19 contains the menu specifications. The first column contains the menu name and the option names. The ampersand places an underline under the following letter. Column B contains the names of the macros that run when you choose an option. Column C is not used in Excel for Windows. Column D contains messages that are displayed in the status bar when the option is highlighted. Column E is blank in this case, but could contain calls to custom help.

The range D1:D5 contains the macro that displays the new menu. The range D7:D9 contains the macro that restores the normal Excel menu bar.

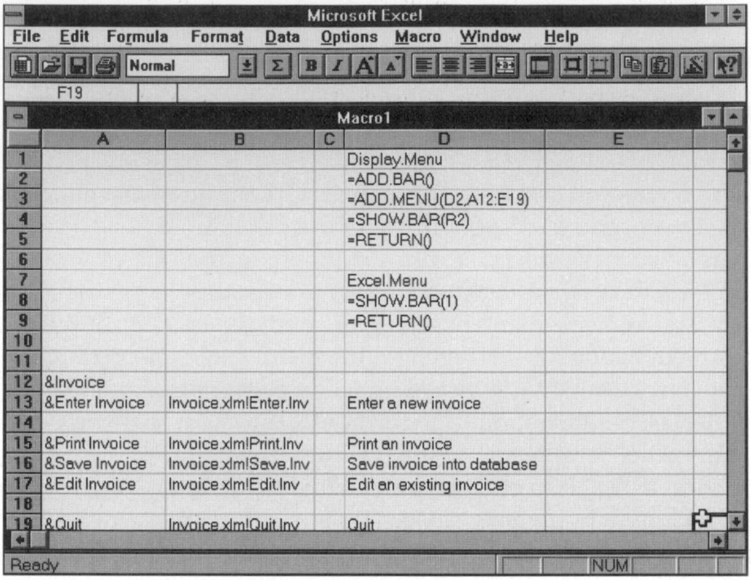

Figure M-4.   *Specifications and macros for a sample custom menu*

See Also

ADD.BAR	Adds a menu bar	Macro Function
ADD.MENU	Adds a menu to a bar	Macro Function
SHOW.BAR	Displays a menu bar	Macro Function

MERGE.STYLE(*name*)

Macro Function

The MERGE.STYLE macro function performs the same action as choosing the Format Style menu command then clicking on the Merge button. The *name* argument is the name of the document that contains the styles that you want to merge with the active document. If the active document contains styles with names identical to those in the document identified by *name*, a dialog box appears asking if you want to replace the existing style.

See Also

FORMAT STYLE	Defines cell formats as styles	Menu Command

MESSAGE(*logical, [message-string]*)

Macro Function

MESSAGE displays the message specified in the *message-string* argument in the message area of the status bar, if the *logical* argument is TRUE. The status bar will show regular command help messages if the *logical* argument is FALSE.

See Also

| ALERT | Displays a message in a dialog box | Macro Function |
| BEEP | Causes your computer to beep | Macro Function |

MID(*string, offset-number, number-of-characters*)

Function

MID returns the specified number of characters in the middle of a string, beginning with the character specified in the *offset-number* argument. The *string* argument can be a literal, a reference to a cell containing a string, or a formula that evaluates to a string.

Example

=MID(H15,FIND(" ",H15)+1,LEN(H15)−FIND(" ",H15)) can be used to separate the first and last names in the string in H15. The first FIND function returns the position of the first space in the string and adds 1 to it to identify the start of the second word. The LEN function returns the number of characters in the string and subtracts the number of characters to the first space. As a result, the MID function returns the number of characters in the string that follows the space—normally the last name.

See Also

FIND	Preforms a case-sensitive string search	Function
LEFT	Returns the left end of a string	Function
RIGHT	Returns the right end of a string	Function
SEARCH	Performs a non-case-sensitive string search	Function

MIN(*list*)

Function

MIN returns the smallest number in the list. The *list* argument can contain numbers, formulas, or references to cells containing numbers or formulas.

M-N

Example

=MIN(A7,H19,50) compares the numbers contained in cells A7 and H19 and the number 50 and returns the smallest of them.

See Also

DMIN	Finds the minimum in a database	Function
MAX	Finds the maximum in a list	Function

MINUTE(*time-serial-number*)

Function

MINUTE returns the minutes from a time serial number. The resulting value is an integer from 1 to 59.

Example

=MINUTE(NOW()) returns the current minute of the day.

See Also

DAY	Returns the day given a serial number	Function
HOUR	Returns the hour given a serial number	Function
MONTH	Returns the month given a serial number	Function
NOW	Returns the current date and time	Function
SECOND	Returns the second given a serial number	Function
WEEKDAY	Returns the day of week given a serial number	Function
YEAR	Returns the year given a serial number	Function

MINVERSE(*numeric-square-array*)

Function

MINVERSE returns the matrix inverse of a *numeric-square-array*. The inverse of an array is an array. You must highlight an array (range) of equal size in which you want the result placed and press CTRL-SHIFT-ENTER after typing the function.

Example

Figure M-5 shows an array in cells A1:C3, and the result of selecting the range D1:F3, then entering the formula =MINVERSE(A1:C3) into cell D1.

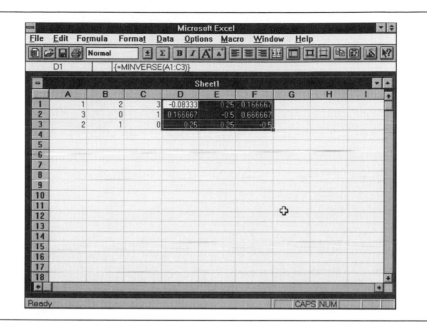

Figure M-5. *The matrix inverse of range A1:C3, returned in range D1:F3*

The matrix inverse of the array in cells A1:C3 is returned in cells D1:F3. This array can also be displayed as {-0.08333,0.25,0.166667; 0.166667,-0.5,0.666667;0.25,0.25,-0.5}.

If you do not highlight an array before typing the function, the cell into which the formula is entered will contain -0.08333. If you check the type, you will see that it is an array. (-TYPE(MINVERSE(A1:C3)) returns 64, the array type.) If you want to specify certain elements in the array, use the INDEX function (=INDEX(MINVERSE (A1:C3),2,2) returns -0.5.)

See Also

MDETERM	Returns the determinant of an array	Function
MMULT	Returns the product of two arrays	Function
TRANSPOSE	Transposes an array	Function

MIRR(*range, investment-rate, interest-rate*)

Function

MIRR returns the modified internal rate of return for a series of cash flows contained in the array *range*. Excel considers both the investment rate and the interest rate

M-N

received on reinvestment when calculating the modified internal rate of return. The *investment-rate* argument is the interest rate that is paid on money used for investments. The *interest-rate* argument is the interest rate received on investments. The first cell in the range usually contains a negative number for the initial investment or outflow of cash; positive numbers are inflows. The internal rate of return is the interest rate that gives a series of cash flows a net present value of zero.

Example

=MIRR(A2:A10,10%,13%) estimates the modified internal rate of return for the cash flows that are contained in cells A2 to A10. It uses 10% as the investment rate and 13% as the interest rate.

See Also

IRR	Returns the internal rate of return	Function
XNPV	Returns the present value	Function

MMULT(*range1,range2*)

Function

MMULT returns the product resulting from the matrix multiplication of two ranges of numbers. The *range1* and *range2* arguments must be arrays of the same size and shape and the result is an array of the same size and shape. You must highlight a range of the correct size for the result, enter the function, and press CTRL-SHIFT-ENTER.

Example

=MMULT(A1:B2,C1:D2) returns the matrix product of range A1:B2 and range C1:D2. The result is shown In Figure M-6; in this example, the cell range E1:F2 was highlighted before the formula was entered, so the result appears in that range.

See Also

MDETERM	Returns the determinant of a matrix	Function
MINVERSE	Returns the inverse of a matrix	Function
TRANSPOSE	Transposes a matrix	Function

MOD(*X,Y*)

Function

MOD returns the modulus, or remainder, of the value *X* that is divided by *Y*.

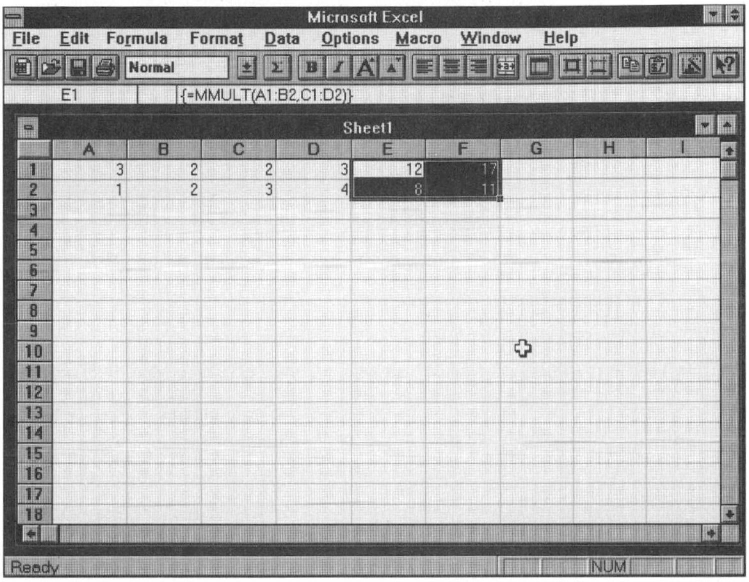

Figure M-6. *The product of matrices A1:B2 and C1:D2, returned in range E1:F2*

Example

=MOD(5,2) returns the value 1.

See Also

| INT | Rounds down to an integer | Function |
| TRUNC | Truncates a number to an integer | Function |

MODE(*X1,[X2],...*)

Function

MODE returns the value that occurs the most frequently in a list of numbers. The list of numbers can be given as numbers separated by commas, an array, or a reference to an array.

Example

=MODE({1,2,3,3,4,5,3,6,3,8}) returns 3.

See Also

AVERAGE	Returns the average of a list of numbers	Function
MEAN	Returns the mean of a list of numbers	Function
MEDIAN	Returns the median of a list of numbers	Function

MONTH(*date-serial-number*)

Function

MONTH returns the month of the year, an integer from 1 to 12, from a date serial number.

Example

=MONTH(NOW()) returns the month of the year for the current date.

See Also

DAY	Returns the day given a serial number	Function
HOUR	Returns the hour given a serial number	Function
MINUTE	Returns the minute given a serial number	Function
NOW	Returns the current date and time	Function
SECOND	Returns the second given a serial number	Function
WEEKDAY	Returns the day of week given a serial number	Function
YEAR	Returns the year given a serial number	Function

MOVE(*[horizontal],[vertical],[window-name]*)
MOVE?(*[horizontal],[vertical],[window-name]*)

Macro Function

MOVE moves the window named by the *window-name* argument (or the current window if the argument is omitted) so that its upper-left corner is positioned according to the *horizontal* and *vertical* arguments (measured in points). With the dialog box version of MOVE?, the arguments, if included, are used as the defaults.

MOVE.TOOL(*from-bar, from-position, [to-bar], [to-position], [copy], [width]*)

Macro Function **New to Version 4.0**

MOVE.TOOL moves a tool from one toolbar to another. It also allows you to adjust the width of a drop-down toolbar. *From-bar* and *to-bar* are the names or numbers of the toolbars. Here are the numbers and names of the built-in toolbars:

Number	Toolbar
1	Standard
2	Formatting
3	Utility
4	Chart
5	Drawing
6	Excel 3.0
7	Macro
8	Macro recording
9	Macro paused

The *to-bar* argument is optional; you don't need to use this argument if you are moving the tool to a different position on the same toolbar.

From-position and *to-position* are numbers that indicate the positions on the toolbars. Positions are numbered starting with 1 on the top or left of the toolbar, depending on the toolbar's orientation. If the position indicated by *to-position* is already occupied, the tool currently in that position is deleted. The *to-position* argument is not used if you are changing the width of a drop-down list.

Copy is a logical value that determines whether the tool is cut or copied from the *from-bar*. If *copy* is TRUE, the tool is copied. If copy is FALSE, the tool is moved.

Width is an optional argument that specifies the width of a drop-down list. If the tool is not a drop-down list, this argument is ignored.

See Also

ADD.TOOL	Adds a tool to a toolbar	Macro Function
COPY.TOOL	Copies a tool to the clipboard	Macro Function
GET.TOOL	Return information about a tool	Macro Function

MOVEAVG(*input,output,[interval],[errors],[chart]*)

Macro Function

MOVEAVG forecasts trends such as sales. MOVEAVG projects forecast values based on the average value of the variable over a certain number of preceding periods.

Input is a reference to the input range containing the data to be analyzed. *Input* must be a single column or a row consisting of at least four cells. *Output* is a reference to the upper-left cell in the output range.

Interval is a number indicating the number of values to use in the interval. The default value for this number is 3.

Errors is a logical value. If *errors* is TRUE, a column of standard errors is included in the output table. If *errors* is FALSE, no standard errors are returned.

Chart is a logical value. If chart is TRUE, a chart is created from the output data. If chart is FALSE, no chart is created. The default value for chart is FALSE.

MOVEAVG is an add-in function. The first time that you use it, you may see a #REF! error while Excel loads the function.

See Also

FORECAST	Returns a linear trend value	Macro Function
GROWTH	Returns an exponential trend value	Macro Function

MROUND(*X, multiple*)

MROUND rounds *X* to a multiple of *multiple*.

Example

=MROUND(17,5) returns 15.

See Also

CEILING	Rounds up to the next integer	Function
FLOOR	Rounds down to the previous integer	Function
ROUND	Rounds to a certain number of digits	Function

MULTINOMIAL(*X1,[X2],...*)

Function

MULTINOMIAL returns the ratio of the factorial of the sum of a list of numbers to the product of the factorials. There can be up to 29 numbers in the list. The formula for MULTINOMIAL for three values is shown here:

$$\text{MULTINOMIAL } (a, b, c) = \frac{(a + b + c)!}{a!\,b!\,c!}$$

MULTINOMIAL is an add-in function. The first time that you use it, you may see a #REF! error while Excel loads the function.

Example

=MULTINOMIAL(3,1,4) returns 280.

See Also

FACT	Returns the factorial of a number	Function
FACTDOUBLE	Returns the double factorial of a number	Function

M-N

N(*range*)

Function

N returns the value of the first cell in the specified *range*. If the cell contains a numeric value, that value is returned. If the cell contains a date, the serial number of the date is returned. If the cell contains a logical TRUE, 1 is returned. If the cell contains anything else, 0 is returned. This function can be used to check for numeric data.

Example

=N(C5:C5) returns the value contained in C5. If C5 contains a logical TRUE, the value returned will be 1; if the cell is empty or if it contains a label, the value returned will be 0.

See Also

| GET.CELL | Returns information about a cell | Macro Function |
| T | Tests for a text string | Macro Function |

NA()

Function

NA returns the value #N/A, which means "not available."

See Also

| ISNA | Tests for an #N/A value | Function |

NAMES([*document*], [*type*], [*match*])

Macro Function

NAMES returns an array containing all the names defined for the *document*. If no *document* is specified, NAMES returns an array of names defined for the active document. *Type* is a number that indicates whether hidden names should be included. The following table specifies the possible values for *type*:

Type	Names Included
1	Non-hidden names only
2	Hidden names only
3	All names

If *type* is omitted, the default value is 1. *Match* is a string that specifies which names you want included. Excel's wildcard characters can be used in the string. If the *match* argument is not given, all names are matched.

Example

=NAMES(,3,"f*") returns all names beginning with the letter *f* that are defined for the active document.

See Also

| DEFINE.NAME | Defines a new name | Macro Function |
| DELETE.NAME | Deletes an existing name | Macro Function |

| LIST.NAMES | Lists names and information | Macro Function |
| SET.NAME | Defines a name as a value | Macro Function |

NEGBINOMDIST(*failures,successes,probability*)

Function   **New to Version 4.0**

NEGBINOMDIST returns the negative binomial distribution. Shown here is the formula for the negative binomial distribution function:

$$nb(x;r,p) = \binom{x+r-1}{r-1} p^r (1-p)^x$$

x = failures
r = successes
p = probability of a success

The negative binomial distribution function calculates the probability that there will be a certain number of *failures* before reaching a certain number of *successes*, depending on the *probability* of success.

Example

=NEGBINOMDIST(20,7,0.2) returns 0.033976.

See Also

| BINOMDIST | Returns the binomial distribution | Function |
| HYPGEOMDIST | Returns the hypergeometric distribution | Function |

M-N

NETWORKDAYS(*start,end,[holidays]*)

Function   **New to Version 4.0**

NETWORKDAYS returns the number of work days between the *start* date and the *end* date. *Start* and *end* must be date serial numbers. A work day is any day not falling on a weekend or holiday. The argument *holidays* is a list of dates that are special holidays. If the *holidays* argument is not given, only standard holidays and weekends will be excluded from the net total of work days.

This function is an add-in function. The first time you use it, you may see a #REF! error while Excel loads the function.

Example

=NETWORKDAYS(DATE(93,12,7),DATE(93,12,10)) returns 4.

See Also

DATE	Returns the serial number of a date	Function
EDATE	Returns the end-of-month date	Function
NOW	Returns the serial number of the current date	Function
WORKDAY	Returns the workday *n* days after a date	Function

NEW(*[type]*,*[chart]*,*[workbook]*)
NEW?(*[type]*,*[chart]*,*[workbook]*)

Macro Function

NEW performs the same action as choosing the File New menu command. NEW opens a new Excel document. *Type* is the type of document to open. *Type* can be either the text string name of a template, or one of the codes listed here:

Type	Document
1	Worksheet
2	Chart
3	Macro sheet
4	International macro sheet
5	Workbook

If the *type* argument is not given, the default is to open the same document type as the currently active document. *Chart* is a number that indicates the organization of data, or that instructs Excel to display a dialog box. The dialog box asks for a chart organization. Below are the possible values for *chart* and their descriptions.

Chart	Action
0	Displays a dialog box
1	Identifies the first row or column as the first series
2	Indicates that the first row or column contains category labels
3	Indicates that the chart is a scatter chart, and that the first row or column contains x values

If *chart* is omitted, the default value is 1. The *workbook* argument is a logical value. If *workbook* is TRUE, the new document is added to the open workbook. If *workbook* is FALSE, it is not added. If *workbook* is not given, the default value is FALSE.

Example

=NEW(3) opens a new macro sheet.

See Also

FILE NEW	Equivalent command	Menu Command
NEW.WINDOW	Opens a new window for an existing document	Macro Function
OPEN	Opens a new document	Macro Function

NEW.WINDOW()

Macro Function

NEW.WINDOW performs the same action as the New Window command on the Window menu. NEW.WINDOW opens a new window for the active document.

Example

=NEW.WINDOW() opens a new window.

See Also

ARRANGE.ALL	Arranges and synchronizes windows	Macro Function
WINDOW.MOVE	Moves a window	Macro Function
WINDOW NEW WINDOW	Equivalent command	Menu Command
WINDOW.SIZE	Sizes a window	Macro Function

M-N

NEXT()

Macro Function

NEXT terminates a FOR-NEXT loop or a WHILE-NEXT loop. If the condition controlling the loop is still met, NEXT causes the macro to execute the loop again; if the condition is not met, NEXT terminates the loop.

See Also

FOR	Begins a FOR-NEXT loop	Macro Function
FOR.CELL	Begins a FOR.CELL-NEXT loop	Macro Function
WHILE	Begins a WHILE loop	Macro Function

NOMINAL(*rate, periods*)

Function   **New to Version 4.0**

NOMINAL returns the nominal annual interest rate. *Rate* is the effective interest rate, and *periods* is the number of compounding periods per year.

This function is an add-in function. The first time you use it, you may see a #REF! error while Excel loads the function.

Example

=NOMINAL(8.1234%,12) returns 0.078358 or 7.8%.

See Also

EFFECT	Returns the effective interest rate	Function

NORMDIST(*X, mean, standard-deviation, cumulative*)

Function   **New to Version 4.0**

NORMDIST calculates the normal distribution for the specified *mean* and *standard-deviation*. *X* is a value for which you want to calculate the normal distribution. *Cumulative* is a logical value. If *cumulative* is TRUE, NORMDIST uses the *cumulative* distribution formula. If *cumulative* is FALSE, NORMDIST uses the probability mass function.

Example

=NORMDIST(10,9,2,TRUE) returns 0.691462.

See Also

NORMINV	Returns the inverse of the normal cumulative distribution	Function

| NORMSDIST | Returns the standard normal cumulative distribution | Function |
| ZTEST | Returns the two-tailed P value | Function |

NORMINV(*probability, mean, standard-deviation*)

Function   **New to Version 4.0**

NORMINV returns the inverse of the normal cumulative distribution. *Probability* is the probability of the normal distribution. *Mean* is the arithmetic mean of the normal distribution. *Standard-deviation* is the standard deviation of the normal distribution.

Example

=NORMINV(0.691462,9,2) returns 9.999999.

See Also

NORMDIST	Returns the normal distribution	Function
NORMSDIST	Returns the standard normal cumulative distribution	Function
STANDARDIZE	Returns a normalized value	Function

NORMSDIST(*X*)

Function   **New to Version 4.0**

NORMSDIST returns the standard normal cumulative distribution for *X*. NORMSDIST uses a mean of 0 and a standard deviation of 1.

Example

=NORMSDIST(2) returns 0.97725.

See Also

NORMDIST	Returns the normal distribution	Function
NORMSINV	Returns the inverse of the standard normal cumulative distribution	Function
STANDARDIZE	Returns a normalized value	Function

M-N

NORMSINV(*probability*)

Function   New to Version 4.0

NORMSINV calculates the inverse of the standard normal cumulative distribution (given the *probability*), with a mean of 0 and a standard deviation of 1.

Example

=NORMSINV(0.97725) returns 1.999997.

See Also

NORMDIST	Returns the normal distribution	Function
NORMINV	Returns the inverse of the normal cumulative distribution	Function
NORMSDIST	Returns the standard normal cumulative distribution	Function
STANDARDIZE	Returns a normalized value	Function

NOT(*X*)

Function

NOT returns the opposite of *X*, where *X* must evaluate to a logical TRUE or a logical FALSE.

Example

=NOT(FALSE) returns TRUE.

See Also

AND	Returns the logical AND	Function
OR	Returns the logical OR	Function

NOTE(*[text]*, *[cell]*, *[start]*, *[number]*)
NOTE?()

Macro Function

NOTE performs the same action as choosing the Formula Note menu command. NOTE adds a note to a *cell* or replaces characters in a note. *Text* is the note, given as a text string. *Cell* is the cell to which you want to attach the note. *Start* is the starting position in the text string. *Number* is the number of characters in the text string, beginning at *start*, that you want to add. If *text* is omitted, the default is " " (the empty string). If *cell* is omitted, the default is the active cell. If *start* is omitted, the starting position is assumed to be 1. If *number* is omitted, the default number of characters added is the entire string given by *text*.

If the version with the question mark is used (NOTE?), a dialog box appears where you can enter the note.

Example

=NOTE("Record sales for John",!$B$67) attaches a new note to the cell B67 that says "Record sales for John".

See Also

GET.NOTE	Returns a note from a cell	Macro Function
SOUND.NOTE	Adds a sound note	Macro Function

NOW()

Function

NOW returns the serial number of the current date and time. The serial number is divided into two sections. The number to the left of the decimal place represents the date, and the number to the right of the decimal place represents the time.

See Also

DATE	Returns the serial number of a date	Function
TODAY	Returns the serial number of the current date	Function

NPER(*interest, payment, present-value, [future-value], [type]*)

Function

NPER returns the number of periods for an investment, given the *payment* amount and the *interest* rate. *Future-value* is an optional argument. If it is omitted, it is assumed that the future value of a loan is $0. If it is included, it is the balance that you wish to obtain after the last payment is made. *Present-value* is the present value of the loan.

Type is an optional argument. A *type* of 0 means that payments are due at the end of the period. A *type* of 1 means that payments are due at the beginning of the period. If the *type* argument is omitted, it is assumed to be of type 0.

Example

=NPER(1.8%,–180,–1000,55500) returns 100. The interest rate is 1.8 percent per month, the payments are $180, the present value is $1000 (the cost of the investment), and the future value is $55,500. The number of payments is 100.

See Also

FV	Returns the future value	Function
IPMT	Returns the interest payment	Function
PMT	Returns the payment	Function
PPMT	Returns the principle payment	Function
PV	Returns the present value	Function
RATE	Returns the interest rate	Function

NPV(*interest,range*)

Function

NPV returns the net present value of a series of cash flows contained in the *range* discounted at the given *interest* rate.

Example

=NPV(.08,C15:C25) returns the net present value of the cash flows contained in cells C15 through C25, discounted at 8 percent.

See Also

FV	Returns the future value	Function
IPMT	Returns the interest payment	Function
PMT	Returns the payment	Function
PPMT	Returns the principle payment	Function
PV	Returns the present value	Function
RATE	Returns the interest rate	Function

OBJECT.PROPERTIES(*[placement]*, *[print]*)

Macro Function   **New to Version 4.0**

OBJECT.PROPERTIES sets certain properties for the selected object or objects. (This macro function replaces the Excel 3.0 PLACEMENT macro function.) *Placement* is a number that indicates how the objects are moved and sized. Here are the possible values for *placement*:

Placement	Description
1	Moved and sized with cells under objects
2	Moved (not sized) with cells under objects
3	Neither moved nor sized with cells under objects

If *placement* is omitted, the way that the object is moved and sized remains the same.
If *print* is TRUE, the objects are printed with the document. If *print* is FALSE, the objects are not printed. If *print* is omitted, the default value is TRUE.

See Also

CREATE.OBJECT	Creates a new object	Macro Function
FORMAT.MOVE	Moves an existing object	Macro Function
FORMAT.SIZE	Sizes an existing object	Macro Function

OBJECT.PROTECTION(*[locked]*, *[text]*)

Macro Function

OBJECT.PROTECTION sets the protection status for the selected object. *Locked* is TRUE if you want to lock the selected object. *Locked* is FALSE if you want to unlock the selected object. If *locked* is omitted, the protection status remains unchanged.

The *text* argument is only relevant if the selected object is a text box or a button. If so, *text* sets the protection status of the text. If *text* is TRUE, the text is locked and cannot be changed. If *text* is FALSE, the text can be changed. The default value for *text* is TRUE.

See Also

PROTECT.DOCUMENT	Sets the protection status of a document	Macro Function

OCT2BIN(*X,[characters]*)

Function   **New to Version 4.0**

OCT2BIN converts a number *X* from octal to binary, and returns the result in *characters* number of places. For example, if *characters* is 8, there will always be eight characters in the result, which will be padded with 0's if necessary.

OCT2BIN is an add-in function. The first time that you use it, you may see a #REF! error while Excel loads the function.

Example

=OCT2BIN(4,8) returns 00000100.

See Also

BIN2OCT	Converts binary to octal	Function
DEC2BIN	Converts decimal to binary	Function
DEC2OCT	Converts decimal to octal	Function
HEX2BIN	Converts hexadecimal to binary	Function
HEX2OCT	Converts hexadecimal to octal	Function

OCT2DEC(*X*)

Function   **New to Version 4.0**

OCT2BIN converts a number *X* from octal to decimal.

This is an add-in function. The first time that you use it, you may see a #REF! error while Excel loads the function.

Example

=OCT2DEC(10) returns 8.

See Also

BIN2DEC	Converts binary to decimal	Function
BIN2OCT	Converts binary to octal	Function
DEC2OCT	Converts decimal to octal	Function
HEX2DEC	Converts hexadecimal to decimal	Function
HEX2OCT	Converts hexadecimal to octal	Function

OCT2HEX(X, [characters])

Function   **New to Version 4.0**

OCT2HEX converts a number X from octal to hexadecimal, and returns the result in *characters* number of places. For example, if *characters* is 8, there will always be eight characters in the result, which will be padded with 0's if necessary.

OCT2HEX is an add-in function. The first time that you use it, you may see a #REF! error while Excel loads the function.

Example

=OCT2HEX(4,8) returns 00000004.

See Also

BIN2OCT	Converts binary to octal	Function
BIN2HEX	Converts binary to hexadecimal	Function
DEC2HEX	Converts decimal to hexadecimal	Function
DEC2OCT	Converts decimal to octal	Function
HEX2OCT	Converts hexadecimal to octal	Function

ODD(X)

Macro Function   **New to Version 4.0**

ODD rounds X away from zero to the nearest odd integer. If X is positive, ODD rounds up. If X is negative, ODD rounds down.

Examples

=ODD(8) returns 9.
=ODD(−8) returns −9.

See Also

CEILING	Rounds up to the nearest integer	Function
EVEN	Rounds away from zero to the nearest even integer	Function
FLOOR	Rounds down to the nearest integer	Function
ROUND	Rounds to a specified number of digits	Function

ODDFPRICE(*settlement, maturity, issue, coupon, rate, yield, redemption, frequency, [basis-code]*)

Macro Function   **New to Version 4.0**

ODDFPRICE calculates the price per $100 face value of a security with an odd first period. An odd first period means that the first period is shorter or longer than normal.

Settlement is the security's settlement date. *Maturity* is the security's maturity date. *Issue* is the security's issue date. *Coupon* is the security's first coupon date. *Settlement, maturity, issue,* and *coupon* should all be given as date serial numbers.

Rate is the security's interest rate. *Yield* is the security's annual yield. *Redemption* is the value per $100 face value of the security. *Frequency* is a number indicating the number of payments per year. The possible values for *frequency* are listed here:

Frequency	Payment
1	Annual
2	Semi-annual
4	Quarterly

The *basis-code* is a number that indicates the day count basis. The possible values for *basis-code* are listed here:

Basis-Code	Day Count
0	30/360
1	Actual/Actual
2	Actual/360
3	Actual/365

If *basis-code* is omitted, the default value is 0.

ODDFPRICE is an add-in function. The first time that you use it, you may see a #REF! error while Excel loads the function.

Example

=ODDFPRICE(date(93,6,1),date(93,12,31),date(93,1,1),date(93,7,1),.105,2000,105, 1,1) returns 54.73315. This shows that a security with a June 1, 1993 settlement date, a December 31, 1993 maturity date, a January 1, 1993 issue date and a July 1, 1993 first coupon date, and a 10 percent interest rate, a $2,000 annual yield, a $105 redemption value, annual payments, and an actual/actual day count basis has a price of $54.73315 per $100 face value.

See Also

| ODDFYIELD | Returns the yield of a security with an odd first period | Function |
| ODDLPRICE | Returns the price of a security with an odd last period | Function |

ODDFYIELD(*settlement, maturity, issue, coupon, rate, price, redemption, frequency, [basis-code]*)

Macro Function   **New to Version 4.0**

ODDFYIELD calculates the yield of a security with an odd first period. An odd first period means that the first period is shorter or longer than normal.

Settlement is the security's settlement date. *Maturity* is the security's maturity date. *Issue* is the security's issue date. *Coupon* is the security's first coupon date. *Settlement, maturity, issue,* and *coupon* should all be given as date serial numbers.

Rate is the security's interest rate. *Price* is the security's price. *Redemption* is the value per $100 face value of the security. *Frequency* is a number indicating the number of payments per year. The possible values for *frequency* are listed here:

Frequency	Payment
1	Annual
2	Semi-annual
4	Quarterly

The *basis-code* is a number that indicates the day count basis. The possible values for *basis-code* are listed here:

Basis-Code	Day Count
0	30/360
1	Actual/Actual
2	Actual/360
3	Actual/365

If *basis-code* is omitted, the default value is 0.

ODDFYIELD is an add-in function. The first time that you use it, you may see a #REF! error while Excel loads the function.

Example

=ODDFYIELD(date(93,6,1),date(93,12,31),date(93,1,1),date(93,7,1),.10,100,150,1,1) returns 126.5019. This shows that a security with a June 1, 1993 settlement date, a December 31, 1993 maturity date, a January 1, 1993 issue date and a July 1, 1993 first coupon date, and a 10 percent interest rate, a $100 price, a $150 redemption value, annual payments, and an actual/actual day count basis has a yield of $126.5019.

See Also

ODDFPRICE	Returns the price of a security with an odd first period	Function
ODDLYIELD	Returns the yield of a security with an odd last period	Function

ODDLPRICE(*settlement, maturity, coupon, rate, yield, redemption, frequency, [basis-code]*)

Macro Function **New to Version 4.0**

ODDLPRICE calculates the price per $100 face value of a security with an odd last period. An odd last period means that the last period is shorter or longer than normal.

Settlement is the security's settlement date. *Maturity* is the security's maturity date. *Coupon* is the security's first coupon date. *Settlement, maturity,* and *coupon* should all be given as date serial numbers.

Rate is the security's interest rate. *Yield* is the security's annual yield. *Redemption* is the value per $100 face value of the security. *Frequency* is a number indicating the number of payments per year. The possible values for *frequency* are listed here:

Frequency	Payment
1	Annual
2	Semi-annual
4	Quarterly

The *basis-code* is a number that indicates the day count basis. The possible values for *basis-code* are listed here:

Basis-Code	Day Count
0	30/360
1	Actual/Actual

Basis-Code	Day Count
2	Actual/360
3	Actual/365

If *basis-code* is omitted, the default value is 0.

ODDLPRICE is an add-in function. The first time that you use it, you may see a #REF! error while Excel loads the function.

Example

=ODDLPRICE(date(93,8,1),date(93,12,31),date(93,7,1),.10,200,90,1,1) returns 0.27794. This shows that a security with an August 1, 1993 settlement date, a December 31, 1993 maturity date, a July 1, 1993 last coupon date, a 10 percent interest rate, a $200 annual yield, a $90 redemption value, annual payments, and an actual/actual day count basis has a price of $0.27794 per $100 face value.

See Also

ODDFPRICE	Returns the price of a security with an odd first period	Function
ODDLYIELD	Returns the yield of a security with an odd last period	Function

ODDLYIELD(*settlement, maturity, coupon, rate, price, redemption, frequency, [basis-code]*)

Macro Function   **New to Version 4.0**

ODDLYIELD calculates the yield of a security with an odd last period. An odd last period means that the last period is shorter or longer than normal.

Settlement is the security's settlement date. *Maturity* is the security's maturity date. *Coupon* is the security's first coupon date. *Settlement, maturity,* and *coupon* should all be given as date serial numbers.

Rate is the security's interest rate. *Price* is the security's price. *Redemption* is the value per $100 face value of the security. *Frequency* is a number indicating the number of payments per year. The possible values for *frequency* are listed here:

Frequency	Payment
1	Annual
2	Semi annual
4	Quarterly

The *basis-code* is a number that indicates the day count basis. The possible values for *basis-code* are listed here:

Basis-Code	Day Count
0	30/360
1	Actual/Actual
2	Actual/360
3	Actual/365

If *basis-code* is omitted, the default value is 0.

ODDLYIELD is an add-in function. The first time that you use it, you may see a #REF! error while Excel loads the function.

Example

=ODDLYIELD(date(93,8,1),date(93,12,31),date(93,7,1),.10,2000,20000,1,1) returns 21.60767. This shows that a security with an August 1, 1993 settlement date, a December 31, 1993 maturity date, a July 1, 1993 last coupon date, and a 10 percent interest rate, a $2,000 price, a $20,000 redemption value, annual payments, and an actual/actual day count basis has a yield of $21.60767.

See Also

ODDFYIELD	Returns the yield of a security with an odd first period	Function
ODDLPRICE	Returns the price of a security with an odd last period	Function

OFFSET(*reference,row-offset,column-offset,[height],[width]*)

Macro Function

OFFSET returns a reference offset from the *reference* given. The *row-offset* and *column-offset* arguments are used to find the upper-left corner of the reference to be returned. OFFSET returns a reference *width* wide and *height* tall. If the *width* and *height* arguments are not given, the default value for each argument is 1.

Example

=SELECT(OFFSET(A1,2,2,2,2)) selects the range C3:D4.

See Also

ABSREF	Returns an absolute reference	Function
RELREF	Returns a relative reference	Function

ON.DATA(*[document]*, *[macro]*)

Macro Function

ON.DATA causes the macro to start whenever the remotely referenced document receives data from another application, if the *macro* argument is included. ON.DATA is disabled if the *macro* argument is not included. If the *document* argument is omitted, the macro starts whenever a document not already controlled by an ON.DATA function receives data.

Example

=ON.DATA("INDATA.XLS","Process") starts the macro "Process" when the document "INDATA.XLS" receives data from another application.

See Also

ERROR	Enables or disables error checking	Macro Function
INITIATE	Opens a channel to an application	Macro Function
ON.ENTRY	Starts a macro when data is entered	Macro Function

ON.DOUBLECLICK(*[document]*, *[macro]*)

Macro Function   New to Version 4.0

ON.DOUBLECLICK causes the macro to start whenever you double-click on any cell or object on the specified document, if the document is a worksheet or a macro sheet. ON.DOUBLECLICK causes the macro to start whenever you double-click on any item on the document if the document is a chart. If the *document* argument is omitted, the macro runs whenever you double-click on any worksheet, macro sheet, or chart that isn't already controlled by an ON.DOUBLECLICK function. If the *macro* argument is omitted, ON.DOUBLECLICK is turned off for the specified document.

Example

=ON.DOUBLECLICK("JUNE.XLS","sort") starts the macro "sort" when you double-click on any cell or object on JUNE.XLS.

See Also

ASSIGN.TO.OBJECT	Assigns a macro to an object	Macro Function
ON.WINDOW	Starts a macro when a window is activated	Macro Function

ON.ENTRY(*[document], [macro]*)

Macro Function

ON.ENTRY causes the specified macro to start whenever you enter data on any cell or object on the document, if the document is a worksheet or a macro sheet. If the *document* argument is omitted, the specified macro runs whenever you enter data on any worksheet or macro sheet that isn't already controlled by an ON.ENTRY function. If *macro* is omitted, ON.ENTRY is turned off for the specified document.

Example

=ON.ENTRY("JUNE.XLS","sort") starts the macro "sort" when any data is entered on the worksheet JUNE.XLS.

See Also

ASSIGN.TO.OBJECT	Assigns a macro to an object	Macro Function
ON.WINDOW	Starts a macro when a window is activated	Macro Function

ON.KEY(*key, [macro]*)

Macro Function

ON.KEY causes the specified macro to start whenever the key or key combination is pressed. The key or key combination must be given as a string. If you want to use a non-alphanumeric key, place the name of the key inside curly braces. Here are some special codes for keys that are coded with characters other than their key names:

ALT	%
BACKSPACE	{BACKSPACE} or {BS}
BREAK	{BREAK}
CAPS LOCK	{CAPSLOCK}
CLEAR	{CLEAR}
COMMAND	*

CTRL	^
DEL	{DELETE} or {DEL}
DOWN ARROW	{DOWN}
END	{END}
ENTER	~ OR {ENTER}
ESC	{ESC} OR {ESCAPE}
HELP	{HELP}
HOME	{HOME}
INS	{INSERT}
LEFT ARROW	{LEFT}
NUM LOCK	{NUMLOCK}
PGDN	{PGDN}
PGUP	{PGUP}
PRINT SCREEN	{PRTSC}
RETURN	{RETURN}
RIGHT ARROW	{RIGHT}
SCROLL LOCK	{SCROLLLOCK}
SHIFT	+
TAB	{TAB}
UP ARROW	{UP}
F1 - F15	{F1} - {F15}

Example

ON.KEY("+{PGUP}","REC.XLM!MonthEnd") starts MonthEnd when SHIFT-PGUP is pressed.

See Also

CANCEL.KEY	Disables macro interruption	Macro Function
ERROR	Enables or disables error checking	Macro Function

ON.RECALC(*[document]*, *[macro]*)

Macro Function   **New to Version 4.0**

ON.RECALC causes the macro to start whenever the document is recalculated, if the *macro* argument is included. ON.RECALC is disabled if the *macro* argument is not included. If the *document* argument is omitted, the macro starts whenever a document not already controlled by an ON.RECALC function is recalculated.

Example

=ON.RECALC("JUNE.XLS","control") starts the macro "control" whenever JUNE.XLS is recalculated.

See Also

CALCULATE.DOCUMENT	Recalculates the active documents	Macro Function
CALCULATE.NOW	Recalculates all open documents	Macro Function
CALCULATION	Sets calculation option	Macro Function

ON.TIME(*time, macro, [wait], [logical]*)

Macro Function

ON.TIME causes the *macro* to start at the specified time, if the *logical* argument is TRUE. Previous requests to start the macro at the specified time are ignored if the *logical* argument is FALSE. If the *logical* argument is omitted, the default value is TRUE. The *time* argument can be a time, or a date and a time. If it is just a time, the macro runs every day at the same time. If Excel can't start the macro at the specified time, it keeps trying for the amount of time specified by the *wait* argument. The default value for *wait* is the maximum time.

Example

=ON.TIME("9:00:00 PM","batch") starts the macro "batch" at 9:00 P.M.

See Also

NOW	Returns the current date and time	Function

ON.WINDOW(*[window-name], macro*)

Macro Function

ON.WINDOW causes the *macro* to start whenever the window specified by *window-name* is activated. Both arguments must be given as strings. If no *window-name* is given, the macro is started whenever any window is activated.

Example

=ON.WINDOW("JUNE.XLS","setup") runs the macro "setup" whenever the window named JUNE.XLS is activated.

See Also

GET.WINDOW	Returns information about a window	Macro Function
WINDOWS	Returns a list of all windows	Macro Function

OPEN(*file*, *[links]*, *[read-only]*, *[delimiter]*, *[protect-pw]*, *[write-pw]*, *[no-message]*, *[type]*, *[custom]*, *[logical]*)
OPEN?(*[file]*, *[links]*, *[read-only]*, *[delimiter]*, *[protect-pw]*, *[write-pw]*, *[no-message]*, *[type]*, *[custom]*, *[logical]*)

Macro Function

OPEN performs the same action as the Open option on the File menu. The *file* argument must be given as a string. In the dialog box version (with the question mark), the *file* argument can contain Excel wildcards, so that you can control the files listed in the dialog box that appears.

The *links* argument allows you to update references to the file. *Links* can be one of the following numbers:

Links	References Updated
0	None
1	External references only
2	Remote references only
3	External and remote references

The *read-only* argument corresponds to the Read Only check box in the Open dialog box, which is shown here:

O

Set *read-only* to TRUE to turn the check box on; set it to FALSE to turn the check box off.

Delimiter is a number that indicates the delimiter used when opening files. Here are the possible values for *delimiter:*

Delimiter	Description
1	Tab
2	Comma
3	Space
4	Semicolon
5	None
6	Custom

If *delimiter* is omitted, the current delimiter remains unchanged.

Protect-pw is the password required to protect or unprotect a document. If the *protect-pw* argument is omitted and a password is required, you will see a dialog box requesting the password.

Write-pw is the password required to open a write-protected document with write privileges. If a password is required and none is given, a dialog box will request the password.

No-message is a logical value. If the *no-message* argument is TRUE, Excel will not display a message alerting you that the file is read-only. If *no-message* is FALSE, Excel will display a message when you open a read-only file. The default for *no-message* is FALSE.

Type is a number that indicates the type of operating system on which a text file originated. This table lists the possible values for *type:*

Type	Operating System
1	Macintosh
2	Windows (ANSI)
3	MS-DOS (PC-8)

If *type* is omitted, the file is assumed to have been created in the current operating system environment.

Custom is a custom delimiter used when opening files. *Custom* is a text string, or a reference to a text string. This argument is ignored unless *delimiter* is 6.

Logical indicates whether or not to add the file to the open workbook. If *logical* is TRUE, the file is added. If *logical* is FALSE, the file is not added. The default value for *logical* is FALSE.

Example

=OPEN("C:\WORK\JUNE.XLS",2,,1,"chinock") opens the file JUNE.XLS, updates the remote references, uses tabs as delimiters, and gives the password "chinock".

See Also

CLOSE	Closes the active window	Macro Function
FILE NEW	Equivalent command	Menu Command
FOPEN	Opens a text file	Macro Function
OPEN.LINKS	Opens linked documents	Macro Function

OPEN.LINKS(*document-list,[read-only],[type]*)
OPEN.LINKS?(*[document-list],[read-only],[type]*)

Macro Function

OPEN.LINKS performs the same action as the Links option on the File menu. The *document-list* argument must be a list of text strings that are document names, references, or arrays that contain names or references. In the dialog box version (with the question mark), the document names are listed in the dialog box that appears.

The *read-only* argument corresponds to the Read Only check box in the File Links dialog box. In the dialog box version, if a value is given for the *read-only* argument, it is used as the default for the dialog box that appears.

The *type* is a number that indicates the type of link. This table lists the possible values for *type:*

Type	Link
1	Microsoft Excel
2	DDE
5	Subscriber (Macintosh)
6	Publisher (Macintosh)

Example

OPEN.LINKS(LINKS()) opens the files that are linked to the current document.

See Also

CHANGE.LINK	Changes links	Macro Function

| GET.LINK.INFO | Returns information about a link | Macro Function |
| LINKS | Returns a list of all links | Macro Function |

OPTIONS

Menu

The Options menu is the catch-all menu for options that don't fit elsewhere. It lets you specify what areas of the worksheet are to be printed and to identify repeated titles on a printout. It also allows you to set manual page breaks, to determine how your screen will look, and to protect a document (worksheet, chart, or macro sheet) or window from being overwritten. The Options menu also lets you set how Excel calculates a worksheet; force the recalculation of a worksheet at any time; change overall defaults like the display of the status bar, toolbars, scroll bars, and formula bar; and change the type of menus. This menu also provides spell checking and access to add-in functions. The Options menu is shown here:

OPTIONS ADD-INS

Menu Command   New to Version 4.0

The Add-Ins option in the Options menu provides access to add-in macros. The Add-In Manager dialog box, shown here, lists add-in macros that have already been loaded, and allows you to add, remove, or change the add-in macros. The macros that are listed in the dialog box are loaded automatically when you start Excel. If there are add-ins that you don't use and memory is a consideration, you can remove the unused add-ins using this menu command. You can also add new add-in macros from the Excel library, or you can add your own custom add-in macro.

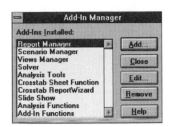

Some functions in Excel 4.0 are actually add-in macros. The first time you use these functions, you may see a #REF! error while Excel loads the macro. If the add-in macro is not installed, you will need to load it by clicking on the Add button and opening the appropriate file in the Excel library.

See Also

ADD-INS	Explains add-in macros	Concept
ANALYSIS TOOLPAK	Explains the Analysis Toolpak	Concept
OPTIONS ANALYSIS TOOL	Accesses the Analysis Toolpak	Menu Command

OPTIONS ANALYSIS TOOLS

Menu Command   **New to Version 4.0**

The Analysis Tools option in the Options menu provides access to Excel's Analysis Toolpak. The Analysis Toolpak is a set of financial and engineering functions that you can load as needed. (They are not loaded automatically to conserve memory.) To use a function from the Analysis Toolpak, choose the Analysis Tools option from the Options menu. Then choose the tool that you want to use from the resultant dialog box, which is shown here:

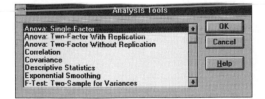

See Also

ADD-INS	Explains add-in macros	Concept
ANALYSIS TOOLPAK	Explains the Analysis Toolpak	Concept

OPTIONS CALCULATE DOCUMENT

Menu Command   **Prior to Version 4.0**

➤   *Shortcut Key:*   SHIFT-F9

The Calculate Document option only appears when you hold down the SHIFT key while you choose the Options menu. The Calculate Document option allows you to calculate the active worksheet, chart, or macro sheet. The calculations are done according to the settings Update Remote References and Precision As Displayed in the Calculation Options dialog box. Excel normally performs calculations on your document automatically. If you set the calculation to Manual in the Calculation Options dialog box, you must use the Calculate Document or Calculate Now option from the Options menu to tell Excel to calculate the document.

OPTIONS CALCULATE NOW

Menu Command   **Prior to Version 4.0**

➤   *Shortcut Key:*   F9

The Calculate Now option on the Options menu lets you calculate all open documents at once. This option also allows you to calculate a formula in the formula bar and replace it with the result. To calculate formulas in all open documents, simply choose the Calculate Now option from the Options menu, making sure that the formula bar is not active. To calculate a formula in the formula bar, choose the Calculate Now option from the Options menu while the formula bar is active and the formula in the formula bar begins with an equal sign.

OPTIONS CALCULATION

Menu Command

The Calculation option on the Options menu lets you control the calculation and recalculation of open documents. Choose this option if you want to turn off automatic recalculation. Choosing the Calculation option from the Options menu brings up the following dialog box:

This dialog box has three sections: Calculation, Iteration, and Sheet Options. Each of these sections has several options, as described here:

CALCULATION	There are three options within the Calculation box:
Automatic	Automatically performs all needed recalculations to your document. This is the default setting for Excel.
Automatic Except	Tells Excel to recalculate everything automatically except formulas within tables.
Tables	When you want to calculate the tables, use the Calc Now button or the Calc Document button.
Manual	Tells Excel not to recalculate your documents until you press the Calc Now or Calc Document button.
ITERATION	Lets you control the number of iterations Excel performs on a recalculation. You can specify the maximum number of iterations in the Maximum Iterations text box. Alternatively, you can enter a value in the Maximum Change text box that tells Excel to iterate until the maximum change in any value is less than the number you specify. If the Iteration box is turned off, Excel's defaults are 100 iterations and a maximum value of 0.001.

Maximum Iterations	Lets you specify the maximum number of iterations Excel will perform when recalculating a document if the Iterations box is turned on. If the Iterations box is turned off, Excel's defaults are 100 iterations and a maximum value of 0.001.
Maximum Change	Lets you specify the number at which Excel will stop iterating when all values change less than that amount, when the Iterations box is turned on. If the Iterations box is turned off, Excel's defaults are 100 iterations and a maximum value of 0.001.
SHEET OPTIONS	The sheet options check boxes are described here:
Update Remote References	Updates formulas with remote references every time the document is recalculated. When the box is turned off, formulas with remote references are not updated each time the document is recalculated.
Precision As Displayed	Causes Excel to store the calculated values in cells exactly as displayed. If this box is turned off, Excel stores the calculated values in cells with a precision of 15 digits. If you recalculate your worksheet with the Precision As Displayed box turned on, and then turn the box off, your values will *not* be restored to full precision of 15 digits.
1904 Date System	Causes dates to be calculated using the 1904 system if turned on, and the 1900 system if turned off. Dates are stored in Excel as serial numbers. A serial number of 1 will produce a date of 1/1/1900 in the 1900 system, and a date of 1/1/1904 in the 1904 system. The usual format is 1900, but if you import a file from another application and your dates are off by 4 years, turn the 1904 Date System box on.

Save External Link Values	Causes external link values to be saved with the worksheet.
Alternate Expression Evaluation	Causes expressions and text strings to be treated as they would in Lotus 1-2-3.
Alternate Formula Entry	Converts formulas entered in Lotus 1-2-3 format to Excel format.
Calc Now Button	Recalculates all open documents.
Calc Document Button	Recalculates the active document.

See Also

CALCULATION   Equivalent function   Macro Function

OPTIONS COLOR PALETTE

Menu Command   **New to Version 4.0**

The Color Palette option on the Options menu allows you to customize the color palette for the document. There are 16 colors built into Excel. You can modify these colors by adjusting their shade or intensity. You can apply a color palette created in another document to your active document. The Color Palette dialog box is shown in Figure O-1.

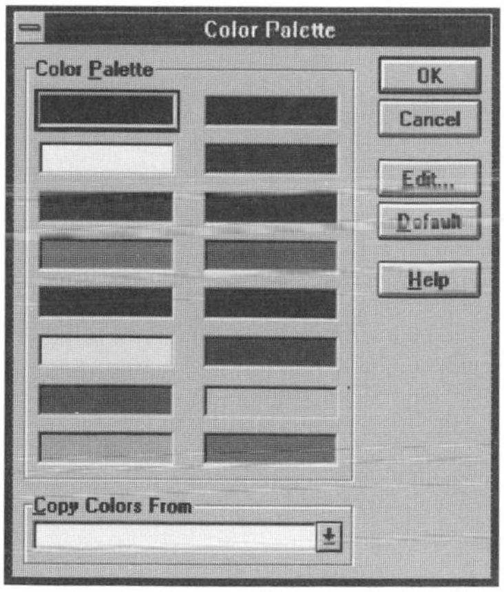

Figure O-1.   *The Color Palette dialog box*

The Edit button brings up another dialog box in which you can customize the color palette. The Default button returns the Color Palette to its original state.

See Also

COLOR.PALETTE   Equivalent function   Macro Function

OPTIONS DISPLAY

Menu Command

The Display option on the Options menu allows you to change the active worksheet's display. Choosing this option brings up the following dialog box:

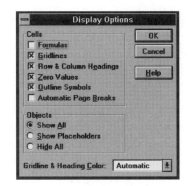

This dialog box allows you to set the display alternatives. The items in the dialog box are described here.

Formulas	If the Formulas check box is turned on, cells containing formulas display the formulas rather than the values to which the formulas evaluate. If the Formulas box is turned off, values are displayed rather than formulas.
Gridlines	Displays or hides grid lines on your worksheet.
Row & Column Headings	Displays or hides row and column headings on your worksheet.
Zero Values	If the Zero Values check box is turned on, zero values are displayed on your worksheet. If this box is turned off, blank cells appear in place of zero values.
Outline Symbols	Displays or hides outline symbols.

Automatic Page Breaks	Displays or hides the automatic page breaks set by Excel.
Show All	Displays all graphic objects, text boxes, etc.
Show Placeholders	Displays placeholders instead of objects, text boxes, etc.
Hide All	Hides all graphics objects, text boxes, etc.
Gridline & Heading Color	Allows you to choose colors for your grid lines and headings. You can set the box to automatic, or specify a color.

See Also

DISPLAY	Equivalent command	Menu Command

OPTIONS FREEZE PANES

Menu Command   **Prior to Version 4.0**

The Freeze Panes option only appears on the Options menu if the Full Menus option is activated. The Freeze Panes option allows you to tell Excel not to scroll parts of your worksheet when you have used the Control Split option to split your worksheet. If you have a vertical split, the pane or panes to the left of the split do not scroll horizontally. If you have a horizontal split, the pane or panes above the split do not scroll vertically.

See Also

FREEZE.PANES	Equivalent command	Macro Function

OPTIONS FULL MENUS

Menu Command   **Prior to Version 4.0**

The Full Menus option on the Options menu tells Excel to display all the menus with all options available. Once you choose the Full Menus option, the Short Menus option appears in its place on the Options menu.

See Also

OPTIONS SHORT MENUS	Related command	Menu Command

OPTIONS GROUP EDIT

Menu Command   New to Version 4.0

The Group Edit option on the Options menu allows you to designate a group of documents and edit them simultaneously. To create a group, choose the Group Edit option from the Options menu. Then hold down the CTRL key while clicking on the document names that you want included in the group. All open documents are listed in the dialog box. Once you have selected the desired documents, click on OK. Now, when you format one document, all documents in the group will be formatted simultaneously.

See Also

FORMAT MENU OPTIONS   Options for formatting   Menu Commands
                           your document

OPTIONS PROTECT DOCUMENT

Menu Command

The Protect Document option on the Options menu allows you to prevent alterations from being made to your worksheet. You can set cell protection options with the Format Cell Protection option. If you turn off the Gridlines option with the Display option on the Options menu, all protected cells will appear underlined. Choosing the Protect Document option brings up the following dialog box:

The items in the Protect Document dialog box are described here:

Password	The Password text box allows you to enter a password for your document. If you protect your document with a password, you may want to write it down and store it in a safe place. If you forget your password, there is no way to find it and no way to access your document.
Cells	Turning on the Cells check box prevents the cells on the worksheet from being changed.

Objects	Turning on the Objects check box prevents the objects on the worksheet from being changed.
Windows	Turning on the Windows check box prevents the worksheet's windows from being changed. If a window has been protected with the Windows option, you can close the window only by using the File Close option.

See Also

PROTECT.DOCUMENT   Equivalent function   Macro Function

OPTIONS REMOVE PAGE BREAK

Menu Command

The Remove Page Break option on the Options menu allows you to remove page breaks that you set with the Set Page Break option on the Options menu. It will not remove automatic page breaks. The Set Page Break option only appears on the Options menu if the active cell is directly above or to the right of a manual page break set with the Set Page Break option. If the active cell is not directly above or to the right of a manual page break, the Set Page Break option appears on the Options menu instead of the Remove Page Break option.

See Also

OPTIONS SET PAGE   Related command   Menu Command
BREAK

OPTIONS SET PAGE BREAK

Menu Command

The Set Page Break option on the Options menu allows you to set page breaks manually. The page break will appear above and to the left of the active cell. You can only remove manual page breaks with the Remove Page Break option.

See Also

OPTIONS REMOVE   Related Command   Menu Command
PAGE BREAK

OPTIONS SET PRINT AREA

Menu Command

The Set Print Area option on the Options menu allows you to select only part of your worksheet to print. You can select one block or use the SHIFT-F8 technique to make multiple selections. Multiple selections will be printed one section at a time. If you want to delete your Print Area, you must delete the named object Print_Area with the Formula Define Name – Delete option. If you do not set a print area, the entire worksheet will be printed.

If you use print titles in conjunction with a print area, make sure that your print titles selection doesn't overlap your print area selection. If they do overlap, your print titles will be printed twice, once as the print titles and once as the print area.

See Also

OPTIONS SET PAGE BREAK	Sets manual page breaks	Menu Command
OPTIONS SET PRINT TITLES	Sets print titles	Menu Command

OPTIONS SET PRINT TITLES

Menu Command

The Set Print Titles option on the Options menu allows you to set selected columns and/or rows to be printed on every page. For example, if you have column headings in row 1, you could select the row 1 and choose the Set Print Titles option. Even if your worksheet is many pages long, the column headings in row 1 will be printed at the top of every page. Row headings work the same way. You can think of row and column headings that you define as a custom version of Excel's row numbers and column letters. Row and column headings are useful for making multiple page documents readable.

When you select a print titles area, you must select the *entire* row or column. You can have more than one row or column in the print titles area, but they must be together on the worksheet. If you want to select both rows and columns as the print titles area, use the SHIFT-F8 method to make a multiple selection. If you want to delete the print titles area that you set with Set Print Titles, you must delete it with the Formula Define Name – Delete option.

If you use print titles in conjunction with a print area, make sure that your print titles selection doesn't overlap your print area selection. If they do overlap, your print titles will be printed twice, once as the print titles, and once as the print area.

See Also

OPTIONS SET PRINT AREA   Sets the print area   Menu Command

OPTIONS SHORT MENUS

Menu Command   **Prior to Version 4.0**

The Short Menus option on the Options menu tells Excel to display the menus with the most frequently used options only. Once you choose the Short Menus option, the option Full Menus appears in its place on the Options menu.

See Also

OPTIONS FULL MENUS   Related command   Menu Command

OPTIONS SPELLING

Menu Command   **New to Version 4.0**

The Spelling option on the Options menu allows you to check the spelling of the entire worksheet or of selected cells. If you want to check the entire worksheet, make sure that only one cell is selected. If you want to check a range, select the range before choosing the Spelling option from the Options menu. Choosing Spelling brings up the following dialog box:

The Spelling dialog box lets you change or ignore the individual word, or all matching words throughout the document. The items in the Spelling dialog box are described here:

Change To	The Change To box contains the word that will replace the misspelled word if you click on the Change button. You can type in a correction here, select a new word from the Suggestions list box, or simply click on Change to accept the default suggestion.
Suggestions	The Suggestions box contains a list of words that is likely to include the correct version of the misspelled word.
Add Words To	The Add Words To box lists the available dictionaries. If you want to add a word to a dictionary, select the appropriate dictionary here and then click on the Add button.
Ignore	If the word in question is spelled the way that you want it, clicking on the Ignore button ensures that no change will be made.
Change	When you click on the Change button, the misspelled word is replaced by the word that appears in the Change To box.
Add	Click on Add to add the word to the dictionary that appears in the Add Words To box.
Suggest	Click on the Suggest button to display a list of suggested alternate spellings in the Suggestions list box. This option appears grey if the Always Suggest check box is turned on.
Ignore All	Click on this button to ignore all instances of the word in question.
Change All	Click on this button to change all instances of the word in question to the word that appears in the Change To box.
Ignore Words in UPPERCASE	Turn this check box on to have the spell checker ignore all uppercase words in the document.
Always Suggest	Turn this check box on to have the spell checker always suggest alternative spellings for misspelled words.

OPTIONS TOOLBARS

Menu Command   **New to Version 4.0**

The Toolbars option on the Options menu allows you to control which toolbars are displayed on your screen. Choosing Toolbars brings up the following dialog box:

You can display, hide, or reset built-in toolbars, or use the Customize dialog box to customize a toolbar. The Reset button resets a toolbar that has been customized to its original state. See the TOOLBARS, CUSTOM entry for an explanation of how to create a custom toolbar or modify an existing toolbar.

See Also

TOOLBARS, CUSTOM	Explains custom toolbars	Concept
TOOLS, CUSTOM	Explains custom tools	Concept

OPTIONS UNFREEZE PANES

Menu Command   **Prior to Version 4.0**

The Unfreeze Panes option on the Options menu tells Excel to unfreeze panes that you froze with the Freeze Panes option on the Options menu. The Unfreeze Panes option only appears on the Options menu after you choose the Freeze Panes option. Once you choose the Unfreeze Panes option, the Freeze Panes option appears once again on the Options menu.

See Also

OPTIONS FREEZE PANES	Related command	Menu Command

OPTIONS UNPROTECT DOCUMENT

Menu Command

The Unprotect Document option on the Options menu only appears on the Options menu if the Full Menus option is activated. This option allows you to unprotect a document that you protected with the Protect Document option on the Options menu. Choosing Unprotect Document displays a dialog box requesting your password. You have to know your password in order to unprotect your document.

See Also

OPTIONS PROTECT DOCUMENT   Related command   Menu Command

OPTIONS WORKSPACE

Menu Command

The Workspace option on the Options menu allows you to set various options that apply to your entire Excel session. Choosing this option displays the Workspace Options dialog box shown in Figure O-2.

The items in the Workspace Options dialog box are described here:

Fixed Decimal	If this check box is turned on, Excel uses the number in the Places box to automatically insert decimal places in numbers you enter on your worksheet.
Places	If the Fixed Decimal check box is turned on, Excel uses the number in the Places box to automatically insert a decimal place in a number. If you put a 2 in the Places box and then type the number 300, Excel will enter 3.00 in the cell. If you put a –2 in the Places box and type the number 300, Excel will enter 30,000 in the cell. Only numbers that you enter without a decimal point are affected. If you type the number 3.9, 3.9 will appear in the cell.
R1C1	If the R1C1 check box is turned on, cell references are displayed in the format R1C1. If this box is turned off, cell references are displayed in the format A1. The cell B5 in format A1 appears as $B$5. In R1C1 format, B5 appears as R2C5. Notice that both rows and columns are numbered.
Status Bar	Displays or hides the status bar.
Info Window	Displays or hides the Info window. The Info window contains information about the active cell or the worksheet, including the note attached to the cell, if one exists.
Scroll Bars	Displays or hides scroll bars. Scroll bars allow you to move around your worksheet quickly with a mouse. If the Scroll Bars box is turned off, you can see more of your worksheets but cannot use the scroll bars.

Formula Bar	Displays or hides the formula bar. If the Formula Bar check box is turned off, the formula bar is not displayed, even when you are entering or editing a formula.
Note Indicator	If the Note Indicator check box is turned on, a small box appears in the corner of the cells containing notes.
Alternate Menu or Help Key	This box allows you to enter a character that will let you access the menu. Normally, you access the menu with the ALT key or the / (slash) key. If you want to access the menu with another key, type it in this box. If you turn on the Microsoft Excel Menus button, the alternate key will activate the Excel menu bar. If you turn on the Lotus 1-2-3 Help button, the alternate key will activate Help for Lotus 1-2-3 users.
Ignore Remote Requests	If this check box is turned on, Excel ignores requests from other Dynamic Data Exchange (DDE) requests. If you want to link an Excel document with another Windows application, turn off this box.
Move Selection After Enter	When this check box is turned on, the active cell is automatically moved down one row after you type in data and press ENTER.
Cell Drag and Drop	When this check box is turned on, you can move and copy cells by dragging them with the mouse.

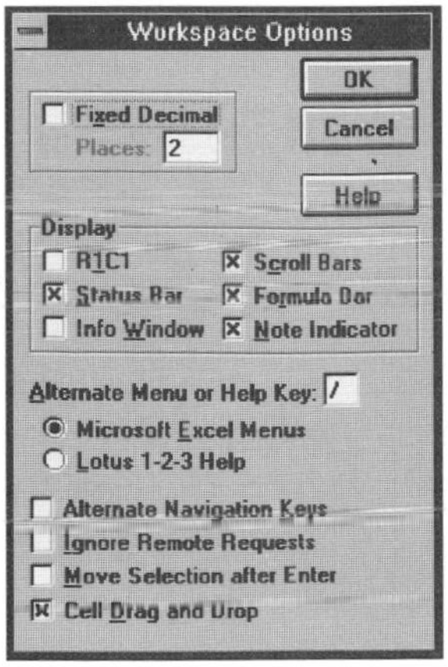

Figure O-2.   *The Workspace Options dialog box*

OR(*x1,x2,...xN*)

Function

OR returns the logical OR of the arguments *x1* through *xN*, which all must evaluate to logical values. You can have up to 30 arguments. If any of the arguments evaluate to TRUE, OR returns TRUE. If all the arguments evaluate to FALSE, OR returns FALSE.

Example

=OR(1=2,3=3,5=10) returns TRUE.

See Also

AND	Returns the logical AND	Function
NOT	Returns the opposite logical value	Function

OUTLINE(*[auto],[rows],[cols],[create]*)
OUTLINE?(*[auto],[rows],[cols],[create]*)

Macro Function

The OUTLINE macro function performs the same action as the Outline option on the Formula menu. OUTLINE creates an outline for your document. The arguments correspond to the check boxes in this dialog box:

Auto corresponds to the Automatic Styles check box. If *auto* is TRUE, automatic styles are applied to the outline. *Rows* corresponds to the Summary Rows Below Detail check box. If *rows* is TRUE, the summary information is located below the detail information. *Cols* corresponds to the Summary Columns To Right of Detail check box. If *cols* is TRUE, the summary information is located to the right of the detail information. *Create* is either 1 or 2. If *create* is 1, an outline is created. If *create* is 2, outline styles are applied to the selection. Supplying no *create* argument is equivalent to clicking on the OK button in the dialog box.

See Also

FORMULA OUTLINE	Equivalent command	Menu Command

OVERLAY(*type*,*[stacked]*,*[100%]*,*[vary-by-cat]*,*[overlapped]*,*[drop-lines]*,
[hi-lo-lines],*[overlap%]*,*[cluster%]*,*[pie-angle]*,*[series]*,*[auto]*)
OVERLAY?(*[type]*,*[stacked]*,*[100%]*,*[vary-by-cat]*,*[overlapped]*,
[drop-lines],*[hi-lo-lines]*,*[overlap%]*,*[cluster%]*,*[pie-angle]*,*[series]*,*[auto]*)

Macro Function

OVERLAY performs the same action as the Overlay option on the Format menu in
Excel version 2.2 or earlier. OVERLAY creates an overlay chart. The *type* argument
can have the following values:

Type	Chart
1	Area
2	Bar
3	Column
4	Line
5	Pie
6	Scatter

The *stacked, 100%, vary-by-cat, overlapped, drop-lines,* and *hi-lo-lines* arguments
correspond to check boxes. If one or more of these arguments are TRUE, they are
checked. The *overlap%, cluster%,* and *pie-angle* arguments are numbers. Arguments
that do not apply to a particular chart type are ignored for that type.

The OVERLAY function is included for compatibility with earlier versions of
Excel. With newer versions, use the FORMAT.OVERLAY macro function.

See Also

FORMAT.OVERLAY	Equivalent function	Macro Function

OVERLAY.CHART.TYPE(*type*)

Macro Function

OVERLAY.CHART.TYPE is the same as the Excel for the Apple Macintosh function
OVERLAY(type-1). This macro function is included for compatibility. It is the same
as DELETE.OVERLAY if the type argument is 0.

See Also

DELETE.OVERLAY	Related function	Macro Function

P

PAGE.SETUP(*[header]*,*[footer]*,*[l-margin]*,*[r-margin]*,*[top-margin]*,
[bottom-margin],*[headings]*,*[gridlines]*,*[h-center]*,*[v-center]*,
[orientation],*[paper-size]*,*[scale]*,*[page-number]*,*[page-order]*,
[bw-cells])
PAGE.SETUP?(*[header]*,*[footer]*,*[l-margin]*,*[r-margin]*,*[top-margin]*,
[bottom-margin],*[headings]*,*[gridlines]*,*[h-center]*,*[v-center]*,
[orientation],*[paper-size]*,*[scale]*,*[page-number]*,*[page-order]*,
[bw-cells])

Macro Function

PAGE.SETUP performs the same action as the Page Setup option on the File menu.
This argument profile is used for worksheets and macro sheets. (There is another
PAGE.SETUP argument profile for charts, detailed in the next entry.)

The *header* and *footer* arguments should be given as strings, and can include the
formatting codes listed here:

Code	Action
&B	Turns bold on or off
&C	Centers the following characters
&D	Prints the current date
&F	Prints the document name
&I	Turns italics on or off
&L	Left-aligns the following characters
&P	Prints the page number

Code	Action
&P+*number*	Prints the page number plus *number*
&P−*number*	Prints the page number minus *number*
&R	Right-aligns the following characters
&S	Turns overstrike on or off
&T	Prints the current time
&U	Turns underlining on or off
&&	Prints an ampersand (&)
& *font*	Prints the following characters in *font*
&*nn*	Prints the following characters in font size *nn*
&N	Prints the total number of pages

The margin arguments should be given as numbers. The *headings* argument and the *gridlines* argument are logical values; if they are TRUE the headings and grid lines are included. *H-center* and *v-center* are logical values; if they are TRUE the output is centered horizontally and vertically on the page.

Orientation is a number that determines the orientation of the output. If *orientation* is 1, the output is printed in portrait mode. If *orientation* is 2, the output is printed in landscape mode. If *orientation* is not included, the orientation remains unchanged. *Paper-size* is a number that indicates the size of the paper. The following table lists the possible values for *paper-size*:

Paper-Size	Description
1	Letter
2	Small letter
3	Tabloid
4	Ledger
5	Legal
6	Statement
7	Exccutive
8	A3
9	A4
10	Small A4
11	A5
12	B4
13	B5

P

Paper-Size	Description
14	Folio
15	Quarto
16	10×14
17	11×17
18	Note
19	ENV9
20	ENV10
21	ENV11
22	ENV12
23	ENV14
24	C sheet
25	D sheet
26	E sheet

Scale indicates how to shrink or enlarge the document on the page. *Scale* can be a number that is a percentage increase or decrease of the original size. *Scale* can also be a two-item array, where the first number is the number of pages on which to fit the document horizontally, and the second number is the number of pages on which to fit the document vertically. *Scale* can also be a logical value. If *scale* is TRUE, the document is scaled to fit on a single page.

Page-number is a number that sets the page number of the first page. *Page-order* is a number that indicates the order in which the pages will be printed. If *page-order* is 1, the pages are printed top to bottom, and then right. If *page-order* is 2, the pages are printed left to right, and then down.

Bw-cells is a logical value. If *bw-cells* is TRUE, Excel prints in black and white. If *bw-cells* is FALSE, Excel prints in color (on a color printer).

If any arguments are omitted, the corresponding setting remains unchanged.

The dialog box version (with the question mark) displays a dialog box. The arguments are used as default values for the dialog box that appears.

See Also

FILE PAGE SETUP	Equivalent Command	Menu Command
GET.DOCUMENT	Returns information about a document	Macro Function
PRINT	Prints the active document	Macro Function
WORKSPACE	Changes workspace settings	Macro Function

PAGE.SETUP(*[header]*,*[footer]*,*[l-margin]*,*[r-margin]*,*[top-margin]*,
[bottom-margin],*[size]*,*[h-center]*,*[v-center]*,*[orientation]*,*[paper-size]*,
[scale],*[page-number]*)
PAGE.SETUP?(*[header]*,*[footer]*,*[l-margin]*,*[r-margin]*,*[top-margin]*,
[bottom-margin],*[size]*,*[h-center]*,*[v-center]*,*[orientation]*,*[paper-size]*,
[scale],*[page-number]*)

Macro Function

PAGE.SETUP performs the same action as the Page Setup option on the File menu.
This argument profile is used for charts. (There is another PAGE.SETUP argument
profile for worksheets and macro sheets, detailed in the previous entry.)

The *header, footer, l-margin, r-margin, top-margin, bottom-margin, h-center, v-center,
orientation, paper-size, scale,* and *page-number* arguments are exactly the same as in the
worksheet and macro sheet profile. The *size* argument is a number that indicates how
to size the chart. The possible values for *size* are listed here:

Size	Description
1	Screen size
2	Fit to page
3	Full page

See Also

FILE PAGE SETUP	Equivalent Command	Menu Command
GET.DOCUMENT	Returns information about a document	Macro Function
PRINT	Prints the active document	Macro Function
WORKSPACE	Changes workspace settings	Macro Function

PARSE(*[string]*,*[ref]*)
PARSE?(*[string]*,*[ref]*)

Macro Function

PARSE performs the same action as the Parse option on the Data menu. PARSE
separates the text in the current selection and places the result in the range indicated
by *ref. String* is the parse line in the form of a text string. The parse line uses square
brackets to indicate how the text should be distributed. If *string* is omitted, Excel
guesses how to distribute the text. *Ref* is the reference to the upper-left cell of the
range where you want to place the resulting parsed data. In the dialog box version

(with the question mark), the argument, if included, is used as a default value for the dialog box that appears.

See Also

MID	Returns the middle of a string	Function
SEARCH	Performs a non-case-sensitive search	Function

PASTE(*[ref]*)

Macro Function

PASTE performs the same action as the Paste option on the Edit menu. PASTE places the object or selection that you identified using the CUT or COPY function in the destination specified with *ref*. If *ref* is omitted, the identified object or selection is pasted to the current selection.

COPY	Copies a selection or an object	Macro Function
CUT	Cuts a selection or an object	Macro Function
PASTE.SPECIAL	Pastes attributes of a selection or an object	Macro Function

PASTE.LINK()

Macro Function

PASTE.LINK performs the same action as the Paste Link option on the Edit menu. PASTE.LINK pastes copied data or objects and establishes a link between the destination document and the source document. The source of the data or objects may be an Excel worksheet or may be another application. Objects or data pasted in the destination with PASTE.LINK will update when the source is updated.

See Also

COPY	Copies a selection or an object	Macro Function
CUT	Cuts a selection or an object	Macro Function
PASTE	Pastes a selection or an object	Macro Function
PASTE.SPECIAL	Pastes attributes of a selection or an object	Macro Function

PASTE.PICTURE()

Macro Function

PASTE.PICTURE pastes onto the worksheet a picture of whatever is in the Clipboard.

See Also

| COPY.PICTURE | Places a picture of the selection in the Clipboard | Macro Function |
| PASTE.PICTURE. LINK | Pastes and links a picture of the last selection | Macro Function |

PASTE.PICTURE.LINK()

Macro Function

PASTE.PICTURE.LINK performs the same action as the Camera Tool on the Utility toolbar. PASTE.PICTURE.LINK pastes onto the current document a linked picture of whatever is in the Clipboard. The source of the picture and the destination are linked, so when you change the picture at the source, these changes will be reflected in the destination.

See Also

| COPY.PICTURE | Places a copy of the selected picture into the Clipboard | Macro Function |
| PASTE.PICTURE | Pastes a picture from the Clipboard | Macro Function |

PASTE.SPECIAL(*attribute, operation, skip-blanks, transpose*)
PASTE.SPECIAL?(*[attribute], [operation], [skip-blanks], [transpose]*)

Macro Function   (Argument Profile 1)

PASTE.SPECIAL performs the same action as the Paste Special option from the Edit menu. It pastes certain attributes of a selection that has been identified with the CUT or COPY function. PASTE.SPECIAL also allows you to combine the data in the destination range with the data identified with the CUT or COPY function by performing an arithmetic operation on the numbers if you are pasting onto worksheets or macro sheets.

There are four argument profiles for PASTE.SPECIAL. The profile you should use depends on the documents you are working with:

Argument Profile	Use
1	Pasting from a worksheet to a worksheet
2	Pasting from a worksheet to a chart
3	Pasting from a chart to a chart
4	Pasting from another application

Make sure that you use the correct version of PASTE.SPECIAL for your situation. In the dialog box versions (with the question marks), the arguments (when included) are used as default values for the dialog boxes that appear.

Argument profile 1 is used to paste from a worksheet to a worksheet. The *attribute* argument allows you to specify which worksheet items you want to paste. Possible values for *attribute* are listed here:

Attribute	Items To Be Pasted
1	All
2	Formulas
3	Values
4	Formats
5	Notes

The *operation* argument allows you to choose the operation to be performed on the paste range.

Operation	Description
1	None
2	Addition
3	Subtraction
4	Multiplication
5	Division

The *skip-blanks* argument is a logical value. If it is TRUE, blanks will not be pasted. If it is FALSE, blanks will be pasted.

The *transpose* argument is also a logical value. If it is TRUE, the rows and columns of the selection will be transposed. If it is FALSE, the selection is pasted the same way it was copied.

PASTE.SPECIAL(*rowcol, series, categories, replace*)
PASTE.SPECIAL?(*[rowcol], [series], [categories], [replace]*)

Macro Function   **(Argument Profile 2)**

Argument profile 2 of PASTE.SPECIAL is used to paste from a worksheet to a chart.

The *rowcol* argument is a number that indicates whether the series are in rows or in columns. If *rowcol* is 1, the series are in rows. If *rowcol* is 2, the series are in columns.

Series is a logical argument. If *series* is TRUE, the labels in the first row or column of the selection are used as the series names. If *series* if FALSE, the data in the first row or the first column is used as the first data points.

Categories is also a logical value. If *categories* is TRUE, the contents of the first row or column are used as the categories for the chart. If *categories* is FALSE, the contents of the first row or column of the selection are used as the first data series.

Replace is a logical value. If *replace* is TRUE, Excel replaces existing categories with information from the copied cell range. If *replace* is FALSE, no categories are replaced.

PASTE.SPECIAL(*paste*)
PASTE.SPECIAL?(*[paste]*)

Macro Function   **(Argument Profile 3)**

Argument profile 3 of PASTE.SPECIAL is used to paste from a chart to a chart. The *paste* argument indicates what part of the chart to paste. The following table gives the possible values for *paste*:

Paste	Chart Items
1	All
2	Formats
3	Data series

PASTE.SPECIAL(*data-type, logical*)
PASTE.SPECIAL?(*[data-type], [logical]*)

Macro Function   **(Argument Profile 4)**

Argument profile 4 of PASTE.SPECIAL is used to paste from another application.

The *data-type* argument is a text string that is a valid data type. For example, "Text" is a valid data type. The *logical* argument should be TRUE if you want to link the source to the pasted data, and FALSE otherwise.

P

PASTE.TOOL(*bar,position*)

Macro Function   **New to Version 4.0**

The PASTE.TOOL function performs the same action as the Paste Tool Face option on the Edit menu. PASTE.TOOL pastes a tool face from the Clipboard to a toolbar. The *bar* argument is the name or the number of the toolbar onto which you want to paste the tool face. The possible values for *bar* are listed here:

Bar	Toolbar
1	Standard
2	Formatting
3	Utility
4	Chart
5	Drawing
6	Excel 3.0
7	Macro
8	Macro recording
9	Macro paused

The *position* argument is the position on the toolbar where you want to place the tool face. *Position* is numbered starting with 1 at the left or top of the toolbar, depending on the toolbar's orientation.

Example

=PASTE.TOOL(7,2) copies the tool face in the Clipboard (put there with the COPY.TOOL function) to the Macro toolbar at position 2.

See Also

COPY.TOOL   Copies a tool face to the Clipboard   Macro Function

PATTERNS(*[area]*,*[fcolor]*,*[bcolor]*)
PATTERNS?(*[area]*,*[fcolor]*,*[bcolor]*)

Macro Function   **(Argument Profile 1)**

PATTERNS performs the same action as the Patterns option on the Format menu. PATTERNS formats the selected cells, objects, or chart items with patterns. In the dialog box versions (with the question marks), any arguments included are used as default values for the dialog boxes that appear.

There are eight argument profiles for PATTERNS. The profile you should use depends on the item you are formatting.

Argument Profile	Items To Be Formatted
1	Cells
2	Lines or arrows on worksheets or charts
3	Arcs, ovals, rectangles, pictures, and text boxes on worksheets and macro sheets
4	Bars, columns, pie slices, plot areas, and text labels on charts
5	Chart axes
6	Drop lines, grid lines, hi-lo lines, lines on a line chart, and picture charts
7	Data lines on charts
8	Picture chart markers

Make sure that you use the correct version of PATTERNS for your situation. Argument profile 1 is used for formatting cells.

The *area* argument is a number corresponding to the patterns available in the Patterns drop-down list box within the Patterns dialog box, shown in Figure P-1.

The *fcolor* and *bcolor* arguments are numbers that correspond to the 16 available colors listed in the Foreground and Background drop-down list boxes in the Patterns dialog box. The *fcolor* argument sets the foreground color and the *bcolor* argument sets the background color.

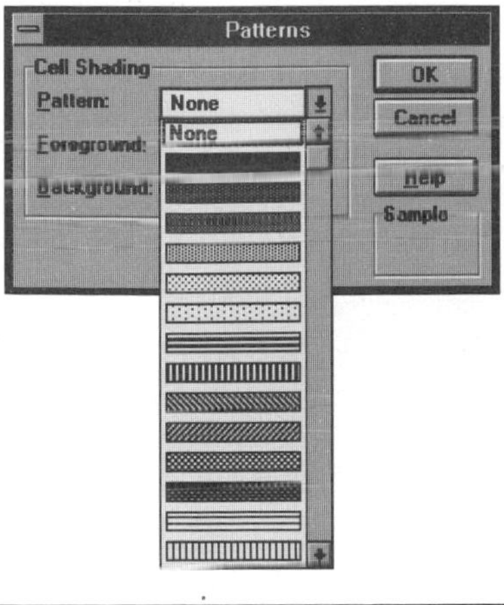

Figure P-1. *The Patterns drop-down list box*

PATTERNS(*[auto-line]*,*[line-style]*,*[line-color]*,*[line-weight]*,
[arrowhead-width],*[arrowhead-length]*,*[arrowhead-type]*)
PATTERNS?(*[auto-line]*,*[line-style]*,*[line-color]*,*[line-weight]*,
[arrowhead-width],*[arrowhead-length]*,*[arrowhead-type]*)

Macro Function   **(Argument Profile 2)**

Argument profile 2 of PATTERNS is used for formatting lines or arrows on worksheets or charts. The arguments correspond to the options in the Patterns dialog box
that appears when you select a line or arrow, then choose the Patterns option from
the Format menu. The dialog box (with an arrow selected) is shown here:

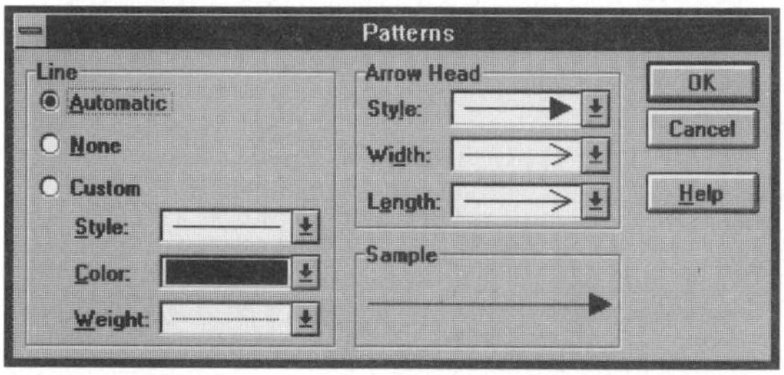

The *auto-line* argument is a number that specifies the line settings. The possible
values for *auto-line* are listed here:

Auto-Line	Description
0	Custom
1	Automatic
2	None

The *line-style* argument is a number from 1 to 8 corresponding to one of the eight
line styles available in the Patterns dialog box.

The *line-color* argument is a number from 1 to 16 corresponding to one of the 16
colors available in the Patterns dialog box.

Line-weight is a number from 1 to 4 corresponding to one of the four line weights
available in the Patterns dialog box. The possible values for *line-weight* are listed here:

Line-Weight	Description
1	Hairline
2	Thin

Line-Weight	Description
3	Medium
4	Thick

Arrowhead-width is a number from 1 to 3 that sets the width of the arrowhead. The possible values for *arrowhead-width* are listed here:

Arrowhead-Width	Description
1	Narrow
2	Medium
3	Wide

Arrowhead-length is a number from 1 to 3 that sets the length of the arrowhead. The possible values for *arrowhead-length* are listed here:

Arrowhead-Length	Description
1	Short
2	Medium
3	Long

Arrowhead-type is a number from 1 to 3 that sets the type of arrowhead. The possible values for *arrowhead-type* are listed here:

Arrowhead-Type	Description
1	No head
2	Open head
3	Closed head

PATTERNS(*[auto-border]*, *[border-style]*, *[border color]*, *[border-weight]*, *[shadow]*, *[auto area]*, *[pattern]*, *[foreground]*, *[background]*, *[rounded]*)
PATTERNS?(*[auto-border]*, *[border-style]*, *[border-color]*, *[border-weight]*, *[shadow]*, *[auto-area]*, *[pattern]*, *[foreground]*, *[background]*, *[rounded]*)

Macro Function   **(Argument Profile 3)**

Argument profile 3 of PATTERNS is used for formatting arcs, ovals, rectangles, pictures, and text boxes on worksheets and macro sheets.

The *auto-border* argument is a number from 0 to 2 that indicates the border settings. The possible values for *auto-border* are listed here:

Auto-Border	Description
0	Custom
1	Automatic
2	None

Border-style is a number from 1 to 8 corresponding to one of the eight border styles available in the Patterns dialog box.

Border-color is a number from 1 to 16 corresponding to one of the 16 colors available in the Patterns dialog box.

Border-weight is a number from 1 to 4 corresponding to one of the four border widths available in the Patterns dialog box. The possible values for *border-weight* are listed here:

Border-Weight	Description
1	Hairline
2	Thin
3	Medium
4	Thick

Shadow is TRUE or FALSE. If *shadow* is TRUE, a shadow is added to the selection. If *shadow* is FALSE, no shadow is added.

Auto-area is a number from 0 to 2 that indicates the area settings. The possible values for *auto-area* are listed here:

Auto-Area	Description
0	Custom
1	Automatic
2	None

Pattern is a number corresponding to one of the available patterns in the Patterns dialog box. *Foreground* is a number from 1 to 16 corresponding to one of the 16 available foreground colors listed in the Patterns dialog box. *Background* is a number from 1 to 16 corresponding to one of the 16 available background colors listed in the Patterns dialog box.

Rounded is TRUE or FALSE. If it is TRUE, the corners of the selection are rounded. If it is FALSE, the corners are not rounded.

PATTERNS(*[auto-border]*,*[border-style]*,*[border-color]*,*[border-weight]*, *[shadow]*,*[auto-area]*,*[pattern]*,*[foreground]*,*[background]*,*[invert]*, *[apply-to-all]*)
PATTERNS?(*[auto-border]*,*[border-style]*,*[border-color]*,*[border-weight]*, *[shadow]*,*[auto-area]*,*[pattern]*,*[foreground]*,*[background]*,*[invert]*, *[apply-to-all]*)

Macro Function   **(Argument Profile 4)**

Argument profile 4 of PATTERNS is used for formatting bars, columns, pie slices, plot areas, and text labels on charts.

Invert is a logical value. If the item represents a negative number, the pattern is inverted if *invert* is TRUE. If *invert* is FALSE, the pattern is not inverted when representing negative numbers.

Apply-to-all is a logical value. If *apply-to-all* is TRUE, the formatting changes are applied to all items similar to the selected item. If *apply-to-all* is FALSE, the formatting is applied only to the selection.

PATTERNS(*[auto-line]*,*[line-style]*,*[line-color]*,*[line-weight]*, *[major-ticks]*,*[minor-ticks]*,*[tick-labels]*)
PATTERNS?(*[auto-line]*,*[line-style]*,*[line-color]*,*[line-weight]*, *[major-ticks]*,*[minor-ticks]*,*[tick-labels]*)

Macro Function   **(Argument Profile 5)**

Argument profile 5 of PATTERNS is used for formatting chart axes.

Major-ticks and *minor-ticks* are numbers from 1 to 4 that set the major and minor tick mark types. The possible values for *major-ticks* and *minor-ticks* are listed here:

Ticks	Description
1	None
2	Inside
3	Outside
4	Cross

Tick-labels is a number from 1 to 4 that set the position of the tick labels. The possible values for *tick-labels* are listed here:

Tick-Labels	Description
1	None
2	Low

P

Tick-Labels	Description
3	High
4	Next to axes

PATTERNS (*[auto-line]*, *[line-style]*, *[line-color]*, *[line-weight]*)
PATTERNS? (*[auto-line]*, *[line-style]*, *[line-color]*, *[line-weight]*)

Macro Function   **(Argument Profile 6)**

Argument profile 6 of PATTERNS is used for formatting picture charts, as well as drop lines, grid lines, hi-lo lines, lines on line charts. For descriptions of the arguments in profile 6, see the PATTERNS entry for argument profile 2.

PATTERNS (*[auto-line]*, *[line-style]*, *[line-color]*, *[line-weight]*,
[auto-marker], *[marker-style]*, *[foreground]*, *[background]*, *[apply-to-all]*)
PATTERNS? (*[auto-line]*, *[line-style]*, *[line-color]*, *[line-weight]*,
[auto-marker], *[marker-style]*, *[foreground]*, *[background]*, *[apply-to-all]*)

Macro Function   **(Argument Profile 7)**

Argument profile 7 of PATTERNS is used for formatting data lines on charts.

The *auto-marker* argument is a number from 0 to 2 that indicates the marker setting. The possible values for *auto-marker* are listed here:

Auto-Marker	Description
0	Custom
1	Automatic
2	None

The *marker-style* argument is a number from 1 to 9 that corresponds to one of the nine available marker styles shown in the Patterns dialog box.

For descriptions of the other arguments in profile 7, review the preceding PATTERNS entries.

PATTERNS (*[type]*, *[units]*, *[apply-to-all]*)
PATTERNS? (*[type]*, *[units]*, *[apply-to-all]*)

Macro Function   **(Argument Profile 8)**

Argument profile 8 of PATTERNS is used for formatting picture chart markers.

The *type* argument is a number that indicates the type of picture being used. The possible values for *type* are listed here:

Type	Description
1	Picture is stretched to reach a value
2	Picture is stacked to reach a value
3	Picture is stacked and units are specified

If the *type* argument is set to 3, the units of the scaled stacked picture chart are set with the *units* argument. If *type* is anything but 3, this argument is ignored.

Apply-to-all is a logical value. If *apply-to-all* is TRUE, the formatting changes are applied to all items similar to the selected item. If *apply-to-all* is FALSE, the formatting is applied only to the selection.

See Also

FORMAT.FONT	Applies a font to selected text	Macro Function
FORMAT PATTERNS	Equivalent command	Menu Command
FORMAT.TEXT	Formats text	Macro Function

PAUSE(*[no-resume]*)

Macro Function   **New to Version 4.0**

PAUSE causes a macro to pause. You may want to pause a macro so that you can work directly with Excel or enter data. You can run other macros while a macro is paused.

The *no-resume* argument indicates whether or not to display the Resume toolbar when you pause the macro. If *no-resume* is TRUE, the Resume toolbar is not displayed. If *no-resume* is FALSE, the Resume toolbar is displayed.

When you want to resume the macro, you can click on the Resume button on the toolbar or choose the Macro Resume menu option.

See Also

HALT	Halts all macros	Macro Function
MACRO RESUME	Resumes a paused macro	Menu Command
RESUME	Resumes a paused macro	Macro Function
STEP	Allows single-step movement through a macro	Macro Function

P

PEARSON(*independent, dependent*)

Function   **New to Version 4.0**

PEARSON calculates the product moment correlation coefficient, which is a dimensionless index ranging from −1.0 to 1.0 reflecting the extent of the linear relationship between an independent data set and a dependent data set. *Independent* is an array of independent values. *Dependent* is an array of dependent values.

Example

=PEARSON({8,6,4,3,2},{6,7,8,4,5}) returns 0.393919.

See Also

INTERCEPT	Returns the intercept	Function
LINEST	Returns linear trend parameters	Function
SLOPE	Returns the slope	Function

PERCENTILE(*data, K*)

Function   **New to Version 4.0**

PERCENTILE returns the *K*th percentile value from the *data* set. *Data* can be given as either a range or an array.

Example

=PERCENTILE({1,3,5,7,9},0.5) returns 5.

See Also

LARGE	Returns the *K*th largest value	Function
MAX	Returns the largest value	Function
MEDIAN	Returns the median	Function
MIN	Returns the smallest value	Function

PERCENTRANK(*data, X, [sig]*)

Function   **New to Version 4.0**

PERCENTRANK returns the percentage rank of *X* in the data set. *Data* can be given as either a range or an array. *Sig* is an optional argument that indicates the number of significant digits returned in the result. If *sig* is omitted, the default value is 3.

Example

=PERCENTRANK({1,3,5,7,9},2) returns 0.125.

See Also

LARGE	Returns the *K*th largest value	Function
MAX	Returns the largest value	Function
MEDIAN	Returns the median	Function
MIN	Returns the smallest value	Function

PERMUT(*total, group*)

Function   **New to Version 4.0**

PERMUT returns the number of permutations of the total number of objects. *Group* is the number of objects in each permutation.

The equation for PERMUT is as follows.

$$P_{k,n} = \frac{n!}{(n-k)!}$$

Example

=PERMUT(20,2) returns 380.

See Also

COMBIN	Returns the number of possible combinations	Function

P

PI()

Function

Returns the value π which is approximately 3.14159265359, the ratio of the circumference of a circle to its diameter.

Example

=PI() * 8^2 returns 201.06, which is the area of a circle whose radius is 8.

See Also

COS	Returns the cosine of a number	Function
SIN	Returns the sine of a number	Function
TAN	Returns the tangent of a number	Function

PMT(*interest, number-of-periods, present-value, [future-value], [type]*)

Function

PMT returns the payment amount for a loan given the interest and the loan terms. *Interest* represents the interest rate. *Number-of-periods* is the number of payment periods in the life of the loan. *Present-value* is the current value of the loan. *Future-value* is an optional argument. If it is omitted, the future value of the loan is assumed to be $0. If it is included, it represents the balance that you wish to obtain after the last payment is made. *Type* is an optional argument. A *type* of 1 means that payments are due at the beginning of the period. A *type* of 0 means that payments are due at the end of the period. If the *type* argument is omitted, type 0 is assumed.

Example

=PMT(10%/12,12,0,9000) returns –716.24.

=PMT(10%/12,48,9000) returns –228.26.

See Also

FV	Returns the future value	Function
IPMT	Returns the interest payment	Function
NPER	Returns the number of payment periods	Function

PPMT	Returns the principle payment	Function
PV	Returns the present value	Function
RATE	Returns the interest rate	Function

POISSON(*X, mean, cum*)

Function   **New to Version 4.0**

POISSON returns the Poisson probability distribution given *X* (the number of events) and the mean. *Cum* is a logical value that determines the form of the POISSON function used. If *cum* is TRUE, the POISSON function determines the probability that the number of random events will occur between 0 and *X*. If *cum* is FALSE, POISSON determines the probability mass function that *X* number of events will occur.

Example

=POISSON(3,8,TRUE) returns 0.04238.

See Also

| EXPONDIST | Determines the exponential distribution | Function |

POKE(*channel, item-name, document*)

Macro Function

POKE causes the data in the specified document to be sent to the item name in the application connected to the specified channel. The channel must have been opened by the INITIATE function. If the *channel* number is not valid, POKE returns a #VALUE! error. If the user presses the ESCAPE key before the application answers, POKE returns a #DIV/0! error. If the application refuses POKE's request, POKE returns a #REF! error.

See Also

INITIATE	Initiates a channel to an application	Macro Function
REQUEST	Gets data from another application	Macro Function
TERMINATE	Terminates a channel to another application	Macro Function

P

PPMT(*interest, period, number-of-periods, present-value, [future-value], [type]*)

Function

PPMT returns the principle payment amount for a loan given the interest and the loan terms. The *period* argument is the period for which you want to find the principle payment. *Period* must be a number between 1 and *number-of-periods*. *Number-of-periods* is the total number of payment periods. *Present-value* is the value of the loan at this time. *Future-value* is an optional argument. If this argument is omitted, the future value of the loan is assumed to be $0. If it is included, it represents the balance that you wish to obtain after the last payment is made. *Type* is an optional argument. A *type* of 1 means that payments are due at the beginning of the period. A *type* of 0 means that payments are due at the end of the period. If the *type* argument is omitted, it is assumed to be of *type* 0.

Example

=PPMT(10%/12,1,48,9000) returns −153.26.

See Also

FV	Returns the future value	Function
IPMT	Returns the interest payment	Function
NPER	Returns the number of payment periods	Function
PPMT	Returns the principle payment	Function
PV	Returns the present value	Function
RATE	Returns the interest rate	Function

PRECISION(*[logical]*)

Macro Function

Using PRECISION is the same as choosing the Calculation option on the Options menu then clicking on the Precision As Displayed check box in the Calculation dialog box. PRECISION determines how values are saved in cells. If *logical* is TRUE, values are stored with 15 digits of precision. If *logical* is FALSE, values in cells are stored as they are displayed.

See Also

FORMAT.NUMBER	Formats numbers in the selection	Macro Function
WORKSPACE	Sets workspace settings	Macro Function

PREFERRED()

Macro Function

PREFERRED performs the same action as the Preferred option on the Gallery menu. It sets the format of the active chart to the preferred chart type. You can set the preferred chart type with the SET.PREFERRED function or the Set Preferred option on the Gallery menu.

See Also

GALLERY PREFERRED	Equivalent Command	Menu Command
GALLERY SET PREFERRED	Sets the preferred chart type	Menu Command
SET.PREFERRED	Sets the preferred chart type	Macro Function

PRESS.TOOL(*bar,position,[down]*)

Macro Function   **New to Version 4.0**

PRESS.TOOL causes the tool identified by the *bar* and *position* arguments to move either up or down on the toolbar. *Bar* is the name or number of the toolbar. The names and numbers of Excel's built-in toolbars are listed here:

Bar Number	Toolbar Name
1	Standard
2	Formatting
3	Utility
4	Chart
5	Drawing
6	Excel 3.0
7	Macro
8	Macro recording
9	Macro paused

The *position* argument is the position of the tool on the toolbar. Positions are numbered starting with 1 on the left or top, depending on the orientation of the toolbar.

Down is a logical value. If *down* is TRUE, the tool is moved down in the toolbar. If *down* is FALSE, the tool is moved up. If *down* is omitted, the default value is FALSE.

P

See Also

ADD.TOOL	Adds a tool to a toolbar	Macro Function
DELETE.TOOL	Deletes a tool from a toolbar	Macro Function

PRICE(*settlement, maturity, rate, yield, redemption, frequency, [basis-code]*)

Function   **New to Version 4.0**

PRICE returns the price per $100 face value of a security where interest is paid periodically. *Settlement* is the serial number of the security's settlement date. *Maturity* is the date serial number of the security's maturity date.

The *rate* argument represents the annual coupon rate of the security. *Yield* is the annual yield of the security. *Redemption* is the redemption value per $100 face value of the security. *Frequency* is the frequency of payments. The possible values for *frequency* are as follows.

Frequency	Payment
1	Annual
2	Semi-annual
4	Quarterly

The *basis-code* is the day count basis. The following table lists the possible values for *basis-code*:

Basis-Code	Day Count
0	30/360
1	Actual/Actual
2	Actual/360
3	Actual/365

The default value for *basis-code* is 0.

PRICE is an add-in function. The first time you use it, you may see a #REF! error while Excel loads the function.

Example

=PRICE(DATE(93,6,15),DATE(93,12,15),6%,7%,100,4,0) returns 99.51283. The price per $100 face value of a security whose settlement date is June 15, 1993 and whose maturity date is December 15, 1993, with a coupon rate of 6 percent, a yield of 7 percent, a $100 redemption value, four payments per year, and a 30/360 day count basis, is $99.51.

See Also

DATE	Returns the serial number of a date	Function
YIELD	Returns the yield of a security	Function

PRICEDISC(*settlement, maturity, discount, redemption, [basis-code]*)

Function   **New to Version 4.0**

PRICEDISC returns the price per $100 face value of a discounted security. *Settlement* is the date serial number of the security's settlement date. *Maturity* is the date serial number of the security's maturity date.

The *discount* argument represents the discount rate of the security. *Redemption* is the redemption value per $100 face value of the security. The *basis-code* is the day count basis. The following table lists the possible values for *basis-code*:

Basis-Code	Day Count
0	30/360
1	Actual/Actual
2	Actual/360
3	Actual/365

The default value for *basis code* is 0.

PRICEDISC is an add-in function. The first time you use it, you may see a #REF! error while Excel loads the function.

Example

=PRICEDISC(DATE(93,6,15),DATE(93,12,15),6%,100,0) returns 97. The price per $100 face value of a discounted security whose settlement date is June 15, 1993 and whose maturity date is December 15, 1993, and which has a coupon rate of 6 percent, a $100 redemption value, and a 30/360 day count basis, is $97.

See Also

DATE	Returns the serial number of a date	Function
DISC	Returns the discount rate of a security	Function
YIELDDISC	Returns the yield of a discounted security	Function

P

PRICEMAT(*settlement, maturity, issue, rate, yield, [basis-code]*)

Function   **New to Version 4.0**

PRICEMAT returns the price per $100 face value of a security where interest is paid at maturity. *Settlement* is the date serial number of the security's settlement date. *Maturity* is the date serial number of the security's maturity date. *Issue* is the date serial number of the security's issue date.

The *rate* is the interest rate of the security at the time it was issued. *Yield* is the annual yield of the security.

The *basis-code* is the day count basis. The following table lists the possible values for *basis-code*:

Basis-Code	Day Count
0	30/360
1	Actual/Actual
2	Actual/360
3	Actual/365

The default value for *basis-code* is 0.

PRICEMAT is an add-in function. The first time you use it, you may see a #REF! error while Excel loads the function.

Example

=PRICEMAT(DATE(93,6,15),DATE(93,12,15),DATE(93,1,1),6%,6%,0) returns 99.92039. The price per $100 face value of a security whose interest is paid at maturity, whose settlement date is June 15, 1993, whose maturity date is December 15, 1993, and whose issue date is January 1, 1993, and which has a coupon rate of 6 percent, a 6 percent yield, and a 30/360 day count basis, is $99.92039.

See Also

DATE	Returns the serial number of a date	Function
DISC	Returns the discount rate of a security	Function
YIELDDISC	Returns the yield of a discounted security	Function
YIELDMAT	Returns the yield of a security	Function

PRINT(*[all-or-part], [first-page], [last-page], [number-of-copies],*
[draft-quality], [preview], [attributes], [color], [feed], [quality],
[vertical-quality])
PRINT?(*[all-or-part], [first-page], [last-page], [number-of-copies],*
[draft-quality], [preview], [attributes], [color], [feed], [quality],
[vertical-quality])

Macro Function

PRINT performs the same action as the Print option on the File menu. It prints the
active document. In the dialog box version (with the question mark), the arguments,
if included, are used as default values for the Print dialog box that appears. The Print
dialog box is shown here:

The *all-or-part* argument can be either 1 (print all) or 2 (print part). If the *all-or-part*
argument is 1, the *first-page* and *last-page* arguments are ignored. If the *all-or-part*
argument is 2, the pages from *first-page* to *last-page* are printed.

The *number-of-copies* argument indicates the number of copies of the document
that you want to print. The *draft-quality* and *preview* arguments correspond to the
check boxes in the File Print dialog box. If TRUE, the check box is turned on. If FALSE,
the check box is turned off. If omitted, the status of the check box is unchanged.

The *attributes* argument (only applicable if the document is a worksheet or macro)
determines what *attributes* of the document will be printed, and can have the following
values:

Attributes	Items Printed
1	Worksheet or macro
2	Notes
3	Both

P

The *color* and *feed* arguments are used only in Excel for the Macintosh.

The *quality* argument corresponds to the setting in the Print Quality drop box within the Print dialog box. *Quality* sets the print quality of the output.

The *vertical-quality* argument also corresponds to the setting in the Print Quality drop box, if you have a printer where horizontal and vertical resolution is set separately. *Vertical-quality* sets the vertical resolution of the output.

Example

=PRINT(2,1,3,2,TRUE,FALSE,1) prints two copies of pages 1 through 3 of the active worksheet or macro sheet in draft mode without previewing and without notes.

See Also

FILE PRINT	Equivalent command	Menu Command
PAGE.SETUP	Sets printing options	Macro Function
PRINT.PREVIEW	Previews the printed document	Macro Function
PRINTER.SETUP	Sets the active printer	Macro Function
SET.PRINT.AREA	Sets the print area	Macro Function
SET.PRINT.TITLES	Sets the print titles	Macro Function

PRINT.PREVIEW()

Macro Function   **New to Version 4.0**

PRINT.PREVIEW performs the same action as the Print Preview option on the File menu. PRINT.PREVIEW causes Excel to display the active document on the screen as it would appear when printed.

PRINTER.SETUP(*printer-name*)
PRINTER.SETUP?(*printer-name*)

Macro Function

PRINTER.SETUP performs the same action as the Page Setup option on the File menu. PRINTER.SETUP establishes which printer you will be printing to. Enter the *printer-name* argument as a string precisely as it appears in the Page Setup dialog box, shown in Figure P-2.

In the dialog box version (with the question mark), the arguments, if included, are used as default values for the dialog box that appears.

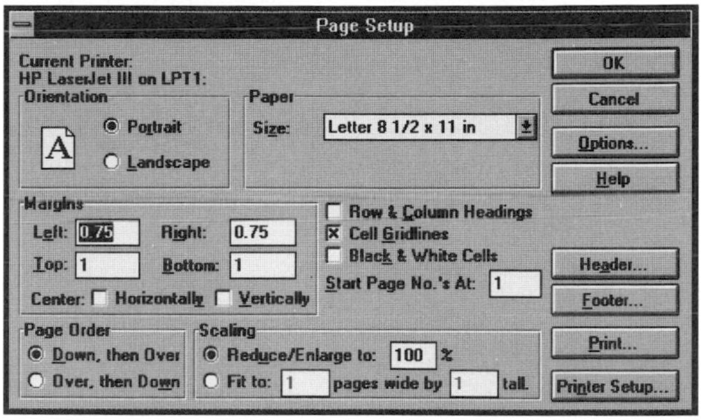

Figure P-2. *The Page Setup dialog box*

See Also

PAGE.SETUP	Sets printing options	Macro Function
PRINT	Prints the active document	Macro Function

PROB(*range,probabilities,lower,[upper]*)

Function   New to Version 4.0

PROB determines the probability that the values in the specified range fall between the lower and upper limits. *Range* is a reference to a range or an array containing numeric x values, and *probabilities* is a reference to a range or an array containing probabilities associated with those values. The values in the probabilities range or array must add up to 1. *Lower* and *upper* are the bounds on the value for which you are determining the probability. If *upper* is omitted, PROB determines the probability that the x values are equal to the *lower* limit.

Example

=PROB({0.2.3.4.5},{0.1,0.2,0.4,0.2,0.1},2) returns 0.2.

See Also

BINOMDIST	Returns the binomial distribution	Function

P

PRODUCT(*x1,x2,...xN*)

Function

PRODUCT returns the product of the arguments *x1* through *xN*. Arguments can be anything but errors or text that cannot be translated into numbers. There can be up to 30 arguments. Each of the arguments can also be a range of cells on the worksheet.

Example

=PRODUCT(1,4,6,2) returns 48. If the numbers (1, 4, 6, 2) were in cells A1 through D1, =PRODUCT(A1:D1) would also return 48.

See Also

FACT	Returns the factorial of an argument	Function
SUM	Returns the sum of a list of numbers	Function

PROMOTE([*rowcol*])
PROMOTE?([*rowcol*])

Macro Function

Using PROMOTE has the same effect as choosing the Promote button. It promotes the current selection in an outline. *Rowcol* determines whether to promote rows or columns. If *rowcol* is 1, rows are promoted. If *rowcol* is 2, columns are promoted. If *rowcol* is omitted, the default value is 1.

See Also

DEMOTE	Demotes the current selection in an outline	Macro Function
SHOW.DETAIL	Expands or collapses an outline	Macro Function
SHOW.LEVELS	Shows specified levels of an outline	Macro Function

PROPER(*string*)

Function

PROPER converts the first letter of all words in a string to uppercase and the remaining letters to lowercase, as in a proper name.

Example

=PROPER("the little RED HEN") would be converted to "The Little Red Hen."

See Also

LOWER	Converts text to lowercase	Function
UPPER	Converts text to uppercase	Function

PROTECT.DOCUMENT(*[contents]*, *[windows]*, *[password]*, *[objects]*)
PROTECT.DOCUMENT?(*[contents]*, *[windows]*, *[password]*, *[objects]*)

Macro Function

PROTECT.DOCUMENT is the same as the Protect Document option on the Options menu if the active document is a worksheet or macro and either or both of the *contents* and *windows* arguments are TRUE. It is the same as the Protect Document option on the Chart menu if the active document is a chart and either or both the *contents* and *windows* arguments are TRUE. It is the same as the Unprotect Document option on the Options menu if the active document is a worksheet or macro and both the *windows* and *contents* arguments are FALSE. It is the same as the Unprotect Document option on the Chart menu if the active document is a chart and both the *windows* and *contents* arguments are FALSE.

The *contents* argument is TRUE if you want to protect the active document's cells or the active chart's chart. If *contents* is FALSE, the active document is unprotected, provided that the appropriate *password* is supplied. The default value for *contents* is TRUE.

If the *windows* argument is TRUE, the document's window cannot be moved or sized. If the *windows* argument is FALSE, the document's window can be moved and sized, provided that the appropriate password is supplied. The default value for *windows* is FALSE.

You use the *password* argument to provide a password if you are unprotecting a document, or to set a new password if you are protecting a document. If you don't set a password when you protect a document, you can unprotect the document without a password.

If the *objects* argument is TRUE, PROTECT protects all locked objects on the worksheet or macro sheet. If the *objects* argument is FALSE, protection is removed from the objects on the worksheet or macro sheet, provided that the appropriate password is supplied. The default value for *objects* is TRUE.

The arguments correspond to the check boxes in the dialog box. In the dialog box version (with the question mark), the arguments, if included, are used as default values for the dialog box that appears.

P

Example

=PROTECT.DOCUMENT(FALSE,FALSE,"dog",FALSE) removes all protection from the document.

See Also

CELL.PROTECTION	Protects or unprotects cells	Macro Function
OPTIONS PROTECT DOCUMENT	Equivalent command	Menu Command
OPTIONS UNPROTECT DOCUMENT	Equivalent command	Menu Command

PTTESTM(*input1,input2,output,[labels],[confidence],[difference]*)

Macro Function   **New to Version 4.0**

PTTESTM determines if the means of the two input samples are equal by performing a paired two-sample student's t-Test, assuming equal variances.

The *input1* and *input2* arguments are ranges where the data is in one column or row, and optionally, labels are included. If labels are included, the input ranges should be two columns or rows wide, where the labels are in the first column or row, and the data in the second column or row. The *labels* argument should be set to TRUE. If no labels are included, the input ranges should be one row or column wide and the *labels* argument should be FALSE. The default value for *labels* is FALSE.

Confidence is the confidence level for the t-Test. If the confidence argument is not given, the default value is 0.05.

Difference is the hypothetical mean difference. If the difference argument is not given, the default value is 0.

PTTESTM is an add-in function. The first time that you use it, you may see a #REF! error while Excel loads the function.

See Also

PTTESTV	Similar function, assuming unequal variance	Macro Function
TDIST	Returns Student's t-distribution	Macro Function
TEST	Returns Student's t-Test	Macro Function

PTTESTV(*input1,input2,output,[labels],[confidence]*)

Macro Function   **New to Version 4.0**

PTTESTV determines if the means of the two input samples are equal by performing a paired two-sample student's t-Test, assuming unequal variances.

The *input1* and *input2* arguments are ranges where the data is in one column or row, and optionally, labels are included. If labels are included, the input ranges should be two columns or rows wide, where the labels are in the first column or row, and the data in the second column or row. The *labels* argument should be set to TRUE. If no labels are included, the input ranges should be one row or column wide and the *labels* argument should be FALSE. The default value for *labels* is FALSE.

Confidence is the confidence level for the t-Test. If the *confidence* argument is not given, the default value is 0.05.

PTTESTV is an add-in function. The first time that you use it, you may see a #REF! error while Excel loads the function.

See Also

PTTESTM	Similar function, assuming equal variance	Macro Function
TDIST	Returns Student's t-distribution	Macro Function
TEST	Returns Student's t-Test	Macro Function

PV(*interest,number-of-periods,payment,[future-value],[type]*)

Function

PV returns the present value of a series of equal payments for a specified term and interest rate. The number of periods and interest rate must be expressed in the same time units (months, years, and so on). *Future-value* is an optional argument. If it is omitted, the *future-value* of a loan is assumed to be $0. If it is included, it is the balance that you wish to obtain after the last payment is made. *Type* is an optional argument. A *type* of 1 means that payments are due at the beginning of the period. A *type* of 0 means that payments are due at the end of the period. If the *type* argument is omitted, it is assumed to be of type 0.

P

Example

=PV(.065/12,120,–1000) returns the present value of $88,068.50 for $1000 invested monthly for 10 years at a 6.5-percent annual interest rate.

See Also

FV	Returns the future value	Function
IPMT	Returns the interest payment	Function
NPER	Returns the number of payment periods	Function
PPMT	Returns the principle payment	Function
RATE	Returns the interest rate	Function

QUARTILE(*array, quartile*)

Function   **New to Version 4.0**

QUARTILE returns a quartile of an array. There can be up to 8191 values in the array. The *quartile* argument indicates which value or values to return. A quartile is a portion of an array that falls within one of four possible percentile groups. The possible values for this argument are listed here:

Quartile	Values Returned
0	Minimum value
1	25th percentile
2	50th percentile
3	75th percentile
4	Maximum value

Example

=QUARTILE({1,2,3,5,6,7,8,9}) returns 3.

See Also

MAX	Returns the maximum value	Function
MEDIAN	Returns the median value	Function
MIN	Returns the minimum value	Function
PERCENTILE	Returns the Kth percentile	Function

QUIT()

Macro Function

QUIT performs the same action as the Exit option on the File menu. It closes Microsoft Excel and also closes any open documents. If any open documents have not been saved, Excel displays a message for each document asking if you want to save that document. However, if you have executed an ERROR(FALSE) function, Excel displays no warning message for unsaved documents.

See Also

ERROR	Enables or disables error checking	Macro Function
FILE.CLOSE	Closes a document	Macro Function
FILE.EXIT	Equivalent command	Menu Command

QUOTIENT(*numerator, denominator*)

Function

QUOTIENT returns the quotient of a division operation given the numerator and denominator. The quotient is the whole number part of the result of dividing the numerator by the denominator.

QUOTIENT is an add-in function. The first time that you use it, you may see a #REF! error while Excel loads the function.

Q, R

Example

=QUOTIENT(7,3) returns 2.

See Also

MOD   Returns the remainder   Function

RADIANS(*angle*)

Function

RADIANS converts an angle measurement from degrees to radians.

This is an add-in function. The first time you use it, you may see a #REF! error while Excel loads the function.

Example

=RADIANS(30) returns 0.523599.

See Also

DEGREES   Converts an angle measurement from radians to   Function
             degrees

RAND()

Function

RAND generates a random number between 0 and 1. If you want a two-digit random number, multiply by 100 (=RAND()*100); if you want a three-digit random number, multiply by 1000.

Example

=RAND() returns a random number between 0 and 1.

See Also

| RANDBETWEEN | Returns a random number between two designated numbers | Function |
| RANDOM | Fills a range with random numbers | Function |

RANDBETWEEN(*lower, upper*)

Function **New to Version 4.0**

RANDBETWEEN returns a random number between the given lower and upper number. Each time the worksheet is recalculated, RANDBETWEEN returns a new random number.

This is an add-in function. The first time you use it, you may see a #REF! error while Excel loads the function.

Example

=RANDBETWEEN(1,10) returns a random number between 1 and 10.

See Also

| RAND | Returns a random number between 0 and 1 | Function |
| RANDOM | Fills a range with random numbers | Function |

RANDOM(*output, [sets], [points], type, [seed], lower, upper*)

Macro Function **(Argument Profile 1)**

The RANDOM macro function fills a range with random numbers or numbers generated from different distributions. There are seven argument profiles for RANDOM. All have the first five arguments in common.

The *output* argument represents the upper-left cell in the range you want to fill.

Sets is an optional argument that indicates how many sets of random numbers you want to generate. The default is the number of columns in the current selection.

Points is an optional argument that indicates how many data points in each set you want to generate. If *points* is omitted, the default is the number of rows in the current selection.

Q, R

The *type* argument controls the type of distribution used. The possible values for type are listed here:

Type	Distribution
1	Uniform
2	Normal
3	Bernoulli
4	Binomial
5	Poisson
6	Patterned
7	Discrete

Seed is optional argument that indicates a number at which to begin random number generation. *Seed* is ignored if *type* is 6 or 7.

Argument profile 1 of RANDOM generates numbers using uniform distribution. The *lower* and *upper* arguments represent boundaries for the distribution.

RANDOM(*output,[sets],[points],type,[seed],mean,st-dev*)

Macro Function   **(Argument Profile 2)**

Argument profile 2 of RANDOM fills a range with numbers generated by normal distribution. The *mean* argument represents the mean, and *st-dev* is the standard deviation.

RANDOM(*output,[sets],[points],type,[seed],probability*)

Macro Function   **(Argument Profile 3)**

Argument profile 3 of RANDOM fills a range with numbers generated by Bernoulli distribution. *Probability* identifies the probability of success for each trial.

RANDOM(*output,[sets],[points],type,[seed],probability,trails*)

Macro Function   **(Argument Profile 4)**

Argument profile 4 of RANDOM fills a range with numbers generated by binomial distribution. The probability of success for each trial is given by the *probability* argument, and the number of trials is given by the *trials* argument.

RANDOM(*output,[sets],[points],type,[seed],lambda*)

Macro Function   **(Argument Profile 5)**

Argument profile 5 of RANDOM fills a range with numbers generated by Poisson distribution. The *lambda* argument is the parameter of the Poisson distribution.

RANDOM(*output,[sets],[points],type,[seed],lower,upper,step,repeat, sequence*)

Macro Function   **(Argument Profile 6)**

Argument profile 6 of RANDOM fills a range with numbers generated by patterned distribution. *Lower* and *upper* are lower and upper bounds for the distribution. The *step* argument represents the increment between the lower and upper bounds.

Repeat is the number of times each value is to be repeated, and *sequence* is the number of times each sequence is to be repeated.

RANDOM(*output,[sets],[points],type,[seed],input*)

Macro Function   **(Argument Profile 7)**

Argument profile 7 of RANDOM fills a range with numbers generated by discrete distribution. *Input* is a two-column range, where the first column contains the values and the second column contains their associated probabilities.

RANK(*X,list,[order]*)

Function   **New to Version 4.0**

RANK returns the rank of a value within a list of values. If the list is ordered, RANK returns the position of the value *X* in the list. *X* is the value for which you want to find the rank. *List* is the list of values given as an array or a reference to a range. *Order* is a logical value. If *order* is TRUE, RANK finds the position of *X* if the list is sorted in descending order. If *order* is FALSE, RANK finds the position of *X* if the list is sorted in ascending order. If *order* is omitted, the default value is TRUE.

Example

=RANK(A1,A1:A4,TRUE) returns 1 if A1:A4 contains the numbers 1, 3, 4, and 7.

RANKPERC(*input, output, [rowcol], [labels]*)

Macro Function   **New to Version 4.0**

RANKPERC determines the percentage rank and order of each value in a set of values and returns the result in a table. *Input* is a reference to the input range. *Output* is a reference to the upper-left cell in the output range. *Rowcol* is either "C" or "R." If *rowcol* is "C," the values in the input range are organized by column. If *rowcol* is "R," the values are organized by row. The default value is "C." Labels is a logical value. If *labels* is TRUE, labels are located in the first row or column of the input range if the data is organized by row or column, respectively. If *labels* is FALSE, there are no labels in the input range. The default value for *labels* is FALSE.

RANKPERC is an add-in function. The first time you use it, you may see a #REF! error while Excel loads the function.

See Also

PERCENTRANK	Returns the percentage rank of *X*	Function
QUARTILE	Returns the quartile	Function

RATE(*number-of-periods, payment, present-value, [future-value], [type], [guess]*)

Function

RATE returns the interest rate given equal payments for a specified number of periods and the present value of a loan. *Future-value* is an optional argument. If it is omitted, the future value of the loan is assumed to be $0. If it is included, it is the balance that you wish to obtain after the last payment is made. *Type* is an optional argument. A *type* of 1 means that payments are due at the beginning of the period. A *type* of 0 means that payments are due at the end of the period. If the *type* argument is omitted, it is assumed to be of type 0. *Guess* is also an optional argument. *Guess* is your estimation of what the rate will be. *Guess* has a default value of 10 percent.

Example

=RATE(120,–300,20000)*12 returns the annual interest rate of 13.12 percent. The result of the RATE function is multiplied by 12 to produce an annual interest rate.

See Also

FV	Returns the future value	Function
IPMT	Returns the interest payment	Function

NPER	Returns the number of periods	Function
PMT	Returns the payment	Function
PPMT	Returns the principle payment	Function
PV	Returns the present value	Function

RECEIVED(*settlement, maturity, investment, rate, [basis-code]*)

Function

RECEIVED returns the amount of money received from a fully invested security at maturity. *Settlement* is the settlement date of the security given as a date serial number. *Maturity* is the maturity date of the security given as a date serial number. *Investment* is the dollar amount invested in the security. *Rate* is the discount rate of the security. *Basis-code* is the day count basis. The possible values for *basis-code* are listed here:

Basis-Code	Day Count
0	30/360
1	Actual/actual
2	Actual/360
3	Actual/365

If *basis-code* is omitted, the default value is 0.

RECEIVED is an add-in function. The first time you use it, you may see a #REF! error while Excel loads the function.

See Also

DATE	Returns the serial number of a date	Function
INTRATE	Returns the interest rate of a security	Function

REFTEXT(*reference, [style]*)

Macro Function

REFTEXT returns the *reference* as text in A1 style if the *style* argument is TRUE, and R1C1 style if the *style* argument is FALSE. The default value for *style* is FALSE.

Example

=REFTEXT(A1,TRUE) returns $A$1.

Q, R

See Also

ABSREF	Returns the absolute reference of a range	Function
DEREF	Returns the values in a range	Function
RELREF	Returns the relative reference of a range	Function

REGISTER(*library, [procedure], [arg-code], [function], [arguments], [macro-type], [category], [shortcut]*)

Macro Function

REGISTER returns a string that is used by CALL. The string that is returned is the register ID of the specified Dynamic Link Library or code. CALL and REGISTER should only be used by experts. Because these functions allow you to access your computer at a low level, they can cause errors in your system if they are used incorrectly.

Library is a text string that specifies the name of the DLL. *Procedure* is a text string that specifies the DLL function name. *Arg-code* is a code that indicates the data type of the value returned and all the input arguments to the DLL function. The codes are listed here:

Arg-Code	Data Type
A	Logical (FALSE=0, TRUE=1) passed by value
B	IEEE 8-byte floating-point passed by value
C	String terminated by null passed by reference
D	Byte-counted string passed by reference
E	IEEE 8-byte floating-point passed by reference
F	String terminated by null passed by reference
G	Byte-counted string passed by reference
H	Unsigned 2-byte integer passed by value
I	Signed 2-byte integer passed by value
J	Signed 4-byte integer passed by value
K	Array passed by reference
L	Logical passed by reference
M	Signed 2-byte integer passed by reference
N	Signed 4-byte integer passed by reference
O	Array passed by reference
P	Excel OPER data structure passed by reference
R	Excel SLOPER data structure passed by reference

Function is a text string that is the name of the function as you want it to appear in the Formula Paste Function dialog box. *Arguments* is a text string of the names of the arguments as you want them to appear in the Formula Paste Function dialog box. Arguments should be separated by commas.

Macro-type is a number that indicates the type of macro. If *macro-type* is 1, the macro is a function macro. If *macro-type* is 2, the macro is a command macro. The default value for *macro-type* is 1.

Category is a number that indicates the function category to which you want the function to belong. This table summarizes the possible values for *category*:

Category	Type of Function
1	Financial
2	Date and time
3	Math and trigonometric
4	Text
5	Logical
6	Lookup and matrix
7	Database
8	Statistical
9	Information
10	Command (macro sheets)
11	Actions (macro sheets)
12	Customizing (macro sheets)
13	Macro Control (macro sheets)
14	User Defined

Shortcut is a character that is used as the shortcut key if the function is registered as a command macro. The shortcut key is a case-sensitive key that can be used to run the command macro.

See Also

CALL	Activates a Dynamic Link Library procedure	Macro Function
UNREGISTER	Unregisters a procedure	Macro Function

Q, R

REGISTER.ID (*module, procedure, [type]*)

Function

REGISTER.ID returns the register ID of the procedure specified by the *module* and *procedure* arguments. *Module* is a text string naming the DLL. *Procedure* is a text string naming the procedure. *Arg-code* is a code that indicates the return data type and the data type of the arguments. The possible values for *arg-code* are the same as those listed under the REGISTER entry.

REGRESS(*dependent, independent, [y-intercept], [labels], [confidence], soutput, [residuals], [std-residuals], [rcharts], [lcharts], routput, [nchart], poutput*)

Macro Function   **New to Version 4.0**

REGRESS executes a linear regression analysis on the independent and dependent data given. *Independent* and *dependent* are references to ranges that contain the x values (independent data) and y values (dependent data). *Y-intercept* is a logical value. If *y-intercept* is TRUE, the y-intercept of the regression line is assumed to be zero. If *y-intercept* is FALSE, the y-intercept is assumed to be nonzero. If *y-intercept* is omitted, the default value is FALSE.

Labels is a logical value that indicates whether labels are included in the two input ranges, *independent* and *dependent*. If *labels* is TRUE, labels are included in the first row or column of both the input ranges. If *labels* is FALSE, no labels are included in the input ranges. If *labels* is omitted, the default value is FALSE.

Confidence is the additional confidence level used by REGRESS. If *confidence* is omitted, the default value is 95 percent.

Soutput is a reference to the upper-left cell in the range for the summary table output.

Residuals is a logical value. If *residuals* is TRUE, residual values are returned in the output table. If *residuals* is FALSE, no residual values are returned. If *residuals* is omitted, the default value is FALSE.

Std-residuals is also a logical value. If *std-residuals* is TRUE, then standardized residual values are returned in the output table. If *std-residuals* is FALSE, no standardized residual values are returned. If *std-residuals* is omitted, the default value is FALSE.

Rcharts is a logical value. If *rcharts* is TRUE, REGRESS creates a chart for every x value in the independent range versus the residual value. If *rcharts* is FALSE, no chart is created. The default value for *rcharts* is FALSE.

Lcharts is a logical value. If *lcharts* is TRUE, REGRESS creates chart regression line fitted to the observed values. If *lcharts* is FALSE, no chart is created. The default value for *lcharts* is FALSE.

Routput is a reference to the upper-left cell in the range for the residuals table output.

Ncharts is a logical value. If *ncharts* is TRUE, REGRESS creates a chart of normal probabilities. If *ncharts* is FALSE, no chart is created. The default value for *ncharts* is FALSE.

Poutput is a reference to the upper-left cell in the range containing the probabilities output table.

See Also

FORECAST	Returns a linear trend forecast	Function
GROWTH	Returns an exponential trend forecast	Function
LINEST	Returns linear trend parameters	Function
LOGEST	Returns exponential trend parameters	Function
TREND	Returns linear trend values	Function

RELREF(*reference,with-respect-to*)

Macro Function

RELREF returns a R1C1 style relative reference as a string, given a reference and a *with-respect-to* argument that is the upper-left corner to which the reference is relative.

Example

=RELREF(B2,A1) returns "R[1]C[1]".

See Also

ABSREF	Returns the absolute reference of a range	Function
DEREF	Returns the values in a range	Function
OFFSET	Returns the offset to a range	Function

REMOVE.PAGE.BREAK()

Macro Function

REMOVE.PAGE.BREAK performs the same action as the Remove Page Break command on the Options menu. REMOVE.PAGE.BREAK removes a page break previously set with SET.PAGE.BREAK. The active cell must be below or to the right of the page break you are trying to remove. REMOVE.PAGE.BREAK removes the page break located directly to the left or above the active cell; it does not remove all page breaks unless the entire document is selected.

See Also

OPTIONS REMOVE PAGE BREAK	Equivalent command	Menu Command
SET.PAGE.BREAK	Sets a page break	Macro Function

Q, R

RENAME.COMMAND(*bar-number, menu-ref, command, name-string*)

Macro Function

RENAME.COMMAND renames a command on a menu with the name specified by the *name-string* argument. *Bar-number* is the number of the menu bar containing the command that you want to rename. The possible values for *bar-number* are listed here:

Bar-Number	Menu Bar
1	Worksheet or macro sheet
2	Chart
3	Null
4	Info
5	Worksheet or macro sheet short menu
6	Chart short menu
7	Cell, toolbar, and workbook shortcut menu
8	Object shortcut menu
9	Chart shortcut menu

Menu-ref identifies the menu containing the command that you want to rename. (Although numbers are quicker to type, menu names are usually easier to remember.) *Command* is the name or number of the command you want to rename.

The *name-string* argument represents the new name for the command. Use the & symbol before the letter you want to use to access the option. The letter following the & symbol will be underlined on the menu.

Example

=RENAME.COMMAND(1,"File","Close","Close &Doc") changes the name of the Close option on the File menu to Close Doc.

See Also

ADD.COMMAND	Adds a new command to a menu	Macro Function
CHECK.COMMAND	Places or removes a check from a command	Macro Function
DELETE.COMMAND	Deletes a command from a menu	Macro Function
ENABLE.COMMAND	Enables or disables a command	Macro Function

REPLACE(*original-string, offset-number, number-of-characters, new-string*)

Function

REPLACE replaces with the new string the specified number of characters in the original string, beginning with the offset number. Either string can be a literal, a reference to a cell containing text, or a formula that evaluates to a string. The *offset-number* argument is the offset from the beginning of the original string at which the replacement is to occur.

If the number of characters specified in the *number-of-characters* argument is the same as the number of characters in the *original-string* argument, the original string will be replaced with the new string. If the number specified in the *offset-number* argument is greater than the number of characters in the original string, the new string is appended to the original string. If the *number-of-characters* argument is 0, the new string will be inserted into the original string. If the new string contains no characters, the original string will be deleted.

Example

=REPLACE("Income Statement",17,0,", as of April, 1993") appends the new string to the original string, resulting in "Income Statement, as of April, 1993."

See Also

FORMULA.REPLACE	Replaces a string throughout a document	Macro Function
MID	Returns a portion of a string	Macro Function
SEARCH	Performs a non-case-sensitive string search	Macro Function
SUBSTITUTE	Substitutes one string for another	Macro Function
TRIM	Removes white space from text	Macro Function

REPLACE.FONT(*font, font-name, size, bold, italic, underlined, strikeout*)

Macro Function

REPLACE.FONT performs the same action as the Font option on the Format menu. This macro function replaces one font with another. This function is included for compatibility with older versions of Excel (version 2.1 or prior). If you want to change the font of the current selection or a specified range, use the FORMAT.FONT function.

Q, R

See Also

FORMAT.FONT   Equivalent function   Macro Function

REPORT.DEFINE(*name,array,[pages]*)

Macro Function   **New to Version 4.0**

REPORT.DEFINE performs the same action as the Print Report command on the File menu. This macro function creates a report of a view or scenario. *Name* is the name of the report you are creating. *Array* is an array of scenario pairs that define the report. *Pages* is a logical value. If *pages* is TRUE, the report will be created with continuous page numbers. If *pages* is FALSE, the page numbers will be reset to 1 for each section of the report. If *pages* is omitted, the default value is TRUE.

REPORT.DEFINE is an add-in function. The first time you use it, you may see a #REF! error while Excel loads the function.

Example

=REPORT.DEFINE("EOY",{"Projected","Actual";"1992","1993"},TRUE) creates a report named EOY that compares the Projected scenario to the Actual scenario and compares the 1992 scenario to the 1993 scenario, and that numbers the pages continuously.

See Also

REPORT.DELETE	Deletes a report	Macro Function
REPORT.GET	Returns information about a report	Macro Function
REPORT.PRINT	Prints a report	Macro Function

REPORT.DELETE(*report*)

Macro Function   **New to Version 4.0**

REPORT.DELETE deletes a report definition defined by the REPORT.DEFINE macro function or the Print Report command on the File menu. *Report* is the name of the report you want to delete.

This is an add-in function. The first time you use it, you may see a #REF! error while Excel loads the function.

Example

=REPORT.DELETE("EOY") deletes the report named "EOY" from the active document.

See Also

REPORT.DEFINE	Defines a report	Macro Function
REPORT.PRINT	Prints a report	Macro Function

REPORT.GET(*type, [report]*)

Macro Function

REPORT.GET returns information about reports defined for the active document. *Type* is a number that indicates the type of information to be returned. The following table lists the possible values for *type*:

Type	Information Returned
1	An array of the active document's reports
2	An array of scenario pairs for the report defined for the active document
3	Returns TRUE if continuous pages are being used for the report

Report is the name of the report. It is only required if *type* is 2 or 3.

REPORT.GET is an add-in function. The first time you use it, you may see a #REF! error while Excel loads the function.

Example

=REPORT.GET(3,"EOY") returns TRUE if the report EOY has continuous page numbers.

See Also

REPORT.DEFINE	Defines a report	Macro Function
REPORT.PRINT	Prints a report	Macro Function

Q, R

REPORT.PRINT(*report, [copies], [logical]*)

Macro Function

REPORT.PRINT prints a report that has previously been defined with the RE-
PORT.DEFINE macro function. *Report* is the name of the report you want to print,
given as a text string. *Copies* is the number of copies of the report you want printed.
Logical determines if a dialog box appears. If *logical* is TRUE, REPORT.PRINT displays
a dialog box asking for the number of copies to print. If *logical* is FALSE, no dialog
box appears. The default value for *logical* is FALSE.

REPORT.PRINT is an add-in function. The first time you use it, you may see a
#REF! error while Excel loads the function.

REPT(*string, number-of-times*)

Function

REPT repeats or duplicates a string the specified number of times. The *string*
argument can be a literal, a reference to a cell containing a label, or a formula that
evaluates to a string.

Example

=REPT("-",20) will print 20 hyphens.

See Also

FILL.DOWN	Fills text down	Macro Function
FILL.LEFT	Fills text left	Macro Function
FILL.RIGHT	Fills text right	Macro Function
FILL.UP	Fills text up	Macro Function
FORMULA.FILL	Fills a range	Macro Function

REQUEST(*channel, item*)

Macro Function

REQUEST returns an array containing information obtained by requesting the item
from the application connected to the specified channel. The *item* argument must
be given as a string. The channel must have been opened by the INITIATE function.
If the channel number is not valid, REQUEST returns a #VALUE! error. If the user
presses the ESCAPE key before the application answers, REQUEST returns a #DIV/0!

error. If the application refuses REQUEST's request, REQUEST returns a #REF! error. If the application is busy, REQUEST returns a #N/A error. You must have Windows 2.0 or higher installed to use this function.

See Also

EXECUTE	Executes a command in another application	Macro Function
INITIATE	Initiates a channel to another application	Macro Function
SEND.KEYS	Sends keystrokes to another application	Macro Function

RESET.TOOL(*bar,position*)

Macro Function   **New to Version 4.0**

RESET.TOOL resets to its original appearance the tool face identified by the *bar* and *position* arguments. *Bar* is the name or number of the toolbar. The bar numbers for the built-in toolbars are listed here:

Bar	Toolbar
1	Standard
2	Formatting
3	Utility
4	Chart
5	Drawing
6	Excel 3.0
7	Macro
8	Macro recording
9	Macro paused

Position is the position of the tool on the toolbar. *Position* is numbered from 1 starting at the top or left of the toolbar, depending on the toolbar's orientation.

Example

=RESET.TOOL("Standard",3) resets the third tool on the standard toolbar to its original appearance.

Q, R

See Also

ADD.TOOL	Adds a tool to a toolbar	Macro Function
DELETE.TOOL	Deletes a tool from a toolbar	Macro Function

RESET.TOOLBAR(*bar*)

Macro Function

RESET.TOOLBAR resets to its original appearance the built-in toolbar identified by *bar*. The *bar* argument can be the name or number of the toolbar you want to reset. (The possible values for *bar* are the same as those listed under RESET.TOOL)

RESET.TOOLBAR returns TRUE if the toolbar is reset successfully, but returns FALSE if you try to reset a custom toolbar.

Example

=RESET.TOOLBAR(3) resets the utility toolbar to its original appearance, and returns TRUE.

See Also

ADD.TOOL	Adds a tool to a toolbar	Macro Function
DELETE.TOOL	Deletes a tool from a toolbar	Macro Function

RESTART(*[stack-level]*)

Macro Function

RESTART removes from the stack the number of return addresses specified by the *stack-level* argument. If *stack-level* is omitted, the default is all addresses on the stack.

See Also

RETURN	Ends a macro	Macro Function

RESULT(*type*)

Macro Function

RESULT defines the type of result that a macro returns. The *type* argument can be any of the following values:

Type	Macro Result
1	Number
2	Text
4	Logical
7	Number, text, or logical
8	Reference
16	Error
64	Array

The default value for *type* is 7.

Example

=RESULT(4) defines the macro to return a logical value.

See Also

RETURN	Ends a macro	Macro Function

RESUME(*[type]*)

Macro Function

RESUME performs the same action as the Resume command on the Macro menu. It starts a paused macro. The *type* argument indicates how to restart the macro. The possible values for *type* are listed here:

Type	Action
1	Restarts where the macro left off, in single-step mode if paused in single-step mode
2	Halts the paused macro
3	Restarts the macro
4	Restarts the macro in single-step mode

If *type* is omitted, the default value is 1.

See Also

HALT	Stops all macros	Macro Function
PAUSE	Pauses a macro	Macro Function

Q, R

RETURN(*[value]*)

Macro Function

RETURN returns the value given as the argument and stops running the macro. If the *value* argument is not supplied, the macro is a command macro.

See Also

HALT	Halts all macros	Macro Function
PAUSE	Pauses a macro	Macro Function
RESULT	Defines the data type returned	Macro Function

RIGHT(*string, [number-of-characters]*)

Function

RIGHT returns the rightmost specified number of characters in a string. The *string* argument can be a literal, a reference to a cell containing a label, or a formula that evaluates to a string. If the *number-of-characters* argument is 0, no characters will be returned. If the *number-of-characters* argument is greater than the number in the string, the entire string will be returned. The *number-of-characters* argument is optional, and has a default value of 1.

Example

=RIGHT("The Month of January",7) returns "January."

See Also

LEFT	Returns the left end of a string	Macro Function
MID	Returns the middle of a string	Macro Function

ROUND(*value, number-of-decimal-places*)

Function

ROUND rounds a value to the specified number of decimal places.

Example

=ROUND(536.8175,3) returns 536.818.

See Also

CEILING	Rounds a number up to the next integer	Function
FLOOR	Rounds a number down to the next integer	Function
TRUNC	Truncates a number to an integer	Function

ROW(*range*)

Function

ROW returns an array of the row numbers (*not* the number of rows) in the specified range. You must highlight a range large enough to receive the resulting array prior to entering the function, and press CTRL-SHIFT-ENTER after typing the function.

Example

=ROW(A1:A4) returns the array {1,2,3,4}. If you highlighted A6:A9 before entering the function and pressed CTRL-SHIFT-ENTER, you would have 1 in A6, 2 in A7, 3 in A8, and 4 in A9.

See Also

COLUMN	Returns an array of column numbers	Function
ROWS	Returns the number of rows in a range	Function

ROW.HEIGHT(*[height], [reference], [default-height], [type]*)
ROW.HEIGHT?(*[height], [reference], [default-height], [type]*)

Macro Function

ROW.HEIGHT performs the same action as the Row Height option on the Format menu. It changes to the specified height the rows in the range referred to by *reference*. If the *reference* argument is omitted, the default is the current selection.

　　Default-height is an optional argument. If *default-height* is TRUE, rows are set to the default height and the *height* argument is ignored. If *default-height* is omitted, the rows are set to the specified height. The default value for *height* is FALSE. *Type* determines whether the rows will be hidden. The following table lists the possible values for *type*:

Type	Action
1	Sets the row height to 0 (hides the row)
2	Redisplays the row by resetting it to its previous height
3	Sets the row to its optimal height

Q, R

The *type* argument is optional; if included, it overrides the other arguments that specify the row height. For example, if *type* is 1, *height* and *default-height* are ignored.

In the dialog box version (with the question mark), the arguments, if included, are used as defaults for the dialog box that appears.

Example

=ROW.HEIGHT(,,TRUE) resets the current selection to the standard row height.

See Also

COLUMN.WIDTH   Sets the column width for a range   Macro Function

ROWS(*range*)

Function

ROWS returns the number of rows in a range or array.

Example

=ROWS(A1:A18) returns the number 18.

See Also

| COLUMNS | Returns the number of columns | Function |
| ROW | Returns an array of row numbers | Function |

RSQ(*Ys, Xs*)

Function   New to Version 4.0

RSQ determines the r^2 value of the linear regression line through the data points given by *Ys* and *Xs*. *Ys* and *Xs* are arrays of data points, or references to ranges that contain data points. The equation for the regression line is as follows.

$$r = \frac{n(\Sigma XY) - (\Sigma X)(\Sigma Y)}{\sqrt{\left[n\Sigma X^2 - (\Sigma X)^2 \right] \left[n\Sigma Y^2 - (\Sigma Y)^2 \right]}}$$

Example

=RSQ({1,4,3,6,5,8},{3,2,5,4,7,9}) returns 0.482552.

See Also

CORREL	Returns the correlation coefficient	Function
LINEST	Returns linear trend parameters	Function
LOGEST	Returns exponential trend parameters	Function
SLOPE	Returns the slope of a linear regression	Function
TREND	Returns linear trend values	Function

RUN(*[reference]*,*[step]*)
RUN?(*[reference]*,*[step]*)

Macro Function

RUN performs the same action as the Run option on the Macro menu. *Reference* is the name of the macro that you want to run, or a number indicating an Auto macro value. *Reference* can have one of the following values:

Reference	Macros To Be Run
1	All Auto_Open macros
2	All Auto_Close macros
3	All Auto_Activate macros
4	All Auto_Deactivate macros

If *reference* is omitted, Excel will run the macro starting at the currently active cell. *Step* is a logical value. If *step* is TRUE, the macro will be run in single-step mode. If *step* is FALSE, the macro will be run normally. The default value for *step* is FALSE.

Example

=RUN(EOM.XLM!Sales) runs the Sales macro on the macro sheet EOM.XLM.

See Also

GOTO	Controls a macro's flow of execution	Macro Function

SAMPLE(*input, output, sampling, rate*)

Macro Function   **New to Version 4.0**

SAMPLE performs a sampling of the input data. *Input* is a reference to the input range. *Output* is a reference to the upper-left cell in the output range. *Sampling* is a text character that indicates the sampling technique used. If *sampling* is "P," periodic sampling is used. If *sampling* is "R," random sampling is used. *Rate* is the sampling rate (if sampling is "P") or the number of samples to take (if sampling is "R".)

See Also

FOURIER	Fourier transformation function	Macro Function

SAVE()

Macro Function

SAVE performs the same action as the Save option on the File menu. SAVE saves the active document on to disk. The SAVE command saves the document with the previously established filename. If you want to change the name of the file when you save it, use the SAVE.AS command.

See Also

FILE SAVE	Equivalent command	Menu Command
SAVE.AS	Names and saves a document	Macro Function
SAVE.WORKBOOK	Saves a workbook	Macro Function

SAVE.AS(*[name]*,*[type]*, *[password]*,*[backup-logical]*,*[write-password]*, *[read-only]*)
SAVE.AS?(*[name]*,*[type]*,*[password]*,*[backup-logical]*,*[write-password]*, *[read-only]*)

Macro Function

SAVE.AS performs the same action as Save As option on the File menu. SAVE.AS allows you to name, protect, and save a document. The *name* argument is the name under which you want to save the document. It can be a full path and filename. If *name* is omitted, the file is saved under the current name.

The *type* argument is the file format with which you want to save the file. The following table summarizes the possible values for *type*:

Type	File Format
1	Normal
2	SYLK
3	Text
4	WKS
5	WK1
6	CSV
7	DBF2
8	DBF3
9	DIF
11	DBF4
15	WK3
16	Microsoft Excel version 2.*x*
17	Template
18	Add-in macro
19	Macintosh text
20	Windows text
21	MS-DOS text
22	Macintosh CSV
23	Windows CSV
24	MS-DOS CSV
25	International macro
26	International add-in macro
29	Microsoft Excel version 3.0

S-T

The default value for *type* is 1.

Password is an optional argument. If a file is saved with a password, it cannot be opened unless that password is supplied. The password should be given as a string, and cannot be more than 15 characters long.

Backup-logical indicates whether the file should be saved with a backup copy. If *backup-logical* is TRUE, a backup file is created each time the file is saved. If *backup-logical* is FALSE, no backup file is created. If *backup-logical* is omitted, the backup status remains unchanged.

If a file has previously been saved as a read-only file, the *write-password* must be supplied in order to save changes to the file. The *write-password* argument is only necessary if the file is read-only.

Read-only is a logical value. If *read-only* is TRUE, the file is saved as a read-only file. If *read-only* is FALSE, the file is saved normally. The default value for *read-only* is FALSE.

In the dialog box version (with the question mark), the arguments, if included, are used as default values for the dialog box that appears.

Example

=SAVE.AS(,,"password") saves the active document with the same name, and provides a password to allow it to be written to disk.

See Also

FILE SAVE AS	Equivalent command	Menu Command

SAVE.TOOLBAR(*[bar]*, *[filename]*)

Macro Function   **New to Version 4.0**

SAVE.TOOLBAR saves the definition for a toolbar. *Bar* is the name or number of the toolbar that you want to save. When you add a toolbar with the ADD.TOOLBAR function, you name the toolbar. Use the same name here to refer to the toolbar you want to save. If you want to save more than one toolbar in a file, put the toolbar names in an array. If the *bar* argument is not given, all the toolbar definitions are saved.

The *filename* is the name of the file in which you want to save the definitions, given as a text string. If *filename* is omitted, the definitions are saved in EXCEL.XLB.

Example

=SAVE.TOOLBAR("Toolbar9","TOOLDEF.XLB") saves the definition for Toolbar9 in the file TOOLDEF.XLB.

See Also

ADD.TOOL	Adds a tool to a toolbar	Macro Function

| ADD.TOOLBAR | Adds a new toolbar | Macro Function |
| OPEN | Opens a file | Macro Function |

SAVE.WORKBOOK(*[name]*, *[type]*, *[password]*, *[backup-logical]*, *[write-password]*, *[read-only]*)
SAVE.WORKBOOK?(*[name]*, *[type]*, *[password]*, *[backup-logical]*, *[write-password]*, *[read-only]*)

Macro Function   **New to Version 4.0**

SAVE.WORKBOOK performs the same action as the Save Workbook option on the File menu. SAVE.WORKBOOK saves the workbook to which the document specified by *name* belongs. If *name* is omitted, the active document's workbook is saved.

The *type* argument is the file format in which you want to save the workbook. The following table summarizes the possible values for *type*:

Type	File Format
1	Normal
2	SYLK
3	Text
4	WKS
5	WK1
6	CSV
7	DBF2
8	DBF3
9	DIF
11	DBF4
15	WK3
16	Microsoft Excel version 2.x
17	Template
18	Add-in macro
19	Macintosh text
20	Windows text
21	MS-DOS text
22	Macintosh CSV
23	Windows CSV
24	MS-DOS CSV
25	International macro

S-T

Type	File Format
26	International add-in macro
29	Microsoft Excel version 3.0

The default value for *type* is 1.

Password is an optional argument. If a workbook is saved with a password, it cannot be opened unless the password is supplied. The password should be given as a string, and cannot be more than 15 characters long.

Backup-logical indicates whether the workbook should be saved with a backup copy. If *backup-logical* is TRUE, a backup workbook file is created each time the file is saved. If *backup-logical* is FALSE, no backup file is created. If *backup-logical* is omitted, the backup status remains unchanged.

If a workbook file has previously been saved as a read-only file, the *write-password* must be supplied in order to save changes to the workbook file. *Write-password* is only necessary if the workbook file is read-only.

Read-only is a logical value. If *read-only* is TRUE, the workbook file is saved as a *read-only* file. If *read-only* is FALSE, the workbook file is saved normally. The default value for *read-only* is FALSE.

In the dialog box version (with the question mark), the arguments, if included, are used as default values for the dialog box that appears.

Example

=SAVE.WORKBOOK(,,"password") saves the active document's workbook with the same name, and provides a password to allow it to be written to disk.

See Also

FILE SAVE AS	Equivalent command	Menu Command

SAVE.WORKSPACE(*[name]*)
SAVE.WORKSPACE?(*[name]*)

Macro Function   **Prior to Version 4.0**

SAVE.WORKSPACE performs the same action as the Save Workspace option on the File menu. *Name* should be given as a string. The default for the *name* argument is "RESUME.XLW".

In the dialog box version (with the question mark), the argument, if included, is used as a default value for the dialog box that appears.

Example

=SAVE.WORKSPACE() saves the workspace under the name "RESUME.XLW".

SCALE(*[cross-at]*, *[categories-per-tick-labels]*, *[categories-per-ticks]*, *[cross-between]*, *[cross-at-max-category]*, *[reverse-order]*)
SCALE?(*[cross-at]*, *[categories-per-tick-labels]*, *[categories-per-ticks]*, *[cross-between]*, *[cross-at-max-category]*, *[reverse-order]*)

Macro Function   **(Argument Profile 1)**

SCALE performs the same action as the Scale option on the Format menu. SCALE changes the scaling, formatting, or position of an axis. There are five argument profiles for SCALE; the one you will use depends on the axis that you want to scale.

Argument profile 1 of SCALE changes the X-axis scaling, formatting, or position if the selected item is a category axis (X axis) and the chart is not a scatter chart.

Cross-at, categories-per-tick-labels, and *categories-per-ticks* should be given as numbers appropriate for each argument. *Cross-at* determines where the X axis will cross the Y axis. The default value for *cross-at* is 1.

Categories-per-tick-labels determines how many categories are between tick labels. The default value is 1.

Categories-per-ticks determines how many categories are between tick marks. The default value is 1.

Cross-between is only used if the *categories-per-tick-labels* is set to something other than 1. *Cross-between* is a logical value. If *cross-between* is TRUE, the X axis crosses the Y axis between categories. If *cross-between* is FALSE, the X axis crosses the Y axis as a category.

Cross-at-max-category is a logical value. If *cross-at-max-category* is TRUE, the Y axis crosses the X axis at the maximum category and the *cross-at* argument is ignored. If *cross-at-max-category* is FALSE, the Y axis crosses the X axis as defined by the *cross-at* argument. The default for *cross-at-max-category* is FALSE.

Reverse-order is a logical value. If *reverse-order* is TRUE, the category order is reverse. If *reverse-order* is FALSE, the category order remains the same. The default value for *reverse-order* is FALSE.

SCALE(*[minimum]*, *[maximum]*, *[major-unit]*, *[minor-unit]*, *[axis-cross]*, *[log-scale]*, *[reverse-order]*, *[cross-at-max-category]*)
SCALE?(*[minimum]*, *[maximum]*, *[major-unit]*, *[minor-unit]*, *[axis-cross]*, *[log-scale]*, *[reverse-order]*, *[cross-at-max-category]*)

Macro Function   **(Argument Profile 2)**

Argument profile 2 of SCALE changes the Y-axis scaling, formatting, or position if the selected item is a value axis (Y axis) and the chart is two-dimensional. You can also use argument profile 2 to change either value axis on a scatter chart.

Minimum, maximum, major-unit, minor-unit, and *axis-cross* correspond to settings in the Format Scale dialog box. They can be set to TRUE to activate the default settings, or they can be numbers.

S-T

Log-scale is a logical value. If *log-scale* is TRUE, the axis is scaled logarithmically. If *log-scale* is FALSE, the axis is scaled normally. If *log-scale* is omitted, the scaling of the axis remains unchanged.

Reverse-order and *cross-at-max-category* are the same as described above for argument profile 1.

SCALE(*[categories-per-tick-labels]*, *[categories-per-ticks]*, *[reverse-order]*, *[cross-between]*)
SCALE?(*[categories-per-tick-labels]*, *[categories-per-ticks]*, *[reverse-order]*, *[cross-between]*)

Macro Function   **(Argument Profile 3)**

Argument profile 3 of SCALE changes the X-axis scaling, formatting, or position if the selected item is a category axis (X axis) and the chart is three-dimensional.

Categories-per-tick-labels, *categories-per-ticks*, *reverse-order*, and *cross-between* are described above in argument profile 1.

SCALE(*[series-per-tick-labels]*, *[series-per-ticks]*, *[reverse-order]*)
SCALE?(*[series-per-tick-labels]*, *[series-per-ticks]*, *[reverse-order]*)

Macro Function   **(Argument Profile 4)**

Argument profile 4 of SCALE changes the X-axis scaling, formatting, or position if the selected item is a series axis (Y axis) and the chart is three-dimensional.

Series-per-tick-labels and *series-per-ticks* should be given as numbers appropriate for each argument.

Series-per-tick-labels determines how many series are between tick labels. The default value is 1.

Series-per-ticks determines how many series are between tick marks. The default value is 1.

Reverse-order is a logical value. If *reverse-order* is TRUE, the series order is reversed. If *reverse-order* is FALSE, the series order remains the same. The default value for *reverse-order* is FALSE.

SCALE(*[minimum]*, *[maximum]*, *[major-unit]*, *[minor-unit]*, *[axis-cross]*, *[log-scale]*, *[reverse-order]*, *[cross-at-min-category]*)
SCALE?(*[minimum]*, *[maximum]*, *[major-unit]*, *[minor-unit]*, *[axis-cross]*, *[log-scale]*, *[reverse-order]*, *[cross-at-min-category]*)

Macro Function   **(Argument Profile 5)**

Argument profile 5 of SCALE changes the X-axis scaling, formatting, or position if the selected item is the Z axis and the chart is three-dimensional.

Minimum, maximum, major-unit, minor-unit, log-scale and *reverse-order* are described above.

Axis-cross is the value where the Z axis crosses the XY plane. If *axis-cross* is omitted, the value where the Z axis crosses the XY plane remains unchanged.

Cross-at-min-category is a logical value. If it is TRUE, the Z axis crosses the XY plane at the minimum value. If it is FALSE, the Z axis crosses the XY plane as defined by *axis-cross.*

See Also

AXES	Shows or hides axes	Macro Function
GRIDLINES	Turns grid lines on or off	Macro Function

SCENARIO.ADD(*name,[array]*)

Macro Function   **New to Version 4.0**

SCENARIO.ADD performs the same action as choosing the Scenario Manager option from the Formula menu and clicking on the Add button. SCENARIO.ADD adds a scenario to your worksheet. A scenario is a set of input values on a worksheet that is being used as a model. Each set of input values is a different scenario of the model.

Name is the name of the scenario you are defining. *Array* is an array of input values. The input values must be in the same order as the input cells. The order of the input cells is defined using the SCENARIO.CELLS macro function.

See Also

FORMULA SCENARIO MANAGER	Manages scenarios	Menu Command
REPORT.DEFINE	Defines a report	Macro Function

SCENARIO.CELLS(*reference*)
SCENARIO.CELLS?()

Macro Function   **New to Version 4.0**

SCENARIO.CELLS performs the same action as defining input cells by choosing the Scenario Manager option from the Formula menu and editing the Changing Cells box. SCENARIO.CELLS defines which worksheet cells you are using as input cells. Each scenario that you create will place different values in the input cells you define here. *Reference* is a reference to all the input cells. If your input cells are not in a single range, use commas to separate the reference, and add an extra set of parentheses.

S-T

Example

=SCENARIO.CELLS((!\$A\$1,!\$B\$14,!C\$28)) defines cells A1, B14, and C28 of the active worksheet as input cells.

See Also

| FORMULA SCENARIO MANAGER | Manages scenarios | Menu Command |
| REPORT.DEFINE | Defines a report | Macro Function |

SCENARIO.DELETE(*name*)

Macro Function   **New to Version 4.0**

SCENARIO.DELETE performs the same action as choosing the Scenario Manager option from the Formula menu and clicking on the Delete button. SCENARIO.DELETE deletes the scenario referred to by *name*.

See Also

| FORMULA SCENARIO MANAGER | Manages scenarios | Menu Command |
| REPORT.DEFINE | Defines a report | Macro Function |

SCENARIO.GET(*type*)

Macro Function   **New to Version 4.0**

SCENARIO.GET returns information about the scenarios defined for your active worksheet. *Type* is a number that indicates the type of information that you want returned. The possible values for *type* are listed here:

Type	Information Returned
1	A horizontal array of scenario names.
2	A reference to the input cells.
3	A reference to the result cells.
4	A two-dimensional array of scenario values. Each row in the array represents a different scenario.

See Also

| FORMULA SCENARIO MANAGER | Manages scenarios | Menu Command |

REPORT.DEFINE	Defines a report	Macro Function

SCENARIO.SHOW(*name*)

Macro Function   **New to Version 4.0**

SCENARIO.SHOW performs the same action as choosing the Scenario Manager option from the Formula menu and clicking on the Show button. SCENARIO.SHOW displays the result of the input associated with the scenario *name* applied to the model worksheet.

See Also

FORMULA SCENARIO MANAGER	Manages scenarios	Menu Command
REPORT.DEFINE	Defines a report	Macro Function

SCENARIO.SHOW.NEXT()

Macro Function   **New to Version 4.0**

SCENARIO.SHOW.NEXT performs the same action as choosing the Scenario Manager option from the Formula menu, selecting the next scenario that has been defined, and then clicking on the Show button. SCENARIO.SHOW.NEXT displays the next scenario applied to the model.

See Also

FORMULA SCENARIO MANAGER	Manages scenarios	Menu Command
REPORT.DEFINE	Defines a report	Macro Function

SCENARIO.SUMMARY(*reference*)
SCENARIO.SUMMARY?(*reference*)

Macro Function

SCENARIO.SUMMARY performs the same action as choosing the Scenario Manager option from the Formula menu and clicking on the Summary button. SCENARIO.SUMMARY creates a summary table of the result of applying each different scenario to the model. *Reference* is a reference to all the cells you want included in the summary table. If your output cells are not in a single range, use commas to separate the *reference*, and add an extra set of parentheses.

Example

=SCENARIO.SUMMARY((!$A$1,!$B$14,!C$28)) creates a table comparing the cells A1, B14, and C28 with all the scenarios applied to the model.

See Also

| FORMULA SCENARIO MANAGER | Manages scenarios | Menu Command |
| REPORT.DEFINE | Defines a report | Macro Function |

SEARCH(*search-string, string, [start-position]*)

Function

Beginning at the *start-position* of a string, SEARCH searches the string for a match to the *search-string* and returns the position where the match is found. The *search-string* and *string* can be literals, formulas that evaluate to strings, or references to cells containing strings. The search is not case-sensitive and will find letters when the case is not identical. *Start-position* is an optional argument with a default value of 1.

Example

=SEARCH("no", A6,6) would result in the value of 8 in the string "yes no no yes no" in cell A6.

See Also

FIND	Case-sensitive search	Function
MID	Returns the middle of a string	Function
REPLACE	Replaces text in a string	Function

SECOND(*time-serial-number*)

Function

SECOND returns the seconds given a time serial number. The result is an integer from 0 to 59.

Example

=SECOND(NOW()) returns the number of seconds in the current time.

See Also

HOUR	Returns the hour of a time serial number	Function
MINUTE	Returns the minute of a time serial number	Function
NOW	Returns the serial number of the current time	Function

SELECT(*[range]*, *[active-cell]*)

Macro Function   **(Argument Profile 1)**

SELECT selects cells, ranges, objects, or chart items. There are three argument profiles for SELECT. The one you will use depends on what you want to select.

Argument profile 1 of SELECT performs the same action as selecting a cell or range on a worksheet or macro sheet. The active cell must be within the specified range. If *range* is omitted, the *active-cell* argument should be given as a relative cell reference.

Example

=SELECT(,R[1]C[1]) activates the cell down one row and over one column from the current active cell.

SELECT(*object*, *[replace]*)

Macro Function   **(Argument Profile 2)**

Use this form of SELECT if you want to select objects on a worksheet or macro sheet. The *object* argument is the name of the object you want to select given as text. The *object* name should be given exactly as returned by CREATE.OBJECT. If you want to select more than one object, separate the object names with commas. The last object listed will be the active object.

Replace is a logical value. If *replace* is TRUE, the objects identified by the *object* argument will replace currently selected objects. If *replace* is FALSE, the objects identified by the *object* argument will be added to the currently selected objects. The default value for *replace* is TRUE.

S-T

SELECT(*code,[point]*)

Macro Function   (Argument Profile 3)

This form of SELECT performs the same action as selecting an item on a chart. The *code* argument indicates which item you want to select on the chart. The *code* can be any of the following strings:

Code	Item Selected
"Arrow *n*"	The *n*th arrow
"Axis 1"	The main chart's value axis
"Axis 2"	The main chart's category axis
"Axis 3"	The overlay chart's value axis
"Axis 4"	The overlay chart's category axis
"Chart"	The whole chart
"Corners"	The corners of a three-dimensional chart
"Down Bar 1"	The main chart down bar
"Down Bar 2"	The overlay chart down bar
"Dropline 1"	The drop lines for the main chart
"Dropline 2"	The drop lines for the overlay chart
"Floor"	The floor of a three-dimensional chart
"Gridline 1"	The major grid lines for the value axis
"Gridline 2"	The minor grid lines for the value axis
"Gridline 3"	The major gridlines for the category axis
"Gridline 4"	The minor grid lines for the category axis
"Gridline 5"	The major grid lines for the series axis
"Gridline 6"	The minor grid lines for the series axis
"Hiloline 1"	The hi-lo lines for the main chart
"Hiloline 2"	The hi-lo lines for the overlay chart
"Legend"	The legend
"Plot"	The plot area
"Series line 1"	The main chart series line
"Series line 2"	The overlay chart series line
"S*n*"	The series *n*
"S*n*P*m*"	The data corresponding to the series *n* and data point *m*

Code	Item Selected
"Text Axis 1"	The main chart value axis label
"Text Axis 2"	The main chart category axis label
"Text Axis 3"	The main chart series axis label
"Text n"	The nth floating text item
"Text Sn"	The text attached to the series n
"Text SnPm"	The text attached to the series n and the point m
"Title"	The chart title
"Up Bar 1"	The main chart up bar
"Up Bar 2"	The overlay chart up bar
"Walls"	The back of a three-dimensional chart

The *point* argument is only needed if the code is "SnPm." *Point* is a logical value. If *point* is TRUE, only a single point is selected. If *point* is FALSE and there is more than one series, the entire series is selected.

See Also

FORMAT.MOVE	Moves objects	Macro Function
FORMAT.SIZE	Sizes objects	Macro Function

SELECT.END(*direction*)

Macro Function

SELECT.END selects the cells to the end of the range in a specified direction. If the *direction* argument is 1, using SELECT.END is the same as pressing CTRL-LEFT ARROW. If the *direction* argument is 2, using SELECT.END is like pressing CTRL-RIGHT ARROW. If the *direction* argument is 3, using SELECT.END is the same as pressing CTRL-UP ARROW. If the *direction* argument is 4, using SELECT.END is the same as pressing CTRL-DOWN ARROW.

SELECT.LAST.CELL()

Macro Function

SELECT.LAST.CELL selects the last cell in the worksheet. The last cell in the worksheet is the intersection of the last column used and the last row used.

S-T

SELECT.SPECIAL(*attributes, [type], [levels]*)

Macro Function

SELECT.SPECIAL performs the same action as the Select Special option on the Formula menu. *Attributes* specifies the attributes that you want to select. The *attributes* argument can have any of the following values:

Attributes	Description
1	Notes
2	Constants
3	Formulas
4	Blanks
5	Present range
6	Present array
7	Row differences
8	Column differences
9	Precedents
10	Dependents
11	Last cell
12	Visible cells
13	All objects

If the *attributes* argument is set to constants (2) or formulas (3), you can set the *type* argument to numbers (1), text (2), logicals (3), or errors (16) to control which constants or formulas are selected. The *levels* argument is used to specify which levels are selected if the *attributes* argument is set to precedents (9) or dependents (10). The *levels* argument can be set to either 1 (direct) or 2 (all).

SELECTION()

Macro Function

SELECTION returns the current selection's identifier. The identifier will be a name followed by a number. The following table summarizes the possible names SELECTION will return depending on the selection's type:

Item	Identifier
Imported graphic	Picture n
Linked graphic	Picture n
Chart picture	Picture n
Linked chart	Chart n
Worksheet range	Picture n
Linked range	Picture n
Text box	Text n
Button	Button n
Rectangle	Rectangle n
Oval	Oval n
Line	Line n
Arc	Arc n
Group	Group n
Freehand drawing	Drawing n

If SELECTION is used with REFTEXT, the current selection's external reference is returned.

Example

=REFTEXT(SELECTION()) returns the current selection's external cell reference as text.

See Also

REFTEXT	Returns an external reference	Macro Function
SELECT	Selects specified objects or cells	Macro Function

SEND.KEYS(*string, [logical]*)

Macro Function

SEND.KEYS sends the specified *string* to the active application as virtual keystrokes. If you want to use a nonalphanumeric key, place the name of the key inside curly braces. Here are some special codes for keys that are coded with characters other than their key names. If the *logical* value is TRUE, Excel waits for the string to be

S-T

processed as keystrokes before going on. If the *logical* value is FALSE, Excel continues without waiting.

Key	Referred to By
ALT	%
CTRL	^
DOWN ARROW	{DOWN}
ENTER	~ OR {ENTER}
ESC	{ESC} OR {ESCAPE}
LEFT ARROW	{LEFT}
PGDN	{PGDN}
PGUP	{PGUP}
PRINT SCRNT	{PRTSC}
RIGHT ARROW	{RIGHT}
SHIFT	+
UP ARROW	{UP}

See Also

APP.ACTIVATE	Activates another application	Macro Function
EXECUTE	Executes a command in another application	Macro Function

SEND.MAIL()
SEND.MAIL?()

Macro Function

SEND.MAIL sends mail using Microsoft Mail. Both forms of the function open a dialog box where you enter the address and the message. This function is only available if you have Microsoft Windows Simple Mail.

SEND.TO.BACK()

Macro Function   **New to Version 4.0**

SEND.TO.BACK sends selected objects to the back, or behind objects that aren't selected.

See Also

BRING.TO.FRONT   Brings selected objects to the front   Macro Function

---

SERIES(*[name], [categories], values, order*)

Chart Function

SERIES is used in charts to define series. This function cannot be used on macro sheets or worksheets. The *name* is the name of the series, and is optional. *Categories* is a reference to the cells that contain the category labels, or the x values for scatter charts. *Values* is a reference to the cells that contain the values in the series. *Order* is an integer that represents the plot order.

See Also

EDIT.SERIES   Edits a series   Macro Function

SERIESSUM(*X, power, step, coefficients*)

Function   New to Version 4.0

SERIESSUM calculates the sum of a power series. *X* is the value on which to perform the power series. *Power* is the power to which the first term is raised. *Step* is the amount each exponent is increased for each successive term. *Coefficients* is a set of coefficients given as a range or an array. The formula for SERIESSUM is shown here:

$$\text{SERIES}(x, n, m, a) = a_1 x^n + a_2 x^{(n+m)} + a_3 x^{(n+2m)}$$

$$+ \ldots + a_i x^{(n+(i-1)m)}$$

X represents the input value, *n* is the power of the first term, *m* is the amount each power is increased for each successive term, and $a1$, $a2$, ... ai are the coefficients for each term.

SERIESSUM is an add-in function. The first time you use it, you may see a #REF! error while Excel loads the function.

Example

=SERIESSUM(3,1,2,{3,4,5,6}) returns 14454.

See Also

SUM   Sums a range of values   Function

S-T

SET.CRITERIA()

Macro Function

SET.CRITERIA performs the same action as the Set Criteria option on the Data menu. SET.CRITERIA defines the selected range to be the criteria range. The criteria is used by database functions and commands to find, delete, or extract particular records from a database.

See Also

DATA SET CRITERIA   Equivalent command   Menu Command

SET.DATABASE()

Macro Function

SET.DATABASE performs the same action as the Set Database option on the Data menu. SET.DATABASE defines the currently selected range to be a database.

See Also

DATA SET DATABASE   Equivalent command   Menu Command

SET.EXTRACT()

Macro Function

SET.EXTRACT performs the same action as the Set Extract option on the Data menu. SET.EXTRACT defines the currently selected range to be the extract range.

SET.NAME(*name, [refers-to]*)

Macro Function

SET.NAME causes the *name* to be set to the value or reference specified by the *refers-to* argument, if the *refers-to* argument is included. If the *refers-to* argument is omitted, the name is deleted.

Example

=SET.NAME("cost",1000) sets the name cost to be the value 1000.

See Also

DEFINE.NAME	Defines a name	Macro Function

SET.PAGE.BREAK()

Macro Function

SET.PAGE.BREAK performs the same action as the Set Page Break option on the Options menu. SET.PAGE.BREAK sets a manual page break to the left of and above the active cell.

See Also

OPTIONS SET PAGE BREAK	Equivalent command	Menu Command
REMOVE.PAGE.BREAK	Removes a manual page break	Macro Function

SET.PREFERRED()

Macro Function

SET.PREFERRED performs the same action as the Set Preferred option on the Gallery menu. SET.PREFERRED sets the preferred chart type to be the format of the active chart.

See Also

GALLERY SET PREFERRED	Equivalent command	Menu Command
PREFERRED	Formats the active chart to the preferred type	Macro Function

SET.PRINT.AREA()

Macro Function

SET.PRINT.AREA performs the same action as the Set Print Area option on the Options menu. SET.PRINT.AREA defines the currently selected range to be the print area. To undefine the print area, you must delete the print area name by using the Formula Define Name menu command.

S-T

See Also

OPTIONS SET PRINT AREA	Equivalent command	Menu Command
PRINT	Prints a document	Macro Function

SET.PRINT.TITLES(*[columns], [rows]*)

Macro Function

SET.PRINT.TITLES performs the same action as the Set Print Titles option on the Options menu. SET.PRINT.TITLES defines the currently selected range to be the print titles.

Columns is a reference to the columns that you want to use as print titles. *Rows* is a reference to the rows that you want to use as print titles. If the *columns* and *rows* arguments are not supplied, the current selection is used.

See Also

OPTIONS SET PRINT TITLES	Equivalent command	Menu Command

SET.UPDATE.STATUS(*link, status, [type]*)

Macro Function

SET.UPDATE.STATUS defines the update status of a link to be manual or automatic. *Link* is the pathname and filename of the link for which you want to set the *status*. *Status* is 1 if you want to update the link automatically, and 2 if you want to update the link manually. *Type* is the type of link. Currently the only type available is 2, which represents a Dynamic Date Exchange link. The default value for *type* is 2.

See Also

GET.LINK.INFO	Returns information about a link	Macro Function
UPDATE.LINK	Updates a link	Macro Function

SET.VALUE(*reference, values*)

Macro Function

SET.VALUE sets the value in the cell or cells on the macro sheet referred to by the *reference* argument. The value used is the one specified by the *values* argument. If there is already a formula in the cell or cells, the formula is not changed. If *reference* refers to a range, *values* must be a range that is the same size as that range.

See Also

| DEFINE.NAME | Defines a name on a worksheet | Macro Function |
| FORMULA | Enters values on a worksheet | Macro Function |

SHORT.MENUS(*[logical]*)

Macro Function   **Prior to Version 4.0**

If the *logical* value is TRUE, SHORT.MENUS performs the same action as the Short Menus option on the Options menu. If the *logical* value is FALSE, SHORT.MENUS performs the same action as the Full Menus option on the Options menu. If no *logical* argument is given, SHORT.MENUS toggles between short and full menus.

SHOW.ACTIVE.CELL()

Macro Function

Using SHOW.ACTIVE.CELL is the same as pressing CTRL-BACKSPACE or choosing the Show Active Cell option from the Formula menu. SHOW.ACTIVE.CELL adjusts the window so that the active cell is visible.

See Also

| ACTIVE.CELL | Returns the active cell's reference | Macro Function |
| FORMULA.GOTO | Selects the cell or range specified | Macro Function |

SHOW.BAR(*bar*)

Macro Function

SHOW.BAR displays the menu bar specified by *bar. Bar* must be either the number of a built-in menu bar or a number that is returned by ADD.BAR if you want to show a custom menu bar. To show a built-in menu bar, use one of the following numbers:

Bar	Menu Bar
1	A full menu bar for a worksheet or macro
2	A full menu bar for a chart

Bar	Menu Bar
3	A menu if there is no window active
4	An Info window menu
5	A short menu bar for a worksheet or macro
6	A short menu bar for a chart

See Also

| ADD.BAR | Adds the specified menu bar | Macro Function |
| DELETE.BAR | Deletes the specified menu bar | Macro Function |

SHOW.CLIPBOARD()

Macro Function

SHOW.CLIPBOARD displays the current contents of the Clipboard in a new window.

SHOW.DETAIL(*rowcol, number, [expand]*)

Macro Function   **New to Version 4.0**

SHOW.DETAIL expands or collapses the detail of an outline.

Rowcol is a number that indicates whether you want to expand or collapse rows or columns. If *rowcol* is 1, rows are expanded or collapsed. If *rowcol* is 2, columns are expanded or collapsed.

Number is the number of the row or column that you want to expand or collapse. If you are in A1 mode, columns are referred to by numbers rather than letters.

Expand is a logical value. If *expand* is TRUE, the outline is expanded. If *expand* is FALSE, the outline is collapsed. If *expand* is omitted, expanded outlines are collapsed and collapsed outlines are expanded.

Example

=SHOW.DETAIL(1,3,TRUE) expands the detail under row 3.

See Also

| SHOW.LEVELS | Displays levels of an outline | Macro Function |

SHOW.INFO(*logical*)

Macro Function

SHOW.INFO activates the Info window if the *logical* argument is TRUE. It activates the document linked to the Info window if the *logical* argument is FALSE.

Example

=SHOW.INFO(TRUE) displays the Info window.

See Also

GET.CELL	Returns information about a cell	Macro Function

SHOW.LEVELS(*[row]*,*[col]*)

Macro Function

SHOW.LEVELS shows a certain number of levels of an outline. *Row* specifies how many row levels to display and *col* specifies how many column levels to display. If the *row* argument is omitted, no row levels are displayed. If the *col* argument is omitted, no column levels are displayed.

See Also

SHOW.DETAIL	Expands or collapses an outline	Macro Function

SHOW.TOOLBAR(*bar,visible,position,[X],[Y],[width]*)

Macro Function   New to Version 4.0

SHOW.TOOLBAR displays or hides the toolbar specified by *bar*. *Bar* is the number or name of a toolbar, or an array containing the numbers or names of the toolbars you want to display. The built-in toolbars have the following numbers and names:

Bar	Toolbar
1	Standard
2	Formatting
3	Utility

S-T

Bar	Toolbar
4	Chart
5	Drawing
6	Excel 3.0
7	Macro
8	Stop Recording
9	Macro Paused

Visible is a logical value. If *visible* is TRUE, the toolbar is displayed. If *visible* is FALSE, the toolbar is hidden.

Position is a number that indicates the location of the toolbar. The following table summarizes the possible values for *position*:

Position	Description
1	Top
2	Left
3	Right
4	Bottom
5	Floating

X and *Y* indicate the exact location of the toolbar. If *position* is 1, 2, 3, or 4, *X* and *Y* are measured from the top and left of the home position in points. If position is 5, *X* and *Y* are measured from the bottom and right edge of the nearest toolbar to the top left edge of the floating toolbar in points. A point is 1/72 of an inch.

Width is an optional argument that represents the width of the toolbar in points. If *width* is omitted, the standard toolbar width is used.

See Also

ADD.TOOLBAR   Adds a toolbar   Macro Function

SIGN(*X*)

Function

SIGN returns 1 if *X* is a positive number, −1 if *X* is negative, and 0 if *X* is zero.

Examples

=SIGN(5) returns 1.

=SIGN(–5) returns –1.
=SIGN(0) returns 0.

See Also

ABS	Returns the absolute value of a number	Function

SIN(*X*)

Function

SIN calculates the sine of an angle *X* measured in radians. (Radians equals degrees multiplied by PI()/180.)

Example

=SIN(B18) calculates the sine of the radian value in B18.

See Also

COS	Returns the cosine of an angle	Function
PI	Returns pi	Function
TAN	Returns the tangent of an angle	Function

SINH(*X*)

Function

SINH returns the hyperbolic sine of an angle *X* measured in radians. (Radians equals degrees multiplied by PI()/180.)

Example

=SINH(2) returns 3.62686.

See Also

ASINH	Inverse hyperbolic sine function	Function
COSH	Hyperbolic cosine function	Function
SIN	Returns the sine of an angle	Function
TANH	Hyperbolic tangent function	Function

S-T

SIZE(*window-width,window-height,[window-name]*)
SIZE?(*[window-width],[window-height],[window-name]*)

Macro Function   **Prior to Version 4.0**

SIZE performs the same action as the Size command on the Control menu. It sizes the window specified by *window-name* according the *window-width* and *window-height* arguments, given in points. If the *window-name* argument is omitted, the default is the current window.

In the dialog box version (with the question mark), the arguments, if included, are used as defaults for the dialog box that appears.

The SIZE function is included for macro compatibility with older versions of Excel. Use the WINDOW.SIZE function to size windows.

See Also

WINDOW.SIZE	Equivalent function	Function

SKEW(*X1,[X2],...*)

Function   **New to Version 4.0**

SKEW returns a distribution's degree of asymmetry around the mean. The arguments *X1, X2,* and so on are the values for which you want to determine the skew. You can include up to 30 arguments.

Example

=SKEW(1,3,4,3,6,5,7,3,2,9,5) returns 0.613717.

See Also

STDEV	Calculates the standard deviation	Function
VAR	Calculates the variance	Function

SLIDE.COPY.ROW()

Macro Function   **New to Version 4.0**

SLIDE.COPY.ROW copies selected rows from the active document, which must be a slide show, and places them on the Clipboard. Each slide in a slide show is stored in a row. SLIDE.COPY.ROW returns TRUE if rows are successfully copied, and FALSE otherwise.

SLIDE.COPY.ROW is an add-in function. You may need to load the Slide Show add-in macro to use it.

SLIDE.CUT.ROW()

Macro Function   **New to Version 4.0**

SLIDE.CUT.ROW cuts selected rows from the active document, which must be a slide show, and places them in the Clipboard. Each slide in a slide show is stored in a row. SLIDE.COPY.ROW returns TRUE if rows are successfully cut, and FALSE otherwise.

SLIDE.CUT.ROW is an add-in function. You may need to load the Slide Show add-in macro to use it.

SLIDE.DEFAULTS(*[effect]*,*[speed]*,*[time]*)

Macro Function   **New to Version 4.0**

SLIDE.DEFAULTS sets the default characteristics of the active slide show document. *Effect* is a number that specifies the transition effect between slides. The transition effect options are listed in the Effect list box in the Edit Slide dialog box.

Effects are numbered starting with 1 at the top. If you omit the *effect* argument, the previously set default remains in effect.

Speed is a number between 1 and 10 indicating the speed of the transition. If you omit the *speed* argument, the previously set default remains in effect.

Time is the amount of time in seconds that each slide is displayed. If *time* is 0, you can advance slides by clicking the mouse or using the keyboard.

SLIDE.DEFAULTS is an add-in function. You may need to load the Slide Show add-in macro to use it.

SLIDE.DELETE.ROW()

Macro Function   **New to Version 4.0**

SLIDE.DELETE.ROW deletes selected rows from the active document, which must be a slide show. Each slide in a slide show is stored in a row. SLIDE.DELETE.ROW returns TRUE if rows are successfully deleted, and FALSE otherwise.

SLIDE.DELETE.ROW is an add-in function. You may need to load the Slide Show add-in macro to use it.

S-T

SLIDE.EDIT(*[effect], [speed], [time], [sound]*)
SLIDE.EDIT?(*[effect], [speed], [time], [sound]*)

Macro Function   **New to Version 4.0**

SLIDE.EDIT sets the characteristics of the active slide show document. *Effect* is a number that specifies the transition effect between slides. The transition effect options are listed in the Effect list box in the Edit Slide dialog box.

Effects are numbered starting with 1 at the top. If you omit the *effect* argument, the previously set default remains in effect.

Speed is a number between 1 and 10 indicating the speed of the transition. If you omit the *speed* argument, the previously set default remains in effect.

Time is the amount of time in seconds that each slide is displayed. If *time* is 0, you can advance slides by clicking the mouse or using the keyboard.

Sound is the name of the file that contains the sound you want played while the slide is displayed.

In the dialog box version (with the question mark), the arguments, if included, are used as defaults for the dialog box that appears.

SLIDE.EDIT is an add-in function. You may need to load the Slide Show add-in macro to use it.

SLIDE.GET(*type, [name], [slide]*)

Macro Function   **New to Version 4.0**

SLIDE.GET returns information about a particular slide in a slide show. *Name* is the name of the slide show. If *name* is omitted, it is assumed to be the active slide show. *Slide* is the number of the slide about which you want information. If *slide* is omitted, either it is assumed to be the slide associated with the active cell or, if you want information about a slide show, it is ignored.

Type is a number that indicates the type of information that you want returned about a slide or about the whole slide show. The possible values for *type* are listed here:

Type	Information Returned
1	The number of slides in the slide show
2	An array containing the first and last slide numbers in the selection
3	The slide show add-in macro version
4	The number of the transition effect

Type	Information Returned
5	The name of the transition effect
6	The speed of the transition effect
7	The time a slide is displayed in seconds
8	The name of the sound file

SLIDE.GET is an add-in function. You may need to load the Slide Show add-in macro to use it.

SLIDE.PASTE(*[effect]*, *[speed]*, *[time]*, *[sound]*)
SLIDE.PASTE?(*[effect]*, *[speed]*, *[time]*, *[sound]*)

Macro Function　　　　　　　　　　　　　　　　**New to Version 4.0**

SLIDE.PASTE pastes the slides in the Clipboard to the active slide show and sets the characteristics as specified. *Effect* is a number that specifies the transition effect between slides. The transition effect options are listed in the Effect list box in the Edit Slide dialog box.

Effects are numbered starting with 1 at the top. If *effect* is omitted, the previously set default remains in effect.

Speed is a number between 1 and 10 indicating the speed of the transition. If *speed* is omitted, the previously set default remains in effect.

Time is the amount of time in seconds that each slide is displayed. If *time* is 0, you can advance slides by clicking the mouse or using the keyboard.

Sound is the name of the file that contains the sound you want played while the slide is displayed.

In the dialog box version (with the question mark), the arguments, if included, are used as defaults for the dialog box that appears.

SLIDE.PASTE is an add-in function. You may need to load the Slide Show add-in macro to use it.

SLIDE.PASTE.ROW()

Macro Function　　　　　　　　　　　　　　　　**New to Version 4.0**

SLIDE.PASTE.ROW pastes previously cut or copied rows to the active document, which must be a slide show. Each slide in a slide show is stored in a row. SLIDE.PASTE.ROW returns TRUE if the rows are successfully pasted, and FALSE otherwise.

SLIDE.PASTE.ROW is an add-in function. You may need to load the Slide Show add-in macro to use it.

S-T

SLIDE.SHOW(*[first-slide], [repeat], [db-title], [keys], [options]*)
SLIDE.SHOW?(*[first-slide], [repeat], [db-title], [keys], [options]*)

Macro Function **New to Version 4.0**

SLIDE.SHOW starts the slide show of the active document, which must be a slide show. *First-slide* is the number of the first slide that you want displayed. The default value for *first-slide* is 1.

Repeat is a logical value. If *repeat* is TRUE, the slide show will repeat after it is done. If *repeat* is FALSE, the slide show is not repeated. The default value for *repeat* is FALSE.

Db-title, an optional argument, is a text string that is used as the title for the dialog boxes displayed during the slide show.

Keys is a logical value. If *keys* is TRUE, navigation keys are enabled during the slide show. If *keys* is FALSE, navigation keys are disabled. The default value for *keys* is TRUE.

Options is a logical value. If *options* is TRUE, the Slide Show Options dialog box is displayed when you press the ESC key during the slide show. If *options* is FALSE, the dialog box is disabled. The default value for *options* is TRUE.

In the dialog box version (with the question mark), the arguments, if included, are used as defaults for the dialog box that appears.

SLIDE.SHOW is an add-in function. You may need to load the Slide Show add-in macro to use it.

See Also

SLIDE.COPY.ROW	Copies a slide from a slide show	Macro Function
SLIDE.CUT.ROW	Cuts a slide from a slide show	Macro Function
SLIDE.DEFAULTS	Sets slide show defaults	Macro Function
SLIDE.DELETE.ROW	Deletes a row from a slide show	Macro Function
SLIDE.EDIT	Edits a slide	Macro Function
SLIDE.GET	Returns information about a slide show	Macro Function
SLIDE.PASTE	Pastes slides from the Clipboard	Macro Function
SLIDE.PASTE.ROW	Pastes a row from the Clipboard	Macro Function

SLN(*cost, salvage, life*)

Function

SLN returns the depreciation expense of an asset for a specified period using the straight-line depreciation method. Enter the *cost* of the asset, its expected *salvage* value, and the expected asset *life*.

Example

=SLN(5000,300,10) returns the annual depreciation expense of $470 for a machine that costs $5,000 and is expected to be worth $300 in 10 years.

See Also

DDB	Returns the double-declining balance depreciation	Function
SYD	Returns the sum-of-year's digits depreciation	Function
VDB	Returns the declining balance depreciation	Function

SLOPE(*dependent, independent*)

Function

SLOPE returns the slope of the linear regression line defined by the dependent and independent data points. Dependent (y values) and independent (x values) are arrays or ranges that contain values.

Example

({2,3,5,4,6,5,7,8},{5,6,7,6,8,9,5,9}) returns 0.635762.

See Also

INTERCEPT	Returns the intercept	Function
LINEST	Returns linear trend parameters	Function
LOGEST	Returns exponential trend parameters	Function
TREND	Returns linear trend values	Function

SMALL(*array, K*)

Function   New to Version 4.0

SMALL returns the *K*th smallest value in the *array*. The *K*th smallest value is in the position *K* if the *array* is sorted in an ascending order.

Example

=SMALL({1,2,3,5,4,5,6,8},4) returns 4.

S-T

See Also

LARGE	Returns the *K*th largest value	Function
MAX	Returns the maximum value	Function
MIN	Returns the minimum value	Function

SOLVER.ADD(*left, relationship, [right]*)

Macro Function   **New to Version 4.0**

Using SOLVER.ADD is the same action as choosing the Solver option on the Formula menu and clicking on the Add button in the Solver Parameters dialog box. The Solver Parameters dialog box is shown here:

SOLVER.ADD adds a constraint to the solver problem. The *left* argument is the left side of the constraint. *Left* is a reference to a cell or a range of cells. *Relationship* is a number that represents the arithmetic relationship between the left and right sides of the constraint. The possible values for *relationship* are listed here:

Relationship	Arithmetic Relationship
1	<=
2	=
3	>=
4	Integer

Right is the right side of the constraint. *Right* can be a value or a reference to one or more cells. If *right* is a reference, the size of the range must be equal to the size of the range referred to by *left*. If *relationship* is 4, SOLVER.ADD tests whether the right side of the constraint is an integer or integers, and the *left* argument is ignored.

SOLVER.ADD is an add-in function. You may need to install the Solver add-in macro if it is not available.

SOLVER.CHANGE(*left, relationship, [right]*)

Macro Function   **New to Version 4.0**

Using SOLVER.CHANGE is the same as choosing the Solver option from the Formula menu and clicking on the Change button in the Solver Parameters dialog box.

SOLVER.CHANGE changes the right side of a constraint. The *left* argument is the left side of the constraint. *Left* is a reference to a cell or a range of cells. *Relationship* is a number that represents the arithmetic relationship between the left and right sides of the constraint. The possible values for *relationship* are listed here:

Relationship	Arithmetic Relationship
1	<=
2	=
3	>=
4	Integer

SOLVER.CHANGE matches the *left* and *relationship* arguments to an existing constraint, and changes the right side of the constraint as given by the *right* argument. If no match is found, SOLVER.CHANGE returns the value 4.

Right is the right side of the constraint. *Right* can be a value or a reference to one or more cells. If *right* is a reference, the size of the range must equal the size of the range referred to by *left*.

SOLVER.CHANGE is an add-in function. You may need to install the Solver add-in macro if it is not available.

SOLVER.DELETE(*left, relationship, [right]*)

Macro Function   **New to Version 4.0**

Using SOLVER.DELETE is the same as choosing the Solver option from the Formula menu and clicking on the Delete button in the Solver Parameters dialog box.

SOLVER.DELETE deletes a constraint from the Solver problem. The *left* argument is the left side of the constraint. *Left* is a reference to a cell or a range of cells. *Relationship* is a number that represents the arithmetic relationship between the left and right sides of the constraint. The possible values for *relationship* are listed here:

Relationship	Arithmetic Relationship
1	<=
2	=

S-T

Relationship	Arithmetic Relationship
3	>=
4	Integer

Right is an optional argument representing the right side of the constraint. SOLVER.DELETE matches the *left* and *relationship* arguments to an existing constraint, and deletes the constraint. If no match is found, SOLVER.DELETE returns a 4, and no constraint is deleted.

SOLVER.DELETE is an add-in function. You may need to install the Solver add-in macro if it is not available.

SOLVER.FINISH(*[keep], [report]*)
SOLVER.FINISH?(*[keep], [report]*)

Macro Function   **New to Version 4.0**

SOLVER.FINISH finishes the Solver problem by displaying a dialog box asking if you want to keep the solution. The arguments are used as default values in the dialog box. *Keep* is 1 if you want to keep the solution, and 2 if you want to discard the solution. *Report* is an array that contains numbers indicating the type of report to produce. Possible values in the *report* array are listed here:

Report	Description
{1}	Answer report
{2}	Sensitivity report
{3}	Limit report

The *report* array can contain more than one of these values.

SOLVER.FINISH is an add-in function. You may need to install the Solver add-in macro if it is not available.

SOLVER.GET(*type, [name]*)

Macro Function   **New to Version 4.0**

SOLVER.GET returns information about the current Solver problem. *Type* is a number that indicates the type of information you want returned. The following table lists the possible values for *type*:

Type	Information Returned
1	The Set Cells reference.
2	1 if Equal To is set to Max, 2 if it is set to Min, and 3 if it is set to Value Of.
3	The Value Of value.
4	The By Changing Cells reference.
5	The number of constraints defined.
6	The left sides of all the constraints in an array.
7	The relationships between all the constraints in an array of numbers. Returns 1 for <=, 2 for =, 3 for >=, 4 for integer.
8	The right sides of all the constraints in a text array.
9	Maximum calculation time.
10	Maximum iterations.
11	Precision.
12	Integer tolerance value.
13	TRUE if the Assume Linear Model check box is on; otherwise FALSE.
14	TRUE if the Show Iteration Results check box is on; otherwise FALSE.
15	TRUE if the Automatic Scaling check box is on; otherwise FALSE.
16	1 for tangent estimates; 2 for quadratic estimates.
17	1 if derivatives are forward; 2 if derivatives are central.
18	1 if the search type is Quasi-Newton; 2 if the search type is is Conjugate Gradient.

Name is an optional argument. *Name* is the name of the document on which the scenario is located. If *name* is omitted, it is assumed to be the active document.

SOLVER.GET is an add-in function. You may need to install the Solver add-in macro if it is not available.

SOLVER.LOAD(*reference*)

Macro Function   **New to Version 4.0**

SOLVER.LOAD loads a Solver problem that has previously been saved on a worksheet. Use SOLVER.SAVE to save a Solver problem. *Reference* is a reference to the range where the specifications are stored.

S-T

SOLVER.LOAD is an add-in function. You may need to install the Solver add-in macro if it is not available.

SOLVER.OK([set-cell], [value], [target], [by-changing-cells]**)**
SOLVER.OK?([set-cell], [value], [target], [by-changing-cells]**)**

Macro Function   **New to Version 4.0**

SOLVER.OK sets options for the current Solver problem. The arguments correspond to the options in the Solver Parameters dialog box.

Set-cell corresponds to the Set Cell box. *Set-cell* is a reference to a cell on the worksheet that you want to set to a value.

Value is a number that indicates what value you want the cell referred to by *set-cell* to achieve. If *value* is 1, *set-cell* is maximized. If *value* is 2, *set-cell* is minimized. If *value* is 3, *set-cell* is matched to the value given by the *target* argument. *Target* is the value that you want *set-cell* to achieve if *value* is 3.

By-changing-cells is a range or multiple cell reference to the cells that you want to allow to vary in order to achieve the desired result in the cell referred to by *set-cell*.

In the dialog box version (with the question mark), the arguments, if included, are used as defaults for the dialog box that appears.

SOLVER.OK is an add-in function. You may need to install the Solver add-in macro if it is not available.

SOLVER.OPTIONS([max-time], [iterations], [precision], [assume-linear-model], [step], [estimates], [derivatives], [search], [tolerance], [scaling]**)**

Macro Function   **New to Version 4.0**

SOLVER.OPTIONS sets options for the Solver problem. The arguments correspond to options in the Solver Parameters dialog box.

Max-time corresponds to the Max Time box, and limits the time that the Solver can spend solving the problem. *Iterations* corresponds to the Iterations box, and limits the number of iterations allowed.

Precision corresponds to the Precision box, and defines the precision of the solution. *Precision* should be a number between 0 and 1.

Assume-linear-model is a logical value and corresponds to the Assume Linear Model check box. If *assume-linear-model* is TRUE, a linear model is assumed and the Solver may find a solution faster. If *assume-linear-model* is FALSE, a linear model is not assumed.

Step is a logical value, and corresponds to the Show Iteration Results check box. If *step* is TRUE, the Solver pauses after each iteration; if *step* is FALSE it does not.

Estimates defines the estimates option. If *estimates* is 1, tangent estimates are used. If *estimates* if 2, quadratic estimates are used.

Derivatives defines the derivatives options. If *derivatives* is 1, forward derivatives are used. If *derivatives* is 2, central derivatives are used.

Search defines the search option. If *search* is 1, Quasi-Newton search is used. If *search* is 2, Conjugate Gradient search is used.

Tolerance is the integer tolerance to be used if there are integer constraints.

Scaling is a logical value that corresponds to the Use Automatic Scaling check box. If *scaling* is TRUE, automatic scaling is turned on; if *scaling* is FALSE, it is not.

SOLVER.OPTIONS is an add-in function. You may need to install the Solver add-in macro if it is not available.

SOLVER.RESET()

Macro Function   **New to Version 4.0**

SOLVER.RESET resets the Solver by removing all constraints and changing all options to their defaults.

This is an add-in function. You may need to install the Solver add-in macro if it is not available.

SOLVER.SAVE(*reference*)

Macro Function   **New to Version 4.0**

SOLVER.SAVE saves the current specifications and options for the Solver in the worksheet location referred to by *reference*. *Reference* is a reference to the upper-left cell in the range where you want to store the specifications.

SOLVER.SAVE is an add-in function. You may need to install the Solver add-in macro if it is not available.

SOLVER.SOLVE([*finish*], [*show*])

Macro Function   **New to Version 4.0**

SOLVER.SOLVE executes the Solver with the current settings and constraints, and returns an integer that indicates the status of the solution.

Finish is a logical value. If *finish* is TRUE, no dialog box is displayed when a solution is found. If *finish* is FALSE, a dialog box is displayed upon completion.

S-T

Show is an optional argument. *Show* is the name of a custom macro that you want to call when a solution is found. If no *show* argument is given, the Show Trial Solution dialog box is displayed when a solution is found. This argument is only used if the Show Iteration Result check box is turned on.

SOLVER.SOLVE is an add-in function. You may need to install the Solver add-in macro if it is not available.

See Also

FORMULA SOLVER	Equivalent command	Menu Command
SOLVER.ADD	Adds a constraint	Macro Function
SOLVER.CHANGE	Modifies a constraint	Macro Function
SOLVER.DELETE	Deletes a constraint	Macro Function
SOLVER.FINISH	Finishes a Solver problem	Macro Function
SOLVER.GET	Returns information about a Solver problem	Macro Function
SOLVER.LOAD	Loads a Solver problem	Macro Function
SOLVER.OK	Sets Solver options	Macro Function
SOLVER.OPTIONS	Sets Solver parameters	Macro Function
SOLVER.RESET	Resets the Solver	Macro Function
SOLVER.SAVE	Saves a Solver problem	Macro Function

SORT(*sort-by, primary-key, primary-order, [secondary-key], [secondary-order], [third-key], [third-order]*)
SORT?(*[sort-by], [primary-key], [primary-order], [secondary-key], [secondary-order], [third-key], [third-order]*)

Macro Function

SORT performs the same action as the Sort option on the Data menu. SORT sorts the current selection as defined by the arguments. The *sort-by* argument should be 1 if you want to sort by rows, or 2 if you want sort by columns.

The *primary-order, secondary-order,* and *third-order* arguments should be 1 for ascending and 2 for descending. The *primary-key, secondary-key,* and *third-key* arguments should be references to the rows or columns you want to sort.

In the dialog box version (with the question mark), the arguments, if included, are used as default values for the dialog box that appears.

SOUND.NOTE(*[reference]*,*[erase]*)
SOUND.NOTE(*[reference]*,*[file]*)

Macro Function   **New to Version 4.0**

SOUND.NOTE attaches a sound note to a cell, or erases a sound note from a cell. There are two argument profiles for this function. The first version of SOUND.NOTE records or erases a note, and the second version attaches an imported sound note to a cell.

Reference is a reference to the cell that you want to record a sound note for or erase a sound note from. If *reference* is omitted, it is assumed to be the active cell.

In the first argument profile, *erase* is a logical value. If *erase* is TRUE, the sound note is erased. If *erase* is FALSE, the Record dialog box is displayed where you can record your sound note. The default value for *erase* is FALSE.

In the second argument profile, *file* is the name of the file that contains the sound note you want to import.

See Also

NOTE	Creates or modifies a text note	Macro Function
SOUND.PLAY	Plays a sound note	Macro Function

SOUND.PLAY(*[reference]*,*[file]*)

Macro Function   **New to Version 4.0**

SOUND.PLAY plays a sound note. You can either play a sound note that is attached to a cell, or a sound note from a file.

Reference is a reference to the cell for which you want to play a sound note. If *reference* is omitted, it is assumed to be the active cell.

File is the name of the file that contains a sound note. If *reference* is included, the *file* argument is ignored.

See Also

NOTE	Creates or modifies a text note	Macro Function
SOUND.NOTE	Attaches or erases a sound note	Macro Function

S-T

SPELLING(*[dictionary]*, *[ignore-uppercase]*, *[always-suggest]*)

Macro Function   **New to Version 4.0**

SPELLING performs the same action as the Spelling option on the Options menu. SPELLING spell checks all the words in the current selection. The Spelling dialog box is shown here:

Dictionary is the filename of the dictionary that you want to use. If *dictionary* is omitted, the currently active dictionary is used.

Ignore-uppercase is a logical value. If *ignore-uppercase* is TRUE, words that are all uppercase are not checked. If *ignore-uppercase* is FALSE, all words are checked. If *ignore-uppercase* is omitted, the status of the *ignore-uppercase* setting remains unchanged.

Always-suggest is a logical value. If *always-suggest* is TRUE, a list of suggested words appears when an incorrect spelling is found. If *always-suggest* is FALSE, no spelling alternatives are presented. If *always-suggest* is omitted, the status of the *always-suggest* setting remains unchanged.

See Also

OPTIONS SPELLING	Equivalent command	Menu Command
SPELLING.CHECK	Checks the spelling of a word	Macro Function

SPELLING.CHECK(*word,[dictionary],[ignore-uppercase]*)

Macro Function   **New to Version 4.0**

SPELLING.CHECK performs a spell check on a specified word. *Word* is the word you want to check given as a text string. SPELLING.CHECK returns TRUE if the word is spelled correctly, and FALSE otherwise.

Dictionary is the file name of the dictionary that you want to use. If *dictionary* is omitted, the currently active dictionary is used.

Ignore-uppercase is a logical value. If *ignore-uppercase* is TRUE, words that are all uppercase are not checked. If *ignore-uppercase* is FALSE, all words are checked. If *ignore-uppercase* is omitted, the status of the *ignore-uppercase* setting remains unchanged.

See Also

OPTIONS SPELLING	Equivalent command	Menu Command
SPELLING	Checks the spelling of a selection	Macro Function

SPLIT(*horizontal, vertical*)

Macro Function

SPLIT performs the same action as the Split option on the Window menu. SPLIT divides the active window into panes. The *horizontal* and *vertical* arguments, which are measured in rows and columns, tell SPLIT where to split the window.

See Also

FREEZE.PANES	Freezes or unfreezes window panes	Macro Function
WINDOW SPLIT	Equivalent command	Menu Command

SQRT(*X*)

Function

SQRT returns the square root of a positive value *X*.

Example

=SQRT(B55) returns the square root of the value in B55.

See Also

PI	Returns the value of PI	Function
SQRTPI	Related function	Function

S-T

SQRTPI(X)

Function   **New to Version 4.0**

SQRTPI returns the square root of a positive value X multiplied by PI.

    This is an add-in function. The first time that you use it, you may see a #REF! error while Excel loads the function.

Example

=SQRTPI(B55) returns the square root of the product of value in B55 and PI.

See Also

PI	Returns the value of PI	Function
SQRT	Returns the square root of a number	Function

STANDARDIZE(X, *mean*, *standard-deviation*)

Function

STANDARDIZE normalizes X from a distribution defined by the *mean* and the *standard-deviation* arguments.

Example

=STANDARDIZE(80,75,.9) returns 5.555556.

See Also

NORMDIST	Returns the normal cumulative distribution	Function
NORMSDIST	Returns the standard normal cumulative distribution	Function
ZTEST	Performs a z-test	Function

STDEV(*list*)

Function

STDEV returns the sample standard deviation of the values itemized in the list. The list can contain any combination of numbers, formulas, or references to cells containing numbers or formulas. Use STDEVP when the number of items in the list is large. Use STDEV when the number is small.

Example

=STDEV(A14:A20) returns the sample standard deviation of the values contained in the range A14 to A20.

See Also

STDEVP   Returns the standard deviation of whole population   Function

STDEVP(*list*)

Function

STDEVP returns the population standard deviation of the values itemized in the specified list. The list can contain any combination of numbers, formulas, or references to cells containing numbers or formulas. Use STDEVP when the number of items in the list is large. Use STDEV when the number is small.

Example

=STDEVP(A14:H120) returns the population standard deviation of the values contained in the range A14 to H120.

See Also

STDEV   Returns the standard deviation of a sample   Function

STEP()

Macro Function

STEP displays the Single Step dialog box. Using this dialog box, you can step through the macro, halt the macro, or continue executing the macro. You can also go to a particular line in the macro, step into or step over a particular line, evaluate the current line, or pause the macro. The Single Step dialog box is shown here:

S-T

See Also

HALT	Halts all macros	Macro Function
RUN	Starts a macro	Macro Function

STEYX(*dependent, independent*)

Function

New to Version 4.0

STEYX calculates the regression and returns the amount of error for a single value of X (an independent point) in the prediction of Y (dependent data). *Dependent* and *independent* are ranges or arrays of dependent (X) and independent (Y) data sets.

Example

=STEYX({1,3,4,5,6},{4,5,6,7,3}) returns 2.213594.

See Also

INTERCEPT	Returns the intercept of a linear regression	Function
LINEST	Returns linear trend parameters	Function
LOGEST	Returns exponential trend parameters	Function
SLOPE	Returns the slope of a linear regression	Function

SUBSTITUTE(*original-string, old-sub-string, new-sub-string, [instance-number]*)

Function

SUBSTITUTE replaces the string specified by *old-sub-string* with the string specified by *new-sub-string* in the *original-string*. The *original-string* specification can be a literal, a reference to a cell containing a label, or a formula that evaluates to a string. The *optional-instance* number argument allows you to specify which instance of the *old-sub-string* you want to replace with the *new-sub-string*.

Example

=SUBSTITUTE("Income Statement","Statement","Projection") returns "Income Projection".

See Also

REPLACE	Similar function	Function
TRIM	Cleans text by removing spaces	Function

SUM(*ref1,[ref2],...*)

Function

SUM returns the sum of the values contained in the references. *Ref1, ref2,* and so on can be references to cells, references to ranges, or actual values.

Example

=SUM(A1:A5,C6:C18) returns the sum of the values in the range A1 through A5 and C6 through C18.

See Also

AVERAGE	Returns the average of the values	Function
PRODUCT	Returns the product of the values	Function
SUMPRODUCT	Returns the sum of the products	Function

SUMPRODUCT(*array1,array2,[array3],...*)

Function

SUMPRODUCT returns the sum of the products of the specified arrays. *Array1, array2,* and so on are arrays of the same size.

Example

=SUMPRODUCT({1,2;2,3;3,4},{3,4;4,5;5,6}) returns 73.

See Also

MMULT	Returns the product of two arrays	Function
PRODUCT	Returns the product of the values	Function
SUM	Returns the sum of the values	Function

S-T

SUMSQ(*list*)

Function

SUMSQ returns the sum of the squares of the values in *list*. *List* is a list of up to 30 numbers.

Example

=SUMSQ(5,7) returns 74.

See Also

SUM	Returns the sum of the values	Function
SUMPRODUCT	Returns the sum of the products	Function

SUMXMY2(*array1,array2*)

Function

SUMXMY2 returns the sum of the squares of differences in values in *array1* and *array2*. The equation for SUMXMY2 is shown here:

$$\text{SUMXMY2} = \Sigma \ (x - y)^2$$

Example

=SUMXMY2({1,2;2,3;3,4},{3,4;4,5;5,6}) returns 24.

SUMX2MY2(*array1,array2*)

Function

SUMX2MY2 returns the sum of the difference of the squares of values in *array1* and *array2*. The equation for SUMX2MY2 is shown here:

$$\text{SUMXMY2} = \Sigma \ (x^2 - y^2)$$

Example

=SUMX2MY2({1,2;2,3;3,4},{3,4;4,5;5,6}) returns 84.

SUMX2PY2(*array1, array2*)

Function

SUMX2PY2 returns the sum of the sum of the squares of values in *array1* and *array2*. The equation for SUMX2PY2 is shown here:

$$SUMX2PY2 = \Sigma \ (x^2 + y^2)$$

Example

=SUMX2PY2({1,2;2,3;3,4},{3,4;4,5;5,6}) returns 170.

SYD(*cost, salvage, life, period*)

Function

SYD returns the depreciation expense for a given period of an asset using the sum-of-the-year's digits depreciation method. Enter the *cost* of the asset, its expected *salvage* value and expected *life*, and the *period* for which the depreciation is to be calculated.

Example

=SYD(5000,300,10,5) returns the depreciation expense of $512.73 for the fifth year, for a machine that costs $5000 and is expected to have a salvage value of $300 at the end of a 10-year life using the sum of the year's digits method.

See Also

DDB	Returns the double-declining balance depreciation	Function
SLN	Returns the straight-line depreciation	Function

T

T(*X*)

Function

T returns *X* as text if *X* is text or refers to text. Otherwise, T returns the empty string. This function is not necessary in Excel because Excel functions requiring a text string will automatically convert a number to an empty string. The T function is only used for compatibility with other programs.

Example

=T("January") returns "January" while =T(1234) returns "" (the empty string).

See Also

CELL	Returns information about a cell	Function
N	Returns the argument as a number	Function
VALUE	Converts text to a number	Function

TABLE(*[row]*, *[column]*)
TABLE?(*[row]*, *[column]*)

Macro Function

The TABLE function is the same as the Table option on the Data menu. TABLE creates a table based on row and column inputs. The *row* and *column* arguments should be external or R1C1 style references to single cells, which are the row and column inputs. If only one of the arguments is given, TABLE creates a one-input table.

In the dialog box version (with the question mark), the arguments, if included, are used as default values for the dialog box that appears.

TAN(*X*)

Function

TAN returns the tangent of a value, *X*, measured in radians. (Degrees multiplied by PI()/180 equals radians.)

Example

=TAN(H28) returns the tangent of the angle in H28.

See Also

ATAN	Returns the arctangent	Function
COS	Returns the cosine	Function
PI	Returns the value of PI	Function
SIN	Returns the sine	Function
TANH	Returns the hyperbolic tangent	Function

TANH(*X*)

Function

TANH returns the hyperbolic tangent of a value, *X*, measured in radians. (Degrees multiplied by PI()/180 equals radians.)

Example

=TANH(H28) returns the hyperbolic tangent of the angle in H28.

See Also

ATAN	Returns the arctangent	Function
COS	Returns the cosine	Function
PI	Returns the value of PI	Function
SIN	Returns the sine	Function
TAN	Returns the tangent	Function

S-T

TBILLEQ(*settlement, maturity, rate*)

Function   New to Version 4.0

TBILLEQ returns a Treasury bill's bond-equivalent yield, given the settlement and maturity dates and the discount rate. *Settlement* and *maturity* should be given as date serial numbers.

TBILLEQ is an add-in function. The first time you use it, you may see a #REF! error while Excel loads the function.

Example

=TBILLEQ(DATE(93,8,1),DATE(94,2,1),10%) returns 0.106804, or 10.68%, which is the bond-equivalent rate of a Treasury bill with an August 1, 1992 settlement date, a February 1, 1993 maturity date, and a 10-percent discount rate.

See Also

DATE	Returns the serial number of a date	Function
TBILLPRICE	Returns a T-bill's price per $100	Function
TBILLYIELD	Returns a T-bill's yield	Function

TBILLPRICE(*settlement, maturity, rate*)

Function   New to Version 4.0

TBILLPRICE returns a Treasury bill's price per $100 face value, given the settlement and maturity dates and the discount rate. *Settlement* and *maturity* should be given as date serial numbers.

TBILLPRICE is an add-in function. The first time you use it, you may see a #REF! error while Excel loads the function.

Example

=TBILLPRICE(DATE(93,8,1),DATE(94,2,1),10%) returns 94.88889, which is the price per $100 face value of a Treasury bill with an August 1, 1992 settlement date, a February 1, 1993 maturity date, and a 10-percent discount rate.

See Also

DATE	Returns the serial number of a date	Function

| TBILLEQ | Returns a T-bill's bond-equivalent yield | Function |
| TBILLYIELD | Returns a T-bill's yield | Function |

TBILLYIELD(*settlement, maturity, price*)

Function   **New to Version 4.0**

TBILLYIELD returns a Treasury bill's yield, given the settlement and maturity dates and the Treasury bill's price per $100 face value. *Settlement* and *maturity* should be given as date serial numbers.

TBILLYIELD is an add-in function. The first time you use it, you may see a #REF! error while Excel loads the function.

Example

=TBILLYIELD(DATE(93,8,1),DATE(94,2,1),94.89) returns 0.105362 or 10.54%, which is the yield of a Treasury bill with an August 1, 1992 settlement date, a February 1, 1993 maturity date, and a $94.89 price per $100 face value.

See Also

DATE	Returns the serial number of a date	Function
TBILLEQ	Returns a T-bill's bond-equivalent yield	Function
TBILLYIELD	Returns a T-bill's yield	Function

TDIST(*X, degrees, tails*)

Function   **New to Version 4.0**

TDIST determines the student's t-distribution of a value X given the *degrees* of freedom. *Tails* is a number that indicates which distribution to return. If *tails* is 1, a one-tailed distribution is returned. If *tails* is 2, a two-tailed distribution is returned.

Example

=TDIST(3,70,1) returns 0.001869.

See Also

| PTTESTV | Performs a two-tailed t-Test | Macro Function |
| TTEST | Performs a student's t-Test | Macro Function |

TERMINATE(*channel*)

Macro Function

TERMINATE closes the DDE channel (previously opened with the INITIATE function). TERMINATE returns a #VALUE! error if it can't close the channel. You must have the full version of Windows (2.0 or higher) to use this function.

INITIATE	Opens a channel to another application	Macro Function

TEXT(*X, format*)

Function

TEXT returns the value *X* as text in the Excel format given by the *format* argument. The *format* argument is a text string that specifies the number format that you want to use. The *format* argument should be given as a text string.

Example

=TEXT(5.458,"$0.00") returns "$5.46".

See Also

DOLLAR	Converts *X* to a currency text string	Function
FIXED	Converts *X* to a decimal text string	Function
T	Converts *X* to text	Function

TEXT.BOX(*text, object, [start], [number]*)

Macro Function

TEXT.BOX changes the text inside a text box. *Text* is the text string with which you want to replace the existing text. *Object* is the name of the text box with the text you want to change, given as a string. *Start* is the starting character number in the existing text string where you want to begin the replacement. *Number* is the number of characters in the existing string that you want to replace. If *start* and *number* are omitted, the entire string is replaced.

Example

=TEXT.BOX("Run Macro Now","Button 2") replaces the text string in Button 2 with "Run Macro Now".

See Also

CREATE.OBJECT	Creates an object	Macro Function
GET.OBJECT	Returns information about an object	Macro Function

TEXTREF(*reference-string,[style]*)

Macro Function

TEXTREF converts the *reference-string* into an A1 style reference if *style* is TRUE. TEXTREF converts the *reference-string* into a R1C1 style reference if *style* is FALSE. If *style* is omitted, the default value is FALSE.

Examples

=TEXTREF("A1",TRUE) returns the reference $A$1.
=TEXTREF("R1C1",FALSE) returns the reference R1C1.

See Also

LEFT	Returns the left end of a text string	Function
MID	Returns the middle of a text string	Function
REFTEXT	Converts a reference to a text string	Macro Function
RIGHT	Returns the right end of a text string	Function

TIME(*hour, minutes, seconds*)

Function

TIME returns the time serial number for the stated hour, minutes, and seconds. The *hour* can be a number from 1 to 23; *minutes* can be a number from 0 to 59; and *seconds* can be a number from 0 to 59.

Example

=TIME(15,15,0) returns 0.635417, the time serial number for 3:15 P.M.

S-T

See Also

HOUR	Returns the hour from a time serial number	Function
MINUTE	Returns the minute from a time serial number	Function
NOW	Returns the current date and time serial number	Function
SECOND	Returns the second from a time serial number	Function

TIMEVALUE(*string*)

Function

TIMEVALUE returns the time serial number for a string of characters that is in an Excel time format. The *string* can be a reference to a cell containing a label, a string of characters, or a formula that results in a string. This function is used to convert labels or data from another application into a time serial number that can be used in calculations.

Example

=TIMEVALUE("10:15 AM") returns 0.427083, the time serial number of 10:15 A.M.

See Also

DATEVALUE	Converts text to a date serial number	Function
HOUR	Returns the hour from a time serial number	Function
MINUTE	Returns the minute from a time serial number	Function
NOW	Returns the current date and time serial number	Function
SECOND	Returns the second from a time serial number	Function

TINV(*probability, degrees*)

Function   New to Version 4.0

TINV determines the inverse of a Student's t-distribution given the *degrees* of freedom and the *probability*.

Example

=TINV(0.06123,70) returns 1.902422.

See Also

PTTESTV	Performs a two-tailed t-Test	Macro Function
TTEST	Performs a student's t-Test	Macro Function

TODAY()

Function

TODAY returns the date serial number of the current date.

See Also

DATE	Returns the date serial number of a given date	Function
NOW	Returns the current date and time serial number	Function

TOOLS, CUSTOM

Concept

Excel provides an easy way to customize tools. The simplest way to create a custom tool is to write a macro and assign the macro to an existing tool or a new tool.

To create a custom tool, choose the Options Toolbars menu command. The Toolbars dialog box opens, as seen here:

Click on the Customize button to open the Customize dialog box. Pick the tool you want to assign a custom macro to. The Custom category has a set of tool faces that you can use for new tools. You can also assign a custom macro to an existing tool. The Customize dialog box is shown here:

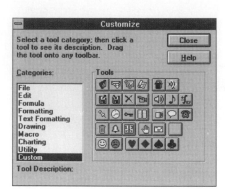

Click on the desired tool face and drag it to the toolbar on which you want the custom tool. The Assign To Tool dialog box automatically opens, as seen here:

From this dialog box, you can pick a macro that has already been written, or click on the Record button to record a new macro. Once you have assigned or recorded the macro, click on OK in the Assign To Tool dialog box to close it; then click on the Close button in the Customize dialog box. Now, every time you click on the tool, the macro you assigned to the tool will run.

See Also

OPTIONS TOOLBARS	Related menu command	Menu Command
TOOLBARS, CUSTOM	Explains customizing toolbars	Concept

TOOLBARS, CUSTOM

Concept

Excel allows you to create customized toolbars. You can put any built-in or custom tools on a custom toolbar.

To create a custom toolbar, choose the Toolbars option from the Options menu. The Toolbars dialog box opens, as seen here:

Type the name of the new toolbar in the Toolbar Name box; then choose the Customize button. The button will open the Customize dialog box. A new toolbar will appear on your screen. It will be small because there are no tools assigned to it yet. Choose a tool from the Customize dialog box and drag it to the new toolbar. Repeat this process until you have placed all the desired tools on your new toolbar. Then click on Close to close the Customize dialog box.

All built-in tools are listed on a command card in the back of this book.

See Also

OPTIONS TOOLBARS	Related menu command	Menu Command
TOOLS, CUSTOM	Explains customizing tools	Concept

TRANSPOSE(*array*)

Function

TRANSPOSE returns the transposition of an array. When you transpose an array, the first row of the given array becomes the first column of the resulting array, the second row becomes the second column, and so on. Since the result is an array, you must highlight a range of the correct size to hold the results, enter the formula, and then press CTRL-SHIFT-ENTER.

Example

=TRANSPOSE(A1:C2) returns {1, 2; 4, 3; 6, 7} if A1:C2 contains the numbers shown in Figure T-1.

See Also

MDETERM	Returns the determinant of a matrix	Function
MINVERSE	Returns the matrix inverse	Function
MMULT	Multiplies two matrices	Function

S-T

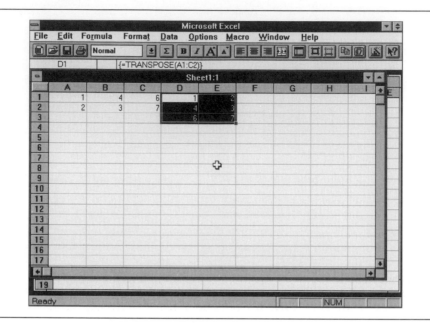

Figure T-1.   *The result of using the TRANSPOSE function*

TREND(*y-array,[x-array],[new-x-array],[constant]*)

Function

TREND returns an array that describes a straight line fit to the data stored in the *y-array*, and optionally, the *x-array*. If the *x-array* argument is omitted, the *x-array* is assumed to be {1, 2, :.}. *New-x-array* represents the new *x* values for which you want to find the *y* values. If the *new-x-array* argument is omitted, it is assumed to be the same as the *x-array* argument. TREND must be entered as an array formula, by first highlighting a range large enough to hold the resulting array, then typing the formula, and finally pressing CTRL-SHIFT-ENTER or pressing CTRL-SHIFT and then clicking with the mouse. The array returned by TREND describes the straight line fit with coordinates. If you want a straight line array described by a y-intercept and a slope, use LINEST.

Example

=TREND(B1:B5) returns the array {296, 316, 336, 356, 376}, if the cells in B1:B5 contain the values shown in Figure T-2.

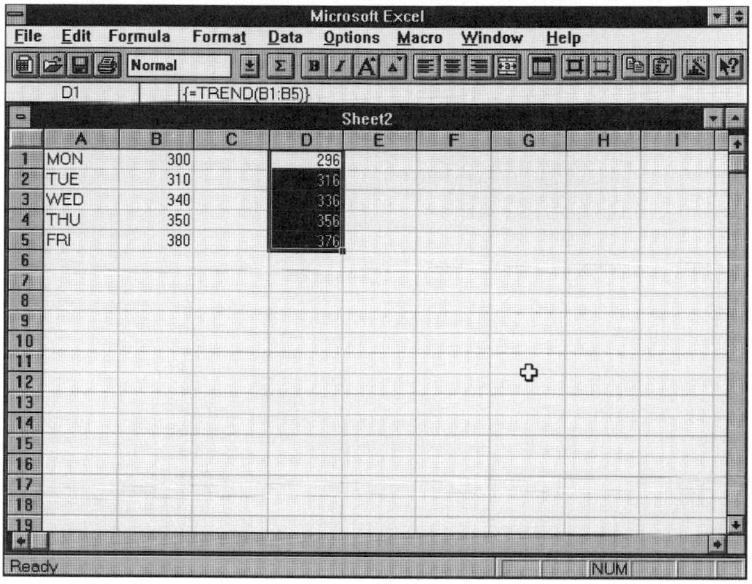

Figure T-2.   *The result of using the TREND function*

See Also

FILL.AUTO	Fills the current selection	Macro Function
LINEST	Returns the parameters of a line	Function

TRIM(*string*)

Function

TRIM returns the *string* with all the spaces removed except for a single space between each word.

Example

=TRIM("Stars   and   Stripes") returns "Stars and Stripes".

See Also

CLEAN	Removes unprintable characters	Function
SUBSTITUTE	Substitutes one string for another	Function

S-T

TRIMMEAN(*array, percentage*)

Function   **New to Version 4.0**

TRIMMEAN excludes a percentage of data points from the array and returns the mean of the remaining points. *Percentage* is the percentage of data points to trim. The data points are excluded from either end of the array.

TRIMMEAN

({1,2,3,4,5,3,4,8,6,1,2},0.15) returns 3.545455.

See Also

AVERAGE	Averages a list of values	Function
GEOMEAN	Returns the geometric mean of a data set	Function
MEDIAN	Returns the median of a list of values	Function

TRUE()

Function

TRUE returns the logical value TRUE, which is equal to 1.

Example

=IF(NAME="Smith",TRUE,FALSE) returns TRUE or 1 if the NAME range contains Smith. Otherwise, it returns FALSE or 0.

See Also

FALSE	Returns a logical FALSE	Function

TRUNC(*X, [number]*)

Function

TRUNC returns the number *X*, with the number of digits specified to the right of the decimal place intact, and the rest of the numbers to the right of the decimal place removed. If the *number* argument is omitted, all digits to the right of the decimal place are removed.

Example

=TRUNC(4.567) returns 4.

See Also

CEILING	Rounds up to the nearest integer	Function
FLOOR	Rounds down to the nearest integer	Function
ROUND	Rounds to a specified number of digits	Function

TTEST(*array1, array2, tails, type*)

Function   **New to Version 4.0**

TTEST determines the probability that two samples (*array1* and *array2*) came from the same underlying population with the same mean. *Tails* indicates the number of distribution tails in the student's t-Test. If *tails* is 1, one-tailed distribution is used. If *tails* is 2, two-tailed distribution is used.

Type is a number that indicates the type of t-Test. If *type* is 1, a paired test is used. If *type* is 2, a homoscedastic (two-sample equal variance) test is used. If *type* is 3, a heteroscedastic (two-sample unequal variance) test is used.

Example

=TTEST({1,2,3,5,6,7},{3,4,5,2,6,8},2,2) returns 0.621356.

See Also

PTTESTV	Performs a two-tailed t-Test	Macro Function
TDIST	Returns t-Test distribution	Macro Function

TTESTM(*input1, input2, output, [labels], [confidence], [difference]*)

Macro Function   **New to Version 4.0**

TTESTM executes a two-sample student's t-Test for means, assuming equal variances.

The *input1* and *input2* arguments are ranges where the data is in one column or row, and optionally, labels are included. If labels are included, the input ranges should be two columns or rows wide, where the labels are in the first column or row, and the data in the second column or row. The *labels* argument should be set to TRUE.

If no labels are included, the input ranges should be one row or column wide and the *labels* argument should be FALSE. The default value for *labels* is FALSE.

Output is the upper-left cell of the range where you want to place the result.

Confidence is the confidence level for the t-Test. If the confidence argument is not given, the default value is 0.05.

Difference is the hypothetical mean difference. If the difference argument is not given, the default value is 0.

TTESTM is an add-in function. The first time that you use this function, you may see a #REF! error while Excel loads the function.

See Also

PTTESTV	Similar function, assuming unequal variance	Macro Function
TDIST	Student's t-distribution function	Macro Function

TYPE(*X*)

Function

TYPE returns the type of the argument *X*. The following table summarizes the possible return types:

Return Type	X
1	Number
2	Text
4	Logical
16	Error
64	Array

Examples

=TYPE(ROW(A1:C3)) returns 64 because row is an array function.
=TYPE(BOB) returns 16 because BOB is not enclosed in quotation marks.

See Also

GET.CELL	Returns information about a cell	Macro Function

UNDO()

Macro Function

UNDO performs the same action as the Undo option on the Edit menu. UNDO reverses the last action you performed, if that action is reversible.

See Also

EDIT UNDO   Equivalent command   Menu Command

UNGROUP()

Macro Function

UNGROUP performs the same action as the Ungroup option on the Format menu. UNGROUP separates grouped objects.

UNHIDE(*window name*)

Macro Function

UNHIDE performs the same action as the Unhide option on the Window menu. UNHIDE displays a hidden window identified by *window-name*. *Window-name* is the name of the window you want to unhide, given as a text string.

Example

=UNHIDE("MONTHEND.XLS") unhides the window containing the document MONTHEND.XLS.

See Also

GET.WINDOW	Returns information about a window	Macro Function
HIDE	Hides a window	Macro Function

UNLOCKED.NEXT()

Macro Function

UNLOCKED.NEXT performs the same action as pressing the TAB key to move to the next unlocked cell.

See Also

CELL.PROTECTION	Protects or unprotects cells	Macro Function
PROTECT.DOCUMENT	Protects or unprotects a document	Macro Function

UNLOCKED.PREV()

Macro Function

UNLOCKED.PREV performs the same action as pressing the SHIFT-TAB key combination to move to the previous unlocked cell.

See Also

CELL.PROTECTION	Protects or unprotects cells	Macro Function
PROTECT.DOCUMENT	Protects or unprotects a document	Macro Function

UNREGISTER(*register-id*)
UNREGISTER(*DLL-name*)

Macro Function

UNREGISTER unregisters a Dynamic Link Library or code resource. There are two argument profiles for this function. The first version unregisters a function code resource identified by the *register-id* argument, which is the register ID returned by the REGISTER function. The second version unregisters a DLL identified by the *DLL-name* argument.

See Also

CALL	Calls a DLL procedure	Macro Function
REGISTER	Registers a code resource	Macro Function
REGISTER.ID	Returns a resource's register ID	Macro Function

UPDATE.LINK(*[link]*, *[type]*)

Macro Function

UPDATE.LINK performs the same action as choosing the Links option from the File menu, selecting a link, and clicking on the Update button. UPDATE.LINK updates a link to a supporting document. Any information on the current document that is obtained from the linked supporting document is updated.

Link is the name of the linked document, given as a text string. If *link* is omitted, links to the active document are updated. *Type* is the type of the linked document. If *type* is 1, the link is to another Excel document. If *type* is 2, the link is to a DLL. If *type* is omitted, the default value is 1.

See Also

CHANGE.LINK	Changes a link	Macro Function
FILE LINKS	Equivalent command	Menu Command
GET.LINK.INFO	Returns information about a link	Macro Function
OPEN.LINKS	Opens linked documents	Macro function

UPPER(*string*)

Function

UPPER returns the *string* in all uppercase letters.

Example

=UPPER("January") returns JANUARY.

See Also

LOWER	Returns a string in lowercase letters	Function
PROPER	Returns a string with leading caps	Function

U-Z

VALUE(*string*)

Function

VALUE returns the *string* as a number, if possible. If it is not possible to convert the *string* into a number, VALUE returns the error #VALUE!.

Example

=VALUE("$5,480.00") returns 5480.

See Also

DOLLAR	Returns a value as a dollar text string	Function
FIXED	Returns a value formatted with decimals	Function
TEXT	Returns a value as formatted text	Function

VAR(*list*)

Function

VAR returns the sample variance of the values itemized in the *list*. The *list* can contain any combination of numbers, formulas, or references to cells containing numbers or formulas. Use VARP when the number of items in the *list* is large. Use VAR when the number is small.

Example

=VAR(A14:A20) returns the sample variance of the values contained in the range A14 through A20.

See Also

VARP	Returns the variance of a population	Function

VARP(*list*)

Function

VARP returns the population variance of the values itemized in the *list*. The *list* can contain any combination of numbers, formulas, or references to cells containing numbers or formulas. Use VARP when the number of items in the *list* is large. Use VAR when the number is small.

Example

=VARP(A14:H120) returns the population variance of the values contained in the range A14 through H120.

See Also

VAR	Returns the variance of a sample	Function

VDB(*cost, salvage, life, start, end, [rate], [no-switch]*)

Function

VDB determines the depreciation of an asset for a period using the variable-declining balance method. *Cost* is the original cost of the asset. *Salvage* is the salvage value of the asset once it is fully depreciated.

   Start and *end* are the first and last periods over which you want to find the depreciation. *Life* is the total number of periods over which the asset is depreciated. *Start*, *end*, and *life* must be given in the same unit. For example, if you supply a *start* value in months, you must do the same for *end* and *life*.

   Rate is the rate of decline that is used. For example, if *rate* is 2, the double-declining balance method is used. The default value for *rate* is 2.

   No-switch is a logical value. If *no-switch* is FALSE, VDB switches to straight-line depreciation if the depreciation exceeds the declining balance. If *no-switch* is TRUE, no switch in method takes place. The default value for *no-switch* is FALSE.

Example

=VDB(3000,300,60,0,12) returns $1,002.71, the first year's depreciation of a $3,000 dollar asset with a $300 dollar salvage value depreciated over 5 years.

U-Z

See Also

DB	Returns the double-declining depreciation	Function
SLN	Returns the straight-line depreciation	Function
SYD	Returns the sum-of-year's digits depreciation	Function

VIEW.3D(*[elevation],[perspective],[rotation],[axes],[height],[autoscale]*)
VIEW.3D?(*[elevation],[perspective],[rotation],[axes],[height],[autoscale]*)

Macro Function

VIEW.3D performs the same action as the 3-D View option on the Format menu, which appears on the Format menu when the active document is a chart. VIEW.3D manipulates the view of the active three-dimensional chart.

Elevation is a number between −90 and 90 that specifies the degree of viewing elevation. If *elevation* is 90, the view is from directly above. If *elevation* is 0, the view is straight on. If *elevation* is −90, the view is from directly below. The default value for *elevation* is 25.

Perspective is a number that specifies the perspective of the chart. *Perspective* can be any number between 0 and 100%. The higher the perspective percentage, the closer the view appears. The default value for perspective is 30%.

Rotation is a number that specifies the *rotation* around the Z axis. *Rotation* can be any number between 0 and 360, unless the chart is a three-dimensional bar chart, where *rotation* is limited to a number between 0 and 44.

Axes is a logical value that determines whether the axes will remain fixed or will rotate with the chart. If *axes* is TRUE, the axes remains fixed. If *axes* is FALSE, the axes rotate with the chart. If *axes* is omitted, axes has the following default values:

Chart Type	Axes Default
Three-dimensional	FALSE
Not three-dimensional	TRUE
Three-dimensional bar charts	TRUE
Three-dimensional pie charts	Ignored

Height is a number between 5 and 500 that specifies the height of the chart with respect to the base. *Height* is a percentage of the length of the base. If *height* is omitted, the default value is 100.

Autoscale is a logical value. If *autoscale* is TRUE, the chart is scaled automatically. If *autoscale* is FALSE, the chart is not scaled automatically. If *autoscale* is omitted, the status of the autoscale setting remains the same.

In the dialog box version (with the question mark), the arguments, if included, are used as default values in the dialog box that appears.

Example

=VIEW.3D(10,90,30,FALSE) changes the view of the active chart to be slightly elevated, a close perspective, a 30-degree rotation, rotating axes, and a height equal to the base.

See Also

FORMAT.MAIN   Formats the main chart   Macro Function

VIEW.DEFINE(*name,[print],[rowcol]*)

Macro Function   **New to Version 4.0**

VIEW.DEFINE performs the same action as choosing the View option on the Window menu and clicking on the Add button. VIEW.DEFINE adds a new view or replaces an existing view.

Name is the name of the view you are defining, given as a text string.

Print is a logical value. If *print* is TRUE, print settings are saved with the view. If *print* is FALSE, no print settings are saved. The default value is TRUE.

Rowcol is a logical value. If *rowcol* is TRUE, row and column settings are saved with the view. If *rowcol* is FALSE, row and column settings are not saved. The default value of *rowcol* is TRUE.

VIEW.DEFINE is an add-in function. If it is not available, install the View Manager add-in function.

See Also

VIEW.DELETE   Deletes a view   Macro Function
VIEW.GET   Returns information about a view   Macro Function
VIEW.SHOW   Displays a view   Macro Function
WINDOW VIEW   Equivalent command   Menu Command

VIEW.DELETE(*name*)

Macro Function   **New to Version 4.0**

VIEW.DELETE performs the same action as choosing the View option on the Window menu, choosing a view, and then clicking on the Delete button. VIEW.DE-LETE deletes the view identified by the *name* argument. *Name* is the name of the view given as a text string.

VIEW.DELETE is an add-in function. If it is not available, install the View Manager add-in function.

U-Z

VIEW.GET(*type, [name]*)

Macro Function   **New to Version 4.0**

VIEW.GET returns information about views that have been defined. *Type* is a number that indicates the type of information that you want returned. The possible values for *type* are listed here:

Type	Information Returned
1	The names of the views defined in an array
2	TRUE if the view identified by name includes print settings; otherwise FALSE
3	TRUE if the view identified by name includes row and column settings; otherwise FALSE

The *name* argument is only required if type is 2 or 3. *Name* is the name of the view about which you want information.

VIEW.GET is an add-in function. If it is not available, install the View Manager add-in function.

VIEW.SHOW(*name*)
VIEW.SHOW?(*[name]*)

Macro Function   **New to Version 4.0**

VIEW.SHOW performs the same action as choosing the View option from the Window menu, selecting a view, and clicking on the Show button. VIEW.SHOW displays the window identified by *name. Name* is the name of the view you want to show, given as a text string.

In the dialog box version (with a question mark), the arguments, if included, are used as defaults for the dialog box that appears.

VIEW.SHOW is an add-in function. If it is not available, install the View Manager add-in function.

VLINE(*X*)

Macro Function

VLINE performs the same action as scrolling *X* number of rows in the currently active window. If *X* is a negative number, VLINE scrolls up. If *X* is a positive number, VLINE scrolls down.

See Also

HLINE	Scrolls horizontally by line	Macro Function
HPAGE	Scrolls horizontally by page	Macro Function
HSCROLL	Scrolls horizontally	Macro Function

VLOOKUP(*X,range,column*)

Function

VLOOKUP returns an entry from a two-dimensional vertical lookup table. Excel searches the left column of a range for the largest value that is less than or equal to *X*. Then Excel retrieves from that row the contents of a second cell, which is in the specified column. A vertical lookup table is a range of cells in which the ascending overall values are in a column. Figure V-1 is an example of a vertical lookup table.

If the value of *X* is not exactly equal to a value in the left column, VLOOKUP finds the closest value that is not larger than *X*. *Column* is the number of the column where the value is to be retrieved. The first (leftmost) column is considered to be column 1.

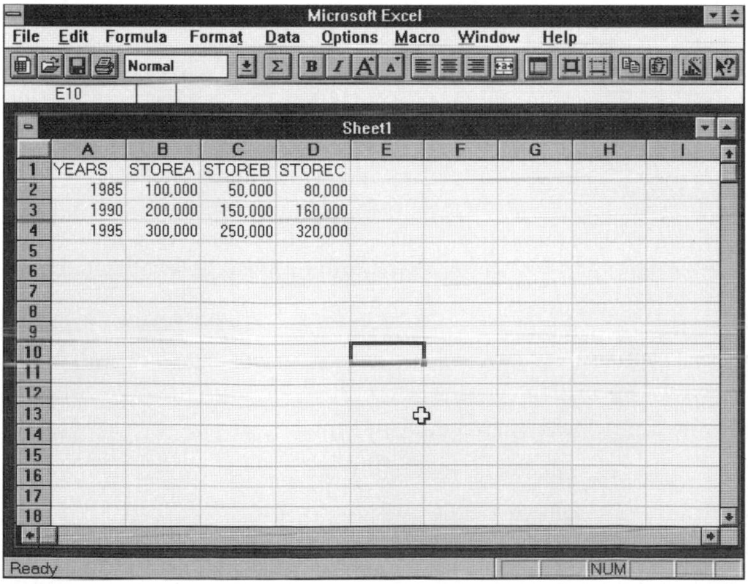

Figure V-1. *A vertical lookup table*

Example

=VLOOKUP(1990,SALES,3) would search for the value 1990 in the first column of the SALES range (SALES is the table in Figure V-1) and return the value that is in column 3. This is 150,000.

See Also

HLOOKUP	Horizontal lookup function	Function

VOLATILE(*[logical]*)

Macro Function   **New to Version 4.0**

VOLATILE defines the custom function to be volatile or nonvolatile. If *logical* is TRUE, the function that the statement VOLATILE appears in is a volatile function. If *logical* is FALSE, the function is nonvolatile. If *logical* is omitted, the default value is TRUE. The VOLATILE function must appear at the end of the function macro, before RESULT and ARGUMENT.

See Also

ARGUMENT	Specifies the arguments of a function	Macro Function
RESULT	Specifies the data type of the return value	Macro Function

VPAGE(*X*)

Macro Function

VPAGE performs the same action as scrolling *X* number of pages vertically in the currently active window. If *X* is a negative number, VPAGE scrolls up. If *X* is a positive number, VPAGE scrolls down.

See Also

HLINE	Scrolls horizontally by line	Macro Function
HPAGE	Scrolls horizontally by page	Macro Function
VLINE	Scrolls vertically by line	Macro Function

VSCROLL(*scroll-to, [logical]*)

Macro Function

VSCROLL performs the same action as scrolling to the row given by the *scroll-to* argument if the *logical* value is TRUE. If the *logical* argument is FALSE, the *scroll-to* argument should be given as a fraction between 0 and 1. If *scroll-to* is 0, VSCROLL scrolls to the top edge. If *scroll-to* is 1, VSCROLL scrolls to the bottom edge. Any fraction in between 0 and 1 causes VSCROLL to scroll to the appropriate column.

See Also

HLINE	Scrolls horizontally by line	Macro Function
HPAGE	Scrolls horizontally by page	Macro Function
VLINE	Scrolls vertically by line	Macro Function

WAIT(*X*)

Macro Function

WAIT stops the execution of a macro until the time specified by *X*. The argument *X* should be given as a time serial number, as text that represents a time, or as a formula that returns a time serial number. If you want to resume execution before the specified time is up, you can press the ESC key.

Example

–WAIT("12:30 AM") stops the macro until 12:30 A.M.

Example

=WAIT(NOW()+"00:10:00") stops the macro for 10 minutes.

See Also

NOW	Returns the serial number of the current date and time	Function
ON.TIME	Starts a macro at a specified time	Macro Function

WEEKDAY(*date-serial-number*)

Function

WEEKDAY returns the day of the week corresponding to the *date-serial-number*. The day of the week is given as a number from 1 to 7 for Sunday to Saturday.

Example

=WEEKDAY(DATE(93,4,5)) returns 2, which is Monday.

See Also

DAY	Returns the day of the month	Function
NOW	Returns the serial number of the current date and time	Function
TODAY	Returns the serial number of the current date	Function

WEIBULL(*X, alpha, beta, cum*)

Macro Function   **New to Version 4.0**

WEIBULL calculates the Weibull distribution for the value *X*, given *alpha* and *beta* as two parameters for the distribution. *Cum* is a number that indicates which form of the Weibull distribution function to use. If *cum* is TRUE, the cumulative distribution function shown here is used:

$$F(x; \alpha, \beta) = 1 - e^{-(x/\beta)^{\alpha}}$$

If *cum* is FALSE, the probability density function shown here is used:

$$f(x; \alpha, \beta) = \frac{\alpha}{\beta^{\alpha}} x^{\alpha-1} e^{-(x/\beta)^{\alpha}}$$

Example

=WEIBULL(200,50,100,TRUE) returns 1.

See Also

EXPONDIST	Returns the exponential distribution	Function

WHILE(*logical*)

Macro Function

Starts a WHILE-NEXT loop. The loop is executed until the *logical* argument is FALSE. *Logical* is an expression that evaluates to TRUE or FALSE. The macro executes the WHILE statement, and if the expression evaluates to TRUE, all the statements below the WHILE statement are executed until the statement NEXT is reached. When NEXT is reached, the macro returns to the WHILE statement and evaluates the expression again. When the expression evaluates to FALSE, the macro skips all the statements between the WHILE and NEXT statements and begins executing the statement immediately below the NEXT statement.

See Also

IF	IF statement	Function
LOOPING	Explains looping	Concept
NEXT	Ends a WHILE loop	Macro Function

WINDOW

Menu

The Window menu allows you to open another window on the same worksheet, to arrange all open windows so they can be seen on the screen, to hide or unhide a window, to add and display different views of a window, to reduce or enlarge a window, to split a window, to freeze panes in the active window, and to choose among open windows. The Window menu is shown here:

WINDOW ARRANGE

Menu Command   **New to Version 4.0**

The Arrange option on the Window menu allows you to arrange windows on your screen and control the synchronization of scrolling. When you choose the Arrange option from the Window menu, this dialog box appears.

The Arrange options in the dialog box are described here:

Tiled	All open windows are arranged in a tiled fashion. (Selecting this option is like choosing Window Arrange All in versions of Excel prior to version 4.)
Horizontal	All open windows are arranged horizontally with even space. (In other words, all windows are stacked one on top of another.)
Vertical	All open windows are arranged vertically with even space. (In other words, all windows are lined up from left to right.)

None	The window arrangement is not changed. (If you want to change the synchronization of windows without changing their sizes and locations, use this option.)

The Windows Of Active Document check box indicates which windows you want to affect. If the check box is selected, only those windows that are part of the active document are affected. If the check box is not selected, all open windows are affected.

If the Windows Of Active Document check box is selected, the following two options become available:

Sync Horizontal	Synchronizes the scrolling of the active document's windows horizontally
Sync Vertical	Synchronizes the scrolling of the active document's windows vertically

See Also

WINDOW ARRANGE ALL	Equivalent command prior to version 4	Menu Command

WINDOW ARRANGE ALL

Menu Command   **Prior to Version 4.0**

The Arrange All option on the Window menu rearranges all your open windows so that they all appear on your screen without overlapping. The space on the screen will be divided as evenly as possible between the windows. This option is especially useful when you have several overlapping windows open and you lose track of a window. This will make all your windows appear on the screen at once. Then you can start over and resize and position the windows where you want them.

See Also

WINDOW ARRANGE	Equivalent command for version 4	Menu Command

WINDOW FREEZE PANES

Menu Command   **New to Version 4.0**

The Freeze Panes option on the Window menu freezes the top and/or left panes in the active window. Freezing a pane or panes prevents scrolling. If the active window

U-Z

is not already divided into separate panes, Window Freeze Panes creates panes to the top and left of the active cell and then freezes those panes. To unfreeze panes, use the Unfreeze Panes option on the Window menu.

WINDOW HIDE

Menu Command

The Hide option on the Window menu hides the active window. The document in the window is still open, and you can reference it the same way you would reference any other open document. If it is a protected document (see OPTIONS PROTECT DOCUMENT), Excel asks you for a password when you hide it and again when you unhide it. To unhide windows, use the Unhide option on the Window menu.

WINDOW.MAXIMIZE(*[name]*)

Macro Function   New to Version 4.0

WINDOW.MAXIMIZE performs the same action as pressing CTRL-F10 or double-clicking on the title bar. WINDOW.MAXIMIZE maximizes the active window so that it fills the entire screen. The *name* argument is the name of the window you want to maximize given as text. If *name* is omitted, the active window is maximized.

WINDOW.MINIMIZE(*[name]*)

Macro Function   New to Version 4.0

WINDOW.MINIMIZE performs the same action as clicking on the minimize button. WINDOW.MINIMIZE minimizes the active window to an icon. The *name* argument is the name of the window you want to minimize given as text. If *name* is omitted, the active window is minimized.

WINDOW MORE WINDOWS

Menu Command

The More Windows option only appears on the Window menu if you have more than nine windows open. If you have more than nine windows open and you choose the

More Windows option, a dialog box appears with all of the windows you have open in an Activate box. You can select one of the windows and click on OK to have Excel activate that window.

WINDOW.MOVE(*[X],[Y],[name]*)
WINDOW.MOVE?(*[X],[Y],[name]*)

Macro Function   **New to Version 4.0**

WINDOW.MOVE moves the window identified by *name* to the position determined by the *X* and *Y* values given. *Name* is the name of the window you want to move, given as a text string. If *name* is omitted, it is assumed to be the active window. *X* and *Y* are the horizontal and vertical positions to which you want to move the upper-left corner of the window. *X* and *Y* are measured in points from the left and top of the screen.

In the dialog box version (with a question mark), the mouse pointer turns into a four-headed cross.

See Also

WINDOW.SIZE   Sizes a window   Menu Command

WINDOW NEW WINDOW()

Menu Command

The New Window option on the Window menu allows you to create an additional window for the active document. The two windows will be completely independent of each other. With two windows into the same document, you can see two different areas of your spreadsheet at once.

WINDOW.RESTORE(*[name]*)

Macro Function   **New to Version 4.0**

WINDOW.RESTORE performs the same action as pressing CTRL-F5, double-clicking on the title bar (if the window is maximized), or double-clicking on the icon (if the window is minimized). WINDOW.RESTORE restores a maximized or minimized window to its size and location prior to being maximized or minimized. The *name* argument is the name of the window you want to restore given as text. If *name* is omitted, the active window or icon is restored.

U-Z

WINDOW SHOW DOCUMENT

Menu Command

➤   *Shortcut Key:* CTRL-F2

The Show Document option only appears on the Window menu when the Info window is the active window. The Show Document option allows you to return to the active document.

WINDOW SHOW INFO

Menu Command   **Prior to Version 4.0**

➤   *Shortcut Key:* CTRL-F2

The Show Info option only appears on the Window menu when the Full Menus option is activated and the active document is a worksheet or macro sheet. The Info window shows the following information about the active document:

Cell	The active cell
Formula	The formula in the active cell
Value	The value to which the active cell evaluates
Format	The format of the active cell
Protect	The cell protection of the active cell
Names	The names defined for the active cell
Precedents	The cells to which the formula in this cell refers
Dependents	The cells that refer to the active cell
Note	The note attached to the cell

You can control which of these items appear in the Info window by using the Info menu options. The Info menu only appears if the Full Menus option is activated.

WINDOW.SIZE(*width,height,[name]*)
WINDOW.SIZE?(*width,height,[name]*)

Macro Function   **New to Version 4.0**

WINDOW.SIZE changes the size of the window identified by *name* to the size specified
by the *width* and *height* arguments. *Name* is the name of the window whose size you
want to change, given as a text string. If *name* is omitted, the active window is sized.
Width and *height* are the width and height that you want the window to be in points.

In the dialog box version (with a question mark), the mouse pointer turns into a
four-headed cross.

See Also

WINDOW.MOVE   Moves a window   Macro Function

WINDOW SPLIT

Menu Command   **New to Version 4.0**

The Split option on the Window menu splits the active window into separate panes.
The active window is split to the top and left of the active cell. Each pane that is
created can scroll independently. If you want to freeze the panes, use the Freeze Panes
option on the Window menu.

See Also

WINDOW FREEZE PANES   Freezes panes in a   Menu Command
                           document

WINDOW.TITLE(*[title]*)

Macro Function   **New to Version 4.0**

WINDOW.TITLE changes the title at the top of the active window. *Title* is a text string
that is the title as you want it to appear in the active window's title bar. If *title* is omitted,
the name of the document contained in the window is used as the title of the window.

U-Z

WINDOW UNHIDE

Menu Command

The Unhide option on the Window menu allows you to bring a hidden window back into view. If you have only one window hidden and you choose the Window Unhide option, Excel simply unhides it. If you have more than one window hidden and you choose the Window Unhide option, Excel displays a dialog box that allows you to select the window to be revealed.

See Also

WINDOW HIDE   Hides a window   Menu Command

WINDOW VIEW

Menu Command   New to Version 4.0

The View option on the Window menu allows you to add, delete, and display different views of your document. A view provides a different way of displaying and printing your document. The Views dialog box is shown here:

To create a view, click on the Add button. This displays the following dialog box:

The view includes the display settings and window characteristics. Name the view and check the Print Settings box if you want to save print settings with the view. Check the Hidden Rows & Columns check box if you want to save the hidden rows and columns as part of the view.

To delete a view, select the view name that you want to delete from the Views dialog box and click on the Delete button. To display a view, select the view name and click on the Show button.

See Also

VIEW.DEFINE	Adds a view	Macro Function
VIEW.DELETE	Deletes a view	Macro Function
VIEW.GET	Returns information about a view	Macro Function
VIEW.SHOW	Displays a view	Macro Function

WINDOW ZOOM

Menu Command   **New to Version 4.0**

The Zoom option on the Window menu allows you to magnify or reduce a displayed document. Choosing the Zoom command on the Window menu brings up the following dialog box:

You can pick one of the built-in percentages of magnification, or type in your own percentage between 10% and 400% in the Custom box. If you choose the Fit Selection option, the current selection will be magnified to fill the active window.

See Also

ZOOM	Equivalent function	Macro Function

WINDOWS

Concept

Excel is a Windows application, meaning that it requires Microsoft Windows in order to run. Windows provides the interface between you and Excel. The environment

U-Z

consists of a standard screen display, or visual interface, that you use to communicate with Windows applications. Once you learn how to use one Windows application, it is easy to learn other Windows applications. Chapter 1 of this book provides an overview of the Windows environment.

WINDOWS(*[type],[match]*)

Macro Function

WINDOWS returns an array that contains the names of the windows open on your screen. The top window is listed first, the bottom window last.

Type is a numeric value that indicates which window names you want returned. The following table lists the possible values for *type*. (The default value is 1.)

Type	Window Names Returned
1	All windows except add-in windows
2	Add-in windows only
3	All windows

Match is a text string that specifies window names that you want returned, and can include wildcard characters. If *match* is omitted, all the window names are returned.

See Also

ACTIVATE	Activates a named window	Macro Function
DOCUMENTS	Returns the names of open documents	Macro Function
GET.WINDOW	Returns information about a window	Macro Function

WORKBOOK.ACTIVATE(*[name],[new]*)

Macro Function   New to Version 4.0

WORKBOOK.ACTIVATE activates a document specified by the *name* argument, or the workbook contents window if the *name* argument is omitted. *New* is a logical value. If *new* is TRUE, the document is opened in a new window with default sizing. If *new* is FALSE, the document is displayed in a window the same size as the workbook contents window. The default value for *new* is FALSE.

See Also

WORKBOOK.OPTIONS	Sets workbook options	Macro Function

WORKBOOK.ADD(*documents,[workbook],[position]*)
WORKBOOK.ADD?(*documents,[workbook],[position]*)

Macro Function   **New to Version 4.0**

WORKBOOK.ADD adds the specified documents to the workbook. *Documents* is the name of a single document or an array of document names that you want to add to the workbook.

Workbook is the name of the workbook to which you want to add the documents. If *workbook* is omitted, the default is the active workbook.

Position is the position number in the workbook where you want to insert the document or documents. If *position* is omitted, the documents are added to the end of the workbook.

WORKBOOK.COPY(*documents,[workbook],[position]*)

Macro Function   **New to Version 4.0**

WORKBOOK.COPY copies the specified documents in the active workbook to another workbook. *Documents* is the name of a single document or an array of document names that you want to copy to the specified workbook.

Workbook is the name of the workbook into which you want to copy the documents. If *workbook* is omitted, the documents are copied to a new window that isn't part of a workbook.

Position is the position number in the workbook where you want to insert the document or documents. If *position* is omitted, the documents are added to the end of the workbook.

WORKBOOK.MOVE(*documents,[workbook],[position]*)

Macro Function   **New to Version 4.0**

WORKBOOK.MOVE moves the specified documents in the active workbook to another workbook. *Documents* is the name of a single document or an array of document names that you want to move to the specified workbook.

Workbook is the name of the workbook to which you want to move the documents. If the *workbook* argument is omitted, the documents are moved to a new window that isn't part of a workbook.

Position is the position number in the workbook where you want to insert the document or documents. If *position* is omitted, the documents are added to the end of the workbook.

U-Z

WORKBOOK.OPTIONS(*document,[bind],[new]*)

Macro Function   **New to Version 4.0**

WORKBOOK.OPTIONS sets options for the document. *Bind* is a logical value. If *bind* is TRUE, the document is bound. If *bind* is FALSE, the document is unbound. If *bind* is omitted, the status of the bind setting is not changed.

New is a new name for the document. If *new* is omitted, the default new name is the document name.

WORKBOOK.SELECT(*[names],[active]*)

Macro Function   **New to Version 4.0**

WORKBOOK.SELECT selects the documents identified by *names* in the active workbook. *Names* is an array of names that you want to select in the workbook. If no *names* argument is given, nothing is selected. *Active* is the name of the document that you want to be the active document. If *active* is omitted, the first document selected becomes the active document.

See Also

GET.WORKBOOK   Returns information about a workbook   Macro Function

WORKDAY(*start,days,[holiday]*)

Function   **New to Version 4.0**

WORKDAY returns a date serial number of the date that is a specified number of workdays after the start date. *Start* is a serial number, and *days* is a number indicating how many workdays, before or after the start date, the date for which you want to know the date serial number falls. *Holiday* is an optional argument. *Holiday* is an array of any special holiday date serial numbers that you want to exclude from what are considered workdays.

Example

=WORKDAY(DATE(93,6,1),30) returns 7/13/93, which is 30 workdays after June 1, 1993.

See Also

DATE   Returns the serial number for a date   Function

| NOW | Returns the serial number of the current date and time | Function |

WORKGROUP(*[names]*)

Macro Function   **New to Version 4.0**

WORKGROUP performs the same action as the Group Edit option on the Options menu. WORKGROUP creates a group of worksheets and macro sheets that you specify in the *names* array. If *names* is omitted, WORKGROUP regroups the most recently created group.

See Also

| OPTIONS GROUP EDIT | Equivalent command | Menu Command |

WORKSPACE(*[fixed-decimals],[decimals],[r1c1],[scroll-bars], [formula-bar],[status-bar],[alt-menu-key],[ignore-remote-requests], [enter-move],[tools],[notes],[nav],[menu-key],[drag-drop],[show-info]*)
WORKSPACE?(*[fixed-decimals],[decimals],[r1c1],[scroll-bars], [formula-bar],[status-bar],[alt-menu-key],[ignore-remote-requests], [enter-move],[tools],[notes],[nav],[menu-key],[drag-drop],[show-info]*)

Macro Function

WORKSPACE performs the same action as choosing the Workspace option from the Options menu. The arguments correspond to options in the Workspace Options dialog box, which is shown in Figure W-1.

Fixed-decimals should be TRUE if you want fixed decimals, and FALSE otherwise. If *fixed-decimals* is TRUE, the number of decimals is given by the *decimals* argument.

If *r1c1* is TRUE, R1C1 style referencing is used. If *r1c1* is FALSE, A1 style referencing is used.

If *scroll-bars* is TRUE, scroll bars are displayed. If *scroll-bars* is FALSE, scroll bars are not displayed.

If *formula-bar* is TRUE, the formula bar is displayed. If *formula-bar* is FALSE, the formula bar is not displayed.

If *status-bar* is TRUE, the status bar is displayed. If *status-bar* is FALSE, the status bar is not displayed.

ALT-menu-key is text that indicates the alternate key that activates the menu bar. *ALT-menu-key* is an optional argument.

If *ignore-remote-requests* is TRUE, remote requests are ignored. If *ignore-remote-requests* is FALSE, remote requests are not ignored.

Figure W-1.   *The Workspace Options dialog box*

If *enter-move* is TRUE, the active cell moves one position when the ENTER key is pressed. If *enter-move* is FALSE, the active cell does not move when the ENTER key is pressed.

If *tools* is TRUE, the Standard toolbar is displayed. If *tools* is FALSE, the Standard toolbar is not displayed.

If *notes* is TRUE, a note indicator appears in cells that have notes attached. If *notes* is FALSE, no note indicators are displayed.

If *nav* is TRUE, alternate navigation keys are turned on. If *nav* is FALSE, navigation keys behave normally.

Menu-key is a number that indicates which help is activated. If *menu-key* is 1, Excel help is activated. If *menu-key* is 2, Lotus 1-2-3 help is activated.

If *drag-drop* is TRUE, the Drag and Drop option is turned on. If *drag-drop* is FALSE, Drag and Drop is turned off.

If *show-info* is TRUE, the Info window is displayed. If *show-info* is FALSE, the Info window is not displayed.

If any of the preceding arguments are omitted, the status of the corresponding setting will remain unchanged.

In the dialog box version (with the question mark), the arguments, if included, are used as default values for the dialog box that appears.

See Also

| GET.WORKSPACE | Returns information about a workspace | Macro Function |

XIRR(*payments, dates, [guess]*)

Function   **New to Version 4.0**

XIRR returns the internal rate of return for an irregular schedule of cash flows. *Payments* is an array of numbers that are payments corresponding to payment dates. *Dates* is an array of date serial numbers representing the dates on which the payments were made. *Guess* is an optional argument that is your best guess at the result of XIRR.

XIRR is an add-in function. The first time that you use it, you may see a #REF! error while Excel loads the function.

Example

=XIRR({-2000,300,400,600},{33970,34001,34060,34121}) returns 0.76378.

See Also

IRR	Returns the internal rate of return	Function
NPV	Returns the net present value	Function
XNPV	Returns the net present value (irregular)	Function

XNPV(*rate, payments, dates*)

Function   **New to Version 4.0**

XNPV returns the net present value for an irregular schedule of cash flows. *Rate* is the discount rate. *Payments* is an array of numbers that are payments corresponding to payment dates. *Dates* is an array of date serial numbers representing the dates on which the payments were made.

U-Z

Example

=XNPV(0,08,{-2000,300,400,600},{33970,34001,34060,34121}) returns −728.276.

See Also

IRR	Returns the internal rate of return	Function
NPV	Returns the net present value	Function
XIRR	Returns the internal rate of return (irregular)	Function

YEAR(*date-serial-number*)

Function

YEAR returns the year, a number from 1900 to 2078, from a date serial number.

Example

=YEAR(NOW()) returns the four-digit year for today's date.

See Also

DAY	Returns the day given a date serial number	Function
MONTH	Returns the month given a date serial number	Function
NOW	Returns the serial number of the current day and time	Function
TODAY	Returns the date serial number of the current day	Function

YEARFRAC(*start, end, [basis]*)

Function   **New to Version 4.0**

YEARFRAC returns a fraction representing the number of whole days between the *start* date and the *end* date. *Start* and *end* should be given as date serial numbers. *Basis-code* is the day count basis to use. The following table lists the possible values for *basis-code*.

Basis-Code	Day Count
0	30/360
1	Actual/actual
2	Actual/360
3	Actual/36

The default value for *basis-code* is 1.

Example

=YEARFRAC(DATE(93,5,13),DATE(93,7,3)) returns 0.141667.

See Also

EDATE	Related function	Function
EOMONTH	Returns the end of month serial number	Function
NOW	Returns the serial number of the current date and time	Function

YIELD(*settlement, maturity, rate, price, redemption, frequency, [basis-code]*)

Function   **New to Version 4.0**

YIELD returns the yield of a security where interest is paid periodically. *Settlement* is the date serial number of the security's settlement date. *Maturity* is the date serial number of the security's maturity date.

The *rate* is the annual coupon rate of the security. *Price* is the price per $100 face value of the security. *Redemption* is the redemption value per $100 face value of the security. *Frequency* is the frequency of payments. The possible values for *frequency* are as follows:

Frequency	Payment
1	Annual
2	Semi-annual
4	Quarterly

The *basis-code* is the day count basis. The following table lists the possible values for *basis-code*. The default value is 0.

Basis-Code	Day Count
0	30/360
1	Actual/Actual
2	Actual/360
3	Actual/365

YIELD is an add-in function. The first time you use it, you may see a #REF! error while Excel loads the function.

Example

=YIELD(DATE(93,6,15),DATE(93,12,15),6%,50,100,4,0) returns 1.759439. The yield of a security whose settlement date is June 15, 1993 and maturity date is December 15, 1993, and which has a coupon rate of 6 percent, a price per $100 of $50, a $100 redemption value, 4 payments per year, and a 30/360 day count basis, is 1.759439.

See Also

DATE	Returns the serial number of a date	Function
PRICE	Returns price per $100 of a security	Function

YIELDDISC(*settlement, maturity, price, redemption, [basis-code]*)

Function   **New to Version 4.0**

YIELDDISC returns a discounted security's yield. *Settlement* is the date serial number of the security's settlement date. *Maturity* is the date serial number of the security's maturity date.

    Price is the price per $100 face value of the security. *Redemption* is the redemption value per $100 face value of the security. The *basis-code* is the day count basis. The values for *basis-code* are listed under the YIELD entry earlier in this chapter. The default value for *basis-code* is 0.

YIELDDISC is an add-in function. The first time you use it, you may see a #REF! error while Excel loads the function.

Example

=YIELDDISC(DATE(93,6,15),DATE(93,12,15),75,100,0) returns 0.666667. The yield of a discounted security whose settlement date is June 15, 1993 and maturity date is December 15, 1993, and which has a price per $100 face value of $75, a $100 redemption value, and a 30/360 day count basis, is 67 percent.

See Also

DATE	Returns the serial number of a date	Function
DISC	Returns the discount rate of a security	Function

YIELDMAT (*settlement, maturity, issue, rate, price, [basis-code]*)

Function   **New to Version 4.0**

YIELDMAT returns the yield of a security where interest is paid at maturity. *Settlement* is the date serial number of the security's settlement date. *Maturity* is the date serial number of the security's maturity date. *Issue* is the date serial number of the security's issue date.

The *rate* is the interest rate of the security at the time it was issued. *Price* is the price per $100 face value.

The *basis-code* is the day count basis. The values for *basis-code* are listed under the YIELD entry earlier in this chapter. The default value for *basis-code* is 0.

YIELDMAT is an add-in function. The first time you use it, you may see a #REF! error while Excel loads the function.

Example

=YIELDMAT(DATE(93,6,15),DATE(93,12,15),DATE(93,1,1),6%,80,0) returns 0.113096. A security whose interest is paid at maturity and whose settlement date is June 15, 1993, maturity date is December 15, 1993, and issue date is January 1, 1993, and which has a coupon rate of 6 percent, a $80 per $100 face value price, and a 30/360 day count basis, has a yield of 11.3 percent.

See Also

DATE	Returns the serial number of a date	Function
DISC	Returns the discount rate of a security	Function
YIELDDISC	Returns the yield of a discounted security	Function

U-Z

Z

ZOOM([*mag*])

Macro Function   **New to Version 4.0**

ZOOM performs the same action as the Zoom option on the Window menu. ZOOM magnifies or reduces the active window as indicated by the *mag* argument. *Mag* can be any number from 10 to 400 representing an enlargement or reduction percentage. *Mag* can also be a logical value. If *mag* is TRUE, the current selection is enlarged to fill the active window. If *mag* is FALSE, the document is restored to 100% magnification. The default value for *mag* is TRUE.

See Also

WINDOW ZOOM   Equivalent command   Menu Command

ZTEST(*array, X, [sigma]*)

Macro Function   **New to Version 4.0**

ZTEST calculates the two-tailed P-value of a z-test of the value *X*. *X* is the value you want to test. *Array* is the array of values you want to test *X* against. *Sigma* is the population standard deviation. If *sigma* is omitted, the default value is the sample standard deviation.

Example

=ZTEST({1,2,4,5,6,7,4,7,8},4) returns 0.130134.

See Also

NORMDIST	Returns the normal distribution	Function
STANDARDIZE	Returns a normalized value	Function

ZTESTM(*input1, input2, output, [labels], [confidence], [difference], var1, var2*)

Macro Function   **New to Version 4.0**

ZTESTM executes a two-sample z-Test for means, assuming known variances.

The *input1* and *input2* arguments are ranges where the data is in one column or row, and optionally, labels are included. If labels are included, the input ranges should be two columns or rows wide, where the labels are in the first column or row, and the data in the second column or row. The *labels* argument should be set to TRUE. If no labels are included, the input ranges should be one row or column wide and the *labels* argument should be FALSE. The default value for *labels* is FALSE.

Output is the upper-left cell of the range where you want to place the result.

Confidence is the confidence level for the t-Test. If the confidence argument is not given, the default value is 0.05.

Difference is the hypothetical mean difference. If the *difference* argument is not given, the default value is 0.

Var1 and *var2* are the variances of *input1* and *input2*.

ZTESTM is an add-in function. The first time that you use it, you may see a #REF! error while Excel loads the function.

See Also

PTTESTV	Similar function, assuming unequal variance	Macro Function
TDIST	Student's t-distribution function	Macro Function

Part III

Appendixes

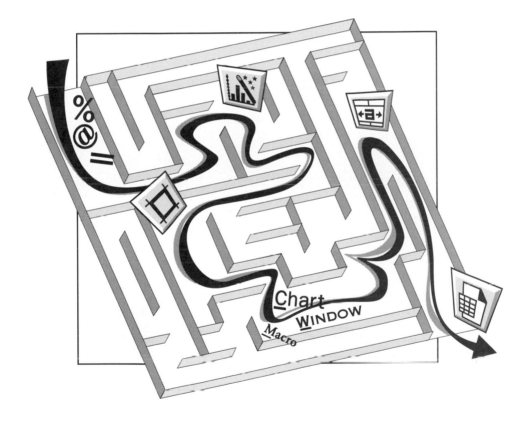

Appendix *A*

Installing Windows and Excel

Windows and Excel can operate with many combinations of computers, disks, displays, and printers. Installation instructions might have been very complex were it not for the Setup programs that come with both Windows and Excel. These programs do most of the work for you. You need only to determine what equipment you have, and then run the Setup programs, answering the questions that appear on your screen.

This appendix describes how to start and use both the Windows and the Excel Setup programs. It also explains how to prepare a disk directory for storing the data you create in Excel, and how to start and leave the Windows and Excel programs.

The minimum system requirements for running Windows 3.1 and Excel 4 are an Intel 80286 or higher processor and 2MB of memory. Of course, you will achieve much faster performance, and be able to take full advantage of the multitasking abilities of Windows 3.1, if you have an Intel 80386 or 80486 processor and increased memory. You will need at least 10MB of free hard disk space to load Windows, and an additional 11MB for a full Excel setup. In addition, your system must be running MS-DOS or PC-DOS version 3.1 or higher.

There are two pieces of optional hardware that will help you get the most out of Excel. A mouse is highly recommended, although technically not required. Both Excel and Windows are designed so that the mouse is the quickest way to maneuver throughout their many windows, menus, and features. Keyboard commands, in most instances, should be looked at as secondary alternatives to using the mouse. A printer is the other device that is extremely useful, though not absolutely necessary, when running Windows and Excel. Without a printer you might find it frustrating not to be able to see your work on paper. Most popular printers are supported by Windows and Excel.

This appendix is written for users of Windows 3.1 and Excel 4. While most of what is said here may be true for other versions of either product, users of those versions should be on the lookout for the differences.

Preparing To Store Data

When you use Excel, you create documents that you will want to use again later. To preserve this data, you store it in files on a disk. The files are preserved when you turn the computer off. The programs that comprise Windows and Excel are also stored in disk files.

You can store the data on either floppy disks or your hard disk. From the standpoints of both speed and ease of use, it is best to store data, in addition to the programs, on your hard disk. Since hard disks store so much information, they should be divided into directories, which are sections of the disk that you establish for particular purposes and name according to your needs. To prepare for storing the data you will create with Excel, you should create one or more directories.

Creating Directories on a Hard Disk

To store the program files on a hard disk, the Windows and Excel Setup programs automatically create directories for you, or use directories that you create and name. The default name for the Windows directory is \WINDOWS, and for Excel it is \EXCEL.

You can use existing Excel directories to hold your data files, but it is easier to locate and access your data files if you create separate directories to organize your work. If you want to create your own data directory to hold Excel data files, use the following instructions. Your computer should be turned on, and you should be at an operating system prompt such as C> or C:\>.

1. Type **cd** and press ENTER to make sure you are in the root directory.

2. Type **md\sheet** (short for worksheet) and press ENTER to create a directory named SHEET. (You can use a different directory name, but this book assumes that SHEET will be the directory for your data files.)

Copying Your Disks

To protect the original floppy disks that contain the Windows and Excel software, you need to make copies, or backups, of these disks before installing the programs. (The Microsoft licenses allow you to make one copy for this purpose.) You will need the same number of new or reusable disks as there are disks in the original programs. (The number of disks depends on whether you are using 5.25-inch or 3.5-inch disks.) You will need to make a copy of each of the original disks, and each disk will be copied onto its own separate backup disk.

You can copy floppy disks in several ways. Since you need only a single floppy drive to run Windows and Excel, instructions are given for using a single floppy drive to copy the original disks. If you wish to use a different method of copying, do so.

The DISKCOPY command used here permanently removes all existing information on the disk. When reusing a disk, make sure you have saved any needed information that may be on it.

1. Count the number of disks that came with both Windows and Excel and note their type: 5.25-inch 360KB, 5.25-inch 1.2MB, 3.5-inch 720KB, or 3.5-inch 1.44MB. 360KB and 720KB disks are labeled DSDD (for double-sided double-density), and 1.2MB and 1.44MB disks are labeled DSHD (double-sided high-density). Obtain and have handy the same number and type of new or reusable disks.

CAUTION: If you use reusable disks, you must be willing to lose all the information currently on them. Their contents will be overwritten during the DISKCOPY operation.

2. If necessary, turn on your computer. You should already have DOS installed on your hard drive, and should also have a basic understanding of how to enter commands from your keyboard, of the capacity of your disk drives, and of how your disk drives are labeled (A, B, C, and so on). If not, consult a basic DOS text.

3. You should be at the DOS prompt (for example C> or C:\>) and in the root directory. If you have been using your computer and/or don't know which directory you are in, type **cd** to return to the root directory

4. Be sure your backup disks (the ones you are copying onto) are the same size as the disks that came with Windows and Excel. Insert the first Excel or Windows program disk into the floppy-disk drive. This appendix assumes that your floppy-disk drive is drive A. If you are using a different drive, just substitute that drive letter in any relevant instructions.

5. At the DOS prompt, type **diskcopy a: a:** and press ENTER. You'll see the message "Insert SOURCE diskette in drive A: Press any key when ready." The source

diskette is the Excel or Windows disk being copied. Since it is already in the drive, you can just press ENTER.

6. When you see the message "Insert TARGET diskette in drive A:", remove the Excel or Windows disk and insert the first new or reusable disk to which you wish to copy. If the disk is a new, unformatted disk, you will see a message, "Formatting while copying", telling you that the disk is also being formatted.

7. Soon you'll again see "Insert SOURCE diskette in drive A:". You must remove the first new or reusable disk and reinsert the first Excel or Windows disk. Then you'll see the message "Insert TARGET diskette in drive A:" telling you to remove the first Excel or Windows disk and reinsert the first new or reusable disk. This will be repeated a couple of times.

Remember that "SOURCE" refers to the disk from which you are copying and is the original Excel or Windows disk, and "TARGET" refers to the disk to which you are copying and is the new or reusable disk that will hold the backup copy. The disk copying process takes several passes, so you must insert and remove each of the disks several times.

8. After several passes, you will see the message "Copy another diskette (Y/N)?". Type **y** and press ENTER.

9. Once again, you will see the message "Insert SOURCE diskette in drive A:". Remove the disk from drive A that is now the copy of the first Excel or Windows disk, label it similarly to the original disk, insert the second Excel or Windows original disk in drive A, and press ENTER.

10. Repeat steps 6 through 9 until you have copied all of the disks that come with your Windows and Excel packages.

11. When you have copied all the disks, type **n** and press ENTER in response to "Copy another diskette (Y/N)?". You will be returned to the DOS prompt. Remove the last copied disk from drive A and label it.

When you have copied all the program disks, protect the new disks to prevent them from being changed or infected with a virus. To protect a 3.5-inch floppy disk, first turn it on its back so you can see the metal hub in the center. Then, with the metal end away from you, slide the small black plastic rectangle in the lower-right corner toward the outer edge of the disk. This will leave a hole you can see through. To protect a 5.25-inch disk, place an adhesive tab over the notch on the upper-right corner of the disk. Once a disk is protected, you cannot change it until you reverse the protection process.

Place your original Windows and Excel disks in a safe location, and use them only when you have to make additional copies. For the installation process that follows, use the copies you just made.

Running Windows Setup

Running the Windows Setup program is very simple. As a matter of fact, you can do it with only a few instructions (assuming that your computer is turned on and that you are at the main DOS prompt):

1. Place the Windows Setup disk in drive A (or another floppy-disk drive) and close the drive door.

2. Type **a:** and press ENTER to make drive A current. (If you are using a different drive, type that drive letter in place of a.)

3. Type **setup** and press ENTER to start the Setup program.

4. Press ENTER again to begin Setup.

5. Press ENTER one final time to start Express Setup.

NOTE: Express Setup is a quick and easy way of installing Windows. If you are an experienced user who wants to control how Windows is installed, you can choose Custom Setup by typing **c.** *Express Setup is sufficient for most users.*

Windows Express Setup will begin copying files. Follow the instructions that appear on your screen.

You can install as many printers as you have available, but the first one you choose will be the default—the one used automatically—unless you choose otherwise. When you have selected a printer (by using DOWN ARROW to move the highlight to it), click on the Install button or press ALT-I. Then click on the port that your printer will use (LPT1, COM1, etc.), or use DOWN ARROW to move the highlight to it, and click on the Install button or press ENTER to complete installing your first printer.

Use Printers in the Main group Control Panel to install a second or third printer. For certain printers—laser printers in particular—you must also specify setup options. To do this, choose Setup from the Printers dialog box (click on Setup or press ALT-S). Change the Printer setup options to suit your needs.

During Windows Setup, you will be asked if you want to run a tutorial on how to use Windows and the mouse. If you are a new user of Windows, you may want to take a break in the setup process to run the tutorials. If you choose to continue the Setup program, you can always run the tutorials later from the Program Manager Help menu. In this case, complete Setup by clicking on Skip Tutorial.

Starting Windows

When you complete the Setup program, you are asked if you want to reboot your computer or return to DOS. Click on the Reboot icon. At the DOS prompt, type **win** and press ENTER to load Windows.

Once Windows is loaded, a screen similar to the one shown in Figure A-I appears. The initial screen shows the Main group of Windows system applications under the Program Manager. Your next task is to run the Excel Setup program.

Running Excel Setup

You must run the Excel Setup program under Windows; in other words, Windows must be running before Excel Setup can run. (If you've followed the steps outlined in the last section, Windows should be running.) To install Excel, follow these instructions:

1. Place the Excel Disk 1 ("Setup") in drive A or any other floppy-disk drive and close the drive door.

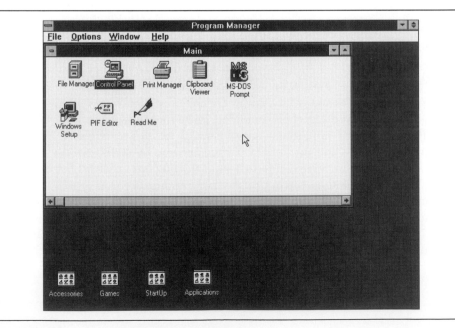

Appendix A-I.   *The initial Windows screen*

2. Move the mouse pointer until it is on the word "File" on the left end of the menu bar (the second bar from the top of the screen). Press and release the left mouse button to "click on" and open the file menu. From the keyboard, you can press ALT-F to achieve the same result.

3. Move the mouse pointer to the Run option on the File menu, and click the mouse to choose that option; alternatively, you can type **r** if you're using the keyboard.

4. Type **a:\setup** and press ENTER to start the Excel Setup program.

As in the Windows Setup program, there are installation options for Excel. Complete Installation is the easiest and most comprehensive. Custom Installation allows you to change the directory path and name and install optional files. The options and contents are listed here:

Option	Contents
Microsoft Excel	Excel programs and the ReadMe and Help files
Excel Tutorial	Files used to run the Excel lessons
Dialog Editor	An application that helps you build dialog boxes
Macro Translator	An application for translating 1-2-3 macros into Excel macros
Macro Library	A library of ready-to-use macros
Excel Solver	An application for goal-seeking analysis
Q+E	An application used to bring information from external database tables into Excel

You can get additional information on each optional file from the Setup Information window. The Minimum Installation installs the programs and files needed to run just Excel. Since you don't install the options, Minimum Installation saves approximately 6MB of disk space. This book assumes that you will perform a Complete Installation. The next series of steps will complete the installation of Excel.

5. Click on the Complete Installation icon. You will be prompted for each installation disk in its turn. Excel and all of its subdirectories and files are installed in C:\EXCEL.

6. Click on No when asked if you want to know about Lotus 1-2-3 usage in Excel. You can view this information from the Help menu after you have loaded Excel.

7. Click on Update to have Excel added to the PATH statement of your system's AUTOEXEC.BAT file.

8. When Setup is complete you will get a message to that effect. Click on OK or press Enter. A new group window entitled "Microsoft Excel 4.0" will appear on the screen, as shown in Figure A-II.

Starting Excel

To start Excel, you must open the Excel group window. Since you no longer need to use the Main group window, you'll close it first.

1. Make the Excel group window smaller by dragging its lower-right corner toward the upper-left corner until you can see the Main group. Then click on the Main group window to activate it.

2. Click on the Minimize button in the upper-right corner of the Main group window (the downward-pointing triangle). Alternatively, you can press ALT-SPACEBAR and RIGHT ARROW from the keyboard to open the Main group's Control menu, and then type **n** to choose Minimize.

3. To start Excel, double-click on the Excel application icon or press ENTER if it is already highlighted. If the Excel icon is not already highlighted, press LEFT ARROW or RIGHT ARROW to move the highlight to the Excel application icon.

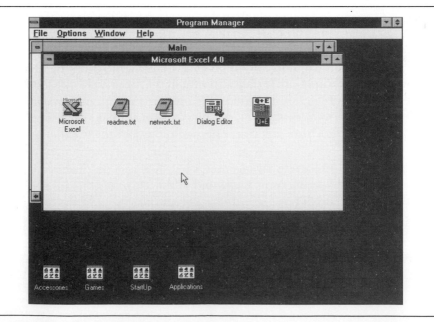

Appendix A-II.   *The Excel group window*

4. When you start Excel for the first time, you are offered three short lessons:

The Basics   Provides the necessary steps to get you using
                               Excel 4 quickly

What's New   Provides an overview of Excel 4's new features

For Lotus 1-2-3 Users   Shows how to use Lotus 1-2-3 skills in Excel

Click on a lesson button if you want to view that lesson, or click on the Exit To
Microsoft Excel button at the bottom of the screen to go directly to the normal
Excel screen, which is shown in Figure A-III.

Leaving Excel and Windows

When you are ready to leave Excel and return to the DOS prompt, follow these
instructions:

1. Double-click on the Control-menu box in the upper-left corner of the Excel
   window (not the Sheet1 window), or press ALT-SPACEBAR and type **c.** You will
   leave Excel and return to Windows.

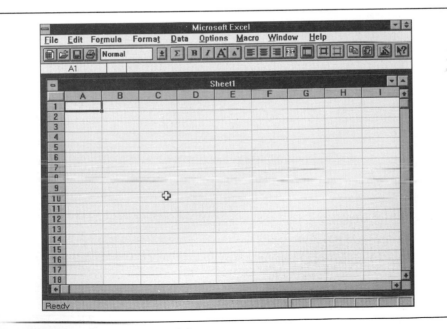

Appendix A-III.   *The normal Excel 4 screen*

2. Double-click on the Control-menu box in the upper-left corner of the Program Manager window (not the Excel group window), or press ALT-SPACEBAR and type **c.**

3. You will be asked if you want to end your Windows session. If you exit Windows now, the layout and contents of the final Program Manager window will be saved. The default is to save these changes when you exit Windows. If you don't want to save changes to the Program Manager window, you can change the default by selecting the Options menu and clicking on the Save Changes check box to turn the option off. From this point on (until you reactivate the Save Changes option), any changes made to the Program Manager window will be lost when you exit Windows.

4. Click on OK or press ENTER, and you will be returned to DOS.

Appendix *B*

The Excel Character Set

NO.	CHAR.	NO.	CHAR.	NO.	CHAR.	NO.	CHAR.
0		15		30		45	-
1		16		31		46	.
2		17		32		47	/
3		18		33	!	48	0
4		19		34	"	49	1
5		20		35	#	50	2
6		21		36	$	51	3
7		22		37	%	52	4
8		23		38	&	53	5
9		24		39	'	54	6
10		25		40	(	55	7
11		26		41	)	56	8
12		27		42	*	57	9
13		28		43	+	58	:
14		29		44	,	59	;

With the =CHAR(NO.) function, if you place a number in the function, the character to its right is returned.

NO.	CHAR.	NO.	CHAR.	NO.	CHAR.	NO.	CHAR.
60	<	91	[	122	z	153	
61	=	92	\	123	{	154	
62	>	93	]	124	|	155	
63	?	94	^	125	}	156	
64	@	95	_	126	~	157	
65	A	96	`	127		158	
66	B	97	a	128		159	
67	C	98	b	129		160	
68	D	99	c	130		161	¡
69	E	100	d	131		162	¢
70	F	101	e	132		163	£
71	G	102	f	133		164	¤
72	H	103	g	134		165	¥
73	I	104	h	135		166	¦
74	J	105	i	136		167	§
75	K	106	j	137		168	¨
76	L	107	k	138		169	©
77	M	108	l	139		170	ª
78	N	109	m	140		171	«
79	O	110	n	141		172	¬
80	P	111	o	142		173	–
81	Q	112	p	143		174	®
82	R	113	q	144		175	¯
83	S	14	r	145	'	176	°
84	T	115	s	146	'	177	±
85	U	116	t	147	"	178	²
86	V	117	u	148	"	179	³
87	W	118	v	149	•	180	´
88	X	119	w	150	–	181	µ
89	Y	120	x	151	—	182	¶
90	Z	121	y	152		183	·

With the =CHAR(NO.) function, if you place a number in the function, the character to its right is returned.

NO.	CHAR.	NO.	CHAR.	NO.	CHAR.	NO.	CHAR.
184	,	202	Ê	220	Ü	238	î
185	¹	203	Ë	221	Ý	239	ï
186	º	204	Ì	222	Þ	240	ð
187	»	205	Í	223	ß	241	ñ
188	¼	206	Î	224	à	242	ò
189	½	207	Ï	225	á	243	ó
190	¾	208	Ð	226	â	244	ô
191	¿	209	Ñ	227	ã	245	õ
192	À	210	Ò	228	ä	246	ö
193	Á	211	Ó	229	å	247	÷
194	Â	212	Ô	230	æ	248	ø
195	Ã	213	Õ	231	ç	249	ù
196	Ä	214	Ö	232	è	250	ú
197	Å	215	×	233	é	251	û
198	Æ	216	Ø	234	ê	252	ü
199	Ç	217	Ù	235	ë	253	ý
200	È	218	Ú	236	ì	254	þ
201	É	219	Û	237	í	255	ÿ

With the =CHAR(NO.) function, if you place a number in the function, the character to its right is returned.

Index

THE EXCEL KEYBOARD COMMANDS

Excel Command	Keypress
Abort an entry before finishing	ESC
Activate the Control menu	ALT-SPACEBAR
Activate the menu bar	ALT or F10
Activate the shortcut menu	SHIFT-F10
Apply currency format to the current selection	CTRL-SHIFT-$
Apply date format to the current selection	CTRL-SHIFT-#
Apply decimal format to the current selection	CTRL-SHIFT-!
Apply exponential format to the current selection	CTRL-SHIFT-^
Apply general format to the current selection	CTRL-SHIFT-~
Apply percent format to the current selection	CTRL-SHIFT-%
Apply time format to the current selection	CTRL-SHIFT-@
Bold (toggle)	CTRL-B
Border the current selection	CTRL-SHIFT-&
Calculate the active document	SHIFT-F9
Calculate all open documents	F9
Close the active document	CTRL-F4
Copy the current selection	CTRL-INS
Cut the current selection	SHIFT-DEL
Delete the current character (Edit mode)	DEL
Delete the current selection	CTRL-- (Hyphen)
Delete the previous character (Edit mode)	BACKSPACE
Enter data in the selected range	Type the first entry, press ENTER, type the next entry, press ENTER, and repeat until the range is full.

Excel Command (*continued*)	Keypress (*continued*)
Enter the current date	CTRL-;
Enter the current time	CTRL-:
Erase the current selection	DEL
Erase formulas in the current selection	CTRL-DEL
Exit from Excel	ALT-F4
Fill a cell with a character	Type a backslash followed by the character, then press ENTER.
Fill down	CTRL-D
Fill right	CTRL-R
Fill the selected range with data	Type the entry, then press CTRL-ENTER.
Find next	F7
Find previous	SHIFT-F7
Help	F1
Help (context-sensitive)	SHIFT-F1
Hide columns in the current selection	CTRL-0
Hide rows in the current selection	CTRL-9
Insert cells	CTRL-SHIFT-+ (Plus sign)
Italic (toggle)	CTRL-I
Maximize the active window	CTRL-F10
Minimize the active window	CTRL-F9
Move the active window	Press CTRL-F7, then use arrow keys.
Move one screen down	PGDN
Move one screen left	CTRL-PGUP
Move one screen right	CTRL-PGDN
Move one screen up	PGUP

Excel Command (*continued*)	Keypress (*continued*)
Move one cell at a time	Arrow keys
Move to cell A1	CTRL-HOME
Move to the first cell in a row	HOME
Move to the last cell in a row	END
Move to the last cell on the worksheet	CTRL-END
Normal font; apply to the current selection	CTRL-1
Open a new chart	ALT-F1 or F11
Open a new macro sheet	ALT-CTRL-F1
Open a new worksheet	ALT-SHIFT-F1 or SHIFT-F11
Open the Define Name dialog box	CTRL-F3
Open the Find dialog box	SHIFT-F5
Open the Goto dialog box	F5
Open the Note dialog box	SHIFT-F2
Open the Open dialog box (open a file)	ALT-CTRL-F2 or CTRL-F12
Open the Save As dialog box	ALT-F2 or F12
Paste	SHIFT-INS
Paste a function	SHIFT-F3
Paste a name	F3
Print the active document	ALT-CTRL-SHIFT-F2 or CTRL-SHIFT-F12
Remove borders from selection	CTRL-SHIFT-–– (Hyphen)
Repeat the last action	ALT-ENTER
Restore the active window	CTRL-F5
Save the active document	ALT-SHIFT-F2 or SHIFT-F12
Select a non-contiguous range	Select the first range, then press the CTRL key while selecting additional ranges with the mouse.

Excel Command (*continued*)	Keypress (*continued*)
Select one screen down	SHIFT-PGDN
Select one screen left	CTRL-SHIFT-PGUP
Select one screen right	CTRL-SHIFT-PGDN
Select one screen up	SHIFT-PGUP
Select the next class of item in a chart	UP ARROW
Select the next item in a chart	RIGHT ARROW
Select the previous class of item in a chart	DOWN ARROW
Select the previous item in a chart	LEFT ARROW
Select the whole column	CTRL-SPACEBAR
Select the whole row	SHIFT-SPACEBAR
Select the whole worksheet	CTRL-SHIFT-SPACEBAR
Select to the beginning of the current row	SHIFT-HOME
Select to the last cell in the current row	END, then SHIFT-ENTER
Size the active window	Press CTRL-F8, then use arrow keys.
Strikeout (toggle)	CTRL-5
Switch to the next window	CTRL-F6
Switch to the next window pane	F6
Switch to the previous window	CTRL-SHIFT-F6
Switch to the previous window pane	SHIFT-F6
Turn Add mode on or off	SHIFT-F8
Turn Extend mode on or off	F8
Turn on Edit mode	F2
Underline (toggle)	CTRL-U
Undo the last action	CTRL-Z
Unhide columns in the current selection	CTRL-SHIFT-)
Unhide rows in the current selection	CTRL-SHIFT-(